A Computer Science Tapestry

Exploring Programming and Computer Science with C++

McGRAW-HILL SERIES IN COMPUTER SCIENCE

SENIOR CONSULTING EDITOR
C. L. Liu, *University of Illinois at Urbana-Champaign*

CONSULTING EDITOR
Allen B. Tucker, *Bowdoin College*

Fundamentals of Computing and Programming

Computer Organization and Architecture

Computers in Society/Ethics

Systems and Languages

Theoretical Foundations

Software Engineering and Database

Artificial Intelligence

Networks, Parallel and Distributed Computing

Graphics and Visualization

The MIT Electrical and Computer Science Series

FUNDAMENTALS OF COMPUTING AND PROGRAMMING

*Abelson and Sussman: Structure and Interpretation of Computer Programs

Astrachan: A Computer Science Tapestry: Exploring Programming and Computer Science with C++

Bergin: Data Abstraction: The Object-Oriented Approach Using C++

Heileman: Data Structures, Algorithms, and Object-Oriented Programming

Kamin and Reingold: Programming with Class: A C++ Introduction to Computer Science

Kernighan and Plauger: The Elements of Programming Style

Smith and Frank: Introduction to Programming Concepts and Methods with Ada

*Springer and Friedman: Scheme and the Art of Programming

Tremblay and Bunt: Introduction to Computer Science: An Algorithmic Approach

Tucker, Bernat, Bradley, Cupper, and Scragg: Fundamentals of Computing I: Logic, Problem Solving, Programs, and Computers

Tucker, Cupper, Bradley, Epstein and Kelemen: Fundamentals of Computing II: Abstraction, Data Structures, and Large Software Systems

*Co-published by the MIT Press and The McGraw-Hill Companies, Inc.

A Computer Science Tapestry

Exploring Programming and Computer Science with C++

Owen L. Astrachan

Department of Computer Science
Duke University

The McGraw-Hill Companies, Inc.
New York St. Louis San Francisco Auckland Bogotá Caracas
Lisbon London Madrid Mexico City Milan Montreal New Delhi
San Juan Singapore Sydney Tokyo Toronto

McGraw-Hill

A Division of The McGraw·Hill Companies

A COMPUTER SCIENCE TAPESTRY
Exploring Programming and Computer Science with C++

This book is printed on acid-free paper.

3 4 5 6 7 8 9 0 DOC DOC 9 0 9 0 8 7

ISBN 0-07-002036-1

This book was set in Palatino by Publication Services.
The editor was Eric M. Munson;
the production supervisor was Annette Mayeski.
The cover was designed by Karen K. Quigley.
Cover art: Anni Albers, *Black-White-Gold I,* 1950, Pictorial Weaving, 32″ × 25″;
Collection the Josef and Anni Albers Foundation/ARS, NY © 1996;
Photo: Tim Nighswander.
Project supervision was done by Publication Services.
R. R. Donnelley & Sons Company was printer and binder.

Astrachan, Owen L.
    A computer science tapestry : exploring programming and computer science with C++/   /   Owen L. Astrachan.
        p.   cm. – (McGraw-Hill series in computer science)
    Includes bibliographical references and index.
    ISBN 0-07-002036-1
    1. C++ (Computer program language) 2.   Electronic digital computers–Programming.   I.   Title.   II.   Series: McGraw-Hill computer science series.
    QA76.73.C153A83   1997
    005.13′3–dc21   96-44011

http://www.mhcollege.com

About the Author

Owen L. Astrachan is Associate Professor of the Practice of Computer Science at Duke University and the department's Director of Undergraduate Studies. After receiving his A. B. degree from Dartmouth College, he taught high school for seven years before returning to graduate school. He received his Ph.D. in Computer Science from Duke in 1992. Professor Astrachan was a member of the Duke programming team that placed fourth in the world in the ACM programming contest in 1989 and coached the third place team in 1994. He was the chief Reader for the Advanced Placement Computer Science Exam from 1990 to 1994. Professor Astrachan has written many technical and pedagogical articles and is the Principal Investigator in two NSF-sponsored educational programs: "The Applied Apprenticeship Approach: An Object-Oriented/Object-Based Framework for CS2" and "CURIOUS: Center for Undergraduate Education and Research: Integration through Performance and Visualization". A well-regarded teacher, Professor Astrachan received the 1995 Robert B. Cox Distinguished Teaching in Science Award.

To my teachers, colleagues, and friends, especially to those who are all three, for educating, arguing, laughing, and helping.

To my family.

Most of all, to Laura.

Contents

3 C++ Programs: Input/Process/Output   81

4 Building Programs and Solving Problems   111

III   DESIGN, USE, AND ANALYSIS: BUILDING ON THE FOUNDATION

9 Characters, Strings, and Streams: Abstraction and Information Hiding   427

Introduction

The Tapestry Viewed from Afar

This book is designed for a first course[1] in computer science that uses C++ as the language by which programming is studied. My goal in writing the book has not been to adopt a "hot" new language[2] and use it in ways otherwise similar to so many introductory programming texts. I have tried to exploit the best features of C++ in the context of studying programming, program design and construction, and computer science. My intent is that mastering the material presented here will provide

1. A strong grounding in the design, construction, and analysis of programs.
2. A means for honing problem-solving skills associated with the study of computer programming.
3. An introduction to computer science that gives the student more of an idea of what the discipline is about than a "traditional" introductory programming book does.

In particular, this is a book designed to teach programming using C++, not a book designed to teach C++. Nevertheless, I expect students who use this book will be reasonably adept C++ programmers. Object-oriented programming is not a programmer's panacea, although it can make some jobs much easier. To mix metaphors, learning to program is a hard task, no matter how you slice it—it takes time to master, just as bread takes time to rise.

The material here is grounded in the concept that the study of computer science should be part of the study of programming. It is also based on the idea that program *design* is a very difficult task for novices to master, but that program *enhancement* or *modification* (a much more manageable skill) permits beginning programmers to develop programming skills in the context of meaningful programs. Most importantly, this book takes the view that the study of computer science should involve hands-on activity and should be fun. The study of programming must cover those areas that are acknowledged as fundamental to computer science, but it should do so in such a way that the foundation that is constructed during this study can be used to study current

---

[1] This first course has traditionally been called CS1 after early ACM guidelines.
[2] If that were the goal, I would have to discard three years of work and switch from C++ to Java.

trends that change, and it should do so in a way that enables students to want to learn more. Support for this position can be found in several places; I offer two quotes that express my sentiments quite well.

> Having surveyed the relationships of computer science with other disciplines, it remains to answer the basic questions: What is the central core of the subject? What is it that distinguishes it from the separate subjects with which it is related? What is the linking thread which gathers these disparate branches into a single discipline? My answer to these questions is simple—it is the art of programming a computer. It is the art of designing efficient and elegant methods of getting a computer to solve problems, theoretical or practical, small or large, simple or complex. It is the art of translating this design into an effective and accurate computer program. This is the art that must be mastered by a practising computer scientist; the skill that is sought by numerous advertisements in the general and technical press; the ability that must be fostered and developed by computer science courses in universities.
>
> C. A. R. Hoare
> "Computer Science" (reprinted in [Hoa89])

A supporting view is expressed in the following quote:

> Programming is unquestionably the central topic of computing.
>
> In addition to being important, programming is an enormously exciting intellectual activity. In its purest form, it is the systematic mastery of complexity. For some problems, the complexity is akin to that associated with designing a fine mechanical watch, i.e., discovering the best way to assemble a relatively small number of pieces into a harmonious and efficient mechanism. For other problems, the complexity is more akin to that associated with putting a man on the moon, i.e., managing a massive amount of detail.
>
> In addition to being important and intellectually challenging, programming is a great deal of fun. Programmers get to build things and see them work. What could be more satisfying?
>
> John V. Guttag
> "Why Programming Is Too Hard and What to Do about It" in [MGRS91]

Programming and Computer Science

This is more than a book about programming. Although its principal focus is on programming using C++, this is also a book about computer science. However, this is neither a book that adopts what some have called a "breadth-first" approach to computer science, nor is it a book primarily designed to teach object-oriented programming in the first course (although glimpses of both approaches will be evident).

I believe that a one-semester course that attempts to cover programming to the same extent as is done in a traditional Pascal, C, or C++ CS1 course and, at the same time, attempts to cover at even a superficial level the core areas of computer science is most likely doomed to failure. There is simply too much material to be covered.

At the same time, there has been an unfortunate though well-motivated tendency in many colleges and universities to move from Pascal-based courses to C-based courses. There are many good reasons for this change, but there is a fundamental pedagogical flaw to using C in a first course that more than counterbalances all the good reasons that so many have propounded: C is not designed to insulate the novice programmer from the machine. Thus, it is a disaster when used in a first course.[3]

Of course, these statements not only border on hyperbole—they embrace it with open arms. Nevertheless, watching students struggle with the many idiosyncrasies of C while trying to develop and master general principles of programming has not been a pretty sight. I did just that for several years before switching to C++ in the first course. At one level, the approach used in this book is the approach I adopted initially in my courses, because C++ is simply a much better C. At a superficial level, its I/O support and its support of more than one mode of parameter passing (by value and by reference) free students from worrying about pointers in the first week of the course. At a deeper level, C++, with its support of objects and libraries, allows students to make use of supplied code in a standard and useful way.

Introductory courses are evolving to take advantage of new and current trends in software engineering and programming language design. One of these trends comprises object-oriented design and object-oriented programming or OOP. Some schools will adopt the approach that learning object-oriented principles should be the focus of a first programming course. Although this approach certainly has some merit, students in the first course traditionally have a very difficult time with the *design* of programs. I believe that attempting to cover program design in addition to object design will not be as conducive to a successful programming experience as will using object-oriented concepts in the context of learning to program by reading programs before writing them. This may seem a subtle distinction, but if the focus of the course is on learning about the design and use of both objects and programs, there may be a tendency to delve too quickly and too deeply into the details of C++.

The approach taken in this book is that C++ and OOP permit students with little or no programming background to make great strides towards developing foundational knowledge and expertise in programming. In subsequent courses students will hone the skills that are first learned in the study of the material in this book and will expand the coverage of computer science begun here. Computer science is not just programming, and students in a first course in computer science must be shown something of what the discipline is about. At the same time, programming provides a means of relating the subdisciplines that compose compter science. Many of the examples and programs in this book

---

[3]It is possible to use C in a first course in a reasonable way, but the only example of doing this that I have seen is in a book by Eric Roberts [Rob95]. Using C++ is much simpler than using C.

rely on the use of classes, code, and libraries that are documented and supplied. It is possible that these examples could be studied using C rather than C++, but this would be very cumbersome and difficult to do in anything but an ad hoc manner specific to this book at best.

A major tenet of the approach used here is that students should read, modify, and extend programs before designing and writing from scratch. This is enabled to a large extent by using the object-oriented features of C++ whenever appropriate. However, neither I nor the book are compelled to delve into design methodologies and features of OOP; C++ is a tool to be used rather than studied. One of the most important ideas underlying the use of classes and objects in C++, and one of the most important concepts in computer science, is the idea of *abstraction.*

> Its [computer science's] study involves development of the ability to abstract the essential features of a problem and its solution, to reason effectively in the abstract plane, without confusion by a mass of highly relevant detail. The abstraction must then be related to the detailed characteristics of computers as the design of the solution progresses; and it must culminate in a program in which all the detail has been made explicit; and at this stage, the utmost care must be exercised to ensure a very high degree of accuracy. At all stages the programmer must be articulate about his activity. The need for abstract thought together with meticulous accuracy, the need for imaginative speculation in the search for a solution, together with a sound knowledge of the practical limitations of the tools available for its implementation, the combination of formal rigour with a clear style for its explanation to others—these are the combinations of attributes which should be inculcated and developed in a student by any university academic discipline; and which must be developed in high degree in students of computer science.
>
> C. A. R. Hoare
> (reprinted in [Hoa89])

Students and teachers of computer science are not obliged to understand the IEEE standards for floating-point numbers in order to write code that uses such numbers. Although at one time a deep understanding of machine architecture was necessary in order to write programs, this is no longer the case. Just as Hoare exhorts the programmer to be articulate about his or her activity, this book is designed to bring the novice programmer and student of computer science to a point where such behavior is possible. The use of C++ provides a mechanism for doing so in which details can be revealed if and when it is appropriate to do so and hidden otherwise.

Programming in C++

Although this book uses C++ as a tool to be used rather than studied, students coming out of a first course must be well prepared for subsequent courses in computer science and other disciplines. Therefore, the essential features of C++ must be used, studied, and mastered. The syntactic and semantic features of C++ sufficient for an introductory course will be thoroughly covered. It has been our experience in using this material that it is easier to move from C++ to C than vice versa. With this in mind, no coverage is given to C topics such as the kind of I/O done using `printf` and `scanf`.

Many thought and programming exercises are integrated in the text, particularly in the pause and reflect sections. These exercises are designed to make students think about what they're doing and to cover some of the messier language details in thought-provoking and interesting ways. Online materials accessible via the World Wide Web will provide supporting programming lab assignments.

A Closer View of the CS Tapestry

This book is different from most other introductory programming contexts in that

■ C++ is used without assuming any programming background.

■ A wide range of computer science topics is incorporated into the programs studied.

■ Whenever possible, the computer is exploited—small programs do not necessarily equate with toy programs.

■ A large number of classes, programs, and libraries is supplied with the book—students learn to read, modify, and enhance programs before writing them from scratch.

■ String and vector classes are used rather than pointer-based implementations, which are more C-based. The string and vector classes are consistent with the proposed ANSI standard C++ classes. Students should be able to use the standard string class in place of the class used in this book with little problem. The string and vector classes are also consistent with the classes designed for use in the Advanced Placement Computer Science course.

How to Use the Book

I do not cover every section of the book in my courses, and instructors who class-tested the book indicated that they skip some sections as well. Different institutions will cover some topics in more detail than others. In particular, Chapter 10 is not a prerequisite for the chapters that follow it, except that it introduces recursion, which is used in Section 11.4 in discussing quicksort. Recursion is also used in the coverage of linked lists and trees in Chapter 12, although linked lists can be studied without recursion. The excursion sections are not prerequisites for any of the material appearing later in the book, so these sections are optional as well. Chapter 8 and Chapter 9 can be covered in the opposite order for teachers who want to have covered streams and characters before arrays and vectors. In our course we don't cover the material explaining the built-in array type except in a cursory manner. The `Vector` and `Matrix` classes are much easier for students to use, since they hide all relationship with pointers.

Thanks

Many people have contributed to this book and the material in it, and I hope that many more will. I must single out several people who have offered criticisms and suggestions that have been extremely useful during the development of the material here: Rich Pattis (University of Washington) and Dave Reed (Dickinson College). At Duke, Susan Rodger taught using a draft, waited patiently while chapters were revised, and offered a nearly uncountable number of exercises, improvements, and programs. Her efforts have been very important in the development of this material. Greg Badros (then at Duke) reviewed the entire manuscript and offered absolutely wonderful suggestions; he astonished me with his perspicacity. In the fall of 1995 David Levine used the book at Gettysburg College and made many constructive suggestions based on this use. In the fall of 1996 Dee Ramm learned and taught using the final draft, and made many useful suggestions. Through the auspices of McGraw-Hill, Marjorie Anderson offered wonderful suggestions for improving the quality of the material here. Although I haven't vanquished the passive voice, any progress is due to her diligence, and all stylistic blunders are my own.

Thanks to Publication Services, especially to Rhonda Zachmeyer. The entire project was overseen and shepherded by Eric Munson and Holly Stark. Their tireless efforts are much appreciated.

In addition, the following people have reviewed the material and offered many useful suggestions (if I've left someone out, I apologize): Gail Chapman, Educational Testing Service; Mike Clancy, University of California at Berkeley; David Kay, University of California at Irvine; Clayton Lewis, University of Colorado; Bob Noonan, College of William and Mary; Richard Prosl, College of William and Mary; Stephen Schach, Vanderbilt University; Andrew Holey, St. John's University; David Levine, Gettysburg College; David Teague, Western Carolina University; Robert Plantz, Sonoma State University; Arthur Farley, University of Oregon; David Mutchler, Rose-Hulman Institute of Technology; Deganit Armon, University of California at Riverside; Stuart Reges, University of Arizona; Jerry Mead, Bucknell University; Beth Katz, Millersville University; Margaret Reek, Rochester Institute of Technology; Beth Weiss, University of Arizona; Jeff Naughton, University of Wisconsin; Robert Anderson, University of Houston; John Barr, Ithaca College; Henry Leitner, Harvard University; Richard Pattis, University of Washington; Donald Gotterbarn, East Tennessee State University; and Judy Mullins, University of Missouri–Kansas City.

Students in the Fall 1994 CPS 06 and 08 courses at Duke suffered through a draft of the material here. Several of them offered useful suggestions that appear in this draft. In particular Travis Pouarz and Derek Mims combed the material for errors and offered useful improvements. Students in the Spring 1995 CPS 08 course had to make due with a version of the book with no index. Nevertheless, several students made useful suggestions. In particular, Jay Kamm found many errors, even looking at code that wasn't in the book and offering suggestions.

Students in the Fall 1995 CPS 06 course had a book with an index, but the pages fell out. These students persevered, and new books arrived. In the interim several students combed the book for typos. I cannot possibly thank them all enough, but one stands out for her diligence: Christine Hong found countless errors and made many suggestions for improvement. Mackenzie Steele offered several quotations in addition to finding errors.

Development

The ideas and exercises in this book have been tested in the first course for majors at Duke during the 1993–1994 and 1994–1995 academic years. A draft form of the book has been used in all courses since the fall of 1994.

Several schools used a beta edition of the book, and the feedback from these schools has been incorporated into the final version. These schools include the University of Iowa, Rose-Hulman Institute of Technology, Gettysburg College, St. John's College (Minnesota), Mills College, and the University of California, Berkeley.

Versions of all the programs used in the book are available for Macintosh, DOS, and Unix machines. The software is currently available via anonymous ftp from `ftp.cs.duke.edu` in `pub/ola/book/code`. It is also accessible using Netscape or other Web browsers via

`http://www.cs.duke.edu/~ola/book.html.`

Although beta editions of the book have been through extensive classroom testing, there are undoubtedly errors that persist. Occasional slips of tongue (or keyboard) have almost certainly crept into the manuscript. Nevertheless, all code has been compiled and executed and is reproduced in this work directly from the sources; it is not retyped. The material here is intended to provide complete coverage for many different kinds of introductory computer science courses based on C++.

I am anxious to correct all the errors and fuzzy, incoherent, or otherwise incomprehensible passages for the first (and hopefully not last) edition of the book. I am not anxious to hear about misplaced commas and semicolons. I haven't mastered comma placement and will leave this to the experts. I would be ecstatic to hear about methods that might improve certain sections, or comments about sections that caused problems even without suggestions for improvement.

Please send all comments by email to

`ola@cs.duke.edu`

I will try to acknowledge all mail received. Materials for the book are also accessible via the World Wide Web from the URL

`http://www.cs.duke.edu/~ola/book.html`

A mailing list is available for discussing any aspects of the book or the course. To subscribe, send email with the message

```
subscribe tapestry
```

as the message body to

```
majordomo@acpub.duke.edu
```

To unsubscribe, send the message

```
unsubscribe tapestry
```

to the same address. To send mail to the list, use the address

```
tapestry@acpub.duke.edu
```

Details

This beta version of the book was prepared using LaTeX on Sun SPARCstation computers and a Micron Pentium-based machine running Linux. Pictures were "drawn" using xfig and exported as PostScript files. Photos were found on the World Wide Web using Netscape and converted to PostScript using XV.

Sometimes I used the Programming Loom to weave part of this Tapestry. The loom weaves virtual computer images as shown below.

This image is copyright ©Aaron Sundance Cobb and used by permission.

To paraphrase Newton, the work in this book is not mine alone; I have stood on the shoulders of giants. Of course Newton paraphrased Robert Burton, who said, "A dwarf standing on the shoulders of a giant may see farther than a giant himself." The styles used in several books serve as models for different portions of this text. In particular, Eric Roberts' *The Art and Science of C* [Rob95] provided style guidelines for formatting; the book *A Logical Approach to Discrete Math* [GS93] by David Gries and Fred B. Schneider motivated the biographies; books by Bjarne Stroustrup [Str94, Str91] and Scott Meyers [Mey92] were indispensable in delving into C++. Rick Mercer's C++ book [Mer94] provided a good example of how to do things well and simply. I've borrowed ideas from almost all of the textbooks I've read in eighteen years of teaching, so I acknowledge them en masse.

Thanks to Duke University and the Computer Science Department for providing an atmosphere in which teaching is rewarded and this book is possible.

Finally, thanks to Laura for always understanding.

Owen L. Astrachan

A Computer Science Tapestry

Exploring Programming and Computer Science with C++

Computer Science and Programming

The computer is no better than its program.
ELTING ELMORE MORISON
Men, Machines and Modern Times

Science and technology, and the various forms
of art, all unite humanity in a single and
interconnected system.
ZHORES MEDVEDEV
The Medvedev Papers

I want to reach that state of condensation of
sensations which constitutes a picture.
HENRI MATISSE
Notes d'un Peintre

The objective of this chapter—and, in part, of this entire book—is to introduce you to computer science. Ideally, therefore, we would begin with a simple definition that could be expanded and refined throughout the book. Unfortunately, it is difficult to answer the question "What is computer science?" This situation is not unique to computer science. For example, we might say that biology is the study of life. But that doesn't explain much about the content of such subdisciplines as animal behavior, immunology, or genetics—all of which are part of biology. Nor does it explain much about the contributions that these disciplines make to biology in general. Similarly, is English the study of grammar and spelling, the reading of Shakespeare's plays, or the writing of poems and stories? In many cases it is easier to consider the subfields within an area of study than it is to define the area of study. So it is with computer science.

1.1 What Is Computer Science?

In some respects, computer science is a new discipline; it has grown and evolved along with the growth of computing technology and the cheaper, faster, and more accessible processing power of modern-day computers. As recently as 1970, many colleges and universities did not even have departments of computer science. But computer science has benefited from work done in such older disciplines as mathematics, psychology, electrical engineering, physics, and linguistics. Computer science inherits characteristics from all these fields in ways that we'll touch on in this book, but the thread that links these and the many subdisciplines of computer science is computer programming.

Some people prefer the term used in many European languages, *informatics*, over what is called *computer science* in the United States. Computer science is more the study of managing and processing information than it is the study of computers. Computer science is more than programming, but programming is at the core of information processing and computer science.

This book will guide you through the study of the design, building, and analysis of computer programs. Although you won't become an expert by working through this book, you will lay a foundation on which expertise can be built. Wherever possible, the programming examples will solve problems that are difficult to solve without a computer: a program might find the smallest of 10,000 numbers, rather than the smallest of 2 numbers. Longer examples are taken from various core areas of computer science. As this is a book about the design and analysis of computer programs, it must be used in conjunction with a computer. Reading alone cannot convey the same appreciation that using, reading, and writing programs can.

The Tapestry of Computer Science

This chapter introduces computer science using a tapestry metaphor. A tapestry has much in common with computer science. A tapestry has many intricate scenes that form a whole. Similarly, computer science is a broad discipline with many intricate subdisciplines. In studying a tapestry, we can step back and view the work as a whole, move closer to concentrate on some particularly alluring or colorful region, and even study the quality of the fabric itself. We'll similarly explore computer science—studying some things in detail, but stepping back to view the whole when appropriate. We'll view programs as tapestries too. You'll study programs written by others, add to these programs to make them more useful, and write your own programs. You'll see that creating and developing programs is not only useful but is immensely satisfying, and often entertaining as well.

Several unifying threads run through a tapestry, and the various scenes and sections originate from and build on these threads. Likewise in computer science, we find basic themes and concepts on which the field is built and that we use to write programs and solve problems. In this chapter we introduce the themes of computer science, which are like the scenes in a tapestry, and the concepts, which are like the unifying threads.

Contexture is a word meaning both "an arrangement of interconnected parts" and "the act of weaving (assembling) parts into a whole." It can apply to tapestries and to computer programming. This book uses a contextural approach in which programming is the vehicle for learning about computer science. Although it is possible to study computer science without programming, it would be like studying food and cooking without eating, which would be neither as enjoyable nor as satisfying.

Computer science is *not* just programming. Too often this is the impression left after an initial exposure to the field. I want you to learn something of what a well-read and well-rounded computer scientist knows. You should have an understanding of what has been done, what might be done, and what cannot be done by programming a computer. After a brief preview of what is ahead, we'll get to it.

1.2   Algorithms

In order to develop an initial understanding of the themes and concepts that make up the computer science tapestry, we'll work through an example. Consider two similar tasks of arranging objects into some predetermined order:

1.   A hand of cards (arrange by rank and suit)
2.   100,000 exams (arrange by six-digit student ID number)

Card players often do the first task because it makes playing much simpler than if the cards in their hands are arranged in a random order. The second task is part of the administration of the Advanced Placement exams given each year to high school students. Many people are hired to sort the exam booklets by student ID number before the scores are entered into a computer. In both cases people are doing the arranging. The differences in the scale of the tasks and the techniques used to solve them will illuminate the study of computer science and problem solving.

Arranging 13 Cards

A hand of cards might look like this:

Most people arrange cards in order by suits (spades, hearts, diamonds, and clubs), and within suit by rank (2, ..., 10, J, Q, K, A) with little thought. In fact, many people perform a slightly different sequence of steps in arranging different hands of cards, modifying their basic technique depending on the order in which the cards are dealt. However, if you are asked to describe the process of arranging a hand of cards to someone who has never seen cards before, the task becomes difficult. The careful description of such processes

ALAN TURING (1912–1954)

Alan Turing was one of the founders of computer science, studying it before there were computers! To honor his work, the highest achievement in the field of computer science—and the equivalent in stature to a Nobel prize—is the Turing award, given by the Association for Computing Machinery (the ACM).

Figure I.I   Alan Turing.

In 1937, Turing published the paper *On Computable Numbers, with an Application to the Entscheidungsproblem.* In this paper he invented an abstract machine, now known as a *Turing Machine,* that is (theoretically) capable of doing any calculation that today's supercomputers can. He used this abstract machine to show that there are certain problems in mathematics whose proofs cannot be found. This also shows that there are certain problems that cannot be solved with any computer. In particular, a program cannot be written that will determine whether an arbitrary program will eventually stop. This is called the **halting problem**.

During World War II, Turing was instrumental in breaking a German coding machine called the *Enigma*. He was also very involved with the design of the first computers in England and the United States. During this time, Turing practiced one of his loves—long-distance running. A newspaper account had this to say of his second-place finish (by 1 foot) in a 3-mile race in a time of 15:51. "Antithesis of the popular notion of a scientist is tall, modest, 34-year-old bachelor Alan M. Turing. . . . Turing is the club's star distance runner . . . [and] is also credited with the original idea for the Automatic Computing Engine, popularly known as the Electronic Brain."

Turing was also fond of playing "running-chess," in which each player alternated moves with a run around Turing's garden. Turing was gay and, unfortunately, the 1940s and 50s were not a welcome time for homosexuals. He was found guilty of committing "acts of gross indecency" in 1952 and sentenced to a regimen of hormones as a "cure." More than a year after finishing this "therapy," and with no notice, Turing committed suicide in 1954.

For a full account of Turing's life see [Hod83] (in the bibliography, at the end of the book).

Arrange cards into four groups by suit: spades, hearts, clubs, diamonds
Sort each group. To sort a group:

For each rank (2, 3, 4, ..., 10, J, Q, K, A) put the 2 first,
followed by the 3, the 4, ..., followed by the 10, J, Q, K, A

(if any rank is missing, skip it)

Figure 1.2   Arranging cards in order.

is one of the fundamental parts of computer science. The descriptions are called
algorithms and are the focus of much study in computer science and in this
book. Algorithms are often compared to recipes used in cooking: they are step-
by-step plans used in some process (arranging cards or baking bread) to arrive
at some end (a sorted hand of cards or a loaf of bread). Although this analogy
is apt, cooking often allows for a larger margin of error than do algorithms
that are to be implemented on a computer. Phrases like "beat until smooth,"
"sauté until tender," and "season to taste" are interpreted differently by cooks.
A more appropriate analogy may be seen with the instructions that are used to
knit a sweater or make a shirt. In such tasks, precise instructions are given and
patterns must be followed or else a sweater with a front larger than the back or
a shirt with mismatched buttons and buttonholes may result.

The algorithm for sorting cards shown in Fig. 1.2 is both correct and concise,
two traits to strive for in writing algorithms. The instructions to sort a group are
applicable to all groups, not just to the spades or to the diamonds. Instructions
that apply in more than one situation are much more versatile than instructions
that apply in a single situation.

You can easily determine that the hand below is sorted correctly, in part
because there are so few cards in a hand and because grouping cards by suit
makes it easier to see if the cards are sorted. Verifying that the algorithm is
correct in general is much more difficult than verifying that one hand of cards
is sorted.

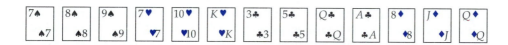

For example, suppose that an algorithm correctly sorts 1,000 hands of cards.
Does this guarantee that the algorithm will sort all hands? No, it's possible that
the next hand might not be sorted even though the first 1,000 hands were. This
points out an important difference between verifying an algorithm and testing an algorithm. A verified algorithm has been proved to work in all situations.

```
repeat the following until all 80 numbers (exams) have been arranged

    scan the list of numbers (exams) looking for the smallest number

    move this smallest number (exam) to another pile of exams
          that are maintained and arranged from smallest to largest
```

Figure I.3   Sorting exams.

A tested algorithm has been rigorously tried with many examples to establish confidence that it works in all situations.

Arranging 100,000 exams

Arranging 100,000 exams by ID number is a much more cumbersome task than arranging 13 cards. Imagine being confronted with 100,000 exams to sort. Where would you begin? This task is more time-consuming and more prone to error than arranging cards. Although you probably don't need a precise description of the card-arranging algorithm in order to sort cards correctly, you'll need to think carefully about developing an algorithm to sort 100,000 exams using 40 people as assistants. Utilizing these "computational assistants" requires communication and organization beyond what is needed to arrange 13 cards in one person's hand. A sample of 80 student ID numbers is shown here:

```
684856 889772 672029 662497 118183 452603 637238 249262 617834 396939
711566 170616 483595 613046 361999 231519 695368 689831 346006 539184
834866 273022 712077 816735 540778 975985 950610 846581 931662 625487
241881 683140 962328 967250 976490 697982 892616 328294 891958 809200
546689 132403 284930 239722 953522 877640 942451 779184 432203 170054
278827 821759 131232 952606 547825 385646 880295 816645 375695 763399
936335 220935 532496 660514 968749 622883 733644 781924 728308 977754
504839 447210 436554 228952 696894 266047 347759 641842 330856 422176
```

These represent a small fraction of the number of exam booklets that must be arranged. Consider the algorithmic description in Fig. 1.3. If this algorithm is implemented correctly, it will result in 80 numbers arranged from smallest to largest. If we had a computer to assist with the task, this might be an acceptable algorithm. (We'll see later that there are more efficient methods for use on a computer but that this is a method that works and is simple to understand.) We might be tempted to use it with 80 exams, but with 100,000 exams it would be extremely time-consuming and would make inefficient use of the resources at our disposal since using 40 people to find the smallest exam number is a literal waste of time.

1.3   Computer Science Themes and Concepts

The sorting example provides a context for the broad set of themes and concepts that make up computer science.

Theory, Language, Architecture

Three areas mentioned in [Ble90] as forming the core of computer science serve nicely as the essential themes, linking the various scenes of the computer science tapestry together. These themes are shown in Fig. 1.4. Although we can develop algorithms for both sorting tasks, it would be useful to know if there are better algorithms or if there is a "best" algorithm in the sense that it can be proven to be the most efficient. Determining whether an algorithm is "better" than another may not be relevant for arranging cards because a nonoptimal algorithm will probably still work quickly. However, a "good" algorithm is very relevant when arranging 100,000 exams. Developing algorithms and evaluating them is the part of computer science known as **theory**.

If the algorithms are to be implemented on a computer or used by people (who are in some sense "computational engines"), there must be a language in which the algorithms are expressed. We have noted that cooking recipes, while similar to algorithms, often leave room for ambiguity. Although English (or other **natural languages**) may at some point become a viable language in which to "instruct" computers, specialized computer languages are needed now. Many programming languages exist, and often the choice of language has a large impact on how well a program is written and on how fast it is developed. Languages are necessary in order to implement algorithms on specific kinds of computers.

Although both these arranging tasks are similar, an algorithm for one may be inappropriate for the other. Viewing a person as a computational resource (or *processor*), we see that the card-arranging task is done using one processor while the exam-arranging task is done using several processors. Just as some people can sort cards more quickly than others, some computer processors are faster and work differently than other processors. The term **architecture** is used to describe how a computer is put together just as it is used to describe how a building is put together. One active research area in computer science involves developing algorithms and architectures for multiprocessor computing systems.

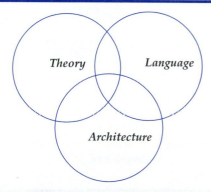

| **Figure 1.4** | Essential computer science themes. |

Abstractions, Models, and Complexity

In this section we continue out contextural approach, whereby we weave the essential themes into the fabric that is computer science and the scenes that make up its tapestry. In addition to the themes of theory, language, and architecture, we'll often refer to several of the recurring concepts presented in [Tuc91]. These form part of the foundation on which computer science is built; they are shown in Fig. 1.5.

Both sorting tasks involve arranging things, yet the complexity of the second task makes it imperative that an efficient algorithm be used if the goal is to be achieved within a reasonable time frame. Both **efficiency** and **complexity** are parts of the computer science tapestry we are studying. In programming and computer science, these terms concern how difficult a problem is and the computational resources, such as time and memory, that a problem requires.

We have avoided many of the details inherent in these examples that might be of concern as rough ideas evolve into detailed algorithms. If 40 people are sorting exams we might be concerned, for example, with how many are left-handed. This might affect the arrangement of the exams as they are physically moved about during the sorting process. Some playing cards are embellished with beautiful designs; it might be necessary to explain to someone who has never played cards that these designs are irrelevant in the arrangement process. In general these levels of detail are examples of **levels of abstraction** (Fig. 1.5). In one sense this entire chapter mirrors the fact that we are viewing the computer science tapestry at a very high level of abstraction, with few details. Each subsequent chapter of this book involves a study of some aspect of the tapestry at a level of greater detail.

Finally, both these tasks involve numbers. We all have an idea of what a number is, although the concept of number may be different to a mathematician and to an accountant. In computer science conceptual ideas must

Figure 1.5   Recurring concepts.

often be formalized in order to be well understood. For example, telling someone playing hide-and-go-seek to start counting from 1 and to stop when they reach the "last number" is an interesting way to teach the concept of infinity. The finite memory of computers, however, imposes a limit on the largest number that can be represented. This difference between **conceptual and formal models** is a concept that will recur and that completes the three concepts in Fig. 1.5, forming common threads of the computer science tapestry.

Pause to reflect

1.1 The *New Hacker's Dictionary* defines *bogo-sort* as described here.

> **Bogo-sort:** Repeatedly throw a hand of cards in the air, picking them up at random, and stopping the process when examining the hand reveals the cards are in order.

Using this "algorithm," what is the minimum number of "throws" that yields a sorted hand? What is the danger of using this algorithm?

1.2 In the algorithm for sorting cards, nothing is stated about forming a hand from each of the separate suits. Does something need to be stated? Is too much left as "understood by the player" so that someone unfamiliar with cards couldn't use the algorithm?

1.3 Write a concise description of the method or algorithm you use to sort a hand of cards.

1.4 Suppose that the 80 student ID numbers listed in the text are sorted. Is it a simple matter to verify that the numbers are in the correct order? Consider the same question for 100,000 numbers.

1.4   Language, Architecture, and Programs

Language is necessary for expressing algorithms. For computers, a precise programming language is necessary. In this section we briefly touch on the process by which an algorithm is transformed from an idea into a working computer program. This process is the same regardless of the kind of computer being used.

The final computer program differs from machine to machine in the same manner that the same idea is expressed differently in German than it is in English. Consider the German word *Geländesprung* defined:

> **Geländesprung:** a jump made in skiing from a crouching position with the use of both poles.

An idea whose expression requires many English words can be expressed in a single German word. Different computers can offer the same economy of expression; what one computer might do in a single instruction can require several instructions (and a corresponding increase in time to execute the instructions) on another computer. For example, so-called **supercomputers** can add 100 numbers with a single instruction. On ordinary computers, one instruction can add only two numbers.

Charles Antony (Tony) Richard Hoare (b. 1934)

Perhaps best known for his invention of the sorting algorithm he modestly named Quicksort, Hoare has made profound contributions to many branches of computer science, especially in programming and programming languages. Hoare received the ACM Turing award in 1980. In his award address he had this to say about learning from failure: "I have learned more from my failures than can ever be revealed in the cold print of a scientific article and now I would like you to learn from them, too. Besides, failures are much more fun to hear about afterwards; they are not so funny at the time." In a collection of

Figure 1.6   C.A.R. Hoare.

essays [Hoa89], Hoare describes the programmer of the current era as part apprentice and part wizard; he urges that computer science education should focus on both theoretical foundations and practical applications. In his last essay of that collection he states "I salute the bravery of those who accept the challenge of being the first to try out new ideas; and I also respect the caution of those who prefer to stick with ideas which they know and understand and trust."

Hoare may not like C++; it is too big, too full of features, and it doesn't have a formal foundation. According to his World Wide Web page, he set himself the following tasks for his 1993–1994 sabbatical year.

- To become acquainted with Visual Basic™.
- To establish a consultancy with a company that successfully maintains a program of over 10 million lines.
- To complete a work on unification of theories of programming.
- To start new work on a range of scientific theories of computational phenomena.

In describing computer science as, in part, an engineering discipline, Hoare states

> ... the major factor in the wider propagation of professional methods is education, an education which conveys a broad and deep understanding of theoretical principles as well as their practical application, an education such as can be offered by our universities and polytechnics.

For more information, see [Hoa89].

High- and Low-level Languages

> High thoughts must have high language.
> ARISTOPHANES
> *Frogs*

How do computers work? We don't need to know this to use computers just as we don't need to know how internal combustion engines work to drive a car. A little knowledge, however, can help to demystify what a computer is doing when it executes a program. A computer can be viewed from many levels, from the transistors that make up its circuits to the programs that are used to design the circuits.

At the lowest level, computers respond to electric signals at an extremely fast rate. Computers react to whether electricity is flowing or not; the computer merely responds to switches that are in one of two states: on or off. This method of using two states involves what is termed the **binary number system,** or the **base 2 system.** This system is based on counting using only the digits 0 and 1. The base 10 system, with which you are most familiar, uses the digits 0 through 9.

There are hundreds of different kinds of computers. You may have used Apple Macintosh computers, which are built using a computer chip called the *Power-PC*™, or another kind of computer based on the Intel *Pentium*™ chip. These chips are the foundation on which a computer is built. The chip determines how fast the computer runs and what kinds of software can be used with the computer. Since computers are constructed from different components and have different underlying architectures, they may respond differently to the same sequence of zeros and ones. Just as *chat* means "to converse informally" in English and means "a small domesticated feline (cat)" in French, so might *00010100111010* instruct one computer to add two numbers and another computer to print the letter *q*.

Rather than instruct computers at this level of zeros and ones, languages have been developed that allow ideas to be expressed at a higher level—in a way more easily understood by people. In addition to being more easily understood, these high-level languages can be translated into particular sequences of zeros and ones for particular computers. Just as translators can translate English into both Japanese and Swahili, so can translating computer programs translate a high-level language into a low-level language for a particular computer. The concept of higher level programming languages was a breakthrough. The first computers were "programmed" literally by flipping switches by hand or physically rewiring the computer to create different on/off states corresponding to a program. The use of higher level languages made programming easier (although it is still an intellectually challenging task) and helped to make computer use more prevalent.

The computer language used in this book is called C++.[1] This language has its roots in the C programming language, which was developed in the 1970s.

---

[1] This is pronounced as "see plus plus."

The language C is a high-level language[2] that allows low-level concepts to be expressed more readily than some other high-level languages. For example, in C it is easy to write a program to change a single bit (a 0 or a 1) in the computer's memory. This is hard, if not impossible, to do in other high-level languages, such as Pascal.

We're not studying C++ because it permits one bit to be changed. We're studying C++ because with it several programming styles are possible. In particular, it can be used with a style of programming called *object-oriented programming*, often abbreviated as OOP. We will use OOP throughout this book, but it will be an aid to our study of programming and computer science rather than the principal focus. We'll explore OOP briefly at the end of this chapter.

The intricacies of C++ are such that mastering the entire language, as well as the concepts of object-oriented programming, is a task too daunting and difficult for beginning programmers. In this book we present a significant subset of C++ and use it to write programs that permit the study of essential areas of computer science. At the same time the power of C++ is exploited where possible to allow you to create more complicated programs than would be feasible using other languages. Don't be disheartened that you won't learn absolutely all of C++ in this book—you'll be building a foundation on which subsequent study can add. The few parts of the language that aren't covered are mostly "short-cuts" that can be replaced using features of the language that are in the book.

A concrete example. To illustrate the difference between high- and low-level languages, we'll study how a C++ program is translated into a low-level language. The low-level language of 0's and 1's that a computer understands is called **machine language**. Because different computers have different machine languages, a program is needed to translate the high-level C++ language into machine language. A **compiler** is a program that does this translation. Often the compiling process involves an intermediate step wherein the code is translated into **assembly language**.

To keep the example simple, we'll use a program that accepts two numbers as input and prints the result of multiplying the numbers. The C++ program is shown in Fig. 1.7. For example, if the program user enters 7 and 12, the program prints 84. We will not discuss the C++ instructions here; we use the program only to illustrate the differences between high- and low-level languages.

The world is full of C++ compilers. Compilers exist for various kinds of computers, sizes of programs, and amounts of money. The code in this book has been tested using three different compilers but was developed primarily with one called *GNU g++*. This compiler runs on many different kinds of computers and is free. The assembly code generated by the g++ compiler is shown in

---

[2]Although some computer scientists might take exception to this statement, C is clearly a much higher level language than machine or assembly language.

```
#include <iostream.h>

main()
{
    int x,y,z;
    cin >> x >> y;
    z = x * y;
    cout << z;
}
```

Figure 1.7   Program to multiply two numbers.

Fig. 1.8 for two different computers: a DEC 3100 and a Sun SPARCstation[3]; there is one column of assembly code for each machine. Note that although the programs are of roughly the same length, there are few similarities in the assembly instructions. Among the instructions are *ld, call,* and *nop* for the Sun assembly and *jal, lw,* and *move* for the DEC. The important point of Fig. 1.8 is that you do *not* need to worry about assembly code in order to write programs in

```
_main:                                              main:
        call    ___main,0                           jal     __main
        nop                                         la      $4,cin
        add     %fp,-20,%o1                         addu    $5,$fp,16
        sethi   %hi(_cin),%o2                       jal     __rs__7istreamRi
        or      %o2,%lo(_cin),%o0                   move    $16,$2
        call    ___rs__FR7istreamRi,0              addu    $2,$fp,20
        nop                                         move    $4,$16
        add     %fp,-24,%o1                         move    $5,$2
        call    ___rs__FR7istreamRi,0              jal     __rs__7istreamRi
        nop                                         lw      $2,16($fp)
        ld      [%fp-20],%o0                        lw      $3,20($fp)
        ld      [%fp-24],%o1                        mult    $2,$3
        call    .umul,0                             mflo    $2
        nop                                         sw      $2,24($fp)
        st      %o0,[%fp-28]                        la      $4,cout
        sethi   %hi(_cout),%o1                      lw      $5,24($fp)
        or      %o1,%lo(_cout),%o0                  jal     __ls__7ostreami
        ld      [%fp-28],%o1                        move    $2,$0
        call    ___ls__FR7ostreaml,0               j       $L230
        nop                                         j       $L230
```

Figure 1.8   Assembly code using g++   (Sparc on left, DEC on right).

---

[3]The characteristics of these machines are not important, but the same compiler runs on both machines, which facilitates a comparison.

C++ or in any other high-level language. It is comforting to know that we can ignore most of the low-level details in writing programs and studying computer science and, perhaps, enticing to know that the details are there for those who are interested.

Creating and Developing Programs

How is a computer program created? Usually a problem arises whose solution requires computation. An algorithm for the solution is developed into a running program in several steps. The steps that lead to the program's execution on a computer are also important. The process of developing an idea into an algorithm that is eventually realized as a working computer program is illustrated in Fig. 1.9. The problem is for the sake of illustration; it requires a program to multiply two numbers.

From problem to algorithm.   Consider the steps labeled 1 and 2 in Fig. 1.9. The problem of multiplying two specific numbers (1285 and 57) has been generalized to the problem of multiplying two arbitrary numbers (Y and Z). The two views of the problem, one concrete and one general, represent two levels of abstraction. A solution to the general problem will be useful for any two numbers, not just for 1285 and 57. If you can develop a general solution, useful in many situations, it is usually worth it. Sometimes, however, a solution to a specific problem is needed and solving a general version would take too long or be too difficult.

To write a program for solving this general problem, we must develop an algorithm for multiplication. Consider multiplying rational numbers (fractions), integers, real numbers, and complex numbers as illustrated in Fig. 1.10.

You may not be familiar with each of these types of numbers, but each uses a different method for multiplication. If we're going to write a program to multiply, we'll need to determine what **type** of number is being used. The general form of $X \times Y$ can be used to express multiplication regardless of which type of number is multiplied. One of the advantages of C++ is that this conceptual similarity in notation is formalized in code: the same symbol, *, can be used to multiply many types of numbers.

In addition to the type of number, considerations in the development of the algorithm might include the size of the numbers being multiplied (an efficient algorithm would be more important if the numbers were hundreds of digits long as opposed to three digits long), how many times numbers will be multiplied, and whether the result of multiplying the numbers can exceed the memory constraints of the computer. Although it's impossible for numbers to get "too big" conceptually, the inherent finiteness of a computer's memory requires that a formal model of computation take this into account.

From algorithm to program.   In step 3 we translate the algorithm into the high-level language C++. The name *operator* * has been given to the C++ instructions that perform the multiplication. Translating the algorithm into code requires a knowledge of the programming language's syntax—the symbols and characters used in the language—as well as the meaning, or semantics, of these characters.

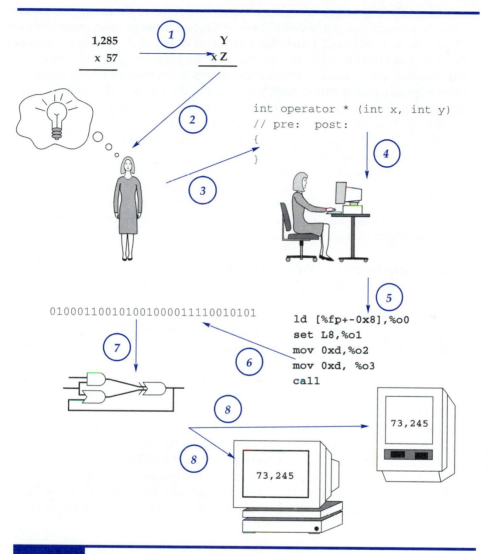

Figure 1.9   The steps of translation from problem to program.

Rational	Integer	Real	Complex
3/4*8/9	1,285*57	3.14*6.023	(3+5i)*(2-7i)
2/3	73,245	18.91222	41-11i

Figure 1.10   Multiplying different types of numbers.

Once the algorithm is represented in a high-level language, a program must be entered into a computer. Step 4 consists of more than merely typing characters at a keyboard. Often the realization of the algorithm as a computer program has errors that become apparent as the program is tested. Testing can indicate that errors exist; removing the errors is another problem. Errors are often euphemistically called *bugs*.[4] This makes the process of removing errors **debugging**. Testing and debugging can uncover errors in the original algorithm in addition to errors in the C++ representation of the algorithm.

As you become more experienced at programming you can employ techniques called **defensive programming**: attempting to ensure that your programs are robust and error-free as part of the design process rather than relying on testing and debugging exclusively. Many computer scientists are currently developing methods that will permit programs to be proved correct in the same manner that mathematical theorems are proved. Although we will not use such formal methods in our study, we introduce some of the techniques.

From high-level program to low-level program. In step 5, the high-level C++ program is translated into a lower-level language called **assembly language**. The name is derived from the notion of assembling the individual low-level instructions available on a particular computer into a form understandable by people. Although some programming is still done directly in assembly, the process of translation from high-level to low-level has been refined enough that programming at this level is often unnecessary.

Step 6 shows the translation of assembly language to **machine language**, the language of zeros and ones that a particular computer understands. Specific assembly language and machine language instructions differ according to the kind of computer being used (as shown in Fig. 1.8), as opposed to high-level languages like C++, which are the same on various computers. The process of translation illustrated by steps 5 and 6 is accomplished by a computer program called a **compiler** and the process is called **compiling**. A compiler translates code written in a high-level language into machine language. This translation process often includes an intermediate step in which the code is translated into assembly language.

Executing machine language. At the lowest level, the zeros and ones of machine language code cause switches to be turned on and off in the computer. These switches are extremely small and can be switched on and off quite rapidly. Technological advances have enabled transistors, which function as switches, to become increasingly smaller and faster. Switches are often represented by the diagrams in step 7.

---

[4]The derivation of the word *bug* is open to debate. Thomas Edison was reported to have discovered a "bug" in his phonograph in 1889. A literal example is the moth trapped in one of the first computers, the Harvard Mark II. The moth was placed into the system's logbook with the annotation "First actual case of bug being found" and is now on display in the Naval Museum in Dahlgren, Virginia.

The execution of a program is separate and different from the compilation of the program. Compiling a C++ program yields a low-level program, whereas executing a machine language program results in the computer performing the tasks represented by the compiled machine code.

Coming full circle: Displaying the results. Most current computers, and certainly the computers you will be using as you study computer science with this book, have

---

GRACE MURRAY HOPPER (1906–1992)

Figure 1.11   Grace Hopper.

Grace Hopper was one of the first programmers of the Harvard Mark I, the first programmable computer built in the United States. In her words she was "the third programmer on the world's first large-scale digital computer" [G95]. This work was done while she was in the Navy in the last years of World War II. It was while working on the Mark II that Hopper was involved with the first documented computer "bug": the famous moth inside one of the computer's relays that led to the use of the term *debugging*.

She developed the first compiler, called A-0, while working for Remington Rand in 1952. Until that time, many people believed that computers were only good for "number crunching," that computers were not capable of programming—which is what a compiler does: it produces a working program from a higher-level language.

Hopper returned to naval duty, after a period of retirement, in 1967, at the age of 60. She remained on active duty for 19 more years and was promoted to commodore in 1983 and to admiral in 1985.

She was a proponent of innovative thinking and kept a clock on her desk that ran counterclockwise to show that things could be done differently. Although very proud of her career in the Navy, Hopper had little tolerance for bureaucracies: "It's better to show that something can be done and apologize for not asking permission, than to try to persuade the powers that be at the beginning."

The Grace M. Hopper award for contributions to the field of computer science is given each year by the ACM (Association for Computing Machinery) for work done before the age of 30. In 1994 this award was given to Bjarne Stroustrup for his work in inventing and developing the language C++.

For more information see [Sla87], from which some of this biography is taken.

a screen to display what happens when a program is run. Whether the program is a word processor or a C++ program for multiplying numbers, output is generally displayed on the screen. Note that the screens on the computers in Figure 1.9 display the answer to the original problem: $1285 \times 57 = 73{,}245$.

1.5   Language and Program Design

One of the "eternal truths" of computer science and the computer industry is

Software is harder than hardware.

This statement means that new computers (hardware) are developed at a faster pace and more easily than new programs (software). There is certainly some truth to this, although new programming languages and new design methods have been developed in an attempt to alleviate this disparity. Many people believe that object-oriented programming, or OOP, will be of great assistance in making software easier to develop. OOP allows pieces of code to be reused in other contexts more easily. Computer scientists disagree about what OOP is and whether it is appropriate for use in an introductory course. By using a carefully chosen subset of C++, it is certainly possible to develop a mastery of basic programming concepts as well as an understanding and appreciation of OOP.

To try to understand what OOP is about, I use an analogy (suggested in [McC93]) that comes from construction (see Fig. 1.12). Suppose you decide to build a birdhouse; you can probably nail some boards together in a couple of hours and provide a useful dwelling for your favorite flyers. You may not put much thought into the design of the house, although if you don't you may waste some wood. (A carpenter's adage is "measure twice, cut once.") Next suppose you're designing a doghouse for your favorite pet. You might take more care; you're probably more concerned with whether Rover gets wet than whether your neighborhood bluejay is inconvenienced by rain. You may buy a kit—a precut set of materials and plans for constructing the doghouse. Nevertheless, this is probably a day-long project, *if* you're used to using saws and hammers.

What about building a house? If you've been involved with house building, you know that it can take a long time, requiring contractors, plumbers, electricians, and usually a lot of headaches. However, it is certainly possible to build a house yourself. Most of the pieces of a house come prebuilt. For houses that don't use prebuilt pieces and instead require custom manufacturing, the price of construction can be very high. Finally, consider building a skyscraper such as the Empire State Building. Such a building requires careful planning and is much more complex than a typical family dwelling. Yet hundreds of such tall buildings are designed and built each year.

Off-the-Shelf Components

Using off-the-shelf components is one of the reasons that constructing large buildings is possible. The phrase *off-the-shelf* is used to mean a component

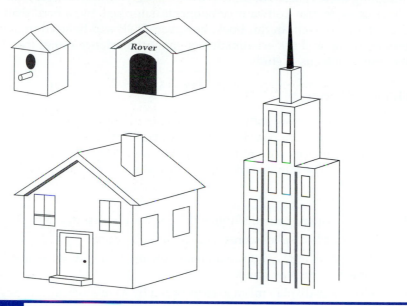

Figure 1.12   Birdhouses and skyscrapers.

that is manufactured in large quantity and that can be used in a variety of situations. Nails are no longer handcrafted by blacksmiths, and even houses can be purchased in a kit form. These components are often inexpensive but serve as well (or better) than custom-built components. The same is true of building computers. One of the reasons that computers get less expensive every year is that the pieces that make up a computer get cheaper as more are produced—this is sometimes called *economy of scale.* Viewed differently, the key is *not* to do all the work yourself but to use what others provide.

Of course, off-the-shelf components don't always work. A roof of a bird-house is different from the roof of the house you live in even though both share some common characteristics. It would be very useful to be able to order a standard roof, but then to be able to customize it easily to fulfill your specific needs.

In this book you will be using others' code in the writing of your own code, and you will be reusing the code you write for yet other programs. Code reuse is increasingly important, partly because of the graphical user interfaces (window systems) that are popular on computers. These interfaces are time-consuming to program but are very similar from program to program, so the potential for code reuse is great.

One of the goals of object-oriented programming is to provide **objects** to make code development easier. Objects are like off-the-shelf software compo-nents. You can imagine that using such objects might be much simpler than designing them yourself. Building a house from a kit is much simpler than designing the kit itself. The same is true of programming and program design—it's simpler to use software components supplied by others than to write everything yourself. In this book, however, OOP will be used in our study of programming and the examination of computer science rather than becoming the principal focus of study.

Using Components

As an example of how software components might be useful, consider digital clocks, electronic scoreboards, the display on a CD player, and a car's odometer. All of these devices require the display of numerals that are manipulated in some fashion. The numerals displayed are different according to how the device is used:

- Clocks display time; the numerals represent hours, minutes, seconds.
- Scoreboards display scores (points) as well as time.
- CD players display information on how many tracks are available on a CD (some also display time).
- Odometers display mileage as recorded by a car's wheels.

It should be possible for the computer programs controlling these displays to share (reuse) the code that displays numerals, differing only in how it is determined what numerals should be displayed and, perhaps, where the numerals are displayed.

Object-oriented programming involves reusable components. In C++ the word **class** refers to a family of components sharing common characteristics. A class allows **operations** that are used to manipulate the **objects** that are components of the class. For example, the class *four-door sedan* describes many makes and models of car. A specific four-door sedan, the one in my driveway, is an object of the generalized "four-door sedan class." All objects in this class share the common characteristic of having four doors and being sedans. They share other characteristics too, such as having a steering wheel, an engine, and four wheels. These characteristics are shared by all cars, not just four-door sedans. Operations allowed by the class *four-door sedan* include being driven, storing luggage, and consuming fuel.

As another example, the display of a numeral might be a different class than the value being displayed. A numeral display class might support operations such as assigning a value to be displayed and actually "drawing" the numeral. Other classes, such as a clock class or a timer class, could supply the values to be displayed. As an example of how simple it is to use such classes, repeated execution of the following C++ code generates a graphically displayed countdown timer.

```
num.SetValue(counter.GetValue());
num.Display();
counter.Tick();
```

The following displays appear as the program is run:

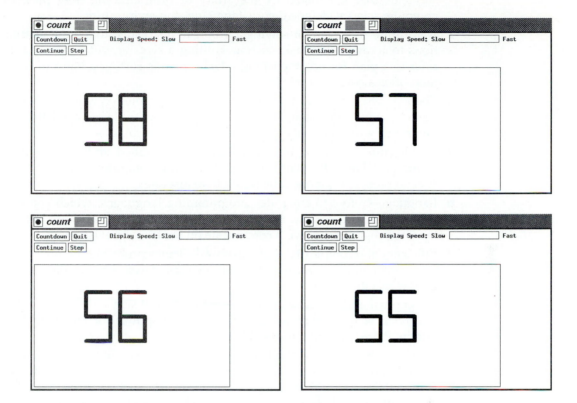

In the code fragment, *num* is a component, or object, of the display class. There are two operations that the display class allows: setting the value to be displayed and displaying the value. These are referred to in the code fragment by *SetValue* and *Display*, respectively. The component, or object, *counter* is from a countdown timer class. It is used with two of the operations it allows: *Tick* and *GetValue*. Each time the three statements above are executed, *num* will display a different value. This is because *Tick* will cause the counter to "tick," or change values, and because the value displayed is the one brought forth by *GetValue*, which obtains the value from the counter. At this point the details of C++ syntax are not important, but it is not too difficult to get some understanding of the code.

1.6 Chapter Review

This chapter provides an introduction to the field of computer science and places programming properly within the field. In subsequent chapters you'll begin the process of augmenting and constructing programs. The important concepts introduced in this chapter are outlined here.

- Computer science—is more than the study of computers. It includes many subfields that are linked by the study of programming. Key parts of computer science include theory, language, and architecture.

- Algorithm—is a plan for solving a problem. It's related to a set of instructions to accomplish a task, such as knitting a sweater, but we'll use it to refer to a plan for accomplishing a task, such as sorting a hand of cards (and often a computer will be involved).

- Theory—refers to underlying mathematical principles on which computer science is built. For example, being able to compare different algorithms to determine which is most efficient relies on theoretical tools.

- Architecture—refers to how a computer is designed and put together. Computers have different architectures: some computers rely on using several processors at one time rather than just one.

- Language—refers to computer programming languages, which come in many forms and flavors. Both high- and low-level languages are used in writing programs, but we'll concentrate on the high-level language C++.

- Efficiency and complexity—refer to how difficult a problem is to solve using a computer and how various algorithms compare in solving problems (e.g., in how fast they run).

- Conceptual and formal models—refer to different ways of thinking. Programs can be thought of as instructions for a computer, but a mathematical notion of programming is possible too.

- Levels of abstraction—refer to different ways of observing. An idea can be turned into an algorithm, which is implemented as a C++ program, which is executed as a machine-language program. The same idea is viewed at many different levels and has particular characteristics depending on the level.

- Compiler—is a computer program that translates a high-level language such as C++ into a low-level language that can be executed on a computer.

- Bug—is a mistake in a program. Finding such mistakes is called debugging.

- Object-oriented programming—is a method of programming that, in a nutshell, relies on the use of off-the-shelf software components.

- Class—is a family of objects sharing common characteristics. The integers are a class of numbers; four-door sedans are a class of cars.

1.7   Exercises

1.1 The process of looking up a word in a dictionary is difficult to describe in a precise manner. Write an algorithm that can be used to find the *page* in a dictionary on which a given word occurs (if the word is in the dictionary). You may assume that each page of the dictionary has guide words indicating the first and last words on the page, but you should assume that there are no thumb indices on the pages (so you cannot turn immediately to a specific letter section).

1.2 Suppose that you have 10 loads of laundry, one washer, and one dryer. Washing a load takes 25 minutes, drying a load takes 25 minutes, and folding the clothes in

BJARNE STROUSTRUP (b. 195?)

Bjarne Stroustrup is truly the "father" of C++. He began its design in 1979 and is still involved with both design and implementation of the language. His interests span computer science, history, and literature. In his own words:

> ...C++ owes as much to novelists and essayists such as Martin A. Hansen, Albert Camus, and George Orwell, who never saw a computer, as it does to computer scientists such as David Gries, Don Knuth, and Roger Needham. Often, when I was tempted to outlaw a feature I personally disliked, I refrained from doing so because I did not think I had the right to force my views on others.

Stroustrup notes that it is as difficult to define what a programming language is as to define computer science.

> Is a programming language a tool for instructing machines? A means of communicating between programmers? A vehicle for expressing high-level designs? A notation for algorithms? A way of expressing relationships between concepts? A tool for experimentation? A means of controlling computerized devices? My view is that a general-purpose programming language must be all of those to serve its diverse set of users.

> For his work in the design of C++, Stroustrup was awarded the 1994 ACM Grace Murray Hopper award, given for fundamental contributions made to computer science by work done before the age of 30. Most of this material is taken from [Str94].

a load takes 10 minutes, for a total of 1 hour per load (assuming that the time to transfer a load is built into the timings given.) All the laundry can be done in 10 hours using the method of completing one load before starting the next one. Devise a method for doing all 10 loads in less than 10 hours by making better use of the resources. Carefully describe the method and how long it takes to do the laundry using the method.

1.3 Suppose that student ID numbers consist of two digits. The exams are sorted in a large room. Consider the following description of a sorting algorithm:

> Make 100 "in-boxes" labeled 00 to 99.
> Divide the exams among the people participating in the sort.
> Have each person put an exam in the correct box according to ID number.
> Collect the exams from the boxes in order (00–99).

This method will work correctly. Try to modify the method to work with four-digit ID numbers and six-digit ID numbers. In making the modification, assume you have only 100 boxes. (Hint: Consider examining only two digits at a time.)

1.4 The steps labeled 1–7 in Fig. 1.9 illustrate the design, development, realization, and implementation of a computer program to multiply two numbers. Consider the following problem:

> **Develop a recipe for a chocolate cake with chocolate icing that tastes delicious and makes you swoon.**

Develop analogs or parallels to the steps 1–7 for developing such a recipe. Write a detailed description of the process you might go through to develop a recipe—*not* what the recipe is.

1.5 Assume that a young friend of yours knows how to multiply any two one-digit numbers (i.e., knows the times tables). Write an explanation (algorithm) of how to multiply an *n*-digit number by a one-digit number. Can you extend this algorithm into one that can be used to multiply two many-digit numbers (such as 1285 and 57, as shown in Fig. 1.9)?

1.6 There are many different high-level programming languages. Common languages include Pascal, FORTRAN, Scheme, BASIC, and COBOL. Can you think of a reason as to why there are many languages as opposed to a single language? Why is more than one language in use today?

1.7 (Suggested by a description in *Computer Architecture*, by Blaauw and Brooks.) Consider clocks and watches as examples of different "architectures" used for telling time. For clocks and watches that have hands and dials, write an outline of an algorithm that can be used to tell time. How is the architecture of a wristwatch (with hands) similar to that of a grandfather clock? How is it different? What features of the face of a watch are essential for telling time? In particular, are numbers needed on the face of a watch in order to tell time? Make a listing of different watch faces and try to distill the essential features of a watch face into a few descriptive sentences.

Consider the inner workings of watches: list at least three different methods used to "run" a watch. How are different levels of abstraction illustrated by the concept of a watch?

How is a digital watch different from a watch with hands? How is it similar?

1.8 C++ (and other high-level language) programs are written in a language that is a compromise between natural languages such as English and the language of zeros and ones, which is "spoken" by computers. Consider musical compositions written for different instruments or groups of musicians. Is music written in a high-level language or a low-level language? Are there different languages for expressing musical compositions as there are different natural languages and different computer languages? Why?

1.9 Suppose that you are playing in a large field with several friends and one of you discovers that a house key has been lost. Write an algorithm for finding the key that is designed to find it as quickly as possible. Write another algorithm designed to take a long time to find the key. Can you reason about whether your algorithms are the best possible or worst possible algorithms for this particular task?

How is this task related to how you look for a key when you have misplaced it inside your house?

1.10 The code below on the left is generated on a Sun SPARCstation using the g++ compiler, as is the code on the left side of Fig. 1.8. The code on the right below is generated using a different compiler on the same workstation. The code on the left is generated with the *optimize* option to the compiler set. This option causes the compiler to try to generate more "intelligent" code. The compilation process takes longer, but the resulting code may run faster.

What is similar in these two versions of g++-generated assembly code and what is different? Can you find instructions that would be common to all the different assembly codes? Why do you think different compilers generate different code for the same program (even on the same machine)?

```
_main:                                      _main:
        call ___main,0                              call      __main,0
        mov 0,%i0                                   nop
        sethi %hi(_cin),%o0                         sub       %fp,0x4,%o1
        or %o0,%lo(_cin),%o0                        set       _cin,%o0
        call ___rs__FR7istreamRi,0                  call      ___rs__7istreamFRi,2
        add %fp,-20,%o1                             nop
        call ___rs__FR7istreamRi,0                  sub       %fp,0x8,%o1
        add %fp,-24,%o1                             call      ___rs__7istreamFRi,2
        ld [%fp-20],%o0                             nop
        call .umul,0                                ld        [%fp+-0x4],%o0
        ld [%fp-24],%o1                             ld        [%fp+-0x8],%o1
        mov %o0,%o1                                 call      .mul,2
        sethi %hi(_cout),%o0                        nop
        call ___ls__FR7ostreaml,0                   st        %o0,[%fp+-0xc]
        or %o0,%lo(_cout),%o0                       set       _cout,%o0
                                                    ld        [%fp+-0xc],%o1
                                                    call      ___ls__7ostreamFi,2
                                                    nop
```

1.11 The cards that were used in the context of sorting in this chapter (ace, king, queen, etc.) provide a good example of an object. If a card is one object, and a hand and deck are other objects composed of card objects, list a few operations that might be useful in manipulating cards, hands, and decks.

1.12 Vending machines are objects composed of several different objects. Pick a specific kind of vending machine and list several objects that are used to "make up" the vending machine (e.g., buttons used to specify items to be bought). For each object, and for the vending machine as a whole, list several operations that might be useful in reasoning about or manipulating the objects.

Are there some characteristics that all vending machines have in common? Are there classes of vending machines, each of which differs fundamentally from other kinds of vending machines?

PART I

FOUNDATIONS OF C++ PROGRAMMING

C++ Programs: Form and Function

Scientists build to learn; engineers learn to build.
FRED BROOKS

tem·plate (tĕm′ plĭt) *n.* A pattern, . . . used as a guide in making something accurately . . .
The American Heritage Dictionary

Art is the imposing of a pattern on experience, and our aesthetic enjoyment in recognition of the pattern.
Dialogues of Alfred North Whitehead (June 10, 1943)

It is a bad plan that admits of no modification.
Publilius Syrus, Maxim 469

To learn to write programs, you must write programs and you must read programs. Although this statement may not seem profound, it is a lesson that is often left unpracticed and, subsequently, unmastered. In thinking about the concepts presented in this chapter, and in practicing them in the context of writing C++ programs, you should keep the following three things in mind.

1. Programming has elements of both art and science. Just as designing a building requires both a sense of aesthetics and a knowledge of structural engineering, designing a program requires an understanding of programming aesthetics, knowledge of computer science, and practice in software engineering.

2. Use the programs provided as templates when designing and constructing programs of your own—use what's provided along with your own ingenuity. When some concept is unclear, stop to work on it and think about it before continuing. This work will involve experimenting with the

programs provided. Experimenting with a program means reading, executing, testing, and modifying the program. When you experiment with a program, you can try to find its weak points and its strengths.

3. Practice.

This book is predicated on the belief that you learn best by doing new things and by studying things similar to the new things. This technique applies to learning carpentry, learning to play a musical instrument, or learning to program a computer. Not everyone can win a Grammy award and not everyone can win the Turing award,[1] but becoming adept programmers and practitioners of computer science is well within your grasp.

Ultimately programs are a means of expressing algorithms in a form that computers execute. Before studying complicated and large programs, it's necessary to begin with the basics of what a program is, how programs are executed, and what C++ programs can do. However, understanding a program *completely* requires a great deal of experience and knowledge about C++. We'll use some simple programs to illustrate basic concepts. Try to focus on the big picture of programming; don't get bogged down by every detail. The details will eventually become clearer, and you'll master them by studying many programming examples.

2.1   Simple C++ Programs

In this section we introduce simple C++ programs to demonstrate how to use the C++ language. These programs produce **output**; they cause characters to be displayed on a computer screen. The first C++ program is *hello.cc*, Prog. 2.1. This program is based on the first program in the book [KR78], written by the inventors of C; and it is the first program in [Str87], written by the inventor of C++. It doesn't convey the power of C++, but it's a tradition for C and C++ programmers to begin with this program.

All programs have names, in this case *hello*, and suffixes, in this case *.cc*. In this book all programs have the suffix *.cc*, which is one convention (other suffixes used include *.cpp* and *.cxx*). In a Windows/DOS/Macintosh environment the suffix *.cpp* is normally used. If this program is compiled and executed, it generates the material shown in the box labeled "output."

Program 2.2, *hello2.cc*, produces output identical to that of Prog. 2.1. We'll look at why one of these versions might be preferable as we examine the structure of C++ programs. In general, given a specific programming task there are many, many different programs that will perform the task.

Syntax and Semantics

Programs are run by computers, not by humans. There is often much less room for error when writing programs than when writing English. In particular,

---

[1]The former is awarded for musical excellence, the latter for excellence in computer science.

Program 2.1   hello.cc

```cpp
#include <iostream.h>

//traditional first program
// author: Owen Astrachan, 12/28/93
//          modified          12/29/95

int main()
{
    cout << "Hello world" << endl;

    return 0;
}
```

OUTPUT

```
prompt> hello
Hello world
```

Program 2.2   hello2.cc

```cpp
#include <iostream.h>

// traditional first program
// uses user-defined function
// author: Owen Astrachan, 12/28/93
//          modified          12/29/95
void
Hello()
{
    cout << "Hello world" << endl;
}

int main()
{
    Hello();

    return 0;
}
```

hello2.cc

DENNIS RITCHIE (b. 1941)

Dennis Ritchie developed the C programming language and codeveloped the UNIX operating system. For his work with UNIX, he shared the 1983 Turing award with the codeveloper, Ken Thompson. In his Turing address, Ritchie writes of what computer science is.

> Computer science research is different from these [physics, chemistry, mathematics] more traditional disciplines. Philosophically it differs from the physical sciences because it seeks not to discover, explain, or exploit the natural world, but instead to study the properties of machines of human creation. In this it is analogous to mathematics, and indeed the "science" part of computer science is, for the most part, mathematical in spirit. But an inevitable aspect of computer science is the creation of computer programs: objects that, though intangible, are subject to commercial exchange.

Ritchie completed his doctoral dissertation in applied mathematics but didn't earn his doctorate because "I was so bored, I never turned it in." In citing the work that led to the Turing award, the selection committee mentions this:

> The success of the UNIX system stems from its tasteful selection of a few key ideas and their elegant implementation. The model of the UNIX system has led a generation of software designers to new ways of thinking about programming.

For more information see [Sla87, ACM87].

you'll need to be aware of certain rules that govern the use of C++. These rules fall into two broad categories: rules of syntax and rules of semantics.

What are syntax and semantics? In English and other natural languages, syntax is the manner in which words are used to construct sentences and semantics is the meaning of the sentences. We'll see that similar definitions apply to syntax and semantics in C++ programs. Before reviewing rules for C++ programs, we'll look at some rules that govern the use and construction of English words and sentences:

■ Rules of spelling:

> *i* before *e* except after *c* or when sounding like $\bar{a}$ as in . . . *neighbor* and *weigh*.

■ Rules of grammar:

> "with *none* use the singular verb when the word means 'no one' . . . a plural verb is commonly used when *none* suggests more than one thing or person—'None are so fallible as those who are sure they're right' " [SW89].

■ Rules of style:

> "Avoid the use of qualifiers. *Rather, very, little, pretty*—these are the leeches that infest the pond of prose, sucking the blood of words" [SW89].

Similar rules exist in C++. One difference between English and C++ is that the meaning, or **semantics,** of a poorly constructed English sentence can be understood although the syntax is incorrect:

> Its inconceivable that someone can study a language and not know whether or not a kind of sentence—the ungainly ones, the misspelled ones, those that are unclear—are capable of understanding.

This sentence has at least four errors in spelling, grammar, and style; its meaning, however, is still discernible.

In general, programming languages demand more precision than do natural languages such as English. A missing semicolon might make an English sentence fall into the run-on category. A missing semicolon in a C++ program can stop the program from working at all.

We'll illustrate the important syntactic details of a C++ program by studying *hello.cc* and *hello2.cc*, Progs. 2.1 and 2.2. We'll then extend these into a typical and general program framework. Four rules for C++ program syntax and style will also be listed. A useful tool for checking the syntax of programs is the C++ compiler, which indicates whether a program has the correct form— that is, whether the program statements are "worded correctly." You should *not* worry about memorizing the syntactic details of C++ (e.g., where semicolons go). The details of the small subset of C++ covered in this chapter will become second nature as you read and write programs.

All the C++ programs we'll study in this book have the format shown in Fig. 2.1 and explained below. Although this format will be used, the spacing of each line in a program does not affect whether a program works. The amount of **white space** and the blank lines between functions help make programs easier for humans to read but do not affect how a program works. *White space* is a general term that in computer science refers to the space, tab, and return keys.

1. Programs begin with the appropriate #include statements.[2] Each include statement provides access, via a **header** file with a .h suffix, to a **library** of useful functions. We normally think of a library as a place from which we can borrow books. A programming library consists of off-the-shelf programming tools that programmers can borrow. These tools are used by programmers to make the task of writing programs easier.

    In most C++ programs it is necessary to import information from such libraries into the program. In particular, the information necessary for output (and input) is stored in the iostream library, accessible by including the header file <iostream.h>, as shown in Fig. 2.1. If a

---

[2]The # sign is read as either "sharp" or "pound"; I usually say "pound-include" when reading to myself or talking with others.

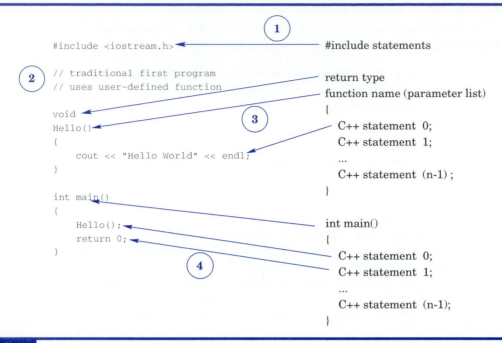

Figure 2.1   Format of a C++ program.

program performs no output (and no input), it isn't necessary to include `<iostream.h>`.

2. All programs should include comments describing the purpose of the program. As programs get more complex, the comments become more intricate. For the simple programs studied in this chapter, the comments are brief. The compiler ignores comments; programmers put comments in programs for human readers. C++ comments extend from a double slash, `//`, to the end of the line. Another style of commenting permits multiline comments—any text between `/*` and `*/` is treated as a comment. It's important to remember that people read programs, so writing comments should be considered mandatory although programs will work without them.

3. Zero, one, or more **programmer-defined** functions follow the `#include` statements and comments. Prog. 2.2, *hello2.cc,* has two programmer-defined functions, named `Hello` and `main`. Prog. 2.1, *hello.cc,* has one programmer-defined function, named `main`. In general, a function is a way of grouping C++ statements together so that they can be referred to by a single name. The function is an abstraction used in place of the statements. As shown in Fig. 2.1, each user-defined function consists of the function's **return type,** the function's **name,** the function's **parameter list,** and the statements that make up the function's **body.** For the function `Hello` the return type is `void`, the name of the function is `Hello`, and there is an empty parameter list. There is only one C++ statement in `Hello`.

The return type of the function main is int. In C++, an int represents an integer; we'll discuss this in detail later. The name of the function is main and it too has an empty parameter list. There are two statements in the function body; the second statement is return 0. We'll also discuss the return statement in some detail later. The last statement in the function main of each program you write should be return 0.

4. Every C++ program must have exactly one function named **main.** The statements in main are executed first when a program is run. Some C++ compilers will generate a warning if the statement return 0 is not included as the last statement in main (such statements are explained in the next chapter). It's important to spell main with lowercase letters. A function named Main is different from main because names are case-sensitive in C++. Finally, the return type of main should be specified as int for reasons we'll explore in Chapter 4.[3]

Since program execution begins with main, it is a good idea to start reading a program beginning with main when you are trying to understand what the program does and how it works.

Pause to reflect

2.1. Find four errors in the ungainly sentence given above whose semantics (meaning) is understandable despite the errors. Are humans better "processors" than computers because of the ability to comprehend "faulty" phrases? Explain your answer.

2.2. Find two syntax errors and one semantic error in the sentence "There is three things worng with this sentence."

2.3. Given the four rules for C++ programs, what is the smallest legal C++ program? (Hint: it doesn't produce any output, so it doesn't need a #include statement.)

2.4. No rules are given about using separate lines for C++ functions and statements. What happens if the main function is changed as shown below? Are the rules given above violated? Will this program compile and execute?

```
int main () { Hello(); return 0; }
```

2.2 How a Program Works

Computer programs execute sequences of statements often producing some form of output. Statements are executed whether the program is written in a high- or low-level language. Determining what statements to include in a program is part of the art and science of programming. Developing algorithms and classes, and the relationship between classes, is also part of this art and science.

---

[3]Some books use a return type of void for main. According to the C++ standard, this is not legal; the return type *must* be int.

OUTPUT

```
Goodbye cruel planet
```

Figure 2.2   Output from modified *hello.cc.*

When you execute a program, either by typing the name of the program at a prompt or using a mouse to click on "run" in a menu, the execution starts in the function `main`. When the program is running it uses the processor of the computer; when the program is finished it returns control of the processor to the operating system. The explicit `return  0` statement in `main` makes it clear that control is returning to the operating system.

The output of Prog. 2.1, *hello.cc,* results from the execution of the statement beginning `cout  <<` followed by other characters, followed by other symbols. This statement is in the body of the function `main`. The characters between the double quotation marks appear on the screen exactly as they appear between the quotes in the statement. (Notice that the quotes do not appear on the screen.) If the statement

```
cout << "Hello world" << endl;
```

is changed to

```
cout << "Goodbye cruel planet" << endl;
```

then execution of the program *hello.cc* results in the output shown in Fig. 2.2.

Flow of Control

In every C++ program, execution begins with the first statement in the function `main`. After this statement is executed, each statement in `main` is executed in turn. When the last statement has been executed, the program is done. Several uses of `<<` can be combined into a single statement as shown in *hello.cc,* Prog. 2.1. Note that `endl` indicates that an end-of-line is to be output (hence "end ell"). For example, if the statement

```
cout << "Hello world" << endl;
```

is changed to

```
cout << "Goodbye" << endl << "cruel planet" << endl;
```

then execution of the program *hello.cc* results in the output shown in Fig. 2.3, where the first `endl` forces a new line of output. This modified output could be generated by using two separate output statements:

```
cout << "Goodbye" << endl;
cout << "cruel planet" << endl;
```

Since each statement is executed one after the other, the output generated will be the same as that shown in Fig. 2.3.

Figure 2.3   Output from (newly) modified *hello.cc.*

In C++, statements are terminated by a semicolon. This means that a single statement can extend over several lines since the semicolon is used to determine when the statement ends.

```
cout << "Goodbye"        << endl
     << "cruel planet" << endl;
```

Just as run-on sentences in English can obscure the meaning, long statements in C++ can be hard to read. Keeping statements on one line when possible is a good programming rule-of-thumb.

Function calls. If a statement invokes, or **calls**, a function—such as when the statement Hello(); in main invokes the function Hello in Prog. 2.2—then each of the statements in the called function is executed. For example, while the statements in the function Hello are executing, the statements in main are suspended, waiting for the statements in Hello to finish. When all the statements in a function have executed, **control** returns to the statement after the call to the function. In Prog. 2.2 this is the statement return 0 after the function call Hello(). When the last statement in a program has executed, control returns from main to the computer just as control returns from Hello to main when the last statement in Hello is executed. If the return 0 statement in main is missing, control will still return to the computer.

In the case of Prog. 2.2, three statements are executed:

1. the call Hello(); in the function main
2. the statement cout << "Hello World" << endl; in the function Hello
3. the statement return 0; in main

The execution of the second statement above results in the appearance of 11 "visible" characters on the computer's screen (note that a space is a character just as the letter *H* is a character).

Output streams. To display output, the **standard output stream** cout is used. This stream is accessible in a program via the included library <iostream.h>. If this header file is not included, a program cannot make reference to the stream cout. You can think of an output stream as a stream of objects in the same way that a brook or a river is a stream of water. Placing objects on the output stream causes them to appear on the screen eventually just as placing a toy boat on a stream of water causes it to flow downstream. Objects are placed on the output stream using <<, the **insertion operator,** so named since it is used to insert values onto an output stream. Sometimes this operator is read as "put-to." The word cout is pronounced "see-out."

2.3   What Can Be Output?

Computers were originally developed as number crunchers, machines used for solving large systems of equations. Not surprisingly, numbers still play a large part in programming and computer science. The output stream cout can be used for the output of numbers and words. In Prog. 2.1 characters appeared on the screen as a result of executing statements that use the standard output stream cout. Sequences of characters appearing between quotes are called **string literals.** Characters include letters a–z (and uppercase versions), numbers, symbols such as !+$%&*, and many other nonvisible "characters," such as the backspace key, the return key, and in general any key that can be typed from a computer keyboard. String literals cannot change during a program's execution. The number 3.14159 is a numeric literal (it approximates the number π). In addition to string literals, it is possible to output numeric literals and arithmetic expressions. For example, if the statement

```
cout << "Hello world" << endl;
```

is changed to

```
cout << "Goodbye" << endl << "cruel planet #" << 1 + 2 << endl;
```

then execution of the program *hello.cc* results in the output shown in Fig. 2.4. The arithmetic expression 1 + 2 is evaluated and 3, the result of the evaluation, is placed on the output stream. To be more precise, each of the chunks that follow a << are evaluated and cause the output stream to be modified in some way. The string literal "Goodbye" evaluates to itself and is placed on the output stream as seven characters. The arithmetic expression 1 + 2 evaluates to 3, and the character 3 is placed on the output stream. Each endl begins a new line on the output stream.[4]

The C++ compiler ensures that arithmetic expressions are evaluated correctly and, with the help of the stream library, ensures that the appropriate characters are placed on the output stream.

Changing the output statement in *hello.cc* to the statement below results in the output shown in Fig. 2.5. The symbol * is used to multiply two values, and the number 0.62137 is the number of miles in 1 kilometer.

---

[4]An endl also flushes the output buffer. Some programmers think it is bad programming to flush the output buffer just to begin a new line of output. The escape sequence \n can be used to start a new line.

OUTPUT

```
Goodbye
cruel planet #3
```

Figure 2.4   Output from modified *hello.cc.*

OUTPUT

```
The radius of planet #3 is 6378.38 km
which is 3963.33 miles,
```

Figure 2.5   Output from further modified *hello.cc.*

```
cout << "The radius of planet #" << 1+2
     << " is " << 6378.38 << " km," << endl
     << "which is " << 6378.38 * 0.62137 << " miles" << endl;
```

The capability of the output stream to handle strings, numbers, and other objects we will encounter later makes it very versatile.

Pause to reflect

2.5. Suppose that the body of the function `Hello` is as shown here:

```
cout << "PI = " << 3.14159 << endl;
```

What appears on the screen? Would the output of

```
cout << "PI = 3.14159" << endl;
```

be the same or different?

2.6. We've noted that more than one statement may appear in a function body:

```
void
Hello()
{
    cout << "PI  = " << 3.14159 << endl;
    cout << "e   = " << 2.71828 << endl;
    cout << "PI*e = " << 3.14159 * 2.71828 << endl;
}
```

What appears on the screen if the function `Hello` above is executed?

2.7. If the third `cout` `<<` statement in the previous problem is changed to

```
cout << "PI*e = 3.14159 * 2.71828" << endl;
```

what appears on the screen? Note that this statement puts a single string literal onto the output stream (followed by an `endl`). Why is this output different from the output in the previous question?

2.8. What does the computer display when the statement

```
cout << "1 + 2 = 5" << endl;
```

is executed? Can a computer generate output that is incorrect?

2.9. What modifications need to be made to the output statement in Prog. 2.1 (the *hello.cc* program) to generate the following output:

```
I think I think, therefore I think I am
```

2.10. All statements in C++ are terminated by a semicolon. Is the user-defined function

```
void
Hello()
{
    cout << "Hello World" << endl;
}
```

a statement? Why? Is the function call `Hello()` in `main` a statement?

2.11. If body of the function `main` of Prog. 2.2 is changed as shown in the following, what appears on the screen?

```
cout << "I rode the scrambler at the amusement park"
     << endl; Hello();
```

2.4   Using Functions

The flow of control in *hello.cc*, Prog. 2.1, is different from *hello2.cc*, Prog. 2.2. The use of the function `Hello` in *hello2.cc* doesn't make the program better or more powerful; it just increases the number of statements that are executed: a function call as well as an output statement. In this section we'll explore programs that use functions in more powerful ways. I say *powerful* in that the resulting programs are easier to modify and are useful in more applications than when functions are not used. Using functions can make programs longer and appear to be more complicated, but sometimes more complicated programs are preferred because they are more general and are easier to modify and maintain. Using functions to group statements together is part of managing the complex task of programming.

We'll now investigate Prog. 2.3 (*makehead.cc*) in which several `cout <<` statements are used in the user-defined function `Head`. In *makehead.cc* the body of the main function consists of a call of the user-defined function `Head` and the statement `return 0`.

For the moment we will assume that all user-defined functions are constructed similarly to the manner in which the function `main` is constructed except that the word `void` is used before each user-defined function. This

<hr>

Program 2.3   makehead.cc

<hr>

```
#include <iostream.h>

// print a head, use of functions

void
Head()
{
    cout << "  ||||||||||||||||||  " << endl;
    cout << "  |                |  " << endl;
    cout << "  |    o    o      |  " << endl;
    cout << "  _|              |_ " << endl;
    cout << " |_            _| " << endl;
    cout << "  |   |_____|    |  " << endl;
    cout << "  |              |  " << endl;

}

int main()
{
    Head();
    return 0;
}
```

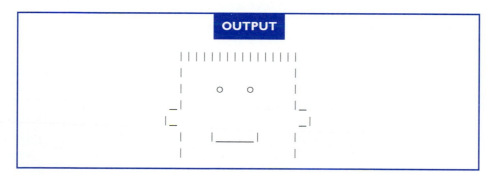

OUTPUT

is precisely how the syntactic properties of functions were given in Sec. 2.1. The word void will be replaced with other words in later examples of user-defined functions; for example, we've seen that int is used with the function main.

At this point the usefulness of functions may not be apparent in the programs we've presented. In the program *parts.cc* that appears as Prog. 2.4, many functions are used. If this program is run, the output is the same as the output generated when *makehead.cc*, Prog. 2.3, is run. The usefulness of functions should become more apparent when the body of main is modified to generate new "heads." This program is longer than the previous programs and may be harder for you to understand. You should begin reading the program starting with the function main. Starting with main you can then move to

Program 2.4   parts.cc

```
#include <iostream.h>

// procedures used to print different heads

void
PartedHair()
// prints a "parted hair" scalp
{
    cout << "  ||||||||/////////// " << endl;
}

void
Hair()
// prints a "straight-up" or "frightened" scalp
{
cout << "  |||||||||||||||||  " << endl;
}

void
Sides()
// prints sides of a head -- other functions should use distance
// between sides of head here as guide in creating head parts (e.g., eyes)
{
    cout << "  |                |  " << endl;
}

void
Eyes()
// prints eyes of a head (corresponding to distance in Sides)
{
    cout << "  |    o    o    |  " << endl;
}

void
Ears()
// prints ears (corresponding to distance in Sides)
{
    cout << " _|                |_ " << endl;
    cout << "|_                _|" << endl;
}

void
Smile()
// prints smile (corresponding to distance in Sides)
{
    cout << "  |    |_____|    |  " << endl;
}

int main()
{
    Hair();
    Sides();
    Eyes();
    Ears();
    Smile();
    Sides();
    return 0;
}
```

```
int main()
{
    Hair();
    Sides(); Sides(); Sides();
    Eyes();
    Ears();
    Smile();
    Sides(); Sides(); Sides();
    return 0;
}
```

OUTPUT

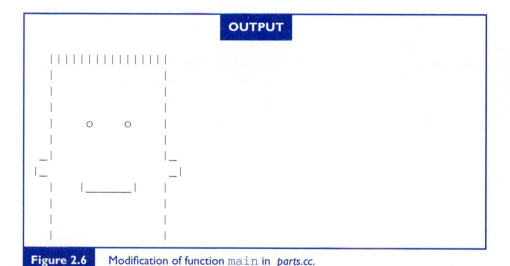

Figure 2.6   Modification of function `main` in *parts.cc*.

reading the functions called from `main`, and the functions that these functions call, and so on. If each call of the function `Sides` in the body of `main` is replaced with three calls to `Sides`, then the new body of `main` and the output generated by the body are as shown in Fig. 2.6. Although *parts.cc*, Prog. 2.4, is more complicated than *makehead.cc*, Prog. 2.3, it is easier to modify. Creating heads with different hairstyles or adding a nose is easier when *parts.cc* is used, because it is clear where the changes should be made because of the names of the functions. It's also possible not only to have more than one hairstyle appear in the same program, but to change what is displayed. For example, adding a nose can be done using a function `Nose`:

```
        void Nose()
        // draw a mustached nose
        {
            cout << "  |        O        |  " << endl;
            cout << "  |      |||||      |  " << endl;
        }
```

On the other hand, the original program clearly showed what the printed head looks like; it's not necessary to run the program to see this. As you gain experience as a programmer, your judgment as to when to use functions will get better.

Pause to reflect

2.12. If you replace the call to the function Hair by a call to the function PartedHair, what kind of picture is output? How can one of the hair functions be modified to generate a flat head with no hair on it? What picture results if the call Hair() is replaced by Smile()?

2.13. Design a new function named Bald that gives the head drawn the appearance of baldness (perhaps a few tufts of hair on the side are appropriate).

2.14. Modify the function Smile so that the face either frowns or shows no emotion. Change the name of the function appropriately.

2.15. What functions should be changed to produce the head shown below? Modify the program to draw such a head.

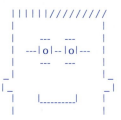

2.5   Functions with Parameters

Program 2.4, *parts.cc*, showed that the use of user-defined functions enabled the program to be more versatile than the program *makehead.cc*. Nevertheless, the program had to be reedited and recompiled to produce new "heads." In this section and the next chapter, you will learn design methods that allow programs to be useful in more contexts.

What Is a Parameter?

In all the programs studied so far, the insertion operator << has been more useful than any user-defined function. The insertion operator is versatile because it can be used to write *any message* to the screen. Any sequence of characters between quotes (recall that such a sequence is termed a string literal) and any arithmetic expression can be inserted onto an output stream using the << operator.

- ```
  cout << "Hello world" << endl;
  ```
- ```
  cout << "Goodbye cruel planet" << endl;
  ```

- `cout << " ||||||||///////// " << endl;`
- `cout << "The square of 10 is " << 10*10 << endl;`

The $<<$ operator can be used to output various things just as the addition operator + can be used to add them. It's possible to write user-defined functions that have this same kind of versatility. You've probably used a calculator with a square root button: $\sqrt{}$. When you find the square root of a number using this button, you're invoking the square root function with an **argument**. In the mathematical expression $\sqrt{101}$, the 101 is the argument of the square root function. Functions that take arguments are called **parameterized functions.** The parameters serve as a means of controlling what the functions do—setting a different parameter results in a different outcome just as $\sqrt{101}$ has a different value than $\sqrt{157}$. The words *parameter* and *argument* are synonyms in this context.

To see how parameters are useful in making functions more general, consider an (admittedly somewhat loose) analogy to a CD player. It is conceivable that one might put a CD of Gershwin's *Rhapsody in Blue* in such a machine and then glue the machine shut. From that point on, the machine becomes a "Gershwin player" rather than a CD player. One can also purchase a "weather box," which is a radio permanently tuned to a weather information service. Although interesting for determining whether to carry an umbrella, the weather box is less general-purpose than a normal (tunable) radio in the same way that the Gershwin player is less versatile than a normal CD player. In the same sense, the $<<$ operator is more versatile than the Head function in Prog. 2.3, which always draws the same head.

Functions with parameters are more versatile than functions without parameters although there are times when both kinds of function are useful. Functions that receive parameters must receive the correct kind of parameter or they will not execute properly (often such functions will not compile). Continuing with the CD analogy, suppose that you turn on a CD player with no CD in it. Obviously nothing will be played. Similarly, if it were possible to put a cassette tape into a CD player without damaging the player, the CD player would not be able to play the cassette. Finally, if a 2.5-inch mini-CD is forced into a normal CD player, still nothing is played. The point of this example is that the "parameterized" CD player must be used properly—the appropriate "parameter" (a CD, not a cassette or mini-CD) must be used if the player is to function as intended.

An Example of Parameterization: Happy Birthday

Suppose you are faced with the unenviable task of writing a program that displays the song "Happy Birthday" to a set of quintuplets named Grace, Alan, John, Ada, and Blaise.[5] The desired output is reproduced in Fig. 2.7. In designing the program, we employ a concept called **iterative enhancement**, whereby a

---

[5]Coincidentally, these are the first names of five pioneers in computer science: Grace Hopper, Alan Turing, John von Neumann, Ada Lovelace, and Blaise Pascal.

OUTPUT

```
Happy birthday to you.
Happy birthday to you.
Happy birthday dear Grace.
Happy birthday to you.

Happy birthday to you.
Happy birthday to you.
Happy birthday dear Alan.
Happy birthday to you.

Happy birthday to you.
Happy birthday to you.
Happy birthday dear John.
Happy birthday to you.

Happy birthday to you.
Happy birthday to you.
Happy birthday dear Ada.
Happy birthday to you.

Happy birthday to you.
Happy birthday to you.
Happy birthday dear Blaise.
Happy birthday to you.
```

Figure 2.7   "Happy Birthday" for quintuplets.

---

rough draft of the program is repeatedly refined until the desired program is finished.

A naive, first attempt with this problem might consist of 24 cout << statements; that is, 5 "verses" × 4 lines per verse + 4 blank lines (note that there is one blank line between each verse so that there is one less blank line than there are verses). Such a program would yield the desired output—but even without much programming experience this solution should be unappealing to you. Indeed, the effort required to generate a new verse in such a program is the same as the effort required to generate a verse in the original program. Nevertheless, such a program has at least one important merit: it is easy to make work. Even though "cut-and-paste" techniques are available in most text editors, it is very likely that you will introduce typos using this approach.

We want to develop a program that mirrors the way people sing "Happy Birthday." You don't think of a special song *BirthdayLaura* to sing to a friend Laura and *BirthdayDave* for a friend Dave. You use one song and fill in (with a parameter!) the name of the person who has the birthday.

```
#include <iostream.h>

// first attempt at birthday singing

void
Sing()
{
    cout << "Happy birthday to you" << endl;
    cout << "Happy birthday to you" << endl;
    cout << "Happy birthday dear  " << endl;
    cout << "Happy birthday to you" << endl;
    cout << endl;
}

int main()
{
    Sing(); Sing(); Sing(); Sing(); Sing();
    return 0;
}
```

```
                                  OUTPUT

 Happy birthday to you
 Happy birthday to you
 Happy birthday dear
 Happy birthday to you

 Happy birthday to you
 Happy birthday to you
 Happy birthday dear
 Happy birthday to you

 Happy birthday to you
 Happy birthday to you
 Happy birthday dear
 Happy birthday to you

 Happy birthday to you
 Happy birthday to you
 Happy birthday dear
 Happy birthday to you

 Happy birthday to you
 Happy birthday to you
 Happy birthday dear
 Happy birthday to you
```

We need to print five copies of the song. We will design a function named Sing whose purpose is to generate the birthday song for each of the quintuplets. Initially we will leave the name of the quintuplet out of the function so that five songs are printed, but no names appear in the songs. Once this program works, we'll use parameters to add a name to each song. This technique of writing a preliminary version, then modifying it to lead to a better version, is one that is employed throughout the book. It is the heart of the concept of iterative enhancement.

The first pass at a solution is *bday.cc*, Prog. 2.5. Execution of this program yields a sequence of printed verses close to the desired output, but the name of each person whose birthday is being celebrated is missing. One possibility is to use five different functions (SingGrace, SingAlan, etc.), one function for each verse, but this isn't really any better than just using 24 cout statements. We need to parameterize the function Sing so that it is versatile enough to provide a song for each quintuplet. This is done in Prog. 2.6, which generates exactly the output required and shown in Fig. 2.7. Note that the statement

```
cout << "Happy birthday dear " << endl;
```

from Prog. 2.5 has been replaced with

```
cout << "Happy birthday dear " << person << endl;
```

Program 2.6   bday2.cc

```cpp
#include <iostream.h>
#include "CPstring.h"

// working birthday program

void
Sing(string person)
{
    cout << "Happy birthday to you" << endl;
    cout << "Happy birthday to you" << endl;
    cout << "Happy birthday dear " << person << endl;
    cout << "Happy birthday to you" << endl;
    cout << endl;
}

int main()
{
    Sing("Grace");
    Sing("Alan");
    Sing("John");
    Sing("Ada");
    Sing("Blaise");
    return 0;
}
```

bday2.cc

This statement can be spread over several lines without affecting its behavior.

```
cout << "Happy birthday dear "
     << person
     << endl;
```

Because only one endl is used in the output statement, only one line of output is written.

Passing Parameters

When the function call Sing("Grace") in main is executed, the string literal "Grace" is the argument **passed** to the string parameter *person*. This is diagrammed by the solid arrow in Fig. 2.8. When the statement cout << "Happy birthday dear " << person << endl" in Sing is executed, the parameter person is replaced by its value, as indicated by the dashed arrow in Fig. 2.8. In this case the value is the string literal "Grace". Since person is not between quotes, it is not a string literal. As shown in Fig. 2.8, the parameter person is represented by a box. When the function Sing is called, the value that is passed to the parameter is stored in this box. Then each statement in the function is executed sequentially. After the last statement, cout << endl, executes, control returns from the function Sing to the statement that follows the function call Sing("Grace"). This means that the statement Sing("Alan") is executed next. This call passes the argument "Alan", which is stored in the box associated with the parameter person.

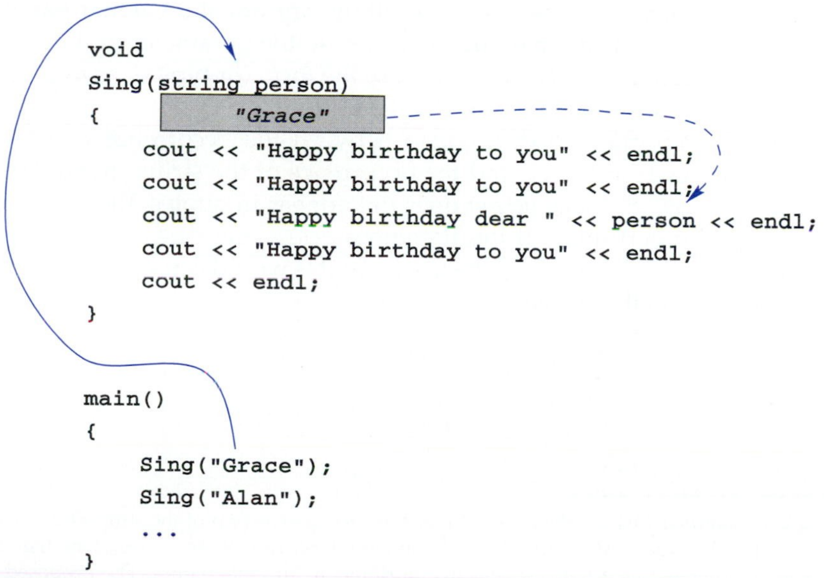

```
void
Sing(string person)
{          "Grace"    - - - - - - - - - - - - - - -
    cout << "Happy birthday to you" << endl;
    cout << "Happy birthday to you" << endl;
    cout << "Happy birthday dear " << person << endl;
    cout << "Happy birthday to you" << endl;
    cout << endl;
}

main()
{
    Sing("Grace");
    Sing("Alan");
    ...
}
```

Figure 2.8   Parameter passing.

If you review the format of a C++ function given in Fig. 2.1, you'll see that each function has a parameter list. In a parameter list, each parameter must include the name of the parameter and the **type** of the parameter. In the definition of Sing the parameter is given the name *person*. The parameter has the type string. Recall that a string is any sequence of characters and that string literals occur between double quotes. All parameters must have an indication as to their structure—that is, what type of thing the parameter is. A parameter's type determines what kinds of things can be done with the parameter in a C++ program.

The type string is not part of standard C++ but is made accessible by using the appropriate include directive:

```
#include "CPstring.h"
```

at the top of the program.[6] Include directives are necessary to provide information to the compiler about different types, objects, and classes used in a program, such as output streams and strings. Standard include files found in all C++ programming environments are indicated using angle brackets, as in #include <iostream.h>. Include files that are supplied by the user rather than by the system are indicated using double quotes, as in #include "CPstring.h".

There is a vocabulary associated with all programming languages. Mastering this vocabulary is part of mastering programming and computer science. To be precise about explanations involving parameterized functions, I will use the word **parameter** to refer to usage within a function and in the function header (e.g., *person*). I will use the word **argument** to refer to what is passed to the function (e.g., *"Grace"* in the call Sing("Grace").) Another method for differentiating between these two is to call the argument an **actual parameter** and to use the term **formal parameter** to refer to the parameter in the function header. The adjective *formal* is used because the form (or type — as in string) of the parameter is given in the function header.

It also is important to distinguish between the occurrence of *person* in the statement cout << ... and the occurrence of the string literal "Happy birthday dear ". Since *person* does not appear in quotes, the value of the parameter *person* is printed. If the statement cout << "person" was used rather than cout << person, the use of quotes would cause the string literal *person* to appear on the screen.

```
Happy birthday to you
Happy birthday to you
Happy birthday dear person
Happy birthday to you
```

---

[6]An implementation of strings, the file *CPstring.cc*, is provided as part of the supporting materials included with this book. The name *String.h* isn't used because there is a system file *string.h* and some environments are not case-sensitive in differentiating file names. The proposed ANSI C++ standard includes a string class. The class string used in this book is compatible with the proposed standard. You may be able to use #include<string> or #include<cstring.h> to access this standard class, but the *CPstring.h* header file will work too.

The use of the parameter's name causes the value of the parameter to appear on the screen. The value of the parameter is different for each call of the function *Sing*. The parameter is a **variable** capable of representing values in different contexts just as the variable x can represent different values in the equation $y = 5 \cdot x + 3$.

2.16. In the following sequence of program statements, is the string literal `"Me"` an argument or a parameter? Is it an actual parameter?

Pause to reflect

```
cout << "  A Verse for My Ego" << endl;
Sing("Me");
```

2.17. What happens with your compiler if the statement `Sing("Grace")` is changed to `Sing(Grace)`? Why?

2.18. What modifications should be made to Prog. 2.6 to generate a song for a person named *Bjarne*?

2.19. What modifications should be made to Prog. 2.6 so that each song emphasizes the personalized line by ending it with three exclamation points?

```
Happy birthday dear Bjarne !!!
```

2.20. What happens if the name of the formal parameter *person* is changed to *celebrant* in the function `Sing`? Does it need to be changed everywhere it appears?

2.21. What call of function `Sing` would generate a verse with the line shown here?

```
Happy birthday dear Mr. President
```

2.22. What is the purpose of the final statement `cout << endl;` in function `Sing` in the birthday programs?

2.23. What is a minimal change to the Happy Birthday program that will cause each verse (about one person) to be printed three times before the next verse is printed three times (rather than once each) for a total of 15 verses? What is a minimal change that will cause all five verses (for all five people) to be printed, then all five printed again, and then all five printed again for a different ordering of 15 verses?

2.24. It is possible to write the Happy Birthday program so that the body of the function `Sing` consists of a single statement. What is that statement? Why is the use of several statements better than the use of one statement?

2.6   Functions with Several Parameters

In this section we will investigate functions with more than one parameter. As a simple example, we'll use the children's song *Old MacDonald*, partially reproduced in Fig. 2.9. We would like to write a C++ program to generate

ADA LOVELACE (1816–1853)

Ada Lovelace, daughter of the poet Lord Byron, had a significant impact in publicizing the work of Charles Babbage. Babbage's designs for two computers, the Difference Engine and the Analytical Engine, came more than a century before the first electronic computers were built but anticipated many of the features of modern computers.

Lovelace was tutored by the British mathematician Augustus De Morgan. In [McC79], she is portrayed as "an attractive and charming flirt, an accomplished musician, and a passionate believer in physical exercise. She combined these last two interests by practicing her violin as she marched around the family billiard table for exercise."

Lovelace translated an account of Babbage's work into English. Her translation, and the accompanying notes, are credited with making Babbage's work accessible. Of Babbage's computer she wrote, "It would weave algebraic patterns the way the Jacquard loom weaved patterns in textiles."

Lovelace was instrumental in popularizing Babbage's work, but she was not one of the first programmers as is sometimes said. The programming language Ada is named for Ada Lovelace. For more information see [McC79, Gol93, Asp90].

OUTPUT

```
Old MacDonald had a farm, Ee-igh, ee-igh, oh!
And on his farm he had a cow, Ee-igh, ee-igh, oh!
With a moo moo here
And a moo moo there
Here a moo, there a moo, everywhere a moo moo
Old MacDonald had a farm, Ee-igh, ee-igh, oh!

Old MacDonald had a farm, Ee-igh, ee-igh, oh!
And on his farm he had a pig, Ee-igh, ee-igh, oh!
With a oink oink here
And a oink oink there
Here a oink, there a oink, everywhere a oink oink
Old MacDonald had a farm, Ee-igh, ee-igh, oh!
```

Figure 2.9   At old MacDonald's barnyard.

the output shown in Fig. 2.9. As always, we will strive to design a general program, useful in writing about, for example, ducks quacking, hens clucking, or horses neighing. In designing the program we first look for similarities and differences in the verses to determine what parts of the verses should be parameterized. We'll ignore for now the ungrammatical construct of *a oink*. The only differences in the two verses are the name of the animal, cow and pig, and the noise the animal makes, moo and oink, respectively. Accordingly, we design two functions: one to "sing" about an animal and another to "sing" about the animal's sounds, in Prog. 2.7, *oldmac1.cc.*

This program produces the desired output but is cumbersome in many respects. To generate a new verse (e.g., about a quacking duck) we must write a new function and call it. In contrast, in the happy-birthday-generating program (2.6), a new verse could be constructed by a new call rather than by writing a new function and calling it. Also notice that the flow of control in Prog. 2.7 is more complex than in Prog. 2.6. We'll look carefully at what happens when the function call Pig() in main is executed. The passing of arguments is diagrammed in Fig. 2.10. There are four statements in the body of the function Pig. The first statement, the function call Refrain(), results in

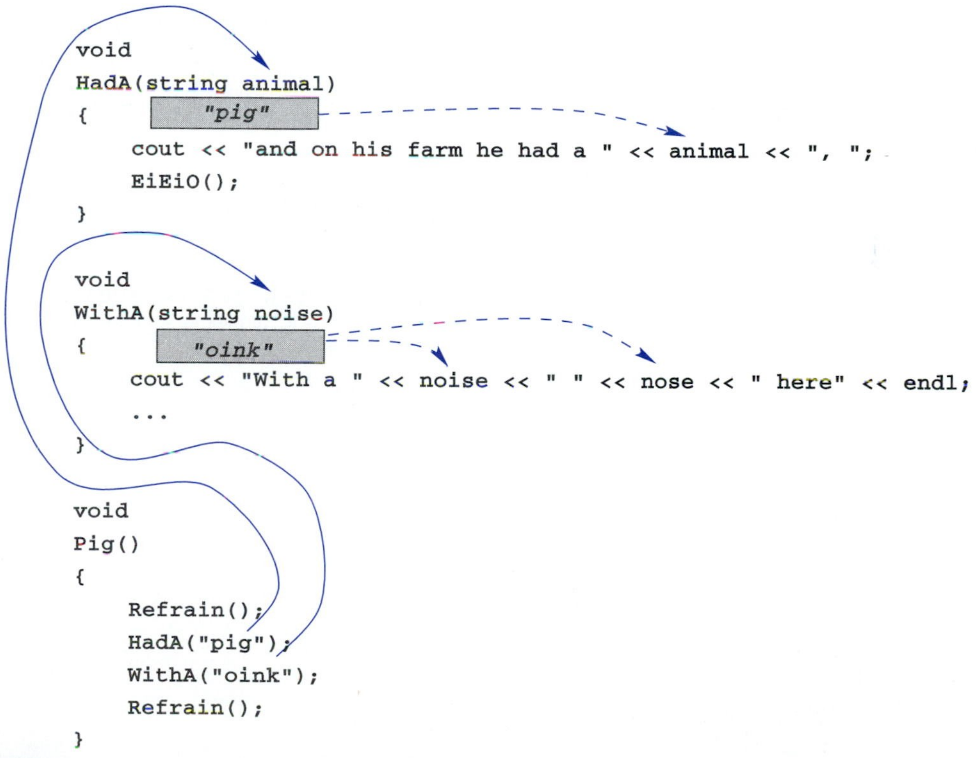

Figure 2.10   Passing two parameters.

```cpp
#include <iostream.h>
#include "CPstring.h"

// working version of old macdonald
// single parameter procedures

void
EiEio()
{
    cout << "Ee-igh, Ee-igh, oh!" << endl;
}

void
Refrain()
{
    cout << "Old MacDonald had a farm, ";
    EiEio();
}

void
HadA(string animal)
{
    cout << "And on his farm he had a " << animal << ", ";
    EiEio();
}

void
WithA(string noise)
// the principal part of a verse
{
    cout << "With a " << noise << " " << noise << " here" << endl;
    cout << "And a " << noise << " " << noise << " there" << endl;

    cout << "Here a " << noise << ", "
         << "there a " << noise << ", "
         << " everywhere a " << noise << " " << noise << endl;
}

void
Pig()
{
    Refrain();
    HadA("pig");
    WithA("oink");
    Refrain();
}

void
Cow()
{
```

```
        Refrain();
        HadA("cow");
        WithA("moo");
        Refrain();
}

int main()
{
        Cow();
        cout << endl;
        Pig();
        return 0;
}
```

oldmac1.cc

two lines being printed (note that `Refrain` calls the function `EiEiO`). When `Refrain` finishes executing, control returns to the statement following the function call `Refrain();` this is the second statement in `Pig`, the function call `HadA("pig")`. The argument `"pig"` is passed to the (formal) parameter `animal` and then statements in the function `HadA` are executed. When the function `HadA` finishes, control returns to the third statement in `Pig`, the function call `WithA("oink")`. As shown in Fig. 2.10 this results in passing the argument `"oink"`, which is stored as the value of the parameter `noise`. After all statements in the body of `WithA` have executed, the flow of control continues with the final statement in the body of the function `Pig`, another function call `Refrain()`. After this call finishes executing, `Pig` has finished and the flow of control continues with the statement following the call of `Pig()` in the main function. This is the statement `return 0` and the program finishes execution.

This program works, but it needs to be redesigned to be used more easily. This redesign process is another stage in program development. Often a programmer redesigns a working program to make it "better" in some way. In extreme cases a program that works is thrown out because it can be easier to redesign the program from scratch (using ideas learned during the original design) rather than trying to modify a program. Often writing the first program is necessary to get the good ideas used in subsequent programs.

In this case we want to dispense with the need to construct a new function rather than just a function call. To do this we will combine the functionality of the functions `HadA` and `WithA` into a new function `Verse`. When writing a program, you should look for similarities in code segments. The bodies of the functions in `Pig` and `Cow` have the same pattern:

```
        Refrain()
        call to HadA(...)
        call to WithA(...)
        Refrain()
```

Incorporating this pattern into the function `Verse`, rather than repeating the pattern elsewhere in the program, yields a more versatile program.

In general, a user-defined function can have any number of parameters, but once written this number is fixed. The final version of this program, Prog. 2.8,

Program 2.8   oldmac2.cc

```
#include <iostream.h>
#include "CPstring.h"

// working version of old macdonald
// procedures with more than one parameter

void
EiEio()
{
    cout << "Ee-igh, Ee-igh, oh!" << endl;
}

void
Refrain()
{
    cout << "Old MacDonald had a farm, ";
    EiEio();
}

void
HadA(string animal)
{
    cout << "And on his farm he had a " << animal << ", ";
    EiEio();
}

void
WithA(string noise)
// the principal part of a verse
{
    cout << "With a " << noise << " " < noise << " here" << endl;
    cout << "And a " << noise << " " < noise << " there" << endl;

    cout << "Here a " << noise << ", "
    cout << "there a " << noise << ", "
    cout << " everywhere a " << noise << " " << noise << endl;
}

void
Verse(string animal, string noise)
{
    Refrain();
    HadA(animal);
    WithA(noise);
    Refrain();
}

int main()
{
    Verse("pig","oink");
    cout <<  endl;
    Verse("cow","moo");
    return 0;
}
```

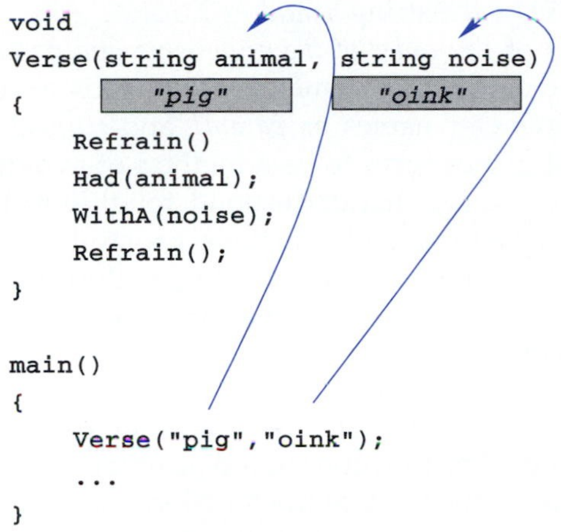

```
void
Verse(string animal, string noise)
{          "pig"          "oink"

    Refrain()
    Had(animal);
    WithA(noise);
    Refrain();

}


main()
{

    Verse("pig","oink");
    ...

}
```

Figure 2.11   Passing multiple parameters.

is shorter and more versatile than the first version, Prog. 2.7. By looking for a way to combine the functionality of functions HadA and WithA, we modified a program and generated a better one. Often as versatility goes up so does length. When the length of a program decreases as its versatility increases, we're on the right track.

I will sometimes use the word *elegant* as a desirable program trait. Prog. 2.8 is elegant compared to Prog. 2.7 because it is easily modified to generate new verses.

Note that it is the order in which arguments are passed to a function that determines their use, not the actual values of the arguments or the names of the parameters. This is diagrammed in Fig. 2.11. In particular, the names of the parameters have nothing to do with their purpose. If *animal* is replaced everywhere it occurs in Prog. 2.8 with *vegetable,* the program will produce exactly the same output. Furthermore, it is the order of the parameters in the function header and the corresponding order of the arguments in the function call that determines what the output is. In particular, the function call

```
Verse("cluck","hen");
```

OUTPUT

```
And on his farm he had a cluck, Ee-igh, ee-igh, oh!
With a hen hen here
And a hen hen there
Here a hen, there a hen everywhere a hen hen
```

Figure 2.12   Parameters passed in the wrong order.

would generate a verse with the lines shown in Fig. 2.12 since the value of the parameter *animal* will be the string literal `"cluck"`.

The importance of the *order of the arguments and parameters* and the lack of importance of the names of parameters often leads to confusion. Although the use of such parameter names as *param1* and *param2* (or, even worse, *x* and *y*) might at first glance seem to be a method of avoiding such confusion, the use of parameter names that correspond roughly to their purpose is far more useful as the programs and functions we study get more complex. In general, parameters should be named according to the purpose just as functions are named. Guidelines as to using lowercase and uppercase characters are provided at the end of this chapter.

Pause to reflect

2.25. Write a function for use in Prog. 2.7 that produces output for a gobbling turkey. The function should be invoked by the call `Turkey`, which appears in the body of the function `main`.

2.26. Is it useful to have a separate function `EiEiO`?

2.27. How would the same effect of the function `Turkey` be achieved in Prog. 2.8?

2.28. If the order of the parameters of the function `Verse` is reversed so that the header is

```
void Verse(string noise, string animal)
```

but no changes are made in the body of `Verse`, then what changes (if any) must be made in the calls to `Verse` so that the output does not change?

2.29. What happens if the statement `Verse("pig","cluck");` is included in the function `main`?

2.30. The statement `Verse("lamb");` will not compile. Why?

2.31. What happens if you include the statement `Verse("owl",2)` in the function `main`? What happens if you include the statement `Verse("owl",2+2)`?

Stumbling block

You must be careful organizing programs that use functions. Although we have not discussed the order in which functions appear in a program, the order is important to a degree. Program 2.9 is designed to print a two-line message. As written, it will not compile.

When this program is compiled using the g++ compiler, the compilation fails with the error messages

```
order.cc: In function 'void  Hi (class string)':
order.cc:8: warning: implicit declaration of function 'Greetings'
ld: Undefined symbol
   _Greetings
collect: ld returned 2 exit status
```

With the Turbo C++ compiler the compilation fails, with the error message

```
Error order.cpp 8: Function 'Greetings' should have a prototype
```

Program 2.9   order.cc

```
#include <iostream.h>
#include "CPstring.h"

// order of procedures is important

void Hi (string name)
{
    cout << "Hi " << name << endl;
    Greetings();
}

void Greetings()
{
    cout << "Things are happening inside this computer" << endl;
}

int main()
{
    Hi("Fred");
    return 0;
}
```

OUTPUT

```
Hi Fred
Things are happening inside this computer
```
(intended output, but the program doesn't run)

These messages are generated because the function `Greetings` is called from the function `Hi` but occurs physically after `Hi` in Prog. 2.9. In general, functions must appear (be defined) in a program before they are called.

*Stumbling
block*

Syntax: function prototype

```
return type

function (type name, type name, ...);
```

This requirement that functions appear before they're called is too restrictive. Fortunately, there is an alternative to placing an entire function before it's called. It's possible to put information about the function before it's called rather than the function itself. This information is called the **signature** of a function, often referred to as the function's **prototype.** Rather than requiring that an entire function appear before it is called, only the prototype need appear. The prototype indicates the order and type of the function's parameters as well as the function's return type. The prototype for the function Hi is

```
void Hi (string name);
```

The prototype of the Verse function in Prog. 2.8 is different:

```
void Verse (string animal, string noise);
```

Just as arguments and parameters must match, so must a function call match the function's prototype. In the call to Greetings made from Hi, the compiler doesn't know the prototype for Greetings. If a function header appears physically before any call of the function, then a prototype is not needed. However, in larger programs it can be necessary to include prototypes for functions at the beginning of a program. In either case the compiler sees a function header or prototype before a function call so that the matching of arguments to parameters can be checked by the compiler.

It's not necessary to include the name of each parameter in the prototype, only the type. It's often useful to include the name, so the examples in this book will normally include both a parameter's type and name in the prototype.

The function main has a return type of int, but all other functions we've used so far have a return type of void. Void functions do not return

---

Program 2.10   order2.cc

```
#include <iostream.h>
#include "CPstring.h"

// illustrates function prototypes

void Hi(string);
void Greetings();

void Hi (string name)
{
    cout << "Hi " << name << endl;
    Greetings();
}

void Greetings()
{
    cout << "Things are happening inside this computer"
        << endl;
}

int main()
{
    Hi("Fred");
    return 0;
}
```

order2.cc

a value. Later you will encounter functions that return many different types. The default return type in C++ is `int`. Thus the error messages generated by the g++ compiler warn of an "implicit declaration" of the function `Greetings`, meaning that the default return of an integer is assumed. Since there is no function `Greetings` with such a return type, the "undefined symbol" message is generated.

The error message generated by the Turbo C++ compiler is more informative and indicates that a prototype is missing. Program 2.10 has function prototypes. Note that the prototype for function `Hi` is not necessary since the function appears before it is called. Some programmers include prototypes for all functions, regardless of whether the prototypes are necessary. In this book we use prototypes when necessary but won't include them otherwise.

2.7 Program Style

The style of indentation used in the programs in this chapter is used in all programs in the book. In particular, each statement within a function or program body is indented four spaces. As programs get more complex in subsequent chapters, the use of a consistent indentation scheme will become more important in ensuring ease of understanding. I recommend that you use the indentation scheme displayed in the programs here. If you adopt a different scheme you must use it consistently.

Indentation is necessary for human readers of the programs you write. The C++ compiler is quite capable of compiling programs that have no indentation, have multiple statements per line (instead of one statement per line as we have seen so far), and that have function names like `He553323xlo3`.

Identifiers

The names of user-defined functions, parameters, and variables are **identifiers**— a means of referral both for program designers and for the compiler. Examples of identifiers include *Hello, person,* and *Sing.* Just as good indentation can make a program easier to read, I recommend the use of identifiers that indicate to some degree the purpose of the item being labeled by the identifier. As noted above, the use of *animal* is much more informative than *param1* in conveying the purpose of the parameter to which the label applies. In C++ an identifier consists of any sequence of letters, numbers, and the underscore character (_). Identifiers may not begin with a number. And identifiers are *case-sensitive* (lower- and uppercase letters): the identifier *verse* is different from the identifier *Verse.* Although some compilers limit the number of characters in an identifier, the C++ standard specifies that identifiers can be arbitrarily long.

Traditionally, C programmers use the underscore character as a way of making identifiers easier to read. Rather than the identifier `partedhair`, one would use `parted_hair`. Some recent studies indicate that using upper- and lowercase letters to differentiate the parts of an identifier can make them easier to read. In this book I adopt the convention that all user-defined functions and

Table 2.1   C++ keywords

asm	float	static
auto	for	static_cast
bool	friend	struct
break	goto	switch
case	if	template
catch	inline	this
char	int	throw
class	long	true
const	mutable	try
const_cast	namespace	typedef
continue	new	typeid
default	operator	typename
delete	private	union
do	protected	unsigned
double	public	using
dynamic_cast	register	virtual
else	reinterpret_cast	void
enum	return	volatile
explicit	short	wchar_t
extern	signed	while
false	sizeof	

types[7] begin with an uppercase letter. Uppercase letters are also used to separate subwords in an identifier, e.g., `PartedHair` rather than `parted_hair`. Parameters (and later variables) begin with lowercase letters although uppercase letters may be used to delimit subwords in identifiers. For example, a parameter for a large power of ten might be `largeTenPower`. Note that the identifier begins with a lowercase letter, which signifies that it is a parameter or a variable. You may decide that `large_ten_power` is more readable. As long as you adopt a consistent naming convention, you shouldn't feel bound by conventions I employ in the code here.

In many C++ implementations identifiers containing a double underscore (__) are used in the libraries that supply code (such as `<iostream.h>`), and therefore identifiers in your programs must avoid double underscores. In addition, differentiating between single and double underscores: (_ and __) is difficult.

Finally, some words have special meanings in C++ and cannot be used as user-defined identifiers. We will encounter most of these **keywords,** or **reserved** words, as we study C++. A list of keywords is provided in Table 2.1.

---

[7]The type `string` used in this chapter is not built into C++ but is supplied as a user-defined type. In C++, however, it's possible to use user-defined types just like built-in types.

2.8   Chapter Review

In this chapter we studied the form of C++ programs, how a program executes, and how functions can make programs easier to modify and use. We studied programs that displayed songs having repetitive verses so that an efficient use of functions would reduce our programming efforts. At the same time, the verses had sufficient variation to make the use of parameters necessary in order to develop clean and elegant programs—programs that appeal to your emerging sense of programming style.

- C++ programs have a specific form:
  - `#include` statements to access libraries
  - comments about the program
  - user-defined functions
  - one function named `main`
- Libraries make "off-the-shelf" programming components accessible to programmers. System library names are enclosed between < and >, as in `<iostream.h>`. Libraries that are part of this book and nonsystem libraries are enclosed in double quotation marks, as in `"CPstring.h"`.
- Output is generated using the insertion operator, <<, and the standard output stream, `cout`. These are accessible by including the proper header file `<iostream.h>`.
- Strings are sequences of characters. The type `string` is not a built-in type but is accessible via the header file `"CPstring.h"`.
- Functions group related statements together so that the statements can be executed together, by calling the function.
- Parameters facilitate passing information between functions. The value passed is an *argument*. The "box" that stores the value in the function is a *parameter*.
- Iterative enhancement is a design process by which a program is developed in stages. Each stage is both an enhancement and a refinement of a working program.
- In designing programs, look for patterns of repeated code that can be combined into a parameterized function to avoid code duplication, as we did in `Verse` of Prog. 2.8.
- Prototypes are function signatures that convey to the compiler information that is used to determine if a function call is correctly formed.
- Identifiers are names of functions, classes, and parameters. Identifiers should indicate the purpose of what they name. Your programs will be more readable if you are consistent in capitalization and underscores in identifiers.

2.9   Exercises

2.1 Add a function `Neck` to Prog. 2.4 that can be used to generate output similar to that shown in Fig. 2.13.

Figure 2.13   Use of function *Neck*.

Figure 2.14   A surprised head.

2.2 Modify the appropriate functions in Prog. 2.4 to display the head shown in Fig. 2.14.

2.3 Write a program whose output is the text of Prog. 2.1. Note that the output is a program!

OUTPUT

```
#include <iostream.h>

int main()
{
    cout << "Hello  world" << endl;
    return 0;
}
```

To display the character " you'll need to use **escape sequence.** An escape sequence is a backslash (\) followed by one character. The two-character escape sequence represents a single character; the escape sequence \ " is used to print one quotation mark. The statement

```
cout << "\"Hello\" " << endl;
```

can be used to print the characters "Hello" on the screen, including the quotation marks! Be sure to comment your program-writing program appropriately.

```
                            OUTPUT

That's the way
Uh-huh Uh-huh
I like it
Uh-huh Uh-huh

That's the way
Uh-huh Uh-huh
I like it
Uh-huh Uh-huh
```

Figure 2.15 KC and the Sunshine Band's magnum opus.

2.4 A popular song performed by KC and the Sunshine Band repeats many verses using the words "That's the way Uh-huh Uh-huh I like it Uh-huh Uh-huh," as illustrated in Fig. 2.15. Write a program that generates four choruses of the song.

2.5 Write a program that generates the verses of a children's song shown in Fig. 2.16. Don't worry about the ungrammatical qualities inherent in the use of "goes" and "go" in your first attempt at writing the program. You should include a function

```
                            OUTPUT

The wheel on the bus goes round round round
round round round
round round round
The wheel on the bus goes round round round
All through the town

The wipers on the bus goes swish swish swish
swish swish swish
swish swish swish
The wipers on the bus goes swish swish swish
All through the town

The horn on the bus goes beep beep beep
beep beep beep
beep beep beep
The horn on the bus goes beep beep beep
All through the town

The money on the bus goes clink clink clink
clink clink clink
clink clink clink
The money on the bus goes clink clink clink
All through the town
```

Figure 2.16 The bus song.

with two parameters capable of generating any of the verses when the appropriate arguments are passed. Strive to make your program "elegant."

Is it possible to generate a verse of the song based on the lines

```
The driver on the bus goes move on back
move on back
move on back
```

with small modifications? How many parameters would the `Verse` function of such a song have?

2.6 Consider the song about an old woman with an insatiable appetite, one version of which is partially reproduced in the following.

OUTPUT

```
There was an old lady who swallowed a fly
I don't know why she swallowed a fly
Perhaps she'll die.

There was an old lady who swallowed a spider
That wiggled and jiggled and tiggled inside her
She swallowed the spider to catch the fly
I don't know why she swallowed a fly
Perhaps she'll die.

There was an old lady who swallowed a bird
How absurd to swallow a bird
She swallowed the bird to catch the spider
That wiggled and jiggled and tiggled inside her
She swallowed the spider to catch the fly
I don't know why she swallowed a fly
Perhaps she'll die.
```

This song may be difficult to generate via a program using just the predefined output stream `cout`, the operator `<<`, and user-defined parameterized functions. Write such a program or sketch its solution and indicate why it might be difficult to write a program for which it is easy to add new animals while maintaining program elegance. You might think about adding a verse about a cat (imagine that!) that swallows the bird.

2.7 In a song made famous by Bill Haley and the Comets, the chorus is

```
One, two, three o'clock, four o'clock rock
Five, six, seven o'clock, eight o'clock rock
Nine, ten, eleven o'clock, twelve o'clock rock
We're going to rock around the clock tonight
```

Rather than using words to represent time, you are to use numbers and write a program that will print the chorus above but with the line

```
1, 2, 3 o'clock, 4 o'clock rock
```

as the first line of the chorus. Your program should be useful in creating a chorus that could be used with military time; i.e., another chorus might end thus:

```
21, 22, 23 o'clock, 24 o'clock rock
We're going to rock around the clock tonight
```

You should use the arithmetic operator + where appropriate and strive to make your program as succinct as possible, calling functions with different parameters rather than writing similar statements.

2.10 A Computer Science Excursion: Program Complexity

An important concept studied in computer science is **complexity.** In computer science this word does not mean *intricate*, *knotty*, or *complicated*, which are typical English synonyms. Rather, *complexity* refers to the concept of measuring computational resources, such as the time or memory required by an algorithm. Consider, for example, the process of looking up a word in a dictionary or a name in a phonebook. We use the alphabetical listing of entries to develop a method or algorithm for looking up entries. How many pages does one need to look at to find the page with the name of a given person in the Manhattan phone book? How many words are examined, on the average, when looking up a word in a dictionary that has no thumb indices? How hard is it to arrange words that are in random order into alphabetical order? These are the kinds of questions that people who study complexity in computer science ask (and answer). More concretely, it is very easy to determine if a number is even; the last digit provides enough information. Determining if the number of digits is even is harder because we must count the digits. Determining whether 123 and 393819383928393928 are even is simple. Determining whether such numbers have an even number of digits is difficult and gets increasingly more difficult as the numbers get larger.

Although complexity is addressed in subsequent chapters, we will get a jump on these ideas by studying programs that generate output. Specifically, we want to study properties of programs defined below in reasoning about a class of programs, each of which generates output.

- number of lines
- number of functions
- number of function calls

Rather than use songs, we will print a person's name. The complexity results apply to song-printing programs as well.

Printing Names

Consider printing a name on the screen eight times. One method for doing this (for someone named Alan Turing) is illustrated in Prog. 2.11. This program

Program 2.11   names.cc

```cpp
#lincude <iostream.h>

void PrintNames()
{
    cout << "Alan Turing" << endl;
    cout << "Alan Turing" << endl;
    cout << "Alan Turing" << endl;
    cout << "Alan Turing" << endl;
    cout << "Alan Turing" << endl;
    cout << "Alan Turing" << endl;
    cout << "Alan Turing" << endl;
    cout << "Alan Turing" << endl;
}

int main()
{
    PrintNames();
    return 0;
}
```

OUTPUT

```
Alan Turing
Alan Turing
Alan Turing
Alan Turing
Alan Turing
Alan Turing
Alan Turing
Alan Turing
```

has eight statements that generate output. Extending the program to print 128 names is an unenviable task given the programming tools we've studied so far.[8] It requires the addition of 120 `cout << "..." << endl;` statements if we naively use the method of Prog. 2.11. We will study some alternatives that allow us to increase the number of names printed by a large amount with relatively few additions to the program, but first we will study Prog. 2.11.

We begin with an investigation of how the number of names printed increases with the addition of one `cout << "..." << endl` statement. We have already noted that the addition of 120 such statements increases the number of names printed to 128. In general, if there are n such statements there will be n names printed.

---

[8]Writing this program will be straightforward after learning about loops.

Table 2.2 Output linear in the size of the program

	2	3	8	128	1,000	n	**no. of statements**
`cout << "..." << endl;`	2	3	8	128	1,000	n	**lines printed**
PrintNames	16	24	64	1,024	8,000	$8 \cdot n$	**lines printed**

If, instead of adding `cout << "..." << endl;` statements to `PrintNames`, we add `PrintNames` function calls to `main()`, how does the number of names printed change? With two calls, 16 names are printed and with three calls, 24 names are printed. In general, with n calls, $8 \cdot n$ names are printed. This information is summarized in Table 2.2, where the increase in number of names printed is shown as the number of each type of statement is increased (assuming the original Prog. 2.11 is used).

This same information is shown graphically in Fig. 2.17. Although increasing the number of `PrintNames` calls generates more names than increasing the number of `cout << "..." << endl;` statements by the same amount, note that the shape of the "curves" is the same: a straight line. This shape is one we return to in later analysis of the complexity of both programs and

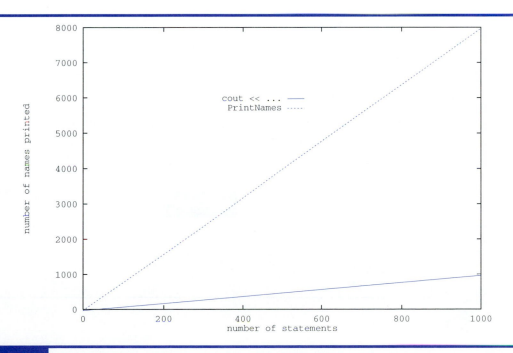

Figure 2.17 Adding one statement.

algorithms. It gives rise to the term **linear** as in *the number of names printed increases linearly with the number of statements.* Computer scientists use **big-Oh** notation[9] to describe complexity and write $O(n)$ to describe the number of lines printed by a program that has n lines. The O is used to describe the shape of the curve—in this case, linear. It doesn't mean that an n-line program generates n lines of output but that the size of the output is linear with respect to the size of the program.

Both methods of modifying Prog. 2.11 result in a program whose output size is linear with respect to the number of lines in the program. Both methods yield $O(n)$ lines of output for an n-line program.

Note that to print one million names would require the use of either one million `cout << "..." << endl;` statements or 125,000 calls of function *PrintNames* using the methods outlined above. The "short" million-name printing program (125,000 function calls) is a program of 125,018 lines (including blank lines). To print this program (assuming 66 lines per page) would require almost 2000 sheets of paper and yield a program listing 7.5 inches thick. Note that this is the thickness of the *program,* not the output of the program (which would be more than 7.5 inches thick).

Program 2.12   sqname.cc

```
#include <iostream.h>

void PrintNames()
{
    cout << "Alan Turing" << endl;
    cout << "Alan Turing" << endl;
}

int main()
{
    PrintNames();
    PrintNames();
    return 0;
}
```

OUTPUT

```
Alan Turing
Alan Turing
Alan Turing
Alan Turing
```

---

[9]We will develop an in-depth definition of big-Oh later; we're just trying to develop intuition at this point.

Table 2.3 Addition of two statements: half `cout`, half function calls

4	6	8	128	1,000	n	**no. of statements**
4	9	16	4,096	250,000	$(n/2)^2$	**lines printed**

More names, fewer statements. Consider Prog. 2.12, which is a version of Prog. 2.11 designed to print four names.

Suppose we add statements to Prog. 2.12; but rather than adding statements to either function `PrintNames` or to the function `main` as was done previously, we add one statement in both places, i.e., both a `cout << "..." << endl` statement and a `PrintName` call. Some careful thought should reveal that such a program (consisting of three `cout << "..." << endl` statements and three function calls) will yield nine lines of output—three lines per function call. If we continue this process of adding both one `cout << "..." << endl` statement and one function call in the main-program body (thus adding two statements each time), we get a sequence of programs that print an increasing number of names as summarized in Table 2.3.

To print one million names would require one of these programs consisting of 2010 lines (1000 `cout << ...` statements, 1000 `PrintNames` calls, and 10 other lines—see Prog. 2.12). Such a program would require only 30 sheets of paper and would yield a program listing 0.12 inch thick, a stark contrast to the million-name printing program patterned after Prog. 2.11.

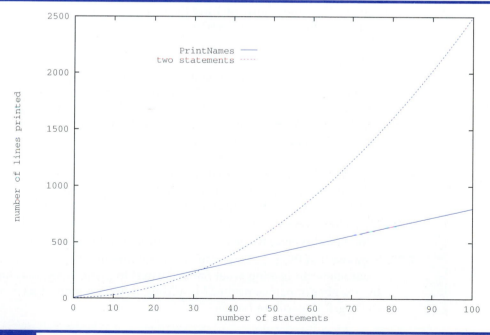

Figure 2.18   Adding two statements compared to one function call.

A comparison of the two program types is graphed in Fig. 2.18. The graph compares the addition of two statements (one `cout << ...` statement and one function call) to the addition of one function call in the function `main`.

Note that for programs of roughly 30 statements or less a program patterned after Prog. 2.11 prints more names than a program patterned after Prog. 2.12. But the "superiority" of the latter type of program is clearly shown as the number of statements increases. The shape of the curve labeled *two statements* in Fig. 2.18 is **quadratic** as opposed to the linear shape of the curve labeled *PrintNames*. In general, if the expression used to describe the size of the output (e.g., number of names printed) based on an input of size n (e.g., number of statements) is a multiple of n, as in n, $8 \cdot n$, $100 \cdot n$, the term *linear* is used to describe the relationship. If the expression requires squaring n, as in $(n/2)^2$, $n^2/100$, $50 \cdot n^2$, the term *quadratic* is used. Using big-Oh notation, the size of the output is $O(n^2)$ for a program of n lines.

Pause to reflect

2.32. If the listing of the program that prints one million names is 7.5 inches thick (see the 125,000-function call program above), how thick is the listing of a similar program that prints two million names? three million names?

2.33. Based on the data in Table 2.2, how thick is the program listing for a program with one million `cout << "..." << endl;` statements?

2.34. If the two types of program illustrated in Fig. 2.18 are used to print one billion names, how thick are the respective program listings (one billion is a thousand millions)?

Still more names, still fewer statements. In Prog. 2.13 we decrease the number of `cout << "..." << endl` statements needed to print eight names (compared to Prog. 2.11). Modifying Prog. 2.13 to print 12 names is a simple task (it can be done by adding one function call). By using still more functions, however, we can double the number of names written with relative ease. Program 2.14 indicates how this is done to print 16 names.

Pause to reflect

2.35. How many lines are printed if function `Names2` in Prog. 2.13 consists of three calls to `PrintNames`? four calls? five calls? Is this relationship of calls to lines printed linear, quadratic, or something different?

2.36. If two function calls are added to Prog. 2.13, what two calls should be added (and where) to maximize the number of lines printed?

2.37. Suppose that Prog. 2.12 is modified so that function `PrintNames` has a parameter indicating what name (string) to print. Does this change the number of names printed? Is adding the same kind of parameter to Prog. 2.13 easier or harder?

Note that Prog. 2.14 has six more lines of text than Prog. 2.13 but that the number of names printed has doubled. This trend continues in the following

---

Program 2.13　names2.cc

Program 2.13　names2.cc

```
#include <iostream.h>

void PrintNames()
{
    cout << "Alan Turing" << endl;
    cout << "Alan Turing" << endl;
}

void Names2()
{
    PrintNames();
    PrintNames();
}

int main()
{
    Names2();
    Names2();
    return 0;
}
```

OUTPUT

```
Alan Turing
Alan Turing
Alan Turing
Alan Turing
Alan Turing
Alan Turing
Alan Turing
Alan Turing
```

programs—by adding six lines of text (one new function with a blank line) the number of names written doubles.

By continuing to add new functions whose bodies consist of two calls to another function we can continue to double the number of names written. By adding a function Names4 that calls Names3, and a function Names5 that calls Names4, as shown in Prog. 2.15, we have a program that can print 64 names. Note that Prog. 2.15 consists of 38 lines[10] (including blank lines between

---

[10]To keep the listing of the program short, void is on the same line as the function name to which it refers.

Program 2.14   names3.cc

```cpp
#include <iostream.h>

void PrintNames()
{
    cout << "Alan Turing" << endl;
    cout << "Alan Turing" << endl;
}

void Names2()
{
    PrintNames();
    PrintNames();
}

void Names3()
{
    Names2();
    Names2();
}

int main()
{
    Names3();
    Names3();
    return 0;
}
```

OUTPUT

```
Alan Turing
Alan Turing
Alan Turing
Alan Turing
Alan Turing
Alan Turing
Alan Turing
Alan Turing
Alan Turing
Alan Turing
Alan Turing
Alan Turing
Alan Turing
Alan Turing
Alan Turing
Alan Turing
```

Program 2.15 bigname.cc

```cpp
#include <iostream.h>

void PrintNames()
{
    cout << "Alan Turing" << endl;
    cout << "Alan Turing" << endl;
}

void Names2()
{
    PrintNames();
    PrintNames();
}

void Names3()
{
    Names2();
    Names2();
}

void Names4()
{
    Names3();
    Names3();
}

void Names5()
{
    Names4();
    Names4();
}

int main()
{
    Names5();
    Names5();
    return 0;
}
```

OUTPUT

```
Alan Turing
Alan Turing
Alan Turing
Alan Turing
Alan Turing
Alan Turing
Alan Turing
Alan Turing
Alan Turing
Alan Turing
Alan Turing
```

functions). Although we have shown the output of Prog. 2.15, we do not expect that most output devices will display the small font we have shown here or have "stretchable" screens, capable of displaying all the output at once.

The data shown in Table 2.4 indicate the number of functions other than main, the number of lines in the program (including blank lines, but treating void as part of the name of each user-defined function), the number of C++ statements (cout << . . . and function calls, but not including the return 0 in main), and the number of lines of output for Progs. 2.13 through 2.15 with some data given for a program not shown.

Note that the number of lines in the program is one more than three times the number of statements. (Is this a linear or a quadratic relationship?) To print one million names (actually slightly more) using this type of program requires

Table 2.4   Increasing the number of functions

program	functions	lines	statements	lines printed
Program 2.13	2	20	6	8
Program 2.14	3	26	8	16
Program 2.15	5	38	12	64
(not shown)	10	68	22	2,048

19 functions, 40 statements, and therefore a program of 121 lines. Note that the listing of the program will fit on two pages and be 0.008 inch thick (based on the same paper thickness used in previous calculations). This multifunction method is compared graphically to the quadratic two-statement method in Fig. 2.19. The shape of the curve labeled *multi-func* is called **exponential.** Note that the graph only compares the two curves on programs of fewer than 16 statements. If the range of data plotted on the *x*-axis is increased, the curve labeled *two statements* is obscured by the rapid growth of the exponential curve (imagine comparing 128-statement programs—see Table 2.5.)

Table 2.5 recasts the data of Table 2.4 in the same style as Tables 2.3 and 2.2. When the output is related linearly to the input (Table 2.2), a 128-statement

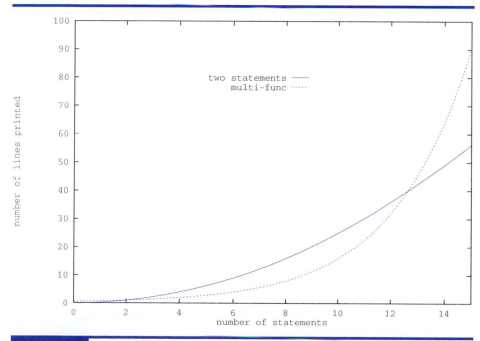

Figure 2.19   Exponential and quadratic methods.

Table 2.5   Adding functions

6	8	22		128	n	**no. of statements**
8	16	2,048	18,446,744,073,709,551,616		$2^{n/2}$	**lines printed**

program generates 1,024 lines of output. In contrast, when the output is related quadratically (Table 2.3), a 128-statement program generates 4,096 lines of output. A multifunction 128-statement program (Table 2.5) generates a quantity of lines so large as to be unpronounceable if not incomprehensible—if printed, the output would generate a listing that would reach to the sun *and back* more than 90 times! The size of the output is $O(2^n)$ for a program of n lines.

To compare all three methods of printing names we use another method of graphing, as shown in Fig. 2.20. In this graph a different type of scaling is used to better illustrate the differences of the three methods over a wider range of numbers. The y-axis is shown with a **logarithmic** scale so that the shape of the curves is more easily discernible. Some of the numbers on the y-axis are labeled with numbers written in scientific notation. The number labeled `1e+06` represents 1×10^6, or one million, lines printed. For programs with a very small number of statements, the method that grows linearly (labeled *Print-Names*) prints more names for a given number of statements (as was indicated in Fig. 2.18) and the quadratic method (labeled *two statements*) prints more names

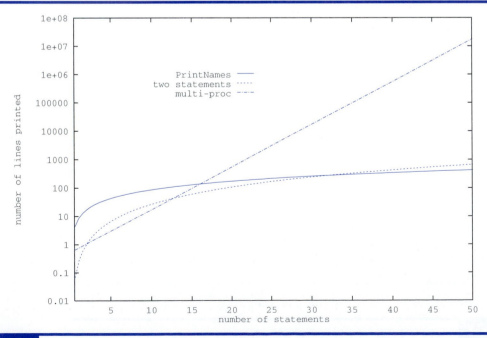

Figure 2.20   Comparing three methods of printing names.

than the exponential method. But as the number of statements increases, the exponential method prints many more names than either the linear or quadratic methods. Note that the linear and quadratic curves cross near a 30-statement program. This reinforces the graphical data shown in Fig. 2.18.

Excursion Exercises

2.8 Suppose the body of function `PrintNames` in Prog. 2.11 is modified so that it consists of three `cout << "..." << endl;` statements rather than eight. If the program is then modified by adding successively more calls of `PrintNames` in the body of `main` (leaving the number of `cout <<` statements at 3), how many names will be printed when there are 10 such calls? when there are 128 such calls? when there are n such calls?

How thick is the program listing of such a program that prints one million lines?

2.9 In the method of increasing the number of statements (two at a time) used in Prog. 2.12, the statements were equally divided between `cout << ...` statements and calls to the function `PrintNames`. Suppose a similar method is used but that Prog. 2.13 is modified so that statements are added three at a time divided equally among `cout <<` statements, calls to the function `PrintNames`, and calls to the function `Names2`.

Supply the numbers missing in Table 2.6, which indicates how many names are printed for programs built based on this pattern. How thick is the listing of the smallest such program that prints at least one million lines?

2.10 A computer network is equipped with a high-speed printer capable of printing 100,000 lines of text per minute. It will require 10 minutes to print one million names using such a printer ($1,000,000 \div 10 = 100,000$). A student runs a program based on Progs. 2.13 and 2.15 that contains 20 functions (see Table 2.4) and directs the output to the printer. How long will the printer take to finish printing the output? How many sheets of paper will be used (assuming 66 lines of text per page)?

2.11 Consider a program similar to Prog. 2.15 except that each function has five function calls (or 5 `cout << ...` statements for function `PrintNames`). Create a table similar to Table 2.4 based on such a program. How many lines of code are in the smallest program that prints at least one million lines of output?

2.12 Modify Prog. 2.11, *names.cc,* by adding a function call `PrintNames()` as the last line of the function *PrintNames* so that in some sense the function calls itself. Execute this modified program and count how many lines of output it generates.

Table 2.6 Adding three different statements: one-third `cout <<`, one-third `PrintNames`, one-third `Names-2`

6	9	12	15	45	126	999	n	no. of statements
8	27			3,375				lines printed

C++ Programs: Input/Process/Output

GIGO—Garbage In, Garbage Out
Common computer aphorism

GIGO—Garbage In, Gospel Out
New Hacker's Dictionary

Civilization advances by extending the number
of important operations which we can
perform without thinking about them.
ALFRED NORTH WHITEHEAD
An Introduction to Mathematics

The memory of all that—
No, no! They can't take that away from me.
IRA GERSHWIN
They Can't Take That Away from Me

The song-writing and head-drawing programs in Chapter 2 generated the same output for all executions unless the programs were modified and recompiled. These programs do not respond to a user of the program at **run time,** meaning while the programs are running or executing. The solutions to many programming problems require input from program users during execution. Therefore, we must be able to write programs that process input during execution. A typical framework for many computer programs is one that divides a program's execution into three stages.

1. Input—information is provided to the program.
2. Process—the information is processed.
3. Output—the program displays the results of processing the input.

This **input/process/output (IPO)** model of programming is used in the simple programs we'll study in this chapter as well as in million-line programs that forecast the weather and predict stock market fluctuations. Breaking a program into parts, implementing the parts separately, and then combining the parts into a working program is a good method for developing programs. This is often called **divide and conquer;** the program is divided into pieces, each piece is implemented, or "conquered," and the final program results from combining the conquered pieces. We'll employ divide and conquer together with iterative enhancement when designing classes and programs.

3.1   The Input Phase of Computation

Two runs of a modified version of Prog. 2.8 are in the following output box. Input entered by the user (you) is shown in italics. The computing environment used displays `prompt>` as a cue to the user to enter a command—in this case, the name of a program. Prompts may be different in other computing environments.

OUTPUT

```
prompt>  macinput

Enter the name of an animal: cow
Enter noise that a cow makes: moo

Old MacDonald had a farm, Ee-igh, ee-igh, oh!
And on his farm he had a cow, Ee-igh, ee-igh, oh!
With a moo moo here
And a moo moo there
Here a moo, there a moo, everywhere a moo moo
Old MacDonald had a farm, Ee-igh, ee-igh, oh!

prompt> macinput

Enter the name of an animal: hen
Enter noise that a hen makes: cluck

Old MacDonald had a farm, Ee-igh, ee-igh, oh!
And on his farm he had a hen, Ee-igh, ee-igh, oh!
With a cluck cluck here
And a cluck cluck there
Here a cluck, there a cluck, everywhere a cluck cluck
Old MacDonald had a farm, Ee-igh, ee-igh, oh!
```

Each run of the program produces different output according to the words you enter. If the function `main` in Prog. 2.8 is modified as shown in the code segment in Prog. 3.1, the modified program generates the runs shown above.

Program 3.1   macinput.cc

```
//  see program oldmac2.cc for function Verse
int main()
{
    string animal;
    sting noise;

    cout << "Enter the name of an animal: ";
    cin >> animal;

    cout << "Enter noise that a " << animal << " makes: ";
    cin >> noise;

    cout << endl;
    Verse(animal,noise);
    return 0;
}                                                          macinput.cc
```

The Input Stream, `cin`

We'll investigate each statement in `main` of Prog. 3.1. In a run of the program, you enter information and the program reacts to that information by printing a verse of Old MacDonald's Farm that corresponds to the entered data. In C++, information you enter comes from the input stream `cin` (pronounced "cee-in"). Just as the output stream, `cout`, generates output, the input stream accepts input values used in a program. In the run of Prog. 3.1, the output statement

```
        cout << "Enter the name of an animal: "
```

is *not* followed by an `endl`. As a result, your input appears on the same line as the words that prompt you to enter an animal's name.

When you enter input, it is taken from the input stream using the **extraction** operator, `>>` (sometimes read as "takes-from"). When the input is taken, it must be stored someplace. Program **variables,** in this case `animal` and `noise`, are used as a place for storing values. This is diagrammed in Fig. 3.1.

Variables

The following statements from Prog. 3.1 **define** two `string` variables, named *animal* and *noise.*

```
        string animal;
        string noise;
```

These variables are represented in Fig. 3.1 as shaded boxes that store the variable values in computer memory. The value stored in a variable can be used just as the values stored in a function's formal parameters can be used within the function (see Fig. 2.8). Parameters and variables are similar; each has a name

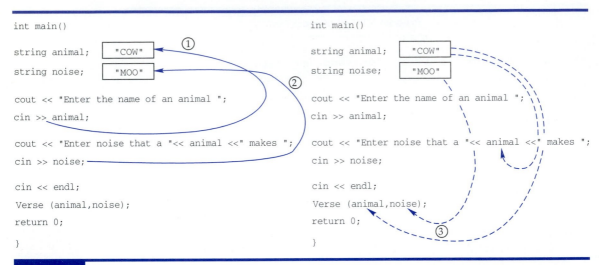

Figure 3.1   Using variables for input.

such as `animal` or `noise` and an associated storage location. Parameters are given initial values, or **initialized,** by calling a function and passing an argument. Variables are often initialized by accepting input from the user.

Variables in a C++ program must be **defined** before they can be used. Sometimes the terms *allocate* and *create* are used instead of *define*. Sometimes the word **object** is used instead of *variable*. For the moment you should think of *variable* and *object* as synonyms. Just as all formal parameters have a type or class, all variables in C++ have a type or class that determines what kinds of operations can be performed with the variable. The variable `animal` has the type or class `string`.

In the run of Prog. 3.1 diagrammed in Fig. 3.1, values taken from the input stream are stored in a variable's memory location. The variable `animal` gets a value in the statement labeled 1; the variable `noise` gets a value in the statement labeled 2. The value of `animal` is used to prompt the user; this is shown by the dashed arrow. The arrow labeled 3 shows the values of both variables used as arguments to the function `Verse`. In the interactive C++ environments used in the study of this book, the user must often press the return (enter) key before an input statement completes execution and stores the entered value in `animal`. This allows the user to make corrections (using arrow keys or a mouse, for example) before the final value is stored in memory.

An often-used metaphor associates a variable with a mailbox. Mailboxes usually have names associated with them (either 206 Main Street, or the Smith residence) and offer a place in which things can be stored. Perhaps a more appropriate metaphor associates variables with dorm rooms.[1] For example, a room in a fraternity or sorority house (say, ΨΥ or ΔΔΔ) can be occupied by any

----

[1]This was suggested by Deganit Armon.

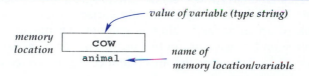

Figure 3.2   Variable as named memory location.

member of the fraternity or sorority but *not* by members of other residential groups.[2] The occupant of the room may change just as the value of a variable may change, but the type of the occupant remains the same, just as a variable's type remains fixed once it is defined. Thus we think of variables as named memory storage locations capable of storing a specific type of object. In the foregoing example the name of one storage location is `animal` and the type of object that can be stored in it is a `string`; for example, the value `cow` can be stored as shown in Fig. 3.2.

> **Syntax: Variable definition**
>
> *type name;*   **OR**
> *type name$_1$,name$_2$,... , name$_k$;*

In this book we'll define each variable in a separate statement as was done in Prog. 3.1. It's possible to define more than one variable in a single statement. For example, `string animal,noise;` defines two `string` variables. In C++, variables can be defined anywhere, but they must be defined before they're used. Some programmers prefer to define all variables immediately after a left brace, {. Others define variables just before they're first used. (We'll have occasion to use both styles of definition.) When all variables are defined at the beginning of a function, it is easy to find a variable when reading code. Thus when one variable is used in many places, this style makes it easier to find the definition than searching for the variable's first use. Another version of the code in Prog. 3.1 is shown in the following block of code with an alternate style of variable definition:

```
int main()
{
    cout << "Enter the name of an animal ";
    string animal;
    cin >> animal;

    cout << "Enter noise that a " << animal << " makes ";
    string noise;
    cin >> noise;

    cout << endl;
    Verse(animal,noise);
    return 0;
}
```

---

[2]The room could certainly not be occupied by independents or members of the opposite sex except in the case of co-ed living groups.

Before the statement `cin >> animal` in Prog. 3.1 is executed, the contents of the memory location associated with the variable `animal` are undefined. You can think of an undefined value as garbage. Displaying an undefined value probably won't cause any trouble, but it might not make any sense. In more complex programs, accessing an undefined value can cause a program to crash.

> **Program Tip: Be careful that every variable is given a value before being used for the first time in an expression or an output statement, or as an argument in a function call.**
>
> One way of doing this is to define variables just before they're used for the first time; that way you won't define lots of variables at the beginning of a function and then use one before it has been given a value. Alternatively, you can define all variables at the beginning of a function and program carefully.

Pause to reflect

3.1. If you run Prog. 3.1, *macinput.cc*, and enter *baah* for the name of the animal and *sheep* for the noise, what is the output? What happens if you enter *rooster* for the name of the animal and *cock a doodle doo* for the noise (you need to run the program to find the answer)? What if *cock-a-doodle-doo* is entered for the noise?

3.2. Why is there no `endl` in the statement

```
cout << "Enter the name of an animal ";
```

and why is there a space after the ell in `animal`?

3.3. Write (and test) a function *main* for Prog. 2.6 (the Happy Birthday program) that prompts the user for the name of a person for whom the song will be "sung."

3.4. What happens if the statement `cin >> noise;` is removed from Prog. 3.1 and the program is run?

3.2   Processing Numbers

All the examples we've studied so far have used strings. Although many programs manipulate strings and text, numbers are used extensively in computing and programming. In this section we'll discuss how to use numbers for input, processing, and output. As we'll see, the syntax for the input and output of numbers is the same as for strings, but processing numbers requires a new set of symbols based on those you learned for ordinary math.

Just as printing "Hello World" is often used as a first program, programs that convert temperature from Fahrenheit to Celsius are commonly used to

Program 3.2   fahrcels.cc

```
#include <iostream.h>

//  illustrates i/o of ints and doubles
//  illustrates arithmetic operations

int main()
{
    int ifahr;
    double dfahr;

    cout << "enter a Fahrenheit temperature ";
    cin >> ifahr;
    cout << ifahr << " = "
         << (ifahr - 32) * 5/9
         << " Celsius" << endl;

    cout << "enter another temperature ";
    cin >> dfahr;
    cout << dfahr << " = "
         << (dfahr - 32.0) * 5/9
         << " Celsius" << endl;

    return 0;
}
```

OUTPUT

prompt> *fahrcels*
enter a Fahrenheit temperature *40*
40 = 4 Celsius
enter another temperature *40*
40 = 4.44444 Celsius

illustrate the use of numeric literals and variables in C++ programs.[3] Prog. 3.2 shows how this is done.

Two variables are defined in Prog. 3.2, ifahr and dfahr. The type int represents an integer, what we think of mathematically as a value from the set of numbers ... $-3, -2, -1, 0, 1, 2, 3, \ldots$. The type double represents what is called a **floating-point** number in computer science and a *real number* in mathematics. Floating-point numbers have a decimal point; examples include $\sqrt{17}$, 3.14159, and 2.0. In Prog. 3.2 the input stream cin extracts an integer value entered by

---

[3]Note, however, that using a computer program to convert a single temperature is probably overkill. This program is used to study the types int and double rather than for its intrinsic worth.

the user with the statement `cin >> ifahr;` and stores the entered value in the variable `ifahr`. A floating-point number entered by the user is extracted and stored in the variable `dfahr` by the statement `cin >> dfahr;`. Except for the name of the variable, both these statements are identical in form to the statements in Prog. 3.1 that accepted strings entered by the user. When writing programs using numbers, the type `double` should be used for all variables and calculations that might have decimal points.[4] The type `int` should be used whenever integers, or numbers without decimal points, are appropriate.

Numeric Data

Although there is no largest integer in mathematics, the finite memory of a computer limits the largest and smallest `int` values in C++. On many microcomputers, the values of an `int` can range from −32,768 to 32,767. When workstations are used, the typical range of `int` values is −2,147,483,648 to 2,147,483,647. You don't need to remember these limits; in Sec. 9.8 we'll discuss why the limits have particular values. The smaller range of `int` values is really too small to do many calculations. For example, the number of seconds in a day is 86,400, far exceeding the value that can be stored in an `int` using C++ on most microcomputers. To alleviate this problem the type `long int` should be used instead of `int`. The variable `ifahr` could be defined to use this modified `long int` type as `long int ifahr;`.

Program 3.3 shows the limitations of the type `int`. The run adjacent to the program listing is from a workstation. The same run on a microcomputer generates a much different set of results, as shown.

Microcomputer OUTPUT

```
prompt> daysecs
how many days: 31
31 days = -8576 seconds
prompt> daysecs
how many days: 365
365 days = 13184 seconds
prompt> daysecs
how many days: 13870
13870 days = -23296 seconds
```

If the definition `int days` is changed to `long int days`, then the runs will be the same on both kinds of computers.

---

[4]The type `float` can also be used for floating-point numbers. We will not use this type, since most standard mathematical functions use `double` values. There is little reason to use `float` except to save memory, and this kind of saving is usually not necessary.

```
#include <iostream.h>

// converts days to seconds
// illustrates integer overflow

int main()
{
    int days;

    cout << "how many days: ";
    cin >> days;
    cout << days << " days = "
         << days*24*60*60
         << " seconds" << endl;

    return 0;
}
```

OUTPUT

```
prompt> daysecs
how many days: 31
31 days = 2678400 seconds
prompt> daysecs
how many days: 365
365 days = 31536000 seconds
prompt> daysecs
how many days: 13870
13870 days = 1198368000 seconds
```

Program Tip: As a guideline, when using microcomputers, use the type `long int` **instead of the type** `int` **in any program that uses integer values above 5,000.** This will help ensure that the output of the program is correct. When computers and compilers that use 32-bit integers (see Sec. 9.8) become more common, this will not be necessary.

It's also possible to use the type `double` instead of either `int` or `long int`. In mathematics, real numbers can have an infinite number of digits after a decimal point. For example, $1/3 = 0.333333\ldots$ and $\sqrt{2} = 1.41421356237\ldots$, where there is no pattern to the digits in the square root of two. Data represented using `double` values are approximations since it's not possible to have an infinite number of digits. When the definition of `days` is changed to double days the program generates the same results on both workstations and microcomputers.

OUTPUT

```
prompt> daysecs
how many days: 31
31 days = 2.6784e+06 seconds
prompt> daysecs
how many days: 365
365 days = 3.1536e+07 seconds
prompt> daysecs
how many days: 13870
13870 days = 1.19837e+09 seconds
```

The output in this run is shown using **exponent,** or **scientific,** notation. The expression 2.6784e+06 is equivalent to 2,678,400. The e+06 means "multiply by 10^6." The same run results if the definition int days is used, but the output statement is changed as shown below.

```
<< days*24.0*60*60 << " seconds" << endl;
```

We'll explore why this is the case in the next section.

Arithmetic Operators

Although the output statements in *fahrcels.cc*, Prog. 3.2, are the same except for the name of the variable storing the Fahrenheit temperature, the actual values output by the statements are different. This is because arithmetic performed using int values behaves differently than arithmetic performed using double values. An **operator,** such as +, is used to perform some kind of computation. Operators combine **operands** as in 15 + 3; the operands are 15 and 3. An **expression** is a sentence composed of operands and operators, as in $(X - 32)*5/9$. In this expression, X, 32, 5, and 9 are operands. The symbols −, *, and / are operators.

To understand why different output is generated by the following two expressions when the same value is entered for both ifahr and dfahr, we'll need to explore how arithmetic expressions are evaluated and how evaluation depends on the types of the operands.

```
(ifahr - 32) * 5/9           (dfahr - 32.0) * 5/9
```

The division operator / yields results that depend on the types of its operands. For example, what is 7/2? In mathematics the answer is 3.5, but in C++ the answer is 3. This is because division of two integer quantities (in this case, the literals 7 and 2) is defined to yield an integer. The value of 7.0/2 is 3.5 because division of double values yields a double. When an operator has more than one use, the operator is **overloaded.** In this case the division operator is overloaded since it works differently with double values than with int values.

Table 3.1 The Arithmetic Operators

symbol	meaning	example
*	multiplication	3*5*x
/	division	5.2/1.5
%	mod/remainder	7 % 2
+	addition	12+x
−	subtraction	35-y

The arithmetic operators available in C++ are shown in Table 3.1. Most should be familiar to you from your study of mathematics except, perhaps, for the modulus operator, %. The modulus operator % yields the remainder when one integer is divided by another. For example, a calculation showing remainders is diagrammed in Fig. 3.3. Executing the statement

```
cout << "47 divides 1347 " << 147/47 << " times, with remainder "
<< 1347 % 47 << endl;
```

would print

```
47 divides 1347 28 times, with remainder 31
```

because $1347 = 28 * 47 + 31$.

In general the result of p % q (read this as "p mod q") for two integers should be a value r with the property that p = x*q + r where x = p/q. The % operator is often used to determine if one integer divides another—that is, divides with no remainder, as in 4/2 or 27/9. If x % y = 0, there is a remainder of zero when x is divided by y, indicating that y evenly divides x. The examples below illustrate several uses of the modulus operator.

```
25 % 5 = 0        13 % 2 = 1        4 % 3 = 1
25 % 6 = 1        13 % 3 = 1        4 % 4 = 0
48 % 8 = 0        13 % 4 = 1        4 % 5 = 4
48 % 9 = 3        13 % 5 = 3        5 % 4 = 1
```

If either p or q is negative, however, the value calculated may be different on different systems. As a rule, avoid negative values when using the % operator, or check the documentation of the programming environment you use. In any case, the C++ standard requires that a = (a/b)*b + a%b.

Figure 3.3 Using the modulus operator.

Evaluating Expressions

The following rules are used for evaluating arithmetic expressions in C++ (these are standard rules of arithmetic as well):

1. Evaluate all parenthesized expressions first, with nested expressions evaluated "inside-out."

2. Evaluate expressions according to **operator precedence:** evaluate *, /, and % before + and −.

3. Evaluate operators with the same precedence left to right—this is called left-to-right **associativity.**

We'll use these rules to evaluate the expression (ifahr - 32) * 5/9 when ifahr has the value 40 (as in the output of Prog. 3.2).

1. Evaluate (ifahr - 32) first; this is 40 − 32, which is 8. (This is rule 1 above: evaluate parenthesized expressions first).

2. The expression is now 8 * 5/9 and * and / have equal precedence so are evaluated left to right (rule 3 above). This yields 40/9, which is 4.

In the last step above 40/9 evaluates to 4. This is because in integer division any fractional part is truncated, or removed. Thus although 40/9 = 4.444... mathematically, the fractional part .444... is truncated, leaving 4.

At this point it may be slightly mysterious why Prog. 3.2 prints 4.44444 when the expression (dfahr - 32.0) * 5/9 is evaluated. The subexpression (dfahr - 32.0) evaluates to the real number 8.0 rather than the integer 8. The expression (dfahr - 32) would evaluate to 8.0 as well because subtracting an int from a double results in a double value. Similarly, the expression 8.0 * 5/9 evaluates to 40.0/9, which is 4.44444, because when / is used with double values or a mixed combination of double and int values, the result is a double. The evaluation of both expressions from Prog. 3.2 is diagrammed in Fig. 3.4. This means that if the first cout << statement in Prog. 3.2 is modified

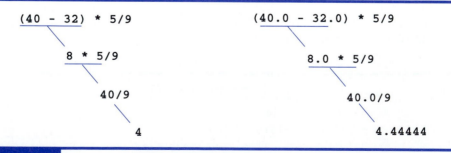

Figure 3.4   Evaluating arithmetic expressions.

Program 3.4   express.cc

```
#include <iostream.h>

// illustrates problems with evaluating
// arithmetic expressions

int main()
{
    double dfahr;

    cout << "enter a Fahrenheit temperature ";
    cin >> dfahr;
    cout << dfahr << " = "
         << 5/9 * (dfahr - 32.0)
         << " Celsius" << endl;

    return 0;
}
```

OUTPUT

```
prompt> express
enter a Fahrenheit temperature 40.0
40.0 = 0 Celsius
prompt> express
enter a Fahrenheit temperature 37.33
37.33 = 0 Celsius
```

so that the 5 is replaced by 5.0, as in `(ifahr - 32) * 5.0/9`, then the expression will evaluate to 4.44444 when 40 is entered as the value of `ifahr` because 5.0 is a `double` whereas 5 is an `int`.

Often arithmetic is done by specialized circuitry built to add, multiply, and do other arithmetic operations. The circuitry for `int` operations is different from the circuitry for `double` operations, reflecting the different methods used for multiplying integers and reals. When numbers of different types are combined in an arithmetic operation, one circuit must be used. Thus when `8.0 * 5` is evaluated, the 5 is **converted** to a `double` (and the double circuitry would be used). Sometimes the word **promoted** is used instead of *converted*.

Pitfalls with evaluating expressions. Because arithmetic operators are overloaded and because we're not used to thinking of arithmetic as performed by computers, some expressions yield results that don't meet our expectations. Referring to Prog. 3.4, we see that in the run of *express.cc* the answer is 0, because the value of the expression 5/9 is 0 since integer division is used. It might be a better idea to use 5.0 and 9.0 since the resulting expression should use `double` operators. If an arithmetic expression looks correct to you but it yields results that are not correct, be sure that you've used parentheses properly, that you've taken `double` and `int` operators into account, and that you have accounted for operator precedence.

Pause to reflect

3.5. If the output expressions in Prog. 3.2 are changed as shown in the following (with parentheses added to the `double` expression in the same way), the value printed by both statements will be 0. Why is this?

```
(ifahr - 32) * (5/9)
```

3.6. What is printed (and why) if parentheses are not used in either of the expressions in Prog. 3.2?

```
ifahr - 32 * 5/9
```

3.7. If the expression using `ifahr` is changed to

```
(ifahr - 32.0) * 5/9
```

what will the output be if the value of 40 is entered? Why?

3.8. What modifications are needed to change Prog. 3.2 so that it converts degrees Celsius to Fahrenheit rather than vice versa?

3.9. If *daysecs.cc*, Prog. 3.3, is used with the definition `long int day`, but the output is changed to `<< 24*60*60*days << endl`, then the program behavior on a microcomputer changes as shown here. The output is incorrect.

OUTPUT

```
prompt> daysecs
how many days: 31
31 days = 646784 seconds
prompt> daysecs
how many days: 365
365 days = 7615360 seconds
```

Explain why the change in the output statement makes a difference. (Hint: consider rule 3 for evaluating expressions.)

3.10. The quadratic formula, which gives the roots of a quadratic equation, is

$$\frac{-b \pm \sqrt{b^2 - 4ac}}{2a}$$

The roots of $2x^2 - 8x + 6$ should be 3 and 1, where $a = 2$, $b = -8$, $c = 6$, and $\sqrt{b^2 - 4ac} = 4$. Explain why the statements below print 12 and 4 instead of 3 and 1.

```
cout << (8 + 4)/2*2 << endl;
cout << (8 - 4)/2*2 << endl;
```

JOHN KEMENY (1926–1992)

Figure 3.5   John Kemeny.

John Kemeny, with Thomas Kurtz, invented the programming language BASIC (Beginner's All-purpose Symbolic Instruction Code). The language was designed to be simple to use but as powerful as FORTRAN, one of the languages with which it competed when first developed in 1964. BASIC went on to become the world's most popular programming language.

Kemeny was a research assistant to Albert Einstein before taking a job at Dartmouth College. At Dartmouth he was an early visionary in bringing computers to everyone. Kemeny and Kurtz developed the Dartmouth Time Sharing System, a method that allowed hundreds of users to use the same computer "simultaneously".

Kemeny was an inspiring teacher. While serving as president of Dartmouth College he still taught at least one math course each year. With a cigarette in a holder and a distinct, but very understandable, Hungarian accent, Kemeny was a model of clarity and organization in the classroom.

In a book published in 1959, Kemeny wrote the following, comparing computer calculations with the human brain. It's interesting that his words are still relevant more than 35 years later.

> When we inspect one of the present mechanical brains we are overwhelmed by its size and its apparent complexity. But this is a somewhat misleading first impression. None of these machines compare with the human brain in complexity or in efficiency.... It is true that we cannot match the speed or reliability of the computer in multiplying two ten-digit numbers, but, after all, that is its primary purpose, not ours. There are many tasks that we carry out as a matter of course that we would have no idea how to mechanize.

For more information see [Sla 87, AA85].

3.3   Case Study: Pizza Slices

In this section we'll look at one program in some detail. The program uses the types int and double in calculating several statistics about different sizes of pizza.

Pizza Statistics

Pizzas can be ordered in several sizes. Some pizza parlors cut all pizzas into eight slices, whereas others get more slices out of larger pizza pies. In many situations it would be useful to know what size pie offers the best deal in terms of cost per slice or cost per square inch of pizza. Prog. 3.5, *pizza.cc*, provides a first attempt at a program for determining information about pizza prices.

Program 3.5   pizza.cc

```
#include <iostream.h>

// find the price of one slice of pizza
// and the price per square inch
//
// Owen Astrachan
// January 10, 1995
//

void SlicePrice(int radius, double price)
// compute pizza statistics
{
    // assume all pizzas have 8 slices

    cout << "sq in/slice = ";
    cout << 3.14159*radius*radius/8 << endl;

    cout << "one slice: $" << price/8 << endl;

    cout << "$" << price/(3.14159*radius*radius);
    cout << " per sq. inch" << endl;
}

int main()
{
    int radius;
    double price;

    cout << "enter radius of pizza ";
    cin >> radius;

    cout << "enter price of pizza ";
    cin >> price;

    SlicePrice(radius, price);
```

```
    return 0;
}
```

```
                            ◦OUTPUT

prompt> pizza
enter radius of pizza 8
enter price of pizza 9.95
sq in/slice = 25.1327
one slice: $1.24375
$0.0494873 per sq. inch

prompt> pizza
enter radius of pizza 10
enter price of pizza 11.95
sq in/slice = 39.2699
one slice: $1.49375
$0.0380381 per sq. inch
```

The function `SlicePrice` is used for both the processing and the output steps of computation in *pizza.cc*. The input steps take place in `main`. Numbers entered by the user are stored in the variables `radius` and `price` defined in `main`. The values of these variables are sent to

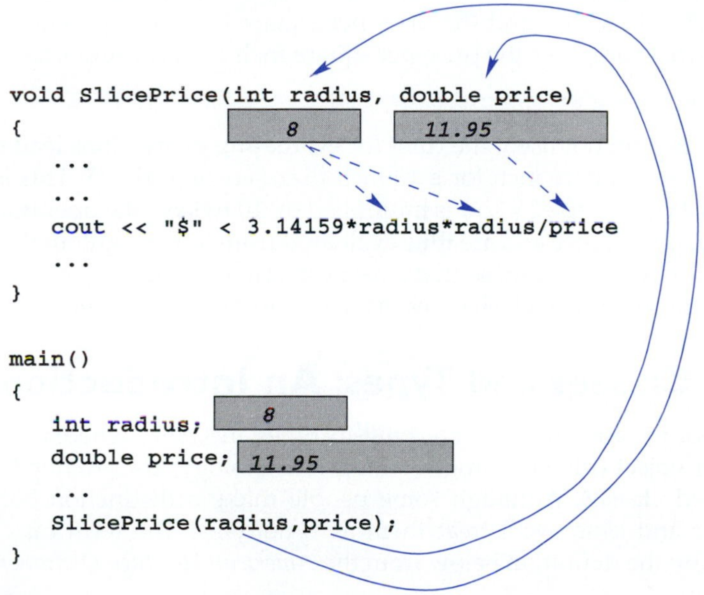

Figure 3.6   Passing variable values.

`SlicePrice` for processing. This is diagrammed in Fig. 3.6. If the order of the parameters in the call `SlicePrice(radius,price)` is changed to `SlicePrice(price,radius)`, the compiler issues a warning:

```
pizza.cc: In function 'int main()':
pizza.cc:35: warning: 'double' used for argument 1 of 'SlicePrice(int, double)'
```

It's not generally possible to pass a `double` value to an `int` parameter without losing part of the value, so the compiler issues a warning. For example, passing 11.95 as the argument for the parameter `radius` results in a value of 11 for the parameter because `double` values are truncated when stored as integers . This is called **narrowing** of values. If an argument of 11.0 is passed to an `int` parameter, the parameter will have the value of 11; so it is possible to store a `double` value in an `int` variable. Until we discuss how to convert values of one type to another type, you should be sure that the type of an argument matches the type of the corresponding formal parameter. Since different types may use different amounts of storage and may have different internal representations in the computer, it is a good idea to take steps to ensure that types match properly.

Program Tip: When the compiler issues a warning, interpret the warning as an indication that your program is not correct. Although the program may still compile and execute, the warning indicates that something isn't proper with your program.

The area of a circle is given by the formula $\pi \times r^2$, where r is the radius of the circle. This formula is used in `SlicePrice` to determine the number of square inches in a slice and the price per square inch. The parentheses in the statement that computes the price per square inch are very important.

```
cout << "$" << price/(3.14159*radius*radius)
```

If parentheses are not used, the rules for evaluating expressions lead to a value of $380.381 per square inch for a 10-inch pizza costing $11.95. This is because the value of `price/3.14159` is multiplied by 10 twice—the operators / and * have equal precedence and are thus evaluated from left to right. In the exercises you'll modify this program so that a user can enter the number of slices as well as other information. Such changes make the program useful in more settings.

3.4   Classes and Types: An Introduction

The types `int` and `double` are built-in types in C++, whereas `string` is a class. In object-oriented programming terminology, user-defined types are often called **classes.** Although some people make a distinction between the terms *type* and *class,* we'll treat them as synonyms. The term *class* is apt as indicated by the definition below from the *American Heritage Dictionary:*

class 1. A set, collection, group, or configuration containing members having or thought to have at least one attribute in common

---

Program 3.6 fly.cc

```
#include <iostream.h>
#include "balloon.h"

// illustrates use of Balloon class
// balloon (guided by auto-pilot) ascends, cruises, descends

int main()
{
    Balloon montgolfier;
    int rise;                   // how high to fly      (meters)
    int duration;               // how long to cruise   (seconds)


    cout << "Welcome to the windbag emporium." << endl;
    cout << "You'll rise up, cruise a while, then descend." << endl;
    cout << "How high (in meters) do you want to rise: ";
    cin >> rise;

    cout << "How long (in seconds) do you want to cruise: ";
    cin >> duration;

    montgolfier.Ascend(rise);           // ascend to specified height
    montgolfier.Cruise(duration);       // cruise for specified time steps
    montgolfier.Descend(0);             // come to earth

    return 0;
}
```

fly.cc

All variables of type, or class, `string` share certain attributes that determine how they can be used in C++ programs. As we've seen in several examples, the types `int` and `double` represent numbers with different attributes. In the discussion that follows, I'll sometimes use the word **object** instead of the word *variable.* You should think of these as synonyms. The use of classes in object-oriented programming gives programmers the ability to write programs using off-the-shelf components. In this section we'll examine a programmer-defined class that simulates a computer-guided hot-air balloon (see Prog. 3.6). You won't know all the details of how the simulated balloon works, but you'll still be able to write a program that guides the balloon. This is also part of object-oriented programming: using classes without knowing exactly how the classes are implemented, that is, without knowing about the code used "behind the scenes." Just as many people drive cars without understanding exactly what a spark plug does or what a carburetor is, programmers can use classes without knowing the details of how the classes are written.

A fundamental property of a class is that its behavior is defined by the functions by which objects of the class are manipulated. Knowing about these functions should be enough to write programs using the objects; intimate knowledge of how the class is implemented is not necessary. This should make sense since you've worked with `double` variables without knowledge of how `double` numbers are stored in a computer.

In *fly.cc*, Prog. 3.6, an object (variable) `montgolfier`[5] of type, or class, `Balloon` is defined and used to simulate a hot-air balloon rising, cruising for a specified duration, and then descending to earth. Two different runs are shown in the following ouputs.

OUTPUT

```
prompt> fly
Welcome to the windbag emporium.
You'll rise up, cruise a while, then descend.
How high (in meters) do you want to rise: 20
How long (in seconds) do you want to cruise: 10

***** (Height = 0) Ascending to 20 meters *****

0 meters  Burn! ...
10 meters  Burn! ...

***** Cruising at 20 meters  with margin +/- 5 for 10 time-steps *****

20 meters (time step 0)
20 meters (time step 1)     wind-shear bump up 5 meters
25 meters (time step 2)     wind-shear drop 2 meters
23 meters (time step 3)
23 meters (time step 4)     wind-shear bump up 1 meters
24 meters (time step 5)     wind-shear drop 2 meters
22 meters (time step 6)
22 meters (time step 7)     wind-shear bump up 2 meters
24 meters (time step 8)     wind-shear bump up 3 meters too high!  Woooosh!
17 meters (time step 9)

***** (Height = 17) Descending to 0 meters *****

17 meters  Woooosh!
7 meters  Woooosh!
```

---

[5]The Montgolfier brothers were among the first to use hot-air balloons.

OUTPUT

```
prompt> fly
Welcome to the windbag emporium.
You'll rise up, cruise a while, then descend.
How high (in meters) do you want to rise: 20
How long (in seconds) do you want to cruise: 10


***** (Height = 0) Ascending to 20 meters *****

0 meters   Burn! ...
10 meters  Burn! ...


***** Cruising at 20 meters  with margin +/- 5 for 10 time-steps *****

20 meters (time step 0)    wind-shear drop 2 meters
18 meters (time step 1)    wind-shear drop 4 meters too low!  Burn! ...
24 meters (time step 2)    wind-shear drop 1 meters
23 meters (time step 3)
23 meters (time step 4)    wind-shear bump up 3 meters too high!  Woooosh!
16 meters (time step 5)
16 meters (time step 6)    wind-shear drop 3 meters too low!  Burn! ...
23 meters (time step 7)    wind-shear drop 1 meters
22 meters (time step 8)    wind-shear bump up 4 meters too high!  Woooosh!
16 meters (time step 9)    wind-shear bump up 4 meters


***** (Height = 20) Descending to 0 meters *****

20 meters   Woooosh!
10 meters   Woooosh!
```

Clearly there is something going on behind the scenes since the statements in Prog. 3.6 do not appear to be able to generate the output shown. In the next chapter we'll study how the `Balloon` class works; at this point we'll concentrate on understanding the three function calls in Prog. 3.6.

Member Functions

We have studied several programs with user-defined functions. In *macinput.cc*, Prog. 3.1, the function `Verse` has two `string` parameters. In *pizza.cc*, Prog. 3.5, the function `SlicePrice` has one `int` parameter and one `double` parameter. In Prog. 3.6 , *fly.cc*, three function calls are made; the functions called are *Ascend*, *Cruise*, and *Descend*. Together, these functions define the behavior of a `Balloon` object—access to such an object is through these functions only. These functions are applied to the object *montgolfier* as indicated by the "dot" syntax as in

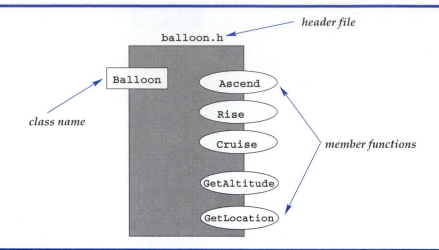

Figure 3.7   Interface diagram for Balloon class.

```
montgolfier.Ascend(rise);
```

which is read as "*montgolfier dot ascend rise*." These functions are referred to as **member functions** in C++. In other object-oriented languages, functions that are used to manipulate objects of a given class are often called **methods.** In this example, the object montgolfier invokes its member function Ascend with rise as the argument.

Note that definitions of these functions do *not* appear in the text of Prog. 3.6 before they are called. The prototypes for these functions are made accessible by the statement

```
#include "balloon.h"
```

which causes the information in the **header file** *balloon.h* to be included in Prog. 3.6. The header file is an interface to the class Balloon. Sometimes an **interface diagram** is used to summarize how a class is accessed. The diagram shown in Fig. 3.7 is modeled after diagrams used by Grady Booch [Boo91] and Rick Mercer [Mer94].

Each member function[6] is shown in an oval, and the name of the class is shown in a rectangle. Full details about the member function prototypes as well as what they do are found in the header file. The interface diagram serves as a reminder of what the names of the member functions are.

Reading Programs

One skill you should begin to learn is how to read a program and the supporting documentation for the program. Rich Pattis, the author of *Karel the Robot*, argues

---

[6]We will not use the functions GetAltitude and GetLocation now but will return to them in a later chapter.

that you should read a program carefully, not like a book but like a contract you desperately want to break. The idea is that you must pay close attention to the "fine print" and not just read for plot or characterization. Sometimes such minute perusal is essential, but it is often possible to gain a general understanding without such scrutiny.

The header file *balloon.h* is shown in Prog. 3.7.

Program 3.7   balloon.h

```
#ifndef _BALLOON_H
#define _BALLOON_H

// class for balloon manipulation using simulated auto pilot
// written: 8/29/93   (based on an idea of Dave Reed)
// modified: 8/30/94, 12/29/94, 11/3/95

// member function explanation:
//
// Ascend: balloon ascends to height specified by parameter
//         in a sequence of burns.  Each burn raises the
//         altitude by 10 meters
//
// Cruise: balloon cruises at current altitude for a number of time
//         steps specified by parameter.  Random wind-shear can cause
//         balloon to rise and fall, but vents and burns keep the
//         balloon within +/- 5 meters of the altitude at which cruising
//         starts
//
// Descend:   balloon descends to height specified by parameter in a
//            sequence of vents.  Each vet drops the balloon 10 meters,
//            or to the ground (if less than 10 meters to the ground)
//
//
// int GetAltitude: returns altitude (in meters)
//
// int GetLocation: returns how many time steps taken

#include "rando.h"

class Balloon
{
  public:
    Balloon();                      // constructor

          // change where balloon is (up,down,"forward")

    void Ascend(int);               // ascend so altitude >= parameter
    void Descend(int);              // descend so altitude <= parameter
    void Cruise(int);               // cruise for parameter time steps
```

```
                    // retrieve balloon's location

     int GetAltitude();                   // returns height above ground
     int GetLocation();                   // returns how cruise "steps" taken

   private:
     int myAltitude;                      // altitude (height) of balloon
     int myCruiseSteps;                   // number of time steps cruised
     RandGen myRand;                      // random number generator

     void Burn();                         // go up (some amount)
     void Vent();                         // go down (some amount)
     void BurnMessage();                  // message printed when burning
     void VentMessage();                  // message printed when venting
     void AltitudeMessage();              // message to print current altitude
     void AdjustAltitude();               // adjust altitude randomly
};

#endif    // _BALLOON_H defined
```

balloon.h

There are three important details of this header file.

1. Comments provide users and readers of the header file with an explanation of what the member functions do.

2. Member functions are declared in the **public** section of a class definition and may be called by a user of the class as is shown in Prog. 3.6. We'll discuss the special member function `Balloon` later. The other functions, also shown in the interface diagram in Fig. 3.7, each have prototypes showing they take one `int` parameter except for `GetAltitude` and `GetLocation`.

3. Functions and data in the **private** section are *not* accessible to a user of the class. As a programmer using the class, you may glance at the private section, but the compiler will prevent your program from accessing what's in the private section. Definitions in the private section are part of the class's implementation, *not* part of the class's interface. As a user, or **client,** of the class, your only concern should be with the interface, or public section.

Private and Public

The declaration of the class `Balloon` in Prog. 3.7 shows that the parts of the class are divided into two sections: the private and the public sections. The public section is how an object of a class appears to the world, how the object behaves. Objects are manipulated in programs like Prog. 3.6, *fly.cc,* by calling the object's public member functions. The private member functions like `Burn` and `AdjustAltitude` exist only to help implement the public functions. This is a hard concept to understand. Imagine a company that publishes a list of its company phone numbers. For security reasons, some numbers are accessible only by those calling from within the company building. An outsider can get a copy of the company phonebook and see the inaccessible phone numbers, but the company switchboard will allow only calls from within the building to go through to the inaccessible numbers.

In general, the designation of what should be private and what should be public is a difficult task. At this point, the key concept is that access to a class is via the public functions. Some computer scientists consider it a drawback of C++ that information in the private section can be seen and read, but many languages suffer from the same problem. To make things simple, you should think of the private section as invisible until you begin to design your own classes.

There are often variables in the private section. These variables, such as `myAltitude`, define an object's **state**—the information that determines the object's characteristics. In the case of a `Balloon` object, the altitude of the balloon, represented by the `int` variable `myAltitude`, is part of this state. Knowledge of the private section isn't necessary to understand how to use `Balloon` objects.

The public section describes the interface to an object, that is, what a client or user needs to know to manipulate the object. In a car, the brake pedal is the interface to the braking system. Pressing the pedal causes the car to stop, regardless of whether antilock brakes, disc brakes, or drum brakes are used. In general, the public interface provides "buttons" and "levers" that a user can push and pull to manipulate the object as well as dials that can be used to read information about the object state.

All header files we'll use in this book will have statements similar to the `#ifndef _BALLOON_H` statement and others that begin with the # sign, as shown in *balloon.h.* For the moment we'll ignore the purpose of these statements; they're necessary but are not important to the discussion at this point. The `ifndef` statement makes it impossible to include the same header file more than once in the same program. We'll see why this is important when programs get more complex.

3.5   Compiling and Linking

In Chapter 1 we discussed the differences between **source code,** written in a high-level language like C++, and machine code, written in a low-level language specific to one kind of computer. The compiler translates the source code into machine code. Another step is almost always necessary in making an executable program. Code from libraries needs to be **linked** together with the machine code to form an executable program. For example, when the header file `<iostream.h>` is used, the code that implements input and output streams must be linked. When the header file `"balloon.h"` is used, the code that implements the balloon class must be linked. This process of compiling and linking is illustrated in Fig. 3.8.

The compiler translates source code into machine, or **object,** code. The word *object* here has nothing to do with object-oriented programming; think of it as a synonym for *machine code.* In some environments object code has a `.o` extension; in other environments it has a `.obj` extension. The different object files are linked together to form an executable program. Sometimes you may not be aware that linking is taking place. But when you develop more complex programs, you'll encounter errors in the linking stage. For example, if you try to

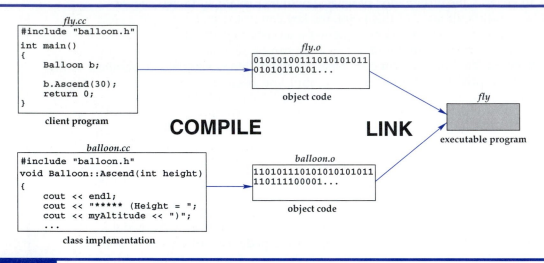

Figure 3.8   Compiling and linking.

compile *fly.cc*, Prog. 3.6, you *must* link-in the code that implements the balloon class. The implementation of the class is declared in *balloon.h* and is found in the file *balloon.cc.* The corresponding object code, as translated by the compiler, is in *balloon.o.* It's often convenient to group several object files together in a code **library.** The library can be automatically linked into your programs so that you don't need to take steps to do this yourself.

Pause to reflect

3.11. Some pizza parlors cut larger pies into more pieces than small pies: a small pie might have 8 pieces, a medium pie 10 pieces, and a large pie 12 pieces. Modify the function `SlicePrice` so that the number of slices is a parameter. The function should have three parameters instead of two. How would the function `main` in Prog. 3.5 change to accommodate the new `SlicePrice`?

3.12. In *pizza.cc*, what changes are necessary to allow the user to enter the diameter of a pizza instead of the radius?

3.13. Based on the descriptions of the member functions given in the header file `balloon.h` (Prog. 3.7), why is different output generated when Prog. 3.6 is run with the same input values? (Run the program and see if the results are similar to those shown above.)

3.14. What would the function `main` look like of a program that defines a `Balloon` object, causes the balloon to ascend to 40 meters, cruises for 10 time-steps, ascends to 80 meters, cruises for 20 time-steps, then descends to earth?

3.15. What do you think happens if the following two statements are the only statements in a modified version of Prog. 3.6?

```
montgolfier.Ascend(50);
montgolfier.Ascend(30);
```

What would happen if these statements are reversed (first ascend to 30 meters, then to 50)?

DONALD KNUTH (b. 1938)

Donald Knuth is perhaps the best-known computer scientist and is certainly the foremost scholar of the field. His interests are wide-ranging, from organ playing to word games to typography. His first publication was for *MAD* magazine, and his most famous is the three-volume set *The Art of Computer Programming.*

In 1974 Knuth won the Turing award for "major contributions to the analysis of algorithms and the design of programming languages." In his Turing award address he says:

> The chief goal of my work as educator and author is to help people learn how to write *beautiful* programs. My feeling is that when we prepare a program, it can be like composing poetry or music; as Andrei Ershov has said, programming can give us both intellectual and emotional satisfaction, because it is a real achievement to master complexity and to establish a system of consistent rules.

Figure 3.9   Donald Knuth.

In discussing what makes a program "good," Knuth says:

In the first place, it's especially good to have a program that works correctly. Secondly it is often good to have a program that won't be hard to change, when the time for adaptation arises. Both of these goals are achieved when the program is easily readable and understandable to a person who knows the appropriate language.

Of computer programming Knuth says:

We have seen that computer programming is an art, because it applies accumulated knowledge to the world, because it requires skill and ingenuity, and especially because it produces objects of beauty.

For more information see [Sla87, AA85, ACM87].

3.6   Chapter Review

In this chapter we studied the input/process/output model of computation and how input is performed in C++ programs. We also studied numeric types and operations and a user-defined class, `Balloon`. The importance of reading programs and documentation in order to be able to modify and write programs was stressed.

- Input is accomplished in C++ using the extraction operator, `>>`, and the standard input stream, `cin`. These are accessible by including `<iostream.h>`.

- Variables are memory locations with a name, a value, and a type. Variables must be defined before being used in C++. Variables can be defined anywhere in a program in C++, but we'll define most variables at the beginning of the function in which they're used.

- Numeric data represent different kinds of numbers in C++. We'll use two types for numeric data: `int` for integers and `double` for floating-point numbers (real numbers, in mathematics). If you're using a microcomputer, you should use the type `long int` instead of `int` for quantities over 5,000.

- Operators are used to form arithmetic expressions. The standard math operators in C++ are `+ - * / %`. In order to write correct arithmetic expressions you must understand operator precedence rules and the rules of expression evaluation.

- Conversion takes place when an `int` value is converted to a corresponding `double` value when arithmetic is done using both types together.

- Classes are types, but are defined by a programmer rather than being built into the language like `int` and `double`. The interface to a class is accessible by including the right header file.

- Member functions manipulate or operate on classes. Only member functions defined in the public section of a class definition can be used in a client program.

- A class is divided into two sections, the private section and the public section. Programs that use the class access the class by the public member functions.

- Executable programs are created by compiling source code into object code and linking different object files together. Sometimes object files are stored together in a code library.

3.7   Exercises

3.1 Write a program that prompts the user for a first name and a last name and that prints a greeting for that person. For example:

```
enter first name Owen
enter last name Astrachan
Hello Owen, you have an interesting last name: Astrachan.
```

3.2 Write a program that prompts the user for a quantity expressed in British thermal units (Btu) and that converts it to joules. The relationship between these two units of measure is given by: $1 \text{ joule} = 9.48 \times 10^{-1} \text{ Btu}$.

3.3 Write a program that prompts the user for a quantity expressed in knots and that converts it to miles per hour. The relationship needed is that $1 \text{ knot} = 101.269 \text{ ft/min}$ (and that $5{,}280 \text{ ft} = 1 \text{ mile}$).

3.4 Write a program using the operators / and % that prompts the user for a number of seconds and then determines how many hours, minutes, and seconds this represents. For example, 20,000 seconds represents 5 hours, 33 minutes, and 20 seconds.

3.5 Write a program that prints three verses of the classic song "One hundred bottles of _____ on the wall" as shown here.

OUTPUT

```
56 bottles of cola on the wall
56 bottles of cola
If one of those bottles should happen to fall
55 bottles of cola on the wall
```

The function's **prototype** is

```
void
BottleVerse(string beverage, int howMany)
```

The first parameter, `beverage`, is a string representing the kind of beverage for which a song will be printed. The second parameter, `howMany`, is not a string but is a C++ integer. The advantage of using an `int` rather than a `string` is that arithmetic operations can be performed on `int`s. For example, given the function `BottleVerse` shown below, the function call `BottleVerse("cola",56)` would generate the abbreviated verse shown here.

```
void
BottleVerse(string beverage, int howMany)
{
    cout << howMany << " bottles of "
        << beverage << ", ";
    cout << "one fell, " << howMany - 1
        << " exist" << endl;
}
```

OUTPUT

```
56 bottles of cola, one fell, 55 exist
```

Note how the `string` parameter is used to indicate the specific kind of beverage for which a verse is to be printed. The `int` parameter is used to specify how many bottles are "in use." Note that because `int` parameters support arithmetic operations, the expression `howMany - 1` is always 1 less than the just-printed number of bottles. In the program you write, three verses should be printed. The number of bottles in the first verse can be any integer. Each subsequent verse should use 1 bottle less than the previous verse. The user should be prompted for the kind of beverage used in the song.

3.6 Write a program that calculates pizza statistics, but takes both the number of slices into account and the thickness of the pizza. The user should be prompted for both quantities.

3.7 Write a program that can be used as a simplistic trip planner. Prompt the user for the number of car passengers, the length of the trip in miles, the capacity of the fuel tank in gallons, the price of gas, and the miles per gallon that the car gets. The program should calculate the number of tanks of gas needed, the total price of the gas needed, and the price per passenger if the cost is split evenly.

3.8 Write a program that uses a variable of type `Balloon` that performs the following sequence of actions:

1. Prompt the user for an initial altitude and a number of time steps.
2. Cause the balloon to ascend to the specified altitude, then cruise for the specified time steps.
3. Cause the balloon to descend to half the altitude it initially ascended to, then cruise again for the specified time steps.
4. Cause the balloon to descend to earth (height = 0).

Building Programs and Solving Problems

If *A* equals success, then the formula is
$A = X + Y + Z$. *X* is work. *Y* is play. *Z* is keep
your mouth shut.
ALBERT EINSTEIN
quoted in *SIGACT News*, Vol. 25, No. 1, March
1994

Your "if" is the only peacemaker; much virtue
in "if."
WILLIAM SHAKESPEARE
As You Like It, V, iv

Leave all else to the gods.
HORACE
Odes, Book I, Ode ix

In the programs studied in Chapter 3, statements executed one after the other
to produce output. This was true both when all statements were in `main`
or when control was transferred from `main` to another function, as it was
in `SlicePrice` in *pizza.cc*, Prog. 3.5. However, code behind the scenes in
fly.cc, Program 3.6, executed differently in response to the user's input and to
a simulated wind-shear effect. Many programs require nonsequential control.
For example, transactions made at automatic teller machines (ATMs) process an
identification number and present you with a screen of choices. The program
controlling the ATM executes different code depending on your choice—for
example, either to deposit money or to get cash. This type of control is called
selection: a different code segment is selected and executed based on interaction
with the user or on the value of a program variable.

Another type of program control is **repetition:** the same sequence of C++
statements executes over and over, usually with different values for some of
the variables in the statements. For example, printing a yearly calendar requires

printing a calendar for each month. Your program could call a `PrintMonth` function twelve times:

```
PrintMonth("January", 31);
PrintMonth("February", 29);
PrintMonth("March", 31);
//...
PrintMonth("November",30);
PrintMonth("December",31);
```

Here the name of the month and the number of days in the month are arguments passed to `PrintMonth`. Alternatively, you could construct the `PrintMonth` function to determine the name of the month as well as the number of days in the month given the year and the number of the month (with January = 1, February = 2,..., December = 12). This could be done for the year 2000 by repeatedly executing the following statement and assigning values of $1, 2, \ldots, 12$ to `month`:

```
PrintMonth(month, 2000);
```

In this chapter we'll study methods for controlling how the statements in a program are executed and how this control is used in constructing functions and classes. To do this we'll expand our study of arithmetic operators, introduced in the last chapter, to include operators for other kinds of data. We'll also study C++ statements that alter the flow of control within a program. Finally, we'll see how functions and classes can be used as a foundation on which we'll continue to build as we study how programs are used to solve problems.

4.1   The Assignment Operator

In the next three sections we'll use a program that makes change using U.S. coins to study relational and assignment statements and conditional execution. We'll use the same program as the basis for what could be a talking cash register.

The program shows how values can be stored in variables using the **assignment operator,** =. This operator is used to assign values for each kind of coin and to reset the value of the variable `amount` so that change will be correctly calculated.

A run of *change.cc,* Prog. 4.1, shows how change is made using quarters, dimes, nickels, and pennies.

The **assignment** operator = stores values in variables. The expression on the right-hand side of the = is evaluated, and this value is stored in the memory location associated with the

> **Syntax: assignment operator =**
>
> *variable = expression*

variable named on the left-hand side of the =. The use of the equal sign to assign values to variables can cause confusion, especially if you say "equals" when you read an expression like `quarters = amount/25`. Operationally, the value on the right is stored in `quarters`, and it would be better to write `quarters ←` `amount / 25`. The assignment statement can be read as *"The memory location of the variable quarters is assigned the value of amount/25,"* but that is cumbersome

```cpp
#include <iostream.h>

// make change in U.S. coins
// Owen Astrachan, 1/2/96

int main()
{
    int amount;
    int quarters, dimes, nickels, pennies;

    // input phase of program

    cout << "make change in coins for what amount: ";
    cin >> amount;

    // calculate number of quarters, dimes, nickels, pennies

    quarters = amount/25;
    amount = amount - quarters*25;

    dimes = amount/10;
    amount = amount - dimes*10;

    nickels = amount/5;
    amount = amount - nickels*5;

    pennies = amount;

    // output phase of program

    cout << "# quarters =\t" << quarters << endl;
    cout << "# dimes =\t"    << dimes    << endl;
    cout << "# nickels =\t"  << nickels  << endl;
    cout << "# pennies =\t"  << pennies  << endl;

    return 0;
}
```

OUTPUT

```
prompt> change
make change in coins for what amount: 87
# quarters =    3
# dimes =       1
# nickels =     0
# pennies =     2
prompt> change
make change in coins for what amount: 42
# quarters =    1
# dimes =       1
# nickels =     1
# pennies =     2
```

(at best). If you can bring yourself to say "gets" for =, you'll find it easier to distinguish between = and == (the boolean equality operator). Verbalizing the process by saying "*Quarters gets amount divided by twenty-five*" will help you understand what's happening when assignment statements are executed.

The statement amount = amount - quarters*25 updates the value of the variable amount. The right-hand side of the statement is evaluated first. The value of this expression, amount - quarters*25, is stored in the variable on the left-hand side of the assignment statement—that is, the variable amount. This process is diagrammed in Fig. 4.1 when amount is 87.

A sequence of assignments can be chained together in one statement:

$$x = y = z = 13;$$

This statement assigns the value 13 to the variables x, y, and z. The statement is interpreted as x = (y = (z = 13)). The value of the expression (z = 13) is 13, the value assigned to z. This value is assigned to y, and the result of the assignment to y is 13. This result of the expression (y = 13) is then assigned to z. Parentheses aren't needed in the statement x = y = z = 13, because the assignment operator = is **right-associative:** in the absence of parentheses the rightmost = is evaluated first. In contrast, the subtraction operator is **left-associative,** so the expression 8 - 3 - 2 is equal to 3, because it is evaluated as (8 - 3) - 2 rather than 8 - (3 - 2): here the leftmost - is evaluated first. Most operators are left-associative.

Escape sequences. The output of *change.cc* is aligned using a tab character '\t'. The tab character prints one tab position, ensuring that the amounts

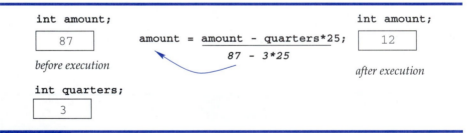

Figure 4.1   Updating amount: amount = amount - quarters*25.

Table 4.1   Escape Sequences in C++

Escape sequence	Name	Description
\t	Tab	Move cursor to next tab stop
\n	Newline	Move cursor to next line
\"	Double quote	Prints a double quote
\\	Backslash	Prints a backslash
\'	Single quote	Prints a single quote
\a	Bell	"Prints" (sounds) a bell or alert

of each kind of coin line up. The backslash and `t` to print the tab character are an example of an **escape sequence.** Common escape sequences are given in Table 4.1 Each escape sequence prints a single character. For example, `cout << "\"\\\'\""` `<< endl` prints the four-character string `"\'"`.

4.2   Choices and Conditional Execution

I shall set forth from somewhere, I shall make
the reckless choice
ROBERT FROST
"The Sound of the Trees"

In this section we'll alter Prog. 4.1 so that it doesn't print those coins not used in giving change. We'll also move the output part of the program to a separate function. By parameterizing the output and using a function, we make it simpler to incorporate modifications to the original program.

Program 4.2   change2.cc

```cpp
#include <iostream.h>
#include "CPstring.h"

// make change in U.S. coins
// Owen Astrachan, 1/2/96

void Output(string coin, int amount)
{
    if (amount > 0)
    {
        cout << "# " << coin << " =\t" << amount << endl:
    }
}

int main()
{
    int amount;
    int quarters, dimes, nickels, pennies;

    // input phase of program

    cout << "make change in coins for what amount: ";
    cin >> amount;

    // calculate number of quarters, dimes, nickels, pennies

    quarters = amount/25;
    amount = amount - quarters*25;

    dimes = amount/10;
    amount = amount - dimes*10;
```

```
nickels = amount/5;
amount = amount - nickels*5;

pennies = amount;

// output phase of program

Output("quarters",quarters);
Output("dimes",dimes);
Output("nickels",nickels);
Output("pennies",pennies);

return 0;
}
```

OUTPUT

```
prompt> change2
make change in coins for what amount: 87
# quarters =     3
# dimes =        1
# pennies =      2
```

In the function `Output` an `if` statement is used for **conditional execution**—that is, `if` makes the execution depend on the value of `amount`. In the C++ statement

```
if (amount > 0)
{
    cout << "# " << coin << " =\t" << amount << endl;
}
```

the **test expression** `(amount > 0)` controls the `cout << ...` statement so that output appears only if the value of the `int` variable `amount` is greater than zero.

The `if/else` Statement

An `if` statement contains a test expression and a **body:** a group of statements within curly braces { and }. These statements are executed *only* when the test expression, also called a **condition** or a **guard,** is true. The test *must* be enclosed by parentheses. In the next section we'll explore oper-

Syntax: if statement

```
if (test expression)
{
    statement list;
}
```

ators that can be used in tests, including `<`, `<=`, `>`, and `>=`.

The body of the `if` statement can contain any number of statements. The curly braces that are used to delimit the body of the `if` statement aren't needed when there's only one statement in the body, but we'll always use them as part of a defensive programming strategy designed to ward off bugs before they appear.

Program 4.3 shows that an `if` statement can have an `else` part, which also controls, or guards, a body of statements within curly braces { and } that is executed when the test is false. If the value of `response` is something other than `"yes"`, then the `cout << ...` statements associated with the `if` section are not executed, and the statements in the `else` section of the program are executed instead. In particular, if the user enters `"Yes"` or `"yup"`, then the program takes the same action as when the user enters `"no"`. Furthermore, the answer `"Yes"` is also

---

Program 4.3   broccoli.cc

```
#include <iostream.h>
#include "CPstring.h"

// illustrates use of if-else statement

int main()
{
    string response;

    cout << "Do you like broccoli [yes/no]> ";
    cin >> response;
    if ("yes" == response)
    {
        cout << "Green vegetables are good for you" << endl;
        cout << "Broccoli is good in Chinese food as well" << endl;
    }
    else
    {
        cout << "De gustibus non disputandum" << endl;
        cout << "(There is no accounting for taste)" << endl;
    }

    return 0;
}
```

OUTPUT

```
prompt> broccoli
Do you like broccoli [yes/no]> yes
Green vegetables are good for you
Broccoli is good in Chinese food as well

prompt> broccoli
Do you like broccoli [yes/no]> no
De gustibus non disputandum
(There is no accounting for taste)
```

treated like the answer `"no"` rather than `"yes"`, because a capital letter is different from the equivalent lower-case letter. As we saw in Prog. 4.1, *change.cc,* the rules of C++ do *not* require an `else` section for every `if`. The `else` section in Prog. 4.3 could be removed, leaving the following function `main`:

```
int main()
{
        string response;

        cout << "Do you like broccoli [yes/no]> ";
        cin >> response;
        if ("yes" == response)
        {
                cout << "Green vegetables are good for you" << endl;
                cout << "Broccoli is good in Chinese food as well" << endl;
        }
         return 0;
}
```

In this modified program, if the user enters any string other than `"yes"`, nothing is printed.

Any kind of statement can appear in the body of an `if/else` statement, including other `if/else` statements. We'll discuss formatting conventions for writing such code after we explore the other kinds of operators that can be used in the test expressions that are part of `if` statements.

Sometimes it is convenient to have an **empty** `if` or `else` body: one with no statements. Usually this can be avoided by changing the test used with the `if`, such as from `<` to `>=`.

> **Syntax: if/else statement**
>
> ```
> if (test expression)
> {
>         statement list;
> }
> else
> {
>         statement list;
> }
> ```

4.3   Operators

We've seen arithmetic operators such as `+`, `*`, `%`, the assignment operator `=`, and the `<` operator used in `if/else` statements. In this section we'll study the other operators available in C++.

Relational Operators

> Comparisons are odious.
> JOHN FORTESCUE
> *De Laudibus Legum Angliae,* 1471

The expressions that form the test of an `if` statement are built from different operators. In this section we'll study the **relational operators,** which are used to determine the relationships between different values. Relational operators are listed in Table 4.2.

Table 4.2   The Relational Operators

Symbol	Meaning	Example
==	Equal to	if ("yes" == response)
>	Greater than	if (salary > 30000)
<	Less than	if (0 < salary)
!=	Not equal to	if ("yes" != response)
>=	Greater than or equal to, $\geq$	if (salary >= 10000)
<=	Less than or equal to, $\leq$	if (20000 <= salary)

The parenthesized expression that serves as the test of an `if` statement can use any of the relational operators shown in Table 4.2. The parenthesized expressions evaluate to true or false and are called **boolean** expressions, after the mathematician George Boole. Boolean expressions have one of two values: **true** or **false.** In C++ programs, any nonzero value is considered "true," and zero-valued expressions are considered "false." In 1994 the committee developing standards for C++ approved a new built-in type **bool**, for which valid values are *true* and *false.* Many compilers have not yet implemented this type; we'll use it, however, because it will be implemented by all compilers supporting the draft C++ standard.[1] We'll use `true` and `false` as values rather than zero and one, but remember that zero is the value used for false in C++.

The relational operators < and > behave as you might expect when used with `int` and `double` values. In the following statement the variable `salary` can be an `int` or a `double`. In either case the phrase about minimum wage is printed if the value of `salary` is less than 10.0.

```
if (salary < 10.0)
{
    cout << "you make below minimum wage" << endl;
}
```

When `string` values are compared, the behavior of the inequality operators < and > is based on a dictionary order, sometimes called **lexicographical** order:

```
string word;
cout << "enter a word: ";
cin >> word;
if (word < "middle")
{
    cout << word << " comes before middle" << endl;
}
```

---

[1]If you're using a compiler that doesn't support `bool` as a built-in type, you can use `#include"bool.h"` supplied with the code from this book to get access to a programmer-defined version of type `bool`.

In the foregoing code fragment, entering the word `"apple"` generates the following output.

```
apple comes before middle
```

Entering the word `"zebra"` would cause the test (`word < "middle"`) to evaluate to false, so nothing is printed. The comparison of strings is based on the order in which the strings would appear in a dictionary, so that `"A"` comes before `"Z"`. Sometimes the behavior of string comparisons is unexpected. Entering `"Zebra"`, for example, generates this output:

```
Zebra comes before middle
```

This happens because capital letters come before lower-case letters in the ordering of characters used on most computers.[2]

To see how relational operators are evaluated, consider the output of these statements:

```
cout << (13 < 5) << endl;
cout << ("Apple" != "apple") << endl;
cout << (5 + 1 < 6 * 2) << endl;
```

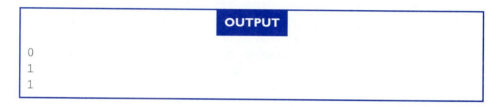

```
OUTPUT

0
1
1
```

The value of `13 < 5` is false, which is zero; the value of `"Apple" != "apple"` is true, which is one; and the value of `6 < 12` is true, which

Table 4.3   Precedence of C++ Operators

	Operators	Descriptions
	`!`	Logical negation
Higher	`*`, `/`, `%`	Arithmetic multiplication, division, and modulus
precedence	`+`, `-`	Arithmetic addition and subtraction
	`<<`, `>>`	Stream insertion and extraction
	`<`, `<=`, `>`, `>=`	Relational less than (or equal), greater than (or equal)
Lower	`==`, `!=`	Relational equality (equals), inequality (not equals)
precedence	`&&`	Logical AND
	`||`	Logical OR
	`=`, `+=`, `-=`, `*=`, `/=`, `%=`	Assignment operators

---

[2]We'll explore the ASCII character set, which is used to determine this ordering, in Chapter 9.

is one. In the last output statement, the arithmetic operations are executed first, because they have higher precedence than relational operators. You've seen precedence used with arithmetic operators; for example, multiplication has higher precedence than addition, so that $3 + 4 \times 2 = 11$. You can use parentheses to bypass the normal precedence rules. The expression $(3 + 4) \times 2$ evaluates to 14 rather than 11.

The precedence of operators in C++ is described fully in Table 4.3. The operators with the highest precedence are listed first; operators with lower precedence appear at the bottom. Operators that we haven't mentioned yet are discussed in the sections that follow.

Program Tip: When you write expressions in C++ programs, use parentheses liberally.

Trying to uncover precedence errors in a complex expression can be very tiring. Looking for precedence errors is often the last place you'll look when trying to debug a program. As part of defensive programming, use parentheses rather than relying exclusively on operator precedence.

Because execution of an `if` statement depends only on whether the test is true or false (nonzero or zero), the following code is legal in C++:

```
if (6 + 3 - 9)
{
    cout << "great minds think alike" << endl;
}
else
{
    cout << "fools seldom differ" << endl;
}
```

These statements cause the string "fools seldom differ" to be output, because the expression $(6 + 3 - 9)$ evaluates to 0, which is false in C++. Although this code is legal, it is not necessarily good code. It is often better to make the comparison explicit, as in

```
if (x != 0)
{
    DoSomething();
}
```

rather than relying on the equivalence of "true" and any nonzero value:

```
if (x)
{
    DoSomething();
}
```

which is equivalent in effect, but not in clarity. There are situations, however, in which the second style of programming is clearer. When such a situation arises, I'll point it out.

Logical Operators

As we will see (for example, in *usemath.cc*, Prog. 4.6, page 134), it can be necessary to check that a value you enter is in a certain range (e.g., not negative). In *change.cc*, Prog. 4.1, the program should check to ensure that the user's input is valid (e.g., between 0 and 99). The following code implements this kind of check.

```
if (choice < 0)
{
    cout << "illegal choice" << endl;
}
else if (choice > 99)
{
    cout << "illegal choice" << endl;
}
else
{
    // choice ok, continue
}
```

This code has the drawback of duplicating the code that's executed when the user enters an illegal choice. Suppose a future version of the program will require the user to reenter the choice. Modifying this code fragment would require adding new code in two places, making the likelihood of introducing an error larger. In addition, when code is duplicated, it is often difficult to make the same modifications everywhere the code appears.

Logical operators allow boolean expressions to be combined, as follows:

```
if (choice < 0 || choice > 99)
{
    cout << "illegal choice" << endl;
}
else
{
    // choice ok, continue
}
```

The test now reads, "If choice is less than zero or choice is greater than ninety-nine." The test is true (nonzero) when either `choice < 0` or `choice > 99`. The operator `||` is the **logical OR** operator. It evaluates to true when either or both of its boolean arguments is true.

The **logical AND** operator `&&` operates on two boolean expressions and returns true only when both are true. The preceding test for valid input can be rewritten using logical AND as follows:

```
if (0 <= choice && choice <= 99)
{
    // choice ok, continue
}
else
{
    cout << "illegal choice" << endl;
}
```

Table 4.4 The Logical Operators

A	B	A && B	A || B	!A
False (0)	False (0)	False (0)	False (0)	True (1)
False (0)	True (1)	False (0)	True (1)	True (1)
True (1)	False (0)	False (0)	True (1)	False (0)
True (1)	True (1)	True (1)	True (1)	False (0)

Be careful when translating English or mathematics into C++ code. The phrase "choice is between 0 and 99" is often written in mathematics as $0 \le$ choice ≤ 99. In C++, relational operators are left-associative, so the following if test, coded as it would be in mathematics, will evaluate to true for *every* value of choice.

```
if (0 <= choice <= 99)
{
    // choice ok, continue
}
```

Since the leftmost <= is evaluated first, the test is equivalent to ((0 <= choice) <= 99) and the value of the expression (0 <= choice) is either false (0) or true (1), both of which are less than or equal to 99, thus satisfying the second test.

There is also a unary operator ! that works with boolean expressions. This is the **logical NOT operator.** The value of !expression is false if the value of expression is true, and true when the value of expression is false. The two expressions below are equivalent.

```
x != y          !(x == y)
```

Because ! has a very high precedence, the parentheses in the expression on the right are necessary (see Table 4.3).

The logical operators are summarized in Table 4.4.

Short-Circuited Evaluation

The following statement is designed to print a message when a grade-point average is higher than 90%:

```
if (scoreTotal/numScores > 0.90)
{
    cout << "excellent!  very good work" << endl;
}
```

This code segment might cause a program to exit abnormally[3] if the value of numScores is zero, because the result of division by zero is not defined. The

---

[3]The common phrase for such an occurrence is **bomb,** as in "The program bombed." If you follow good defensive programming practices, your programs should not bomb.

abnormal exit can be avoided by using another `if` statement (the approach required in languages such as Pascal):

```
if (numScores > 0)
{
    if (scoreTotal/numScores > 0.90)
    {
        cout << "excellent!  very good work" << endl;
    }
}
```

However, in C++ and C another approach is possible:

```
if (numScores != 0 && scoreTotal/numScores > 0.90)
{
    cout << "excellent!  very good work" << endl;
}
```

The subexpressions in an expression formed by the logical operators `&&` and `||` are evaluated from left to right. Furthermore, the evaluation automatically

---

CLAUDE SHANNON (b. 1916)

Claude Shannon founded **information theory**—a subfield of computer science that is used today in developing methods for encrypting information. Encryption is used to store data in a secure manner so that the information can be read only by designated people.

In his 1937 master's thesis, Shannon laid the foundation on which modern computers are built by equating Boolean logic with electronic switches. This work enabled hardware designers to design, build, and test circuits that could perform logical as well as arithmetic operations. In an interview in [Hor92], Shannon responds to the comment that his thesis is "possibly the most important master's thesis in the century" with "It just happened that no one else was familiar with both those fields at the same time." He then adds a wonderful non sequitur: "I've always loved that word 'Boolean.'"

Shannon is fond of juggling and riding unicycles. Among his inventions are a juggling "dummy" that looks like W.C. Fields and a computer THROBAC: Thrifty Roman Numeral Backward Computer.

Although much of Shannon's work has led to significant advances in the theory of communication, he says:

I've always pursued my interests without much regard for financial value or the value to the world; I've spent lots of time on totally useless things.

Shannon's favorite food is vanilla ice cream with chocolate sauce. Shannon received the National Medal of Science in 1966. For more information see [Sla87, Hor92].

stops as soon as the value of the entire test expression can be determined. In the present example, if the expression `numScores != 0` is false (so that `numScores` is equal to 0), the entire expression must be false, because when `&&` is used to combine two boolean subexpressions, both subexpressions must be true (nonzero) for the entire expression to be true (see Table 4.4). When `numScores == 0`, the expression `scoreTotal/numScores > 0.90` will *not* be evaluated, avoiding the potential division by zero.

Similarly, when `||` is used, the second subexpression will not be evaluated if the first is true, because in this case the entire expression must be true—only one subexpression needs to be true for an entire expression to be true with `||`. For example, in the code

```
if (choice < 1 || choice > 3)
{
    cout << "illegal choice" << endl;
}
```

the expression `choice > 3` is not evaluated when `choice` is 0. In this case, `choice < 1` is true, so the entire expression must be true.

The term **short-circuited evaluation** describes this method of evaluating boolean expressions. The short circuit occurs when some subexpression is not evaluated because the value of the entire expression is already determined. We'll make extensive use of short-circuited evaluation (also called "lazy evaluation") in writing C++ programs.

Arithmetic Assignment Operators

C++ has several operators that serve as "contractions," in the grammatical sense that "I've" is a contraction of "I have ." These operators aren't necessary, but they can simplify and shorten code that changes the value of a variable. For example, several statements in *change.cc*, Prog. 4.1, alter the value of `amount`.

```
amount = amount - quarters*25;
```

This statement can be rewritten using the operator `-=`.

```
amount -= quarters*25;
```

Similarly, the statement `number = number + 1`, which increments the value of `number` by one, can be abbreviated using the `+=` operator: `number += 1;`. In general, the statement *variable = variable + expression;* has exactly the same effect as the statement *variable += expression;*

Using such assignment operators can make programs easier to read. Often a long variable name appearing on both sides of an assignment operator `=` will cause a lengthy expression to wrap to the next line and be difficult to read. The arithmetic assignment operators summarized in Table 4.5 can alleviate this problem.

It's not always possible to use an arithmetic assignment operator as a contraction when a variable appears on both the left and right sides of an assignment statement. The variable must occur as the *first* subexpression on the right side. For example, if `x` has the value zero or one, the statement `x =`

Table 4.5   Arithmetic Assignment Operators

Symbol	Example	Equivalent
+=	x += 1;	x = x + 1;
*=	doub *= 2;	doub = doub * 2;
-=	n -= 5;	n = n - 5;
/=	third /= 3;	third = third / 3;
%=	odd %= 2;	odd = odd % 2;

`1 - x` changes the value from one to zero and vice versa. This statement cannot be abbreviated using the arithmetic assignment operators.

4.4   Block Statements and Defensive Programming

Following certain programming conventions can lead to programs that are more understandable (for you and other people reading your code) and more easily developed.

In this book we follow the convention of using **block delimiters,** { and }, for each part of an `if/else` statement. This is shown in *change2.cc,* Prog. 4.2 (page 115). It is possible to write the `if` statement in Prog. 4.2 without block delimiters:

```
if (amount > 0)
    cout << "# " << coin << " =\t" << amount << endl;
```

The test of the `if` statement controls the output statement so that it is executed only when `amount` is greater than zero.

As we've seen, it is useful to group several statements together so that all are executed precisely when the test of an `if/else` statement is true. To do this, a **block** (or **compound**) **statement** is used. A block statement is a sequence of one or more statements enclosed by curly braces, as shown in Prog. 4.2. If no braces are used, a program may compile and run, but its behavior might be other than expected. Consider the following program fragment:

```
int salary;
cout << "enter salary ";
cin >> salary;
if (salary > 30000)
    cout << salary << " is a lot to earn " << endl;
    cout << salary*0.55 << " is a lot of taxes << endl;
cout << "enter # of hours worked ";
...
```

Two sample runs of this fragment follow:

```
                         OUTPUT

enter salary  31000
31000 is a lot to earn
17050.00 is a lot of taxes
enter # of hours worked
. . .


enter salary  15000
8250.00 is a lot of taxes
enter # of hours worked
. . .
```

Note that the indentation of the program fragment might suggest to someone reading the program (but not to the compiler!) that the "lot of taxes" message should be printed only when the salary is greater than 30,000. However, the taxation message is *always* printed. The compiler interprets the code fragment as though it were written this way:

```
int salary;
cout << "enter salary ";
cin >> salary;
if (salary > 30000)
{
    cout << salary << " is a lot to earn " << endl;
}
cout << salary*0.55 << " is a lot of taxes " << endl;
cout << "enter # of hours worked ";
```

When 15000 is entered, the test `salary > 30000` evaluates to false, and the statement about "a lot to earn" is not printed. The statement about a "lot of taxes", however, is printed, because it is not controlled by the test.

Indentation and spacing are ignored by the compiler, but they are important for people reading and developing programs. For this reason, we will always employ braces { } and a block statement when using `if`/`else` statements, even if the block statement consists of only a single statement.

Defensive Programming Conventions

This convention of always using braces is an example of a **defensive programming** strategy: writing code to minimize the potential for causing errors. Suppose you decide to add another statement to be controlled by the test of an `if` statement that is initially written without curly braces. When the new statement is added, it will be necessary to include the curly braces that delimit a block statement, but that is easy to forget to do. Since the missing braces can

Program 4.4   noindent.cc

```
#include <iostream.h>
#include "CPstring.h"
int main() { string response; cout
<< "Do you like C++ programming [yes/no]> "; cin >> response;
        if ("yes" == response) { cout <<
"It's more than an adventure, it can be a job"
                        << endl; } else { cout
<< "Perhaps in time you will" << endl; } return     0;}
```

noindent.cc

cause a hard-to-detect error, we adopt the policy of including them even when there is only a single statement controlled by the test.

In this book the left curly brace { always follows an if/else on the next line after the line on which the if or else occurs. The right curly brace } is indented the same level as the if/else to which it corresponds. Other indentation schemes are possible; another common convention is as follows:

```
if ("yes" == response) {
   cout << "Green vegetables are good for you" << endl;
   cout << "Broccoli is good in Chinese food as well" << endl;
}
```

You can adopt either convention, but your boss (professor, instructor, etc.) may require a certain style. If you're consistent, the style isn't that important.

To see that indentation makes a difference, note that *noindent.cc,* Prog. 4.4, compiles and executes without error but that no consistent indentation style has been used. Notice that the program is much harder for people to read, although the computer "reads" it with no trouble.

Stumbling block

Confusion between the equality operator == and the assignment operator = can lead to hard-to-locate bugs in a program. A coding convention outlined here can help to alleviate these bugs, but you must keep the distinction between = and == in mind when writing code. Some compilers are helpful in this regard and issue warnings about "potentially unintended assignments."

The following program fragment is intended to print a message depending on a person's age:

```
string age;
cout << "are you young or old [young/old]: ";
cin >> age;
if (age = "young")
{
    cout << "not for long, time flies when you're having fun";
}
```

```
else
{
    cout << "hopefully you're young at heart";
}
```

If the user enters `old`, the message beginning "not for long..." is printed. Can you see why this is the case? The test of the `if`/`else` statement should be read as "if age gets young." The string literal `"young"` is assigned to `age`, and the result of the assignment is nonzero (it is `"young"`, the value assigned to `age`). Because anything nonzero is regarded as true, the statement within the scope of the `if` test is executed.

You can often prevent such errors by putting constants on the left of comparisons as follows:

```
if ("young" == age)
```

If the assignment operator is used by mistake, as in `if ("young" = age)`, the compiler will generate an error.[4] It is much better to have the compiler generate an error message than to have a program with a bug in it.

Putting constants on the left in tests is a good defensive programming style that can help to trap potential bugs and eliminate them before they creep into your programs.

Cascaded `if`/`else` Statements

Sometimes a sequence of `if`/`else` statements is used to differentiate among several possible values of a single expression. Such a sequence is called **cascaded.** An example is shown in *days4.cc,* Prog. 4.5.

It's possible to write the code in *days4.cc* using **nested** `if`/`else` statements as follows. This results in code that is much more difficult to read than code using cascaded `if`/`else` statements.

```
if ("september" == month)
{
    days = 30;
}
else
{
    if ("april" == month)
    {
        days = 30;
    }
    else
    {
```

---

[4]On one compiler the error message "error assignment to constant" is generated. On another, the less clear message "sorry, not implemented: initialization of array from dissimilar array type" is generated.

```
#include <iostream.h>
#include "CPstring.h"

// illustrates cascaded if/else statements
// Owen Astrachan 1/2/1996

int main()
{
    string month;
    int days = 31;            // default value of 31 days/month

    cout << "enter a month (lowercase letters): ";
    cin >> month;

    // 30 days hath september, april, june, and november

    if ("september" == month)
    {
        days = 30;
    }
    else if ("april" == month)
    {
        days = 30;
    }
    else if ("june" == month)
    {
        days = 30;
    }
    else if ("november" == month)
    {
        days = 30;
    }
    else if ("february" == month)
    {
        days = 28;
    }

    cout << month << " has " << days << " days" << endl;

    return 0;
}
```

OUTPUT

```
prompt>  days4
enter a month (lowercase letters):  january
january has 31 days
prompt>  days4
enter a month (lowercase letters):  april
april has 30 days
prompt>  days4
enter a month (lowercase letters):  April
April has 31 days
```

```
        if ("june" == month)
        {
            days = 30;
        }
        else
        {
            if ("november" == month)
            {
                days = 30;
            }
            else
            {
                if ("february" == month)
                {
                    days = 28;
                }
            }
        }
    }
}
```

Whenever a sequence of `if`/`else` statements like this is used to test the value of one variable repeatedly, we'll use cascaded `if`/`else` statements. The rule of using a block statement after an `else` is not (strictly speaking) followed, but the code is much easier to read. Because a block statement follows the `if`, we're not violating the spirit of our coding convention.

4.1. The statements altering amount in *change.cc*, Prog. 4.1, can be written using the mod operator `%`. If amount = 38, then amount/25 == 1, and amount % 25 == 13, which is the same value as 38 − 25*1. Rewrite the program using the mod operator. Try to use an arithmetic assignment operator.

Pause to reflect

4.2. Describe the output of Prog. 4.3 if the user enters the string `"Yes"`, the string `"yup"`, or the string `"none of your business"`.

4.3. Modify *broccoli.cc*, Prog. 4.3 (page 117), to include an `if` statement in the `else` clause so that the "taste" lines are printed only if the user enters the string `"no"`. Thus you might have lines such as

```
if ("yes" == response)
{

}
else if ("no" == response)
{

}
```

4.4. Using the previous modification, add a final `else` clause (with no `if` statement) so that the output might be as follows:

```
                          OUTPUT

Do you like broccoli [yes/no]>  no
De gustibus non disputandum
(There is no accounting for good taste)
```

```
                          OUTPUT

Do you like broccoli [yes/no]>  nope
Sorry, only responses of yes and no are recognized
```

4.5. Write a sequence of if/else statements using > and, perhaps, < that prints a message according to a grade between 0 and 100, entered by the user. For example, high grades might get one message and low grades might get another message.

4.6. Why is days given a "default" value of 31 in *days4.cc*, Prog. 4.5?

4.7. How can *days4.cc*, Prog. 4.5, be modified to take leap years into account?

4.8. Explain why the output of the statement cout << (9 * 3 < 4 * 5) << endl; is 0, but the output of cout << (9 * (3 < 4) * 5) << endl; is 45. Why are the parentheses needed?

4.9. What is output by the statement cout << (9 * 5 < 45) << endl? What about the statement cout << (9*5 < 45 < 30) << endl;? What does the output of the last statement depend on?

4.10. Write a code fragment in which a string variable grade is assigned one of three states: "High Pass", "Pass", and "Fail" according to whether an input integer grade is between 80 and 100, between 60 and 80, or below 60, respectively. It may be useful to write the fragment so that a message is printed and then modify it so that a string variable is assigned a value.

Stumbling block

Using the block delimiters { and } in all cases when writing if/else statements can prevent errors that are very difficult to find because the indentation, which conveys meaning to a reader of the program, is ignored by the compiler when code is generated. Using block delimiters also helps in avoiding a problem that results from a potential ambiguity in computer languages such as C++ that use if/else statements (C and Pascal have the same ambiguity, for example).

The following code fragment attempts to differentiate odd numbers less than zero from other numbers. The indentation of the code conveys this meaning, but the code doesn't execute as intended:

```
if (x % 2 == 1)
   if (x < 0)
   cout << " number is odd and less than zero" << endl;
else
   cout << " number is even " << endl;
```

What happens if the `int` object x has the value 13? The indentation seems to hint that nothing will be printed. In fact, the string literal `"number is even"` will be printed if this code segment is executed when x is 13. The segment is read by the compiler as though it is indented as follows:

```
if (x % 2 == 1)
    if (x < 0)
        cout << " number is odd and less than zero" << endl;
    else
        cout << " number is even " << endl;
```

The use of braces makes the intended use correspond to what happens. Nothing is printed when x has the value 13 in

```
if (x % 2 == 1)
{
    if (x < 0)
        cout << " number is odd and less than zero" << endl;
}
else
{
    cout << " number is even " << endl;
}
```

As we have noted before, the indentation used in a program is to assist the human reader. The computer doesn't require a consistent or meaningful indentation scheme. Misleading indentation can lead to hard-to-find bugs where the human sees what is intended rather than what exists.

One rule to remember from this example is that an `else` always corresponds to the most recent `if`. Without this rule there is ambiguity as to which `if` the `else` belongs; this is known as the **dangling-else** problem. Always employ curly braces { and } when using block statements with `if/else` statements (and later with looping constructs). If braces are always used, there is no ambiguity, because the braces serve to delimit the scope of an `if` test.

4.5 Functions That Return Values

> Civilization advances by extending the number
> of important operations which we can perform
> without thinking about them.
> ALFRED NORTH WHITEHEAD
> *An Introduction to Mathematics*

In Chapter 3 we studied programmer-defined functions, such as `SlicePrice` in *pizza.cc*, Prog. 3.5 (page 96), whose prototype is

```
void SlicePrice(int radius, double price)
```

The return type of `SlicePrice` is `void`. Many programs require functions that have other return types. You've probably seen mathematical functions on hand-held calculators such as $\sin(x)$ or $\sqrt{x}$. These functions are different from the function `SlicePrice` in that they return a value. For example, when you use a calculator, you might enter the number 115, then press the square-root key. This displays the value of $\sqrt{115}$ or 10.7238. The number 115 is an **argument** to the square root function. The value returned by the function is the number 10.7238. Program 4.6 is a C++ program that processes information in the same way: users enter a number, and the square root of the number is displayed.

Control flow from *usemath.cc* is shown in Fig. 4.2. The value 115, entered by the user and stored in the variable `value`, is copied into a memory location associated with the parameter `x` in the function `sqrt`. The square root of 115 is calculated, and a **return** statement in the function `sqrt` returns this square root, which is used in place of the expression `sqrt(value)` in the `cout` statement. As shown in Fig. 4.2, the value 10.7238 is displayed as a result.

The function `sqrt` is accessible by including the header file `<math.h>`. Table 4.6 lists the functions accessible from this header file. In the sample output of *usemath.cc*, Prog. 4.6, the square roots of floating-point numbers aren't always exact. For example, $\sqrt{100.001} = 10.0000499998$, but the

---

Program 4.6   usemath.cc

```
#include <iostream.h>
#include <math.h>

// illustrates use of math function returning a value

int main()
{
    double value;
    cout << "enter a positive number ";
    cin >> value;
    cout << "square root of " << value << " = " << sqrt(value) << endl;

    return 0;
}
```

OUTPUT

```
prompt>   usemath
enter a positive number   115
square root of 115 = 10.7238

prompt>   usemath
enter a positive number   100.001
square root of 100.001 = 10

prompt>   usemath
enter a positive number   -16
square root of -16 = NaN
```

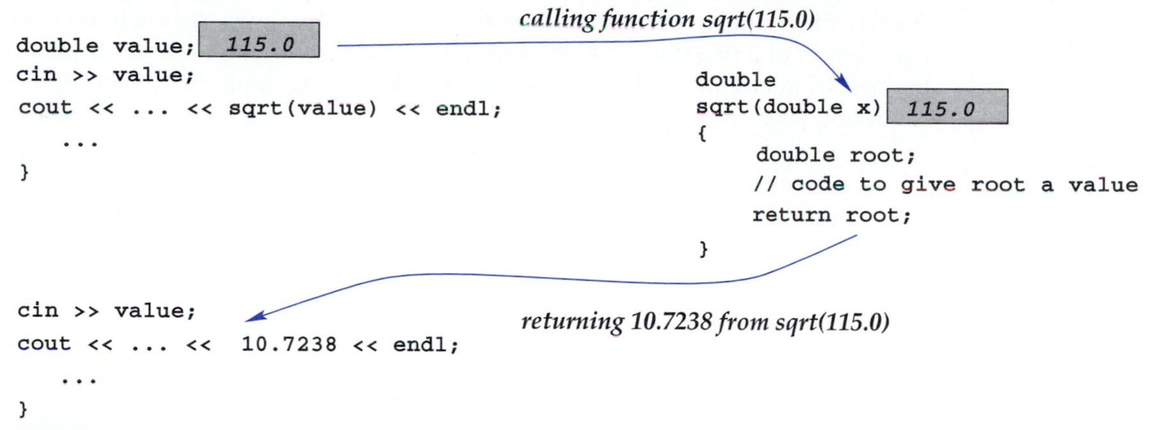

calling function sqrt(115.0)

```
double value;  115.0
cin >> value;
cout << ... << sqrt(value) << endl;                          double
   ...                                                        sqrt(double x)  115.0
}                                                             {
                                                                 double root;
                                                                 // code to give root a value
                                                                 return root;
                                                             }

cin >> value;
cout << ... <<   10.7238 << endl;           returning 10.7238 from sqrt(115.0)
   ...
}
```

Figure 4.2 Evaluating the function call `sqrt(115)`.

Table 4.6 Some Functions in `<math.h>`

Function prototype	Returns
`double fabs(double x)`	Absolute value of x
`double log(double x)`	Natural log of x
`double log10(double x)`	Base-10 log of x
`double sin(double x)`	Sine of x (x in radians)
`double cos(double x)`	Cosine of x (x in radians)
`double tan(double x)`	Tangent of x (x in radians)
`double asin(double x)`	Arc sine of x $[-\pi/2, \pi/2]$
`double acos(double x)`	Arc cosine of x $[0, \pi]$
`double atan(double x)`	Arc tangent of x $[-\pi/2, \pi/2]$
`double pow(double x, double y)`	x^y
`double sqrt(double x)`	$\sqrt{x}$, nonnegative square root of x
`double floor(double x)`	Largest integer value not greater than x
`double ceil(double x)`	Smallest integer value not less than x

value displayed is 10. Floating-point values cannot always be exactly determined. Because of inherent limits in the way these values are stored in the computer, the values are rounded off to the most precise values that can be represented in the computer. The resulting **roundoff error** illustrates the theme of *conceptual* and *formal* models introduced in Chapter 1. Conceptually, the square root of 100.001 can be calculated with as many decimal digits as we have time or inclination to write down. In the formal model of floating-point numbers implemented on computers, the precision of the calculation is limited.

Finally, although the program prompts for positive numbers, there is no check to ensure that the user has entered a positive number. In the output shown, the symbol NaN stands for "not a number." Not all compilers will display this value. In particular, on some personal computers, trying to take the square root of a negative number may cause the machine to lock up. It would be best to guard the call sqrt(value) using an if statement such as the following one:

```
if (0 <= value)
{
    cout << "square root of " << value << " = "
        << sqrt(value) << endl;
}
else
{
    cout << "nonpositive number " << value
        << " entered" << endl;
}
```

Alternatively, we could **compose** the function sqrt with the function fabs, which computes absolute values.

```
cout << "square root of " << value << " = "
    << sqrt(fabs(value)) << endl;
```

The result returned by the function fabs is used as an argument to sqrt. Since the return type of fabs is double (see Table 4.6), the argument of sqrt has the right type.

The Math Library <math.h>

In C and C++ several mathematical functions are available by accessing a math library using #include <math.h>.[5] Prototypes for some of these functions are listed in Table 4.6. For a complete listing, consult your system's <math.h> header file.

All of these functions return double values and have double parameters. Integer values can be converted to doubles, so the expression sqrt(125) is legal (and evaluates to 11.18033). The function pow is particularly useful, because there is no built-in exponentiation operator in C++. For example, the statement cout << pow(3,13) << endl can be used to output the value of 3^{13}: three to the thirteenth.

The functions declared in <math.h> are tools that can be used in any program. As programmers, we'll want to develop functions that can be used in the same way. On occasion, we'll develop functions that aren't useful as general-purpose tools but make the development of one program simpler. For example, in *pizza.cc*, Prog. 3.5 (page 96), the price per square inch of pizza is calculated and printed by the function SlicePrice. If the value were returned by the function rather than printed, it could be used to determine

---

[5]On most Unix systems the math library must be specifically linked into a program calling these functions when the program is compiled. A typical command to do this is g++ prime.cc -o prime -lm; the -lm links the math library in. Compilers on PCs like Borland C++ link the math library automatically.

```cpp
#include <iostream.h>

// find the price per square inch of pizza
// to compare large and small sizes for the best value
//
// Owen Astrachan
// January 2, 1996
//

double Cost(double radius, double price)
// postcondition: returns the price per sq. inch
{
    return price/(3.14159*radius*radius);
}

int main()
{
    double smallRadius, largeRadius;
    double smallPrice, largePrice;
    double smallCost, largeCost;

    // input phase of computation

    cout << "enter radius and price of small pizza ";
    cin >> smallRadius >> smallPrice;

    cout << "enter radius and price of large pizza ";
    cin >> largeRadius >> largePrice;


    // process phase of computation

    smallcost = Cost(smallRadius,smallPrice);
    largeCost = Cost(largeRadius,largePrice);

    // output phase of computation

    cout << "cost of small pizza = " << smallCost << " per sq.inch" << endl;
    cout << "cost of large pizza = " << largeCost << " per sq.inch" << endl;

    if (smallCost < largeCost)
    {
        cout << "SMALL is the best value " << endl;
    }
    else
    {
        cout << "LARGE is the best value " << endl;
    }

    return 0;
}
```

```
                            OUTPUT

prompt>  pizza2
enter radius and price of small pizza   6 6.99
enter radius and price of large pizza   8 10.99
cost of small pizza = 0.0618052 per sq.inch
cost of large pizza = 0.0546598 per sq.inch
LARGE is the best value
```

which of several pizzas was the best buy. This is shown in *pizza2.cc*, Prog. 4.7. Encapsulating the calculation of the price per square inch in a function, as opposed to using the expression `smallPrice/(3.14159 * smallRadius * smallRadius)`, avoids errors that might occur in copying or retyping the expression for a large pizza. Using a function also makes it easier to include other sizes of pizza in the same program. If it develops that we've made a mistake in calculating the price per square inch, isolating the mistake in one function makes it easier to change than finding all occurrences of the calculation and changing each one.

From the user's point of view, Prog. 3.5 and Prog. 4.7 exhibit similar, though not identical, behavior. When two programs exhibit identical behavior, we describe this sameness by saying that the programs are identical as **black boxes.** We cannot see the inside of a black box; the behavior of the box is discernible only by putting values into the box (running the program) and noting what values come out (are printed by the program). A black box specifies input and output, but not how the processing step takes place. The `balloon` class and the math function `sqrt` are black boxes; we don't know how they are implemented, but we can use them in programs by understanding their input and output behavior.

In the function `SlicePrice` of *pizza2.cc*, Prog. 4.7, a comment is given in the form of a **postcondition.** A postcondition of a function is a statement that is true when the function finishes executing. Each function in this book will include a postcondition that describes what the function does.

In the `main` function of *pizza2.cc*, the extraction operator `>>` extracts two values in a single statement. Just as the insertion operator `<<` can be used to put several items on the output stream `cout`, the input stream `cin` continues to flow so that more than one item can be extracted.

Pause to reflect

4.11. Write program fragments or complete programs that convert degrees Celsius to degrees Fahrenheit, British thermal units (Btu) to joules (J), and knots to miles per hour. Note that x degrees Celsius equals $(9/5)x + 32$ degrees Fahrenheit; that x J equals $9.48 \times 10^{-4}(x)$Btu; and that 1 knot = 101.269 ft/min (and that 5,280 ft = 1 mile). At first do this *without* using assignment statements, by incorporating the appropriate expressions in output statements. Then define variables and use assignment statements as appropriate. Finally, write functions for each of the conversions.

4.12. Modify *pizza2.cc*, Prog. 4.7, to use the function pow to square radius in the function Cost.

4.13. If a negative argument to the function sqrt causes an error, for what values of x does the following code fragment generate an error?

```
if (x >= 0 && sqrt(x) > 100)
    cout << "big number" << endl;
```

4.14. Heron's formula gives the area of a triangle in terms of the lengths of the sides of the triangle: a, b, and c.

$$\text{Area} = \sqrt{s(s-a)(s-b)(s-c)}$$

where s is the semiperimeter, or half the perimeter $a + b + c$ of the triangle. Write a function TriangleArea that returns the area of a triangle. The sides of the triangle should be parameters to TriangleArea.

4.15. The law of cosines gives the length of one side of a triangle, c, in terms of the other sides a and b and the angle C formed by the sides a and b:

$$c^2 = a^2 + b^2 - 2ab \cos C$$

Write a function SideLength that computes the length of one side of a triangle, given the other two sides and the angle (in radians) between the sides as parameters to SideLength.

4.16. The following code fragment allows a user to enter three integers:

```
int a,b,c;
cout << "enter three integers ";
cin >> a >> b >> c;
```

Add code that prints the average of the three values read. Does it make a difference if the type is changed from int to double? Do you think that >> has the same kind of associativity as =, the assignment operator?

Function Return Types

The functions sqrt and SlicePrice used in previous examples both returned double values. In this section we'll see that other types can be returned.

Determining leap years. Leap years have an extra day (February 29) not present in nonleap years. We use arithmetic and logical operators to determine whether a year is a leap year. Although it's common to think that leap years occur every four years, the rules for determining leap years are somewhat more complicated, because the period of the Earth's rotation around the Sun is not exactly 365.25 days but approximately 365.2422 days.

■   If a year is evenly divisible by 400, then it is a leap year.

■   Otherwise, if a year is divisible by 100, then it is *not* a leap year.

■   The only other leap years are evenly divisible by 4.[6]

For example, 1992 is a leap year (it is divisible by 4), but 1900 is not a leap year (it is divisible by 100), yet 2000 is a leap year, because, although it is divisible by 100, it is also divisible by 400.

The boolean-valued function `IsLeapYear` in Prog. 4.8 uses multiple `return` statements to implement this logic.

Recall that in the expression `(a % b)` the modulus operator `%` evaluates to the remainder when `a` is divided by `b`. Thus, `2000 % 400 == 0`, since there is no remainder when 2000 is divided by 400.

The sequence of cascaded `if` statements in `IsLeapYear` tests the value of the parameter `year` to determine whether it is a leap year. Consider the first run shown above, when `year` has the value 1996. The first test, `year % 400 == 0`, evaluates to false, because 1996 is not divisible by 400. The second test evaluates to false, because 1996 is not divisible by 100. Since $1996 = 4 \times 499$, the third test, `(year % 4 == 0)`, is true, so the value `true` is returned from the function `IsLeapYear`. This makes the expression `IsLeapYear(1996)` in `main` true, so the message is printed indicating that 1996 is a leap year. You may be tempted to write

$$\text{if (IsLeapYear(year) == true)}$$

rather than using the form shown in *useleap.cc*. This works, but the `true` is redundant, because the function `IsLeapYear` is boolean-valued: it is either true or false.

The comments for the function `IsLeapYear` are given in the form of a **precondition** and a postcondition. For our purposes, a precondition is what must be satisfied for the function to work as intended. The "as intended" part is what is specified in the postcondition. These conditions are a *contract* for the caller of the function to read: if the precondition is satisfied, the postcondition will be satisfied. In the case of `IsLeapYear` the precondition states that the function works for any year greater than 0. The function is *not* guaranteed to work for the year 0 or if a negative year such as -10 is used to indicate the year 10 B.C.

It is often possible to implement a function in many ways so that its postcondition is satisfied. Program 4.9 shows an alternative method for writing `IsLeapYear`. Using a black-box test, this version is indistinguishable from the `IsLeapYear` used in Prog. 4.8.

---

[6]These rules correspond to a year length of 365.2425 days. In the *New York Times* of January 2, 1996 (page B7, out-of-town edition), a correction to the rules used here is given. The year 4000 is *not* a leap year, nor will any year that's a multiple of 4000 be a leap year. Apparently this rule, corresponding to a year length of 365.24225 days, will have to be modified too, but we probably don't need to worry that our program will be used beyond the year 4000.

Program 4.8   useleap.cc

```cpp
#include <iostream.h>

// illustrates user-defined function for
// determining leap years

bool IsLeapYear(int year)
// precondition: year > 0
// postcondition: returns true if year is a leap year,
//                else returns false
{
    if (year % 400 == 0)          // divisible by 400
    {
        return true;
    }
    else if (year % 100 == 0)   // divisible by 100
    {
        return false;
    }
    else if (year % 4 == 0)     // divisible by 4
    {
        return true;
    }
    return false;
}

int main()
{
    int year;
    cout << "enter a year ";
    cin >> year;

    if (IsLeapYear(year))
    {
        cout << year
            << " has 366 days, it is a leap year"
            << endl;
    }
    else
    {
        cout << year
            << " has 365 days, it is NOT a leap year"
            << endl;
    }
    return 0;
}
```

```
                            OUTPUT

prompt>   useleap
enter a year   1996
1996 has 366 days, it is a leap year

prompt>   useleap
enter a year   1900
1900 has 365 days, it is NOT a leap year
```

Program 4.9   isleap2.cc

```
bool IsLeapYear(int year)
// precondition: year > 0
// postcondition: returns true (1) if year is a leap year,
//                  else false (0)
{
    return (year % 400 == 0) ||
        ( year % 4 == 0 && year % 100 != 0 );
}
```
isleap2.cc

A boolean value is returned from `IsLeapYear` because the logical operators `&&` and `||` return boolean values. For example, the expression `IsLeapYear(1974)` causes the following expression to be evaluated by substituting 1974 for `year`:

   (1974 % 400 == 0) || (1974 % 4 == 0 && 1974 % 100 != 0);

Since the logical operators are evaluated left to right to support short-circuited evaluation, the subexpression `1974 % 400 == 0` is evaluated first. This subexpression is false, because `1974 % 400` is 374. The rightmost parenthesized expression is then evaluated, and its subexpression `1974 % 4 == 0` is evaluated first. Since this subexpression is false, the entire `&&` expression must be false (why?), and the expression `1974 % 100 != 0` is not evaluated. Since both subexpressions of `||` are false, the entire expression is false, and `false` is returned.

Boolean-valued functions such as `IsLeapYear` are often called **predicates.** Predicate functions often begin with the prefix `Is`. For example, the function `IsEven` might be used to determine whether a number is even; the function `IsPrime` might be used to determine whether a number is prime (divisible by only 1 and itself, e.g., 3, 17); and the function `IsPalindrome` might be used to determine whether a word is a palindrome (reads the same backward as forward, e.g., mom, racecar).

Converting numbers to English. We'll explore a program that converts some integers to their English equivalent. For example, 57 is "fifty-seven" and 14 is "fourteen." Such a program might be the basis for a program that works as a talking cash register, speaking the proper coins to give as change. With speech synthesis becoming cheaper on computers, it's fairly common to encounter a computer that "speaks." The number you hear after dialing directory assistance is often spoken by a computer. There are many home finance programs that print checks; these programs employ a method of converting numbers to English to print the checks. In addition to using arithmetic operators, the program shows that functions can return strings as well as numeric and boolean types, and it emphasizes the importance of pre- and postconditions.

Program 4.10 numtoeng.cc

```
#include <iostream.h>
#include "CPstring.h"

// coverts two digit numbers to English equivalent
// Owen Astrachan, 6/8/95

string DigitToString(int num)
// precondition: 0 <= num < 10
// postcondition: returns english equivalent,
//                e.g., 1->one,...9->nine
{
    if (0 == num)           return "zero";
    else if (1 == num)    return "one";
    else if (2 == num)    return "two";
    else if (3 == num)    return "three";
    else if (4 == num)    return "four";
    else if (5 == num)    return "five";
    else if (6 == num)    return "six";
    else if (7 == num)    return "seven";
    else if (8 == num)    return "eight";
    else if (9 == num)    return "nine";
    else return "?";
}

string TensPrefix(int num)
// precondition: 10 <= num <= 99 and num % 10 == 0
// postcondition: returns ten, twenty, thirty, forty, etc.
//                corresponding to num, e.g., 50->fifty
{
    if (10 == num) return "ten";
    else if (20 == num) return "twenty";
    else if (30 == num) return "thirty";
    else if (40 == num) return "forty";
    else if (50 == num) return "fifty";
    else if (60 == num) return "sixty";
    else if (70 == num) return "seventy";
    else if (80 == num) return "eighty";
    else if (90 == num) return "ninety";
    else return "?";
}
```

```cpp
string TeensToString(int num)
// precondition: 11 <= num <= 19
// postcondition: returns eleven, twelve, thirteen, etc.
//                corresponding to num, e.g., 15 -> fifteen
{
    if (11 == num) return "eleven";
    else if (12 == num) return "twelve";
    else if (13 == num) return "thirteen";
    else if (14 == num) return "fourteen";
    else if (15 == num) return "fifteen";
    else if (16 == num) return "sixteen";
    else if (17 == num) return "seventeen";
    else if (18 == num) return "eighteen";
    else if (19 == num) return "nineteen";
    else return "?";
}

string NumToString(int num)
// precondition: 0 <= num <= 99
// postcondition: returns english equivalent,
//                e.g., 1->one, 13->thirteen
{
    if (0 <= num && num < 10)
    {
        return DigitToString(num);
    }
    else if (10 < num && num < 20)
    {
        return TeensToString(num);
    }
    else if (num % 10 == 0)
    {
        return TensPrefix(num);
    }
    else
    {
    // concatenate tens' digit with ones' digit
        return TensPrefix(10 * (num/10)) + "-" +
            DigitToString(num % 10);
    }
}

int main()
{
    int number;
    cout << "enter number between 0 and 99: ";
    cin >> number;
    cout << number  << " = " << NumToString(number)
        << endl;
    return 0;
}
```

```
                              OUTPUT

prompt>  numtoeng
enter number between 0 and 99:   22
22 = twenty-two

prompt>  numtoeng
enter number between 0 and 99:   17
17 = seventeen

prompt>  numtoeng
enter number between 0 and 99:   103
103 = ?-three
```

The code in the `DigitToString` function does not adhere to the rule of using block statements in every `if`/`else` statement. In this case, using `{}` delimiters would make the program unnecessarily long. It is unlikely that statements will be added (necessitating the use of a block statement), and the form used here is clear.

> **Program Tips: White space usually makes a program easier to read and clearer. Block statements used with** `if`/`else` **statements usually make a program more robust and easier to change.**
>
> However, there are occasions when these rules are not followed. As you become a more practiced programmer, you'll develop your own aesthetic sense of how to make programs more readable.

A new use of the operator + is shown in function `NumToString`. In the final `else` statement, three strings are joined together using the + operator:

```
return TensPrefix(10 * (num/10)) + "-" + DigitToString(num % 10);
```

When used with `string` values, the + operator joins or **concatenates** (sometimes "catenates") the `string` subexpressions into a new `string`. For example, the value of `"apple"` + `"sauce"` is a new `string`, `"applesauce"`. This is another example of operator overloading; the + operator has different behavior for `string`, `double`, and `int` values.

Robust programs. In the sample runs shown, the final input of 103 does not result in the display of `one hundred three`. The value of 103 violates the precondition of `NumToString`, so there is no guarantee that the postcondition will be satisfied. **Robust** programs and functions do not bomb in this case, but either return some value that indicates an error or print some kind of message telling the user that input values aren't valid. The problem occurs in

---

Program 4.11   prompt.cc

```
#ifndef _PROMPT_H
#define _PROMPT_H
#include "CPstring.h"

// facilitates prompting for int, double or string
// Owen Astrachan
// 1/8/95
//
// PromptRange: used for int or double entry
//
// int PromptRange(string prompt, int low, int high)
//                         -- returns int in range [low..high]
// Example:
//   int x = PromptRange("enter weekday",1,7);
//
// generates prompt: enter weekday between 1 and 7
//
// double PromptRange(string prompt, double low, double high)
//                         -- returns int in range [low..high]
// Example:
//    double d = PromptRange("enter value",0.5,1.5);
//
// generates prompt: enter value between 0.5 and 1.5
//
// string PromptString(string prompt)
//                         --returns a string
// Example:
//    string filename = PromptString("enter file name");


int PromptRange(string prompt,int low, int high);
// precondition: low <= high
// postcondition: returns a value between low and high
//               (inclusive)

double PromptRange(string prompt,double low, double high);
// precondition: low <= high
// postcondition: returns a value between low and high
//               (inclusive)

string PromptString(string prompt);
// postcondition: returns string entered by user
#endif
```

prompt.cc

this program because "?" is returned by the function call TensPrefix(10
* (num/10)). The value of the argument to TensPrefix is $10 \times (100/10)$
$== 10 \times 10 == 100$. This value violates the precondition of TensPrefix. If no
final else were included to return a question mark, then nothing would be
returned from the function TensPrefix when it was called with 103 as an
argument. This situation makes the concatenation of "nothing" with the hyphen

and the value returned by `DigitToString(num % 10)` problematic, and the program would terminate, because there is no `string` to join with the hyphen.

Many programs like *numtoeng.cc* prompt for an input value within a range. A function that ensures that input is in a specific range by reprompting would be very useful. A library of three related functions is specified in *prompt.h*, Prog. 4.11. Two functions have the same name, `PromptRange`, although they have different parameter lists and different return types. This is another example of function overloading. Two (or more) functions can have the same name in C++, provided that the parameter lists of the functions are different. It is *not* enough for just the return types to be different; the parameter lists must differ in number or type of parameter. Here is a modified version of `main` that uses `PromptRange`:

```
int main()
{
    int number = PromptRange("enter a number",0,99);
    cout << number << " = " << NumToString(number) << endl;

    return 0;
}
```

OUTPUT

```
prompt>  numtoeng
enter number between 0 and 99:   103
enter a number between 0 and 99:   100
enter a number between 0 and 99:   -1
enter a number between 0 and 99:   99
99 = ninety-nine
```

We don't have enough programming tools to know how to write `PromptRange` (we need loops, studied in the next chapter), but the specifications of each function make it clear how the functions are called. You can treat the functions as black boxes, just as you treat the square-root function *sqrt* in `<math.h>` as a black box.

4.17. Write a function `DaysInMonth` that returns the number of days in a month encoded as an integer with 1 = January, 2 = February,..., 12 = December. The year is needed, because the number of days in February depends on whether the year is a leap year. In writing the function, you can call `IsLeapYear`. The specification for the function is

Pause to reflect

```
 int DaysInMonth(int month,int year)
// precondition: month coded as: 1 = january, ...,
//                               12 = december
// postcondition: returns # of days in month in year
```

4.18. Why are parentheses needed in the argument passed in the expression `TensPrefix(10 * (num/10))`? For example, if `TensPrefix(10 * num/10)` is used, the program generates a non-number when the user enters 22.

4.19. Write a predicate function `IsEven` that evaluates to true if its `int` parameter is an even number. The function should work for positive and negative integers. Try to write the function using only one statement: `return` *expression.*

4.20. Write a function `DayName` whose header is

```
string DayName(int day)
// precondition: 0 <= day <= 6
// postcondition: returns string representing day, with
//                0 = "Sunday", 1 = "Monday", ...,
//                6 = "Saturday"
```

so that the statement `cout << DayName(3) << endl;` prints `Wednesday`.

4.21. Describe how to modify the function `NumToString` in *numtoeng.cc,* Prog. 4.10, so that it works with three-digit numbers.

4.22. In many programs a user is prompted for a yes/no answer; see Prog. 4.3 for an example. A function with header `string YesNo(string prompt)` might be used in different situations as follows (where the left-hand side of each assignment is a `string` variable):

```
response = YesNo("Do you like broccoli");
if ("yes" == response)
   ...

answer = YesNo("Do you want to continue");
if ("no" == response)
   ...
deleteStatus = YesNo("Do you really want to delete this file");
if ("yes" == deleteStatus)
   ...
```

These different uses of `YesNo` generate the following sequence of prompts (with possible user input shown in italics):

OUTPUT

```
Do you like broccoli [yes/no]?  yes
Do you want to continue [yes/no]?  no
Do you really want to delete this file [yes/no]?  no
```

Write the function `YesNo`.

4.23. An Islamic year y is a leap year if the remainder, when $11y + 14$ is divided by 30, is less than 11. In particular, the 2nd, 5th, 7th, 10th,

13th, 16th, 18th, 21st, 24th, 26th, and 29th years of a 30-year cycle are leap years. Write a function `IsIslamicLeapYear` that works with this definition of leap year.

4.24. In the Islamic calendar [DR90] there are also 12 months, which strictly alternate between 30 days (odd-numbered months) and 29 days (even-numbered months), except for the twelfth month, *Dhu al-Hijjah*, which in leap years has 30 days. Write a function `DaysInIslamicMonth` for the Islamic calendar that uses only three `if` statements.

4.6 Classes and Member Functions

In Sec. 3.4 the class `Balloon`, which we used to simulate a hot-air balloon, had member functions `Ascend`, `Descend`, and `Cruise`. In this section we'll introduce some of the member functions for the class `string`.

String Member Functions

The entire header file for the `string` class is given in Appendix A. In Table 4.7 we introduce some useful member functions. If you're using the C++ standard `string` class rather than the class defined in `"CPstring.h"`, you'll have access to many more functions.

If you're using the C++ standard `string` class, you won't be able to use `Contains`, `Upcase`, and `Downcase`. Instead of `Contains`, you can use the standard function `find` (which can also be used as a member function for *CPstring.h* strings). The function `find` returns the int at which the string argument begins rather than a boolean value; the value `NPOS` indicates that the argument is not contained in `str` and corresponds to `Contains` returning `false`. The following are equivalent:

```
if (str.Contains("pest")) ...

if (str.find("pest") != NPOS) ...
```

There are also functions that can be used instead of `Downcase` and `Upcase`: `ToLower` and `ToUpper` are accessible with the header file `"strutils.h"`, as are several other utility functions. You can use the functions in `strutils.h` with string classes defined elsewhere.

Composing functions. Program 4.12, *compose.cc* shows how string functions can be combined using the dot notation for member functions.

The length of the `string` variable `s67` is determined by invoking the member function for the variable: `s67.length()`. The function `NumToString` returns a `string`, so the returned value's length can also be calculated as shown in the initialization of the variable `stuff`:

```
string stuff = big.substr(0,NumToString(90).length());
```

Here the second argument of `substr` must be an `int`, according to the specification in Table 4.7. The evaluation of `NumToString(90).length()`

Table 4.7 String Member Functions

Function prototype	Returns	Example given `str = "tapestry"; t = "TAPES"`
`int length()`	The number of characters	`str.length() == 8`

`string substr(int pos,int len)`	A string of `len` characters beginning at position `pos`. The first character of a string is position zero; the last is `length() - 1`. If `len` specifies more characters than there are, `length() - pos` characters are used (the maximum number that can be used).	`str.substr(0,4) == "tape"`
		`str.substr(5,3) == "try"`
		`str.substr(5,8) == "try"`

`bool Contains(string s)`	`True` if string contains `s` as a substring, otherwise `false`.	`str.Contains("pest") == true` `str.Contains("post") == false`
`int find(string s)`	Position at which `s` begins, or `NPOS` of `s` is not contained (first character has position 0).	`if (str.find("pest") != NPOS)`
`string Downcase()`	Lower-case equivalent (nonalphabetic characters are not affected)	`t.Downcase() == "tapes"` `str.Downcase() == "tapestry"`
`string Upcase()`	Upper-case equivalent (nonalphabetic characters are not affected)	`str.Upcase() == "TAPESTRY"`

Program 4.12   compose.cc

```cpp
#include <iostream.h>
#include "CPstring.h"

// demonstrates function composition
// Owen Astrachan, 1/2/96

// functions from numtoeng.cc appear here

int main()
{
    int number;
    string s67   = NumToString(67);
    string big   = NumToString(99)+NumToString(99);
    string stuff = big.substr(0,NumToString(90).length());

    cout << s67            << " length = "
         << s67.length()            << endl;
    cout << s67.Upcase() << " length = "
         << s67.Upcase().length() << endl;
    cout << big            << " length = "
         << big.length()            << endl;
    cout << stuff          << " length = "
         << stuff.length()          << endl;
    if (big == big.Upcase().Downcase())
    {
        cout << "up and down are equal to original" << endl;
    }
    return 0;
}
```

OUTPUT

```
prompt>  compose
sixty seven length = 11
SIXTY SEVEN length = 11
ninety nineninety nine length = 22
ninety length = 6
up and down are equal to original
```

is shown in Fig. 4.3. A `string`, `"ninety"`, is returned from `NumToString`, and this string's length is 6.

Similarly, the function `Upcase` returns a `string`, so member functions can be applied to the return value of `Upcase`:

```cpp
                    if (big == big.Upcase().Downcase())
```

An upper-case version of `big` is made, the resulting string is made into lower case, and the final string is compared to the original value of `big`.

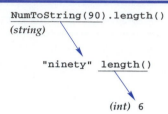

Figure 4.3   Function composition.

Member functions like `length`, which return information about a string but do not alter the string, are called **accessor** member functions. Member functions that can alter an object, as `Upcase` alters a string, are called **mutator** member functions.

RICHARD STALLMAN (b. 1953)

Richard Stallman is hailed by many as "the world's best programmer." Before the term *hacker* became a pejorative, he used it to describe himself as "someone fascinated with how things work, [who would see a broken machine and try to fix it]." Stallman believes that software should be free, that money should be made by adapting software and explaining it, but not by writing it. Of software he says, "I'm going to make it free even if I have to write it all myself."

He is the founder of the GNU software project, which creates and distributes free software tools. The GNU g++ compiler, used to develop the code in this book, is widely regarded as one of the best compilers in the world.

In 1990 Stallman received a MacArthur "genius" award of $240,000 for his dedication and work. He continues this work today as part of the League for Programming Freedom, an organization that fights against software patents (among other things). In an interview after receiving the MacArthur award, Stallman had a few things to say about programming freedom:

> I disapprove of the obsession with profit that tempts people to throw away their ideas of good citizenship....businesspeople design software and make their profit by obstructing others' understanding. I made a decision not to do that. Everything I do, people are free to share. The only thing that makes developing a program worthwhile is the good it does.

4.7   Chapter Review

In this chapter we discussed building functions and classes. Changing the flow of control within functions is important in constructing programs. Encapsulating information in functions that return values, and encapsulating state and behavior in C++ classes, are key concepts in building large programs.

The `if/else` statement can be used to alter the flow of control in a program. You can write programs that respond differently to different inputs by using `if/else` statements. The test in an `if` statement uses relational operators to yield a boolean value whose truth determines what statements are executed. In addition to relational operators, logical (boolean), arithmetic, and assignment operators were discussed and used in several different ways.

The following C++ and general programming features were covered in this chapter:

- The `if/else` statement is used for conditional execution of code. Cascaded `if` statements are formatted according to a convention that makes them more readable.

- A function's return type is the type of value returned by the function. For example, the function `sqrt` returns a `double`. Functions can return values of any type.

- The library whose interface is specified in `<math.h>` supplies many useful mathematical functions.

- Boolean expressions and tests have values of true or false and are used as the tests that guard the body of code in `if/else` statements. The type `bool` is a built-in type in C++ with values of `true` and `false`.

- A block (compound) statement is surrounded by { and } delimiters and is used to group several statements together.

- Relational operators are used to compare values. For example, 3 < 4 is a relational expression using the < operator. Relational operators include `==, !=, <, >, <=, >=`. Relational expressions have boolean values.

- Logical operators are used to combine boolean expressions. The logical operators are `||, &&, !`. Both `||` and `&&` (logical OR and logical AND, respectively) are evaluated using **short-circuit** evaluation.

- Defensive programming is a style of programming in which care is taken to prevent errors from occurring rather than trying to clean up when they do occur.

- Pre- and postconditions are a method of commenting functions; if the preconditions are true when a function is called, the postconditions will be true when the function has finished executing. These provide a kind of contractual arrangement between a function and the caller of a function.

- Several member functions of the `string` class can be used to determine characteristics of strings and to alter string values.

4.8   Exercises

4.1 Write a program that prompts the user for a person's first and last names (be careful; more than one `cin >>` statement may be necessary). The program should print a message that corresponds to the user's names. The program should recognize at least four different names. For example:

```
                          OUTPUT

enter your first name>   Owen
enter your last name>    Astrachan
Hi Owen, your last name is interesting.

enter your first name>   Dave
enter your last name>    Reed
Hi Dave, your last name rhymes with thneed.
```

4.2 Write a program using ideas from the head-drawing program *parts.cc,* Prog. 2.4, that could be used as a kind of police sketch program. A sample run might be as shown below.

```
                          OUTPUT

prompt>   sketch
Choices of hair style follow

(1)   parted
(2)   brush cut
(3)   balding

enter choice:   1
Choices of eye style follow

(1)   beady-eyed
(2)   wide-eyed
(3)   wears glasses

enter choice:   3
Choices of mouth style follow

(1)   smiling
(2)   straightfaced
(3)   surprised

enter choice:   3

            | | | | | | | | / / / / / / / /
            |                   |
            |    ---    ---     |
            |---|o|--|o|---|
            |    ---    ---     |
           _|                   |_
          |_                     _|
            |         o          |
            |                    |
```

4.3 Write a function whose specification is

```
string IntToRoman(int num)
// precondition: 0 <= num <= 10
// postcondition: returns Roman equivalent of num
```

so that `cout << IntToRoman(7) << endl;` would cause `"VII"` to be printed. Note the precondition. Write a program to test that the function works.

4.4 Write a function with prototype `int Min2(int,int)` that returns the minimum value of its parameters. Then use this function to write another function with prototype `int Min3(int,int,int)` that returns the minimum of its three parameters. `Min3` can be written with a single line:

```
return Min2(              );
```

where the two-parameter function is called with appropriate actual parameters. Write a test program to test both functions.

You can then rewrite the minimum functions, naming them both `Min`. In C++, functions can have the same name, if their parameters differ (this is another example of overloading).

4.5 Write a program in which the user is prompted for a real number (of type `double`) and a positive integer and that prints the double raised to the integer power. Use the function `pow` from `<math.h>`. For example:

OUTPUT

```
enter real number   3.5
enter positive power  5
3.5 raised to the power 5 = 525.218
```

4.6 Write a function that allows the user to design different styles of T-shirts. You should allow choices for the neck style, the sleeve style, and the phrase or logo printed on the T-shirt. For example,

---

OUTPUT

```
prompt>  teedesign
Choices of neck style follow

(1) turtle neck
(2) scoop neck (rounded)
(3) vee neck

enter choice: 1
Choices of sleeve style follow

(1) short
(2) sleeveless
(3) long
```

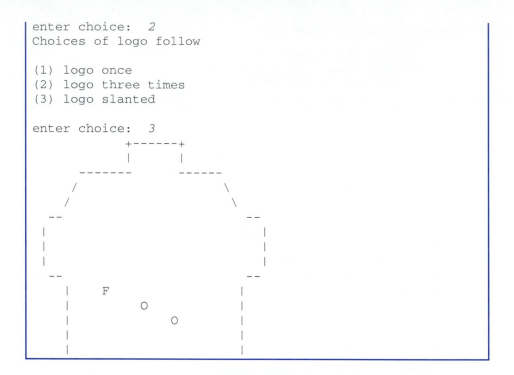

```
enter choice:   2
Choices of logo follow

(1) logo once
(2) logo three times
(3) logo slanted

enter choice:   3
```

4.7 (Advanced) Study the implementation of the `Balloon` class introduced in the last chapter (it's in the file *balloon.cc*). In the member function `AdjustAltitude` there is code that stops the balloon from having a negative altitude. Change this code so that the balloon crashes if the altitude ever gets to be less than zero. To do this, introduce a boolean-valued `int` data field named `balloonOK` that's initialized to 1 in the constructor. If the balloon crashes, this field should be assigned 0 (the balloon is no longer ok). The field is checked in every member function before any code is executed. If the balloon isn't ok, a message should be printed and no code executed.

   An alternate method for modifying the code is to include the header file `<stdlib.h>` and then use a call `exit(0)`, which terminates execution of a program. The prototype for `exit` is in the header file `<stdlib.h>`. Some `int` parameter for `exit` is required.

4.8 Write a program that is similar to *numtoeng.cc,* Prog. 4.10, but that prints an English equivalent for any number less than one million. If you know a language other than English (e.g., French, Spanish, Arabic), use that language instead of English.

4.9 Use the function `sqrt` from the math library[7] to write a function `PrintRoots` that prints the roots of a quadratic equation whose coefficients are passed as parameters. The call

$$\texttt{PrintRoots(1,-5,6);}$$

---

[7]On some systems you may need to link the math library in to get access to the square root function.

might cause the following to be printed:

```
roots of equation 1*x^2 - 5*x + 6 are 2.0 and 3.0
```

Your output doesn't have to look exactly like this.

4.10 (from [Coo87]) The surface area of a person is given by the formula

$$7.184^{-3} \times \text{weight}^{\,0.452} \times \text{height}^{\,0.725}$$

where weight is in kilograms and height is in centimeters. Write a program that prompts for height and weight and then prints the surface area of a person. Use the function pow from <math.h> to raise a number to a power.

4.11 (from [KR96]) The wind chill temperature is given according to a somewhat complex formula derived empirically. The formula converts a temperature (in degrees Fahrenheit) and a wind speed to an equivalent temperature as follows:

$$\text{Equivalent temp} = \begin{cases} \text{Temp} & \text{if Wind} <= 4 \\ 1.6 \times \text{Temp } - 55.0 & \text{if Wind} > 45 \\ 91.4 - (10.45 + 6.69 \times \sqrt{\text{Wind}} - 0.447 \times \text{Wind}) & \text{otherwise} \\ \qquad\qquad \times (91.4 - \text{Temp})/22.0 & \end{cases}$$

Write a program that prompts for a wind speed and a temperature and prints the corresponding wind chill temperature. Use a function WindChill with the following prototype:

```
double WindChill(double temperature, double windSpeed)
// precondition: temperature in degrees Fahrenheit
// postcondition: returns wind-chill index/
//                comparable temperature
```

4.12 (also from [KR96]) The U.S. CDC (Centers for Disease Control—this time, not Control Data Corporation) determine obesity according to a "body mass index," computed by

$$\text{Index} = \frac{\text{Weight in kilograms}}{(\text{Height in meters})^2}$$

An index of 27.8 or greater for men or 27.3 or greater for nonpregnant women is considered obese. Write a program that prompts for height, weight, and sex and that determines whether the user is obese. Write a function that returns the body mass index given the height and weight in inches and pounds, respectively. Note that one meter is 39.37 inches, one inch is 2.54 centimeters, one kilogram is 2.2 pounds, and one pound is 454 grams.

4.13 Write a program that converts a string to its Pig-Latin equivalent. To convert a string to Pig-Latin use the following algorithm:

1. If the string begins with a vowel, add "way" to the string. For example, Pig-Latin for "apple" is "appleway."
2. Otherwise, find the first occurrence of a vowel, move all the characters before the vowel to the end of the word, and add "ay". For example, Pig-Latin for "strong" is "ongstray" since the characters "str" occur before the first vowel.

```
                              OUTPUT

prompt>  pigify
enter string:  strength
strength = engthstray
prompt>  pigify
enter string:  alpha
alpha = alphaway
prompt>  pigify
enter string:  frzzl
frzzl = frzzlay
```

Assume that vowels are a, e, i, o, and u. You'll find it useful to write several functions to help in converting a string to its Pig-Latin equivalent. You'll need to use string member functions `substr`; `find`, `Contains`, or both; and `length`. You'll also need to concatenate strings using +. Finally, to find the first vowel, you may find it useful to write a function that returns the minimum of two values (see Ex. 4.8). You'll need to be careful with the value `NPOS` returned by the string member function `find`. You cannot assume anything about its value. In particular, the actual value may be negative.

4.9   A Computer Science Excursion: Recursion and Exponentiation

During World War II a group of mathematicians in England struggled to determine how a German coding machine called the *Enigma* worked, so that German messages could be intercepted and deciphered. This group, led by Alan Turing (see Sec. 1.1), figured out how the machine operated. This was a very important contribution to the Allied war effort.

Today's businesses and governments rely increasingly on electronic messages and transactions. With powerful computers to assist in electronic spying, many worry that no message is safe from being stolen and deciphered. However, computer scientists have developed methods of data encryption that result in messages that are provably difficult to decrypt or decode.

These techniques of data encryption require that large prime numbers (approximately 150 digits) be manipulated by raising these numbers to large powers.[8] Data encryption is used to prevent people from "spying" on electronic information (see page 212). For example, a 0 sending an electronic message from an office in Europe to an office in Canada might be worried that the message will be intercepted by electronic eavesdroppers. Instead of being sent as **plain text** (i.e., understandable by anyone), the message might be **encrypted** so that it cannot be intercepted and understood.

---

[8]This is part of how *RSA* encryption works; the powers are computed modulo another number m so that the result is constrained to be between 0 and $m - 1$.

Efficient methods for computing x^n, the operation of **exponentiation,** are essential when both x and n are large. In C++, the exponentiation operation is not a built-in operator, as addition, subtraction, multiplication, division, and some others (e.g., the % operator for remainder) are. The library of routines specified in the header file <math.h> does include an exponentiation routine called pow (see Table 4.6), but it is useful for us to examine ways of implementing a function to perform exponentiation. Not only will doing so illuminate concepts of C++; it is sometimes necessary to implement such a function when the one provided in the math library fails (e.g., in raising an object of a user-defined class, such as a fraction or a complex number, to a power).

Exponentiation can be defined in at least two ways. One method uses **iteration** and can be implemented using a while loop, covered in the next chapter. You don't need to understand precisely how a loop works, but it causes a code segment to be executed repeatedly while the loop test is true:

$$a^n = \underbrace{a \times a \times \cdots \times a}_{n \text{ times}}$$

This method is illustrated in the function Power in Prog. 4.13. Note that the expression Power(3,0) correctly evaluates to 1. You should verify this by tracing the code in Prog. 4.13.

Another definition, which is **inductive** or **recursive,** is

$$a^n = \begin{cases} 1 & \text{if } n = 0 \\ a \times a^{(n-1)} & \text{otherwise} \end{cases}$$

A recursive definition or C++ function is one that "calls itself." This method is used in Prog. 4.14. A sample run is shown after the program.

Program 4.13   itpower.cc

```
int
Power(int base, int expo)
// precondition:   expo >= 0
// postcondition:  returns base^expo (base to the power expo)
{
    int result = 1;
    int k=0;

        // iterate 'expo' times, i.e., compute base * base * ... * base

    while(k < expo)
    {
        result = result * base;
        k += 1;
    }
    return result;
}
```

Program 4.14   recexpo.cc

```cpp
#include <iostream.h>

// illustrates recursion and the exponentiation operator

int
Power(int base, int expo)
// precondition:   expo >= 0
// postcondition: returns base^expo (base to the power expo)
{
    if (0 == expo)
    {
        return 1;
    }
    else
    {
        return base * Power(base,expo-1);
    }
}

int main()
{
    int base,expo,result;

    cout << "enter base and exponent: ";
    cin >> base >> expo;

    result = Power(base,expo);

    cout << base << " ** " << expo
         << " = " << result << endl;

    return 0;
}
```

OUTPUT

```
enter base and exponent   25 6
25 ** 6 = 244140625
```

All recursive functions must have a **base case:** a case that does *not* generate a recursive call. Like all recursive functions, Power has a base case that terminates a chain of recursive calls. The base case is typically one that is simple to compute, as it is here (note that $a^0 = 1$ for all nonzero a). The function Power almost exactly mimics the inductive definition of exponentiation given above.

Computing 57^{15} requires 15 multiplications using this method. You might expect that only 14 multiplications are necessary, because in the expression

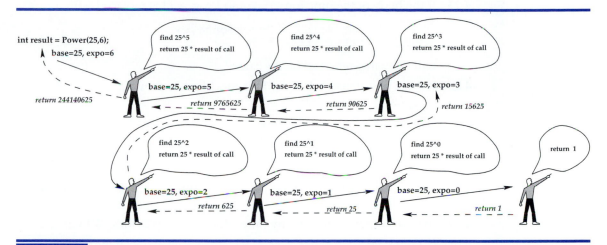

Figure 4.4 Computing 25^6 recursively.

$57 \times 57 \times \cdots \times 57$ there are 15 occurrences of 57 and hence 14 occurrences of the $\times$ sign indicating a multiplication. However, because the base case of this definition occurs when $n = 0$, there is an "extra" multiplication by 1.

You *must* think of the call `Power(base,expo-1)` that occurs in the body of the function `Power` in Prog. 4.14 as the call of *another* function named `Power`, not the same function in which the call occurs. Fig. 4.4 shows how "clones" of the function `Power` each receive different values when the function recurses (calls itself).

Note that each version (clone) of `Power` in Fig. 4.4 executes the same statement to return a value, but because the value returned *to* the function (the result of the function call) is different, a different value is returned *from* the function (the result of the `return` statement). The last function called returns 1 as shown; the function that called the last function returns `25*1`; the function that called the function that called the last function returns `25*25`, and so on.[9]

You do not need to understand completely how the chain of recursive calls works. You must try to understand that the result of a recursive function call, `Power(base,expo-1)`, is used to return the correct value from the function. The correct result is returned by multiplying the recursive result by `base`:

```
return base * Power(base,expo-1);
```

The `Power` functions show that it is possible to write a function either recursively or iteratively. Both versions satisfy the same pre- and postconditions; from a black-box viewpoint, they are the same function.

The next example will show how recursion can be used to code a method that is complicated to code without using recursion.

---

[9]"There once was a lady who swallowed a fly...." Sound familiar?

Pause to
reflect

4.25. If the body of the function `Power` in Prog. 4.14 is replaced with

```
int value = Power(base,expo-1);
return base * value;
```

will the value returned be the same?

4.26. If the `else` clause in Prog. 4.14 is modified as shown,

```
else
{   int result = base * Power(base,expo-1);
    cout << result << endl;
    return result;
}
```

what values will be printed by the call `Power(25,6)`? By the call `Power(3,9)`?

4.27. In terms of `expo`, how many times does the loop in Prog. 4.13 iterate?

4.28. If a statement `cout << expo << endl;` is added at the beginning of the function `Power` in Prog. 4.14, what values are printed by the call `Power(2,14)`? By the call `Power(3,9)`?

4.29. Suppose that the precondition on the function `Power` in the recursive formulation given in Prog. 4.14 is changed to

```
// precondition: expo >= 1
```

and the body is changed as follows so that the function need *not* work correctly for raising a number to the zeroth power. In this case a different base case can reduce the number of multiplications required by one.

```
if (1 == expo)
{
    return base;
}
else
{
    return base * Power(base,expo-1);
}
```

Is this an important savings?

Efficiency and Complexity

You may realize that, although simple to implement, the method of raising a number to a power that we studied in the previous section is not the way that you would do it with pencil and paper. For example, most people will compute 2^{14} by using properties of exponents such as $a^{x+y} = a^x \times a^y$. Thus $2^{14} = 2^{10} \times 2^4 = 1,024 \times 16 = 16,384$, where 2^4 is easy to compute and 2^{10} might be a value remembered because it comes up so often, or it might be computed by $2^{10} = 2^4 \times 2^6$ or something similar.

Given the task of computing 3^{16}, you might break the problem down as shown in Fig. 4.5, where 3^{16} is calculated by computing 3^8 (6,561) and squaring

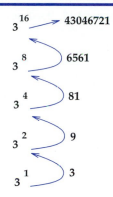

Figure 4.5 Computing 3^{16}.

this number. In turn, 3^8 is calculated by computing 3^4 (81) and squaring it. This process of breaking down a number continues until the simple case of $3^1 = 3$ is reached. Note that only four multiplications are required—one for squaring each of the numbers: $3, 9, 81, 6561$. This is many fewer multiplications than the 16 required by the naïve method used in Prog. 4.14. Translating this method into C++ code is not overly difficult, but it requires some care in examining how many cases there are.

In general, calculating a power such as a^k is very simple when k is an even number. For example, to calculate 12^{100} it is only necessary to know the value of 12^{50} since squaring this number yields the desired result: $12^{50} \times 12^{50} = 12^{100}$. If k is odd, then it is only slightly tricky to calculate a^k. For example, computing 11^{53} could be done using the relationship $11^{53} = 11^{26} \times 11^{27}$. Alternatively, it could be calculated by computing 11^{26} and then using $11 \times 11^{26} \times 11^{26} = 11^{53}$. The advantage of the second method is that once 11^{26} is computed, it need not be computed again. In general, this leads to the following rules for computing exponents:

$$
a^n = \begin{cases}
1 & \text{if } n = 0 \\
a^{(n/2)} \times a^{(n/2)} & \text{if } n \text{ is even} \\
a \times a^{(n/2)} \times a^{(n/2)} & \text{if } n \text{ is odd (note that } n/2 \text{ truncates to an integer)}
\end{cases}
$$

A function `Power` using this method of exponentiation is shown in Prog. 4.15. Note that in this version of `Power`, the parameter `base` is a `double`.

You should think about how this version of `Power` works. One useful way of doing this is to add the statement

```
cout << "exponent = " << expo << " result = "
     << semi*semi << endl;
```

just before the statement `return semi*semi` (you can do this and run the program, or think about what would happen if you did). Here is a run of

Program 4.15   logexpo.cc

```cpp
#include <iostream.h>

// exponentiation using logarithmic number of multiplications
// Owen Astrachan

double Power(double base, int expo)
// precondition: expo >= 0
// postcondition: returns base^expo (base to the power expo)
{
    if (0 == expo)
    {
        return 1.0;                 // correct for zeroth power
    }
    else
    {
        double semi = Power(base,expo/2);
        // build answer from this

        if (expo % 2 == 0)      // even exponent
        {
            return semi*semi;
        }
        else                    // odd exponent
        {
            return base*semi*semi;
        }
    }
}

int main()
{
    int expo;
    double base,result;

    cout << "enter base and exponent: ";
    cin >> base >> expo;

    result = Power(base,expo);

    cout << base << " ** " << expo
         << " = " << result << endl;

    return 0;
}
```

logexpo.cc

Prog. 4.15 modified with the addition of such a `cout` statement:

```
                          OUTPUT

enter base and exponent:   3 32
exponent = 2 result = 9
exponent = 4 result = 81
exponent = 8 result = 6561
exponent = 16 result = 4.30467e+07
exponent = 32 result = 1.85302e+15
3 ** 32 = 1.85302e+15
```

Note that scientific notation is used when the result attains a large enough value. The number $4.30467e+07$ is $4.30467 \times 10^7 = 43,046,700$. The value of 3^{32} is actually $1,853,020,188,851,841$, but some precision is lost because of the way in which `double` values are stored in the computer. Note that if the version of `Power` in Prog. 4.14 is used (where `int` values are used rather than `double` values), the answer printed is $-501,334,399$, because the largest `int` value is not large enough to hold the correct answer.

Measuring performance. For "human calculators" the method outlined in Prog. 4.15 is clearly superior, because it requires fewer multiplications than does the method outlined in Prog. 4.14 and Prog. 4.13. For example, the exponent is divided in half in each recursive call in the statement

$$\text{double semi = Power(base,expo/2);}$$

Thus, raising 2^{1000} generates the recursive call `Power(2,500)` followed by a sequence of calls with `expo` values of

$$250, 125, 62, 31, 15, 7, 3, 1, 0$$

for a total of 11 calls (including the original call). Recall that $125/2 = 62$, because integer division truncates in C++. Since each call requires at most two multiplications (why?), there are a maximum of 24 multiplications.

In contrast, the first method covered requires 1,000 multiplications to calculate 2^{1000}. In theory, then, the second method is "better" if the measurement used is the number of multiplications required. What remains to be seen, however, is whether the theoretical results are realized in practice. To determine this, I used a class (described below) that permits parts of a program to be timed. The results of calculating powers of three from 3^0 to 3^{300} using three different methods are displayed in Fig. 4.6. The methods used are the iterative method of Prog. 4.13 (labeled `itpower`), the method used in Prog. 4.15 (labeled `LogPower`), and the function `pow` in `<math.h>`. As indicated, the time shown is for 10,000 executions of the calculation 3^x. For example, to calculate 3^{300} using Prog. 4.13 requires approximately 3 seconds, meaning that to calculate 3^{300} *once* using this method requires approximately 0.0003 second (compared to 0.000126

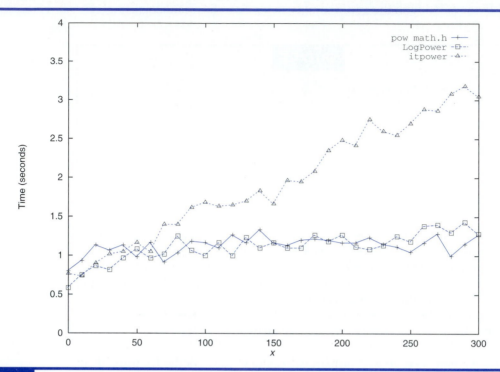

Figure 4.6   Comparing three methods of exponentiation for 10,000 iterations of 3^x.

for the other methods). What can we conclude from the results shown in this graph? The method used in Prog. 4.15 is about as fast as the method used by the library routine in <math.h>. The naïve method is certainly slower, but given that it takes only 0.0003 second to compute 3^{300}, does this matter? The answer is: *It depends.* It depends on how many operations are being performed. If the operation of raising a number to a power is performed only 10,000 times, the difference between about 1.26 seconds and 3 seconds may be inconsequential. However, if the same operation is performed 10 million times, the times required by each method are approximately 1,260 seconds and 3,000 seconds, respectively. The faster method represents a savings of 29 minutes, which may be very significant. So, the answer to "Which method is better?" is "It depends."

A Timer Class

We would like to combine a theoretical analysis with an **empirical analysis** when evaluating the performance of different algorithms. A theoretical analysis uses mathematical tools to analyze properties of paper-and-pencil algorithms. An empirical analysis uses a computer to determine how an implementation of an algorithm behaves in practice.

We have noted that using the naïve method of raising a number to a power requires approximately 1,000 multiplications to compute 2^{1000}, whereas a method that uses only 10 multiplications to compute 2^{1000} is very easy to code. Theoretically the algorithm requiring fewer multiplications is better, in that it should execute faster because fewer arithmetic operations are required. In many cases, however, a slow algorithm is more than fast enough for practical purposes. For example, if a multiplication requires one microsecond (one-millionth of a second), which is not uncommon on many computers, then 1,000 multiplications require only one one-thousandth of a second—certainly not enough time to get a cup of coffee while a number is raised to a power.

Program 4.16   ctimer.cc

```
#ifndef _CTIMER_H
#define _CTIMER_H

// a class that can be used to "time" parts of programs
// or as general timer
//
// operations are:
//
//      Start() : starts the timer
//      Stop()  : stops the timer
//      ElapsedTime() : returns the elapsed time between
//                      start and the last stop
//      CumulativeTime(): returns cumulative total of all
//                      "laps" (timed intervals), i.e., sum of
//                      calls to ElapsedTime
//      Reset()    : resets cumulative time to 0
//                   so "removes" history of timer
//
//

class CTimer{
   public:
      CTimer();                  // constructor
      void Reset();              // reset timer to 0
      void Start();              // begin timing
      void Stop();               // stop timing
      double ElapsedTime();      // between last start/stop
      double CumulativeTime();   // total of all times since reset
   private:
      long myStartTime,myEndTime;
      double myElapsed;          // time since start and last stop
      double myCumulative;       // cumulative of all "lap" times
};

#endif       // _CTIMER_H not defined
```

ctimer.cc

In this case, it may be useful to time a program or algorithm to see how long it takes to run in practice, or **empirically**—that is by experimenting with the program. To make the timing process more simple, we will introduce a timer class that can be used in any program. The header file for the timer class is given as Prog. 4.16.

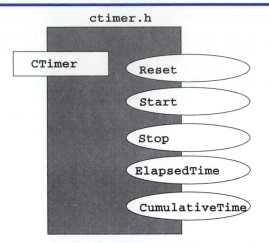

ctimer.h

CTimer

Reset

Start

Stop

ElapsedTime

CumulativeTime

Figure 4.7   Interface diagram for CTimer class.

Examining the class. The class CTimer works like a stopwatch. It can be started, stopped, and reset, and it reports how long it takes sections of a program to run. An interface diagram is shown in Fig. 4.7. The data in the private section are used to keep track of the internal state of the timer and are not important in understanding how the timer is used. All but one of the public member functions are used in *timeexpo.cc*, Prog. 4.17 (page 170), which was used to generate the data shown in the graph in Fig. 4.6.

OUTPUT

```
prompt>  timeexpo
enter base and exponent:  5 100
enter number of iterations  10000
time (linear) = 1.18329
average = 0.000118329
to compute 5**100 = 7.88861e+69
time (logarithmic) = 1.19995
average = 0.000119995
to compute 5**100 = 7.88861e+69
prompt>  timeexpo
enter base and exponent:  5 100
enter number of iterations  10000
time (linear) = 1.34995
average = 0.000134995
to compute 5**100 = 7.88861e+69
```

```
time (logarithmic) = 1.01663
average = 0.000101663
to compute 5**100 = 7.88861e+69
```

Note that the times displayed for these runs differ from one execution of the program to the next. This happens for a variety of reasons:

- The timer is only accurate to a certain degree—it "ticks" in coarse steps, which can be rounded off to give different results.

- The program may "compete" with other programs when running in certain environments. In some computing environments the computer runs one program for a little while, then runs another, then switches back. This can account for a program taking a different amount of time for one run than for another.

The times just found were obtained using a Sun SPARCstation. When the same tests are run from a machine based on a 486/33 chip, the timings are different as follows:

```
                        OUTPUT
enter base and exponent:   5 100
enter number of iterations  10000
time (linear) = 4.89011
average = 0.000489
to compute 5**100 = 7.888609e+69
time (logarithmic) = 1.813187
average = 0.000181
to compute 5**100 = 7.888609e+69
```

There is a drastic difference in the time required for the naïve (linear) method from one machine to another. This may be due in part to the machine and in part to the different compilers used on each machine.

Another run of Prog. 4.17 follows. In this run, timings are for computing 5^{1000} rather than 5^{100}. Note that this value is too large for even the type `double`. As a result, the machine prints *Infinity* as the value of computing 5^{1000}. On some machines and with some compilers, computing such a large number can cause the machine to "hang" or cease to work. On machines supporting a standard for `double` values,[10] symbolic names such as "Infinity" are given to certain

---

[10]This is the IEEE floating-point standard.

invalid expressions:

OUTPUT

```
prompt>  timeexpo
enter base and exponent:  5 1000
enter number of iterations  10000
time (linear) = 6.16642
average = 0.000616642
to compute 5**1000 = Infinity
time (logarithmic) = 1.59994
average = 0.000159994
to compute 5**1000 = Infinity
```

Note that this run shows more clearly (and more in line with the run computing 5^{100} on the 486 machine) the superiority of the logarithmic method over the linear method.

Here is Prog. 4.17, used in comparing the different methods for raising a number to a power and used to illustrate the use of the class CTimer:

Program 4.17   timeexpo.cc

```
#include <iostream.h>
#include "ctimer.h"

// illustrates timing code and comparing algorithms used
// for exponentiation
// Owen Astrachan

double LogPower(double base, int expo)
// precondition: expo >= 0
// postcondition: returns base^expo (base to the power expo)
{
    if (0 == expo)
    {
        return 1.0;                    // correct for zeroth power
    }
    else
    {
        double semi = LogPower(base,expo/2);
        // build answer from this

        if (expo % 2 == 0)        // even exponent
        {
            return semi*semi;
        }
        else                      // odd exponent
        {
```

```
            return base*semi*semi;
        }
    }
}

double Power(double base,int expo)
// precondition:  expo >= 0
// postcondition: returns base^expo (base to the power expo)
{
    double result = 1;
    while (expo > 0)
    {
        result *= base;
        expo -= 1;
    }
    return result;
}

int main()
{
    int expo,iter;
    double base,result;

    cout << "enter base and exponent: ";
    cin >> base >> expo;

    cout << "enter number of iterations ";
    cin >> iter;

    CTimer timer;               // used for timing code segments

    int k=0;
    while (k < iter)            // time naive method
    {
        timer.Start();
        result = Power(base,expo);
        timer.Stop();
        k += 1;
    }
    cout << "time (linear) = " << timer.CumulativeTime()
         << endl;
    cout << "average = " << timer.CumulativeTime()/iter
         << endl;
    cout << "to compute " << base << "**" << expo
         << " = " << result << endl;

    timer.Reset();             // reset to time next method
    k = 0;
    while (k < iter)           // time logarithmic method
    {
        timer.Start();
        result = LogPower(base,expo);
        timer.Stop();
        k += 1;
    }
```

```
    cout << "time (logarithmic) = "
        << timer.CumulativeTime() << endl;
    cout << "average = " << timer.CumulativeTime()/iter
        << endl;
    cout << "to compute " << base << "**" << expo <<
        " = " << result << endl;

    return 0;
}
```

timeexpo.cc

In Prog. 4.17 the timer is started and stopped in statements that bracket each call of a function that computes one number raised to the power of another. In particular, the execution of the statement k += 1; is *not* included in the timings. Note also that the timer is reset between the loops that are used in timing each different function. If the statement timer.Reset() is left out, the result reported by the second call of the method (member function) CumulativeTime would include the timings of the linear method as well.

Excursion Exercises

4.14 Calculate the exact number of recursive calls generated by calling the function Power in Prog. 4.15 using

```
    double result = Power(0.25,2100);
```

Can you think of a method that can be used so that the program prints this number? As a hint, suppose that a statement

```
        recursiveCalls += 1;
```

is placed just before the recursive call to Power. Why can't the value of the variable recursiveCalls be printed within the function Power and yield a correct result? Where should the variable recursiveCalls be initialized?

To do this exercise, the variable will need to be defined as a **global variable**, between the #include statements and the first function used in the program.

```
            #include <iostream.h>

            int recursiveCalls = 0;

            double
            Power(double base, int expo)
            // precondition: expo >= 0
            ...
```

Since such a variable is defined outside of any function, it is accessible within all functions.

Variables used for bookkeeping chores such as the one in this exercise are good candidates for global variables, because they must often be accessible in many functions (think of each recursively invoked function as a separate function). Modify Prog. 4.15 so that it counts the number of times a recursive call is made. Then use this modified version (and a modified function main) to calculate and print the number of times `Power` is invoked in calculating 3.0^n as n varies from 0 to 500 in increments of 10.

4.15 It is often claimed that recursive functions are "inferior" to iterative functions because each function call takes time. It is true that calling a function takes more resources than incrementing a variable by one, but how much more time? Write and test a program that uses both the iterative and recursive versions of the naïve method for raising a number to a power shown in Prog. 4.13 and Prog. 4.14, respectively. Use a timer to time each function. How much overhead does the recursive version have?

4.16 A common measure of the performance of computers used for scientific calculations, such as weather prediction or simulating flow for the design of an airplane wing, is *flops*, or floating-point operations per second. A floating-point operation involves the type `double` (or the other C++ type `float`).

Write and test a program to determine the flops rate of the machine you use. Use

$$val = 3.5 * 1.3;$$

for a floating-point operation (where `val` is of type `double`). What happens if you replace 3.5 with a variable of type `double`? Answer the same question but use an integer operation rather than a floating-point operation. Which is faster on the machine you use?

4.17 The **Fibonacci**[11] sequence of numbers occurs often in computer science and in nature. The sequence is given by

$$1, 1, 2, 3, 5, 8, 13, 21, 34, 55, 89, \ldots$$

where each number after the first two is the sum of the preceding two numbers. (What is the next number after 89?) In this sequence the first two Fibonacci numbers have the value 1.

This sequence can be calculated iteratively using three variables. If variables `first` and `second` hold the values of the "last two" Fibonacci numbers, then the next number can be calculated using three variables as shown:

```
int next = first + second;
first = second;
second = next;
```

The nth Fibonacci number $F(n)$ can also be calculated using the mathematical definition

$$F(n) = \begin{cases} 1 & \text{if } n = 0 \text{ or } n = 1 \\ F(n-1) + F(n-2) & \text{otherwise} \end{cases}$$

which gives rise to a recursive function:

```
int Fib(int n)
// precondition: 0 <= n
```

---

[11]Pronounced "fib-oh-notch-ee," the pen name of Leonardo da Pisa (c. 1170–c. 1250), who discovered this sequence.

```
// postcondition: returns n-th Fibonacci number
{
    if (0 == n || 1 == n)
    {
        return 1;
    }
    else
     {
        return Fib(n-1) + Fib(n-2);
    }
}
```

Write and test a program that uses both the iterative and recursive methods to calculate the first 15 Fibonacci numbers. Time each method for determining the numbers. Can you account for the difference in times?

Iteration with Programs and Classes

"What IS the use of repeating all that stuff," the Mock Turtle interrupted, "if you don't explain it as you go on? It's by far the most confusing thing I ever heard!"

LEWIS CARROLL
Alice's Adventures in Wonderland

I shall never believe that God plays dice with the world.

ALBERT EINSTEIN
Einstein, His Life and Times, Philipp Frank

The if/else statement selects different code fragments depending on values calculated at run time by the program. In this chapter we will study control statements called **loops,** which are used to execute code segments repeatedly. Repetition significantly extends the kinds of programs we can write. We will also study several classes that extend the domain of problems we can solve using programming solutions. For example, we'll see a short program that prints a calendar for any month in any year. Printing a calendar requires repetition in printing each day of the week and a class that helps determine the weekday on which the first day of a month falls.

To extend the range of problems and programs, we will use some basic design guidelines that help in designing programs and classes. As classes and programs get larger and more complicated, these design guidelines will help in managing the complexity that comes with harder and larger problems.

In the first part of the chapter we'll introduce a new class and discuss how classes are designed and implemented. We'll use this class to motivate and study control statements used for looping or repeated execution of code. We'll study several applications using loops and classes to gain an understanding of how to design and implement functions, classes, and programs.

5.1   Random Numbers and *N*-Sided Dice

In this section you'll learn about a programmer-defined class, named `Dice`, that permits the computer to simulate the kind of dice used in board games. The class simulates dice with any number of sides, not just common six-sided dice. It's even possible to have one-sided dice and million-sided dice, both of which are easy to simulate but hard to carve. Six- and twelve-sided dice are shown in the following figure:

The class `Dice` is very general and permits simulation of an *N*-sided die for arbitrary *N*.

These simulated dice, and the computer-generated random numbers on which they are based, are part of an application area of computer science called **simulation.** Simulations model real-world phenomena using a computer, which becomes a virtual laboratory for experimenting with models of physical systems without the expense of building the systems. Computer-based simulations are used to design planes, trains, and automobiles; to predict the weather; and to build and design computers and programs. We'll study simulation in more detail in the next chapter, but we'll use the `Dice`[1] class to study program and class construction.

C++ classes encapsulate **state** and **behavior.** The behavior of a class is what the class does. Behavior is often described with verbs: cats eat, sleep, and play; dice are rolled. The state of a class depends on physical properties. For example, dice have a fixed number of sides. Class behavior is defined by public member functions; these are shown in Fig. 5.1 for the `Dice` class.

To use variables of class `Dice`, you must put `#include"dice.h"` at the beginning of a program (the file *dice.h* is Prog. 5.2 on page 180). Program 5.1, *roll.cc*, is a simple program that uses all three member functions of the class `Dice`. In *roll.cc* two `Dice` objects[2] are defined, one for a six-sided die and one for a twelve-sided die. The six-sided die is rolled twice, and the twelve-sided die is rolled three times.

Let us examine each part of *roll.cc*. At the beginning of the program two `Dice` objects, named `cube` and `dodeca`, are defined.

```
Dice cube(6);          // six-sided die
Dice dodeca(12);       // twelve-sided die
```

When an object is **defined,** memory is allocated for the object, and the object's state is initialized. When a built-in variable is defined, the variable's state may

---

[1]The word *dice* is the plural form of the word *die,* but a class named `Die` seems somewhat macabre. Also, using `Dice` prevents professors from jokingly saying "Die Class" to their students.

[2]Think of the words *object* and *variable* as synonyms. "Variable" is often used for built-in types and "object" for programmer-defined types.

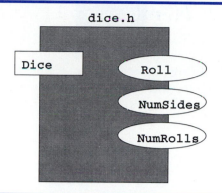

dice.h

Dice

Roll

NumSides

NumRolls

Figure 5.1   Interface diagram for `Dice` class.

Program 5.1   roll.cc

```cpp
#include <iostream.h>
#include "dice.h"

// simple program illustrating use of Dice class
// roll two dice, print results
// Owen Astrachan, 8/9/94

int main()
{
    Dice cube(6);               // six-sided die
    Dice dodeca(12);            // twelve-sided die

    cout << "rolling " << cube.NumSides() << " sided die"
         << endl;
    cout << cube.Roll() << endl;
    cout << cube.Roll() << endl;
    cout << "rolled " << cube.NumRolls() << " times"
         << endl;

    cout << "rolling " << dodeca.NumSides() << " sided die"
         << endl;
    cout << dodeca.Roll() << endl;
    cout << dodeca.Roll() << endl;
    cout << dodeca.Roll() << endl;
    cout << "rolled " << dodeca.NumRolls() << " times"
         << endl;
    return 0;
}
```

```
                              OUTPUT

prompt> roll
rolling 6 sided die
5
3
rolled 2 times
rolling 12 sided die
8
1
12
rolled 3 times

prompt> roll
rolling 6 sided die
1
6
rolled 2 times
rolling 12 sided die
8
9
2
rolled 3 times
```

be uninitialized. For programmer-defined types such as Dice, initialization takes place when the Dice variable is defined. As a programmer using the Dice class, you do not need to be aware of how a Dice object is initialized or what is in the private section of the Dice class. However, as you begin to design your own classes, you'll need to develop an understanding of how the state of an object is reflected by its private data and how member functions use private data. Class state is usually defined by private data, which are not accessible to **client** programs. A client program is a program like *roll.cc*, Prog. 5.1, that uses a class as opposed to implementing the class. The state and behavior of the Dice class are summarized in Fig. 5.2.

Using Constructors to Initialize

When an object like cube is defined in *roll.cc*, in some sense the object "springs to life." The technical word that describes object initialization and definition is **construction.** Construction initializes the state of an object. For programmer-defined classes like Dice, a special member function, called a **constructor,** performs this initialization. In this book, all classes will have at least one constructor.[3] The constructor of the Dice class requires a parameter that

---

[3]It is possible to design a class with no constructor, but all classes in this book have at least one constructor.

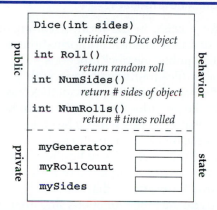

Figure 5.2   Class diagram for `Dice` class.

specifies how many sides an object has. This is the purpose of the 6 in `Dice`
`cube(6)` and the 12 in `Dice dodeca(12)`.

After `cube` and `dodeca` are defined and the constructor of each of them
has been executed, private state variables have values as shown in Fig. 5.3. (The
value of `myGenerator` is shown in gray because we haven't discussed the
class `RandGen`.) Each `Dice` object has its own state. You can see the different
states in the output of *roll.cc*, Prog. 5.1; the number of times each simulated die
is rolled is different, so is the number of sides. These values are accessible in the
client program using the public member functions `NumRolls` and `NumSides`,
respectively. Keep in mind that the public member functions prescribe the
behavior of the class from an outsider's view. Public member functions may
make it possible to affect the state or to learn about the values of the state, but
the state is not accessible in client programs like *roll.cc* unless member functions
are provided that return this state information.

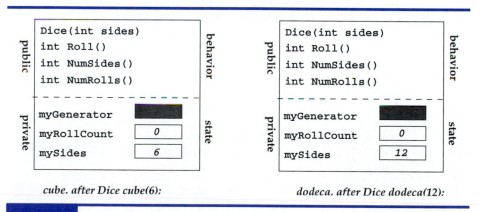

cube. after Dice cube(6):   *dodeca. after Dice dodeca(12):*

Figure 5.3   After `Dice` constructors have executed.

Class Documentation: The Interface

The documentation for a class, in the form of comments in the **header file** in which the class is declared, furnishes information about the constructor's parameters and about all public member functions.

The names of header files traditionally end with a .h suffix. In this book the name of a header file begins with the name of the class that is declared in the header file. The header file provides the compiler with the information it needs about the form of class objects. In one sense, a header file serves as a manual on how to use a class or some other set of routines (as <math.h> describes math functions such as sqrt). This analogy is not quite exact, however, because we don't need a car manual to drive a car, or a stereo manual to use a stereo, but the compiler *must* know, for example, that the member functions NumSides and Roll are legal Dice member functions and that each returns an int

---

Program 5.2   dice.h

```
#ifndef _DICE_H
#define _DICE_H

//   class for simulating a die (object "rolled" to generate
//   a random number)
//
//   Dice(int sides) -- constructor, sides specifies number of
//                      "sides" for the die, e.g., 2 is a coin,
//                      6 is a 'regular' die
//
//   int Roll() -- returns the random "roll" of the die, a
//                 uniformly distributed random number between
//                 1 and # sides
//
//   int NumSides() -- access function, returns # of sides
//
//   int NumRolls() -- access function, returns # of times
//                     Roll called for an instance of the class

#include "rando.h"                          // for random number generator

class Dice
{
  public:
    Dice(int sides);                        // constructor
    int Roll();                             // return the random roll
    int NumSides();                         // how many sides this die has
    int NumRolls();                         // # times this die rolled
  private:
    RandGen myGenerator;                    // random number generator
    int myRollCount;                        // # times die rolled
    int mySides;                            // # sides on die
};
#endif     // _DICE_H not defined
```

dice.h

value. In any case, we can usually learn much from manuals, so reading them is useful. By reading the header file you can see that three private data variables, `myGenerator`, `myRollCount`, and `mySides`, define the state of a `Dice` object. As the designer and writer of client programs, you do _not_ need to look at the private section of a class declaration. Since client programs can access a class only by calling public member functions, you should take the view that class behavior is described only by public member functions and not by private state.

In C++ a constructor is a member function with the same name as the class. Constructors are functions with no return type. Neither `void`, `int`, `double`, nor any other type can be specified as the return type of a constructor. In later examples we will see how more than one constructor can be useful, but in `dice.h` there is only one constructor for the class `Dice`. If a `Dice` variable is defined without providing arguments to the constructor as shown in Prog. 5.3, an error message will be generated. The error message generated by the g++ compiler is

```
tryroll.cc: In function 'int main()':
tryroll.cc:6: no matching function for call to 'Dice::Dice ()'
tryroll.cc:6: in base initialization for class 'Dice'
```

With Turbo C++ the compiler generates the error message

```
Error TRYROLL.CPP 6: Could not find a match for 'Dice::Dice()'
```

Note that the error messages indicate that the compiler tries to find a constructor with no parameters, `Dice::Dice()`—(the `::` operator will be discussed later)—but cannot find one.

A header file is an **interface** to a class or to a group of functions. The interface is a description of what the behavior of a class is, but not of how the behavior is implemented. You probably know how to use a stereo—at least how to turn one on and adjust the volume. From a user's point of view, the stereo's interface consists of the knobs, displays, and buttons on the front of the receiver, CD player, tuner, and so on. Users don't need to know how many watts per channel an amplifier delivers or whether the tuner uses phase-lock looping. You may know how to drive a car. From a driver's point of view, a car's interface

---

Program 5.3   tryroll.cc

```cpp
#include <iostream.h>
#include "dice.h"

int main()
{
    Dice spinner;

    cout << "# of sides = " << spinner.NumSides() << endl;
    return 0;
}
```
tryroll.cc

is made up of the gas and brake pedals, the steering wheel, and the dashboard dials and gauges. To drive a car you don't need to know whether a car engine is fuel-injected or whether it has four or six cylinders.

The `dice.h` header file is an interface to client programs that use `Dice` objects. Just as you use a stereo without (necessarily) understanding fully how it works, and just as you use a calculator by pressing the $\sqrt{\ }$ button without understanding what algorithm is used to find a square root, a `Dice` object can be used in a client program without knowledge of its private state. As the buttons and displays provide a means of accessing a stereo's features, the public member functions of a class provide a means of accessing (and sometimes modifying) the private fields in the class. The displays on an amp, tuner, or receiver are like functions that show values; the buttons that change a radio station actually change the state of a tuner, just as some member functions can change the state of a class object.

When a stereo is well-designed, one component can be replaced without replacing all components. Similarly, several models of personal computer offer the user the ability to upgrade the main chip in the computer (the Central Processing Unit, or CPU) without buying a completely new computer. In these cases the implementation can be replaced, provided that the interface stays the same. The user won't notice any difference in how the buttons and dials on the box are arranged or in how they are perceived to work. Replacing the implementation of a class may make a user's program execute more quickly, or use less space, or execute more carefully (by checking for precondition violations) but should not affect whether the program works as intended. Since client programs depend only on the interface of a class and not on the implementation, we say that classes provide a method of **information hiding**—the state of a class is hidden from client programs.

Class Documentation: The Implementation

The header file `<math.h>` contains function prototypes, or headers, for functions like `sqrt` and `sin`. The bodies of the functions are not part of the header file. A function prototype provides information that programmers need to know to call the function. A prototype also provides information that enables the compiler to determine if a function is called correctly. The prototype is an interface, just as the class declaration in `"dice.h"` is an interface for users of the `Dice` class.

The bodies of the `Dice` member functions are not part of the header file *dice.h*, Prog. 5.2 (page 180). These function bodies provide an implementation for each member function and are put in a separate file. As a general rule (certainly one we will follow in this book), the name of the **implementation file** will begin with the same prefix as the header file but will end with a `.cc` suffix, indicating that it consists of C++ code.[4]

Like all functions we've studied, a member function has a return type, a name, and a parameter list. However, there must be some way to distinguish

---

[4]A suffix of `.cpp` is used in the code provided for use with PC's and Macintoshes.

Syntax: member function prototype

```
ClassName::ClassName (parameter list)
//constructor (cannot have return type)

return type
ClassName::FunctionName (parameter list)

//nonconstructor member function
```

---

member functions from nonmember functions when the function is defined. The double colon `::` **scope resolution operator** specifies that a member function is part of a given class. The prototype `int Dice::NumSides()` indicates that `NumSides()` is a member function of the `Dice` class. Constructors have no return type. The prototype `Dice::Dice(int sides)` is the `Dice` class constructor. The prototype for the constructor of the `Balloon` class described in *balloon.h,* Prog. 3.7 (page 103), is `Balloon::Balloon()`, since no parameters are required.

As an analogy, when I'm with my family, I'm known simply as `Owen`, but to the world at large I'm `Astrachan::Owen`. This helps identify which of many possible Owens I am; I belong to the `Astrachan` "class."

The implementation of each `Dice` member function is given in *dice.cc,* Prog. 5.4. Each `Dice` member function is implemented with only a few lines of code. The variable `mySides`, whose value is returned by the function `Dice::NumSides`, is not a parameter and is not defined within the function. Similarly, the variable `myRollCount`, incremented within the function `Dice::Roll`, is neither a parameter nor a variable locally defined in `Dice::Roll`.

Program 5.4   dice.cc

```
#include "dice.h"

// implementation of dice class
// written Jan 31, 1994, modified 5/10/94 to use RandGen class

Dice::Dice(int sides)
// precondition:  sides >= 1
// postcondition: all private fields initialized
{
    myRollCount = 0;
    mySides = sides;
}

int Dice::Roll()
// postcondition: number of rolls updated
```

```
//                      random 'die' roll returned
{
    myRollCount += 1;                          // update # of times die rolled
    return myGenerator.RandInt(1,mySides);    // in range [1..mySides]
}

int Dice::NumSides()
// postcondition: return # of sides of die
{
    return mySides;
}

int Dice::NumRolls()
// postcondition: return # of times die has been rolled
{
    return myRollCount;
}
```

dice.cc

The variables `myRollCount` and `mySides` are private variables that make up the state of a `Dice` object. Private variables are sometimes called **data fields, data members,** or **instance variables.** As shown in Fig. 5.3, each instance of the `Dice` class has its own state variables. Each object may have a different number of sides or be rolled a different number of times, so different variables are needed for each object's state. The convention of using the prefix `my` with each private data field emphasizes that the data belongs to a particular object. The variable `cube` in *roll.cc*, Prog. 5.1 (page 177), has a `mySides` field with value six, whereas the `mySides` that is part of the `dodeca` variable has value 12. This is why `dodeca.NumSides()` returns 12 but `cube.NumSides()` returns 6; the member function `NumSides` returns the value of `mySides` associated with the object to which it is applied with `.`, the dot operator.

If the interface (header file) is well designed, you can change the implementation without changing or recompiling the client program.[5] Similarly, once the implementation is written and compiled, it does not need to be recompiled each time the client program changes. For large programs this can result in a significant savings in the overhead of designing and testing a program. With the advent of well-constructed class **libraries** that are available for a fee or for free, users can write programs much more easily and without the need for extensive changes when a new implementation is provided. This process of compiling different parts of a program separately is described in Sec. 3.5.

Pause to reflect

5.1. How do the displays and buttons on a stereo receiver provide an interface to the receiver? If you purchase a component stereo system (e.g., a CD player, a tuner, a receiver, and a cassette deck), do you need to buy a new receiver if you upgrade the CD player? How is this similar to or different from a header file and its corresponding implementation?

---

[5]You *will* need to relink the client program with the new implementation.

5.2. Do you know how a soda-vending machine works (on the inside)? Can you "invent" a description of how one works that is consistent with your knowledge based on using such machines?

5.3. Why are there so many comments in the header file `dice.h`?

5.4. What is the purpose of the member functions `NumSides` and `NumRolls`? For example, why won't the lines

```
Dice tetra(4);
cout << "# of sides = " << tetra.mySides << endl;
```

compile (and what is an alternative that will compile)?

5.5. In the member function `Dice::Roll()` the value returned is specified by `myGenerator.RandInt(1,mySides)`. What type/class of variable is `myGenerator` and where is the class declared?

5.6. What changes to *roll.cc*, Prog. 5.1 (page 177), permit the user to enter the number of sides in the simulated die? Can the user also enter the number of times that the die is tossed?

5.2   Iteration: Testing the Dice Class

When a new class is designed and implemented, it must be tested. Testing usually requires programs specifically designed for testing rather than for general use or for a specific application. For the `Dice` class we'd like to know whether the simulated dice behave as we'd expect real dice to behave. Are the simulated dice truly random? Do the simulated dice conform to the mathematical models that exist for random events such as dice rolls? To test the `Dice` class, we'll develop a program to see whether the theoretical outcomes of rolling dice are matched by the empirical results of the test program.

We'll use a program *rolltest.cc*, designed to toss two six-sided dice and to determine how many rolls are needed to obtain a specific sum. For example, we should expect that fewer rolls of a pair of dice are required to obtain a sum of 7 than to obtain a sum of 2. Furthermore, given that there is exactly one way to obtain a sum of 2 and one way to obtain a sum of 12 (rolling two ones and two sixes, respectively), we should expect the same number of simulated rolls to obtain either the sum of 2 or 12. The program will simulate tossing two dice and record the number of rolls needed to obtain some target between 2 and 12. We'll repeat this experiment several times and output the average number of rolls needed to obtain each sum. We wouldn't be surprised, for example, if a program needed only one roll to obtain a sum of twelve—tossing double sixes does happen. We should be surprised, however, if the experiment of trying for a twelve was repeated 1,000 times and the average number of rolls before rolling a twelve was reported to be 1—this doesn't match either our intuitive expectation or the mathematical expectation of how many rolls it takes to obtain a twelve with two six-sided dice.

We first use *rollsum.cc*, Prog. 5.5, to perform one experiment. Then we'll modify the program to repeat the experiment many times. Developing a

---

Program 5.5   rollsum.cc

```cpp
#include <iostream.h>
#include "dice.h"
#include "prompt.h"

// simulate rolling two dice to obtain specified sum
// Owen Astrachan, 8/9/94

int main()
{
    Dice d1(6);             // define two dice
    Dice d2(6);
    int numRolls = 1;    // # of times dice are rolled
    int targetSum = PromptRange("enter target to roll:",2,12);
    while (d1.Roll() + d2.Roll() != targetSum)
    {
        numRolls += 1;
    }

    cout << "number of rolls needed to get " << targetSum
         << " = " << numRolls << endl;
    return 0;
}
```

OUTPUT

```
prompt> rollsum
roll to get what number with two dice:    7
number of rolls needed to get 7 = 11
prompt> rollsum
roll to get what number with two dice:    7
number of rolls needed to get 7 = 1
```

program in stages, rather than all at once, often makes it easier to determine whether there are mistakes. Making incremental changes to a working program is usually easier than writing a large program and then trying to determine whether the program is correct. This is another example of **iterative enhancement.**

The `while` Loop

> **banana problem**: Not knowing where or when to bring a production to a close. "I know how to spell 'banana', but I don't know when to stop."
> *The New Hacker's Dictionary*

A new control statement, the **while statement,** is used in *rollsum.cc* to execute a group of statements repeatedly. Repeated execution is often called **iteration** or **looping.** The C++ `while` statement is similar syntactically to the `if` statement, but very different semantically. Both statements have tests whose truth determines whether a block of statements is executed. When the test of an `if` statement is true, the block of statements that the test controls is executed once. In contrast, the block of statements controlled by the test of a `while` loop is executed repeatedly, as long as the test is true. In a `while` loop, after execution of the last statement in the **loop body** (the block of statements guarded by the test), the test expression is evaluated again. If it is true, the statements in the loop body are executed again, and the process is repeated until the test becomes false.

The control flow for `if` statements and `while` statements is shown in Fig. 5.4. In a loop, the test is evaluated repeatedly, and the statements guarded by the test are executed until the test becomes false. The test of a loop must be false when the loop exits. Thus, in Prog. 5.5 we can determine that `d1.Roll() + d2.Roll() == targetSum`. To be more precise, we can determine that the values rolled the last time the loop test was evaluated summed to `targetSum`.

The **body** of a `while` loop is the group of statements within the curly braces { and } that is guarded by the parenthesized test. The test is evaluated once before all the statements in the loop body are executed, *not* once after each statement. If the test is true, *all* the statements in the body are executed. After the last statement in the body is executed, the test is evaluated again. If the test evaluates to true, the statements in the loop body are executed again, and this process of test/execute repeats until the test is false. (We will

learn methods for "breaking" out of loops later that invalidate this rule, but it is a good rule to keep in mind when designing loops.)

When writing loops, remember that the loop test is *not* reevaluated after each statement in the loop body, only after the last statement. To ensure that loops do not execute forever, it's important that at least one statement

```
if (test)
{
    statement list;
}
next statement;
```

```
while (test)
{
    statement list;
}
next statement;
```

Figure 5.4 Flow control for `if` and `while` statements.

in the loop changes the values that are part of the test expression. In Prog. 5.5 the values in the loop test change each time, since new rolls of d1 and d2 are made in the loop test.

The variable numRolls in Prog. 5.5, *rollsum.cc*, is not needed, because each Dice variable maintains the number of times it has been rolled as state information. The final output statement can be written as

```
cout << "number of rolls needed to get " << targetSum
     << " = " << d1.NumRolls() << endl;
```

Since the variable numRolls isn't used, the body of the while loop will be empty. All the work is done in the loop test, with each Dice variable tracking how many times it has been rolled.

Infinite Loops

You must be careful when writing loops, because it is possible for a loop to execute forever—a so-called **infinite loop.** As a simple example, consider the loop

```
while (6 != 4)
{
    cout << "this will be printed many times" << endl;
}
```

which will execute forever (or until the user stops the computer), because 6 is not equal to 4, and the truth of the loop test is unchanged by any of the statements in the loop body. On many systems, typing Ctrl-C will stop an infinite loop.

Improving the Test Program

To test the Dice class by rolling two dice 1,000 times rather than just one time, we'll need to use a loop around the code segment that simulates the rolls in *rollsum.cc.* It's often confusing to put one loop inside another loop, so we'll move the loop in *rollsum.cc* into a separate function and call this function 1,000 times from main. This is done in *rollsum2.cc.,* Prog. 5.6:

Program 5.6   rollsum2.cc

```
#include <iostream.h>
#include "dice.h"
#include "prompt.h"

// simulate rolling two dice to obtain specified sum
// repeat the "experiment" specified number of times
// Owen Astrachan, 8/9/94, modified 6/9/95

int NumToRoll(int target);

int main()
{
    int numTimes;                        // for one trial
```

```
    long int totalRolls;          // accumulate for all trials
    int targetSum;                // roll to get this value
    int k;
    targetSum = PromptRange("roll to get what number with two dice:",
        2,12);
    numTimes  = PromptRange("number of experiments",1,20000);

    totalRolls = 0;
    k = 0;
    while (k < numTimes)
    {
        totalRolls += NumToRoll(targetSum);
        k += 1;
    }

    cout << "average # of rolls to obtain " << targetSum;
    cout << " = " << totalRolls/numTimes;
    cout << " (in " << numTimes << " trials)" << endl;

    return 0;
}

int NumToRoll(int target)
// precondition: 2 <= target <= 12
// postcondition: returns # of rolls needed to obtain target
{
    Dice d1(6);
    Dice d2(6);

    int numRolls = 1;     //first time through loop is 1 roll

    while (d1.Roll() + d2.Roll() != target)
    {
        numRolls += 1;
    }

    return numRolls;
}
```

OUTPUT

```
prompt> rollsum2
roll to get what number with two dice: between 2 and 12: 7
number of experiments between 1 and 20000 10000
average # of rolls to obtain 7 = 6 (in 10000 trials)
prompt> rollsum2
roll to get what number with two dice: between 2 and 12: 2
number of experiments between 1 and 20000 10000
average # of rolls to obtain 2 = 36 (in 10000 trials)
prompt> rollsum2
roll to get what number with two dice: between 2 and 12: 12
number of experiments between 1 and 20000 10000
average # of rolls to obtain 12 = 35 (in 10000 trials)
```

The results obtained for trying to roll a two and a twelve are very close. Consulting a book on discrete mathematics provides an answer that is correct theoretically[6] and might further validate these empirical results. The average printed in Prog. 5.6 is rounded off to an integer value (as opposed to a `double` value) because `totalRolls` is a `long int` variable and `numTimes` is an `int`. The result of dividing a `long int` and an `int` value is a `long int` value. Changing the type of `totalRolls` to `double` would yield a more precise average, like 7.3856. A `long int` is used instead of an `int` because the total number of rolls over many trials will exceed the largest `int` value on many computers.

The variable `k` is used in `main` to control how many times the `while` loop iterates. The loop test is true when `k` takes on the values 0, 1, 2, ..., `numTimes` - 1, because the relational operator < is used in the test. A loop designed to repeat a sequence of statements a fixed number of times is called a **counting loop.** Traditionally, a loop that counts to 10 in C++ uses the ten values 0, 1, 2, 3, 4, 5, 6, 7, 8, 9. However, it's possible to start counting at 1 and go up to 10. This could be done in *rollsum2.cc* by initializing `k = 1` before the loop and using the relational operator <= in the loop test.

Pause to reflect

5.7. Modify the loop in *rollsum.cc*, Prog. 5.5, so that the values of the dice rolls are printed. You'll need to define two integer variables to store the values of the dice rolls in order to print them (this can be tricky).

5.8. Write a loop to print the numbers from 1 up to a value entered by the user, one number per line. Modify the loop to print the numbers from the user-entered value down to 1.

5.9. Complete the following loop so that it prints all powers of two less than 30,000, starting with 1 2 4 8 16 ... You can do this by adding a single `*=` statement to the loop.

```
num = 1;
while (num < 30000)
{
    cout << num << endl;


}
```

5.10. How can you determine quickly that the following loop is an infinite loop (and will execute "forever") whenever `num` is less than 100?

```
cout << "enter number ";
cin >> num;
while (num < 100)
{
```

---

[6]Mathematically, the expected number of rolls to obtain either a two or a twelve is 36. This is a property of independent, discrete random variables. The expected number of rolls to obtain a seven is 6.

```
        product = product * num;
        answer = answer + 1;
    }
```

5.11. Write a function that rolls two n-sided dice and returns how many rolls are needed before the dice show the same number—that is, until doubles are rolled.

5.3   Using and Developing Loops

Loops and Mathematical Functions

The first computers were used almost exclusively as "number crunchers"—machines that solved numerical problems and equations. The very word "computer" formerly meant a person employed to perform such extensive calculations. For that reason, one of the first machines to do the job had the name ENIAC, for *Electronic Numerical Integrator And Computer*. This special-purpose computer eventually evolved into a more general machine called UNIVAC, for *Universal Automatic Computer*.

Today the machines we now call "computers" are much more general-purpose, and many people find it difficult to imagine writing without using a word processor, movies without digital special effects, and banking without automatic tellers. All these applications require computers used in ways that at least on the surface don't involve numerical computations. Nevertheless, all information stored in today's computers is represented at some level by a number (even words are "converted" to 0's and 1's when stored in a computer's memory). **Numerical analysis** is a branch of computer science in which mathematical methods for solving many kinds of equations using computers are designed and developed. Although we won't delve deeply into this branch of computer science, we'll use some simple mathematical examples to study some broader concepts.

We'll investigate three mathematical functions: one to calculate the **factorial** of an integer, one to determine whether an integer is **prime,** and one to approximate **square roots** of real numbers. These functions provide simple examples of loops and loop development, reinforce the concept of programmer-defined functions, and introduce functions to which we will return later.

Computing Factorials

The factorial function, usually denoted mathematically as $f(x) = x!$, is used in statistics, probability, and an area of computer science and mathematics called *combinatorics*. One definition of the function is

$$n! = 1 \times 2 \times \cdots \times (n - 1) \times n$$

so that $6! = 1 \times 2 \times 3 \times 4 \times 5 \times 6 = 720$. As a special case, by definition $0! = 1$. Program 5.7 implements and tests a function for computing factorials.

Program 5.7   fact.cc

```
#include <iostream.h>
#include "prompt.h"

// illustrates loop and integer overflow

long int Factorial(int num);

int main()
{
    int highValue = PromptRange("enter max value for factorial",1,30);
    int current = 0;

        // prints factorial tables for numbers from current to highValue
    while (current <= highValue)
    {
        cout << current << "! = " << Factorial(current) << endl;
        current = current + 1;
    }
    return 0;
}

long int Factorial(int num)
// precondition: num >= 0
// postcondition returns num!
{
    long int product = 1;
    int count = 0;

    while (count < num)        // invariant: product == count!
    {
        count += 1;
        product *= count;
    }
    return product;
}
```

OUTPUT

```
prompt> fact
enter max value for factorial between 1 and 30: 17
0! = 1
1! = 1
2! = 2
3! = 6
4! = 24
5! = 120
6! = 720
7! = 5040
```

```
8!  =  40320
9!  =  362880
10! =  3628800
11! =  39916800
12! =  479001600
13! =  1932053504
14! =  1278945280
15! =  2004310016
16! =  2004189184
17! =  -288522240
```

The variable `product` accumulates the result with the statement `product *= count`; this result is returned when the loop finishes executing. The values of the variables `product` and `count` change each time that the loop test is evaluated in computing 6!, as follows:

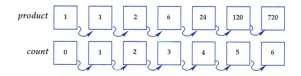

Each time that the loop test is evaluated, the value of the variable `product` is always equal to `(count)!` (that's `count` factorial), as shown. Since 0! = 1 (by definition), this is true the first time the loop test is evaluated as well as after each iteration of the loop body. A statement that is true each time a loop test is evaluated is called a **loop invariant**—the truth of the statement does not vary or change. Loop invariants are useful in reasoning about the correctness of programs that use loops. Since `product == count!` is an invariant, and `product` is returned, we can reason that the `Factorial` function calculates the correct value.

Conceptually, the function `Factorial` in Prog. 5.7 will always return the correct value. However, in practice the correct value may not be returned, as is evident from the foregoing run of the program. Note that 16! < 15!; that 17! is a negative number; and that although 13! = 13 × 12!, the value for 13! ends in a four while 12! ends in a zero. None of these results represents mathematical truth. Because integers stored in a computer have a largest value, it is possible for seemingly bizarre results to occur when this largest value is exceeded. We'll see precisely why this occurs later, but it is important to keep in mind that the limitation on integer values is one of many ways that a computer program can function exactly as it should (although not, perhaps, as intended), but produce unanticipated and often inexplicable results.

Computing Prime Numbers

Prime numbers used to be the domain of pure mathematicians specializing in number theory. Today, they play an increasingly important role in computer science applications. Current **encryption** techniques, used to encode data so that information cannot be read (electronically or visually), are largely based on efficient methods for determining whether a number is prime. Data encryption is a big business, with many ethical and privacy considerations. In addition, writing programs to determine whether numbers are prime is part of the rites of passage one traditionally undergoes in studying programming.

By definition, a number is prime if its only divisors are 1 and the number itself. For example, 5, 7, 53, and 97 are prime, but 91 is not prime, since it is divisible by 7 (and 13). The only even prime number is 2. By convention, 1 is not considered prime.

It seems that we'll need to check divisors of a number N to see whether the number is prime. We could naïvely check all numbers from 1 to N as potential divisors, checking the remainder each time. This method can be improved by checking only potential divisors less than the square root of a number. For example, to determine whether 119 is prime, we check divisors up to 11 (because $11^2 = 121 > 119$). Any number greater than 11 that divides 119 must have a corresponding factor less than 11, since factors come in pairs. Thus 7 and 17 are both factors of 119, but only one factor is needed to show that 119 is not prime (and the second factor is easily obtained by dividing by the first).

We need to be careful. We don't want to check that 1 is a divisor, since it divides every number evenly. We can also avoid testing even numbers as potential divisors, since 2 is the only even number that's prime. The approach used in the boolean-valued function IsPrime shown in Prog. 5.8 tests 0, 1, and 2 explicitly, then uses a loop to check all potential divisors less than the square root of n, the parameter of IsPrime.

Program 5.8   primes.cc

```
#include <iostream.h>
#include <math.h>                    // for sqrt

// program to check for primeness
// Owen Astrachan, 9/25/93, modified 5/9/94

// prototypes

bool IsPrime(int n);               // determines whether n is prime

int main()
{
    int k,low,high;
    int numPrimes = 0;
    cout << "low number> ";
```

```cpp
    cin >> low;

    cout << "high number> ";
    cin >> high;

    cout << "primes between " << low << " and " << high
         << endl;
    cout << "-------------------------------" << endl;

    k = low;
    while (k <= high)
    {
        if (IsPrime(k))
        {
            cout << k << endl;
            numPrimes += 1;
        }
        k += 1;
    }
    cout << "----------------" << endl;
    cout << numPrimes << " primes found between " << low
         << " and " << high << endl;

    return 0;
}


bool IsPrime(int n)
// precondition: n >= 0
// postcondition: returns true if n is prime, else returns false
//                returns false if precondition is violated
{
    if (n < 2)              // 1 and 0 aren't prime
    {                       // treat negative #'s as not prime
        return false;
    }
    else if (2 == n)        // 2 is only even prime number
    {
        return true;
    }
    else if (n % 2 == 0)    // even, can't be prime
    {
        return false;
    }
    else                    // number is odd
    {
        int limit = int(sqrt(n) + 1);  // largest divisor to check
        int divisor = 3;  // initialize to smallest divisor

        while (divisor <= limit)
        {
            if (n % divisor == 0)  // n is divisible, not prime
            {
```

```
                    return false;
            }
            divisor += 2;  // check next odd number
        }
        return true;          // number must be prime
    }
}
```

```
                              OUTPUT

prompt> primes
low number> 1000
high number> 1100
primes between 1000 and 1100
-----------------------------------
1009
1013
1019
1021
1031
1033
1039
1049
1051
1061
1063
1069
1087
1091
1093
1097
-----------------
16 primes found between 1000 and 1100
```

Each return statement in IsPrime exits the function. Flow of control continues with the statement that follows the call of IsPrime. In particular, the return statement in the while loop permits a kind of premature loop exit. As soon as a divisor is found, the function exits and returns false. If control reaches the return statement after the while loop, the loop test must be false; that is, divisor > limit. In this case n is prime.

Program Tip: When a return statement is executed, flow of control immediately leaves the function in which the return is located and continues with the statement that follows the function call. No other statements within the function are executed. One school of thought says that each function should have exactly one return statement. This is always possible, but it often requires the introduction of extra variables or more complicated code. You will find that judicious use of multiple `returns` within one function can make the function simpler to write and easier to reason about.

On some computers the assignment `int limit = sqrt(n) + 1` may cause a warning:

```
primes.cc: In function 'bool IsPrime(int)':
primes.cc:61: warning: initialization to 'int' from 'double'
```

The value returned by `sqrt` is a `double`. Assigning a `double` to an `int` is not always possible, because the largest `double` value may be greater than the largest `int` value. Even though a program compiles, compiler warnings should not be ignored; they are often an indication that you have misused the language. In this case, you can avert the warning by explicitly converting the `double` value to an `int`. This is shown in *primes.cc* in the statement assigning a value to `limit`:

```
int limit = int(sqrt(n) + 1);    // largest divisor to check
```

Using the type `int` like a function call explicitly converts the value `sqrt(n) + 1` into an integer. This is called a **type cast.** The cast prevents the warning, because you, the programmer, explicitly converted one type to another. We'll study casts in more detail in Sec. 6.2.[7]

The value `sqrt(n) + 1` is used instead of `sqrt(n)` because of the limited precision of floating-point numbers. For example, the square root of 49 might be calculated as 6.9999 rather than 7.0. In this case, the assignment `int limit = sqrt(49)` stores the value 6 in `limit`, because the `double` is truncated when it's assigned to an `int`. Adding 1 avoids this kind of problem.

Efficiency Considerations

How important is it to check divisors up to $\sqrt{n}$ rather than n in determining whether a number is prime? People often suggest using $n/2$ rather than n. Is this better than $\sqrt{n}$? These questions are important in determining the efficiency or **complexity** of the algorithm used in `IsPrime`, but they don't affect the correctness of the algorithm. Consider that $\sqrt{50{,}000} = 223.6$, but that $50{,}000/2 = 25{,}000$. This difference means that using $n/2$ as the limit in `IsPrime` could result in approximately 12,388 more numbers being checked as potential divisors in determining that 49,999 is prime (it is). The extra number of

---

[7]As we'll see in Section 6.2, the latest C++ standard has a casting operator `static_cast`, whose use is preferred to the style of cast we've shown here. Not all compilers support `static_cast` at the time of this writing.

divisors is 12,388 rather than 24,776 because only odd numbers are checked as potential divisors in the loop. I timed two versions of Prog. 5.8: one that used `limit = sqrt(n) + 1` and one that used `limit = n/2 + 1`. It took 1.44 seconds to determine that there are 5,133 primes between 1 and 50,000 when the square root limit was used, but 45.78 seconds when the limit based on half of `n` was used. Interestingly, even checking only divisors less than the square root of a number is much too slow for the encryption algorithms that are based on using large prime numbers (see the following box). These encryption algorithms use pairs of large prime numbers, so they need to determine whether 200-digit numbers are prime. The square root of such a number has 100 digits. Testing 10^{100} numbers as potential divisors would require more time than the universe has been in existence. What makes the encryption algorithms feasible? Computer scientists and mathematicians developed efficient methods for determining whether a number is prime. These methods don't actually factor a number; they just yield a yes or no answer to the question "Is this number prime?" However, no one has developed an efficient algorithm for factoring numbers. The keys to the encryption methods used are (1) efficiently determining that a number is prime, and (2) difficulty in factoring the product of the two primes.

Cryptography and Computer Science

Before the 1970s, encryption techniques were largely based on sharing a private key that was used to encrypt messages. Both the sender and the receiver needed to have the private key. This was a potential security leak: how is the key transmitted from one person to another? In old movies couriers transported keys in briefcases strapped to their wrists. Apparently this method was used in real life as well.

In the mid 1970s several people developed **public-key** cryptography. The essence of these methods is that there are two keys: one private and one public. Everyone in the world has access to the public key and can use it to encrypt messages. Only the receiver of the message has the private key, and this key is required to decrypt the message. The keys are numbers and are calculated by choosing two large prime numbers, multiplying them together, and then doing a few other mathematical operations. The August 1977 "Mathematical Games" section of the magazine *Scientific American* explained this method of cryptography and had a challenge from the inventors of the method: Decrypt a message based on factoring the number called RSA-129 (it has 129 digits and is named for the inventors of the encryption method: Rivest, Shamir, and Adleman):

```
114,381,625,757,888,867,669,235,779,976,146,612,010,218,
296,721,242,362,562,561,842,935,706,935,245,733,897,830,
597,123,563,958,705,058,989,075,147,599,290,026,879,543,541
```

The column claimed that it would take 40 quadrillion years to decrypt the message and offered $100.00 to the first person to do it. In 1994, more than

> 1600 computers around the world were put to work for eight months using new factoring methods to factor RSA-129. Coordinated by Arjen Lenstra, the computers used "wasted cycles"—time that the computers would have been otherwise idle—to factor RSA-129. The number was successfully factored, and the message from the *Scientific American* article decrypted. The message was THE MAGIC WORDS ARE SQUEAMISH OSSIFRAGE.
>
> For an illuminating account of the method and history of public-key cryptography, and of a public-domain program called PGP that can be used for encrypting/decrypting, see [Gar95].

Approximating Square Roots

We have studied several functions whose prototypes are given in <math.h>, including the function sqrt, which calculates square roots. In this section we'll develop a function that approximates square roots. Of course you should use the the sqrt function from <math.h> when you need to calculate square roots in a program, but the general topic of approximation is quite important in many areas of computer science. It's also possible that you may need to approximate square roots when the sqrt function is not appropriate, such as when arbitrarily large integers are used (see Sec. 8.8). Finally, this method of approximation, known as **Newton's method,** can be generalized to solve many kinds of equations.

To approximate the square root of a number n using Newton's method, you need to make an initial guess at the root and then refine this guess until it is "close enough." In the code shown in the function Newton from *newton.cc,* Prog. 5.9, the initial approximation for the root is $n/2$. A sequence of approximations is generated by computing the average of root and n/root. In code this is written as follows: [8]

```
root = 0.5 * (root + n/root);
```

Program 5.9   newton.cc

```
#include <iostream.h>
#include <math.h>                    // for sqrt
#include <float.h>                   // for DBL_EPSILON
#include "prompt.h"

// Owen Astrachan, 6/9/96
// illustrates Newton Method's for square roots
// and floating point values/approximation
```

---

[8]The general form of Newton's method relies on a calculation using a function and the function's derivative. The form is root $=$ root $- f(\text{root})/f'(\text{root})$ for a function $f(x)$. To approximate the square root of n, the function $f(x) = x^2 - n$ is used.

```
bool FloatEqual(double lhs, double rhs);
double Newton(double n);

int main()
{
    int iterations = PromptRange("iterations:",1,1000000);
    double low     = PromptRange("low:",0.0,1e30);
    double high    = PromptRange("high:",low,1e30);
    double delta   = (high - low)/iterations;
    double sroot,nroot;

    while (low <= high)   // loop from low to high, increment by delta
    {
        nroot = Newton(low);
        sroot = sqrt(low);

        if (!FloatEqual(sroot,nroot))
        {
            cout << "not float equal: " << low << endl;
            cout << "newt = " << nroot << " sqrt = " << sroot << endl;
        }
        else if (sroot != nroot)
        {
            cout << "not equal: " << low << endl;
            cout << "newt = " << nroot << " sqrt = " << sroot << endl;
        }
        low += delta;
    }
    return 0;
}

bool FloatEqual(double lhs, double rhs)
// postcondition: returns true if lhs == rhs where equality
//                is determined by using relative error, i.e.
//                |lhs-rhs| / min(|lhs|,|rhs|)
{
    const double EPSILON = DBL_EPSILON*10;  // precision for equality

    double flhs = fabs(lhs);             // compute absolute values
    double frhs = fabs(rhs);
    double min = frhs;
    if (flhs < frhs)                     // set minimum of absolute values
    {
        min = flhs;
    }
    if (min < EPSILON)                   // avoid division by zero, check
    {
        return (fabs(lhs-rhs) < EPSILON);
    }
    return (fabs(lhs-rhs)/min < EPSILON);
}

double Newton(double n)
// precondition: n >= 0
// postcondition: returns sqrt(n)
```

```
{
    double root = n/2.0;
    int count = 0;

    if (FloatEqual(0.0,n))              // avoid division by zero
    {
        return 0.0;
    }

    while (!FloatEqual(root*root,n))  // loop until approximation is good
    {
        root = 0.5*(root + n/root);
    }
    return root;
}
```

```
                        OUTPUT

prompt> newton
iterations: between 1 and 1000000: 10
low: between 0 and 1e+30: 0.0
high: between 0 and 1e+30: 1.0
not equal: 0.2000000000000000
        newt = 0.4472135954999580 sqrt = 0.4472135954999579
not equal: 0.3000000000000000
        newt = 0.5477225575051664 sqrt = 0.5477225575051662
not equal: 0.5000000000000000
        newt = 0.7071067811865475 sqrt = 0.7071067811865476
not equal: 0.9999999999999999
        newt = 1.0000000000000000 sqrt = 0.9999999999999999
prompt> newton
iterations: between 1 and 1000000: 10
low: between 0 and 1e+30: 1.0
high: between 0 and 1e+30: 2.0
not equal: 1.5000000000000004
        newt = 1.2247448713915894 sqrt = 1.2247448713915892
not equal: 1.9000000000000008
        newt = 1.3784048752090223 sqrt = 1.3784048752090226
```

Using this method, the square root of 37 is approximated by the sequence of numbers listed in Table 5.1.

When does the sequence of approximations stop, and what is meant by "close enough" in the foregoing description? In the case of finding square roots, we can stop when the approximation squared is equal to n, the number whose square root is sought. However, because floating-point numbers are approximated, it's very dangerous to test for equality using the $==$ operator.

Table 5.1   Approximating the Square Root of 37

Calculate root	Root
Initial guess $37/2$	18.5
$0.5(18.5 + 37/18.5)$	10.25
$0.5(10.25 + 37/10.25)$	6.9298780487804876
using $0.5(\text{root} + n/\text{root})$	6.1345386724324786
	6.0829810283008774
	6.0827625342223959
	6.0827625302982202

Instead, two `double` floating-point numbers should be considered equal when their relative difference is small. The relative difference of two numbers x and y is calculated by the following formula, in which the vertical bars denote absolute value.

$$\frac{|x - y|}{\min(|x|, |y|)}$$

If this relative difference is small enough, two numbers are considered equal. For example, comparing 1000 and 1001 yields $|1000 - 1001|/1000 = 0.001$, whereas comparing 0.1 and 0.2 yields $|0.1 - 0.2|/0.1 = 1$, so in some sense 1000 is closer to 1001 than 0.1 is to 0.2. The function `FloatEqual` in *newton.cc* is used instead of the `==` operator to determine whether two `double` values are equal. The function depends on a constant `DBL_EPSILON` defined in the header file `<float.h>` to minimize differences in floating-point precision in different computing environments. The function `fabs` from `<math.h>` returns the absolute value of a `double` value. The output shows that two numbers can be considered equal using `FloatEqual`, although the numbers are not equal according to the `==` operator.

You can see from the output of Prog. 5.9 that numbers between 0.0 and 1.0 have different behavior than numbers between 1.0 and 2.0. For example, the last number printed for the range 0.0–1.0 is not represented as 1.0 but as 0.9999999999999999. This discrepancy is due to how decimal-based numbers are approximated in computer programs. Again, you do not need to know how the approximation is done, but you should be aware of some of the problems associated with floating-point computations.

Program Tip: In general, do not rely on using the `==` operator to compare two `double` floating-point values for equality. Use a function like `FloatEqual` instead.

Because all floating-point values are approximations of real numbers, you cannot assume that simple mathematical equations such as $1.0 + 10 \times 0.1 = 2.0$ will be true when `double` floating-point numbers are used.

Defining Constants

The `double` identifier `EPSILON` is defined as `const double` in `FloatEqual`. The type modifier **const** means that `EPSILON` is a constant. Because it is constant, `EPSILON` cannot be assigned a new value or changed in any way. For example, if the line

```
EPSILON = 10e-13;
```

is added immediately after the definition of `EPSILON`, the g++ compiler generates the error message

```
newton.cc: In function 'bool FloatEqual(double, double)':
newton.cc:48: assignment of read-only variable 'double const EPSILON'
*** Error code 1
make: Fatal error: Command failed for target 'newton'
```

In general, it is good programming practice to use constants to represent values that do not change during the execution of a program. Some examples of constant definitions are the following:

```
const double PI = 3.14159265;
const double INCHES_PER_CM = 0.39370;
const int January = 1;
const string cpp = "C++";
```

> **Syntax: const variable**
>
> `const` *type identifier = value;*

Using named constants not only improves the readability of a program; it permits edit changes in a program to be localized in one place. For example, if you need a more precise value of π of 3.1415926535897, only one constant is changed (and the program recompiled). Mnemonic names, or names that indicate the purpose they serve, also provide meaning and make it easier to read and understand code. Using the constant `January` instead of 1 in a calendar-making program can make the code much easier to follow. It is a common convention for constant identifiers to consist of all capital letters and to use underscores to separate different words.

Using constants also protects against inadvertent modification of a variable. The compiler can be an important tool in developing code if you use language features like `const` appropriately.

5.12. Assume that the factorial of a negative number is defined to be the factorial of the corresponding absolute value so that, for example, $(-5)! = 5! = 120$. Modify the function `Factorial` in Prog. 5.7 so that the correct value is returned for any value of `num`. Be sure to change the comments.

5.13. Here is another version of `Factorial`; this version is changed only slightly from that given in Prog. 5.7. Does this version pass a black-box test comparing it with the original?

```
int Factorial(int num)
{
    int product = 1;
```

Pause to reflect

```
        int count = 1;

        while (count <= num)
        {
            product *= count;
            count += 1;
        }
        return product;
    }
```

5.14. If the statement `divisor += 2` is changed to `divisor += 1`, does the function `IsPrime` still work as intended?

5.15. What value is returned by the call `IsPrime(1)`? Is this what should be returned?

5.16. It is possible to write a loop without a return from the middle of the loop in the function `IsPrime`. The `while` loop can be replaced by the following:

```
    while (divisor <= limit && n % divisor != 0)
    {
        divisor += 2;
    }
```

What statement is needed after the loop to ensure that the correct value is returned?

5.17. Why is the `if` statement `if (min < EPSILON)` needed in `FloatEqual` from *newton.cc*?

5.18. Write appropriate constant definitions to represent the number of feet in a mile (5,280); the number of ounces in a pound (16); the mathematical constant *e* (2.71828); the number of grams in a pound (453.59); and the number foot-pounds in an erg (1.356×10^7).

5.19. Modify the function `Newton` in *newton.cc* so that the loop terminates when two successive approximations are equal (using `FloatEqual`) rather than when the approximation is close to the actual square root. You'll need to introduce another variable; you can call this `oldRoot`. Loop until `oldRoot` and `loop` are equal.

Numbers Written in English

As another example of a loop we'll use `DigitToString` from *numtoeng.cc*, Prog. 4.10 (page 143), to convert a number to an English equivalent string formed from the digits (Prog. 5.10). For example, 123 is represented by `"one two three"`, and 4017 is represented by `"four zero one seven"`.

We'll need a loop to do two things:

- Extract one digit at a time from the number
- Build up the string one word at a time

The modulus operator `%` makes it easy to determine the rightmost digit of any number. It's difficult to get the leftmost digit, because we don't know how many

---

Program 5.10   digits.cc

```cpp
#include <iostream.c>
#include "CPstring.h"

// illustrates loops, convert a number to a string of English
// digits; i.e., 1346 -> one three four six
// Owen Astrachan, 6/8/95

string DigitToString(int num);
string StringOut(long int number);

int main()
{
    int number;

    cout << "enter an integer: ";
    cin >> number;
    cout << StringOut(number) << endl;

    return 0;
}

string DigitToString(int num)
// precondition: 0 <= num < 10
// postcondition: returns english equivalent,
//                e.g., 1->one,...9->nine
{
    if (0 == num)        return "zero";
    else if (1 == num)   return "one";
    else if (2 == num)   return "two";
    else if (3 == num)   return "three";
    else if (4 == num)   return "four";
    else if (5 == num)   return "five";
    else if (6 == num)   return "six";
    else if (7 == num)   return "seven";
    else if (8 == num)   return "eight";
    else if (9 == num)   return "nine";
    else return "?";
}

string StringOut(long int number)
// precondition: 0 < number
// postcondition: returns string formed from digits written
//                in English; e.g., 123 -> "one two three"
{
    string s = "";
    int digit;
    while (number != 0)
    {
        digit = number % 10;
        s = DigitToString(digit) + " " + s;
```

```
        number / 10;
    }
    return s;
}
```

```
                                    OUTPUT

prompt> digits
enter an integer: 9299338
nine two nine nine three three eight
prompt> digits
enter an integer: 401706
four zero one seven zero six
prompt> digits
enter an integer: -139
? ? ?
prompt> digits
enter an integer: 18005551212
eight two five six eight two zero two eight
prompt> digits
enter an integer: 8005551212
? ? ? ? ? ? ? ? zero
```

digits are in the number. To build the English equivalent, we'll have to build a `string` by concatenating each digit-string in the proper order. Each time a digit is peeled off the number, its corresponding string is concatenated to the front of the `string` being built. The values of the variables `digit`, `number`, and `s`, each time that the loop test `number != 0` is evaluated when `number` is initially 123, are shown in Fig. 5.5.

The first time the loop test is evaluated, `s` represents the empty string `""`: a `string` with no characters. The value of `digit` is undefined because no value has been assigned to `digit`. Since a space is always added af-

```
        while (number != 0)
        {
            digit = number % 10;
            s = DigitToString(digit) + " " + s;
            number /= 10;
        }
```

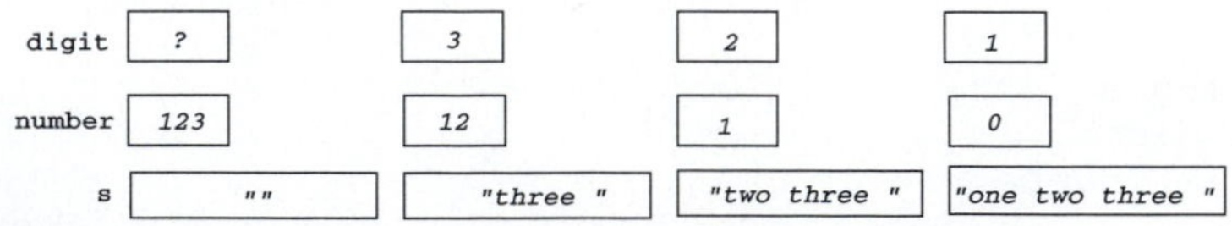

digit	?	3	2	1
number	123	12	1	0
s	""	"three "	"two three "	"one two three "

Figure 5.5   Variable values as loop test is executed.

ter the digit string prepended to the `string` s, there is a space at the end of s. This space won't be "visible" if s is printed, unless another string is printed immediately after s. The space will be included in calculating the length of s, so `StringOut(111).length() == 12`.

Fence Post Problems

The extra space after the last English digit of the `string` made by `StringOut` in Prog. 5.10, *digits.cc,* is undesirable. Spaces should occur between each two digits rather than after each digit. A similar problem occurs with the following loop, intended to print the numbers 1 through 10 separated by commas: `1,2,3,4,5,6,7,8,9,10`. The loop doesn't work properly:

```
int num = 1;
while (num <= 10)
{
    cout << num << ",";
    num += 1;
}
cout << endl;
```

The loop prints `1,2,3,4,5,6,7,8,9,10,` instead (note the trailing comma). The problem here is that the number of numbers is one more than the number of commas, just as the number of digits is one more than the number of spaces in the function *StringOut.*

This kind of problem is often called a **fence post** problem, because a fence (see picture below) has one more fence post than fence crosspieces. In our example, the numbers are the posts and the commas are the crosspieces.

The correct number of posts and crosspieces cannot be printed in a loop that outputs both fences and crosspieces, because the loop generates the same number of each. There are three alternatives: print the first fence post (number) before the loop; print the last post (number) after the loop; or guard the printing of the crosspiece inside the loop. The three approaches are coded as follows:

```
int num = 1;                    int num = 1;
cout << num;                    while (num < 10)
num += 1;                       {
while (num <= 10)                   cout << num << ",";
{                                   num += 1;
    cout << "," << num;         }
    num += 1;                   cout << num << endl;
}
cout << endl;
```

```
int num = 1;
while (num <= 10)
{
    cout << num;
```

```
                    if (num < 10)
                        cout << ",";
                    num += 1;
                }
                cout << endl;
```

In the solution at the top left, the comma is printed before each number is printed in the loop. This requires an increment before the loop as shown or a different initialization of `num`.

Printing the comma after each number requires printing the final number after the loop. This is shown at the top right in the preceding listing by modifying the test to use `<` instead of `<=`.

Both solutions share the problem of code duplication. In the code segment at the top left, `num` is incremented by one in two places. In the segment at the top right, there are two `cout << num` statements. Code duplication often causes maintenance problems, since changes must be made identically in more than one place. The solution on the bottom avoids the code duplication but mimics the loop test inside the loop. Each of these solutions is an acceptable way to solve fence post problems.

Pause to reflect

5.20. Write code that permits the user to enter the number of fence posts in a fence and that then "draws" a fence as shown in the following sample output:

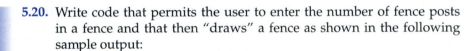

```
OUTPUT


enter number of fence posts:   8
|---|---|---|---|---|---|---|
|---|---|---|---|---|---|---|
```

5.21. Alter the code in the function *StringOut* in Prog. 5.10, *digits.cc,* so that spaces occur between each digit as opposed to after each digit.

5.22. Write a function that returns the number of characters in an `int`, accounting for a minus sign for negative numbers. For example, `NumDigits(1234)` returns 4, and `NumDigits(-1234)` returns 5.

5.23. Write a loop that prints the numbers 1 through 100 with each group of 10 numbers starting on a new line. There should be a space between each of the numbers on a line:

```
1 2 3 4 5 6 7 8 9 10
11 12 13 14 15 16 17 18 19 20
...
91 92 93 94 95 96 97 98 99 100
```

You may find it useful to use the statement

```
if (num % 10 == 0)
{
    cout << endl;
}
```

in the loop body.

5.24. Write a loop using the operator `/=` that calculates how many times a number can be divided in half before 0 is reached. For example, 2 can be divided twice (attaining 1 then 0), 3 can be divided twice, 511 can be divided 9 times, and 512 can be divided 10 times. Use this loop to write a function `IntegerLog` that has two parameters, `number` and `n`, and returns how many times `number` can be divided by `n`.

5.4 Alternative Looping Statements

Writing loops can be difficult. It's not always easy to determine what the loop test should be, what statements belong in the loop body, and how variables should be initialized and updated before, in, and after a loop. Loops tend to have four sections:

- **Initialization:** This step occurs prior to the loop. Variables that need to be initialized are given values prior to the first time the loop test is evaluated.

- **Loop test:** The test determines whether the loop body will be executed. When the loop test is false, the loop body is not executed. If the loop test is always true, an infinite loop results, unless the loop is exited with a `return` statement, as used in `IsPrime` in *primes.cc*, Prog. 5.8.

- **Loop body:** The statements that are executed each time the loop test evaluates to true.

- **Update:** The statements that affect values in the loop test. These statements ensure that the loop will eventually terminate. Values of variables in the loop test will be changed by the update statements.

These sections are diagrammed in Fig. 5.6 for the two loops in *primes.cc*, Prog. 5.8 (page 195).

The `for` Loop

These loops, and the counting loop in `main` of *rollsum2.cc*, Prog. 5.6 (page 188), are often written using an alternative looping construct to the `while` loop. The **for loop** is just a kind of shorthand, or **syntactic sugar**,[9] that can be used instead of a `while` loop. Anything written with one loop can be written with the other and vice versa.

---

[9]The term **syntactic sugar** is used for constructs that don't have a new meaning but are more aesthetically pleasing in some way. Often this means "easier for a human reader to understand."

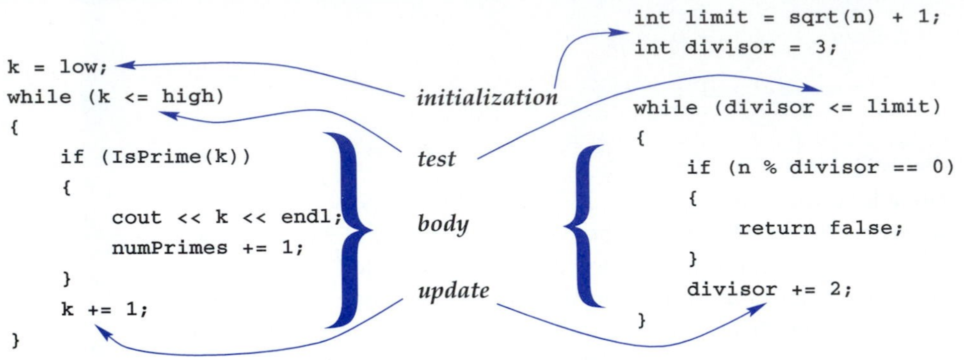

```
                                                         int limit = sqrt(n) + 1;
                                                         int divisor = 3;
k = low;
while (k <= high)             initialization            while (divisor <= limit)
{                                                       {
    if (IsPrime(k))              test                       if (n % divisor == 0)
    {                                                       {
        cout << k << endl;       body                           return false;
        numPrimes += 1;                                     }
    }                                                       divisor += 2;
    k += 1;                      update                  }
}
```

Figure 5.6   The four sections of a loop.

Here is the `while` loop from `main` in *primes.cc*, Prog. 5.8, with the corresponding `for` loop:

```
k = low;                          for(k=low; k <= high; k += 1)
while (k <= high)                 {
{                                     if (IsPrime(k))
    if (IsPrime(k))                   {
    {                                     cout << k << endl;
        cout << k << endl;                numPrimes += 1;
        numPrimes += 1;               }
    }                             }
    k += 1;
}
```

The parentheses following the `for` loop enclose three separate parts of a loop: initialization, test, and update. These parts are separated by semicolons as shown. Block statement delimiters enclose the body of the `for` loop just as they enclose the body of the `while` loop.

The `for` loop offers some economy in terms of lines of code when compared with its `while` loop equivalent. The **initialization** statement is executed only once, before the evaluation of the test for the first time. The **test expression** is evaluated; if it is true, the loop body is executed. After the last statement in the loop body is executed, the **update** statement is executed. The test is then evaluated again, and

> **Syntax: for loop**
>
> for (*initialization*; *test expression*; *update*)
> {
>   *statement list*;
> }

the process continues (without initialization) until the test becomes false. Since all the information in a `for` loop appears at the beginning of the loop, it is often easier to understand than the corresponding `while` loop.

The update statement should change values used in the test expression so that the loop makes progress toward termination.

I adhere to a style of programming in which `for` loops are used only when a bound on the number of iterations is known before the loop is executed. Such loops are sometimes called **definite** loops. Typically, these loops are counting loops—loops that execute a sequence of statements a fixed number of times, as shown in the example above from *primes.cc*. Many C++ programmers use `for` loops exclusively; the economy of code makes programs *appear* shorter. Choosing the style of loop to use should not be a major decision point in developing a program. Sticking with the style adopted in the code used in this book is one way of ensuring that little time is spent on deciding what kind of loop to use. As an example of when I choose *not* to use a `for` loop, a `while` loop from *digits.cc*, Prog. 5.10 (page 205), is shown here on the left with the corresponding `for` loop on the right:

```
while (number != 0)               for(; number != 0; number /= 10)
{                                 {
    digit = number % 10;              s = DigitToString (digit)
                                              + " " + s;
    s = DigitToString(digit)      }
          + " " + s;
    number /= 10;
}
```

This is *not* a counting loop. The number of times the loop body is executed depends on how many times `number` can be divided by ten.[10] This example shows that the initialization part of a `for` loop can be omitted. The other parts of a `for` loop can be omitted too, but omitting the test part results in an infinite loop.

As another example, I would not use a `for` loop in place of the `while` loop in *rollsum.cc*, Prog. 5.5 (page 186).

The Operators ++ and --

Counting loops often require statements such as `k += 1`. Because incrementing by one is such a common operation, C++ includes an operator that can be used in place of `+= 1` to increment a variable by one. The statement

```
k++;
```

can be used in place of `k += 1`. Similarly, the statement `k--` can be used in place of `k -= 1` to decrement a value by one. The operator `++` is the **postincrement** operator, and the operator `--` is the **postdecrement** operator. In all the code in this book, the expression `x++` is used only as shorthand for `x += 1`. Similarly, `x--` is used only as shorthand for `x -= 1`. If you read other books on C++, you may find these operators used as parts of other expressions. For example, the statement `x = z + y++` is legal in C++. This statement stores `z + y` in `x`, and then increments the value of `y` by one. Don't try to use the operator this way—it will invariably get you into trouble. Instead, use `++`

---

[10] Although this number of iterations can be calculated using logarithms, this isn't done in this loop.

and -- only as abbreviations as already described. When used in this way, the statements below on the left affect x the same way: its value is incremented by one. Similarly, the statements on the right decrement x by one.

```
x += 1;                          x -= 1;
x++;                             x--;
++x;                             --x;
```

I don't use the **preincrement operator** ++x or the **predecrement operator** --x in this book. When used in expressions like x = z + ++y, the value of y is incremented first, then the value of z + y is stored in x. Since I don't use ++ and -- except as abbreviations for += 1 and -= 1, I use only the postincrement and postdecrement operators.

An example of a counting for loop using the postincrement operator follows; this is the while loop from main of *primes.cc*, Prog. 5.8:

```
for(k = low; k <= high; k++)
{
    if (IsPrime(k))
    {
        cout << k << endl;
        numPrimes++;
    }
}
```

Pause to reflect

5.25. The function Factorial in *fact.cc* Prog. 5.7 (page 192), uses a while loop to calculate the factorial of a number. Rewrite the function so that a for loop is used instead.

5.26. Write a while loop equivalent to the following for loop:

```
double total = 0.0;
double val;
for(val = 1.0; val < 10000; val *= 1.5)
{
    total += val;
}
```

5.27. Write a for loop equivalent of the following while loop:

```
int k = 1;
int sum = 0;
Dice die(12);
while (k <= num)

{
    sum += die.Roll();
    k += 2;
}
```

5.28. What is printed by the following for loop?

```
int k;
for(k=1024; ;k/=2)
{
    cout << k << endl;
}
```

The `do-while` Loop

Many programs prompt for an input value within a range. For example, Prog. 4.10, *numtoeng.cc,* prompts for an `int` between 0 and 100. As we have seen, the `PromptRange` functions specified in `"prompt.h"` ensure that input is within a range specified by the programmer. Think for a moment about how to write a loop that continually reprompts if input is not within a specific range. Since you must enter a value before any test can determine whether the value is valid, using a `while` loop leads to a fence post problem. Instead, a **do-while** loop can be used. The `do-while` loop works similarly to a `while` loop, but the loop test occurs at the end of the loop rather than at the beginning. This means that the body of a `do-while` loop is executed at least once. In contrast, a `while` loop does not iterate at all if the loop test is false the first time it is evaluated. Here is the body of one of the `PromptRange` functions (from *prompt.cc*):

```
int PromptRange(string prompt,int low, int high)
// precondition: low <= high
// postcondition: returns a value between low and high (inclusive)
{
    int value;
    do
    {
        cout << prompt << " between ";
        cout << low << " and " << high << ": ";
        cin >> value;
    } while (value < low || high < value);

    return value;
}
```

Note that the output statements for the prompt are executed prior to the input statement. If the value entered is not valid, the loop continues to execute until a valid value is entered.

Infinite Loops

Because of errors in design, loops sometimes execute forever. It's fairly common to forget to increment a counter when writing a `while` loop. This is a good reason to use a `for` loop—it's harder to forget the update statement in a `for` loop.

Sometimes, however, it's useful to write seemingly infinite loops with an exit condition from within the loop body. Often it's hard to determine the logic to use in a loop test when complex boolean expressions are used. For example, the `do-while` loop in `PromptRange` uses the boolean operator `||` to determine when to exit the loop. As another example, consider the following loop, which sums user-entered values until the user enters zero:

```
int sum = 0;
int number;
cin >> number;
while (number != 0)
```

```
    {
        sum += number;
        cin >> number;
    }
    cout << "total = " << sum << endl;
```

To evaluate the test `while (number != 0)`, the variable `number` is given a value before the test is evaluated for the first time as well as each time the loop body is executed. Reading an initial value so that the loop test can be evaluated the first time is called **priming** the loop. A word is read again within the loop body before the next evaluation. Eric Roberts, author of *The Art and Science of C,* calls these "loop-and-a-half" loops [Rob95]. Studies show that loop-and-a-half[11] loops are easier for students to write as infinite loops with an exit as follows:

```
while (true)                    // until break from within loop
{
    cin >> number;
    if (number == 0)
    {
        break;                  // OUT OF LOOP
    }
    sum += number;
}
cout << "total = " << sum << endl;
```

Since the loop test is always true, the loop is an infinite loop. There is no way for the test to become false. The **break** statement in the loop causes an abrupt change in the flow of control. When executed, a `break` causes execution to break out of the innermost loop in which the `break` occurs. In the example here, execution continues with the output statement `cout << "total = "` ... when the `break` is executed. As an alternative to `while(true)`, the loop test `for(;;)` is a special C++ idiom that also means "execute forever."

It is easy to carry this style of writing loops to extremes and write only infinite loops with break statements. You should try to write loops with explicit loop tests and use `while(true)` loops only for loop-and-a-half problems or when you're stuck trying to develop the proper loop test.

> **Program Tip:** The `break` **statement causes termination of the innermost loop in which it occurs. Control passes to the next statement after the innermost loop. Use the** `break` **statement judiciously.**
>
> As we'll see in later chapters, loop tests often provide meaningful clues when it becomes necessary to reason about how a loop works and whether or when the loop terminates. A test of `true` doesn't provide many clues. However, used properly, infinite loops avoid code duplication and thus lead to programs that are easier to maintain.

---

[11]It would be nice to say that four out of five programmers surveyed prefer `while (true)`-with-break loops. Studies do indicate [Rob94] that students find it easier to write code using this kind of loop than using a primed `while` loop.

Some programmers find it easier to understand the logic of the following loop than that of the loop used in PromptRange shown previously:

```
while (true)
{
    cout << prompt << " between ";
    cout << low << " and " << high << ": ";
    cin >> value;
    if (low <= value && value <= high) return value;
}
```

The return statement exits the function (and the loop) when the user-entered value is within the specified range. Sometimes it's easier to develop the logic for loop termination, as shown above, than for loop continuation, as shown in the function PromptRange.

Choosing a Looping Statement

The while loop is the kind of loop to use in most situations. For writing definite loops, a for loop may be appropriate. For writing loops that must iterate once, a do-while loop may be appropriate. Given that there are three different kinds of loops, it's natural to wonder whether there are rules that can make the "correct" choice of what kind of loop to apply easier to determine. Since any loop can be made to do the work of any other by using appropriate statements, we won't worry too much about this kind of decision. In summary, however, the following guidelines may prove helpful:

- The while loop is a general-purpose loop. The test is evaluated before the loop body, so the loop body may never execute.
- The for loop is best for definite loops—loops in which the number of iterations is known before loop entry.
- The do-while loop is appropriate for loops that must execute at least once, because the test is evaluated after the loop body.
- Infinite loops, with a break (or return from function) statement, are often useful alternatives, especially when loop priming is necessary or when it's difficult to develop the logic used in the loop test.

In all three types of loop the braces {} that surround the loop body are not required by the compiler if the loop body is a single statement. However, the style guidelines for code in this book require the bodies of loops and if/else statements to be enclosed in braces, even if they consist of single comments.

Nested Loops

In modifying *rollsum.cc*, Prog. 5.5 (page 186), to produce *rollsum2.cc*, Prog. 5.6 (page 188), one loop was replaced by a counting loop with a function call in the body of the counting loop. This was done to avoid using one loop inside another loop, or a so-called **nested loop**. In *primes.cc*, Prog. 5.8, there is a "virtual nested loop," because the loop in the function IsPrime is executed repeatedly by the call from the loop in main. You should think very carefully when you decide that nested loops are necessary, especially if you're using while loops. Nested loops are often necessary when data are printed or processed in a tabular format, but it is often possible to use a single loop with an if statement in the loop body, and one loop is usually easier to code properly than two nested loops are.

An example adapted from [KR96] shows how nested loops can be used to print a table of wind chill values. The effective temperature is significantly decreased when the wind speed is high. For example, a 20 mile-per-hour wind on a 50-degree day reduces the temperature to an equivalent wind chill index of 32 degrees. The desired output is a table of wind speed and temperature, with the wind chill index temperature given as follows:

OUTPUT

```
prompt> windchill
degrees F:   50    40    30    20    10     0   -10   -20   -30   -40   -50   -60

    0 mph:   50    40    30    20    10     0   -10   -20   -30   -40   -50   -60
    5 mph:   47    37    26    16     5    -4   -15   -25   -36   -47   -57   -68
   10 mph:   40    28    15     3    -9   -21   -33   -46   -58   -70   -83   -95
   15 mph:   35    22     8    -4   -18   -31   -45   -58   -72   -85   -99  -112
   20 mph:   32    17     3   -10   -24   -39   -53   -67   -82   -96  -110  -124
   25 mph:   29    14     0   -14   -29   -44   -59   -74   -89  -104  -118  -133
   30 mph:   28    12    -2   -17   -33   -48   -63   -79   -94  -109  -125  -140
   35 mph:   26    11    -4   -20   -35   -51   -67   -82   -98  -113  -129  -145
   40 mph:   25     9    -5   -21   -37   -53   -69   -85  -101  -116  -132  -148
   45 mph:   25     9    -6   -22   -38   -54   -70   -86  -102  -118  -134  -150
   50 mph:   25     9    -7   -23   -39   -55   -71   -87  -103  -119  -135  -151
```

Because the table must be printed one row at a time, a first cut at the code is row-oriented, with one row for each wind speed between 0 and 50 miles per hour:

```
for(windspeed=0; windspeed <= 50; windspeed += 5)
    print a row of temperatures;
```

Printing a row also requires a loop, and this leads to the nested loops shown in *windchill.cc,* Prog. 5.11. Each wind chill temperature is printed by the **inner loop,** in which temperature varies from 50 down to −60 degrees; the inner loop prints a complete row of the table. The inner loop executes completely before one iteration of the **outer loop** has finished.

Because the function WindChill returns a double value and there is no reason to print several numbers after a decimal point in the table, the value

Program 5.11   windchill.cc

```cpp
#include <iostream.h>
#include <math.h>                // for sqrt

// Owen Astrachan
// nested loops to print wind-chill chart
//
// idea: Programming with class by Kamin and Reingold, McGraw-Hill
// formula for wind-chill from
// UMAP Module 658, COMAP, Inc., Lexington, MA 1984, Bosch and Cobb

double WindChill(double temperature, double windSpeed);

int main()
{
    const int WIDTH = 5;
    int temp,wind,chill;

    // print column headings

    cout << "degrees F:";
    for(temp = 50; temp >= -60; temp =-10)
    {
        cout.width(WIDTH);
        cout << temp;
    }
    cout << endl << endl;

    // print table of wind chill temperatures

    for(wind = 0; wind <= 50; wind += 5)
    {
        cout.width(WIDTH);                        // row heading
        cout << wind << " mph:";

        for (temp = 50; temp >= -60; temp -= 10)
        // print the row
        {
            chill = int(WindChill(temp,wind));
            cout.width(WIDTH);
            cout << chill;
        }
        cout << endl;
    }
}

double WindChill(double temperature, double windSpeed)
// precondition: temperature in degrees Fahrenheit
// postcondition: returns wind-chill index/
//                comparable temperature
```

```
{
    if (windSpeed <= 4)   // low wind, temperature unaltered
    {
        return temperature;
    }
    else if (windSpeed <= 45)    // high wind
    {
        return
            91.4 - (10.45 + 6.69*sqrt(windSpeed) - 0.447 *
            windSpeed) * (91.4 - temperature)/22.0;
    }
    else
    {
        return (1.6 * temperature - 55.0);
    }
}
```

windchill.cc

returned by the `WindChill` function is stored in an `int` variable. The value is converted to an `int` using the expression `int(WindChill(temp,wind))` just as the value returned by the function `sqrt` was converted to an `int` in *primes.cc*, Prog. 5.8. In order to make each column of the table line up properly, a member function `width` for the input stream `cout` is used. The argument to `width` specifies a **field width** used to print the next value. Printing a number like 27 in a field width of five requires three extra spaces in addition to the two characters of `27` to pad the output to five characters. If the output occupies three spaces (e.g., the number 123 or the string `"cat"`), then 2 literal blanks ` ` will pad the output to five spaces. If the value being printed requires more than five spaces (e.g., for the number 123456), the entire value is still printed. It's possible to print the right number of spaces by testing the value being printed as follows for a field width 3 used with an integer `num`.

```
if (num < 10)
{
    cout << "  ";         // two spaces
}
else if (num < 100)
{
    cout << " ";          // one space
}
cout << num;
```

Program output should be easy to read, but you should not concentrate on well-formatted output when first implementing a program.

Sometimes it is useful to use the value of the outer loop to control how many times the inner loop iterates. This is shown in *multiply.cc*, Prog. 5.12, which prints the lower half of a multiplication table (the upper half is the same, because multiplication is commutative: $2 \times 5 = 5 \times 2$). Both loops are counting loops. The outer loop, whose loop control variable is `j`, determines how many rows appear in the output. The statement `cout << endl` is executed once each time the body of the outer loop is executed. The number of iterations of

---

Program 5.12   multiply.cc

```cpp
#include <iostream.h>
#include "prompt.h"

// simple illustration of nested loops

int main()
{
    int j,k;
    int limit = PromptRange("number for multiply table",2,15);

    for(j=1; j <= limit; j++)
    {
        for(k=1; k <= j; k++)
        {
            cout.width(3);
            cout << k*j << " ";
        }
        cout << endl;
    }
    return 0;
}
```

```
                        OUTPUT

prompt> multiply
number for multiply table between 2 and 15: 5
   1
   2    4
   3    6    9
   4    8   12   16
   5   10   15   20   25

prompt> multiply
number for multiply table between 2 and 15: 11
   1
   2    4
   3    6    9
   4    8   12   16
   5   10   15   20   25
   6   12   18   24   30   36
   7   14   21   28   35   42   49
   8   16   24   32   40   48   56   64
   9   18   27   36   45   54   63   72   81
  10   20   30   40   50   60   70   80   90  100
  11   22   33   44   55   66   77   88   99  110  121
```

the inner loop is determined by the value of j. As can be seen in the output, the number of entries in each row increases by 1 in each successive row. When j is one, there is one number, 1, in the first row. When j is three, there are three numbers, 3 6 9, in the third row. The width member function ensures that three-digit numbers and two-digit numbers line up properly in columns.

If a break statement is inserted as the last statement of the inner loop, immediately following cout << k*j << " ", the output changes:

OUTPUT

```
prompt> multiply
number for multiply table between 2 and 15: 5
1
2
3
4
5
```

Note that the outer loop is *not* exited early. The break statement causes the inner loop (in which the loop control variable is k) to exit before the loop test k <= j becomes false. This means that the inner loop executes exactly once.

Pause to reflect

5.29. Write a function that rolls three six-sided dice and returns the number of rolls needed before all three dice show the same number. Use an infinite loop with a return statement, but also try to develop a do-while loop with a boolean test using && or || to determine when the loop should terminate.

5.30. Write a loop that accepts input from the user until the number zero is entered. The output should be the number of positive numbers entered and the number of negative numbers entered.

5.31. There is a fence post problem in *multiply.cc*: a space is printed after every number rather than between numbers. Modify the loop so that no space is printed after the last number in a row (*Hint:* it's possible to do this by modifying how width is used).

5.32. Write nested loops to print (a) the pattern of stars on the left and (b) the pattern of stars on the right. The number of rows should be entered by the user; there are *k* stars in row *k*.

```
*                          *
*  *                      *  *
*  *  *                  *  *  *
*  *  *  *              *  *  *  *
*  *  *  *  *          *  *  *  *  *
```

5.5   Variable Scope

In Sec. 3.1. we discussed where variables are defined, and we showed that it is possible to define variables anywhere, not just immediately following a curly brace {. You need to be aware of how the location of a variable's definition affects the use of the variable. For example, the variable numPrimes, defined in main of *primes.cc*, Prog. 5.8, is not accessible from the function IsPrime. A variable defined within a function is **local** to the function and cannot be accessed from another function. Parameters provide a mechanism for passing values from one function to another.

Similarly, a variable defined between two curly braces { } is accessible only within the curly braces. To be more precise, a variable name can be used only from the point at which it is defined to the first right curly brace }. For example, consider the following fragment from the function IsPrime. The variables limit and divisor are accessible only within the else block in which they are defined. The added comment after the else block indicates that these variables cannot be accessed at that point.

```
else                                    // number is odd
{
    int limit = int(sqrt(n) + 1);  // largest divisor to check
    int divisor = 3;   // initialize to smallest divisor

    while (divisor <= limit)
    {
        if (n % divisor == 0)  // n is divisible, not prime
        {
            return false;
        }
        divisor += 2;                   // check next odd number
    }
    return true;                        // number must be prime
}

// comment added: limit and divisor NOT defined here
```

The following code fragment shows a variable count that can only be accessed in the bottom "half" of a loop:

```
    while(total <= limit)
    {
        // count NOT accessible here

        int count = 0;

        // count IS accessible here

    }
    // count NOT accessible here
```

The variable `count` is accessible only from within the loop, and only from its definition to the bottom of the loop. The part of a program in which a variable name is accessible is called the variable name's **scope**.

You should be careful when defining variables in loop bodies (or `if/else` blocks), because these variables will not be accessible outside the loop body. In particular, be careful of `for` loops written as follows:

```
for(int k=0; k < 10; k++)
{
    // loop body
}
// k is NOT accessible here
```

The variable `k` is not, strictly speaking, defined within the curly braces that delimit the body of the loop. Nevertheless, the scope of `k` is local to the loop; `k` cannot be accessed after the loop. Not all compilers support this kind of scoping with `for` loops, but according to the C++ standard the scoping should be supported. It is common to need to access the value of a loop index variable (`k` in the example above) after the loop has finished. In such a case, the loop index cannot be local to the loop.

Scope of Private Variables

The variables defined in the private section of a class declaration are accessible in all member functions of the class. Private variable names are **global** to all member functions, since they can be accessed in each member function. By defining a variable at the beginning of a program and outside of any function, you can make it global to all the functions in a program. This is considered poor programming style, because the proliferation of global variables in large programs makes it difficult to modify one part of the program without affecting another part.

5.6   Case Study: Simulating Gambling Games

A gambling game called *craps* is played with two six-sided dice. There are several different ways of betting on this game, but we won't study them here. Instead, we'll use a program that simulates the playing of thousands of craps games as an example of iterative enhancement. We'll introduce an alternative statement to `if/else` for selection as part of the program.

Selection with the `switch` Statement

In Exercise 4.2 (page 154) a program was described that draws different heads as part of a simulated police sketch program. The following function `Hair` comes from one version of this program:

```
void Hair(int choice)
// precondition: 1 <= choice <= 3
```

```
// postcondition: prints hair in style specified by choice
{
    if (1 == choice)
    {
        cout << "  |||||||////////// " << endl;
    }
    else if (2 == choice)
    {
        cout << "  ||||||||||||||||| " << endl;
    }
    else if (3 == choice)
    {
        cout << "  |_____| " << endl;
    }
}
```

The cascaded if/else statements work well. In some situations, however, an alternative conditional statement can lead to code that is shorter and often more efficient. You shouldn't be overly concerned about this kind of efficiency, but in a program differentiating among 100 choices instead of three the efficiency might be a factor. The statement that provides an alternative method for writing the code in Hair is **switch**:

```
void Hair(int choice)
// precondition: 1 <= choice <= 3
// postcondition: prints hair in style specified by choice
{
    switch(choice)
    {
        case 1:
            cout << "  |||||||////////// " << endl;
            break;
        case 2:
            cout << "  ||||||||||||||||| " << endl;
            break;
        case 3:
            cout << "  |_____| " << endl;
            break;
    }
}
```

Each **case label**, such as case 1, determines what statements are executed based on the value of the expression used in the switch test (in this example, the value of the variable choice). There should be one case label for each possible value of the switch test expression.

All of the labels are *constants* that represent *integer* values known at compile time. Examples include 13, 53 - 7, and true.[12] It's not legal to use

---

[12]Later we'll see that character constants like 'a' can be used also.

double values like 2.718, string values like "spam", or expressions that use variables like 2*choice for case labels in a switch statement. The value of *expression* in the switch test matches a case label, and the corresponding statements are executed. The break causes flow of control to continue with the statement following the switch. If no matching case label is found, the default statements, if present, are executed.

There are no "shortcuts" in forming cases. You cannot write, for example, case 1,2,3: to match either one,

---

Syntax: switch **statement**

```
switch (expression )
{
    case constant₁ :
        statement list;
        break;
    case constant₂ :
        statement list;
        break;
        . . .
    default :
        statement list;
}
```

---

two, or three. For multiple matches, each case is listed separately:

```
case 1 :
case 2 :
case 3 :
    statement list;
        break;
```

In the switch statement shown in Hair, exactly one case statement is executed; the break causes control to continue with the statement following the switch. (Since there is no following statement in Hair, the function exits and the statement after the call of Hair is executed next.) In general, a break statement is required, or control will **fall through** from one case to the next.

Program Tip: It's very easy to forget the break **needed for each** case **statement, so when you write** switch **statements, be very careful.**

As a general design rule, don't include more than two or three statements with each case label. If more statements are needed, put them in a function and call the function. This will make the switch statement easier to read.

A missing break statement often causes hard-to-find errors. If the break corresponding to case 2 in the function Hair is removed, and the value of choice is 2, two lines of output will be printed.

(Warning! Incorrect code follows!)

```
void Hair(int choice)
// precondition: 1 <= choice <= 3
// postcondition: prints hair in style specified by choice
{
    switch(choice)
    {
        case 1:
            cout << "   ||||||||//////////// " << endl;
```

```
            break;
        case 2:
            cout << "  |||||||||||||||  " << endl;
        case 3:
            cout << "  |_____|  " << endl;
            break;
    }
}
```

OUTPUT

```
|||||||||||||||
|_____|
```

Because there is no `break` following the hair corresponding to `case 2`, execution falls through to the next statement, and the output statement corresponding to `case 3` is executed.

The efficiency gained from a `switch` statement occurs because only one expression is evaluated and the corresponding `case` statements are immediately executed. In a sequence of `if/else` statements it is possible for all the `if` tests to be evaluated. As mentioned earlier, it's not worth worrying about this level of efficiency until you've timed a program and know what statements are executed most often. The `switch` statement does make some code easier to read, and the efficiency gains can't hurt.

Simulating Dice Games

Here are rules for one version of the game of craps:

A player rolls two dice. If the sum of the two is 7 or 11, the roller wins at once; if the sum is a 2, 3, or 12, the roller loses at once. If the sum is 4, 5, 6, 8, 9, or 10, the roller rolls again. By repeating the initial number, the roller "makes his or her point" and wins. By rolling a 7 the roller "craps out" and loses. Otherwise, the roller keeps on rolling again until he or she wins or loses.

Program 5.13 simulates one game of craps.

Program 5.13   craps.cc

```
#include <iostream.h>
#include "dice.h"

// simulate one game of craps (rules from W. Weaver,
// Lady Luck, 1982, Doubleday Press --- as given in Charles
// Whitney, Random Processes in Physical Systems, 1990,
// Wiley Interscience)
```

```
// written 5/17/94, modified 6/21/95

// prototypes

int RollTwo();

int main()
{
    int sum;
    int point = RollTwo();       // initial point

    switch (point)
    {
      case 7:
      case 11:
        cout << "natural winner!!" << endl;
        break;
      case 2:
      case 3:
      case 12:
        cout << "craps!! a loser" << endl;
        break;
      default:
        while (true)
        {
            sum = RollTwo();
            if (sum == point)
            {
                cout << "got your point! a winner" << endl;
                break;
            }

            if (sum == 7)
            {
                cout << "loser, lost going for " << point
                    << endl;
                break;
            }
        }

    }
    return 0;
}

int RollTwo()
//postcondition: returns sum of rolling two dice
//               prints values rolled
{
    Dice d(6);
    int first = d.Roll();
    int second = d.Roll();
    cout << "rolling ... " << first << " " << second
        << endl;
    return first + second;
}
```

```
                            OUTPUT

prompt> craps
rolling ... 4 3
natural winner!!
prompt> craps
rolling ... 3 1
rolling ... 5 5
rolling ... 2 5
loser, lost going for 4
prompt> craps
rolling ... 2 1
craps!! a loser
prompt> craps
rolling ... 3 1
rolling ... 3 5
rolling ... 6 3
rolling ... 3 6
rolling ... 3 2
rolling ... 1 3
got your point! a winner
```

In designing *craps.cc* I did not initially include a function `RollTwo`. Instead, I defined a `Dice` variable in `main` to determine the initial "point." The following definitions appeared in the first version of *craps.cc*:

```
Dice d(6);
int point = d.Roll() + d.Roll();          // initial point
```

This program simulated the game correctly, but only the final output was printed. The individual dice rolls were not printed. Since this didn't make as interesting output (or as useful for determining correctness), I had to make a decision about how to print the dice rolls. Separate output statements could accompany each code fragment that rolled a simulated die, but this would make for a cluttered program. In addition, I anticipated wanting to run this program without output. This might be done to simulate 10,000 craps games. For such a program, the output of the dice rolls used in 10,000 craps games is irrelevant and only gets in the way of the data about how many games are won and lost. By isolating the output into a single function, it can be removed easily by actually deleting the line or by **commenting it out** as follows:

```
//  cout << "rolling ... " << first << " " << second << endl;
```

Since the program *craps.cc* was written with the intent of simulating one game of craps, it may be difficult to modify to simulate 10,000 games. The `while(true)` loop that executes as the `default` part of the `switch` statement is near the limit of how much code should be included as part of a label in a `switch` statement. Note that the `break` statements in the `while(true)` loop break out of the loop and *not* out of the `switch` statement. Because the loop is part of the `default` label, which is the last label of the `switch` statement, a `break` statement to break out of the `switch` isn't necessary.

An alternative design uses a function `WinGame` called from `main`. `WinGame` simulates one game, as the code in `main` does in *craps.cc*, Prog. 5.13. By putting this code in another function, simulating two games becomes very easy: simply call the function `WinGame` twice. Program 5.14, *craps2.cc*, is based on code from *craps.cc*. Writing the program to simulate one game lets us focus on whether the simulation is correct. Then we can modify the program to simulate thousands of games. The `while(true)` loop from *craps.cc* has been turned into a do-`while` loop and moved to the function `GetPoint`. This makes the code in `WinGame` much easier to follow. A do-`while` loop is the right loop choice, since it must execute at least once.

Program 5.14   craps2.cc

```cpp
#include <iostream.h>
#include "dice.h"
#include "prompt.h"

// simulate multiple games of craps (rules from W. Weaver,
// Lady Luck, 1982, Doubleday Press --- as given in Charles
// Whitney, Random Processes in Physical Systems, 1990,
// Wiley Interscience
// written 5/17/94, modified 6/21/95, modified 6/25/96

// prototypes

bool GetPoint(int point);
bool WinGame();
int RollTwo();

int main()
{
    int k;
    int gamesWon = 0;
    int simulations = PromptRange("enter # games to simulate",
        1,1000000);

    for(k=0; k < simulations; k++)
    {
        if (WinGame())
        {
            gamesWon++;
        }
    }
    cout << "# of games = " << simulations;
```

```cpp
    cout << " # won = "        << gamesWon << " = ";
    cout << double(gamesWon)/simulations * 100 << "%"
        << endl;
    return 0;
}

bool WinGame()
// postcondition: return true if single game of craps won
//                return false if game lost
{
    int point = RollTwo();              // initial point

    switch (point)
    {
      case 7:
      case 11:
        // cout << "natural winner!!" << endl;
        return true;
        break;
      case 2:
      case 3:
      case 12:
        // cout << "craps!! a loser" << endl;
        return false;
        break;
      default:
        return GetPoint(point);
    }
}

bool GetPoint(int point)
// precondition: 2 <= point <= 12
// postcondition: returns true if point obtained (winner)
//                returns false if 'crapped out'
{
    int sum;
    do
    {
        sum = RollTwo();
    } while (sum != point && sum != 7);

    return (sum == point);
}

int RollTwo()
//postcondition: returns sum of rolling two dice
{
    Dice d(6);
    int first = d.Roll();
    int second = d.Roll();
//  cout << "rolling ... " << first << " " << second
//       << endl;
    return first + second;
}
```

OUTPUT

```
prompt> craps2
enter # games to simulate: 1000
# of games = 1000 # won = 484 = 48.4%
prompt> craps2
enter # games to simulate: 10000
# of games = 10000 # won = 4885 = 48.85%
prompt> craps2
enter # games to simulate: 100000
# of games = 100000 # won = 49619 = 49.619%
```

It's often difficult to develop the proper loop test when there is more than one way for a loop to exit. Using an infinite `while(true)` loop with explicit `break` statements to exit the loop is often easier in an initial design. However, a rule from mathematical logic called **De Morgan's law** can make developing loop tests easier; the rule is described in the next section. The last statement of `GetPoint` returns `true` when the point is obtained and `false` otherwise. You may find it easier to see this if an `if/else` statement is used.

```
if (sum == point) return true;
else              return false;
```

However, since the value of `sum == point` is either `true` or `false`, the value of the expression can be returned.

De Morgan's Law

We use De Morgan's law[13] to find the logical negation, or opposite, of an expression formed with the logical operators `&&` and `||`.

```
! (a && b) == (!a) || (!b)
! (a || b) == (!a) && (!b)
```

The negation of an `&&` expression is an `||` expression, and vice versa. We can use De Morgan's law to develop the loop test used in `GetPoint` from *craps2.cc*, Prog. 5.14, by listing the criteria that should cause the loop to exit. The criteria are explicit in the `while(true)` loop from *craps.cc*:

- Exit if sum == point (and the game is won) **OR**
- Exit if sum == 7 (and the game is lost)

In C++ these termination conditions are

```
(sum == point) || (sum == 7)
```

---

[13] Augustus De Morgan (1806–1871), first Professor of Mathematics at University College, London, as well as teacher to Ada Lovelace (see Sec. 2.5).

A loop test is an expression that is true when the loop should continue; this is the opposite, or the logical negation of the termination condition. Using De Morgan's law, we can see that the negation of the termination conditions forms the loop test:

```
(sum != point) && (sum != 7)
```

This gives a two-step process that helps develop loop tests:

1. List the termination conditions for the loop.
2. Use De Morgan's law to transform termination conditions into the continuation expression that forms the loop test.

 Pause to reflect

5.33. Consider a program designed to accept commands from the user, who is supplied with a menu of commands. An automated teller machine is guided by such a program. For example, commands might be `deposit`, `withdrawal`, `information`, and `quit`. Sketch a loop to accomplish this task, assuming the user keeps entering commands until `"quit"` is entered.

5.34. Why can't a `switch` statement replace the `if/else` statements of *broccoli.cc*, Prog. 4.3?

5.35. Write a loop to count how many times three six-sided dice must be rolled until the values showing are all different. (De Morgan's law may be useful.)

5.36. Rewrite the loop used in `IsPrime` from *primes.cc*, Prog. 5.8, so that a `return` statement is not used from inside the loop; instead, a single `return` statement should return the proper value after the loop exits.

5.7   Chapter Review

In this chapter we discussed how classes are implemented. We also covered different looping and selection statements. Guidelines were given to assist in determining what kind of loop statement should be used and how loops are developed. The important topics covered in this chapter are summarized here.

- Interface (`.h` file) and implementation (`.cc` files) provide an abstraction mechanism for writing and using C++ classes.
- Constructors are member functions that are automatically called to construct and initialize an object.
- Member functions are used to access an object's behavior or to get information about the object's state.
- The `for` loop is an alternative looping construct used for definite loops (where the number of iterations is known before the loop executes for the first time).

- The do-while loop body is always executed once, in contrast to a while loop body, which may never be executed.

- Infinite loops formed using while(true) or for(;;) are often used with break statements to avoid duplicated code and complex loop tests. However, you should be judicious in using break statements, because overreliance on them can lead to code that is hard to understand logically.

- A loop invariant is a statement that helps reason about and develop loops. A loop invariant is true each time the loop test is evaluated, although its truth must often be reestablished during the loop's execution.

- The built-in types int and double represent a limited range of values in computing, compared to the infinite range of values of integers and real numbers in mathematics. You must be careful to take this limited range of values into account when interpreting data and developing programs.

- Often small differences in a program can have a drastic effect on program efficiency. Determining whether a number is prime illustrates some considerations in making a program efficient.

- A return statement causes a function to stop, and control is returned to the calling statement. It is possible and often convenient to use return to exit a function early, much as a break statement is used to exit infinite loops.

- Fence post problems are typical in code that loops. A fence post problem is often solved using a special case before the loop or after the loop.

- The postincrement and postdecrement operators ++ and -- are convenient shortcuts for adding and subtracting one, respectively.

- Variables modified with const have values that do not change. Using such constants can make programs more readable; for example, the constant AVOGADRO or MOLE carries more meaning than 6.023e23.

- A variable is accessible only within its scope, usually delimited by curly braces: { and }. Private data variables in a class are global to all member functions of the class.

- The switch statement is an alternative selection statement. It offers some economy in lines of code and can be more efficient than if/else statements, but switch statements can only be used with integral values.

- The break statement is used with switch statements and to exit loops.

- De Morgan's law is useful in developing loop tests. The law is used to form the logical negation of statements using && and ||.

- Use the convention of beginning the identifier of each private instance variable with the prefix my. This convention helps when you must read and modify code for implementing member functions.

- Write programs using iterative enhancement. Try to add code to a working program rather than writing large amounts of code and then testing.

- Develop test programs when you design and implement classes. Testing should be an integral part of the process of program and class design.

5.8 Exercises

5.1 Write a program that prints a totem pole of random heads. Prompt the user for the number of heads; each head of the totem pole should be randomly drawn by using a `Dice` variable to choose among different choices for hair, eyes, mouth, etc.

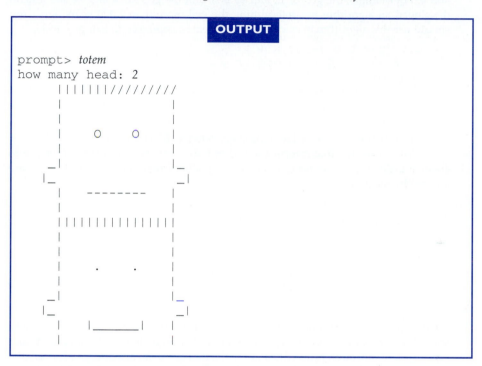

5.2 Write a program modeled after the exercise on page 116 that will print as many verses of the song as the user specifies (both the kind of beverage and the number of bottles should be specified by the user). Try to make the program grammatical so that it doesn't print

> one bottles of sarsaparilla on the wall

(note the incorrect plural of bottle).

5.3 Modify *rollsum2.cc*, Prog. 5.6, so that it calculates the average number of rolls to obtain all possible sums for two *n*-sided dice, where *n* is a value entered by the user. The number of "experiments" should also be entered by the user. Write functions that can be used to minimize the amount of code that appears in `main`. As an example, you might consider a function with the following prototype:

```
double AverageRolls(int target, int numTrials, int numSides)
// precondition: 2 <= target <= 2*numSides
// postcondition: returns average # of rolls needed to obtain
//       the sum 'target' rolling two dice with 'numSides'
//       sides and repeating the experiment 'numTrials' times
```

This function might call a function similar to `NumToRoll` from *rollsum2.cc*.

Can you modify this program easily to work for three n-sided dice rather than two?

5.4 Write a program that finds the greatest common divisor, or gcd, of two numbers. The gcd of two numbers x and y is the largest number that evenly divides both x and y. For example, the gcd of 12 and 42 is 6, and the gcd of 14 and 74 is 2. Euclid developed an algorithm for determining the gcd more than 2,000 years ago. You should use this algorithm in calculating the greatest common divisor of x and y:

```
assign r the value x % y
if r equals 0 then gcd is y
otherwise
    assign x the value y
    assign y the value r
    repeat
```

Using $x = 21$ and $y = 35$ we have the steps listed in Table 5.2.

Write a function that returns the gcd of two numbers, and use the function to create a table of gcds similar to the following table, where the range of x and y are entered by the user.

```
     y
 x | 1  2  3  4  5  6  7
---+----------------------
11 | 1  1  1  1  1  1  1
12 | 1  2  3  4  1  6  1
13 | 1  1  1  1  1  1  1
14 | 1  2  1  2  1  2  7
15 | 1  1  3  1  5  3  1
```

5.5 Write a program to simulate tossing a coin (use a two-sided die). The program should toss a coin 10,000 times (or some number of times specified by the user) and keep track of the longest run of heads or tails that occurs in a sequence of simulated coin flips. Thus, in the sequence HTHTTTHHHHT there is a sequence of 3 tails and a sequence of 4 heads.

To keep track of the runs, four variables—headRun, tailRun, maxHeads, and maxTails—are defined and initialized to 0. These variables keep track of the length of the current head run, the length of the current tail run, and the maximum runs of heads and of tails, respectively. After the statement heads += 1, the value of headRun is incremented. After the statement tails += 1 the value of tailRun is incremented. In addition, these variables must be reset to zero at the appropriate time and the values of the max head run and max tail run variables set appropriately.

Table 5.2 Computing the gcd of Two Numbers

	x	y	r
Initially	21	35	21 % 35 = 21
	35	21	35 % 21 = 14
	21	14	21 % 14 = 7
	14	7	14 % 7 = 0
	Stop, answer is $y = 7$		

5.6 Write a function that simulates a slot machine by printing three randomly chosen strings as the values displayed on by the slot machine. Each string should be chosen randomly from among four different choices, such as `"orange"`, `"lemon"`, `"lime"`, `"cherry"` (but any words will do). Choose the random values eight times and display each choice of three as shown in the following sample run. If the strings are all the same or are all different when the final sequence of these strings appears, then print a message that the user wins; otherwise the user loses.

OUTPUT

```
prompt> slots
Welcome to the slot machine simulation
Here's a spin....
cherry orange cherry
lime    lemon  cherry
lime    lemon  lemon
lime    cherry cherry
lemon  lime    cherry
lemon  lemon  lime
orange lime    lime
you lose!!

prompt> slots
Welcome to the slot machine simulation
Here's a spin....
lime    lime    orange
orange cherry orange
orange cherry lime
cherry orange lime
lime    orange orange
cherry orange lemon
lemon  lemon  lemon
all values equal, you win!!

prompt> slots
Welcome to the slot machine simulation
Here's a spin....
lemon  cherry orange
lemon  orange lemon
cherry orange lime
lime    cherry lime
cherry cherry cherry
orange cherry cherry
orange lime    cherry
all values different, you win!!
```

5.7 Write a program that computes all **twin primes** between two values entered by the user. Twin primes are numbers that differ by two and are both primes, such as 1019 and 1021.

5.8 Write a function with prototype int NumDigits(num) that determines the number of digits in its parameter. Use the ideas of the previous exercise, but be sure that the function works for *all* integer values (including zero, which has one digit, and negative numbers—don't forget about the function fabs).

5.9 Write a boolean-valued predicate function similar to IsPrime that returns true if its parameter is a perfect number and false otherwise. A number is perfect if it is equal to the sum of its proper divisors (i.e., not including itself). For example, $6 = 1 + 2 + 3$ and $28 = 1 + 2 + 4 + 7 + 14$ are the first two perfect numbers. Recall that the expression num % divisor has value 0 exactly when divisor divides num exactly; for example, 30 % 6 == 0 but 30 % 7 = 2. The function should be named IsPerfect.

5.10 Write a function SumOfNums that calculates and returns the sum of the numbers from 1 to *n* (where *n* is a parameter). The statement

```
cout << SumOfNums(100) << endl;
```

should cause 5050 to be printed since $1 + 2 + \cdots + 100 = 5050$. It's possible to write this program without using a loop (such a solution is often attributed to the mathematician C. F. Gauss, who supposedly discovered it when he was a boy).

5.11 Change the return type of the function Factorial (Prog. 5.7, page 192) so that the function returns a double. Why doesn't this change the largest value that can be computed (approximately) correctly?

Change the type of the variable product to double as well, and the function should produce correct values for larger values—determine the largest value for which factorial is approximately correct. (If doubles are represented with 64 bits, the largest correct value is computed for a double less than 200.)

5.12 Write a program that displays the prime factors of a number. The prime factors of 60 are $2 \times 2 \times 3 \times 5$. Use the program to display the prime factors of all numbers between two user-entered numbers.

5.13 It is possible, but somewhat difficult, to write an iterative version of the function Power in Prog. 4.15. The loop used is best described by using an invariant. A loop, with some code missing, follows:

```
double
Power(double base, int expo)
// precondition: expo >= 0
// postcondition: returns base^expo (base to the power expo)
{
    double result = 1.0;
    double a = base;
    double b = expo;

        // invariant:  result * (a^b) = base^expo

    while (b > 0)
    {
        if (expo % 2 == 0)                 // exponent is even
        {
```

```
            b = b / 2;
        }
        else
        {
            b = b - 1;
        }
    }
        // assertion: b == 0

        return result;
}
```

The specified invariant `result` $\times a^b = $ `base`^{expo} must hold each time the loop test is evaluated.

Why is the invariant true the first time the test `b > 0` is evaluated? Why must the assertion `b == 0` be true when the `while` loop has finished iterating?

There are two statements missing—one from the `if` block statement and one from the `else` block statement. Determine what these statements *must* be if the invariant is to be maintained. Test your program, time the version of the function given here, and compare it to the recursive version of the function.

5.14 The following loop sums all numbers entered by the user (and stops when the user enters a nonpositive number).

```
int num;
cin >> num;
int sum = 0;
while (num >= 0)
{
    sum += num;
    cin >> num;
}
```

Explain how the two uses of `cin >>` correspond to a kind of fence post problem. Then write a program based on the foregoing loop to calculate the average of a sequence of nonnegative numbers entered by the user.

5.15 To approximate cube roots using Newton's method, an initial approximation to the cube root is used to generate a sequence of ever closer approximations, just as was done in *newton.cc,* Prog. 5.9, for square roots. Write a program to find the cube root of n using an initial approximation of $n/2$ and the following equation to modify the approximation:

$$(2*\text{root} + \text{x}/(\text{root}*\text{root}))/3.0;$$

Write a program that compares the value returned using this method to the value returned using `pow(n,1.0/3.0)`, which approximates $\sqrt[3]{n}$ using $n^{1/3}$ for several different values of n.

5.16 Write a program that allows the user to play craps but to place a bet before each sequence of dice rolls. Start with an initial bankroll of $500.00. Betting $100.00 and winning increases the bankroll by $100.00; losing decreases the bankroll by $100.00. As a skeleton, use the following Game class and implement each member function.

Include all the member functions in the same file as `main`; for this program there's no reason to use separate `.h` and `.cc`/`.cpp` files.

Here is part of a sample run:

```
                              OUTPUT

prompt> playgame
place your bet for this round
enter wager between 0 and 500: 100
rolling ... 6 5
natural winner!!
you have $600
do you want to continue [yes/no]?: yes
place your bet for this round
enter wager between 0 and 600: 200
rolling ... 5 1
rolling ... 4 5
rolling ... 6 4
rolling ... 5 4
rolling ... 5 2
loser, lost going for 6
you have $400
do you want to continue [yes/no]?: yes
place your bet for this round
enter wager between 0 and 400: 400
rolling ... 6 4
rolling ... 1 2
rolling ... 3 4
loser, lost going for 10
you're busted, game's over
```

```cpp
class Game
{
  public:

    Game();              // initialize state appropriately
    bool Continue();     // returns true if game continues to play
    void MakeBet();      // place a wager for one turn of the game
    void Play();         // play the game once

  private:

    int myBankRoll;      // current bank roll (money in hand)
    int myWager;         // current wager (bet)

    int RollTwo();
};
```

```
                    // implement member functions here
int main()
{
    Game craps;
    do
    {
        craps.MakeBet();
        craps.Play();
    } while (craps.Continue());
    return 0;
}
```

5.17 Write a program similar to the craps-playing program from the previous exercise, but simulate a roulette game rather than a craps game. In roulette you can place bets on which of 38 numbers is chosen when a ball falls into a numbered slot. The numbers range from 1 to 36, with special 0 and 00 slots. The 0 and 00 slots are colored green; each of the numbers 1 through 36 is red or black. The red numbers are 1, 3, 5, 7, 9, 12, 14, 16, 18, 19, 21, 23, 25, 27, 30, 32, 34, and 36. Gamblers can make several different kinds of bet, each of which pays off at different odds as listed in Table 5.3. A payoff of 1 to 1 means that a $10.00 bet earns $10.00 (plus the bet $10.00 back); 17 to 1 means that a $10.00 bet earns $170.00 (plus the $10.00 back). If the wheel spins 0 or 00, then all bets lose except for a bet on the single number 0/00 or on the two consecutive numbers 0 and 00.

  You may find it useful to implement a separate Bet class to keep track of the different kinds of bets and odds. For example, when betting on a number, you'll need to keep track of the number, but betting on red/black requires only that you remember the color chosen.

5.18 Write a program to track the number of times each sum for two 12-sided dice occurs over 10,000 rolls, or more generally, the number of times each sum for two N-sided dice occurs. We'll learn how to do this simply in Chapter 8, but with the programming tools you have, you'll need to write a program to write the program for you! Write a program, named *metadice.cc*, that reads the number of sides of the dice and outputs *a program* that can be compiled and executed. For example, the following function might be part of the program; it defines and initializes variables to track each dice sum:

```
void Definitions(int sides)
// postcondition: variable definitions for c2, c3, ...
//                are output int cX = 0;   2 <= x <= 2*sides
```

Table 5.3   Roulette Bets

Bet	Payoff odds
Red/black	1 to 1
Odd/even	1 to 1
Single number	35 to 1
Two consecutive numbers	17 to 1
Three consecutive numbers	11 to 1

```
{
    int k;
    for(k=2; k <= 2*sides; k++)
    {
        cout << "\t" << "int c" << k << " = 0;" << endl;
    }
    cout << endl << endl;
}
```

OUTPUT

```
prompt> metadice
enter # sides: 5
#include <iostream.h>
#include "dice.h"
int main()
{
        int c2 = 0;
        int c3 = 0;
        int c4 = 0;
        int c5 = 0;
        int c6 = 0;
        int c7 = 0;
        int c8 = 0;
        int c9 = 0;
        int c10 = 0;
program continues here
```

5.9   A Computer Science Excursion: Calendars and a Date Class

In this section we'll study a program that prints calendars for any month of any year. The program uses a programmer-defined class `Date`. Once we've studied the `Date` class, the calendar program will be relatively straightforward. This program could serve as the basis for a larger program that keeps track of schedules and appointments. In general, manipulating and understanding dates and calendars is an integral part of many software products. Careless programming and design can lead to serious problems with such products. In [Neu95] several potential problems with software that manipulates dates and times are illustrated:

■ COBOL (COmmon Business-Oriented Language), a programming language used extensively in business and finance, allocates only two digits for the year part of a date. This will undoubtedly cause problems in switching from December 31, 1999, to January 1, 2000.

- Early releases of the spreadsheet program Lotus 1-2-3 treated 2000 as a nonleap year and 1900 as a leap year when, in fact, the opposite is the case. Later versions of the software corrected the problem for the year 2000, but not for 1900, which remains a leap year according to the software.

- A Washington, DC, hospital computer crashed on September 19, 1989, precisely 32,768 days after January 1, 1900. Note that 32,767 is the largest integer representable by an `int` on typical microcomputers.

Designing robust software is difficult, especially when incorrect assumptions are made about how long and to what purpose the software will be used. We'll develop a program to print a calendar for any month in any year after October, 1752.[14] In order to print the calendar, the day of the week corresponding to the first day of the month must be determined (of course much else must be done too). Some of the tools for making this calculation have been developed already in previous programs: determining the number of days in a month and determining when a year is a leap year.

Rather than use these tools to develop code that calculates the day of the week, we'll use a class `Date`, accessible using the include file `"date.h"`. In making a calendar, not all of the member functions of the `Date` class will be used, and we won't study every member function that appears in *date.h*, Prog. 5.15. Instead, we'll rely on the comments to understand how the member functions that are used behave. We'll discuss some of the other member functions too. The `Date` class is diagrammed in Fig. 5.7 .

Program 5.15   date.h

```
#ifndef _DATE_H
#define _DATE_H

#include "CPstring.h"

// a class for manipulating dates
// written 2/2/94, Owen Astrachan
// modified 1/5/96 to add arithmetic operators and change
//                 names of some member functions
//
// Date class represents a date in the Gregorian calendar
// works only for dates after October, 1752
//
// attempts to construct invalid dates, e.g., 15th month
// or 38th day, result in month == 1, day == 1.  years aren't
// checked for validity
//
```

---

[14]The calendar used in the United States is the *Gregorian* calendar, which went into effect in 1582, but not in the English-speaking world until 1752. Several countries did not adopt this calendar until the 1900s, but it is adopted almost universally today. In-depth and interesting information about calendars can be found in [DR90, RDC93].

```
// Date()        --- construct default date (today)
// Date(long int days) --- construct date given absolute #
//              of days from 1 A.D., e.g., 710,347 =
//              November 12, 1945
// Date(int m,int d,int y) --- constructor requires three
//              parameters: month, day, year, e.g.,
//              Date d(4,8,1956); initializes d to represent
//              the date April 8, 1956.  Full year is required
//
// void SetDate(int m,int d,int y) -- set date according
//              to parameters: month, day, year, e.g.,
//              d.SetDate(1,1,2000); sets date d to January
//              1 in the year 2000
//
// int Month() --- return, respectively, month, day, and year
// int Day()   corresponding to date with 1 = january,
// int Year()  2 = february, ... 12 = december
//
//
// string DayName() --- return string corresponding to day
//              of week either "Monday", "Tuesday", ... "Sunday"
// string MonthName() --- return string corresponding to month
//              either "January", "February",..."December"
//
// int DaysIn() --- return number of days in month
//
//
// long int Absolute() == returns absolute # of date assuming
//              that Jan 1, 1 AD is day 1.  Has property
//              that Absolute() % 7 = k, where k = 0 is sunday
//              k = 1 is monday, ... k = 6 is saturday
//
// string ToString() --- returns string version of date, e.g.,
//              d.SetDate(11,23,1963); then d.ToString()
//              returns string "November 23 1963"
// string DateAscii() -- returns ascii version of date
//              (for backward compatibility)
//
// *********************************************
//         arithmetic operators for dates
// *********************************************
//
// dates support some addition and subtraction operations
//
// Date d(1,1,1960);        // 1960 is a leap year
// d++;                     // d represents January 2, 1960
// d--;                     // d is back to January 1, 1960
// d += 31;                 // d is February 1, 1960
// d -= 32;                 // d is December 31, 1959
// Date d2 = d + 1;         // d2 is January 1, 1960
// Date d3 = 365 + d2;      // d3 is December 31, 1961
// Date d4 = d - 1;         // d4 is December 30, 1959
//
// *********************************************
```

```
class Date
{
  public:
                 // constructors
     Date();                           // date with default value
     Date(long int days);              // date from absolute #
     Date(int m,int d,int y);          // date with specified values

             // accessor functions

     int Month()          const;       // return month of date
     int Day()            const;       // return day of date
     int Year()           const;       // return year of date
     int DaysIn()         const;       // return # of days in month
     string DayName()     const;       // "monday" ... or "sunday"
     string MonthName()   const;       // "january" ... or "december"
     long int Absolute()  const;       // number of days since 1 A.D.
     string ToString()    const;       // string for date in ascii
     string DateAscii()   const;       // string for date in ascii

             // mutator functions

     void SetDate(int m,int d,int y);  // set to specified date
     Date operator ++(int);   // add one day, postfix operator
     Date operator --(int);   // subtract one day, postfix operator
     Date& operator +=(int dx);  // add dx, e.g., jan 1 + 31 = feb 1
     Date& operator -=(int dx);  // subtract dx, e.g., jan 1 - 1 = dec 31

  private:

     int myDay;           // day of week, 0-6
     int myMonth;         // month, 0-11
     int myYear;          // year in four digits, e.g., 1899

     void CheckDate(int m, int d, int y);  // make sure that date is valid
};

Date operator + (const Date & d, int dx); // add dx to date d
Date operator + (int dx, const Date & d); // add dx to date d
Date operator - (const Date & d, int dx); // subtract dx from date d

#endif
```
                                                                    date.h

The member functions of the Date class are described carefully in the header file *date.h*. For this class, however, there are three different constructors. These constructors are used in *usedate.cc*, Prog. 5.16.

Constructors and Other Member Functions

The first line of output from *usedate.cc* will differ depending on the day the program is run. This is because the variable today, defined using the

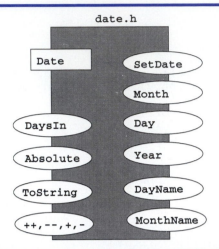

Figure 5.7   Interface diagram for Date class.

parameterless or **default** constructor, constructs a variable with "today's date" according to the documentation in *date.h*, Prog. 5.15. (I ran the program on the summer solstice in 1995). The variable birthDayUS is constructed by calling the three-parameter constructor. According to the documentation in *date.h* the parameters specify the month, day, and year of a Date object. The variable million is constructed using the single-parameter constructor. The documentation in *date.h* indicates that the value of the parameter specifies the absolute number of days from January 1, A.D. 1; one million days from this date is November 28, 2738. Finally, the variable badDate is constructed with an invalid date in March; the invalid date is converted to March 1, as described in the beginning of the header file. Invalid months (i.e., outside the range 1–12) are converted to January.

Classes often have more than one constructor, especially when there is more than one way to specify the value of a class object. The constructors are overloaded just as the arithmetic operator + is overloaded and the function PromptRange in *prompt.h* is overloaded. The compiler can determine which constructor to use since the parameter lists are different.

The member function Date::ToString is used in *usedate.cc* to print a string corresponding to a given date.[15] You may recall that the :: operator specifies the class to which a member function belongs. Other member functions described in the documentation of the header file are mostly straightforward,

---

[15]The function DateAscii is provided for backward compatibility with a previous version of the class Date.

Program 5.16   usedate.cc

```
#include <iostream.h>
#include "date.h"

// show three different Date constructors

void PrintDate(Date d)
{
    cout << d.ToString() << endl;
}

int main()
{
    Date today;
    Date birthDayUS(7,4,1776);
    Date million(1000000);
    Date badDate(3,38,1999);

    PrintDate(today);
    PrintDate(birthDayUS);
    PrintDate(million);
    PrintDate(badDate);

    PrintDate(birthDayUS + 365*200);
    PrintDate(million - 999999);

    birthDayUS++;
    PrintDate(birthDayUS);
    return 0;
}
```

OUTPUT

```
prompt> usedate
June 21 1995
July 04 1776
November 28 2738
March 01 1999
May 17 1976
January 01 0001
July 05 1776
```

with the exception of the overloaded arithmetic operators ++, --, +=, -=, +, and -.

Overloaded Arithmetic Operators

What's the date 90 days after April 1, 1998? The arithmetic operators defined as part of the Date class make this kind of calculation possible as shown in the run of *usedate.cc*. These calculations are easy to implement because of the member function `Date::Absolute`. To find the date that occurs 90 days after April 1, 1998, two statements effectively convert the date into an absolute number of days and back again.

```
Date d(4,1,1998);
Date dPlus90(d.Absolute() + 90);
```

Instead of requiring client programs to do the conversion explicitly, the overloaded arithmetic operators allow `Date` and `int` values to be added and subtracted. Although it makes sense to subtract an `int` from a `Date`, it doesn't make sense to subtract a `Date` from an `int`. In other words, it makes sense to ask what the date is 30 days before October 3rd, but it does not make sense to ask what the date is January 3 before 10. If you examine the header file `"date.h"` carefully, you'll see that there are two functions defined for addition using the + operator, but only one function defined using the – operator. The prototypes from *date.h* are the following.

```
Date operator + (const Date & d, int dx);   // add dx to date d
Date operator + (int dx, const Date & d);   // add dx to date d
Date operator - (const Date & d, int dx);   // subtract dx from date d
```

There are two functions for `operator +`, because we want to be able to write code like `today + 31` and `31 + today`, where `today` is a `Date` variable. Although the + appears between the two numbers, the function called is one of the `operator +` functions declared in *date.h*. Because there is only one `operator -` function declared, the compiler will catch attempts to write `32 - today`. The error message printed with one compiler indicates exactly why this expression will not compile:

```
usedate.cc: In function 'int main()':
usedate.cc:25: no match for 'operator -(int, class Date)'
```

For technical reasons we'll discuss in a later chapter, these three functions (for + and –) are *not* member functions. Even without this technical understanding of some complex C++ programming rules, you can easily write programs like *usedate.cc* that use `Date` variables.

A Calendar-Printing Program

Program 5.17 prompts for a month and year and prints a calendar for that month. The `width` stream function is used to align the dates in a calendar. By altering the field width, the calendar can be made larger.

Program 5.17   calendar.cc

```
#include <iostream.h>
#include "date.h"
#include "prompt.h"

// illustrates use of date class to make calendar
// Owen Astrachan
```

```cpp
const int FIELD_WIDTH = 3;              // space calendar out

void Calendar(int month, int year)
// precondition: 1752 < year and 1 <= month <= 12
// postcondition: print calendar for given month in given year
{

    int k;
    Date d(month,1,year);   // start on first day of month
    int firstDay = d.Absolute() % 7;  // 0=sunday, 1=monday, etc.
    int numDays = d.DaysIn();   // # of days in month

    cout.width(FIELD_WIDTH);

    // print spaces, then month name
    cout << " ";
    cout << d.MonthName() << " " << year << endl;

    cout << " Su Mo Tu We Th Fr Sa" << endl;   // print header
    for(k=0; k < firstDay;k++)
    // print leading blanks
    {
        cout.width(FIELD_WIDTH);
        cout << " ";
    }


        // print rest of days;

    for(k=1; k <= numDays; k++)
    // print every day in month
    {
        cout.width(FIELD_WIDTII);  // print day in field properly
        cout << k;
        if (d.DayName() == "Sunday")
        {
            cout << endl;
        }
        d++;
    }

    if (d.DayName() != "Sunday")
    // finish off last line if necessary
    {
        cout << endl;
    }
}

int main()
{
    int month = PromptRange("enter month",1,12);
    int year  = PromptRange("enter year",1752,2500);
    Calendar(month,year);
    return 0;
}
```

```
                          OUTPUT

prompt> calendar
enter month between 1 and 12:6
enter year between 1752 and 2500:1999

     June 1999
  Su Mo Tu We Th Fr Sa
         1  2  3  4  5
   6  7  8  9 10 11 12
  13 14 15 16 17 18 19
  20 21 22 23 24 25 26
  27 28 29 30
```

The program is well commented to help in understanding how the function `Calendar` works. The task of printing a calendar is divided into three parts:

- Print a header for the calendar (i.e., Su Mo Tu We Th Fr Sa)
- Print the first row of the calendar, which will have "blank" days unless the first day of the month is a Sunday.
- Print a number for each day of the month, starting a new row of the calendar after each Saturday is printed.

A `for` loop prints a number for each day of the month. This loop follows another `for` loop that prints the "blank" days in the first week. The following statement determines the first day of the month:

```
int firstDay = d.Absolute() % 7;  // 0=sunday, 1=monday, etc.
```

This statement assigns a value from the range 0–6 to `firstDay`. The documentation in *date.h*, Prog. 5.15, indicates that `Date::Absolute` returns the absolute number of days corresponding to a given date with January 1, A.D. 1, being day one. Since this day is a Monday,[16] using `% 7` converts the absolute date into the appropriate day of the week. This day is used to begin printing the calendar on the correct day.

The day of the week is obtained using the `Date::DayName` member function. Because the `Date d` variable is incremented using `d++` in each iteration of the `for` loop, the day of the week is automatically updated as well.

---

[16]The *Gregorian* calendar was not in place in the United States until the eighteenth century. The *Julian* calendar was used before that time. Using Monday as January 1 of A.D. 1 is done by counting backwards from the current calendar. By the Julian calendar this is January 3, A.D. 1—a complete description of this can be found in [DR90].

The `if` statement that appears after the `for` loop ensures that the last week of a month is followed by an `endl`.

Pause to reflect

5.37. Using one `Date` variable and the member function `DaysIn` write the boolean-valued function `IsLeapYear` as specified, for example, in *useleap.cc*, Prog. 4.8 (page 141). This can be done by defining one variable and then using a `return` statement that returns the result of a boolean expression that contains only one operator: `==`.

5.38. How would you use a `Date` variable to determine on what day of the week you were born?

5.39. If the one-millionth day is November 28, 2738 (see *usedate.cc*), do we need to worry that the `Date` class is not robust and might cause problems when the absolute number of days since A.D. 1 exceeds the largest value of a `long int`?

5.40. Suppose that a field width of 4 is used instead of 3 in the function `Calendar` in *calendar.cc*. How would the output differ from that when 3 is used?

5.41. What fence post examples are there in the function `Calendar`?

5.42. Make changes to Prog. 5.17 to print a calendar for an entire year rather than for a particular month. Will the program `date.cc` need to be recompiled? Will the program `calendar.cc` need to be recompiled?

C++ Details of the Class `Date` (Optional)

We haven't covered all the features of C++ necessary to understand the syntax used for declaring each member function of the `Date` class. However, as you can see from studying *calendar.cc*, using the expression `d++` to increment a date by one day is easy to understand, even if the function prototype `Date operator ++(int)` is not so easy to understand.

In this section we'll briefly outline some of the syntactic and design issues raised by the `Date` class. You don't need to understand these details to use the `Date` class, but you might want to implement a similar class in the future.

Implementing operators `+=` *and* `+`. It is almost always easiest to implement the operator `+=` first, then use this to implement regular addition using `+`. The `+=` operator must be a member function since it modifies a `Date` object. The following code prints "`January 01 1998`":

```
Date d(12,31,1997);
d += 1;
cout << d.ToString() << endl;
```

It is possible to write `d.operator += (1)` instead of `d += 1`. Note that the `+=` is a member function, since it is applied using dot notation to the variable `d`. In contrast, the `+` operator is not a member function in this case. It doesn't make sense, for example, to write `3.operator + (d)`, since 3 is an int and built-in types cannot have member functions applied to them. To be consistent in using the same style to implement + for both d+3 and 3+d, the + operator is implemented as a nonmember, or **free**, function.

```
Date operator + (const Date & d, int dx)
// postcondition: returns d + dx
{
    Date copy(d);
    copy += dx;
    return copy;
}
```

Note that a copy of the parameter d is made and that this copy is modified using the += operator. For reasons we'll discuss in the next chapter, the parameter d is constant and cannot change. Since d is constant, a copy is used in conjunction with +=. This style of implementing + can always be used whenever the += operator is defined. When operators are overloaded, they should be overloaded consistently with their use on built-in types. This means that users can expect that operator += will be implemented whenever + is implemented and vice versa. Fortunately, that is very easy to do, as shown here.

Implementing operator ++. The postfix increment operator ++ is easy to implement once the += operator is implemented, although the syntax in the member function is somewhat complicated by C++ issues that we will postpone. However, there must be some way to differentiate between the postfix and prefix ++ operators. An unused or dummy int parameter differentiates the postfix ++ from the prefix ++. The member function operator ++ could be implemented as shown here, although its actual implementation in *date.cc* is slightly different.

```
Date Date::operator ++(int)
// postcondition: increment by one
{
    Date hold(Absolute());
    hold += 1;
    SetDate(hold.Month(), hold.Day(), hold.Year());
    return hold;
}
```

In executing d++, first a local variable hold is initialized to the same date as the object being incremented (d in this example). When a member function is invoked from within another member function, as Absolute is invoked from within operator +=, both member functions work on the same object. The variable hold is incremented, and then the month, day, and year of hold are used to change the value of d using SetDate (again, a member function invoked from within a member function).

Excursion Exercises

5.19 The statement in *calendar.cc*, Prog. 5.17, that prints the abbreviations for the days of the week does not use cout.width(). Put this code in a function PrintHeader and modify it so that FIELD_WIDTH is used to print the header as well as the day numbers.

```
cout << " Su Mo Tu We Th Fr Sa" << endl;  // print header
```

5.20 Modify *calendar.cc*, Prog. 5.17, so that it prints labels for each day of the week and puts "boxes" around each day. For example, for April 1996 the calendar might appear as

```
    Su   Mo   Tu   We   Th   Fr   Sa
+---+---+---+---+---+---+---+
|    |  1 |  2 |  3 |  4 |  5 |  6 |
+---+---+---+---+---+---+---+
|  7 |  8 |  9 | 10| 11| 12| 13|
+---+---+---+---+---+---+---+
| 14| 15| 16| 17| 18| 19| 20|
+---+---+---+---+---+---+---+
| 21| 22| 23| 24| 25| 26| 27|
+---+---+---+---+---+---+---+
| 28| 29| 30|    |    |    |    |
+---+---+---+---+---+---+---+
```

but you should let your imagination run wild. Does it make sense for the calendar-printing function to be a member function of the Date class (assuming you could modify the class)?

5.21 Expand the program from the previous exercise so that each day is drawn in a large box:

```
+---------+---------+---------+
|       1 |       2 |       3 |
|         |         |         |
|         |         |         |
|         |         |         |
+---------+---------+---------+
```

Try to write the program so that the user can specify the size of the box.

5.22 Write a program that prompts the user for a year and prints out a calendar for each month of the year. Be sure to reuse code from the chapter or the previous exercise.

5.23 Daylight-saving time causes clocks to be reset in the spring and fall in many (but not all) parts of the United States. Daylight saving begins on the first Sunday of April (set clocks ahead one hour, "spring ahead") and ends on the last Sunday of October (set clocks back one hour, "fall back"). Write a program that shows the number of days in which daylight-saving time is in effect for all years from 1990 to 2010. You may find it useful to write a function that returns the number of daylight-saving days given the year (as a parameter).

5.24 Write a program that finds the number of days between holidays. Choose at least five holidays. The program should print the name of the holiday (e.g., Arbor Day) and the number of days between each two holidays.

5.25 Some people believe that our physical, emotional, and intellectual habits are governed by *biorhythms*. A biorhythm cycle exists for each of these three traits; the length of the cycle differs, but all cycles start when we are born. The physical cycle is 23 days long, the intellectual cycle is 33 days long, and the emotional cycle is 28 days long. The cycles repeat as sine waves, with the period of each wave given by the cycle length. A critical day occurs when all three cycles cross at the equivalent of $y = 0$ if the cycles are plotted on x and y axes. When a cycle is at its peak (e.g., as $\sin(\pi/2)$ is the peak of a sine wave), we are favored for that cycle, so that a peak on the intellectual cycle is a good day to take an exam.

Use the Date class to determine when your next critical day is and when your next peak and low days are for each of the three cycles.

PART II

PROGRAM AND CLASS CONSTRUCTION: EXTENDING THE FOUNDATION

Sequential Access: Streams and Iterators

Nature uses only the longest threads to weave her pattern, so each small piece of the fabric reveals the organization of the entire tapestry.

RICHARD FEYNMAN
QUOTED BY GRADY BOOCH
Object Solutions

The control structures we studied in Chaps. 4 and 5 permit program statements to be executed selectively or repeatedly according to values entered by the user or calculated by the program. In this chapter we'll extend the idea of repetition by processing various data in several applications. A common pattern emerges from all these applications: the pattern of iterating over a sequence of data. Examples of such iteration include processing each word in one of Shakespeare's plays, processing each movement of a simulated molecule, and processing each beat of a simulated heart. Using these applications we'll explore design guidelines for constructing classes and programs.

In particular, we'll cover classes used to read information from files stored on a disk rather than entered from the keyboard. We'll use a standard stream class that behaves in the same way `cin` behaves but that allows data to flow from text files. We'll develop a new class for reading words from files and build on the pattern of iteration developed for the class to develop new classes. Writing programs and functions that use these classes requires a new kind of parameter, called a *reference parameter*, which we'll discuss in some detail.

6.1 Reading Words: Stream Iteration

If you steal from one author, it's plagiarism;
if you steal from many, it's research.
WILSON MIZNER

Word processing programs merely manipulate words and characters, but scholars sometimes use programs that process character data to determine authorship. For example, literary investigators have sought to determine the authorship of Shakespeare's plays and sonnets. Some have argued that they were written by philosopher Francis Bacon or dramatist Christopher Marlowe, but most Shakespearean authorities doubt these claims. To amass evidence regarding the authorship of a literary work, it is possible to gather statistics to create a "literary fingerprint." Such a fingerprint can be based on frequently used words, phrases, or allusions. It can also include a count of uncommon words. Computer programs facilitate the gathering of these data.

In this section, we demonstrate the pattern of iterating over words and characters by simpler, but similar, kinds of programs. These programs will count words and letters—the kind of task that is built into many word processing programs and used when a limit on the number of words in an essay is set, e.g., by newspaper columnists and students writing English papers. We'll first write a program that counts words entered by the user or stored in a text file. A text file is the kind of file in which C++ programs are stored or word processing documents are saved when the latter are saved as plain text.[1]

I'll adopt a three-step process in explaining how to develop the program. As you write and develop programs, you should think about these steps and use them if they make sense. These steps are meant as hints or guidelines, not rules that should be slavishly followed.

Recommended problem-solving and programming steps

1. Think about how to solve the problem with paper, pencil, and brain (but no computer). Consider how to extend the human solution to a computer-based solution. You may find it useful to sketch a solution using **pseudocode,** a mixture of English and C++.

2. If, after thinking about how to solve the problem with a computer (and perhaps writing out a solution), you are not sure how to proceed, pause. Try thinking about solving a related problem whose solution is similar to a program previously studied.

3. Develop a working program or class in an iterative manner, implementing one part at a time before implementing the entire program. This can help localize problems and errors because you'll be able to focus on small pieces of the program rather than the entirety.

We will use these steps to solve the word count problem. First we'll specify the problem in more detail and develop a pseudocode solution. This step will show that we're missing some knowledge of how to read from files, so we'll solve a related problem on the way to counting the words in a text file. After writing a complete program we'll develop a class-based alternative that will provide code that's easier to reuse in other contexts.

---

[1]The adjective *plain* is used to differentiate text files from files in word processors that show font, page layout, and formatting commands. Most word processors have an option to save files as plain text.

A Pseudocode Solution

Counting the words in this chapter or in Shakespeare's play *Hamlet* by hand would be a boring and arduous task. However, it's an easy task for a computer program—simply scan the text and count each word. It would be a good idea to specify more precisely what a "word" is. The first part of any programming task is often a careful **specification** of exactly what the program should do. This may require defining terms such as *word*. In this case, we'll assume that a word is a sequence of characters separated from other words by white space. White space characters in C++ are given in Table 6.1.

The space, tab, and newline characters are white space characters found in typical text files. Except for the space character, each white space character is represented by an escape sequence. The backslash character, \ , is a prefix for escape sequences; it is not printed. Escape sequences represent certain characters such as the tab and carriage return in C++; a table of common escape sequences is given in Table 4.1. To print a backslash requires an escape sequence; \ \ prints as a single backslash.[2]

For this problem, we'll write a pseudocode description of a loop to count words. Pseudocode is a language that has characteristics of C++ (or Pascal, or some other language), but liberties are taken with syntax. Sketching such a description can help focus your attention on the important parts of a program.

```
numWords = 0;
while (words left to read)
{
    read a word;
    numWords++;
}
print number of words read
```

These pseudocode instructions are very close to C++, except for the test of the `while` loop and the statement `read a word`. In fact, we've seen code to read a word using the extraction operator `>>` (e.g., Prog. 3.1, *macinput.cc*). White space separates one string from another when the extraction operator `>>` is

Table 6.1 White Space Characters in C++

Character	C++ representation
Space	' '
Tab	'\t'
Newline	'\n'
Form feed, return, vertical tab (not usually encountered)	'\f' '\r' '\v'

---

[2]Consider buying groceries. Often a plastic bar is used to separate your groceries from the next person's. What happens if you go to a store to buy one of the plastic bars? If the person behind you is buying one too, what can you use to separate your purchases?

used to process input. This is just what we want to read words. As an example, what happens if you type `steel-gray tool-box` when the code below is executed?

```
string first, second;
cout << "enter two words:";
cin >> first >> second;
cout << first << " : " << second << endl;
```

Since the space between the *y* of *steel-gray* and the *t* of *tool-box* is used to delimit the words, the output is the following.

OUTPUT

```
steel-gray : tool-box
```

As another example, consider this loop, which will let you enter six words:

```
string word;
int numWords;
for(numWords=0; numWords < 6; numWords++)
{
    cin >> word;
    cout << numWords << " " << word << endl;
}
```

If you type the words below with a tab character between `it` and `ain't`, the return key pressed after `broke`, and two spaces between `don't` and `fix`,

```
If it        ain't broke,
don't   fix it.
```

the output of the loop above is

OUTPUT

```
0  If
1  it
2  ain't
3  broke,
4  don't
5  fix
```

Although the input typed by the user appears as two lines, the input stream `cin` processes a sequence of characters, not a sequence of words or lines. The characters on the input stream appear as literally a stream of characters (the symbol ⎵ is used to represent a space).

If⎵⎵it\tain\'t⎵⎵broke,\ndon\'t⎵⎵⎵fix it.

There are three different escape characters in this stream: the tab character, \t, the newline character, \n, and the apostrophe character, \'. We don't need to be aware of these escape characters, or any other individual character, to read a sequence of words using the loop shown above. At a low level a stream is a sequence of characters, but at a higher level we can use the extraction operator, >>, to view a stream as a sequence of words.

The extraction operator, >>—when used with String variables—groups adjacent, non–white space characters on the stream to form words as shown by the output of the while loop above. Note that punctuation is included as part of the word broke, because all non–white space characters, including punctuation, are the same from the point of view of the input stream cin. Since the operator >> treats all white space the same, the newline is treated the same as the spaces or tabs between adjacent words. Any sequence of white space characters is treated as white space, as can be seen in the example above, where a tab character space separates it from ain't and two spaces separate don't from fix.

Now that we have a better understanding of how the extraction operator works with input streams, characters, and words, we need to return to the original problem of counting words in a text file. We address two problems: reading an arbitrary number of words and reading from a file. We cannot use a definite loop because we don't know in advance how many words are in a file—that's what we're trying to determine.

Solving a Related Problem

How can a loop be programmed to stop when there are no more words in the input? Step two of our method requires solving a familiar but related problem when confronted with a task whose solution isn't immediately apparent. In this case, suppose that words are to be entered and counted until you enter some specific word signaling that no more words will be entered. The test of a while loop used to solve this task can consist of while (word != LAST_WORD), where LAST_WORD is the special word indicating the end of the input and word holds the value of the string that you enter.

This is an example of a **sentinel** loop—the sentinel is the special value that indicates the end of input. Such loops are classic fence post problems: you must enter a word before the test is made and, if the test indicates there are more words, you must enter another word. Program 6.1 shows such a sentinel loop accepting entries until the user enters the word *end*. The special sentinel value is *not* considered part of the data being processed. Sometimes it's difficult to designate a sentinel value since no value can be singled out as invalid data. In the second run the number of words does not appear immediately after the word *end* is entered since more typing takes place afterward. The number of words is not output until after the return key is pressed, and this occurs several words after the word *end* is entered. This apparent delay is a side effect of **buffered input,** which allows the user to make corrections as input is entered. When input is buffered, the program doesn't actually receive the input and doesn't do any processing until the return key is pressed. The input is stored in

---

Program 6.1   sentinel.cc

```cpp
#include <iostream.h>
#include "CPstring.h"

   // count words in the standard input stream, cin

int main()
{
    const string LAST_WORD = "end";

    string word;
    int numWords = 0;                       // initially, no words

    cout << "type '" << LAST_WORD << "' to terminate input"
         << endl;
    cin >> word;
    while (word != LAST_WORD)            // read succeeded
    {
        numWords++;
        cin >> word;
    }

    cout << "number of words read = " << numWords << endl;
    return 0;
}
```

OUTPUT

```
prompt> sentinel
type 'end' to terminate input
One fish, two
fish, red fish, blue fish
end
number of words read = 8

prompt> sentinel
type 'end' to terminate input
How will the world end--with a bang or a whimper?
number of words read = 4
```

a memory area called a *buffer* and then passed to the program when the line is finished and the return key pressed. Most systems use buffered input, although sometimes it is possible to turn this buffering off.

Although we still haven't solved the problem of developing a loop that reads all words (until none are left), the sentinel loop is a start in the right direction and will lead to a solution in the next section.

Pause to reflect

6.1. The sentinel loop shown here reads integers until the user enters a zero. Modify the loop to keep two separate counts: the number of positive integers entered and the number of negative integers entered. Use appropriate identifiers for each counter.

```
const int SENTINEL = 0;
int count = 0;

int num;
cin >> num;
while (num != SENTINEL)
{
    count += 1;
    cin >> num;
}
```

6.2. Does your system buffer input in the manner described in this section? What happens if Prog. 6.1 is run and the user enters

```
This is the start, this is the end --- nothing
is in between.
```

Why?

6.3. Another technique used with sentinel loops is to force the loop to iterate once. If the statement `cin >> word` before the `while` loop in Prog. 6.1 is replaced with the statement `word = "dummy";`, how should the body of the `while` loop be modified so that the program counts words in the same way?

6.4. Suppose that you want to write a loop that stops after either of two sentinel values is read. Using the technique of the previous problem in which the loop is forced to iterate once by giving a dummy value to the string variable used for input, write a loop that counts words entered by the user until the user enters either the word `end` or the word `finish`. Be sure to use appropriate `const` definitions for both sentinels.

The Final Program: Counting Words

We are finally ready to finish a program that counts all the words in a text file or all the words a user enters. We would like to refine the loop in Prog. 6.1, *sentinel.cc*, so that it reads all input but does not require a sentinel value to identify the last word in the input stream. This will let us calculate the number of words (or characters, or occurrences of the word *the*) in any text file since we won't need to rely on a specific word to be the sentinel last word. This is possible in C++ because the extraction operator not only extracts strings (or numbers) from an input stream, but returns a result indicating whether the extraction succeeds. For example, a code fragment used earlier read the words `steel-gray` and `tool-box` using the statement

```
cin >> first >> second;
```

WILLIAM H. (BILL) GATES (b. 1955)

Bill Gates is the richest person in the United States and CEO of Microsoft. He began his career as a programmer writing the first BASIC compiler for early microcomputers while a student at Harvard. When asked whether studying computer science is the best way to prepare to be a programmer, Gates responded:

> No, the best way to prepare is to write programs, and to study great programs that other people have written. In my case, I went to the garbage cans at the Computer Science Center and I fished out listings of their operating system.
>
> You've got to be willing to read other people's code, then write your own, then have other people review your code.

Gates is a visionary in seeing how computers will be used both in business and in the home. Microsoft publishes best-selling word processors, programming languages, and operating systems as well as interactive encyclopedias for children. Some people question Microsoft's business tactics, but in late 1994 antitrust proceedings did little to deter Microsoft's progress. There is no questioning Gates's and Microsoft's influence on how computers are used.

Although Gates doesn't program anymore, he remembers the satisfaction that comes from programming.

> When I compile something and it starts computing the right results, I really feel great. I'm not kidding, there is some emotion in all great things, and this is no exception.

For more information see [Sla87].

This statement is read, or parsed, by the C++ compiler as though it were written as (cin >> first) >> second; because >> is left-associative. Think of the input stream, cin, as flowing through the extraction operators, >>. The first word on the stream is extracted and stored in first, and the stream continues to flow so that the second word on the stream can be extracted and stored in second. The result of the first extraction, the value of the expression (cin >> first), is the input stream, cin, without the word that has been stored in the variable first.

The most important point of this explanation is that the expression (cin >> first) not only reads a string from cin but returns the stream so that it can be used again, e.g., for another extraction operation. Although it may seem strange at first, the stream itself can be tested to see if the extraction succeeded. The following code fragment shows how this is done.

```
int num;
cout << "enter a number: ";
if (cin >> num)
{
    cout << "valid integer: "   << num << endl;
}
else
{
    cout << "invalid integer: " << num << endl;
}
```

OUTPUT

```
enter a number: 23
valid integer: 23
enter a number: skidoo23
invalid integer: 292232
enter a number: 23skidoo
valid integer: 23
```

The expression (cin >> num) evaluates to true when the extraction of an integer from cin has succeeded. The characters skidoo23 do not represent a valid integer, so the message invalid integer is printed. The integer printed here is a garbage value. Since no value is stored in the variable num when num is defined, whatever value is in the memory associated with num is printed. Other runs of the program may print different values. Note that when 23skidoo is entered, the extraction succeeds and 23 is stored in the variable num. In this case, the characters skidoo remain on the input stream and can be extracted by a statement such as cin >> word, where word is a string variable. The use of the extraction operator to both extract input and return a value used in a boolean test can be confusing since the extraction operation does two things.

Some people prefer to write the if statement using the fail member function of the stream cin.

```
cin >> num;
if (! cin.fail())
{
    cout << "valid integer: "   << num << endl;
}
```

The member function fail returns true when an extraction operation has failed and returns false otherwise. You do not need to use fail explicitly since the extraction operator returns the same value as fail, but some programmers find it clearer to use fail.

Program 6.2 correctly counts the number of words in the input stream cin by testing the value returned by the extraction operator in a while loop.

The test of the while loop is false when the extraction operation fails. When reading strings, extraction fails only when there is no more input. As shown above, input with integers (and doubles) can fail if a noninteger value

Program 6.2   countw.cc

```
#include <iostream.h>
#include "CPstring.h"

    // count words in the standard input stream, cin

int main()
{
    string word;
    int numWords = 0;                        // initially, no words

    while (cin >> word)                      // read succeeded
    {
        numWords++;
    }

    cout << "number of words read = " << numWords << endl;
    return 0;
}
```

countw.cc

is entered. Since any sequence of characters is a string, extraction fails for strings only when there is no more input. You indicate no more input by typing a special character called the **end-of-file** character. This character should be typed as the first and only character on a line, followed by pressing the return key. When UNIX or Macintosh computers are used, this character is Ctrl-D, and on MS-DOS/Windows machines this character is Ctrl-Z. To type this character the control key must be held down at the same time as the D (or Z) key is pressed. Such control characters are sometimes not shown on the screen but are used to indicate to the system running the program that input is over (end of file has been reached).

OUTPUT

```
prompt> countw
How shall I love thee? Let
me count
the ways.
^D
number of words read = 10
```

The end-of-file character was *not* typed as the string ^D but by holding down the Control key and pressing the D key simultaneously.

We'll modify *countw.cc* so that it will count words stored in a text file; then we'll see how to turn this program into a class that makes it a general-purpose programming tool.

6.2   Streams Associated with Files

In Prog. 6.1, *sentinel.cc*, and Prog. 6.2, *countw.cc*, the standard input stream, cin, was used as the source of words. Clearly you can't be expected to type in all of *Hamlet* to count the words in that play. Instead, you need some way to create a stream associated with a text file (rather than with the keyboard and the standard input stream, cin). A class ifstream, accessible by including the file <fstream.h>, is used for streams that are associated with text files. Program 6.3, *countw2.cc*, is a modification of Prog. 6.2 but uses an ifstream variable.

There is a similar class **ofstream** (for *output file stream*) also accessible by including the header file #include <fstream.h>. This class supports the use of the insertion operator, <<, just as ifstream supports extraction, using the >> operator.

In the following runs, the file melville.txt is the text of Herman Melville's *Bartleby, The Scrivener: A Story of Wall-Street*. The file hamlet.txt

---

Program 6.3   countw2.cc

```
#include <iostream.h>
#include <fstream.h>                    // for ifstream
#include "CPstring.h"
#include "prompt.h"

   // count words in a file specified by the user

int main()
{
    string word;
    int numWords = 0;                  // initially, no words
    int sum = 0;                       // sum of all word lengths
    ifstream input;

    string filename = PromptString("enter name of file: ");

    input.open(filename);              // bind input to named file

    while (input >> word)                 // read succeeded
    {
        numWords++;
        sum += word.length();
    }

    cout << "number of words read = " << numWords << endl;
    cout << "average word length = " << sum/numWords << endl;
    return 0;
}
```

is the complete text of William Shakespeare's *Hamlet*. These, as well as other works by Shakespeare, Edgar Allen Poe, Mark Twain, and others, are accessible as text files.[3]

OUTPUT

```
prompt> countw2
enter name of file: melville.txt
number of words read = 14353
average word length = 4

prompt> countw2
enter name of file: hamlet.txt
number of words read = 31956
average word length = 4

prompt> countw2
enter name of file: macbet.txt
number of words read = 0
Floating exception
```

The variable `input` is an instance of the class `ifstream`—an **input file stream**—and supports extraction using `>>` just as `cin` does. The variable `input` is associated, or **bound,** to a particular user-specified text file specified using the member function `ifstream::open()`.

```
input.open(filename);     // bind input to named file
```

The string `filename` that holds the name of the user-specified file is an argument to the member function `ifstream::open()`.[4] Once `input` is bound to a text file, the extraction operator `>>` can be used to extract items from the file (instead of from the user typing from the keyboard as is the case with `cin`). In the example of using Prog. 6.3, file `macbet.txt` has no words. I made a mistake when entering the name of the file to read (I meant to type

---

[3]The files containing these literary works are available with the material that supports this book. These texts are in the public domain, which makes on-line versions of them free.

[4]If the standard string class is used rather than the string class defined in *CPstring.h,* then the syntax used for the open function will be `input.open(filename.c_str())`. The standard string member function `c_str()` returns a C-style string required by the prototype for the function `open()`. The `open()` function may be modified to accept standard strings, but as of the writing of this book compilers do not support this feature and the conversion function `c_str()` must be used. The function `c_str()` works with the *CPstring.h* string class as well, so you can use it in code developed using *CPstring.h* that will be ported later to the standard `string` class.

`macbeth.txt`), which caused the extraction operation to fail because the file does not exist. Because no words were read, the average calculation resulted in a division-by-zero error. On some systems, division by zero can cause the machine to crash. A **robust** program protects against errors. Program 6.3 could be made robust by guarding the average calculation with an `if` statement to check whether `numWords == 0`.

You should always look carefully at program output to determine if it meets your expectations. The average printed for both *Hamlet* and *Melville* is four. This is surprising; you probably do not expect the averages to be exactly the same. To fix this problem we'll need to change how the average is calculated.

Type Casting

Since both `numWords` and `sum` are `int` variables, the result of the division operator, `/`, yields an `int`. How can the correct average be calculated? One method is to define `sum` to be a `double` variable. Since the statement

```
sum += word.length();
```

will correctly accumulate a sum of integers even when `sum` is a `double` variable, this method will work reasonably well. However, it may not be the best method, since the wrong type (`double`) is being used to accumulate the sum of integers. Instead, we can use a **type cast.** This is a method that allows one type to be converted (sometimes called **coerced**) into another type. In this case the statement

```
cout << "average word length = " << double(sum)/numWords << endl;
```

can be used to yield the correct average of 4.705 for *Melville* and 4.362 for *Hamlet*. The expression `double(sum)` shows that the type `double` is used like a function name with an argument `sum`. The result is a `double` that is as close to the integer value of `sum` as possible. Since the result of a mixed-type arithmetic expression is of the highest type (in this case, `double`), 3.5 will be printed. You can also write a cast as `((double) sum)/numWords`. This is the C-style of casting but can be used in C++ and is necessary if the cast is to a type whose name is more than one word, such as `long int`. A cast has higher precedence than arithmetic operators, so `(double) sum/numWords` will also work because `sum` is cast to a `double` value before the division occurs.

The statement

```
cout << "average word length = " << sum/double(numWords) << endl;
```

gives a correct result too since the mixed-type expression yields a result of type `double`.

> **Program Tip: Be careful when casting a value of one type to another.** It is possible that a type cast will result in a value changing.

For example, using Turbo C++ the output of the three statements

```
cout << int(32800.2) << endl;
cout << double(333333333333333) << endl;
cout << int(3.6) << endl;
```

is

```
-32736
9.214908e+08
3
```

The third number printed is easy to explain—casting a double to an `int` **truncates,** or chops off, the decimal places. The first two numbers exceed the range of valid values for `int` and `double`, respectively.

In general, casting is sometimes necessary, but you must be careful that the values being cast are valid values in the type being cast to.

Casting with `static_cast`

Four cast operators have been recently added to C++. In this book the operator `static_cast` will be used.[5] As an example, the statement `cout << double(sum)/numWords << endl;` is written as shown in the following to use the `static_cast` operator.

```
cout << static_cast<double>(sum)/numWords << endl;
```

Your C++ compiler may not support `static_cast`, but this will change soon as the C++ standard is adopted. Using `static_cast` makes casts easier to spot in code and allows one form of cast to be used uniformly; e.g., to cast a `double` to a `long int` the following code is used.

```
cout << static_cast<long int>(32800.2) << endl;
```

A Word-Reading Class Using `ifstream`

The third of the three program development guidelines given in Sec. 6.1 calls for programs to be developed using an iterative process. Sometimes this means redesigning an already working program so that it will be useful in different settings. In the case of Prog. 6.2, *countw.cc,* we want to reimplement the program in a new way to study a programming pattern that we will see on many occasions throughout this book. The resulting program will be longer, but it will yield a C++ class that is easier to modify for new situations than the original program. It will also help us focus on a pattern you can use in other classes and programs: the idea of processing "entries." In this case we'll process all the words in a text file. The same design pattern can be used to process all the prime numbers between 1000 and 9999, all the files in a computer disc directory, and all the tracks on a compact disc.

---

[5]The other cast operators are `const_cast`, `dynamic_cast`, and `reinterpret_cast`; we won't use these in the code in this book.

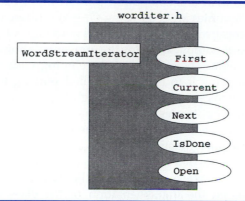

Figure 6.1 `WordStreamIterator` class.

The pattern of iteration over entries is expressed in pseudocode as

```
find the first entry;
while (the current entry is valid)
{
    process the current entry;
    advance to the next entry;
}
```

We'll use a `WordStreamIterator` class to get words one at a time from the text file. The class is diagrammed in Fig. 6.1.

As an example of how to use the class, the function `main` below does the same thing as Prog. 6.2, *countw.cc*. For any input, the output of these two programs is the same.

```
int main()
{
    string word;
    int numWords = 0;               // initially, no words
    WordStreamIterator iter;

    iter.Open(PromptString("enter name of file: "));

    for(iter.First(); ! iter.IsDone(); iter.Next())
    {
        numWords++;
    }
    cout << "number of words read = " << numWords << endl;

    return 0;
}
```

This program fragment may seem more complex than the code in *countw2.cc*, Prog. 6.3. This is often the case; using a class can yield code that is lengthier and more verbose than non–class-based code. However, class-based code is often easier to adapt to different situations. Using classes also makes programs easier to develop on more than one computing platform. For example, if there are differences in how text files are read using C++ on different computers, these differences can be encapsulated in classes and made invisible to programmers who can use the classes without knowing the implementation details. This makes the code more portable. The process of developing code in one computing environment and moving it to another is called **porting** the code. The code fragment above contains a `for` loop. Although this is *not* a definite loop (the number of times the loop iterates isn't known beforehand), it is emblematic of `for` loops and is a common C++ idiom. When the `WordStreamIterator` class is used, the member functions `First`, `IsDone`, and `Next` correspond precisely to the three parts of a `for` loop: initialization, test, and update.

In previous uses of classes—for example, the classes `Dice` and `Balloon`—we have not discussed the implementation of the class member functions in detail. We have focused on how to use classes rather than on how to design classes. In general, designing classes and programs is a difficult task. One design rule that helps is based on building new designs on proven designs. This is especially true when a design pattern can be reused. The entire `WordStreamIterator` interface, implementation, and use are combined in Prog. 6.4. In other programs, the interface, or declaration, of a class is put in a header file with a `.h` suffix. The implementation of the class's member functions is put in a corresponding file with a `.cc` suffix. In this case, however, we have included the interface, implementation, and client code that uses the class in a single file. If we decide that the class `WordStreamIterator` is useful, we can separate the class into an interface (`.h` file) and an implementation (`.cc` file) so that other programs can use the class more easily. I've shown the declaration, implementation, and use of the class `WordStreamIterator` in one program, *countw3.cc,* Prog. 6.4. However, to make the class easier to use in other client programs, a header file *worditer.h* is provided with the code for this book. Program 6.7 (*maxword.cc*), examined later, uses the class by including the header file.

Program 6.4	countw3.cc

```
#include <iostream.h>
#include <fstream.h>
#include "CPstring.h"
#include "prompt.h"

// count words in stream bound to text file
// uses a WordStreamIterator class to hide I/O details

class WordStreamIterator
{
  public:

    WordStreamIterator();
    void Open(string name);             // bind stream to specific text file
    void First();                       // initialize iterator
    string Current();                   // returns current word
```

```
    bool IsDone();                          // true if iterator is done
    void Next();                            // advance to next word

  private:

    string myWord;              // the current word
    bool myDone;                // true if no more words
    ifstream myInput;           // the stream to read from
};

WordStreamIterator::WordStreamIterator()
// postcondition: iterator is initialized, IsDone() == true
{
    myWord = "";
    myDone = true;              // First() must be called
}

void WordStreamIterator::Open(string name)
{
    myInput.open(name);
}

void WordStreamIterator::First()
// postcondition: first word read from stream myInput
{
    myInput.seekg(0);                   // back to beginning
    myInput.clear();                    // clear the stream
    myDone = ! (myInput >> myWord);     // read first word, set state
}


string WordStreamIterator::Current()
// precondition: IsDone() == false
// postcondition: returns current word
{
    return myWord;
}

bool WordStreamIterator::IsDone()
// postcondition: returns true if no words left in stream
//          (all words have been read) otherwise returns false
{
    return myDone;
}

void WordStreamIterator::Next()
// precondition: ! IsDone()
// postcondition: next word from stream myInput read
{
    if (! IsDone())
    {
        myDone = ! (myInput >> myWord);
    }
}

int main()
{
```

```
string word;
int numWords = 0;                // initially, no words
WordStreamIterator iter;

iter.Open(PromptString("enter name of file: "));

for(iter.First(); ! iter.IsDone(); iter.Next())
{
    numWords++;
}
cout << "number of words read = " << numWords << endl;

return 0;
}
```

OUTPUT

prompt> *countw3*
enter name of file: *melville.txt*
number of words read = 14353

Remember that the private data variables myWord, myDone, and myInput encapsulate the state of a WordStreamIterator variable. These data are accessible in each member function of the class WordStreamIterator. As in any well-designed class, the state of a class object is accessible only by using public member functions. As a user of the class, you don't need to know details about how a class is implemented although you may have access to state information using member functions (e.g., Dice::NumSides for the Dice class). As an implementor and designer of classes, you do need to know details about the state. In both situations, it is sometimes important to know certain properties that are associated with a class.

In the case of a WordStreamIterator object, you should know that the member function WordStreamIterator::IsDone will return false unless there is no more input to be read from the ifstream variable myInput. When IsDone returns false, accessing the current word using the Current member function is a valid operation; the stream *is not* done. However, if IsDone returns true, accessing the current word is *not* a valid operation; the stream *is* done. Client programs should not access the current word once IsDone returns true.

The constructor WordStreamIterator::WordStreamIterator leaves the object iter in a state where accessing the current word is *not* valid. In this state the function IsDone will return true. You must call the function First to get any words. The call iter.First reads the first word from the input stream and updates the internal state accordingly. Understanding the last statement in the body of WordStreamIterator::First may be tricky. Here it is again:

```
myDone = ! (myInput >> myWord);
```

This statement is equivalent to

```
myInput >> myWord;
if (myInput.fail())              // extraction failed?
{
    myDone = true;
}
else
{
    myDone = false;
}
```

Extracting a word from `myInput` and storing the word in `myWord` using the extraction operator, `>>`, succeeds unless there are no more words to extract. When there are no more words, the extraction fails, and the expression `(myInput >> word)` has a boolean value of `false`. As long as the extraction succeeds, `myDone` should be `false` to indicate that a word can be examined using the member function `WordStreamIterator::Current`. The unary boolean operator `!` (sometimes pronounced "not") negates the expression so that `myWord` will be false when the extraction succeeds.

The first two statements in `WordStreamIterator::First` reset the stream to the beginning so that the stream can be read more than once. We'll discuss stream functions in more detail in Chap. 9. You don't need to understand the statements; it's enough to know that `First` can be used to reread an input stream from the beginning.

I/O Redirection

UNIX and MS-DOS/Windows machines provide a useful facility for permitting programs that read from the standard input stream, `cin`, to read from files. As we've seen, it's possible to use the class `ifstream` to do this. However, we often use programs written to read from the keyboard and use the stream `cin` to read from files instead. You can use **input redirection** to do this. When you run a program that reads from `cin`, the input can be specified to come from a text file using the symbol < and the name of the text file. Running Prog. 6.2, *countw.cc*, as shown in the following, indicates how input redirection works.

OUTPUT

```
prompt> countw < melville.txt
number of words read = 14353

prompt> countw < hamlet.txt
number of words read = 31956
```

The less-than sign, <, causes the program on the left of the sign (in this case, *countw*) to take its `cin` input from the text file specified on the right of the < sign. The operating system that runs the program recognizes when the text file has "ended" and signals end of file to the program *countw*. This means that no special end-of-file character is stored in the files. Rather, end of file is a state detected by the system running the program.

It is possible to run the word-counting program on its own source code and on a chapter of this book.

OUTPUT

```
prompt> countw < countw.cc
number of words read = 49
prompt> countw < chapter2.tex
number of words read = 24148
```

Among the *words* of Prog. 6.2, *countw.cc*, are `main()`, `{`, `(cin`, and `endl;`. You should examine the program to see if you can determine why these are considered words.

6.3   Finding Extreme Values

> We ascribe beauty to that which is simple,
> which has no superfluous parts;
> which exactly answers its end,
> which stands related to all things,
> which is the mean of many extremes.
> RALPH WALDO EMERSON
> *The Conduct of Life*

The maximum and minimum values in a set of data are sometimes called **extreme** values. In this section we'll examine code to find the maximum (or minimum) values in a set of data. For example, instead of just counting the number of words in Shakespeare's *Hamlet* we might like to know what word occurs most often. Using the `WordStreamIterator` class we can do so, although the program is very slow. Later in the chapter I will introduce a mechanism for speeding up the program. As a preliminary step, we'll look at *mindata.cc*, Prog. 6.5, designed to find the minimum of all numbers in the standard input stream.

The `if` statement compares the value of the number just read with the current minimum value. A new value is assigned to `minimum` only when the newly read number is smaller. However, Prog. 6.5 does not always work as intended, as you may be able to see from the second run of the program. Using the second run, you may reason about a mistake in the program: the variable `minimum` is initialized incorrectly. You may wonder about what happens when the string `"apple"` is entered when a number is expected. As you can see from the output, the program only counts four numbers as read in the second run.

The operator `>>` fails when you attempt to extract an integer but enter a noninteger value such as `"apple"`. The operator `>>` fails in the following situations:

1.   There is no more data to be read (extracted) from the input stream; i.e., all input has been processed.

2.   There was never any data because the input stream was not bound to any file. This can happen when an `ifstream` object is constructed and initialized with the name of a file that doesn't exist or isn't accessible.

3.   The data to be read is not of the correct type, e.g., attempting to read the string `"apple"` into an integer variable.

Program 6.5   mindata.cc

```
#include <iostream.h>

    // determine minimum of all numbers in input stream

int main()
{
    int numNums = 0;                    // initially, no numbers
    int minimum = 0;                    // tentative minimal value is 0

    int number;
    while (cin >> number)
    {
        numNums++;
        if (number < minimum)
        {
            minimum = number;
        }
    }

    cout << "number of numbers = " << numNums << endl;
    cout << "minimal number is " << minimum << endl;
    return 0;
}
```

OUTPUT

```
prompt> mindata
-3 5 2 135 -33 14 3
199 257 -582 9392 78
number of numbers = 19
minimal number is -582

prompt> mindata
20 30 40 50 apple 60 70
number of numbers = 4
minimal number is 0
```

There are two methods for fixing the program so that it will work regardless of what integer values are entered.

■ Initialize `minimum` to "infinity" so the first time the `if` statement is executed the entered value will be less than `minimum`.

■ Initialize `minimum` to the first value entered on the input stream.

We'll elaborate on each of these approaches in turn. The problem with the method used in *mindata.cc* is that the test in the `if` statement will never be true if the user enters only positive numbers.

Largest/Smallest Values

To implement the first approach we'll take advantage of the existence of a largest integer in C++. Since integers (and other types such as `double`) are stored in a computer using a fixed amount of memory, there cannot be arbitrarily large or small values. In the standard system file `<limits.h>`, several useful constants are defined:

```
INT_MAX    INT_MIN    LONG_MAX    LONG_MIN
```

These constants represent, respectively, the largest and smallest `int` values and the largest and smallest `long int` values. Using these constants we can initialize `minimum` from Prog. 6.5 as

```
#include <iostream.h>
#include <limits.h>

    // determine minimum of all numbers in input stream

int main()
{
    int numNums = 0;        // initially, no numbers
    int minimum = INT_MAX; // all values less than this
}
```

The program finds the correct minimum because the `if` test evaluates to true the first time, since any integer value is less than or equal to `INT_MAX`. However, if only values of `INT_MAX` are encountered, the test of the `if` statement will never be true. In this case the program still finds the correct minimum of `INT_MAX`.

Similar constants exist for `double` values; these are accessed by including `<float.h>`. The largest and smallest `double` values are represented by the constants `DBL_MIN` and `DBL_MAX`, respectively.

Initialization: Another Fence Post Problem

Implementing the second approach to the extreme value problem—using the first item read as the initial value for `minimum`—is a typical fence post problem. An item must be read before the loop to initialize `minimum`. Items must continue to be read within the loop. In developing code for this approach, we

---

Program 6.6   mindata2.cc

```
#include <iostream.h>

    // determine minimum of all numbers in input stream
    // illustrates fence post problem: first item is
    // minimum initialization

int main()
{
    int numNums = 0;            // initially, no numbers
    int minimum;                // smallest number entered
    int number;                 // user entered number

    if (cin >> number)          // read in first value
    {
        minimum = number;       // to initialize minimum
        numNums++;
    }
        // read in any remaining values

    while (cin >> number)
    {
        numNums++;
        if (number < minimum)
        {
            minimum = number;
        }
    }

    if (numNums > 0)
    {
        cout << "number of numbers = " << numNums << endl;
        cout << "minimal number is " << minimum << endl;
    }
    else
    {
        cout << "no numbers entered, no minimum found"
            << endl;
    }
    return 0;
}
```

mindata2.cc

---

must decide what to do if no items are entered. What is the minimum of no values? Perhaps the safest approach is to print an error message as shown in Prog. 6.6.

The input statement `cin >> number` is the test of the `if` statement. It ensures that a number has been read. Another approach to using the first number read as the initial value of `minimum` uses an `if` statement in the body of the `while` loop to differentiate between the first number and all other numbers. The value of numNums can be used for this purpose.

```
while (cin >> number)
{
    numNums++;
    if (numNums == 1 || number < minimum)
    {
        minimum = number;
    }
}
```

Many people prefer the first approach because it avoids an extra check in the body of the `while` loop. The check `numNums == 1` is true only once, but it is checked every time through the loop. In general, you should prefer an approach that does not check a special case over and over when the special case can only occur once. On the other hand, the check in the loop body results in shorter code because there is no need to read an initial value for `minimum`. Since code isn't duplicated (before the loop and in the loop), there is less of a maintenance problem because code won't have to be changed in two places. The extra check in the loop body may result in slightly slower code, but unless you have determined that this is a time-critical part of a program, ease of code maintenance should probably be of greater concern than a very small gain in efficiency. There is no single rule you can use to determine which is the best method. As with many problems the best method depends on the exact nature of the problem.

Word Frequencies

We can use the method of finding extreme values from *mindata.cc,* Prog. 6.5, and the `WordStreamIterator` class to find the word that occurs most often in a text file. The idea is to read one word at a time using a `WordStreamIterator` object and to use another iterator to read the entire text file from beginning to end counting how many times the given word occurs. This is shown in Prog. 6.7. Using nested iterators in this way results in a very slow program, since if there are 2000 words in a file, the file will be read 2000 times. We have redundancy because we don't have the programming tools to keep track of whether a word has already been counted; thus we may count how many times *the* occurs over 100 times, for example.

Program 6.7   maxword.cc

```
#include <iostream.h>
#include "worditer.h"
#include "CPstring.h"
#include "prompt.h"

// illustrates nested loops using WordStreamIterator class
// to find the word that occurs most often in a file
//
```

```
// Owen Astrachan
// 2/13/96

int main()
{
    int max = 0;
    string word,maxWord;
    string filename = PromptString("enter file name: ");
    WordStreamIterator outer,inner;

    outer.Open(filename);          // open two iterators
    inner.Open(filename);

    for(outer.First(); ! outer.IsDone(); outer.Next())
    {
        word = outer.Current();    // current word for comparison
        int count = 0;             // count # occurrences

        for(inner.First(); ! inner.IsDone(); inner.Next())
        {
            if (inner.Current() == word)   // found another occurrence
            {
                count++;
            }
        }
        if (count > max)                       // maximal so far
        {
            max = count;
            maxWord = word;
        }
    }
    cout << "word \"" << maxWord << "\" occurs " << max
         << " times" << endl;
    return 0;
}
```

OUTPUT

```
prompt> maxword
enter file name: poe.txt
word "the" occurs 149 times
```

The outer loop, using the iterator `outer`, processes each word from a text file one at a time. The inner loop reads the entire file, counting how many times `word` occurs in the file. Since each object has its own state, the iterator `outer` keeps track of where it is in the input stream, even as the iterator `inner` reads the entire stream from beginning to end.

*Pause to
reflect*

6.5. If *mindata.cc*, Prog. 6.5, is modified so that it reads floating-point numbers (of type `double`) instead of integers, which variables' types change? What other changes are necessary?

6.6. What happens if each of the following statements is used to calculate the average of the values entered in Prog. 6.3? Why?

```
cout << "average word length = "
     << (double) sum/numWords << endl;
cout << "average word length = "
     << (double sum/numWords) << endl;
```

6.7. Write and run a small program to output the largest and smallest integer values on your system.

6.8. Modify *mindata.cc*, Prog. 6.5, and *mindata2.cc*, Prog. 6.6, to calculate the maximum of all values read.

6.9. According to *countw2.cc*, Prog. 6.3, *Hamlet* has 31,956 words and an average word length of 4.362 characters. If a computer can read 200,000 characters per second, provide a rough but reasoned estimate of how long it will take *maxword.cc* to find the word in *Hamlet* that occurs most often.

6.4   Reference Parameters and Class Design

We're now able to calculate the number of words and the average word length in a text file. However, these statistics are not sufficient as a literary fingerprint, a statistic that we aimed to calculate at the beginning of this chapter. We'd like to extend the methods used in *countw2.cc*, Prog. 6.3, to calculate more information about the words in a file, for example, how many small, medium, and large words there are. Unfortunately, all the code in *countw2.cc* is in the function `main`. The use of more than one function in earlier programs helped to simplify program development and enabled sections of code to be used more easily in other contexts. Using more than one function in Prog. 6.3 is difficult, however, because two quantities are computed from the input data: the number of words and the average length of the words. Since functions can return only one value, we're stuck.

We'll discuss two ways of solving this problem, one based on developing a class to calculate literary fingerprints and one that doesn't use a class but uses parameters to pass values back from a function. As a starting point we'll count the number of short, medium, and long words in a file. These three quantities will constitute a kind of "author fingerprint" that might be used to identify certain authors (perhaps Mark Twain used more short words than Herman Melville). Arbitrarily we'll define a short word to have fewer than four letters and a long word to have more than seven letters. We'll develop a program in which changing these values is straightforward.

A Class Solution

We want to calculate the statistics for a text file in one function, but print the statistics in a different function. In general it's a good idea to design functions for a single purpose and not to combine calculation with output. We saw this in early programs with the input/process/output model of computation. It's also a good idea to keep computation out of `main` when possible. Keeping functions simple and single-purposed makes them easier to debug and makes the functions more usable in other contexts. This principle extends beyond programming. Although millions of televisions and VCRs are sold every year, several electronic companies have been unsuccessful in marketing televisions combined with VCRs. What happens, for example, if the VCR breaks? What happens if you want to buy a bigger television but continue to use the VCR? In this case, single-purpose devices are more useful. The same is often true of functions and classes.

We'd like the body of `main` to be something similar to the following fragment.

```
int main();
{
    string filename = PromptString("enter filename: ");
    Calculate(filename);
    PrintStats();
    return 0;
}
```

Obviously this will not work since there is no way for the function `Calculate` to communicate the statistics to `PrintStats` for printing.[6]

Instead, we can make `Calculate` and `PrintStats` member functions of a class. Since all member functions have access to private data, the private data can be assigned values in `Calculate`, which are then printed in `PrintStats`. This also makes it easier to change what kind of statistics are calculated. The member functions are changed, but `main` and the client program are not. A class-based solution is shown in *cfingerp.cc*, Prog. 6.8. Three private `int` fields are used as counters for the number of small, medium, and large words. These data fields are initialized to zero in the constructor and also in the member function `Calculate`. A text file is read in `Calculate`, and the data fields are used to store counts of different word lengths. The function `PrintStats` prints the values and the percentage of the total for each word length.

One disadvantage of the solution using the class `FingerPrint` in *cfingerp.cc* is that client programs cannot access the statistics; they can only print them. Although it's possible to supply member functions `GetSmall`, `GetMedium`, and `GetLarge` to return the number of small, medium, and large words, respectively, this approach is cumbersome and difficult to extend when different statistics are calculated. Instead, we'll use parameters to pass values back from functions.

---

[6]Actually, it's possible to define **global** variables at the beginning of the file and access these variables in every function. It is bad programming practice to use global variables, so we won't take this approach.

Program 6.8   cfingerp.cc

```cpp
#include <iostream.h>
#include <fstream.h>
#include "CPstring.h"
#include "worditer.h"
#include "prompt.h"

// compute authorship fingerprint using a class
// 6/28/96
// author: Owen Astrachan

class FingerPrint
{
  public:
    FingerPrint();                        // constructor
    void Calculate(string filename);      // calculate stats for text file
    void PrintStats();                    // print statistics

  private:
    int mySmall;               // store counters
    int myMedium;              // for different word lengths
    int myLarge;
};

FingerPrint::FingerPrint()
// postcondition: all fields initialized
{
    mySmall = myMedium = myLarge = 0;
}

void FingerPrint::PrintStats()
// postcondition: statistics printed
{
    int total = mySmall + myMedium + myLarge;

    cout << "\t # of small words = \t" << mySmall;
    cout << " =\t" << double(mySmall)*100/total << "%"
        << endl;

    cout << "\t # of medium words = \t" << myMedium;
    cout << " =\t" << double(myMedium)*100/total << "%"
        << endl;

    cout << "\t # of large words = \t" << myLarge;
    cout << " =\t" << double(myLarge)*100/total << "%"
        << endl;
}
```

```
void FingerPrint::Calculate(string filename)
// precondition: filename = name of file that can be opened
//                for reading
// postcondition: statistics have been calculated
{

    const int SMALL_SIZE = 4;        // mySmall words < this many letters
    const int LARGE_SIZE = 7;        // myLarge words > this many letters

    WordStreamIterator wstream;
    wstream.Open(filename);

    mySmall = myMedium = myLarge = 0;              // initialize counters
    for(wstream.First(); ! wstream.IsDone(); wstream.Next())
    {
        if (wstream.Current().length() < SMALL_SIZE)
            mySmall++;
        else if (wstream.Current().length() > LARGE_SIZE)
            myLarge++;
        else
            myMedium++;
    }
}

int main()
{
    string filename = PromptString("enter name of file: ");
    FingerPrint finger;

    finger.Calculate(filename);
    finger.PrintStats();

    return 0;
}
```

OUTPUT

```
prompt> cfingerp
enter name of file: romeo.txt
        # of small words =     9671 =  37.5019%
        # of medium words =   14042 = 54.4517%
        # of large words =     2075 =  8.04638%
```

Reference Parameters

Rather than adding a member function GetStatistics to the class FingerPrint from *cfingerp.cc*, Prog. 6.8, we'll develop a related program that doesn't use a class. In the exercises we'll explore ways to combine these two approaches. We'll write a function FingerPrint to compute the three-value fingerprint of some text file whose name is specified by a `string` parameter passed to the function. The three counters for the number of small, medium, and large words will be passed back from the function `FingerPrint`. In the header of `FingerPrint` in Prog. 6.9, *fingerp.cc,* note that these three parameters are preceded by an ampersand, `&`. Using an ampersand permits values to be passed back from the function to the calling statement. We'll discuss this form of parameter shortly.

Program 6.9   fingerp.cc

```cpp
#include <iostream.h>
#include <fstream.h>
#include "CPstring.h"
#include "worditer.h"
#include "prompt.h"

// compute authorship fingerprint for a sequence of
// files specified by the user
// author: Owen Astrachan, June 15, 1994, modified 6/28/96

const int SMALL_SIZE = 4;    // small words < this many letters
const int LARGE_SIZE = 7;    // large words > this many letters
                             // so SMALL <= medium <= LARGE

const string FILE_SENTINEL = "none";
// string for no more files to process

 // function prototype(s)

void FingerPrint(string filename, int & small, int & medium,
                 int & large);
void Output(string label, int amount, int total);

int main()
{
    string filename;
    int smallCount,mediumCount,largeCount,total;

    while ((filename = PromptString("enter name of file (\""
                    + FILE_SENTINEL + "\" to exit): "))
          != FILE_SENTINEL)
    {
        FingerPrint(filename,smallCount,mediumCount,largeCount);
        total = smallCount + mediumCount + largeCount;

        cout << "data for " << filename << endl;
        Output("small",  smallCount,  total);
        Output("medium", mediumCount, total);
        Output("large",  largeCount,  total);
    }
    return 0;
}
```

```
void FingerPrint(string filename, int & small, int & medium,
                 int & large)
// precondition: filename = name of file that can be opened
//               for reading
// postcondition: small  = # of words of length < SMALL_SIZE
//                medium = # of medium length words
//                large  = # of words of length > LARGE_SIZE
{
    WordStreamIterator wstream;
    wstream.Open(filename);

    small = medium = large = 0;      // initialize counters
    for(wstream.First(); ! wstream.IsDone(); wstream.Next())
    {
        if (wstream.Current().length() < SMALL_SIZE)
        {
            small++;
        }
        else if (wstream.Current().length() > LARGE_SIZE)
        {
            large++;
        }
        else
        {
            medium++;
        }
    }
}

void Output(string label,int amount, int total)
// precondition: total != 0
// postcondition: prints amount, and amount/total nicely
//                formatted
{
    cout << "\t # of " << label << " words = \t" << amount;
    cout << " =\t" << double(amount)*100/total << "%"
        << endl;
}
```

OUTPUT

```
prompt> fingerp
enter name of file ("none" to exit): romeo.txt
data for romeo.txt
        # of small words =     9671 =  37.5019%
        # of medium words =   14042 = 54.4517%
        # of large words =     2075 =  8.04638%
enter name of file ("none" to exit): macbeth.txt
data for macbeth.txt
        # of small words =     6586 =  36.1233%
        # of medium words =    9519 = 52.2104%
        # of large words =     2127 =  11.6663%
```

```
enter name of file ("none" to exit): tempest.txt
data for tempest.txt
          # of small words  =    6428  =   36.9128%
          # of medium words =    8755  =   50.2756%
          # of large words  =    2231  =   12.8115%
enter name of file ("none" to exit): none
```

Although this is only a rudimentary fingerprint, the percentage of small words seems to be consistent across the three Shakespeare plays. However, we would need to gather more statistics before making any conclusions from these data. Note that the function Output is used to isolate formatting details. If the output format changes, it will be easier to make the changes in one place than if the output statements were included in main.

The first parameter of the function FingerPrint represents the name of the file from which data are read. This value is passed into the function. The other parameters are used to pass values back from the function FingerPrint to the statement calling the function. These last three parameters are **reference** parameters; the ampersand appearing between the type and name of the parameter indicates a reference parameter. The diagram in Fig. 6.2 shows how information flows between FingerPrint and the statement that calls FingerPrint from main. The ampersand modifier used for the last three parameters in the prototype of FingerPrint makes these references to integers rather than integers. We'll elaborate on this distinction, but a reference is used as an alias to refer to a variable that has already been defined. The memory for a reference parameter is defined somewhere else, whereas the memory for a nonreference parameter, also called a **value** parameter, is allocated in the function.

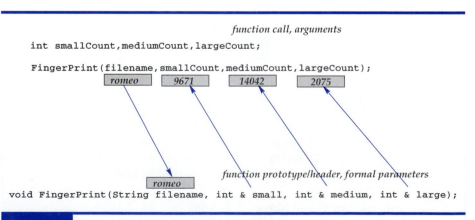

Figure 6.2   Value and reference parameters.

The value of `filename` (*romeo*, in the figure) is copied from `main` into the memory location associated with the parameter `filename` in `FingerPrint`. Once the value is copied, the variable `fileName` defined in `main` and the parameter `filename` in `FingerPrint` are not connected or related in any way. For example, if the value of `filename` in `FingerPrint` is changed, the value of `filename` in `main` is *not* affected. This is very different from the way reference parameters work. As indicated in Fig. 6.2, the storage for the last three arguments in the function call is referenced, or referred to, by the corresponding parameters in `FingerPrint`. For example, the variable `smallCount` defined in `main` is referred to by the name `small` within the function `FingerPrint`. When one storage location (in this case, defined in `main`) has two different names, the term **aliasing** is sometimes used. Whatever happens to `small` in `FingerPrint` is really happening to the variable `smallCount` defined in `main` since `small` refers to `smallCount`. This means that if the statement `small++;` assigns 3 to `small` in `FingerPrint`, the value is actually stored in the memory location allocated in `main` and referred to by the name `smallCount` in `main`. Rich Pattis, author of *Get A-Life: Advice for the Beginning C++ Object-Oriented Programmer* [Pat96] calls reference parameters "voodoo doll" parameters: if you "stick" `small` in `FingerPrint`, the object `smallCount` in `main` yells "ouch."

One key to understanding the difference between the two kinds of parameters is to remember where the storage is allocated. For reference parameters, the storage is allocated somewhere else, and the name of the parameter refers back to this storage. For value parameters, the storage is allocated in the function, and a value is copied into this storage location. This is diagrammed by the leftmost arrow in Fig. 6.2. When reference parameters are used, memory is allocated for the arguments, and the formal parameters are merely new names (used within the called function) for the memory locations associated with the arguments. This is shown in Fig. 6.2 by the arrows that point "up" from the identifiers `small`, `medium`, and `large` that serve as aliases for the memory locations allocated for the variables `smallCount`, `mediumCount`, and `largeCount`.

Program 6.10 and its output show how value and reference parameters work. The value assigned to `number` within the function `DoStuff` does *not* affect the value of the argument `num`. The same does not hold for the reference parameter `word`; the changed value does change the value of the argument `name`.

Program 6.10 pbyvalue.cc

```
#include <iostream.h>
#include "CPstring.h"

// illustrates pass-by-value/pass-by-reference semantics

void
DoStuff(int number, string & word)
```

```
{
    cout << "entering DoStuff " << number << " " << word << endl;
    number *= 2;
    word = "What's up Doc?";

    cout << "exiting DoStuff " << number << " " << word << endl;
}

int main()
{
    int num = 30;
    string name = "Bugs Bunny";

    DoStuff(num,name);
    cout << "end of program " << num << " " << name << endl;
    return 0;
}
```

OUTPUT

```
prompt> pbyvalue
entering DoStuff 30 Bugs Bunny
exiting DoStuff 60 What's up Doc?
end of program 30 What's up Doc?
```

The first line of output prints the values that are passed into `DoStuff`. The value of the parameter `number` in `DoStuff` is the same as the value of `num` in `main` since this value is copied when the argument is passed into the memory location in `DoStuff`. Once the value is copied, there is no relationship between `number` and `num`. This can be seen in the last line of output: `num` is still 30. However, the change to parameter `word` does change `name`; this can be seen in the last line of the output. Values are *not* copied when passed by reference. The identifiers `word` and `name` are aliases for the same memory location.

When a function is called and an argument passed to a reference parameter, the term **call by reference** is used. When an argument is copied into a function's parameter, the term **call by value** is used. Value parameters require time to copy the value and require memory to store the copied value. The time and space used by value parameters can impact a program's performance. Sometimes reference parameters are used to save time and space. Unfortunately, this permits the called function to change the value of the argument—this is the very reason we used reference parameters in Prog. 6.9. You can protect against unwanted change and still have the efficiency of reference parameters when needed. We'll explore this in more depth in Sec. 6.4.

Some programmers use reference parameters only with `void` functions. Functions that modify parameters in addition to returning values can be confusing. The extraction operator is an example of such a function. Extraction has two effects: a value is extracted from an input stream, and the success of the extraction is returned. Because of this we can write loops to extract all numbers in a stream:

```
while (cin >> number) { // process all numbers }
```

Functions or operators that modify parameters and return values have **side effects.** A side effect is an effect that is not the main purpose of a function or is not discernible from the function prototype. Presumably, the main purpose of extraction is to remove an item from an input stream. As a side effect, the success of the extraction (the state of the stream) is returned. Modifying a global variable is another kind of side effect since the modification cannot be determined by examining the function call or prototype. Function side effects are sometimes necessary and should be well documented.

6.10. Suppose that the code in `main` from *mindata.cc,* Prog. 6.5, is moved to a function named `ReadNums` so that the new body of `main` is

*Pause to
reflect*

```
{
    ....
    ReadNums(numNums,minimum);
    cout << "number of numbers = " << numNums << endl;
    cout << "minimal number is " << minimum << endl;
}
```

What is the function header and body of `ReadNums`? How would the function header and body change if only the average of the numbers read is to be returned?

6.11. What is the function header and body of a function `GetName` that prompts for a first and last name and returns two strings, one representing each name?

6.12. Suppose `FingerPrint` in *fingerp.cc,* Prog. 6.9, is modified to calculate the average word length of all the words in a file. How would the function header change? How would the body of the function change?

6.13. Write a function `Roots` having the following function header

```
void
Roots(double a, double b, double c,
      double & root1, double & root2)
// precondition:   a,b,c coefficients of
//                  ax^2 + bx + c
// postcondition:  sets root1 and root2 to roots
//                  of quadratic
```

that uses the quadratic formula,

$$\frac{-b \pm \sqrt{b^2 - 4ac}}{2a}$$

to find the roots of a quadratic. The call `Roots(1,5,6,r1,r2)` would result in r1 and r2 being set to −2 and −3. You'll have to decide what to do if there are no real roots.

6.14. Suppose that a function `Mystery` has only value parameters. What is printed by the following statements? Why?

```
int num = 3;
double top = 4.5;
Mystery(num,top);
cout << num << " " << top << endl;
```

6.15. Two formal parameters can alias the same argument. Explain why 20 is printed by the code fragment below and determine what is printed if `num` is initialized to 3 rather than 8.

```
void Change(int & first, int & second)
{
    first += 2;
    second *= 2;
}

main()
{
    int num = 8;
    Change(num,num);
    cout << num << endl;
}
```

6.16. Strings can be compared alphabetically (also called *lexicographically*) using the operators $<$ and $>$ so that `"apple"` $<$ `"bat"` and `"cabinet"` $>$ `"cabbage"`. What is the function header and body of a function that exhaustively reads input and returns the alphabetically first and last word read?

6.17. It is often necessary to interchange, or swap, the values of two variables. For example, if $a = 5$ and $b = 7$, then swapping values would result in $a = 7$ and $b = 5$. Write the body of the function `Swap` (*Hint:* You'll need to define a variable of type `int`).

```
void Swap(int & a, int & b)
// postcondition: interchanges values of a and b
```

const **Reference Parameters**

Value parameters are copied from the corresponding argument, as shown in *pbyvalue.cc*, Prog. 6.10. For parameters that require a large amount of memory, making the copy takes time (to make the copy) in addition to the memory used for the copy. In contrast, reference parameters are not copied, and thus no extra memory is required and less time is used.

Some programs must make efficient use of time and memory space. Value parameters for large objects are problematic in such programs. Some programmers pass larger objects by reference to be efficient when necessary. However, reference parameters can be used to change the argument passed since the parameter is merely an alias for the memory associated with the argument. Fortunately, C++ has a mechanism that combines the efficiency of

---

Program 6.11   constref.cc

```
#include <iostream.h>
#include "CPstring.h"
#include "prompt.h"

// illustrates const reference parameters
// Owen Astrachan, 7/11/96

void Print(const string & word);

int main()
{
    string word = PromptString("enter a word: ");

    Print("hello world");
    Print(word);
    Print(word + " " + word);

    return 0;
}

void Print(const string & word)
{
    cout << "printing: " << word << endl;
}
```

OUTPUT

```
prompt> constref
enter a word: salacious
printing: hello world
printing: salacious
printing: salacious salacious
```

---

reference parameters with the safety of value parameters.[7] A **constant reference** parameter, often abbreviated as const **reference** parameter, achieves this dual goal of efficiency and safety. A const reference parameter is defined using the const modifier in conjunction with an ampersand as shown in *constref.cc*, Prog. 6.11. Const reference parameters are also called **read-only** parameters.

The parameter word in Print is a const reference parameter. The use of const prevents the code in Print from "accidentally" modifying the value of

---

[7]"Safety" means that it's not possible to change a value parameter so that the argument is also changed. The argument is protected from accidental or malicious changing.

the argument corresponding to word. For example, adding the statement word = "hello" just before the output statement generates the following error message when the g++ compiler is used:

```
constref.cc: In function 'void Print(const class string &)':
constref.cc:23: no matching function for call to 'string::operator = (char[6]) const'
CPstring.h:119: candidates are: string::operator =(const string &)
CPstring.h:118:                   string::operator =(const char *)
*** Error code 1
make: Fatal error: Command failed for target 'constref'
```

In addition, const reference parameters allow literals and expressions to be passed as arguments. In *constref.cc*, the first call of Print passes the literal "hello world", and the third call passes the expression word + " " + word. Literals and expressions can be arguments passed to value parameters since the value parameter provides the memory. However, literals and expressions cannot be passed to reference parameters since there is no memory associated with either a literal or an expression. Fortunately, the C++ compiler will generate a temporary variable for literals and expressions when a const reference parameter is used. If the const modifier is removed from Print in *constref.cc*, the g++ compiler issues a warning:

```
constref.cc: In function 'int main()':
constref.cc:14: warning: initializing non-const 'string &' with 'char *' will use a temporary
constref.cc:8: warning: in passing argument 1 of 'Print(string &)'
...
```

Some compilers will fail to compile *constref.cc* rather than issue a warning.

> **Program Tip: As a general rule, parameters of programmer-defined classes like** string **should be** const **reference parameters rather than value parameters.** Don't worry about adhering to this guideline at all times; some functions require a copy rather than a safe and efficient reference parameter (although such functions are rare). There is no reason to worry about this kind of efficiency for built-in types like int and double; these use relatively little memory, so that a copy takes no more time to create than a reference does and no temporary variables are needed when literals and expressions are passed as arguments.

For some classes a specific function is needed to create a copy. If a class does not supply such a "copy-making" function—actually a special kind of constructor called a **copy constructor**—one will be generated by the compiler. This default copy constructor may not behave properly in certain situations we'll discuss at length later. A brief discussion of copy constructors can be found in Sec. 7.6.

6.5   Chapter Review

In this chapter we studied several data sources that support a pattern of iteration using functions First, IsDone, and Next. Sources of data include ifstream variables: streams bound to files stored on disks. Using classes to process data isn't always the best choice; sometimes a program that doesn't use classes is shorter. However, the idiom of using a class and the three iteration functions can make it easier to develop other programs that iterate over different kinds of data.

Important topics covered include the following.

- Programs are best designed in an iterative manner, ideally by developing a working program and adding pieces to it so that the program is always functional to some degree. Writing pseudocode first is often a good way of starting the process of program development.

- The extraction operator, >>, uses white space to delimit, or separate, one string from another.

- In sentinel loops, the sentinel value is *not* considered part of the data.

- The extraction operator returns a value that can be tested in a loop to see whether the extraction succeeds, so while (cin >> word) is a standard idiom for reading streams until there is no more data (or until the extraction fails). The stream member function fail can be used too.

- Files can be associated with streams using ifstream variables. The extraction operator works with these streams. The ifstream member function open is used to bind a named disk file to a file stream. An ofstream variable is used to associate an output file stream with a named disk file.

- If you enter a nonnumeric value when a numeric value (e.g., an int or a double) is expected, the extraction will fail and the nonnumeric character remains unprocessed on the input stream.

- Types sometimes need to be cast, or changed, to another type. Casting often causes values to change; e.g., when casting from a double to an int, truncation occurs. A new cast operator, static_cast, should be used if your compiler supports it.

- Constants for the largest int and double values are accessible and can be found in the header files <limits.h> and <float.h>, respectively. The constants defining system extreme values are INT_MAX, INT_MIN, LONG_MAX, LONG_MIN, DBL_MAX, and DBL_MIN.

- Finding extreme (highest and lowest) values is a typical fence post problem. Initializing with the first value is usually a good approach, but sometimes a value of "infinity" is available for initialization (e.g., INT_MAX).

- Parameters are passed by value (a copy is made) unless an ampersand, &, is used for pass by reference. In this case the formal parameter identifier is an alias for the memory associated with the associated function argument.

- A variable is **defined** when storage is allocated. A variable is **declared** if no storage is allocated, but the variable's type is associated with the variable's identifier.

- Parameters for programmer-defined classes are often declared as const reference parameters to save time and space while ensuring safety.

6.6 Exercises

6.1 Create a data file in the format

```
firstname lastname testscore
firstname lastname testscore
```

where the first two entries on a line are `string` values and the last entry is an `int` test score in the range 0–100. For example:

```
Owen Astrachan 95
Dave Reed 56
Steve Tate 99
Dave Reed 77
Steve Tate 92
Owen Astrachan 88
Mike Clancy 100
Mike Clancy 95
Dave Reed 47
```

Write a program that prompts for a name and then reads the text file and computes and outputs the average test score for the person whose name is entered. Use the following `while` statement to read entries from an `ifstream` variable `input`.

```
string first, last;
int score;
while (input >> first >> last >> score)
{
    // read one line, process it
}
```

6.2 Create a data file where each line has the format

```
item size retail-price-sold-for
```

For example, a file might contain information from a clothing store (prices aren't meant to be realistic):

```
coat small 110.00
coat large 130.00
shirt medium 22.00
dress tiny 49.00
pants large 78.50
coat large 140.00
```

Write a program that prompts the user for the name of a data file and then prompts for the name of an item, the size of the item, and the wholesale price paid for the item. The program should generate several statistics as output:

- Average retail price paid for the item
- Total profit made for selling the item

- Percentage of all sales accounted for by the specified item and size, both by price and by units sold

- Percentage of all item sales, where the item is the same as specified, both by price and by units sold

For example, in the data file above, if the wholesale price of a large coat is $100.00, then the output should include

- Average retail price for large coats is $135.00.

- Total profit is $70.00.

- Percentage of all sales is one-third (2 out of 6).

- Percentage of all coat sales is two-thirds (2 out of 3).

6.3 Write a program based on the word game *Madlibs*. The input to Madlibs is a vignette or brief story, with words left out. Players are asked to fill in missing words by prompting for adjectives, nouns, verbs, and so on. When these words are used to replace the missing words, the resulting story is often funny when read aloud.

In the computerized version of the game, the input will be a text file with certain words annotated by enclosing the words in brackets. These enclosed words will be replaced after prompting the user for a replacement. All words are written to another text file (use an `ofstream` variable).[8] Since words will be read and written one at a time, you'll need to keep track of the number of characters written to the output file so that you can use an `endl` to finish off, or flush, lines in the output file. For example, in the sample run below, output lines are flushed using `endl` after writing 50 characters (the number of characters can be accumulated using the `string` member function `length`.)

The output below is based on an excerpt from *Romeo and Juliet* annotated for the game. Punctuation must be separated from words that are annotated so that the brackets can be recognized (using `substr`). Alternatively, you could search for brackets using `find` and maintain the punctuation.

The text file `mad.in` is

```
But soft! What [noun] through yonder window [verb] ?
It is the [noun] , and [name] is the [noun] !
Arise, [adjective] [noun] , and [verb] the [adjective] [noun] ,
Who is already [adjective] and [another_adjective] with [emotion]
```

The output is shown on the next page. Because we don't have the programming tools to read lines from files, the lines in the output aren't the same as the lines in the input. In the following run, the output file created is reread to show the user the results.

---

[8] You may need to call the member function `close` on the `ofstream` object. If the output file is truncated so that not all data is written, call `close` when the program has finished writing to the stream.

OUTPUT

```
prompt> madlibs
enter madlibs file: mad.in
name for output file: mad.out
enter noun: fish
enter verb: jumps
enter noun: computer
enter name: Susan
enter noun: porcupine
enter adjective: wonderful
enter noun: book
enter verb: run
enter adjective: lazy
enter noun: carwash
enter adjective: creative
enter another_adjective: pretty
enter emotion: anger
But soft! What fish through yonder window jumps ? It is the computer
, and Susan is the porcupine ! Arise, wonderful book , and run the
lazy carwash , Who is already creative and pretty with anger
```

6.4 Write a program to compute the average of all the numbers stored in a text file. Assume the numbers are integers representing test scores, for example:

```
70 85 90
92 57 100 88
87 98
```

First use the extraction operator, `>>`. Then use a `WordStreamIterator` object. Since `WordStreamIterator::Current` returns a string, you'll need to convert the string to the corresponding integer; i.e., the `string` `"123"` should be converted to the `int` 123. The function `atoi` in `"CPstring.h"` will convert the string.

```
int atoi(string s)
// precondition: s represents an int, e.g., "123", "-457", etc.
// postcondition: returns int equivalent of s
//              returns 0 if s isn't a properly formatted int (e.g., "12a3")
```

6.5 The **standard deviation** of a group of numbers is a statistical measure of how much the numbers spread out from the average (the average is also called the *mean*). A low standard deviation means most of the numbers are near the mean. If numbers are denoted as $(x_1, x_2, x_3, \ldots, x_n)$, then the mean is denoted as $\bar{x}$. The standard deviation is the square root of the **variance**. (The standard deviation is usually denoted by the Greek letter sigma, σ, and the variance is denoted by σ^2.)

The mathematical formula for calculating the variance is

$$\sigma^2 = \frac{1}{n-1}[(x_1 - \bar{x})^2 + (x_2 - \bar{x})^2 + \cdots + (x_n - \bar{x})^2]$$

$$= \frac{1}{n-1}\left[\sum_{i=1}^{n}(x_i - \bar{x})^2\right]$$

Using algebra this formula can be rearranged to yield the formula

$$\sigma^2 = \frac{1}{n-1}\left[\sum_{i=1}^{n} x_i^2 - \frac{1}{n}(\sum_{i=1}^{n} x_i)^2\right]$$

This formula does not involve the mean, so it can be computed with a single pass over all the data rather than two passes (one to calculate the mean, the other to calculate the variance).

Write a program to compute the variance and standard deviation using both formulae. Although these formulae are mathematically equivalent, they often yield very different answers because of errors introduced by floating-point computations. Use the technique from the previous exercise so that you can read a file of data twice using a `WordStreamIterator` object. If the data consist of floating-point values instead of integers, you can use the function `atof` to convert a string to the `double` value it represents, e.g., `atof("123.075") == 123.075`.

6.6 The **hailstone** sequence, sometimes called the **3n + 1** sequence, is defined by a function $f(n)$:

$$f(n) = \begin{cases} n/2 & \text{if } n \text{ is even} \\ 3 \times n + 1 & \text{otherwise, if } n \text{ is odd} \end{cases}$$

We can use the value computed by f as the argument of f as shown below; the successive values of n form the hailstone sequence.[9]

```
while (n != 1)
{
    n = f(n);
}
```

Although it is conjectured that this loop always terminates, no one has been able to prove it. However, it has been verified by computer for an enormous range of numbers. Several sequences are shown below with the initial value of n on the left.

7 22 11 34 17 52 26 13 40 20 10 5 16 8 4 2 1

11 34 17 52 26 13 40 20 10 5 16 8 4 2 1

22 11 34 17 52 26 13 40 20 10 5 16 8 4 2 1

14 7 22 11 34 17 52 26 13 40 20 10 5 16 8 4 2 1

8 4 2 1

9 28 14 7 22 11 34 17 52 26 13 40 20 10 5 16 8 4 2 1

---

[9]It's called a *hailstone sequence* because the numbers go up and down, mimicking the process that forms hail.

Write a program to find the value of *n* that yields the longest sequence. Prompt the user for two numbers, and limit the search for *n* to all values between the two numbers.

6.7   A Computer Science Excursion: Lists

Program 6.7, *maxword*, finds the most frequently occurring word in a text file, but the program is very slow. In this section we'll use the class List to store data in a program. Using lists will speed up the calculation of the most frequently occurring word and open a new domain of problems we'll be able to solve. For example, using *maxword.cc* to calculate that *the* occurs most frequently in Poe's *The Cask of Amontillado* takes three minutes on the computer on my desk. Using lists the program takes less than two seconds.

We'll use a class to implement lists, but in other programming languages lists are fundamental types in the way that int and double are built-in types in C++. For example, one of the oldest languages still in use today is Lisp (for LISt Processing), a language originally designed to support artificial intelligence applications. Lisp and its dialects are still used today for such applications but also to extend text editors (Emacs) and design tools (AutoCAD).

Lists and List Operations

The class List stores sequences of objects. A List can store a sequence of strings, integers, doubles, and all built-in types. It can also store a sequence of dates and other programmer-defined types including lists, so it's possible to have a list of lists of strings, for example. When a list is first defined, it is constructed containing no elements. This is called an **empty list.** You can prepend an item to the front of a list or append an item to the back of a list. You can access the item at the front of a list or the item at the back of a list. Using standard iterating member functions List::First, List::IsDone, List::Next, and List::Current, you can access all the elements in a list.

Program 6.12, *uselist.cc*, shows a simple example using many of the List member functions. Since lists can store different types of elements, the type must be specified when a List variable is defined.

Program 6.12   uselist.cc

```
#include <iostream.h>
#include "list.cc"
#include "CPstring.h"

// illustrate basic list operations

int main()
{
    List<string> fruitList;
    List<int>    intList;
```

```
    fruitList.Append("apple");
    fruitList.Append("banana");
    fruitList.Append("kiwi");
    fruitList.Append("watermelon");

    fruitList.Print();
    fruitList.ChopFront();
    fruitList.Print();
    fruitList.Prepend(fruitList.Back());
    fruitList.Print();

    for(fruitList.First(); ! fruitList.IsDone(); fruitList.Next())
    {
        intList.Append(fruitList.Current().length());
    }
    intList.Print();

    return 0;
}
```

uselist.cc

The output shows a list of four fruits altered by removing the first element then prepending a copy of the last element to the front of the fruit list. A list of integers is formed using the lengths of each string in the fruit list.

OUTPUT

```
prompt> uselist
( apple banana kiwi watermelon )
( banana kiwi watermelon )
( watermelon banana kiwi watermelon )
( 10 6 4 10 )
```

All List operations are declared in the header file *list.h*, which is shown in the appendix of this book. These operations are summarized in the comments from the header file, reproduced here.

```
// a list class that supports insertion at either the front
// or back.  Other operations include testing for containment
// and iterating over all elements of the list.  Iterator
// permits deletion and insertion before current item
//
// mutating functions, change list
//
// void Append(const Type & t)   -- add t to back of list
// void Prepend(const Type & t)  -- add t to front of list
// void ChopFront()              -- remove first element
// void Clear()                  -- make the list empty
//
// accessing functions, get values from list
//
// Type Front()     -- return copy of first element in list
// Type Back()      -- return copy of last element in list
```

```
// bool Contains(const Type & t) -- return true iff list contains t
// int Size(), int Length() -- return # elements in list
// void Print()             -- print list elements
//
// iterating functions:
// First(), IsDone(), Next() -- iterate through all elements
// Type & Current()           -- return element: can modify element
//                               (const version exists too)
// Delete()                   -- delete current item
// InsertBefore(const Type & t) -- insert t before current item
```

The `List` class is different from classes we've used before since it can be used with different types, e.g., `string` and `int` as shown in *uselist.cc*. The type of item stored in a `List` object is specified when the object is defined by including the type between angle brackets, `<` and `>`. Any type or class that has a parameterless (or **default**) constructor can be used. For example, the definition `List<Dice> diceList` will *not* compile, because the `Dice` class has only one constructor that requires an `int` parameter. A list's type is something like a parameter specified when the list is defined, so the `List` class is called a **parameterized class,** or a **templated class.** In the comments from *list.h* reproduced above, `Type` is used as the identifier for the generic kind of item stored in a list. Templated classes can be difficult to use in C++ programs depending on the programming environment you are using. If you look at *uselist.cc* carefully, you'll see the statement `#include "list.cc"` at the beginning of the program. This is not a mistake; the source code stored in the file *list.cc* is included. This is not ideal; we'd like to be able to include only the `.h` interface file, not the implementation. However, many environments require access to the source code when a templated class is used, so we'll adopt this approach when using the `List` class.[10]

Pause to reflect

6.18. The function `ChopHalf` shown here is supposed to remove the first half of a list; i.e., the list (apple banana kiwi watermelon) should be changed to (kiwi watermelon). However, the list is changed to `banana kiwi watermelon`. Explain why and fix the problem.

```
void ChopHalf(List<string> & list)
{
    int k;
    for(k=0; k < list.Length()/2; k++)
    {
        list.ChopFront();
    }
}
```

---

[10]It's possible to define the `List` functions **inline**—within the declaration of the class in the `.h` file. This is the approach we take with the `Vector` class. However, in some environments using inline definitions instantiates all member functions, not just those used in a client program. This would require list items to support operator `==` and operator `<<` even when member functions `Contains` and `Print` are not called.

6.19. Write (and test) a function `Reverse` to reverse the elements in a list of strings.

```
void Reverse(List<string> & list)
// postcondition: elements in list are reversed
```

You can do this by calling `Append`, `Front`, and `ChopFront` in a definite `for` loop that iterates the proper number of times.

6.20. Write a function that returns the sum of all the elements in a list of integers. The function should return 26 for a list representing (5 6 7 8). You'll need to use the `List` iterating member functions.

6.21. Complete the function `ListDouble` below using the member function `InsertBefore` so a list of strings (apple banana kiwi watermelon) is changed to (apple apple banana banana kiwi kiwi watermelon watermelon).

```
void ListDouble(List<string> & list)
// postcondition:   list is "doubled":
//                  (a b c) becomes (a a b b c c)
{
    for(list.First(); ! list.IsDone(); list.Next())
     {
         // add one statement here
     }
}
```

Counting Words

We were motivated to use lists as a way to count how many times each word occurs in a text file. Program 6.13, *wordlist.cc*, is a first step toward a solution to this problem. The program keeps track of unique words—each different word from a text file is stored in a list of strings. When a new word is read, it is stored in the list only if it was not already stored. The function `List::Contains` is used to determine if a word is already stored in the list. Words in the list are not added, so the list stores exactly one occurrence of each different word in a text file.

Program 6.13   wordlist.cc

```
#include <iostream.h>
#include "CPstring.h"
#include "list.cc"
#include "worditer.h"
#include "prompt.h"

// Owen Astrachan, 6/29/96
// use of List class to find unique words in text file

int main()
{
```

```
WordStreamIterator iter;
string word;
List<string> wordList;
string filename = PromptString("enter file name: ");
int count = 0;

iter.Open(filename);

for(iter.First(); ! iter.IsDone(); iter.Next())
{
    word = iter.Current().Downcase();
    if (! wordList.Contains(word))
    {
        wordList.Append(word);
    }
    count++;
}
cout << "total # different words = " << wordList.Length() << endl;
cout << "total # words = " << count << endl;
return 0;
}
```

```
                                         OUTPUT

prompt> wordlist
enter file name: poe.txt
total # different words = 1000
total # words = 2324
prompt> wordlist
enter file name: hamlet.txt
total # different words = 7234
total # words = 31956
prompt> wordlist
enter file name: melville.txt
total # different words = 4103
total # words = 14353
```

Because our goal is to find how many times each different word occurs and not just the number of different words, we must modify *wordlist.cc*. Once we can determine how many times each different word occurs, we can easily calculate the word that occurs most often. To keep track of both words and occurrences, we'll design and implement a new class WordCounter. A WordCounter object stores both a word and the number of times the word occurs. We'll need to access the word and the number of occurrences, and we'll need to increment the number of occurrences. The class is described in Fig. 6.3 and implemented in *maxword2.cc*, Prog. 6.14, below. We'll use a list of WordCounter objects to find statistics about the words in a file. Because we want to use a List<WordCounter> object, we need to supply a parameterless

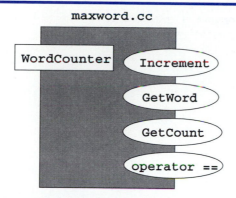

Figure 6.3   WordCounter class.

constructor for WordCounter. We also want to be able to initialize a WordCounter object so that it can represent a word that occurs once. We'll use the Increment member function to change the number of occurrences. The following function Update shows how to add a WordCounter object to a list of WordCounter objects. The comparison operator == is overloaded so that it works with WordCounter objects. When an element is found in wordList, the code increments the number of occurrences and stops searching since the list stores each word exactly once. If the word is not found, it is added to the end of wordList.

```
void Update(List<WordCounter> & wordList, const WordCounter & wc)
// postcondition: word represented by wc is added to wordList if
//                it is not already in wordList.  Otherwise, the
//                count of wc.GetWord() is updated in wordList
{
    for(wordList.First(); ! wordList.IsDone(); wordList.Next())
    {
        if (wordList.Current() == wc)
        {
            wordList.Current().Increment();
            return;
        }
    }
    wordList.Append(wc);
}
```

The new word could also be added to the front of wordList. You'll be asked to reason about whether this is preferable to appending in one of the exercises for this section. The final program, including the declaration and definition of the class WordCounter, is Prog. 6.14. Not all the words are shown in the output, since this would require too much space.

Program 6.14   maxword2.cc

```cpp
#include <iostream.h>
#include "CPstring.h"
#include "list.cc"
#include "worditer.h"
#include "prompt.h"
#include "ctimer.h"

// Owen Astrachan, 7/1/96
// illustrates List class for tracking words and occurrences

class WordCounter
{
  public:
    WordCounter();                      // need default constructor for List
    WordCounter(string word);           // store word with count = 1
    void    Increment();                // bump the counter by 1
    int     GetCount() const;           // return word count
    string GetWord()  const;            // return word
    bool operator == (const WordCounter & rhs);

  private:

    string myWord;      // store word
    int myCount;        // # occurrences of word
};

void Update(List<WordCounter> & wordList,
            const WordCounter & wc);
void Print(const List<WordCounter> & wordList);
void MaxStats(const List<WordCounter> & wordList,
              string & maxWord,
              int & maxOccurrences);
int main()
{
    WordStreamIterator iter;
    string word;
    List<WordCounter> wordList;
    CTimer timer;
    string filename = PromptString("enter file name: ");
    iter.Open(filename);

    // read and store all words

    timer.Start();
    for(iter.First(); ! iter.IsDone(); iter.Next())
    {
        Update(wordList, WordCounter(iter.Current().Downcase()));
    }

    timer.Stop();
    Print(wordList);
```

```
        cout << "total # different words = " << wordList.Length()
            << endl;
        cout << "read and process time = " << timer.ElapsedTime()
            << endl;

        int occurs;
        MaxStats(wordList,word,occurs);
        cout << "max word = \"" << word << "\" # occurrences = "
            << occurs << endl;
}

void Print(const List<WordCounter> & wordList)
// postcondition: words and counts printed, one entry per line
{
    for(wordList.First(); ! wordList.IsDone(); wordList.Next())
    {
        cout << wordList.Current().GetCount() << "\t";
        cout << wordList.Current().GetWord() << endl;
    }
}

void Update(List<WordCounter> & wordList,
            const WordCounter & wc)
// postcondition: word represented by wc is added to wordList
//                if it is not already in wordList.  Otherwise,
//                the count of wc.GetWord() is updated in
//                wordList
{
    for(wordList.First(); ! wordList.IsDone(); wordList.Next())
    {
        if (wordList.Current() == wc)
        {
            wordList.Current().Increment();
            return;
        }
    }
    wordList.Append(wc);
}

void MaxStats(const List<WordCounter> & wordList,
              string & maxWord, int & maxOccurrences)
// postcondition: maxWord = most frequently occurring word in
//     wordList,  maxOccurrences = # times most
//     frequent word occurs
{
    maxOccurrences = 0;
    for(wordList.First(); ! wordList.IsDone(); wordList.Next())
    {
        if (wordList.Current().GetCount() > maxOccurrences)
        {
            maxOccurrences = wordList.Current().GetCount();
            maxWord = wordList.Current().GetWord();
        }
    }
}
```

```
WordCounter::WordCounter()
// postcondition: default wordcounter constructed
{
    myWord = "";
    myCount = 0;
}

WordCounter::WordCounter(string word)
// postcondition: word stored with count of 1
{
    myWord = word;
    myCount = 1;
}

void WordCounter::Increment()
// postcondition: # occurrences incremented by 1
{
    myCount++;
}

int WordCounter::GetCount() const
// postcondition: return # occurrences
{
    return myCount;
}

string WordCounter::GetWord() const
// postcondition: return word
{
    return myWord;
}

bool WordCounter::operator == (const WordCounter & rhs)
// postcondition: return true if word == rhs.word,
// # occurrences is not used for determining equality
{
    return myWord == rhs.myWord;
}
```

OUTPUT

```
prompt> maxword2
enter file name: poe.txt
161     the
1          cask
75       of
3          amontillado
...
1          them.
1          pace
1          requiescat!
```

```
total # different words = 1000
read and process time = 1.73
max word = "the" # occurrences = 161
```

Operator Details

(*The material in this section is not essential to understanding how the* WordCounter *class works but is part of the details of the C++ implementation.*)

Note that each member function of the WordCounter class is very short; in fact, none of the member functions contains more than one statement. Although the WordCounter class is useful for counting word occurrences, it is not a completely general class. For example, you cannot use wordList.Print to print the elements in a list of WordCounter objects. The member function List::Print uses the insertion operator, <<, to print. Since there is no insertion operator defined for the WordCounter class, a separate nonmember function Print is used to print the list.

The overloaded operator, WordCounter::operator ==, compares two WordCounter objects. Only the strings are used to compare objects; the counts are not used. The statement if (wordList.Current() == wc) from *max-word2.cc* is used to compare two WordCounter objects. Since operator == is a member function, the object on the left-hand side of the == is an implicit parameter. To make it clear that operator == is a member function, the statement can be rewritten as if (wordList.Current().operator==(wc)). This makes it clear that wc is an argument passed to operator == whose left-hand side is wordList.Current(). Since operator == is a member function, it can access the private data of any WordCounter object, not just its own data.

Excursion Exercises

6.7 Modify the code in *maxword2.cc* so that items are added to the front of a word list rather than to the back in the function Update. Time both versions of the program for different data files using the CTimer class (defined in *ctimer.h*, Prog. 4.16). You should also try to explain the results of the timings.

6.8 Modify the code in *maxword2.cc* so that the list of WordCounter objects is maintained in sorted order by number of occurrences with the most frequently occurring word first in the list. You can do this by changing the code that increments a WordCounter object when it is found in the list.
   1. Store the current item (the item just incremented) in a local WordCounter variable; then delete the current item.
   2. Traverse the list from the front. The traversal should stop when an item is found that has fewer (or equal) occurrences than the saved/deleted item. Then use InsertBefore to add the saved item back to the list.

There are some special cases that make this code tricky (think about deleting an item from a list with only one element). Time this program and compare its performance to *maxword2.cc*, Prog. 6.14.

6.9 Reimplement `WordCounter::operator ==` in *maxword2.cc*, Prog. 6.14, so that it is not a member function by writing it as

```
bool operator == (const WordCounter & lhs, const WordCounter & rhs)
{
    return lhs.GetWord() == rhs.GetWord();
}
```

Then recompile and run the program comparing the times to those obtained from the original version of *maxword2.cc*. The new program will be significantly slower. Can you account for this difference?

6.10 Write a program similar to *maxword2.cc*, Prog. 6.14, but use more than one list for storing `WordCounter` objects. Use two lists: one for frequent words and one for infrequent words. When searching for a word (e.g., in `Update`), the frequent list is searched first then the infrequent list is searched only if the word is not found in the frequent list. A word is first placed in the infrequent list. When the number of occurrences of a word in the infrequent list reaches a threshold, it is removed and placed on the frequent list.

Try a threshold of 10 initially and see if this speeds up the program. Experiment with different thresholds to see how the program responds to different values.

6.11 Write a program similar to *maxword2.cc*, Prog. 6.14, but use a different method for storing words and occurrences. Instead of using `List<WordCounter>`, you should use

```
    List<List<WordCounter> > wordList;
```

This defines `wordList` as a list of `WordCounter` lists. The space between the `> >` is needed so the compiler won't think there is an insertion operator, `>>`. Each element of `wordList` is a list of `WordCounter` objects. You should have one list for words beginning with the letter *a*, one list for words beginning with *b*, and so on, for at most 26 lists. You can use `s.substr(0,1)` to find the first letter of a string. Remember that `substr` returns a string.

6.12 Write and time (using the class `CTimer` from *ctimer.h*, Prog. 4.16) a program that uses the following approach to find the word that occurs most often in a text file.
1. Read all words from the file into two lists: `unique`, which stores each different word exactly once, and `complete`, which stores every word in the file.
2. Iterate over `unique`, counting how many times each word occurs in `complete` (by using a nested loop to iterate over `complete`).

This method should be much faster than the approach in *maxword.cc*, Prog. 6.7, using `WordStreamIterators`, since the outer iterator loops over many fewer strings and all the strings are in memory instead of being reread from disk. Compare the times found by this program to those of *maxword2.cc*, Prog. 6.14.

Class Design and Implementation via Simulation

When you can measure what you are speaking about, and express it in numbers, you know something about it . . .
LORD KELVIN
Popular Lectures and Addresses

We must never make experiments to confirm our ideas, but simply to control them.
CLAUDE BERNARD
Bulletin of New York Academy of Medicine, vol. IV, p. 997

One tenet of object-oriented programming is that a library of well-designed classes makes it easier to design and write programs. Classes are often easier to reuse in programs than code not using classes. For example, we've used the Dice class in several programs. In almost all programs we've used cout and cin, objects that are part of the hierarchy of stream classes. As programmers and designers, we need to be familiar with what classes are available and with patterns of design that we can use. Reusing concepts is often as important as reusing code.

In this section we'll explore some programs and classes that are simulations of natural and mathematical events. We'll also use the pattern of iteration introduced with the WordStreamIterator class in *countw3.cc,* Prog. 6.4, in designing and using two classes: one for random walks and one for observing random walks. First we'll write a simple program to simulate random walks, then we'll design and implement a class based on this program. Comparing the features of both programs will add to your understanding of object-oriented programming. We'll also study structs, a C++ feature for storing data that can be used instead of a class.

7.1   Random Walks

A random walk is a model built on mathematical and physical concepts that is used to explain how molecules move in an enclosed space. It's also used as the basis for several mathematical models that predict stock market prices. First we'll investigate a random walk in one dimension and then move to higher dimensions.

One-Dimensional Random Walks

Suppose a frog lives on a lily pad and there are lily pads stretching in a straight line in two directions. The frog "walks" by flipping a coin. If the coin comes up heads, the frog jumps to the right, otherwise the frog jumps to the left. This process is repeated for a specific number of steps and then the walk stops. The initial configuration for such a random walk is shown in Fig. 7.1. We can gather several interesting statistics from a random walk when it is complete (and sometimes during the walk). In a walk of n steps we might be interested in how far from the start the frog is at the end of the walk. Also of interest are the furthest points from the start reached by the frog (both east and west or positive and negative if the walk takes place on the x-axis) and how often the frog revisits the "home" lily pad.

We'll use a two-sided `Dice` object to represent the coin that determines what direction the frog jumps. Program 7.1, *frogwalk.cc,* simulates a one-dimensional random walk.

With a graphical display, the frog could be shown moving to the left and right. Alternatively, a statement that prints the position of the frog could be included within the `for` loop. This would provide clues as to whether the program is working correctly. In the current program, the only output is the final position of the frog. Without knowing what this position should be in terms of a mathematical model, it's hard to determine if the program accurately models a one-dimensional random walk.

A RandomWalk Class

Program 7.1, *frogwalk.cc,* is short. It's not hard to reason that it correctly simulates a one-dimensional random walk. However, modifying the program to have more than one frog hopping on the lily pads is cumbersome because the program is not designed to be extended in this way. If we encapsulate the

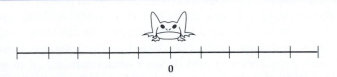

| **Figure 7.1** | Frog at start of random walk. |

Program 7.1   frogwalk.cc

```cpp
#include <iostream.h>
#include "dice.h"
#include "prompt.h"

// simulate one-dimensional random walk
// Owen Astrachan, 8/13/94

int main()
{
    int numSteps = PromptRange("enter # of steps",0,1000000);

    int position = 0;            // "frog" starts at position 0
    Dice die(2);                 // used for "coin flipping"
    int k;
    for(k=0; k < numSteps; k++)
    {
        switch (die.Roll())
        {
          case 1:
            position += 1;     // step to the right
            break;
          case 2:
            position -= 1;     // step to the left
            break;
        }
    }
    cout << "final position = " << position << endl;
    return 0;
}
```

OUTPUT

```
prompt> frogwalk
enter # of steps between 0 and 1000000:  1000
final position = 32
prompt> frogwalk
enter # of steps between 0 and 1000000:  1000
final position = -14
prompt> frogwalk
enter # of steps between 0 and 1000000:  1000
enter # of steps:  1000
final position = 66
```

Figure 7.2   RandomWalk **class.**

state and behavior of a random-walking frog in a class, it will be easier to have more than one frog in the same program. Using a class will also make it easier to extend the program to simulate a two-dimensional walk.

We'll use a RandomWalk class whose interface is shown in Fig. 7.2. Member functions First, IsDone, and Next behave similarly to their counterparts in the WordStreamIterator class (see Prog. 6.4, *countw3.cc*). We use them since the random walk is an iterative process.

A parameter to the RandomWalk constructor specifies the number of steps in the walk. The main function that uses the class is

```
int main()
{
    int numSteps = PromptRange("enter # steps",0,1000000);

    RandomWalk frog(numSteps);
    frog.Simulate();
    cout << "final position = " << frog.GetPosition() << endl;
}
```

In this program an entire simulation takes place at once using the member function Simulate. The output from this program is the same as the output from *frogwalk.cc*. Using the RandomWalk class makes it easier to simulate more than one random walk at the same time. In *frogwalk2.cc*, Prog. 7.2, two random walkers are defined. The program keeps track of how many times the walkers are located at the same position during the walk. It would be very difficult to write this program based on a program *frogwalk.cc* that doesn't use a class. Since the number of steps in the simulation is a parameter to the RandomWalk constructor, variables frog and toad must be defined *after* you enter the number of steps. One alternative would be to have a member function SetSteps used to set the number of steps in the simulation.

Because both random walkers take the same number of steps, it isn't necessary to have checks using both frog.IsDone() and toad.IsDone(), but since both walkers must be initialized using First and updated using Next, we use IsDone for both to maintain symmetry in the code.

```
#include <iostream.h>
#include "prompt.h"
#include "walk.h"

// simulate two random walkers at once
// Owen Astrachan, 6/29/96

int main()
{
    int numSteps = PromptRange("enter # steps",0,1000000);

    RandomWalk frog(numSteps);          // define two random walkers
    RandomWalk toad(numSteps);
    int samePadCount = 0;               // # times at same location

    frog.First();
    toad.First();

    while (! frog.IsDone() && ! toad.IsDone())
    {
        if (frog.GetPosition() == toad.GetPosition())
        {
            samePadCount++;
        }
        frog.Next();
        toad.Next();
    }

    cout << "frog position = " << frog.GetPosition() << endl;
    cout << "toad position = " << toad.GetPosition() << endl;
    cout << "# times at same location = " << samePadCount << endl;
    return 0;
}
```

OUTPUT

```
prompt>  frogwalk2
enter # steps between 0 and 1000000:  10000
frog position = -6
toad position = -26
# times at same location = 87
prompt>  frogwalk2
enter # steps between 0 and 1000000:  10000
frog position = 16
toad position = 40
# times at same location = 392
prompt>  frogwalk2
enter # steps between 0 and 1000000:  10000
frog position = 128
toad position = 20
# times at same location = 4
```

Before examining the interface and implementation of the class `RandomWalk` we'll discuss some design guidelines in building classes.

Class Design Guidelines

1. Identify the behavior of the class first. The behavior will guide you in deciding appropriate member functions.
2. Identify the state of the class after thinking about the behavior. The state will guide you in determining what private data members are needed.

For `RandomWalk` I first decided to use the iteration pattern of `First`, `IsDone`, and `Next`. Since it may be useful to execute an entire simulation without using a one-step-at-a-time approach, I decided to implement a `Simulate` function to do this. As we'll see, it will be easy to implement this function using the iterating member functions. Finally, the class must provide some accessor functions. In this case we need functions to determine the current location of a `RandomWalk` object and to determine the number of steps taken.

Determining what data should be private is not always a simple task. You'll often need to revise initial decisions and add or delete data members as the design of the class evolves. As a general guideline, private data should be an intrinsic part of what is modeled by the class. Also, state information that must be accessed in more than one member function should be private data as opposed to data defined within a member function. For example, the current position of a `RandomWalk` object is certainly an intrinsic part of a random walk. The `Dice` object used to determine the direction to take at each step is not intrinsic. The state of one `Dice` object does not need to be accessed by different member functions. Even if a `Dice` object is used in several member functions, there is no reason the same `Dice` object should be used across more than one function.

When you implement a class you should use the same process of iterative enhancement we used in previous programs. For classes this means you might not implement all member functions at once. For example, you could leave a member function out of the public section at first and add it later when the class is partially complete. Alternatively, you could include a declaration of the function, but implement it as an empty **stub function** with no statements. A stub function for `First` is now shown. There are no statements in the function body; it is a stub that will be filled in later.

```
void RandomWalk::First()
// postcondition: first step of random walk taken
{
}
```

When I implemented `RandomWalk` I realized that there would be code duplicated in `First` and `Next` since both functions simulate one random step. Since it's a good idea to avoid code duplication whenever possible, I decided to factor the duplicate code out into another function that is called from both

First and Next.[1] This kind of **helper function** should be declared in the private section so that it is not accessible to client programs. Member functions, however, can call private helper functions.

The header file *walk.h* is shown in Prog. 7.3. It's not unreasonable to make TakeStep public so that client programs could use either the iteration member functions or the TakeStep function. Similarly you may decide that the function Simulate is superfluous since client programs can implement it by using First, IsDone, and Next (see Prog. 7.4, *walk.cc*). There is often a tension between including too many member functions in an effort to provide as much functionality as possible and too few member functions in an effort to keep the public interface simple and easy to use. There are usually many ways of writing a program, implementing a class, skinning a cat, and walking a frog.

Program 7.3   walk.h

```
#ifndef _RANDOMWALK_H
#define _RANDOMWALK_H

// Owen Astrachan, 6/20/96
// class for implementing a one dimensional random walk
//
// constructor specifies number of steps to take, random walk
// goes left or right with equal probability
//
// two methods for running simulation:
//
// void Simulate()   -- run a complete simulation
//
// First(); ! IsDone(); Next() -- idiom for starting and iterating
//                                one step at a time
//
// accessor functions:
//
// int GetPosition() -- returns x coordinate
//                      (# steps left/right from origin)
//
// int GetSteps()    -- returns total # steps taken

class RandomWalk
{
  public:
    RandomWalk(int maxSteps);  // constructor, parameter = max # steps
    void First();              // take first step of walk
    bool IsDone();             // returns true if walk finished, else false
    void Next();               // take next step of random walk
```

---

[1]Actually, I wrote the code for First and Next and then realized it was duplicated after the fact so I added the helper function.

```
    void Simulate();              // take all steps in simulation

    int GetPosition();            // returns position (x coord) of frog
    int GetSteps();               // returns # of steps taken by frog
  private:
    void TakeStep();              // simulate one step of walk
    int myPosition;               // current x coordinate
    int mySteps;                  // # of steps taken
    int myMaxSteps;               // maximum # of steps allowed

};

#endif                                                        walk.h
```

Program 7.4   walk.cc

```
#include "walk.h"
#include "dice.h"

RandomWalk::RandomWalk(int maxSteps)
// postcondition: all private data fields initialized
{
    myPosition = mySteps = 0;
    myMaxSteps = maxSteps;
}

void RandomWalk::TakeStep()
// postcondition: one step of random walk taken
{
    Dice coin(2);
    switch (coin.Roll())
    {
      case 1:
        myPosition--;
        break;
      case 2:
        myPosition++;
        break;
    }
    mySteps++;
}

void RandomWalk::First()
// postcondition: first step of random walk taken
{
    myPosition = 0;
    mySteps = 0;
    TakeStep();
}
```

```
bool RandomWalk::IsDone()
// postcondition: returns true when random walk is finished
//                i.e., when # of steps taken == max. # of steps
{
    return mySteps >= myMaxSteps;
}

void RandomWalk::Next()
// postcondition: next step in random walk simulated
{
    TakeStep();
}

void RandomWalk::Simulate()
    // postcondition: one simulation completed
{
    for(First(); ! IsDone(); Next())
    {
    // simulation complete using iterator methods
    }
}

int RandomWalk::GetPosition()
// postcondition: returns position of "frog" (x coordinate)
{
    return myPosition;
}

int RandomWalk::GetSteps()
// postcondition: returns number of steps taken by "frog"
{
    return mySteps;
}
```

walk.cc

The RandomWalk member functions are fairly straightforward. All private data are initialized in the constructor, the function TakeStep simulates a random step and updates private data accordingly, and the other member functions are used to simulate a random walk or to access information about a walk, e.g., the current location of the simulated walker. The implementation is shown in Prog. 7.4.

Each member function requires only a few lines of code. The brevity of the functions makes it easier to verify that they are correct. As you design your own classes, try to keep the implementations of each member function short. Using private helper functions can help both in keeping code short and in factoring out common code.

Two-Dimensional Walks

In this section we'll extend the one-dimensional random walk to two dimensions. A two-dimensional random walk is a more realistic model of a large molecule moving in a gas or liquid, although it is still much simpler than the physical forces that govern molecular motion. Nevertheless, the two-dimensional walk provides insight into the phenomenon known as *Brownian motion*, named after the botanist Robert Brown who, in the early 1800s, investigated pollen grains moving in water. His observations were modeled physically by Albert Einstein, whose hypotheses were confirmed by Jean-Baptiste Perrin, who won a Nobel prize for his work.

The class `TwoDimWalk` models a two-dimensional random walk, the implementation and use of which are shown in *brownian.cc,* Prog. 7.5. In two dimensions, a molecule can move in any direction. This direction can be specified by a random number of degrees from the horizontal. A random number between 1 and 360 can be generated by a 360-sided dice. However, using a `Dice` object would constrain the molecule to use a direction that is an integer, $1, 2, 3, \ldots, 360$. We'd like molecules to be able to go in any direction, including angles such as 1.235157 and 102.3392. Instead of using a `Dice` object, we'll use an object from the class *RandGen*, specified in *rando.h.* The *RandGen* class is used in implementing the `Dice` class. In *dice.h,* Prog. 5.2, a private field `myGenerator` of type `RandGen` is defined and then used in the implementation of the `Dice` class. The `RandGen` class can be used to generate a random integer in a range other than $1 \ldots n$, which comes from n-sided dice. It also generates random `double` values. Since the sine and cosine functions `sin` and `cos` from `<math.h>` are needed for this simulation, and since these functions require an angle specified in radians[2] rather than degrees, we need to use random `double` values. We use the member function `RandGen::RandReal` to return a random `double` value between zero and one. The class *rando.h* is described in Program A.1.

The geometry needed to translate a random direction into x and y distances is illustrated thus:

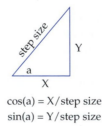

cos(a) = X/step size
sin(a) = Y/step size

If a random angle a is chosen, the distance moved in the X-direction is $\cos(a) \times$ step size as shown in the diagram. The distance in the Y-direction is a similar function of the sine of the angle a. In the member function

---

[2]There are 360 degrees in a circle and 2π radians in a circle. It's not necessary to understand radian measure, but $180° = \pi$ radians. This means that $d° = d(3.14159/180)$ radians.

Program 7.5   brownian.cc

```cpp
#include <iostream.h>
#include <math.h>              // for sin, cos, sqrt
#include "rando.h"
#include "prompt.h"

// simluate two-dimensional random walk
// Owen Astrachan, 6/20/95, modified 6/29/96

class TwoDimWalk
{
  public:
    TwoDimWalk(int maxSteps,
               int size);       // # of steps, size of one step
    void First();               // take first step of walk
    bool IsDone();              // returns true if walk finished, else false
    void Next();                // take next step of random walk
    void Simulate();            // complete an entire random walk

    int GetSteps();             // returns # of steps taken by molecule
    void GetPosition(double &x, // return x and y coordinates
                     double &y);

  private:
    void TakeStep();            // simulate one step of walk
    double myXcoord;            // current x coordinate
    double myYcoord;            // current y coordinate
    int mySteps;                // # of steps taken
    int myStepSize;             // size of step
    int myMaxSteps;             // maximum # of steps allowed
};

TwoDimWalk::TwoDimWalk(int maxSteps,int size)
// postcondition: all private data fields initialized
{
    mySteps = 0;
    myMaxSteps = maxSteps;
    myStepSize = size;
}

void TwoDimWalk::TakeStep()
// postcondition: one step of random walk taken
{
    const double PI = 3.14159265;
    RandGen gen;                        // random number generator
    double randDirection = gen.RandReal() * 2 * PI;

    myXcoord += myStepSize * cos(randDirection);
    myYcoord += myStepSize * sin(randDirection);

    mySteps++;
}
```

```
void TwoDimWalk::First()
// postcondition: first step of random walk taken
{
    mySteps = 0;
    myXcoord = myYcoord = 0.0;
    TakeStep();
}

bool TwoDimWalk::IsDone()
// postcondition: returns true when random walk is finished
//                i.e., when # of steps taken == max. # of steps
{
    return mySteps >= myMaxSteps;
}

void TwoDimWalk::Next()
// postcondition: next step in random walk simulated
{
    TakeStep();
}

void TwoDimWalk::Simulate()
{
    for(First(); ! IsDone(); Next())
    {
        // simulation complete using iterator methods
    }
}

int TwoDimWalk::GetSteps()
// postcondition: returns number of steps taken by molecule
{
    return mySteps;
}

void TwoDimWalk::GetPosition(double & x, double & y)
// postcondition: return molecule's x coordinate
{
    x = myXcoord;
    y = myYcoord;
}

int main()
{
    int numSteps = PromptRange("enter # of random steps",1,1000000);
    int stepSize = PromptRange("size of one step",1,20);
    int trials   = PromptRange("number of simulated walks",1,1000);
    TwoDimWalk molecule(numSteps,stepSize);

    int k;
    double total = 0.0;
    double x,y;
    for(k=0; k < trials; k++)
```

```
    {
        molecule.Simulate();
        molecule.GetPosition(x,y);    // sum distance from origin of molecule
        total += sqrt(x * x + y * y);
    }
    cout << "average distance from origin = " << total/trials << endl;
    return 0;
}
```

OUTPUT

```
prompt>  brownian
enter # of random steps between 1 and 1000000:  1024
size of one step between 1 and 20:  1
number of simulated walks between 1 and 1000:  100
average distance from origin = 26.8131
prompt>  brownian
enter # of random steps between 1 and 1000000:  1024
size of one step between 1 and 20:  4
number of simulated walks between 1 and 1000:  100
average distance from origin = 108.861
```

`TwoDimWalk::TakeStep` these properties are used to update the co-ordinates of a molecule in simulating a two-dimensional random walk. These are the principal differences between the class `RandomWalk` and `TwoDimWalk`: the implementation of the member function `TakeStep`, the addition of another dimension for the position of the random walker (two private data fields rather than one), and the replacement of the function `int RandomWalk::GetPosition()` with the procedure `void TwoDimWalk::GetPosition(double & x, double & y)` since a position now has two dimensions.

If the output of one simulation is printed and used in a plotting program, a graph of the random walk can be made. Two such graphs are shown in Fig. 7.3. Note that the molecule travels in completely different areas of the plane. However, the molecule's final distance from the origin doesn't differ drastically between the two runs. The distance from the origin of a point (x, y) is calculated by the formula $\sqrt{x^2 + y^2}$. The distances are accumulated in Prog. 7.5 so that the average distance can be output.

The paths of the walk shown in Fig. 7.3 are interesting because they are **self-similar.** If a magnifying glass is used for a close-up view of a particular part of the walk, the picture will be similar to the overall view of the walk. Using a more powerful magnifying glass doesn't make a difference; the similarity still exists. This is a fundamental property of **fractals,** a mathematical concept that is used to explain how seemingly random phenomena aren't as random as they initially seem.

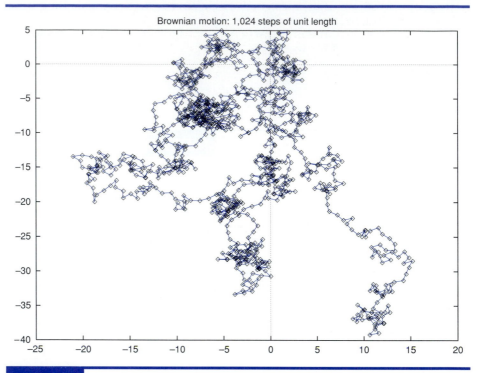

Figure 7.3a   Fractal characteristics of random walks.

The results of both random walks illustrate one of the most important relationships of statistical physics. In a random walk, the distance D from the start of a walk of N steps, where each step is of length L, is given by the equation

$$D = \sqrt{N} \times L$$

The results of the simulated walks above don't supply enough data to validate this relationship, but the data are supportive. In the exercises you'll be asked to explore this further.

Pause to reflect

7.1. Modify *frogwalk.cc*, Prog. 7.1, so the user enters a distance from the origin—say, 142—and the program simulates a walk until this distance is reached (in either the positive or negative direction). The program should output the number of steps needed to reach the distance.

7.2. Only one simulation is performed in Prog. 7.1. The code for that one simulation could be moved to a function. Write a prototype for such a function that returns both the final distance from the start as well as the maximum distance from the start reached during the walk.

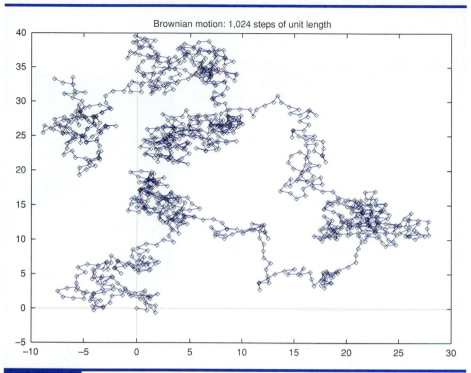

Brownian motion: 1,024 steps of unit length

Figure 7.3b Fractal characteristics of random walks. (*Continued*)

7.3. Can you find an expression for use in *frogwalk.cc,* Prog. 7.1, so that no `switch` or `if/else` statement is needed when the position is updated? For example: `position += die.Roll()` would add either 1 or 2 to the value of `position`. What's needed is an expression that will add either −1 or 1.

7.4. A two-dimensional walk on a lattice constrains the random walker to take steps in the compass point directions: North, East, South, West. How can the class `RandomWalk` be modified to support a frog that travels on lattice points? How can the class `TwoDimWalk` be modified?

7.5. If you modified both random walking classes (`TwoDimWalk` and `RandomWalk`) with code to track the number of times the walker returned to the starting position, either (0,0) or 0 respectively, would you expect the results to be similar?

7.6. Suppose the one-dimensional walker is restricted to walking in a circle instead of on an infinite line. Outline a modification to the class `RandomWalk` so that the number of "lily pads" on a circle is specified as well as the number of steps in a walk. Strive for a modification that entails minimal change to the class.

MARY SHAW

Mary Shaw is Professor of Computer Science at Carnegie Mellon University. Her research interests are in the area of software engineering, a subfield of computer science concerned with developing software using well-defined tools and techniques. In [EL94] Shaw says this about software engineering:

> Science often grows hand-in-hand with related engineering. Initially, we solve problems any way we can. Gradually a small set of effective techniques enters the folklore and passes from one person to another. Eventually the best are recognized, codified, taught, perhaps named. Better understanding yields

Figure 7.4   Mary Shaw.

> theories to explain the techniques, to predict or analyze results, and to provide a base for systematic extension. This improves practice through better operational guidance and tools that automate details. The software developer, thus freed from certain kinds of detail, can tackle bigger, more complex problems.

In discussing her current research interests, Shaw combines the themes of both language and architecture. She describes her research in the following:

> Software now accounts for the the lion's share of the cost of developing and using computer systems. My research is directed at establishing a genuine engineering discipline to support the design and development of software systems and reduce the costs and uncertainties of software production. My current focus is on design methods, analytic techniques, and tools used to construct complete software systems from subsystems and their constituent modules. This is the software architecture level of design, which makes me a software architect. (This is from her World Wide Web home page at Carnegie Mellon.)

In 1993 Shaw received the Warnier prize for contributions to software engineering. Among her publications are guides to bicycling and canoeing in western Pennsylvania.

7.2   Coordinating Several Classes

The fractal output of the two-dimensional random walks shown graphically in Fig. 7.3 was generated by recording the x and y coordinates of the walker and then using a plotting program. In this section we'll develop a class used specifically for observing a one-dimensional random walker. We could modify the class RandomWalk specified in *walk.h*, Prog. 7.3, to record information or observe the walk in some other fashion. However, keeping the walk and the walk observer as separate classes will make it much simpler to develop alternative observer classes. For example, if we have access to graphical user interface classes (a **GUI** framework) we could graph a random walk and update the view on the screen as the walk takes place.

> **Program Tip: As a general guideline do not combine too much functionality in one class. It is often better to separate different behavior into separate classes rather than combining related behavior into a single class.** For example, a random walk and the observer of a random walk are really separate concepts. Although it is possible to combine them into one class, using two classes will make it easier to modify each class separately.

A Walk Observer Class

We'll implement a simple observer class and use it as a springboard to discuss alternative observer classes. The observer class will record information about a walk in a text file. We mentioned the class ofstream used for output streams in Sec. 6.1. We'll see a simple use of this stream in the class WalkObserver whose implementation is declared in *observer.h*, Prog. 7.6. A WalkObserver object is constructed by specifying the name of the text file for storing output. The Update member function will be called from a RandomWalk object to update and record the information about the walk.

The WalkObserver class declared in *observer.h* simply writes the time step and position to the output stream myOutputStream. This creates a file that can be used in a plotting program. The output file stores information in the format below indicating the frog went right, left, left, right, and so on. The first right is at time step one; this results in a position of one and the pair 1 1 stored as the first entry in the output file.

```
1    1
2    0
3   -1
4    0
5   -1
6   -2
```

The WalkObserver class is implemented in *frogwalk3.cc*, which observes two walkers. The program is identical to *frogwalk2.cc*, Prog. 7.2, except for the implementation and use of the class WalkObserver. A modified version of the RandomWalk class that supports observers must be used. This class is named RandomWalkO and is declared in *walko.h*, Prog. 7.7, below. The only difference is that the constructor has a WalkObserver parameter that is used to initialize a private data member.

```
#ifndef _OBSERVER_H
#define _OBSERVER_H

// a class for observing a one-dimensional random walk
// this version records the events of the walk in
// a text file whose name is specified in a parameter to
// the constructor
//
// WalkObserver(const string & filename)-- observer records output
//                                         in the text file "filename"
//
// void Update(int step, int position) --  called by a walking object
//                                         to observe (record) the walk

class WalkObserver
{
  public:

    WalkObserver(const string & filename);  // specify filename
    void Update(int step, int position);    // update information from walker

  private:

    ofstream myOutputStream;                // output stream for data
};

#endif
```

observer.h

```
#ifndef _RANDOMWALKO_H
#define _RANDOMWALKO_H

// Owen Astrachan, 6/20/96
// class for implementing a one dimensional random walk with observer
//
// constructor specifies observer and number of steps to take, random walk
// goes left or right with equal probability, updating the observer
// with each step
//
// two methods for running simulation:
//
// void Simulate()  -- run a complete simulation
//
```

```
// First(); ! IsDone(); Next() -- idiom for starting and iterating
//                                 one step at a time
//
// accessor functions:
//
// int GetPosition() -- returns x coordinate
//                      (# steps left/right from origin)
//
// int GetSteps()    -- returns total # steps taken

#include "observer.h"

class RandomWalkO
{
  public:
    RandomWalkO(WalkObserver & obs,
                int maxSteps); // constructor, set observer and max steps
    void First();              // take first step of walk
    bool IsDone();             // returns true if walk finished, else false
    void Next();               // take next step of random walk

    void Simulate();           // take all steps in simulation

    int GetPosition();         // returns position (x coord) of frog
    int GetSteps();            // returns # of steps taken by frog
  private:
    void TakeStep();           // simulate one step of walk
    int myPosition;            // current x coordinate
    int mySteps;               // # of steps taken
    int myMaxSteps;            // maximum # of steps allowed

    WalkObserver& myObserver;  // observe this walk
};

#endif
```

walko.h

A discussion of the private data member myObserver follows the program
frogwalk3.cc, Prog. 7.8. When you run *frogwalk3.cc*, the output doesn't show that
the observers frogObserver and toadObserver have an effect. However,
two output files, "frog.out" and "toad.out", are created to record data
for the walks simulated by the objects frog and toad, respectively.

Program 7.8   frogwalk3.cc

```
#include <iostream.h>
#include <fstream.h>

#include "prompt.h"
#include "walko.cc"
```

```
#include "observer.h"
// simulate two random walkers at once
// Owen Astrachan, 6/29/96
//
// uses a WalkObserver to monitor each of the random walkers

WalkObserver::WalkObserver(const string & filename)
{
    myOutputStream.open(filename);
}

void WalkObserver::Update(int step, int position)
{
    myOutputStream << step << " " << position << endl;
}

int main()
{
    int numSteps = PromptRange("enter # steps",0,1000000);

    WalkObserver frogObserver("frog.out");
    WalkObserver toadObserver("toad.out");
    RandomWalkO frog(frogObserver,numSteps);   // define two random walkers
    RandomWalkO toad(toadObserver,numSteps);
    int samePadCount = 0;                       // # times at same location

    frog.First();
    toad.First();

    while (! frog.IsDone() && ! toad.IsDone())
    {
        if (frog.GetPosition() == toad.GetPosition())
        {
            samePadCount++;
        }
        frog.Next();
        toad.Next();
    }
    cout << "frog position = " << frog.GetPosition() << endl;
    cout << "toad position = " << toad.GetPosition() << endl;
    cout << "# times at same location = " << samePadCount << endl;
    return 0;
}
```

OUTPUT

```
prompt>  frogwalk3
enter # steps between 0 and 1000000:  10000
frog position = -34
toad position = -48
# times at same location = 48
```

The implementation of the `WalkObserver` class is simple: the output text file is opened in the constructor, and output is stored in the text file in the member function `WalkObserver::Update()`.[3]

I used the output files created by the observers to plot the random walks shown in the run above; the plots are shown in Fig. 7.5*a* and *b*. Figure 7.5*a* is the entire walk of 1000 steps. Figure 7.5*b* shows a zoomed-in view of steps 1–100 where most of the walk crossings take place.

Using and Sharing Observers: Reference Variables

The `WalkObserver` objects `frogObserver` and `toadObserver` are defined in `main` of *frogwalk3.cc,* Prog. 7.8. These objects are passed to the corresponding `RandomWalkO` object when the walker objects are constructed. If you examine the prototype for the `RandomWalkO` constructor in *walko.h,* Prog. 7.7, you'll see that the `WalkObserver` parameter is a reference parameter. This

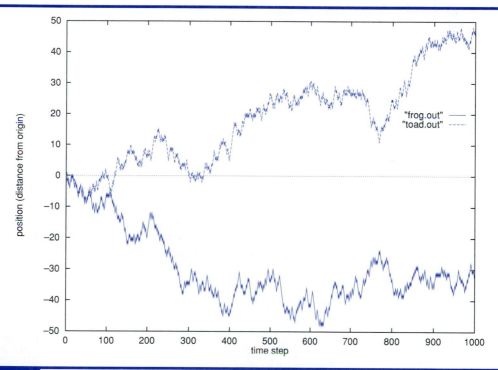

Figure 7.5a   Random walks observed and graphed. (*a*) 1000 steps.

---

[3]Later we'll see that it's sometimes necessary to explicitly close `ofstream` objects to flush all output. In *frogwalk3.cc* the output streams are automatically closed when the program terminates.

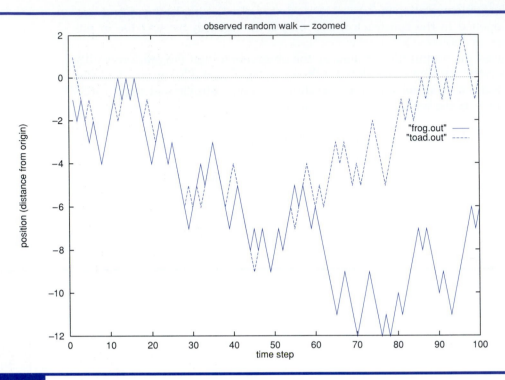

Figure 7.5b   Random walks observed and graphed. (*b*) First 100 steps.

makes sense since you don't want to make a copy of the `frogObserver` for the `frog` walker, you want the `frog` walker to be observed using the observer `frogObserver` defined in `main`. There is more to using the `frogObserver` object than simply passing it by reference. Since each `RandomWalkO` object must contain a data member for its observer, what should the type of the data member be? Using the following definition will not work:

`WalkObserver myObserver;`

With this definition the object `myObserver` will be a copy—there is no way to assign a value to `myObserver` so that it actually references the object `frogObserver` defined in `main`. Note that the value assigned to `myMaxSteps` is a copy of the value of `numSteps` in `main` and not a reference to `numSteps`. Instead, the private data member must be a `reference variable`—a reference to a variable defined elsewhere. This is done using an ampersand just as a reference parameter is indicated using an ampersand:

`WalkObserver & myObserver;`

Using this definition means that `myObserver` must be constructed from an object defined elsewhere, in this case in `main`. A different syntax is used for initializing data members that are reference variables. These data members

Program 7.9   walko2.cc

```cpp
#include "walko.h"
#include "dice.h"

// part of walko.cc, just the member functions that are different
// than the functions for the class RandomWalk

RandomWalkO::RandomWalkO(WalkObserver & obs, int maxSteps)
  : myObserver(obs)
// postcondition: all private data fields initialized
{
    myPosition = mySteps = 0;
    myMaxSteps = maxSteps;
}

void RandomWalkO::TakeStep()
// postcondition: one step of random walk taken
{
    Dice coin(2);
    switch (coin.Roll())
    {
      case 1:
        myPosition--;
        break;
      case 2:
        myPosition++;
        break;
    }
    mySteps++;

    myObserver.Update(mySteps,myPosition);
}
```

walko2.cc

must be initialized in the constructor using an **initializer list.** You can see
how initializer lists work in the implementation of the RandomWalkO class in
walko.cc. Except for the constructor and the private helper function TakeStep,
the member functions are the same as those in the class RandomWalk (see
walk.cc, Prog. 7.4). The changed member functions are shown in *walko2.cc,*
Prog. 7.9.

An initializer list is used in a class constructor to initialize private data
members before the body of the constructor is executed. All reference variables
must be initialized using initializer lists and cannot be initialized in the body
of the constructor. A more complete description of initializer lists is given in
Sec. 7.3. Some programmers prefer to initialize all private variables in initializer
lists. For the class RandomWalkO this is done as follows:

```
RandomWalkO::RandomWalkO(WalkObserver & obs, int maxSteps)
  : myPosition(0),
    mySteps(0),
    myMaxSteps(maxSteps),
    myObserver(obs)
// postcondition: all private data fields initialized
{
    // work done in initializer list
}
```

The `myObserver` data member should be a reference variable for another reason. We might want to share one observer among several walkers. For example, if we had an observer that could show a graphical display of a walker as the walk executes rather than plotted after the fact, we might share one observer between both `frog` and `toad` in *frogwalk3.cc*, Prog. 7.8. If the data member is a copy, then it cannot be shared among different objects, it must be a reference to be shared.[4]

7.3   Language Tools for Designing Classes

In this section we'll discuss enumerated types, initializer lists, and structs. These language constructs help in designing classes that are easy to use, efficient, and modifiable. Enumerated types and structs have counterparts in many programming languages, so their use transcends their implementation in C++. An **enumerated type** allows you to create all the legal values for a new type. For example, a coin type might have the values *heads* and *tails*, and a color spectrum type might have the values *red, orange, yellow, green, blue, indigo*, and *violet*. Using enumerated types makes programs more readable. In C++ a **struct** is similar to a class but is used for storing related data together. Structs are implemented almost exactly like classes, but the word `struct` replaces the word `class`. The only difference between a struct and a class in C++ is that by default all data and functions in a struct are public whereas the default in a class is that everything is private.

Developing a Coin Class

In *frogwalk.cc*, Prog. 7.1, a two-sided `Dice` object simulates a coin. The two-sided die does represent a coin, but uses values of 1 and 2 to represent heads and tails and uses a function `Roll` to represent a coin flip. Rather than using a `Dice` object, we can develop a `Coin` class. Coins are flipped rather than rolled, and they yield values of heads and tails instead of 1 and 2.

Program 7.10 shows the use of the `Coin` class, which is diagrammed in Fig. 7.6. The member function `Coin::Flip()` returns either `heads` or `tails`. These values match our intuition of what a coin should return more closely than 1 and 2. We'll see how values like `heads` and `tails` are defined in the discussion that follows.

---

[4]We'll see later that using pointers permits sharing too.

Program 7.10   flip.cc

```cpp
#include <iostream.h>
#include "coin.h"
#include "prompt.h"

// verify random nature of Coin class, flip coin lots of times

int main()
{
    Coin theCoin;

    long int numFlips = PromptRange("# coin flips",1,1000000);
    long int numHeads = 0;          // number of times 'heads' is flipped
    long int k;

    for(k=0; k < numFlips; k++)
    {
        if (theCoin.Flip() == heads)
        {
            numHeads++;
        }
    }
    cout << "# of heads = " << numHeads << " : "
         << double(numHeads)*100/numFlips << "%" << endl;

    return 0;
}
```

```
                              OUTPUT

prompt>   flip
# coin flips between 1 and 1000000:   10000
# of heads = 4976 : 49.76%
prompt>   flip
# coin flips between 1 and 1000000:   200000
# of heads = 100190 : 50.095%
prompt>   flip2
how many times to flip coin:   500000
# of heads = 250576 : 50.1152%
```

We expect that a coin should yield heads 50% of the time, so the output of *flip.cc* should increase our confidence in the random nature of the `Dice` class on which the `Coin` class is based. Note the expression `if (theCoin.Flip() == heads)` used to determine the outcome of the coin flip. The value `heads` is a value of the enumerated type `FlipValue` defined in *coin.h*, Prog. 7.11. We'll discuss enumerated types in the next section.

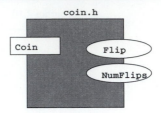

Figure 7.6   Coin class.

Program 7.11   coin.h

```
#ifndef _COIN_H
#define _COIN_H

//   class for simulating a coin (object "tossed" to generate
//                                 a random number 0 or 1)
//
//   Coin() -- constructor
//
//   FlipValue Flip() -- returns the random "flip" of the coin,
//                     either heads or tails with equal probability
//
//   int NumFlips() -- access function, returns # of times Flip called
//                     for an instance of the class

#include "dice.h"

enum FlipValue {heads,tails};        // possible coin flip outcomes

class Coin
{
  public:
    Coin();                   // constructor
    FlipValue Flip();         // return the random flip
    int NumFlips();           // # times this coin flipped
  private:
    Dice myDie;               // will be a two-sided die
};

#endif    // _COIN_H not defined
```
coin.h

Enumerated Types or Enums

The **enumerated type,** or **enum,** defined in *coin.h* and reproduced here creates a new type named `FlipValue`.

```
enum FlipValue {heads,tails};      // possible coin flip outcomes
```

The possible values of the new type `FlipValue` are listed between braces after the name of the type as shown. In this case `heads` and `tails` are the only possible values for a variable or expression whose type is `FlipValue`.

An `enum` introduces a new type whose possible values are defined completely when the enum is defined. Each value of an enum type has an associated integer value; default values of $0, 1, \ldots$ are assigned to each enum value in succession. However, enums are most often used because they let values be represented symbolically rather than numerically. For example, the definition `enum CardSuit {spade, heart, diamond, club};` creates a new type `CardSuit`. The variable definition `CardSuit suit;` creates a variable `suit` whose only possible values are `spade`, `heart`, `diamond`, and `club`. The assignment `suit = spade` is legal; the assignment `suit = 1` is not legal. The integer values associated with `CardSuit` values make `spade` have the value 0 and `club` have the value 3. The statement `cout << suit;` outputs an integer, either 0, 1, 2, or 3. Enums are *not* printed symbolically except, perhaps, in a debugging environment. It's possible to assign explicit values using `enum FlipValue {heads = 2, tails = 5};` so that the value associated with `heads` is 2 and with `tails` is 5. Enums let you use symbolic values in your code, and this can make code easier to read and maintain. Relying on a correspondence between the value 1 and a toss of heads, which would be necessary if enums weren't used, can cause errors since it's easy to forget that 1 means heads and 0 means tails.

> **Syntax: enum definition**
>
> ```
> enum identifier {value,...,
>     value};
>
> enum ident {value = int,...,
>     value = int};
> ```
>
> The *identifier* is used as the name of a new type, all of whose values are listed completely between braces.

The implementation of the `Coin` class declared in *coin.h* is given in *coin.cc*, Prog. 7.12. The member functions rely on the private field `myDie` to simulate a coin. It's possible to move the declaration of the enum `FlipValue` inside the declaration of the class `Coin`. This restricts the type to use as part of the `Coin` class and is better than declaring `FlipValue` outside of the class. By restricting the enum to be used as part of the class, several different classes can use the same enum values. For example, it is not legal to declare the following two enums because the value `orange` cannot be shared among different enumerated types.

```
enum SpectrumValue {red, orange, yellow, green, blue, indigo, violet};
enum FruitKind {orange, apple, cherry, banana};
```

Program 7.12   coin.cc

```cpp
#include "coin.h"

// implementation of coin class

Coin::Coin()
    : myDie(2)
// postcondition: all fields initialized
{
    // nothing needed, private field myDie constructed
}

FlipValue Coin::Flip()
// postcondition: return random coin flip
{
    if (myDie.Roll() == 1)
    {
        return heads;
    }
    return tails;
}

int Coin::NumFlips()
// postcondition: return # of times coin has been flipped
{
    return myDie.NumRolls();
}
```

coin.cc

However, if the enumerated types are moved inside classes Spectrum and Fruit, respectively, then there is no conflict since the values are Spectrum::orange and Fruit::orange, which are different. If the declaration enum FlipValue {heads,tails} is moved into the Coin class declaration, then the if statement in *flip.cc* changes:

```cpp
if (theCoin.Flip() == Coin::heads)
```

Constructors, Declarations, and Initializer Lists

The definitions of each member function of the Coin class are very short since most of the work is done by the Dice class via the private data field myDie. Sometimes the term **instance variable** is used for a private data field. Like all objects, myDie needs to be constructed. In a program, you might write a variable definition such as Dice die(2) that calls the Dice constructor passing the value 2. Variables that are **declared** in the private section of a class must be constructed too. A distinction is made between variable definition and declaration. A definition allocates storage for an object. A declaration tells the type of an object, but doesn't allocate storage. The private section of a class shows the types of the data members, but storage is not allocated until a class object is defined. For example, in the `Dice` class the private data member `mySides` is declared in the header file *dice.h*. No memory is allocated until an object is defined; e.g., `Dice cube(6)` defines an object named `cube`. The object has its own private data, and in particular has `int` instance variables `mySides` and `myRollCount`. The memory for these variables is part of the object `cube`.

For the `Coin` class, the private variable `myDie` must be constructed. You might think at first that the following code can be used; but this code won't work—it looks as if a function named `myDie` is called.

```
Coin::Coin()
{
    myDie(2);
}
```

Instead, a special form of initialization is used to construct private variables. The `Dice` constructor for `myDie` is called explicitly by the `Coin` constructor in the statement

```
Coin::Coin()
  : myDie(2)
```

Here the object `myDie` is constructed similarly to the way it would be defined in a program: `Dice die(2)`, by passing a value to the constructor.

Syntax: initializer list

```
ClassName::ClassName()
     :   myVar1(argument),
         myVar2(argument),
         ...
         myVarN(argument)
{ // begin constructor body ...

         ⋮
```

In general, any number of explicit calls to constructors may appear immediately following the constructor header. These appear after a colon and before the { that marks the beginning of the constructor body in an **initializer list**. Parameters are included in the initializer list constructor calls when needed. An initializer list can include initialization of built-in types as well as programmer-defined types. For example, a class `Game` with instance variables `Dice myDie` and `int myWins` might have this constructor:

```
Game::Game(int sides)
      : myDie(sides),
        myWins(0)
{
    ...
```

The `Game` constructor shown makes `myDie` a dice variable with the number of sides specified by the `Game` constructor parameter `sides`. The private data variable `myWins` is initialized to zero. Other statements may be included in the `Game` constructor body; the fields `myGameDie` and `myWins` will be constructed before these other statements are executed.

It is more efficient and usually better to initialize private variables using an initializer list rather than in the body of a constructor. All non–built-in types will be constructed before the statements in the body of the constructor are executed, so initializing them explicitly helps ensure that private variables have values in the body of the constructor.

Program Tip: When an initializer list is used, the private variables are constructed in the order in which they appear in the class declaration, *not* **in the order they appear in the initializer list.** This can cause bugs if some variables in an initializer use other variable values. In general it is a good design rule to avoid using one private variable value to initialize another. Sometimes this cannot be avoided. In such a case, you must be sure to declare the variables in the right order if an initializer list is used.

When a private data field is constructed, the compiler will automatically call a constructor if necessary. This happened in the class `Dice`, which has instance variable `myGenerator`, an object of the class `RandGen` used to generate random numbers. If you look at the implementation file *dice.cc*, Prog. 5.4, you'll see that no constructor is explicitly called for `myGenerator`. The `Dice` constructor could be written as shown in the following, making the constructor call explicit.

```
Dice::Dice(int sides)
    : myGenerator()
// postcondition: all private fields initialized
{
    myRollCount = 0;
    myNumSides = sides;
}
```

In this case the explicit call to the constructor `myGenerator()` is *not* necessary; the compiler will automatically generate a call of a constructor if the constructor has no parameters. It is good programming style to explicitly call the constructors for each instance variable since often the constructors for such fields will require parameters.

Since the `Coin` class constructor has no parameters, the object `theCoin` is constructed in *flip.cc*, Prog. 7.10, with the definition `Coin theCoin`. It is an error to include an empty parameter list as in the definition `Coin theCoin();`. This would be interpreted by the compiler as the prototype for a function named `theCoin` with no parameters that returns an object of type `Coin`.

structs as Data Aggregates

In the previous chapter we used two different programs for finding literary fingerprints: one that uses a class (*cfingerp.cc*) and one that uses a function with reference parameters (*fingerp.cc*). The function `FingerPrint` in *fingerp.cc*,

Prog. 6.9, has four parameters; its prototype is

```
void FingerPrint(string filename, int & small, int & medium, int & large);.
```

It's easy to think of a more elaborate fingerprint consisting of more data than the number of small, medium, and large words; the parameter list for a modified `FingerPrint` function would quickly become cumbersome. The class approach has the same problem if we want to implement a member function `GetStatistics` to return the fingerprint information; we'll still need several reference parameters. The same problem arises with the member function `GetPosition` from the random walk classes `RandomWalk` and `TwoDimWalk`. In the one-dimensional walk class, `GetPosition` returns a value representing the x-coordinate of the walker object. In the two-dimensional case, `GetPosition` is a `void` function with two reference parameters for returning a walker's x- and y-coordinates. This asymmetry of the `GetPosition` functions might be confusing in a complex simulation.

Instead of using several related parameters, we can group the parameters together so that they can be treated as a single structure. The related data may already be stored in a class as instance variables, but class data are private and thus not accessible to client programs. Object-oriented programmers generally accept the design guideline that all data in a class should be private with accessor and mutator member functions implemented for retrieving and updating the data. Sometimes, rather than using a class to encapsulate both data (state) and behavior, a struct is used. We'll use structs to combine related data together so that the data can be treated as a single unit. A struct used for this purpose is described in the C++ standard as *plain old data,* or *pod.*

For literary fingerprints we can combine the name of the file with the number of small, medium, and large words. Since the combined data have different types, e.g., `string` and `int`, a struct is often called a **heterogeneous aggregate,** a means of encapsulating data of potentially different types into one new type. As a general design rule we won't require any member functions in a struct and will rely on all data fields being public by default. As we'll see, it may be useful to implement some member functions, including constructors, but we won't insist on these as we do for the design and implementation of a new class. In general, we'll use structs when we want to group data (state) and perhaps some behavior (functions) together, but we won't feel obligated to use the same kinds of design rules that we use when we design classes (e.g., all data are private). You should know that other programmers use structs in a different way and do not include constructors or other functions in structs. Since constructors often make programs shorter and easier to develop without mistakes, we'll use them when appropriate.

`structs` for Storing Points

Program 7.13, *points.cc,* is a small program for manipulating points in two dimensions that illustrates how structs are used. Since a struct is used exactly like a class, there aren't any new language features shown in the program.

Program 7.13   points.cc

```cpp
#include <iostream.h>
#include <math.h>

// illustrates structs to define a point in two dimensions
// Owen Astrachan, 7/13/96

struct Point
{
    double x;           // x-coordinate
    double y;           // y-coordinate

    Point();                // constructors
    Point(double xval, double yval);
};

Point::Point()
 : x(0.0), y(0.0)
// postcondition: point initialized at origin
{ }

Point::Point(double xval, double yval)
 : x(xval), y(yval)
// postcondition: point initialized at (xval,yval)
{ }

double Distance(const Point & p, const Point & q);

int main()
{

    Point p;
    Point q(-1.0, 1.0);

    cout << p.x << " " << p.y << endl;

    p.x = 1.3;          // change coordinates of p
    p.y = 2.4;

    cout << p.x << " " << p.y << endl;
    cout << q.x << " " << q.y << endl;
    cout << "distance between = " << Distance(p,q) << endl;

    return 0;
}

double Distance(const Point & p, const Point & q)
// postcondition: returns distance between points p and q
{
    double xdist = p.x - q.x;
    double ydist = p.y - q.y;
    return sqrt(xdist*xdist + ydist*ydist);
}
```

OUTPUT

```
prompt>   points
0  0
1.3  2.4
-1  1
distance between = 2.69258
```

However, the data in a struct are public (by default) so the data can be accessed directly using dot notation rather than by using member functions. Points are passed as const reference parameters following the guidelines established in Sec. 6.4.3 for programmer-defined classes.

The data members of the structs p and q are accessed with a dot notation just as member functions of a class are accessed. However, because the data fields are public, they can be updated and accessed without using member functions. Sometimes the decision to use a struct, versus several variables, versus a class will not be simple. Using a struct instead of several variables makes it easy to add more data at a later time.

> **Program Tip:** If you're designing a class with no behavior, but just data that are accessed and modified, consider implementing the class as a struct. A class should have behavior beyond setting and retrieving the value of each instance variable. Using structs for encapsulating data (with helper functions when necessary, e.g., for construction and printing) is a good compromise when development of a complete class seems like overkill.

In the declaration for the struct Point in *points.cc*, I did not use the prefix my for the instance variables x and y. It's usually a good idea to stay with the convention of using the my prefix, but for something as common as a point the convention of using identifiers x and y outweighs our design rule of using myX and myY.

Operators for structs

Two constructors are implemented for the struct Point in *points.cc*, Prog. 7.13. This makes it simple to define Point variables since values can be passed to the constructor. Note, however, the cumbersome and repetitious code for printing the two Point objects p and q. Fortunately, we can use the insertion operator, <<, to print points. We do this by overloading the operator so it can be used with Point objects. The overloaded insertion operator for Point objects is shown in the following and incorporated into *points2.cc*, Prog. 7.14.

```
ostream & operator << (ostream & output, const Point & p)
// postcondition: p inserted on output as (p.x,p.y)
```

```
                    {
                        output << "(" << p.x << "," << p.y << ")";
                        return output;
                    }
```

For a `Point p`, we can write `cout << p << endl` once the insertion operator is overloaded. The parameter `output` represents any output stream, i.e., either `cout` or an `ofstream` object. After the point p is inserted onto stream `output`, the stream is returned so that a chain of insertions can be made in one statement as shown in *points2.cc*.

Program 7.14   points2.cc

```
#include <iostream.h>
#include <math.h>

// illustrates structs to define a point in two dimensions
// also inline constructors, and operator << overloaded
// Owen Astrachan, 7/13/96

struct Point
{
    double x;           // x-coordinate
    double y;           // y-coordinate
    // constructors
    Point() : x(0.0), y(0.0) {}
    Point(double xval, double yval) : x(xval), y(yval) {}
};

ostream & operator << (ostream & output, const Point & p)
// postcondition: p inserted on ouput as (p.x,p.y)
{
    output << "(" << p.x << "," << p.y << ")";
    return output;     .
}

double Distance(const Point & p, const Point & q);

int main()
{

    Point p;
    Point q(-1.0, 1.0);

    cout << p << " " << q << endl;
    cout << "distance between = " << Distance(p,q) << endl;

    p.x = 1.3;          // change coordinates of p
    p.y = 2.4;
```

```
    cout << p << " " << q << endl;
    cout << "distance between = " << Distance(p,q) << endl;

    return 0;
}

double Distance(const Point & p, const Point & q)
// postcondition: returns distance between points p and q
{
    double xdist = p.x - q.x;
    double ydist = p.y - q.y;
    return sqrt(xdist*xdist + ydist*ydist);
}
```

OUTPUT

```
prompt> points2
(0,0) (-1,1)
distance between = 1.41421
(1.3,2.4) (-1,1)
distance between = 2.69258
```

One other change is made in the `Point` constructors shown in *points2.cc* compared with `points.cc`. The constructors are defined **inline** or within the class declaration rather than outside the class declaration. Any member function can be defined inline, but we do not do this with classes since classes are normally implemented in separate interface and implementation files. We will keep to this design rule of defining class member functions separately and not inline. Sometimes, however, we'll define struct member functions inline, especially when the functions are very short. Compilers can implement some inline functions to be more efficient than an equivalent non-inline function. You should not worry about this kind of efficiency as you begin to program. As you become more adept at programming, you may find applications that require inline definitions for efficiency reasons. For our purposes, we define some struct functions as inline only when they are easier to read.

7.4   Chapter Review

■   When designing and implementing classes, first concentrate on behavior (member functions) then concentrate on state (private data).

■   Use stub functions when you want to test a class (or program) without implementing all the functions at once.

■   Factor out common code accessed by more than one function into another function that is called multiple times. For member functions, make these helping functions private so that they can be called from other member functions but not from client programs.

■ Try to keep the bodies of each member function short so that the functions are easy to verify and modify.

■ The class `RandGen` declared in *rando.h* can be used to generate random `int` and `double` values.

■ Keep classes single purpose. Use more than one class rather than combining different or unrelated behaviors in the same class.

■ Reference variables are used when an object should not be copied or to share one object among several objects (again, a copy must be avoided to share the object).

■ Initializer lists are used to construct private data in a class. You should use initializer lists rather than assigning values in the body of a constructor.

■ Enumerated types, or `enum` types, allow you to define the legal values of a type. Enums make a program more readable since values can be symbolic rather than numeric, for example.

■ Structs are used as heterogeneous aggregates. When related data should be stored together without the programming and design overhead of implementing a class, structs are a useful alternative. Structs are classes in which the data are public by default. Structs can also have constructors and helper functions to make them easier to use.

■ The insertion operator can be overloaded for programmer-defined types.

7.5   Exercises

7.1 A reasonable but rough approximation of the mathematical constant π can be obtained by simulating throwing darts. The simulated darts are thrown at a dartboard in the shape of a square with a quarter-circle in it.

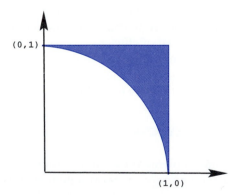

If 1000 darts are thrown at the square, and 785 land in the circle, then $785/1000$ is an approximation for $\pi/4$ since the area of the circle (with radius 1) is $\pi/4$. The approximation for π is $4 \times 0.785 = 3.140$. Write a program to approximate π using this method. Use a unit square as shown in the figure, with corners at (0,0), (1,0),

(1,1), and (0,1). Use the `RandGen` class specified in *rando.h* and the member function `RandReal`, which returns a random `double` value in the range [0..1). For example, the following code segment generates random x and y values inside the square and increments a counter `hits` if the point (x, y) lies within the circle.

```
x = gen.RandReal();
y = gen.RandReal();

if (x*x + y*y <= 1.0)
{
    hits++;
}
```

This works because the equation of the unit circle is $x^2 + y^2 = 1$. Allow the user to specify the number of darts (random numbers) thrown or use a varying number of darts to experiment with different approximations. This kind of approximation is called a **Monte Carlo** approximation.

7.2 A result of Dirichlet (see [Knu81], Sec. 4.5) says that if two numbers are chosen at random, the probability that their greatest common divisor equals 1 is $6/\pi^2$. Write a program that repeatedly chooses two integers at random and calculates the approximation to π. For best results use a `RandGen` variable `gen` (from *rando.h*) and generate a random integer using `gen.RandInt(1,RAND_MAX)`.

7.3 This problem is a simplistic simulation of neutrons in a nuclear reactor (adapted from [BRE71]). Neutrons enter the lead wall of a nuclear reactor and collide with the lead atoms in the wall. Each time a neutron collides with a lead atom it rebounds in a random direction (between 0 and 2π radians) before colliding with another lead atom, reentering the reactor, or leaving the wall. To simplify the simulation we'll assume that all neutrons enter the wall at a right angle; each neutron travels a distance d before either colliding, reentering the reactor, or leaving the wall; and the wall is $3d$ units thick. Figure 7.7 diagrams a wall; the reactor is at the bottom. The neutron at the left reenters the reactor, the neutron in the middle leaves the wall outside the reactor, and the neutron on the right is absorbed in the wall (assume that after 10 collisions within the wall a neutron is absorbed).

If p is the depth of penetration inside the wall, then p is changed after each collision by `p += d * cos(angle)` where `angle` is a random angle (see *brownian.cc*, Prog. 7.5). If $p < 0$, then the neutron reenters the reactor, and if $3d < p$, then the neutron leaves the wall; otherwise it collides with another lead atom or is absorbed.

Write a program to simulate this reactor. Use 10,000 neutrons in the simulation and determine the percentage of neutrons that return to the reactor, are absorbed in the wall, and penetrate the wall to leave the reactor. Use the simulation to determine the minimal wall thickness (as a multiple of d) required so that no more than 5% of the neutrons escape the reactor. To help test your simulation, roughly 26% of the neutrons should leave a $3d$-thick wall and roughly 22% should be absorbed.

7.4 Repeat the simulation from the previous exercise but assume the neutrons enter the wall at a random angle rather than at a right angle. Then implement a neutron observer class that records the movements of a neutron. Record the motion of 10 neutrons and graph the output if you have access to a plotting program.

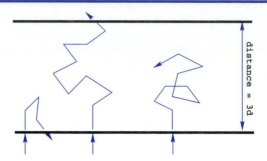

Figure 7.7   Collisions in a nuclear reactor.

7.5 Write a program to test the relationship $D = \sqrt{N} \times L$ from statistical physics, described in Sec. 7.1. Use a one-dimensional random walk and vary both the length of each step L and the number of steps N. You'll need to run several hundred experiments for each value; try to automate the process.

   If you have access to a graphing program, graph the results. If you know about curve fitting, try to fit a curve to the results and see if the empirical observations match the theoretical equation. You can repeat this experiment for the two-dimensional random walk.

7.6 Write a program for two-dimensional random walks in which two frogs (or two molecules) participate at the same time. Keep track of the closest and furthest distances the molecules are away from each other during the simulation. Can you easily extend this to three frogs or four frogs?

7.7 (This exercise requires Excursion Sec. 6.7.) Write a program that simulates n one-dimensional random walkers, where the user enters n. You'll need to modify the class `RandomWalker` so that it has a default parameter in order to create a `List<RandomWalker>` object. Keep track of how many times half of the walkers occupy the same location.

7.8 Modify *fingerp.cc*, Prog. 6.9, to use the following struct `FileStats`.

```
struct FileStats
{
    string filename;            // name of file
    int numSmall;               // # of small words in file
    int numMedium;              // # of medium words in file
    int numLarge;               // # of large words in file
    int total;                  // total # of words
    FileStats(const string & name);      // constructor
};

FileStats::FileStats(const string & name)
    : filename(name)
// postcondition: all fields initialized
```

```
    {
        numSmall = numMedium = numLarge = total = 0;
    }
```

With this constructor, an object must be constructed after the user enters the file name. Add a member function named `Print()` to `FileStats` to print a file's fingerprint or overload the insertion operator, `<<`.

7.6　A Computer Science Excursion: Embedded Real-Time Systems

In this section we'll lay the groundwork for an extended set of exercises based on a class designed to simulate a cardioverter-defibrillator. This is a device that monitors a person's heart rhythms and administers an electric shock when these rhythms indicate that the heart is not functioning correctly. The class is based on an idea of Rich Pattis in [Pat91]. This class is a very loose simulation of a real cardiac monitor. For example, initially the same "shock" is administered for both bradycardia and tachycardia (too slow and too rapid heartbeats, respectively). A cardiac monitor is an example of an **embedded real-time system.** "Real time" means that there can be no delays in the operation of the system; it must function constantly. "Embedded" means that the system is not a general-purpose computing device, but is designed and used for a very specific purpose.

The simulated heart monitor illustrates a key benefit of simulations: model the real world before coping with the real world. In the case of a cardioverter, it would be useful to know of any "bugs" in the design and the use of such pacemakers before testing them with real hearts.

Collaborating Classes: Heart and Monitor

For the purposes of this simulation, a shock to the heart is necessary whenever there are too few or too many beats in a given period. The member function `Heart::Sense()` returns a voltage reading. The value of the voltage reading

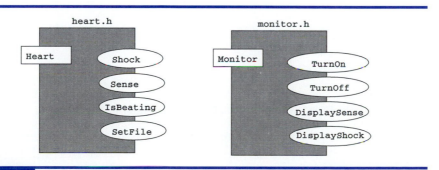

Figure 7.8　　Heart **class.**

represents information about how the heart is beating. The Heart class is diagrammed in Fig. 7.8. The class Monitor is used to monitor the heart similarly to how the Observer class observes a random walk.

Program 7.15, *cardiov.cc*, illustrates the use of the class Heart and the class Monitor. The program prompts for the name of a file storing simulated voltages and then reads and prints the voltages.

Program 7.15   cardiov.cc

```
#include <iostream.h>
#include "heart.h"
#include "monitor.h"
#include "prompt.h"

// skeleton program for heart monitor program
// written: 9/8/93
// modified 1/17/94, 7/1/96
//
// Owen Astrachan

void Operate(Heart & theHeart,Monitor & m);    // do work of heart sensing

int main()
{
    Monitor m;
    Heart theHeart(m);          // initialize heart with monitor

    theHeart.SetFile(PromptString("enter filename: "));
    Operate(theHeart,m);             // monitor the heart

    return 0;
}

void Operate(Heart & theHeart, Monitor & m)
// precondition: heart is properly formed
// postcondition: heart is monitored until all beats have been processed
{

    int newSense;
    m.TurnOn();

    while (theHeart.IsBeating())
    {
        newSense = theHeart.Sense();
        if (newSense < MIN_VOLT || MAX_VOLT < newSense)
        {
            cout << "ERROR: bad voltage reading: " << newSense << endl;
        }
    }
    theHeart.Shock(Heart::SpeedUp);
}
```

```
                              OUTPUT

prompt>  cardiov
enter name of input file>    heart.dat
monitor sense: 1
monitor sense: -1
monitor sense: 2
monitor sense: 3
monitor sense: -4
monitor sense: 11
ERROR: bad voltage reading: 11
monitor sense: 10
monitor sense: 9
monitor sense: -8
monitor sense: -11
ERROR: bad voltage reading: -11
monitor sense: 5
Shocked after 11 senses
SPEED UP
```

Just as the walker class required an observer when constructed in *frog-walk3.cc*, Prog. 7.8, a heart class requires a monitor when constructed. The monitor m is also passed to the function Operate so that m can be turned on during an "operation." If the monitor isn't turned on, the output will not be visible. The Heart variable theHeart is sensed as long as it continues to beat. The heartbeats that appear in the output are not printed directly by *cardiov.cc* but are generated by the Monitor object m. The text file *heart.dat* used in the run of *cardiov.cc* contains the data

```
1 -1 2 3 -4
11 10 9 -8 -11 5
```

The header file *heart.h* for the Heart class (Prog. 7.16) contains documentation about the class's member functions that will be useful in analyzing the behavior of *cardiov.cc*.

Program 7.16 heart.h

```
#ifndef _HEART_H
#define _HEART_H

// class for implementing cardioverter/fibrillator simulation
// from an idea by Rich Pattis (in SIGCSE 90)
//
```

```
// written by Owen Astrachan
// 9/8/93, modified 1/17/94, modified 6/20/96
//
// use/semantics:
//
// Heart(Monitor & m) -- initialize heart to be monitored
//
// int Sense()     -- precondition: heart still beating
//                    i.e., information still available in file (if reading)
//                    postcondition: returns voltage (int) read from file
//                    exception: returns INT_MAX if no data available
//
// void Shock(ShockType)  -- causes heart to be shocked, this causes some
//                    action, and may affect subsequent sense readings
//
// bool IsBeating() -- returns true if heart is beating, false otherwise
//
// void SetFile(string name) -- set up heart to read simulated
//                    voltages from file "name"


#include <limits.h>
#include <fstream.h>
#include "CPstring.h"
#include "monitor.h"

const int MAX_VOLT = 10;               // maximum voltage for heart beat
const int MIN_VOLT = -10;              // minimum voltage for heart beat

class Heart
{
  public:
    enum ShockType {SlowDown,SpeedUp};

    Heart(Monitor & m);           // monitor the heart using monitor m
    void SetFile(const string & name); // specifies file for voltages
    int Sense();                  // return next sensed heart beat value
    void Shock(ShockType s);      // shock the heart
    bool IsBeating();             // return true if heart is beating

  private:

    bool myFromFile;              // true if beats come from file
    ifstream myFile;              // file being read for simulation
    int mySenseCount;             // store # times heart has been sensed
    bool myBeating;               // stores "good" state (still beating)
    int mySense;                  // stores last value read/next value sensed

    Monitor & myMonitor;          // monitor heart via this field
    int SelfSense();              // heart generates its own beat

    Heart (const Heart &);        // pass-by-value prohibited
    Heart & operator = (const Heart &); // no assignment possible
};

#endif  // _HEART_H not defined
```

A Simulated Cardioverter

The function `main` in Prog. 7.15 is fairly straightforward. Because the `Heart` constructor has a `Monitor` reference parameter, the `Monitor` object m must be defined before the `Heart` object `theHeart`. The user is prompted for the name of a file storing numbers representing simulated voltages. The heart is then passed to the user-defined function `Operate`, which checks the voltages of the simulated heart. The formal parameter `theHeart` is passed by reference as indicated in both the prototype of `Operator` and in the function header. It's often useful to pass objects that are instances of a class by reference to save memory and time. It's not possible to use a const reference parameter here because the heart changes: it beats, it is sensed, and it might be shocked.

Reading simulated heart values. The member function `Heart::Sense()` detects a simulated heartbeat. As the documentation in the header file *heart.h*, Prog. 7.16, indicates, when the heart is no longer beating, a value of `INT_MAX` is returned. There are several alternative methods that might be used to signal the end of the simulated heart, and you'll be asked to explore some in the exercises. For example, instead of using the member function `Heart::IsBeating()`, you can test the value returned by `Heart::Sense()` to see if it is equal to `INT_MAX`. The `while` loop test shown here uses the value returned by the assignment operator = in an expression typical of C and C++:

```
while ( (newSense = theHeart.Sense()) != INT_MAX)
```

Copy constructors. In the function `Operate` of Prog 7.15 `theHeart` is monitored by reading values from a file to simulate heart voltages. The stream that represents the file is part of the class `Heart`—it's stored as the `ifstream` instance variable `myFile`. Calling the member function `Heart::Sense()` results in extracting a value from the stream, in this case, reading the file. The state of the object `theHeart` changes as a result of this monitoring: a voltage value has been extracted from the stream of voltages. Because this change should be communicated back to the calling program (in this case, `main`), `theHeart` must be a reference parameter. In general all stream parameters should be passed by reference. We've only seen `ifstream` stream variables, but in later chapters we'll use other kinds of streams. For example, `cin` is an input stream that isn't an `ifstream` object; it's not bound to a file.

Program Tip: Passing streams by value can result in ill-defined program behavior. In general, pass all streams by reference. As another general rule, pass parameters by value, as the default, if the parameter is a built-in type (e.g., `int`), and parameters of user-defined classes by reference (as the default). There are occasions, however, to pass built-in types by reference and user-defined types by value.

When a value parameter is copied, the compiler must be able to generate the copy. For user-defined types, the compiler will try to do the right thing in copying a variable, but as we'll see in a later chapter this default right thing is not always desirable. For this reason, the designer of a class can implement a special constructor that defines how to copy a value when using a value parameter. Such a constructor is called a **copy constructor.** At this point, we're concerned only with the existence of the copy construc-

> **Syntax: copy constructor**
>
> ```
> ClassName::ClassName(const
> ClassName & param-id)
> ```
>
> The constructor used to make a copy when a parameter is passed by value.

tor, not how to implement one. In the file `heart.h`, the copy constructor is declared to be private since the function prototype `Heart::Heart(const Heart &)` appears in the private section. Since a client program cannot access any private data or member functions, the copy constructor is not accessible.

If the prototype (and header) for the function `Operate` in Prog. 7.15 is changed to

```
void Operate(Heart heart, Monitor & m); // do work of heart sensing
```

the program will not compile. The g++ compiler generates the very informative error message

```
heart.h: In function 'int  main ()':
heart.h:37: the constructor 'Heart::Heart (const class Heart&)' is private
cardiov.cc:22: within this context
```

indicating both that constructor is private and that it is called from line 22 in *cardiov.cc*. The Turbo C++ compiler generates the error message

```
Error HEARTMON.CPP 22: 'Heart::Heart(const Heart &)' is not accessible
Error HEARTMON.CPP 22: Type mismatch in parameter 'myHeart' in call Monitor(myHeart)
```

This is also somewhat useful in pinpointing the problem.

Heart rhythms. The purpose of this simulation is to determine whether the heart is beating regularly. A series of voltage readings is taken and the number of heartbeats in a period of beatings determines if the heart is functioning normally. The length of a period is 20 voltage readings, but this may change. The program developed around the `Heart` and `Monitor` classes should be easy to modify to accommodate such changes.

Whenever the voltage changes from positive to negative, or vice versa, the heart beats. This voltage change is the heart contracting and expanding, sending different electronic signals to the monitor. For purposes of the simulation, a reading of zero (0) is positive. If there are fewer than 5 beats in a period, then the heart is not beating enough and should be shocked. If there are more than 10 beats in a period, the heart is beating too rapidly and should be shocked. For each period of senses, it will be necessary to determine whether it is necessary to administer a shock.

Consider the following voltage chart, which shows 22 voltage readings, and the accumulated zero-crossing count (zcc):

sense	*	1	2	3	4	5	6	7	8	9	10	11	12	13	14	15	16	17	18	19	20	21	22
volt.	0	5	9	5	0	−3	0	3	0	−1	0	5	9	5	0	−3	0	3	0	−1	0	−2	9
zcc	0					1	2			3	4					5	6			7	8	1	

Note that the "zeroth" voltage (marked with an * above) is assumed to be positive, so that if the first voltage actually read/sensed is negative then a zero crossing occurs. Also note that in the first period of 20 readings there are 8 zero crossings, and that the first reading in period 21 (a reading of -2) is marked as a zero crossing because the previous reading (in the previous period) is positive.

In modifying the function `Operate` in Prog. 7.15 so that the heart will be shocked appropriately, it will be necessary to track the zero crossings. This will require a counter that is initialized to zero, incremented when a zero crossing occurs, and reset to zero when a period has been monitored. To determine when a zero crossing occurs the most recently monitored voltage (value stored in `newSense`) will need to be compared with the last voltage read. Determining if these values have different signs can be done in many ways:

- using statements such as `if(0 <= newSense && oldSense < 0)`
- using a user-defined function that indicates if its `int` parameter is positive or negative (such a function is typically called `sign` or `sgn`)
- multiplying the values to see if the result is positive indicating that the signs are the same

Implementing the `Heart` Class

The implementation of the `Heart` class is shown below as Prog. 7.17.

Program 7.17   heart.cc

```
#include <iostream.h>
#include <stdlib.h>                // for exit
#include <math.h>
#include "heart.h"
#include "dice.h"
#include "rando.h"
// implementation of heart monitor (cardioverter/defibrillator)
// Owen Astrachan
// written 9/8/93
// extensively modified 1/16/94
```

```
// now supports input from ifstream
// modified 6/95 to add IsBeating member function
// modified 6/96 to add external monitor

Heart::Heart(Monitor & m)
    : myFromFile(false),
      mySenseCount(0),
      myBeating(true),
      myMonitor(m)
// postcondition: heart is initialized to "sense itself"
//                all fields initialized
{

}

void Heart::SetFile(const string & name)
// precondition: text file "name" can be open for reading
// postcondition: heart is set to read data from file "name"
{
    myFile.open(name.c_str());
    myBeating = false;
    myFromFile = true;

    if (myFile.fail())
    {
        cerr << "could not open file " << name << endl;
    }
    else
    {
        if (myFile >> mySense)
        {
            mySenseCount = 0;
            myBeating = true;
        }
        else
        {
            myBeating = false;
        }
    }
}

int Heart::Sense()
// precondition: if reading from file: file specified by myFile has
//               unread numerical data
// postcondition: next heart 'sense' is returned, also monitored
// exception: if int read fails, INT_MAX returned
// side-effect: mySenseCount updated
//              heart is monitored
{
    int value;

    if (myFromFile)                 // reading sense from file?
    {
        if (IsBeating())
        {
            value = mySense;
```

```
                mySenseCount++;
                myFile >> mySense;
                if (myFile.fail())
                {
                    myBeating = false;
                }
            }
            else
            {
                value = INT_MAX;
                myBeating = false;
            }
        }
        else                          // generating own sense
        {
            mySenseCount++;
            value = SelfSense();
        }
        myMonitor.DisplaySense(itoa(value));
        return value;
}

int Heart::SelfSense()
// postcondition: returns a value representing electric signal
// side-effect:   heart is monitored
{
        static RandGen gen;         // for random electrical fluctuations

        int value =  gen.RandInt(MIN_VOLT,MAX_VOLT);

        return value;
}


bool Heart::IsBeating()
// postcondition: returns true if heart is beating;
//                otherwise returns false
{
        return myBeating;
}

void Heart::Shock(ShockType s)
// postcondition: shock method printed
{
        myMonitor.DisplayShock("Shocked after " + itoa(mySenseCount) + " senses");

        if (s == SpeedUp)
        {
            myMonitor.DisplayShock("SPEED UP");
        }
        else
        {
            myMonitor.DisplayShock("SLOW DOWN");
        }
}
```

Like all constructors, the `Heart` constructor must initialize all private data fields. An initializer list is used since this is the preferred method for initializing instance variables and is required in the case of the reference variable `myMonitor`.

An error message is printed in `Heart::SetFile()` if the `ifstream` variable `myFile` cannot be opened. The standard error stream `cerr` is used for this message. Like `cout`, this stream is normally associated with the screen of a computer. It is good practice to write error messages to the `cerr` stream. This is especially important in environments in which I/O redirection (see Sec. 6.2) is used since the stream `cerr` is not redirected in the same way that `cout` is.

The `Sense` function uses the extraction operator, `>>`, to read data and uses `fail` to determine if the extraction succeeds. When the extraction fails, the value `INT_MAX` is returned. The logic of the function is tricky because the extraction stores the next value that will be sensed. This is necessary so that the `Heart::IsBeating()` function will work properly. When the heart is beating, it can be sensed. However, sensing the heart must also set the state for the next sensing. The member function `Heart::Shock()` simply passes a shock message to the instance variable `myMonitor` including how many times the heart has been sensed.

In the exercises we'll explore an alternative for the simulation wherein a `Heart` object generates its own beats. This kind of behavior is supported in the current `Heart` implementation by the member function `SelfSense`. This function is called if the client program has not called `SetFile`. In its current version, the function `SelfSense` returns a random value in the proper voltage range. In the exercises you'll be asked to change this behavior so that voltage readings are more regular. For the moment we'll ignore the definition of `RandGen gen` as a `static` variable; static variables are explained in detail in Sec. 10.5.

Excursion Exercises

7.9 Modify *cardiov.cc,* Prog. 7.15, so that zero-crossing counts are calculated. Plan the modifications carefully and think about difficult cases you'll need to test by developing appropriate test files. When you are satisfied that this part of the program works, add code so that the heart is shocked when it is beating either too slowly or too rapidly based on the values discussed in the text above. Be sure to use constants where appropriate.

7.10 Add an enhancement to the `Heart` class by defining a new member function that can be called when the heart is no longer beating (i.e., the body to which the heart belongs is dead). This method might, for example, print an appropriate message. Also include a member function that can be called when the heart is beating spasmodically, defined by a zero-crossing count of greater than 75% of the voltages in a period (e.g., 15 zcc's when the period is 20).

7.11 Currently, values that are "out of range," i.e., greater than 10 or less than −10, are checked by the client program. Change the responsibility for this range checking so that it belongs to the `Heart` class. As a first step, have out-of-range values converted to the highest or lowest legal voltages depending on whether the out-of-range values are too high or too low. As a second step modify `Heart::Sense()` so that illegal values are skipped. This will require using a loop rather than an `if` statement. Be sure that the loop does not attempt to read past the end of the file in which the simulated voltages are stored.

7.12 Modify `Heart::Sense()` so that the sensed value is returned via a reference parameter. Then change the return value of the function so that it is boolean and returns true whenever the sense succeeded and false otherwise. A loop to sense all values can now be written as

```
int newSense;
while (heart.Sense(newSense))
{
    // process newSense
}
```

This works because the `Sense` method now returns true only if the value assigned to the parameter `newSense` (this isn't necessarily the name of the formal parameter) is valid. Be sure to change the documentation in the header file appropriately.

7.13 Change `Heart::SelfSense()` so that instead of using a random value a sine wave is used to give relatively regular voltage readings. Use a function of the form

$$A \times \sin(f \times mySenseCount)$$

where A is the amplitude of the sine function and f is the frequency. An amplitude of 10 ensures that all readings are between -10 and 10. If the frequency is increased, the heart will beat more rapidly; i.e., there will be more zero crossings. Decreasing the frequency makes the heat beat more slowly. Add instance variables for the amplitude and frequency. Shocking the heart should change the frequency appropriately so that a misbehaving heart is "fixed."

7.14 Using the modification of `Heart::SelfSense()` from the previous exercise, add a random component. There should be a 5% chance that the heart speeds up and a 5% chance that it slows down, for a 10% chance that the beat changes. Use a 100-sided `Dice` object and increase the frequency if it rolls 1–5 and decrease the frequency if it rolls 96–100. Then add a random spike component so that there is 1 chance in 1,000 that the heart stops beating completely.

Arrays, Data, and Random Access

A teacher who can arouse a feeling for one single good action . . . , accomplishes more than he who fills our memory with rows on rows of natural objects, classified with name and form.
GOETHE
Elective Affinities, Book II, Ch. 7

Computers are useless, they can only give you answers
PABLO PICASSO
21st Century Dictionary of Quotations

A compact disc (CD), a computer graphics monitor, and a group of campus mailboxes share a common characteristic, as shown in Fig. 8.1: Each consists of a sequence of items, and each item is accessible independently of the other items. In the case of a CD, any track can be played without regard to whether

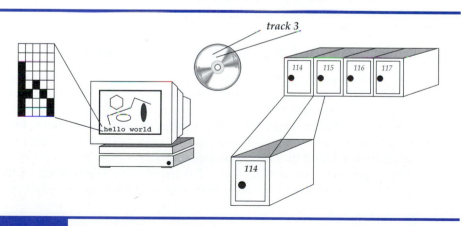

Figure 8.1   Instant/random access.

the other tracks are played. This arrangement is different from the way songs are recorded on a cassette tape, where, for example, the fifth song is accessible only after playing or fast-forwarding past the first four. In the case of a graphics monitor, any individual picture element, or **pixel**, can be turned on or off, or changed to a different color, without concern as to what the values of the other pixels are. The independence of each pixel to display different colors permits images to be displayed very rapidly. The address of a student on many campuses, or a person living in an apartment building, is typically specified by a box number. Postal workers can deliver letters to box 117 without worrying about the location of the first 100 boxes, the last 100 boxes, or any boxes other than 117.

This characteristic of instant access is useful in programming applications. The terminology used is **random access,** as opposed to the **sequential access** to a cassette tape. Most programming languages include a construct that allows data to be grouped together so that each data item is accessible independently of the other items. For example, a collection of numbers might represent test scores; a collection of strings could represent the different words in *Hamlet;* and a collection of strings and numbers combined in a struct might represent the words in *Hamlet* and how many times each word occurs.

We've studied three ways of structuring data in C++ programs: classes, structs, and files accessible using streams.[1] In this chapter you will learn about a data structure called an **array**—one of the most useful data structures in programming. Examples of array use in this chapter include

- Using an array as many counters, e.g., to keep track of how many times all sums of rolling *n*-sided dice occur or to keep track of how many times each letter of the alphabet occurs in *Hamlet.*

- Using an array to store a list of words in a file, keeping track of each different word and then extending this array to track how many times each different word occurs.

- Using an array to maintain a database of on-line information for over 3,000 different CD titles, or alternatively, an on-line address book.

8.1   Arrays and Vectors as Counters

Program 6.9, *fingerp.cc* (page 307), keeps track of the number of "short" and "long words" in any text file. Modifying the program to keep track of several different word lengths would be a cumbersome programming task. For example, six variables are needed to keep track of the number of two-, three-, four-, five-, six-, and seven-letter words in one of Shakespeare's plays. These variables must be defined, initialized, and updated appropriately.

A similar program, *rollsum2.cc*, Prog. 5.6 (page 188), keeps track of the number of times a seven (or any other user-specified number) is rolled in a

---

[1]In Excursion Section 6.7 we studied the class List, which is also used to structure data.

series of dice rolls. Modifying this program to track the number of times each possible dice roll occurs is also cumbersome, as shown in Prog. 8.1, *dieroll.cc*, which calculates the number of times all possible rolls of two four-sided dice occur. You can see that a program for a six-sided die would be very ugly.

Program 8.1   dieroll.cc

```cpp
#include <iostream.h>
#include "dice.h"

// illustrates cumbersome programming
// roll two dice and track occurrences of all possible rolls

const int DICE_SIDES = 4;

int main()
{
    int rolls;
    int twos = 0;          // counters for each possible roll
    int threes = 0;
    int fours = 0;
    int fives = 0;
    int sixes = 0;
    int sevens = 0;
    int eights = 0;

    cout << "how many rolls ";
    cin >> rolls;

    Dice d(DICE_SIDES);
    int k;
    for(k=0; k < rolls; k++)          // simulate all the rolls
    {
        int sum = d.Roll() + d.Roll();
        switch (sum)
        {
          case 2:
            twos++;
            break;
          case 3:
            threes++ ;
            break;
          case 4:
            fours++;
            break;
          case 5:
            fives++;
            break;
          case 6:
            sixes++;
            break;
```

```
            case 7:
              sevens++;
              break;
            case 8:
              eights++;
              break;
        }
    }

    // output for each possible roll # of times it occurred

    cout << "roll\t# of occurrences" << endl;
    cout << "2\t" << twos   << endl;
    cout << "3\t" << threes << endl;
    cout << "4\t" << fours  << endl;
    cout << "5\t" << fives  << endl;
    cout << "6\t" << sixes  << endl;
    cout << "7\t" << sevens << endl;
    cout << "8\t" << eights << endl;

    return 0;
}
```

OUTPUT

```
prompt> dieroll
how many rolls   10000
roll             # of occurrences
2                623
3                1204
4                1935
5                2474
6                1894
7                1246
8                624
```

The code in *dieroll.cc* would be much more compact if loops could be used to initialize the variables and generate the output. We need a new kind of variable that maintains several different values at the same time; such a variable could be used in place of twos, threes, fours, and so on. Most programming languages support such variables; they are called **arrays.** An array structures data together, but has three important properties:

1. An array is a *homogeneous* collection. Each item stored in an array is the same type; for example, all integers, all doubles, or all strings. It is not possible to store both integers and strings in the same array.

2. Items in an array are numbered, or ordered; that is, there is a first item, a fifteenth item, and so on. The number that refers to an item is the item's **index,** sometimes called the **subscript.**

3. An array supports **random access.** The time to access the first item is the same as the time to access the fifteenth item or the hundredth item.

In C++ the built-in array type has many problems; it is difficult for beginning programmers to use and is too closely related to the low-level details of how arrays are implemented in C++. We'll study built-in arrays, but we want to study the concept of homogeneous collections and random access without the hardships associated with using the built-in array type. Instead, we'll use a class that behaves identically to an array from a programming perspective but insulates us from the kind of programming problems that are common with built-in arrays. We'll use a `Vector` class, defined in the header file *vector.h*.[2]

Before studying Prog. 8.2, a program that is similar to *dieroll.cc* but uses a `Vector` to track dice rolls, we'll discuss important properties of the `Vector` class and how to define `Vector` variables.

`Vector` **Definition: An Introduction**

The simplest definition of a `Vector` variable includes the variable's name, the type of item being stored, and an integer value passed to the constructor that indicates how many items the vector can store. The definitions below define a variable `numbers` that can store seven integer values and a variable `words` that can store five string values.

```
Vector<int>    numbers(7);
Vector<string> words(5);
```

Because a `Vector` is a homogeneous collection, you can think of a `Vector` variable as a collection of boxes:

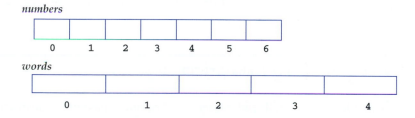

---

[2]There is a class `vector` defined as part of the STL library in the C++ standard. The class `Vector` declared in *vector.h* is consistent with this standard class. There is also a class `apvector`, defined for use in the Advanced Placement computer science course. The `apvector` class is based on the class `Vector`, and all member functions of the `apvector` class are also member functions of the `Vector` class.

Each box or item in the Vector is referenced using a numerical index. In C++ the first item stored in a Vector has index zero. Thus, in the diagram here, the five items in words are indexed from zero to four. In general, the valid indices in a Vector with n elements are $0, 1, \ldots, n - 1$.

An element of a Vector is selected, or referenced, using a numerical index and brackets: [ ]. The following statements store the number 13 as the first element of *numbers* and the string "fruitcake" as the first element of *words* (remember that the first element has index zero):

```
numbers[0] = 13;
words[0] = "fruitcake";
```

Vector variables can be indexed using a loop as follows, where all the elements of numbers are assigned the value zero:

```
int k;
for(k=0; k < 5; k++)
{
    numbers[k] = 0;
}
```

The number of elements in a vector variable is specified by a parameter to the Vector constructor, just as the number of sides of a Dice variable is specified when the Dice variable is constructed, as shown in Fig. 8.2. This value can be a variable whose value is entered by the user; an expression; or, in general, any integer value. More details on defining Vector variables are given in Sec. 8.2.

Vectors and Counting: Rolling Dice

Program 8.2, *dieroll2.cc* uses a Vector to keep track of different dice rolls but otherwise performs the same tasks as Prog. 8.1, *dieroll.cc.*

From a black-box viewpoint there is no difference between the programs *dieroll.cc* and *dieroll2.cc.* The Vector variable diceStats can store nine different integer values. The capacity of diceStats is determined when the variable is defined by the statement Vector<int> diceStats(2*DICE_SIDES+1).

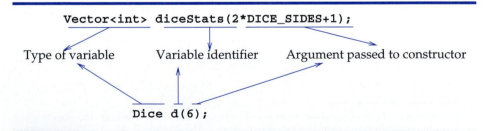

Figure 8.2 Comparing a Vector variable definition to a Dice variable definition. Both variables have names and a constructor parameter.

Program 8.2   dieroll2.cc

```cpp
#include <iostream.h>
#include "dice.h"
#include "vector.h"

// use vector to simulate rolling of two dice
// Owen Astrachan
// March 9, 1994

const int DICE_SIDES = 4;

int main()
{
    int rolls;
    int sum;
    int k;
    Dice d(DICE_SIDES);
    Vector<int> diceStats(2*DICE_SIDES+1); // room for largest dice sum

    cout << "how many rolls ";
    cin >> rolls;

    for(k=2; k <= 2*DICE_SIDES; k++)         // initialize counters to zero
    {
        diceStats[k] = 0;
    }

    for(k=0; k < rolls; k++)                 // simulate all the rolls
    {
        sum = d.Roll() + d.Roll();
        diceStats[sum]++;
    }

    cout << "roll\t\t# of occurrences" << endl;
    for(k=2; k <= 2*DICE_SIDES; k++)
    {
        cout << k << "\t\t" << diceStats[k] << endl;
    }
    return 0;
}
```

OUTPUT

```
prompt> dieroll2
how many rolls 10000
```

```
roll              # of occurrences
2                 623
3                 1204
4                 1935
5                 2474
6                 1894
7                 1246
8                 624
```

There is one major difference between the definition of diceStats as a Vector variable and that of d as a Dice variable: the Vector definition indicates that the Vector contains integers. We'll discuss this in depth after examining other parts of the program.

Because the indexing begins with 0, the last location in a nine-element array has index 8. This is why space for nine integer values is allocated in Prog. 8.2 even though only seven of the locations are accessed in the program—diceStats[2] through diceStats[8]—as shown in Fig. 8.3. The conceptual simplicity of using diceStats[sum] to represent the number of times two dice are rolled more than compensates for the two memory locations that could be saved by defining an array of seven values and using diceStats[sum-2] to store the number of times sum is obtained.

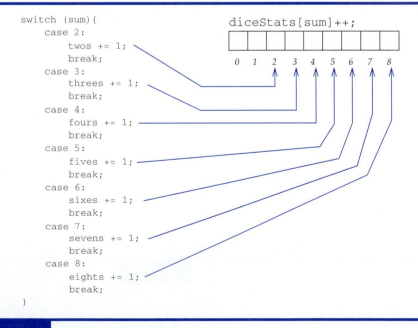

Figure 8.3   Using an array to store counts.

In Fig. 8.3 the `switch` statement used to increment the appropriate counter in Prog. 8.1 is contrasted with the single statement `diceStats[sum]++`, which increments the corresponding array location serving as a counter in Prog. 8.2.

When an array is defined, the values in each array location, or **cell,** are initially undefined. The array cells can be used as variables, but they must be indexed, as shown here for an array named `diceStats` containing nine cells:

```
Vector<int> diceStats(9);
```

| ? | ? | ? | ? | ? | ? | ? | ? | ? | Values undefined
| --- | --- | --- | --- | --- | --- | --- | --- | --- |
index 0 1 2 3 4 5 6 7 8

```
diceStats[1] = 0;
```

| ? | 0 | ? | ? | ? | ? | ? | ? | ? | One value defined
| --- | --- | --- | --- | --- | --- | --- | --- | --- |
index 0 1 2 3 4 5 6 7 8

```
diceStats[1]++;
```

| ? | 1 | ? | ? | ? | ? | ? | ? | ? | One value incremented
| --- | --- | --- | --- | --- | --- | --- | --- | --- |
index 0 1 2 3 4 5 6 7 8

The indexing expression determines which of the many array locations is accessed. Indexing makes arrays extraordinarily useful. One array variable represents potentially thousands of different values, each value specified by the array variable name and the indexing value. The expression `diceStats[1]` is read as "diceStats sub one," where the word "sub" comes from the mathematical concept of a *subscripted* variable such as n_1.

8.2 Defining and Using Vectors/Arrays

`Vector` Definition

When you define a `Vector` variable, you must specify the number of entries, or cells, in the `Vector`. Because vectors are homogeneous collections, you must also specify the type stored in each entry, such as `int`, `string`, or `double`.

The following three statements define two `Vector` variables: one named `numList`, capable of storing 200 values of type `double`, and one named `names`, capable of storing 50 `string` values:

```
const int SIZE = 100
Vector<double> numList(SIZE*2);
Vector<string> names(SIZE/2);
```

The type of value stored in each cell of a `Vector` variable is specified between angle brackets (the less-than and greater-than symbols) before the name of the variable is given. The size of the `Vector` is an argument to the constructor, as illustrated in Fig. 8.2.

The type that is used to define what *kind* of element is stored in each array cell can be any built-in type (e.g., `int`, `double`, `bool`). It can also be a programmer-defined type such as `string`. The only qualification on programmer-defined types is that the type must have a default (or param-

> **Syntax: Vector variable definition**
>
> `Vector<`*type*`>` *name* ;
> `Vector<`*type*`>` *name* (*expression*) ;
> `Vector<`*type*`>` *name* (*expression* ,
>   *value*) ;

eterless) constructor. For example, it is *not* possible to have a definition `Vector<Dice> dielist(10)` for an array of 10 dice elements, because a `Dice` object requires a parameter indicating the number of sides that the `Dice` object has. It is possible to define a vector of `Date` elements (see `"date.h"`, Program 5.15), because there is a default constructor for the `Date` class.

The *expression* in the `Vector` constructor determines the number of cells of the `Vector` variable. This integer expression can use variables, arithmetic operators, and function calls. For example, it is possible to use `Vector<int> primes(int(sqrt(X)));` to allocate a variable named `primes` whose number of cells is given by the (integer) truncated value of the square root of a variable `X`. If no integer expression is used, as in `Vector<int> list`, a vector with zero cells is created. We'll see later that sometimes this is necessary and that the number of cells in a vector can grow or shrink. The third form of constructor initializes all the cells to the value passed as the second argument to the constructor.

`Vector` Initialization

When a `Vector` variable is defined, each element of the vector has an undefined value unless the vector is constructed with an initial value. For example, when a variable is used to represent several counters, as it is in Prog. 8.2, *dieroll2.cc* (page 365), each element of the vector must be initialized to zero. Two `Vector` member functions, shown in Table 8.1, are used to initialize all elements of a vector, although this can be done by client programs too.

The generic type `Item` is used to represent the appropriate type, depending on what kind of `Vector` variable is used. For example, the two statements

Table 8.1   Initializing a `Vector` variable

Function	Description
`Vector(int size, Item fillValue)`	Constructor specifies size of vector and value to be used for all elements of vector
`void Fill(Item fillValue)`	Function used to specify value assigned to every element of a vector

```
Vector<string> names(20);
names.Fill("Fred Brooks");
```

result in the vector `names` containing twenty elements all with the same value: `"Fred Brooks"`. This could also be accomplished using the `Vector` constructor:

```
Vector<string> names(20,"Fred Brooks");
```

The member function `Fill` can be used to change the values of all vector elements after the vector has been defined.

`Vector` **Parameters**

`Vector` variables can be passed as parameters just like any other variable in C++.[3] To illustrate how vectors are used and passed as parameters, we'll study another example in which a vector is used to count several quantities. We'll count how many time each different character occurs in an input file. For example, we can count the number of occurrences of the letter *e* in *Hamlet* using Prog. 8.3, *letters.cc*. Just as a vector of counters was used to count dice rolls in *dieroll2.cc*, Prog. 8.2, a `Vector` of counters is used to track how many time each character occurs in the file.

Program 8.3   letters.cc

```
#include <iostream.h>
#include <fstream.h>           // for ifstream
#include <stdlib.h>            // for exit()
#include <ctype.h>             // for tolower()
#include <limits.h>            // for CHAR_MAX
#include "CPstring.h"
#include "prompt.h"
#include "vector.h"

// count # occurrences of all characters in a file
// written: 8/5/94
// by:      Owen Astrachan

void Print(const Vector<int> & counts, int total);
void Count(istream & input, Vector<int> & counts,
           int & total);
```

---

[3]This is not quite true of arrays, as we'll see later in this chapter; that is another reason to prefer using the `Vector` class to using built-in arrays.

```cpp
int main()
{
    int totalAlph = 0;
    string filename =
        PromptString("enter name of input file: ");
    ifstream input(filename);
    if (input.fail() )
    {
        cout << "could not open file " << filename << endl;
        exit(1);
    }
    Vector<int> charCounts(CHAR_MAX,0); // all initialized to 0

    Count(input,charCounts,totalAlph);
    Print(charCounts,totalAlph);

    return 0;
}

void Count(istream & input, Vector<int> & counts, int & total)
// precondition: input open for reading
//               counts[k] == 0, 0 <= k < CHAR_MAX
// postcondition: counts[k] = # occurrences of character k
//                total = # alphabetic characters
{
    char ch;
    while (input.get(ch))              // read a character
    {
        if (isalpha(ch))            // is alphabetic (a-z)?
        {
            total++;
        }
        ch = tolower(ch);           // convert to lower case
        counts[ch]++;               // count all characters
    }
}

void Print(const Vector<int> & counts, int total)
// postcondition: all values of counts from 'a' to 'z' printed
{
    cout.setf(ios::fixed);     // print 1 decimal place
    cout.precision(1);

    char k;
    for(k = 'a'; k <= 'z'; k++)
    {
        cout << k;
        cout.width(7);
        cout << counts[int(k)] << "   ";
        cout.width(4);
        cout << 100 * double(counts[int(k)])/total << "%"
            << endl;
    }
}
```

```
OUTPUT
```

```
prompt> letters
enter name of input file: hamlet
a    9950    7.6%
b    1830    1.4%
c    2606    2.0%
d    5025    3.9%
e   14960   11.5%
f    2698    2.1%
g    2420    1.9%
h    8731    6.7%
i    8511    6.5%
j     110    0.1%
k    1272    1.0%
l    5847    4.5%
m    4253    3.3%
n    8297    6.4%
o   11218    8.6%
p    2016    1.5%
q     220    0.2%
r    7777    6.0%
s    8379    6.4%
t   11863    9.1%
u    4343    3.3%
v    1222    0.9%
w    3132    2.4%
x     179    0.1%
y    3204    2.5%
z      72    0.1%
```

Counting characters is similar to counting dice rolls: each `Vector` element records the number of occurrences of one character. Characters are discussed in Sec. 9.1, but you don't need to understand the type `char` in detail to understand how to count characters. For all practical purposes, a `char` variable is an integer constrained to have a value between 0 and `CHAR_MAX-1`. Since `char` variables can be used as integers, we can use a `char` variable to index an array. Figure 8.4 shows how we use a vector element with index `'a'` to count the occurrences of `'a'`, an element with index `'b'` to count the b's, and so on. The constant `CHAR_MAX` is defined in `<limits.h>`. We use it to initialize `charCounts`, a `Vector` of counters, in *letters.cc*. The definition of `charCounts` initializes all elements to zero.

```
Vector<int> charCounts(CHAR_MAX,0);
```

Figure 8.4   Counting characters with a vector.

Only the 26 vector elements corresponding to the alphabetic characters 'a' through 'z' are printed. An alternative method of indexing charCounts that uses only 26 array elements rather than CHAR_MAX elements is explored in the Pause/Reflect exercises. To make the output look nice, we use stream member functions to limit the number of places after a decimal point when a double value is printed. These member functions are discussed in Sec. 9.4.

Vector parameters should always be passed by reference, unless you need to pass a copy of the Vector rather than the Vector itself. Avoid copying, because it takes time and uses memory. Some functions require value parameters, but these are rare when Vector parameters are used, so you should use reference parameters almost all the time. Use a const reference parameter, as shown in Print in Prog. 8.3, when a Vector parameter isn't changed. A const reference parameter is efficient and also allows the compiler to catch inadvertent attempts to change the value of the parameter. The parameter counts in the function Print is *not* changed; its contents are used to print the values of how many times each letter occurs.

Program Tip: Vector parameters should be passed by reference (using &) unless a copy of the parameter is required.

Use a const reference parameter as part of a defensive programming strategy when a parameter is not changed, but is passed by reference because of efficiency considerations.

Notice that the for loop in the function Print uses a char variable to index the values between 'a' and 'z'. When ASCII values are used, these indices correspond to array cells 97 to 122 (see Table 9.1 in Chapter 9).

Pause to reflect

8.1. In Prog. 8.1, how many lines must be changed or added to simulate two 12-sided dice? How many lines must be changed or added in Prog. 8.2 to simulate two 12-sided dice?

(*requires Computer Science Excursion, Sec. 2.10*) Is the number of lines added to Prog. 8.1 a linear or a quadratic function of the number of sides on the dice being rolled?

8.2. What changes must be made to Prog. 8.2 to simulate the rolling of three 6-sided dice?

8.3. Write definitions for a `Vector doubVec` of 512 `doubles` and `intVec` of 256 `ints`. Write code to initialize each vector location to twice its index so that `doubVec[13]` = 26.0 and `intVec[200]` = 400.

Is it possible to create a vector of `Balloons` as declared in Prog. 3.7, *balloon.h* (page 103)? Why?

8.4. Write a definition for a `Vector` of strings that stores the names of the computer scientists for whom "Happy Birthday" was printed in Prog. 2.6, *bday2.cc* (page 48). Write a loop that would print the song for all the names stored in the vector.

8.5. Extend the idea of a literary fingerprint by writing a short program (with all code in `main`) that determines how many two-letter, three-letter, ..., up to 15-letter words there are in a text file.

A `Vector` Case Study: Shuffling CD Tracks

Many CD players have an option for "random play." Pressing the random-play or shuffle button causes the tracks on the CD to be "shuffled" and played in some arbitrary order, which may be different each time the CD is played. In this section we'll develop the program *cdshuffl.cc*, Prog. 8.4, to simulate this random-play feature.

We'll need to store the tracks in a `Vector` and rearrange the elements in the `Vector` to simulate the shuffling. We'll want to identify the original track number as well as the title of the track, so we'll use a `struct` to encapsulate this information.

Developing the program. We'll use the following structure, `TrackInfo`, to store information about each track on a CD. All the tracks on a CD are stored in a `Vector<TrackInfo>` object to be manipulated in *cdshuffl.cc*.

```
struct TrackInfo
{
    string info;           // information about CD track
    int     trackNumber;   // the original track number
};
```

Rather than designing, coding, and testing the entire program at once, we'll concentrate first on the three main features of the program: reading, printing, and shuffling CD track information. Before shuffling, we'll need to read and print, so we'll implement these functions first.

Program Tip: Do *not* design, edit, and then compile an entire program at once. Think about the overall design of the entire program, but implement the program in pieces.

As you extend a program by adding new code and new functionality, add to a working program. This will help make the process of finding and fixing errors faster and more straightforward.

To read and print, we'll use the following `main` function:

```
const int MAX_TRACKS = 20;

// function prototypes
void ReadTracks(Vector<TrackInfo> & tracks, int & numTracks);
void PrintTracks(const Vector<TrackInfo> & tracks,
                 int numTracks);

int main()
{
    const MAX_TRACKS = 20;
    int numTracks = 0;
    Vector<TrackInfo> allTracks(MAX_TRACKS);

    ReadTracks(allTracks,numTracks);
    PrintTracks(allTracks,numTracks);
    return 0;
}
```

Writing the functions `ReadTracks` and `PrintTracks` should be straightforward if we know the format of the input data. We'd like to be able to process titles of real CD tracks, but most titles have many words. We'll use input files in the following format (from *The Best of Van Morrison*, 1990, Mercury Records):

```
3:46     Bright Side Of The Road
2:36     Gloria
4:31     Moondance
```

Unfortunately, extraction >> cannot be used to read these titles, because white space separates entries when using the >> operator. We're forced to use a function we have not studied yet; the function `getline` (see Sec. 9.2) reads an entire line from a stream. In other respects `getline` is used like >>, so we won't spend time here discussing `getline`. By testing and debugging the reading and printing functions, we hope to reduce the development time of the program. The functions `ReadTracks` and `PrintTracks` each have an `int` parameter indicating how many tracks are stored in the `Vector` reference parameter `tracks`. Although the `Vector allTracks` has a capacity of 20 tracks, the number of tracks stored is not necessarily the same as the capacity.

> **Program Tip: Functions that have** `Vector` **parameters often require an** `int` **parameter that specifies the number of values actually stored in the** `Vector`.
>
> The number of values stored is often different from the capacity of the `Vector`.

Shuffling tracks. The shuffling algorithm we'll employ is simple and is good theoretically—that is, it really does shuffle things in a random way. In this case each of the possible arrangements, or **permutations,** of the tracks is equally likely to occur.

The basic algorithm consists of picking a track at random to play first. This can be done by rolling an N-sided die, where there are N tracks on the CD, or by using the `RandGen` class used in Prog. 7.5, *brownian.cc* (page 319). Once the first random track is picked, one of the remaining tracks is picked at random to play second. This process is continued until a track is picked for the first track, second track, and so on through the Nth track. Without a `Vector` this would be difficult (though not impossible) to do. Program 8.4, *cdshuffl.cc*, which will be shown shortly, performs this task.

The expression `randTrack = gen.RandInt(k,numTracks-1)` is used in the function `ShuffleTracks` to choose a random track from those remaining. The first time the `for` loop is executed, the value of k is 0, all the tracks are eligible for selection, and the random number is a valid index between 0 and `numTracks-1`. The contents of the `Vector` cell at the randomly generated index are swapped with the contents of the cell with index 0 so that the random-index track is now the first track. The next time through the loop, the random number chosen is between 1 and `numTracks-1` so that the first track (at index 0) cannot be chosen as the random track.

Program 8.4   cdshuffl.cc

```
#include <iostream.h>
#include <fstream.h>              // for ifstream
#include <stdlib.h>               // for exit, atoi
#include "CPstring.h"
#include "prompt.h"
#include "rando.h"
#include "vector.h"

// reads file containing data for a CD (one line/track) as:
//        track time (Min:Sec) Title of Track
// example:
//        3:46     Bright Side Of The Road
//        2:36     Gloria
//        4:31     Moondance
//
// then randomly shuffle tracks and print them
// treat each track as a line of data
//
// Owen Astrachan, August 4, 1994
// modified: September 27,1994, modified 7/13/96

struct TrackInfo
{
    string info;              // information about CD track
```

```
    int     trackNumber;    // the original track number
};

// function prototypes here

void ReadTracks(Vector<TrackInfo> & tracks, int & numTracks);
void PrintTracks(const Vector<TrackInfo> & tracks,
    int numTracks);
void ShuffleTracks(Vector<TrackInfo> & tracks,int numTracks);

int main()
{
    const MAX_TRACKS = 20;
    int numTracks = 0;
    Vector<TrackInfo> allTracks(MAX_TRACKS);

    ReadTracks(allTracks,numTracks);
    ShuffleTracks(allTracks,numTracks);
    PrintTracks(allTracks,numTracks);

    return 0;
}

void ReadTracks(Vector<TrackInfo> & tracks, int & numTracks)
// postcondition: tracks initialized from user-specified file
//                numTracks = # entries in tracks
{
    ifstream input;
    string filename = PromptString("enter name of data file: ");
    input.open(filename);

    if (input.fail())
    {
        cerr << "could not open file " << filename << endl;
        exit(0);
    }

    string trackinfo;       // information about CD track
    numTracks = 0;          // haven't read any tracks yet
    while (getline(input,trackinfo))  // read one line of file
    {
        tracks[numTracks].info = trackinfo;
        tracks[numTracks].trackNumber = numTracks;
        numTracks++;
    }
}

void PrintTracks(const Vector<TrackInfo> & tracks,
    int numTracks)
// precondition: numTracks = # valid entries in tracks
// postcondition: all track information printed
{
    int k;
    for(k=0; k < numTracks; k++)
```

```
        {
            cout << "(" << tracks[k].trackNumber << ")\t"
                    << tracks[k].info << endl;
        }
}

void ShuffleTracks(Vector<TrackInfo> & tracks,int numTracks)
// precondition: numTracks = # of entries in tracks
// postcondition: entries in tracks have been randomly shuffled
{
    RandGen gen;      // for random # generator
    int randTrack;
    TrackInfo temp;
    int k;
    for(k=0; k < numTracks - 1; k++)
    {
        randTrack = gen.RandInt(k,numTracks-1);// random track
        temp = tracks[randTrack];               // swap entries
        tracks[randTrack] = tracks[k];
        tracks[k] = temp;
    }
}
```

OUTPUT

```
prompt> cdshuffl
enter name of data file: vanmor.dat
(8)      3:57     Wonderful Remark
(17)     4:54     Whenever God Shines His Light
(19)     4:44     Dweller On The Threshold
(12)     2:46     Here Comes The Night
(5)      3:04     Brown Eyed Girl
(11)     4:28     And It Stoned Me
(0)      3:46     Bright Side Of The Road
(3)      2:40     Baby Please Don't Go
(10)     3:14     Full Force Gale
(14)     4:05     Did Ye Get Healed
(15)     3:32     Wild Night
(1)      2:36     Gloria
(9)      2:57     Jackie Wilson Said (I'm In Heaven When You Smile)
(6)      4:21     Sweet Thing
(16)     4:40     Cleaning Windows
(7)      3:22     Warm Love
(13)     3:04     Domino
(18)     4:54     Queen Of The Slipstream
(4)      4:19     Have I Told You Lately
(2)      4:31     Moondance
```

Another run of the program shows that the output does change each time the program is run.

OUTPUT

```
prompt> cdshuffl
enter name of data file: vanmor.dat
(10)    3:14     Full Force Gale
(6)     4:21     Sweet Thing
(4)     4:19     Have I Told You Lately
(1)     2:36     Gloria
(18)    4:54     Queen Of The Slipstream
(2)     4:31     Moondance
(16)    4:40     Cleaning Windows
(13)    3:04     Domino
(17)    4:54     Whenever God Shines His Light
(14)    4:05     Did Ye Get Healed
(15)    3:32     Wild Night
(12)    2:46     Here Comes The Night
(19)    4:44     Dweller On The Threshold
(3)     2:40     Baby Please Don't Go
(5)     3:04     Brown Eyed Girl
(11)    4:28     And It Stoned Me
(7)     3:22     Warm Love
(9)     2:57     Jackie Wilson Said (I'm In Heaven When You Smile)
(0)     3:46     Bright Side Of The Road
(8)     3:57     Wonderful Remark
```

Sometimes it is hard to figure out what statements like these (taken from ReadTracks) are all about:

```
tracks[numTracks].info = trackinfo;
tracks[numTracks].trackNumber = numTracks;
```

To decipher such definitions, you must read them inside out, one piece at a time.[4] The [] are used to indicate an entry in a vector. The identifier to the left of them indicates that the name of the Vector is tracks. The identifier numTracks is used to select a particular cell—note that the initial value of numTracks is 0, indicating the first cell.

---

[4]Sometimes the most inside piece isn't obvious, but there are often several places to start.

Now you need to think about what kind of element is stored in the Vector tracks. The information is provided in the function header: it's a Vector of TrackInfo. Now you need to think about what TrackInfo is. It's a struct, so, as with a class, a period or dot . is needed to access one of its fields. The struct TrackInfo has two fields: info and trackNumber. Examining the struct definition at the top of the program may remind you what type each field is. In particular, info is a string. Each line of the file is read into the string variable trackinfo and then stored in the appropriate data field info of a struct in the Vector tracks.

Pause to reflect

8.6. Consider the three functions ReadTracks, PrintTracks, and ShuffleTracks in Prog. 8.4, *cdshuffl.cc*. Why is numTracks a reference parameter in ReadTracks but not in the other functions? Why is tracks a const parameter in PrintTracks and not in the other functions?

8.7. In PrintTracks, why can't the output be generated by the line

```
cout << tracks[k] << endl;
```

8.8. In ShuffleTracks, is it important that the test of the for loop be k < numTracks - 1 instead of k < numTracks? What would happen if the test were changed?

8.9. A different method of shuffling is suggested by the following idea. Pick two random track numbers and swap the corresponding vector entries. Repeat this process 1,000 times (or some other time as specified by a constant). Write code that uses this method for shuffling tracks. Do you have any intuition as to why this method is "worse" than the method used in *cdshuffl.cc*?

8.3　Vectors as Lists

Our first example programs used vectors as counters to determine how many times each of several possible simulated dice rolls occurs and how many times each character in an input file occurs. Vectors can be used to store data other than counts or integers. For example, we can extend the idea of counting words (see Program 6.3, *countw2.cc*) to counting how many times each word in a file occurs. This could be used, for example, to determine how many times the word "the" occurs in any of Shakespeare's plays.[5]

As a preliminary step, we'll investigate two programs that keep track of the different words in a file. These programs do not count how many times each word occurs but keep track of just the different words in a file. If the word

---

[5]A similar problem was solved using the List class in the Excursion, Sec. 6.7.

"the" occurs 203 times, it will be represented just once in the list of different (or unique) words in a given file. To do this requires two steps:

1.   Keep a list, stored in a vector, of all the different words
2.   When a word is read from the file, see whether it is already in the vector; if not, add it to the vector

To determine whether a word is already in the vector, we will use the typical vector/array framework of a `for` loop that iterates over all the elements of a vector.

```
for(k=0; k < numElements; k++)
{
    // process a[k], the kth element
}
```

However, in this case the number of elements stored in the vector will change as new words are read from the file. We'll need to keep track of two things:

1.   The capacity (the maximum number of words that can be stored in the vector)
2.   The number of words that are currently stored in the vector

In *allword.cc*, Prog. 8.5, these quantities are stored in the variables `size` and `numWords`, respectively. In the program, words are read from a file using a `WordStreamIterator` variable (introduced in *countw3.cc*, Prog. 6.4). A function `Search` is used to see whether the word is already stored in the string vector `list`. If a word is not stored, it is added to the end of the `Vector`, and the number of words stored is incremented. Since vectors are indexed starting from zero, `numWords`, the number of words, is also the index of where the next unseen word should be added to the vector `list`.

Note that the `Vector` parameter in the helper functions `Search` and `Print` is a constant reference parameter. The number of words is also passed as a parameter, because the capacity of the vector is not the same as the number of words actually stored in the vector.

The output of the program consists of all words in a file, the number of words, and the number of unique words. The list of all the words in the file is not shown in the sample run; only the counts are shown.

The function `Search` is typical of functions used with vectors; a `for` loop processes all vector elements. The function returns the index of parameter `key` if it occurs in `list` and returns −1 if `key` is not stored in `list`. The number of elements currently stored in `list` is specified by the parameter `count` (note the precondition of the function). This is different from the capacity of `list` (which could be determined using `list.Length()`).

The third of the sample runs uncovers a flaw in the program. When there are more than 2,000 different words in a file, the program tries to access an invalid vector element, and the program terminates abnormally. This is

---

Program 8.5   allword.cc

```cpp
#include <iostream.h>
#include <fstream.h>
#include <stdlib.h>                      // for exit
#include "CPstring.h"
#include "vector.h"
#include "worditer.h"
#include "prompt.h"

// author: Owen Astrachan
//
// lists all words in an input file, but avoids duplicates
//
// 5-11-95

int Search(const Vector<string> & list, int count, string key);
void Print(const Vector<string> & list, int count);

int main()
{
    int size = 2000;
    Vector<string> list(size);
    int numWords = 0;
    int totalWords = 0;
    string word;
    string filename = PromptString("enter name of file:");

    WordStreamIterator wstream;
    wstream.Open(filename);

    for(wstream.First(); ! wstream.IsDone(); wstream.Next())
    {
        totalWords++;
        word = wstream.Current().Downcase();
        if (Search(list,numWords,word) == -1) // not in list, add it
        {
            list[numWords] = word;
            numWords++;
        }
    }
    Print(list,numWords);

    cout << "total words (nonunique): " << totalWords
         << endl;
    return 0;
}

int Search(const Vector<string> & list, int count, string key)
// precondition: count = # of elements in list
// postcondition: returns index at which key occurs in list
//                returns -1 if key does not occur
```

```
{
    int k;
    for(k=0; k < count; k++)
    {
        if (list[k] == key)        // found key in list
        {
            return k;
        }
    }
    return -1;
}

void Print(const Vector<string> & list, int count)
// precondition: count = # of elements in list
// postcondition: all elements of list printed
{
    int k;
    for(k=0; k < count; k++)
    {
        cout << list[k] << endl;
    }
    cout << endl << "# of words = " << count << endl;
}
```

OUTPUT

```
prompt> allword
enter name of file: poe.txt
# of words = 1000
total words (nonunique): 2324

prompt> allword
enter name of file: twain.txt
# of words = 883
total words (nonunique): 2533

prompt> allword
enter name of file: hamlet.txt
Illegal vector index: 2000 (max = 1999)
Abort (core dumped)
```

---

poor programming style. It would be much better to trap such an error and take appropriate action rather than allowing the illegal Vector index. In this situation we could insert an if statement that checks whether the number of elements currently in the array is less than the capacity of the array:

```
if   (numWords < size)
{
    // there is room, add word and increment numWords
}
```

When built-in arrays are used, this is the only option that is available. However, when the `Vector` class is used, another option is possible: a `Vector` can be extended to accommodate more entries. The member function `Vector::SetSize()` resets the capacity of a vector.[6] If a vector contains values when `SetSize` is called, the values will be copied into the newly grown vector. It is also possible to shrink a vector by decreasing its capacity.

A simple use of `SetSize` is illustrated in Fig. 8.5. If `fruit.SetSize(6)` is replaced by `fruit.SetSize(2)`, then the vector `fruit` will have two entries: `"apple"` and `"grape"`.

Using `SetSize` to increase the size of a vector takes memory and time. To appreciate why, consider what happens if you write a list of names on a piece of paper and run out of space. If you can find a bigger piece of paper, you can have a bigger list, but first you must copy all the names from the first list to the new, bigger piece of paper. This is essentially what happens when `SetSize` is called: all the entries in the vector must be copied to a new, larger vector. To minimize the use of this time-consuming and memory-intensive operation, you should try to pick an initial size for a vector that will accommodate most uses. If the size of the vector must increase, it is best to double the size rather than increase it by one element, ten elements, or some other additive factor. This can be done in Prog. 8.5, *allword.cc*, by adding the following lines just before a word is added to `list`:

```
if (numWords >= size) // vector full, "grow" it
{
    size *= 2;
    list.SetSize(size);
}
```

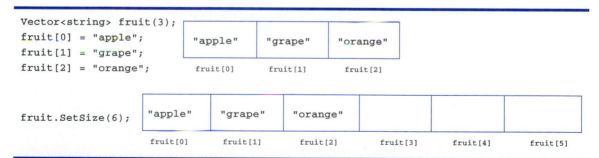

Figure 8.5   "Growing" an array.

---

[6]The C++ standard class (part of STL, the standard template library) uses `resize` for the function that grows vectors. This name can be used in place of `SetSize` for the class declared in `vector.h`, since it supports both names for the function that changes the capacity of a vector.

If this modification is made and the program is recompiled and executed, it can be used to print and count the words in *Hamlet:*

OUTPUT

```
prompt> allword2
enter name of file: hamlet.txt
# of words = 7234
total words (nonunique): 31956
```

Note that the `SetSize` function must be called twice if the initial size of `list` is 2,000 as specified in *allword.cc:* once to increase the capacity to 4,000 and once to increase the capacity to 8,000. Searching a vector repeatedly to see whether a word has already been read is time-consuming. On my computer it takes almost one minute to process all the words in *Hamlet,* but less than one second to read them using *countw2.cc,* Prog. 6.3 (page 265).

Program Tip: The `Vector` **member function** `SetSize` **(or the function** `resize`**) is used to change the capacity of a** `Vector`. **When** `SetSize` **is called, the size of a vector should be doubled or increased by some other multiplicative factor rather than by an additive factor.**

Do not change the number of elements in a vector by adding 1 to the capacity when calling `SetSize`.

The built-in array type does *not* support this kind of growth. The number of elements in a built-in array is fixed when the array is first defined.

8.4   Class Study: Word List

Rather than equip program *allword.cc* with the `SetSize` function and a `Vector` that grows, we'll design a class to implement the behavior of *allword.cc.* Reimplementing this `WordList` class, using new techniques for storing and retrieving words, will be easier than rewriting the functions `Search` and `Print` from *allword.cc.* This is one of the big advantages of writing classes: re-implementation using new techniques is often easier than when a nonclass, several-function program is used.

A class diagram for the `WordList` class is given in Fig. 8.6. A `WordList` object represents a list of words. The `Update` member function is used to add words to the list; the implementation of the function ensures that words are stored only once, as is done in Prog. 8.5, *allword.cc.* The "Get" member functions, `GetUnique` and `GetTotal`, retrieve, respectively, the numbers of unique words and total words stored in a word list. The `Print` member function prints words, just as the `Print` function does in *allword.cc.*

```
            wordlist.h
```

Figure 8.6   Interface diagram for `WordList` class.

A code segment that uses an object of the class `WordList` is shown in Prog. 8.6.

The header file for the `WordList` class is given in Prog. 8.7. Because this class was developed as a demonstration of how to encapsulate state and behavior in a class, rather than as a class to be used in many contexts, the comments are not as extensive as those in header files like *date.h* and *vector.h*. In general, classes that are designed for many users in many contexts must be commented extensively, as the examples in this book have been. Classes designed for one-time use in a program require some comments, perhaps not as extensive as those we've seen in other examples. Of course, a well-designed class may be used in ways unforeseen by the designer or implementer of the class, so erring on the side of including too many comments is better than including too few.

Program 8.6   useword.cc

```cpp
int main()
{
    string word;
    string filename = PromptString("enter filename: ");
    ifstream input;
    input.open(filename);

    WordList wlist(2000);
    while (input >> word)              // reading word succeeded
    {
        wlist.Update(word.Downcase());
    }
    wlist.Print();

    cout << "total words (nonunique): "
         << wlist.GetTotal() << endl;
    return 0;
}
```

useword.cc

```cpp
#include <iostream.h>
#include <fstream.h>
#include <stdlib.h>                  // for exit
#include "CPstring.h"
#include "vector.h"
#include "prompt.h"
#include "ctimer.h"

// author: Owen Astrachan
//
// lists all words in an input file, but avoids duplicates
// uses class WordList to encapsulate behavior
//
// 5-15-95

class WordList
{
  public:
    WordList(int size);               // constructor,  specify size of list
    void Update(const string & word); // update occurrences of word
    int GetUnique();                  // return # of unique words in list
    int GetTotal();                   // return # of total words in list
    void Print();                     // print all words in list
  private:

    int myCount;             // # of entries stored in myList
    int mySize;              // capacity of myList
    int myTotal;             // # of words (nonunique)
    Vector<string> myList;   // storage for strings

    int Search(const string & key); // returns index in myList of key
};

WordList::WordList(int size)
   : myCount(0),
     mySize(size),
     myTotal(0),
     myList(size)
{
    // all work done in initializer list
}

int WordList::Search(const string & key)
// postcondition: returns index at which key occurs in myList
//                returns -1 if key does not occur
{
    int k;
    for(k=0; k < myCount; k++)
    {
```

```
            if (myList[k] == key)       // found key in list
            {
                return k;
            }
        }
        return -1;
}

void WordList::Update(const string & word)
// postcondition: updates occurrence of word
//                adds word to list if not already present
//                increments count of total # of words
{
    int loc = Search(word);

    myTotal++;

    if (loc == -1)                  // not already in list
    {
        if (myCount >= mySize)
        {
            mySize *= 2;
            myList.SetSize(mySize);
        }
        myList[myCount] = word;
        myCount++;
    }
}

void WordList::Print()
// postcondition: all elements of myList printed
{
    int k;
    for(k=0; k < myCount; k++)
    {
        cout << myList[k] << endl;
    }
    cout << endl << "# of words = " << myCount << endl;
}

int WordList::GetUnique()
// postcondition: returns # unique words in list
{
    return myCount;
}

int WordList::GetTotal()
// postcondition: returns total # of words in list
//                same as # of times Update called
{
    return myTotal;
}

int main()
{
```

```
string word;                          // word read from file
string filename = PromptString("enter name of file: ");
ifstream input;
WordList wlist(5000);
CTimer timer;

input.open(filename);
if (input.fail())
{
    cout << "could not open file " << filename << endl;
    exit(0);
}

while (input >> word)          // reading word succeeded
{
    timer.Start();
    wlist.Update(word.Downcase());
    timer.Stop();
}
wlist.Print();

cout << "total words (non-unique): " << wlist.GetTotal()
    << endl;
cout << "total time for update = "
    << timer.CumulativeTime() << endl;
return 0;
}
```

allword3.cc

In most of the examples we've used in this book, class interfaces are declared in a `.h` header file and class implementations are defined in a corresponding file with a `.cc` suffix. The client program that uses the class is another file like Prog. 8.6, *useword.cc.* In this example of implementing a `WordList` class I've included the class interface, implementation, and client code all in one file, Prog. 8.7, *allword3.cc.* It would be better to implement this program using separate interface, implementation, and client files that are compiled and linked into one program, but this isn't required. Developing programs using classes is often easier than developing similar programs in which classes aren't used (as in *allword.cc,* Prog. 8.5). Class-based programs are often easier to modify and extend than those in which classes aren't used. Including all class information in one file is one way of starting to develop a program.

The private `Vector` variable `myList` in the class `WordList` is *not* declared with a default number of entries. A declaration like the one for `myList` will *not* compile:

```
Vector<string> myList(2000);      // storage for strings
```

The class declaration provides an interface; it is *not* executable code. All private variables are constructed when an object of the class is defined; the *class* constructor must construct and initialize the private instance variables. This means that all `Vector` variables in a class or `struct` must be declared (in the private section) *without* a size. The number of elements in such a `Vector` can be set using the `SetSize` member function. The `WordList` constructor could be written as

```
WordList::WordList(int size)
{
    myTotal = myCount = 0;
    mySize = size;
    myList.SetSize(size);
}
```

However, it's better to use an initializer list, as shown in *allword3.cc*, Prog. 8.7. When an initializer list is used, the `WordList` constructor explicitly calls the `Vector` constructor to construct `myList(size)`. Using the constructor is better than using `SetSize`; when `SetSize` is used, the default constructor for `myList` is called before the body of the `WordList` constructor is executed. In general, all of the private variables in a class are constructed before the body of the class's constructor is executed.

The private variable `myList` can be resized if it is full; the code in `WordList::Update()` ensures that there is room in `myList` for adding a new word.

Binary Search

The member function `WordList::Search` in *allword3.cc*, Prog. 8.7 (page 386), implements a **sequential search.** In a sequential search (sometimes called a **linear** search), elements in a list or vector are scanned in sequence, one after the other. Sequential search is necessary, for example, if you want to find the person whose phone number is 555-2622 in your local phone book. Phone books are arranged alphabetically by name rather than numerically by phone number, so you must scan all numbers, one after the other, hoping to find 555-2622. Of course if you were doing this, you could easily miss the number; people aren't good at this kind of repetitive task, but computers are. On the other hand, you can look up John Armstrong's, Nancy Drew's, or Mr. Mxyzptlk's number without scanning every entry. Since name/number pairs are stored alphabetically by name, it's possible to search for a name efficiently. In this section we'll investigate **binary search:** a method of searching that takes advantage of sorted data to speed up search. As we'll see, binary search is not always better than sequential search. Choosing the right searching algorithm depends on the context in which the search will be used.

Binary search is based on the method you may have used in playing a guess-a-number game. Suppose someone thinks of a number between 1 and 100 and will tell you whether your guess is low, high, or correct. You'll probably use 50 as the first guess. This will eliminate half of the numbers from consideration and is considerably more fruitful than guessing 1 (which, invariably, is low). The strategy of guessing the middle number works regardless of the the range of numbers. For example, if someone initially thinks of a number between 1 and 1024, you would guess 512. One guess shrinks the number of possibilities by half, from 1024 to 512. The number of possibilities continues to shrink from 512 to 256, 128, 64, 32, 16, 8, 4, 2, and finally 1. This is a total of 10 guesses to find one of 1024 possible different numbers. Consider what happens if you're told "yes" or "no" rather than high/low, and how this affects your guessing strategy. That example illustrates the difference between binary search and sequential search. Eliminating half of the numbers with one guess, rather than one number, is shown graphically in Fig. 8.7. A `Vector` of 32 elements is shown; the shaded area represents the region of items still being considered after each guess is made.

When binary search is used, each comparison cuts the range of potential matches in half. The total number of guesses will be the number of times the number of initial items can be cut in half. As we've seen, 1024 items require 10 guesses; it's not a coincidence that $2^{10} = 1024$. Doubling the number of items from 1024 to 2048 increases the number of guesses needed by only one, because one guess cuts the list of 2048 down to 1024 and we know that 10 guesses are needed for 1024 items. Again, it's not a coincidence that $2^{11} = 2048$.

Looking up a name in a phone book of 1024 names might require 11 guesses. When there is only one name left to check, it must be checked too, because the name being sought might not be in the phone book (this doesn't happen with the guess-a-number game). How many guesses are needed using binary search to search a list of one million names? As we've seen, this depends on how many times one million can be cut in half. We want to find the smallest number n such that $2^n \geq 1,000,000$; this will tell us how many items must be checked (we might need to add 1 if there's a possibility that the item isn't in the list; this cuts the final list of one item down to a list of zero items). Since $2^{19} = 524,288$ and $2^{20} = 1,048,576$, we can see that 20 (or 21) guesses are enough to find an item using binary search in a list of one million items. If you're familiar with logarithms, you may recall that log functions are the inverse of exponential functions, and therefore that the number of times a number x can be cut in half is $\log_2(x)$, or log base 2 of x. Again, we may need to add 1 if we need to cut a

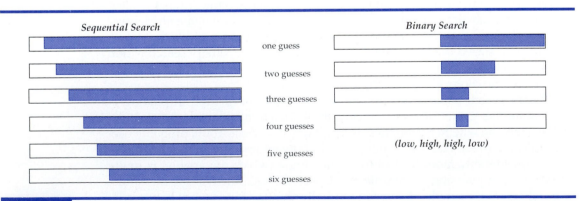

Sequential Search		Binary Search
	one guess	
	two guesses	
	three guesses	
	four guesses	
	five guesses	*(low, high, high, low)*
	six guesses	

Figure 8.7   Comparing sequential (on the left) and binary search.

Table 8.2 Comparing binary and sequential search

	Number of items examined	
List size	Binary search	Sequential search
1	1	1
10	4	10
1,000	11	1,000
5,000	14	5,000
100,000	18	100,000
1,000,000	21	1,000,000

number in half to get down to zero instead of 1. This is the analog of reducing the items down to a zero-element list or a one-element list.

We're more concerned with comparing sequential search and binary search than with the exact number of items examined with binary search. The difference between 20 and 21 items examined is far less important than the difference between 21 items (binary search) and one million items (sequential search). Although it's possible that only one item is examined when a sequential search is used (consider looking up a word like "aardvark" in the dictionary), the worst case is that one million items might need to be examined (consider looking up "zzzz" in a million-word dictionary). Table 8.2 provides a comparison of the number of items that must be examined using sequential and binary search.

Examining 18 items will be much faster than examining 100,000 items, but how much faster? If two strings can be compared in a microsecond (one millionth of a second)—which is very possible on moderately fast computers—both searches will take less than one second. Does it matter that binary search requires 0.000018 seconds and sequential search requires 0.1 seconds? The answer is, "It depends." It probably won't matter to you if you're waiting for a response to appear on a computer monitor, but it may matter if the computer is "waiting" for the search and 100 million searches are necessary. On the computers I used to develop the code in this book, searching for a word in an on-line dictionary of 25,000 words appeared to take no time to me using either sequential or binary search. To be precise, I can type a word in, press Enter, and the word appears on the screen instantaneously. However, I timed how long it would take to search for every word in the dictionary. When sequential search was used, words near the front of the dictionary were found more quickly than words near the end of the dictionary, but it took 377 seconds to search once for each word. When binary search was used it took 0.66 seconds. There's a large difference between roughly half a second and roughly six minutes; that's why the answer to whether binary search or sequential search is better is "It depends."

A version of WordList::Search() that uses binary search follows. Note that the postcondition is the same; this version is equivalent in a black-box sense to the version in *allword3.cc*.

```
int WordList::Search(string key)
// postcondition: returns index at which key occurs in myList
//                 returns -1 if key does not occur
{
    int low = 0;                        // leftmost possible entry
    int high = myCount-1;               // rightmost possible entry
    int mid;                            // middle of current range
    while (low <= high)
    {
        mid = (low + high)/2;
        if (myList[mid] == key)     // found key, exit search
        {
            return mid;
        }
        else if (myList[mid] < key)    // key in upper half
        {
            low = mid + 1;
        }
        else                            // key in lower half
        {
            high = mid - 1;
        }
    }
    return -1;                          // not in list
}
```

Maintaining a Sorted List

Binary search greatly reduces the number of items examined compared to sequential search, but the items must be sorted just as the names in a phone book are sorted. Consider modifying *allword3.cc*, Prog. 8.7 (page 386), to use binary search. Finding a word already stored will require far fewer comparisons than using sequential search. However, when a search is unsuccessful, and a new word is added to `myList` (the `Vector` of strings storing the words), the new word cannot be simply added to the end of the `Vector`. Since the list of words must be maintained in sorted order to enable binary search, words must be moved, or shifted, so that the new word can be added. Suppose, for example, that you keep books arranged alphabetically by author, or a collection of compact discs (CDs) arranged alphabetically by artist. When you get a new book (or a new CD), you'll probably have to move or shift several books to make a spot for the new one. If you're facing a bookshelf, you might start at the rightmost end and slide the books to the right until you find where the new book belongs. This is precisely how strings stored in a `Vector` are moved to make room for a new word when the `Vector` is kept in sorted order. In the following listing the code for doing this in a modified version of function `WordList::Update()` from *allword3.cc*, Prog. 8.7, is shown on the right; the code on the left is the code from the original version of `WordList::Update()`, which adds a new word to the end of `myList`.

```
    // add at end (unsorted)                    // shift to make room
                                                // and add (sorted)
```

```
myList[myCount] = word;
myCount++;
```

```
loc = myCount - 1;
while (0 <= loc &&
       word < myList[loc])
{
    myList[loc+1] = myList[loc];
    loc--;
}
myList[loc+1] = word;
myCount++;
```

The `while` loop shifts elements to the right until the correct location for `word` is found. This shifting is diagrammed in Fig. 8.8 for a `Vector` of eight elements, shown in the diagram as letters rather than words. The value of `myCount` is 8, indicating that there are eight elements in the vector stored in locations with indices $0, 1, \ldots, 7$. When an element is shifted, its value is copied to the right, and the old value remains.[7] This is shown in Fig. 8.8 by using a shaded box to represent the hole left when an item is shifted to the right.

To understand and reason about the loop that shifts elements to the right, we'll concentrate on three properties of the variable `loc`. These properties are

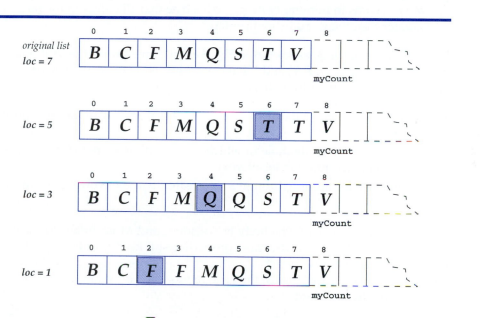

add **D** to vector maintained in sorted order

Figure 8.8   Maintaining a `Vector` in sorted order.

---

[7]Therefore, the analogy of shifting records or CDs is somewhat misleading.

true each time the loop test is evaluated:

- `loc` is the location of the item that will be shifted right if necessary.
- `loc + 1` is the "hole" (location) in which `word` will be stored.
- All items in locations `loc + 2` through location `myCount` are greater than `word`, the item being inserted in sorted order.

You may recall that properties that are true each time a loop test is evaluated are called loop invariants. The first time the loop test is evaluated, `loc == 7`, as shown in Fig. 8.8. Since none of the items stored in the vector have been examined yet, the three properties hold:

- 7 is the location of the item (represented by V) that will be shifted right if necessary.
- 8 is the hole in which word will be stored (for example, if `word` is Z, it is stored in location 8).
- All items in locations 9 through 8 are greater than the word being inserted. In this case the range $9 \ldots 8$ represents an **empty range,** since $9 > 8$. There are no words in this empty range, so it's true that all words in the range are greater than the word being inserted.[8]

When the location is 3, as shown in Fig. 8.8, the three properties still hold. At this point the letters Q, S, T, and V have been shifted to the right, since the loop body has been executed for values of `loc` of $7, 6, 5, 4$.

- 3 is the location of the item (the letter M) that will be shifted right if necessary.
- 4 is the location of the hole in which `word` will be stored (for example, if `word` is P, it is stored in location 4).
- All items in locations 5 through 8 are greater than the word being inserted, D.

Since the loop test is true, the body is executed, and M is shifted to the right. Finally, when `loc == 1`, the three properties still hold (see Fig. 8.8), but the loop test is false, because `word > myList[1]` (since $D > C$). The loop exits, and the new word is inserted in the hole, represented by location `loc + 1`, as described by the invariant.

Case Study: Extended Author Fingerprints

Statistics gleaned from Shakespeare's plays by *fingerp.cc*, Prog. 6.9, didn't provide much data for comparing the works. Using vectors, we can modify that

---

[8]Don't worry too much about this. The key here is that it's impossible to find a word in the range $9 \ldots 8$ that's smaller than the word being inserted. It's impossible because there are no words in the empty range.

program to keep track of how many times individual letters occur in each play, as shown in Prog. 8.3, *letters.cc.* In this section we'll extend *allword3.cc,* Prog. 8.7, to keep track of how many times each word occurs in a file.

Developing the program. The code in *allword3.cc* does most of the work already. However, it tracks how many unique words there are rather than how many times each unique word occurs. We can modify the program to record the number of occurrences of each word by using a Vector of structs rather than a Vector of strings. The struct will have two fields: a string representing a word and an int representing the number of times the word occurs.

```
struct WordStat
{
    string info;                    // the string
    int count;                      // # of times string occurs
};
```

Instead of defining Vector<string> myList, we'll define myList as a Vector<WordStat> in the private section of the class WordList. We still need to alter *allword3.cc* to store values in count for each word. This is a small change of the member function WordList::Update(). If the search for a word fails, the word can be added to myList with an initial count of 1. If the search succeeds, the count value associated with the word is incremented. This is shown in *allword4.cc,* Prog. 8.8. Words are kept in alphabetical order to facilitate a binary search. This requires code in WordList::Update() to shift words when a new word is added to maintain the alphabetical order.

Program 8.8   allword4.cc

```
#include <iostream.h>
#include <fstream.h>
#include <stdlib.h>                 // for exit
#include "CPstring.h"
#include "vector.h"
#include "ctimer.h"                 // for CTimer
#include "strutils.h"               // for StripPunc
#include "prompt.h"

// author: Owen Astrachan
//
// lists all words in an input file, with word counts
// uses class WordList to encapsulate behavior
//
// 5-15-95
```

```
struct WordStat
{
    string info;                   // the string
    int count;                     // # of times string occurs
};


class WordList
{
  public :
    WordList(int size);            // constructor,  specify size of list
    void Update(string word);      // update occurrences of word
    int GetUnique();               // return # of unique words in list
    int GetTotal();                // return # of total words in list
    void Print(ostream & output);  // print all words in list
  private:

    int myCount;                   // # of entries stored in myList
    int mySize;                    // capacity of myList
    int myTotal;                   // # of words (nonunique)
    Vector<WordStat> myList;       // storage for word statistics

    int Search(const string & key); // returns index in myList of key
};

WordList::WordList(int size)
    : myCount(0),
      mySize(size),
      myTotal(0),
      myList(size)
{
    // all work done in initializer list
}


int WordList::Search(const string & key)
// postcondition: returns index at which key occurs in myList
//                returns -1 if key does not occur
{
    int low = 0;
    int high = myCount-1;
    int mid;                       // middle of current range
    while (low <= high)
    {
        mid = (low + high)/2;
        if (myList[mid].info == key)        // found key, exit
        {
            return mid;
        }
        else if (myList[mid].info < key)    // key in upper half
        {
            low = mid + 1;
        }
```

```
            else                          // key in lower half
            {
                high = mid - 1;
            }
        }
        return -1;
}

void WordList::Update(string word)
// postcondition: updates occurrence of word
//                adds word to list if not already present
//                increments count of total # of words
{
    int loc = Search(word);

    myTotal++;

    if (loc == -1)                 // not already in list
    {
        if (myCount >= mySize)
        {
            mySize *= 2;
            myList.SetSize(mySize);
        }
        loc = myCount - 1;          // shift structs right
        while (0 <= loc && word < myList[loc].info)
        {
            myList[loc+1] = myList[loc];
            loc--;
        }
        myList[loc+1].info = word;
        myList[loc+1].count = 1;
        myCount++;
    }
    else
    {
        myList[loc].count++;
    }
}

void WordList::Print(ostream & output)
// postcondition: all elements of myList printed
{
    int k;
    for(k=0; k < myCount; k++)
    {
        output << myList[k].count << "\t"
            << myList[k].info << endl;
    }
    output << endl << "# of words = " << myCount << endl;
}

int WordList::GetUnique()
// postcondition: returns # unique words in list
```

```
{
    return myCount;
}

int WordList::GetTotal()
// postcondition: returns total # of words in list
//                same as # of times Update called
{
    return myTotal;
}

int main()
{
    string word;                       // word read from file
    string filename = PromptString("enter name of file: ");
    ifstream input;
    WordList wlist(1000);
    CTimer timer;

    input.open(filename);
    if (input.fail())
    {
        cout << "could not open file " << filename << endl;
        exit(0);
    }

    while (input >> word)          // reading word succeeded
    {
        word = word.Downcase();
        StripPunc(word);
        timer.Start();
        wlist.Update(word);
        timer.Stop();
    }
    wlist.Print(cout);

    cout << "total words (non-unique): "
         << wlist.GetTotal() << endl;
    cout << "total time for update = "
         << timer.CumulativeTime() << endl;
    return 0;
}
```

OUTPUT

```
prompt> allword4
enter name of input file: melville.txt
1       6
334     a
1       a--premature
```

```
1        abate
...
...
27       your
1        yourn
1        yours
1        yours.-will
4        yourself
2        youth
# of words = 3125
total words (non-unique): 14353
total time for update = 11.09
```

The function `StripPunc` from `"strutils.h"` is used to remove lead-ing and trailing punctuation from a `string`. Other functions declared in `"strutils.h"` include `StripWhite` to strip leading and trailing white space from a `string`, and `ToLower` and `ToUpper`, which are equivalent to the `string` member functions `Downcase` and `Upcase`, respectively, but can be used with `string` classes other than the one defined in `"CPstring.h"`.

Extending the program. If you run *allword4.cc* on several of Shakespeare's plays, you may not see any similarity in the output. One of the problems is that when the statistics printed for each word are printed in alphabetical order, similarities in word frequency are harder to spot than if the data were sorted according to word frequency so that the most frequently occurring word was printed first. We'll explore sorting, and return to this program, in Chapter 11.

8.5 Built-In Arrays (Optional)

In this section we'll study the built-in C++ array type and compare it with the `Vector` class we've used to implement a homogeneous, random-access data structure. The `Vector` class is defined using the built-in C++ array type. Using built-in arrays results in code that will probably execute more quickly than when the `Vector` class is used, because of overhead associated with checking `Vector` indices.

Any integer value can be used to subscript an array, even if the value doesn't represent a valid array location. In some languages (e.g., Pascal), indexing values that do not represent valid array locations cause a program to generate an error message, which can be used to trace the program's behavior. In C and C++, on the other hand, an invalid subscript value can cause unex-pected behavior that can lead to hard-to-find errors. Such invalid subscripts are not checked before being used to index a built-in array. Using the `Vector` class rather than the built-in array type provides some safety when using indexed variables, because indices are checked with the `Vector` class. Arrays in C++

DAVID GRIES

David Gries is a computer scientist and educator at Cornell University. He is well known for his advocation of the use of formal methods in designing and implementing software and in the training of under-graduates in computer science. He has done perhaps more than any one person in making the study of loop invariants and formal methods accessible to students in introductory courses.

In his World Wide Web biography he writes of encounters with recursion when earning his master's degree in 1963: "it was fun, figuring out how to implement recursion efficiently before there were many papers on the topic." In an essay [Gri74] written in 1974 he provides timeless advice:

> It must be made clear that one technique will never suffice (for example, top-down programming). A programmer needs a bag of tricks, a collection of methods for attacking a problem. Secondly, if we are to raise the level of programming, each programmer (no matter how good he feels he is) must become more conscious of the tools and techniques he uses. It is not enough to just program; we must discover how and why we do it.

Figure 8.9   David Gries.

Gries has twins, and in a coincidence of the highest order, the twins were born on the birthday of Gries and his twin sibling. In noting that he is (perhaps) better known for his educational work than his research work, Gries writes, "Do what you are good at; bloom where you are planted." For his work in education Gries was awarded the 1994 IEEE Taylor L. Booth Award, the 1991 ACM SIGCSE award, and the 1995 Karl V. Karlstrom Outstanding Educator Award.

have several properties that, at best, might be described as idiosyncratic, and at worst, are a programmer's nightmare.

To see the difference between arrays and vectors, we'll study the behavior of two programs: one that uses the built-in array type and one that uses the Vector class. Built-in array variables are defined with slightly different syntax compared with Vector variables. A built-in array similar to the Vector diceStats in Prog. 8.2, *dieroll2.cc* (page 365), is defined as follows:

```
int diceStats[2*DICE_SIDES+1];
```

Subscript Errors

Program 8.9 reads numbers until a sentinel of zero is entered. These numbers are stored in an array `list` and the location or index of the largest element is stored in `largeIndex`. A mistake in the logic of the `while` loop can generate an illegal array access, causing incorrect output.

Program 8.9   *badsub.cc*

```cpp
#include <iostream.h>

// illustrates invalid array subscripting
// store values in array and find largest value

int main()
{
    int largeIndex = 0;  // location of largest item in list
    int count = 0;       // number of items in list
    int list[10];

    cout << "enter numbers, 0 to terminate ";
    int num;

    while (cin >> num && num != 0)
    {
        list[count] = num;
        if (num >= list[largeIndex])  // found new largest
        {
            largeIndex = count;  // remember index as well as number
        }
        count++;
    }

    cout << "largest value = " << list[largeIndex];
    cout << " in location " << largeIndex << endl;
    return 0;
}
```

OUTPUT

```
prompt> badsub
enter numbers, 0 to terminate   100 90 80 70 60 50 40 30 0
largest value = 100 in location 0
prompt> badsub
enter numbers, 0 to terminate   21 22 23 23 25 26 27 28 29 30 31 32 33 34 0
largest value = 34 in location 34
```

```
prompt> badsub
enter numbers, 0 to terminate   1 1 1 1 1 1 1 1 1 1 50 13 13 0
largest value = 13 in location 52
prompt> badsub
enter numbers, 0 to terminate   1 1 1 1 1 1 1 1 1 1 100 3 3 0
largest value = 1734965861 in location 100
```

In the sample runs shown here, only the first run has ten or fewer numbers entered. In the second run, 14 numbers are entered. Although the largest number printed by the program is correct, its index is not. In the third run neither the largest number nor the index are correct, although a 13 is entered by the user. In the last run a "garbage" value is printed for the largest number, although the index is a number entered by the user.

> **Program Tip: In addition to generating incorrect data, on many systems an invalid subscript can cause the computer to crash or lock up.**
>
> Be careful when developing programs that use built-in arrays. If you need to use built-in arrays, it's often easier to develop the program using vectors and then substitute arrays for vectors when you are confident the program works.

If the definition `int list[10]` is replaced by `Vector<int> list(10)` in Prog. 8.9, different behavior results. The program, which is available as *badsub2.cc* but not shown here, generates the following output: The input for each run is identical to the input shown in the previous run when *badsub.cc* was executed.

OUTPUT

```
prompt> badsub2
enter numbers, 0 to terminate   100 90 80 70 60 50 40 30 0
largest value = 100 in location 0
prompt> badsub2
enter numbers, 0 to terminate   21 22 23 23 25 26 27 28 29 30 31 32 33 34 0
Illegal vector index: 10 (max = 9)
 failed assertion 'index < length'
prompt> badsub2
enter numbers, 0 to terminate   1 1 1 1 1 1 1 1 1 1 50 13 13 0
Illegal vector index: 10 (max = 9)
 failed assertion 'index < length'
prompt> badsub2
enter numbers, 0 to terminate   1 1 1 1 1 1 1 1 1 1 100 3 3 0
Illegal vector index: 10 (max = 9)
 failed assertion 'index < length'
```

Rather than giving incorrect results, a bad index results in an error message and termination of the program. It is much better to have a program generate an error message than to give incorrect results that may be taken as correct by users. The message "failed assertion" is generated by the `Vector` class and is used to facilitate the use of debuggers when programming.

Defining an Array

In C++ the size of an array must be specified by an expression whose value can be determined at compile time. The three statements below on the left define two arrays: one named `numList`, capable of storing 200 values of type `double`, and one named `names` that can store 50 `string` values. Corresponding `Vector` definitions are given on the right.

```
const int SIZE = 100;            const int SIZE = 100;
double numList[SIZE*2];          Vector<double> numList(SIZE*2);
string names[SIZE/2];            Vector<string> names(SIZE/2);
```

In contrast, the following definition of `numList` is illegal according to the C++ standard, because the value of `size` must be determined at compile time but here is known only at run time. Nevertheless, some compilers may permit such definitions, and in Chapter 12 we will see how to define in a legal manner an array whose size is not known at compile time. There is no compile-time limit on the size of `Vector` variables—only on built-in array variables.

```
int size;
cout << "enter size ";
cin >> size;
double numList[size];            // not legal in standard C++
```

As shown in the foregoing definition `string names[SIZE/2]`, it is possible to define arrays of user-defined types as well as arrays of built-in types. However, as with `Vector` definitions, to define an array of a user-defined type the type must have a default, or parameterless, constructor. For example, the following definition will not compile:

```
#include "dice.h"

Dice days[10];                   // illegal, no default constructor for Dice
```

If the class `Date` as defined in *date.h,* Prog. 5.15 (page 241), is used instead of `Dice`, however, the definition above will compile. The `Date` class supplies a default constructor, which initializes the date to the current date.

Initializing an Array

Arrays can be initialized by assigning values to the individual array locations, using a loop. It is also possible to assign values to individual array locations when an array is defined. For example, the following definitions assign values representing the number of days in each month to `monthDays` and the names of each month to `monthNames`:

```
int monthDays[13] = {0,31,28,31,30,31,30,31,31,30,31,30,31};
string monthNames[13] = {"","January","February","March",
     "April","May","June","July","August",
     "September","October","November","December"};
```

Given these definitions, the output of the statement

```
cout << "number of days in " << monthNames[4] << " is "
     << monthDays[4] << endl;
```

is

OUTPUT

```
number of days in April is 30
```

This kind of initialization is *not* possible with `Vector` variables—only with variables defined using built-in arrays. Note that the zeroth location of each array is unused, so that the *k*th location of each array stores information for the *k*th month rather than storing information for March in the location 2. Again, the conceptual simplicity of this scheme more than compensates for an extra array location.

Although the number of entries in each array (13) is specified in the definitions above, this is not necessary. It would be better stylistically to define a constant `const int NUM_MONTHS = 12;` and use the expression `NUM_MONTHS + 1` in defining the arrays, but no number at all needs to be used, as follows:

```
int monthDays[] = {0,31,28,31,30,31,30,31,31,30,31,30,31};
string dayNames[] = {"Sunday", "Monday", "Tuesday",
     "Wednesday", "Thursday","Friday", "Saturday"};
```

The definition for `dayNames` causes an array of seven strings to be allocated and initialized. The definition of `monthDays` allocates and initializes an array of 13 integers. Since the compiler can determine the necessary number of array locations (essentially by counting commas in the list of values between curly braces), including the number of cells is allowed but is redundant and not necessary.

It is useful in some situations to assign all array locations the value zero as is done in Program 8.2. This can be done when the array is defined, by using initialization values as in the preceding examples, but an alternative method for initializing all entries in an array to zero is

```
int diceStats[9] = 0;
```

The `int` array `diceStats` has 9 locations, all equal to 0. When zero is used to initialize all array locations, the number of locations in the array is *not* redundant as it is in the earlier examples, because there is no comma-separated list of values that the compiler can use to determine the number of array values. This method *cannot* be used to initialize arrays to values other than zero. The definition

```
int units[100] = 1;
```

results in an array with `units[0] == 1`, but all other locations in `units` are zero. When a list of values used for array initialization doesn't have enough values, zeros are used to fill in the missing values. This is essentially what is happening with the shortcut method just given for initializing an array of zeros. I don't recommend this method of initialization; it leads to confusion, because zero is treated differently from other values.

In contrast, `Vector` variables can be initialized so that all entries contain any value, not just zero. This can be done using the two-parameter constructor or the `Vector::Fill` member function, described on page 368.

Arrays as Parameters

Arrays are fundamentally different from other types in C++ in two ways:

1. It is *not* possible to assign one array to another using an assignment operator =.
2. An array passed as a parameter is *not* copied; it is as though the array were passed by reference.

The reason for these exceptions to the normal rules of assignment and parameter passing in C++ (which permit assignment between variables of the same type and use call-by-value for passing parameters) is based on what an array variable name is: a *constant* whose value serves as a *reference* to the first (index 0) item in the array. Since constants cannot be changed, assignments to array variables are illegal:

```
int coins[] = {1,5,10,25};
int bills[] = {1,5,10,20};

coins = bills;        // illegal in C and C++
coins[3] = bills[3];  // legal, assigning to array location
```

Because the array name is a reference to the first array location, it can be used to access the entire contents of the array, with appropriate indexing. Only the array name is passed as the value of a parameter, but the name can be used to change the array's contents even though the array is not explicitly passed by reference. When an array is passed as a parameter, empty brackets [ ] are used to indicate that the parameter is an array. The number of elements allocated for the storage associated with the array parameter does not need to be part of the array parameter. This is illustrated in Prog. 8.10.

Program 8.10   *fixlist.cc*

```cpp
#include <iostream.h>

// illustrates passing arrays as parameters

void Change(int list[], int numElts);
void Print(const int list[], int numElts);

int main()
{
    const int SIZE = 10;

    int numbers[SIZE];
    int k;
    for(k=0; k < SIZE; k++){
        numbers[k] = k+1;
    }

    cout << "before" << endl << "---------" << endl;
    Print(numbers,SIZE);

    cout << endl << "after" << endl << "---------"
        << endl;
    Change(numbers,SIZE);
    Print(numbers,SIZE);
    return 0;
}

void Change(int list[], int numElts)
// precondition: list contains at least numElts cells
// postcondition: list[k] = list[0] + list[1] + ... + list[k]
//                for all 0 <= k < numElts
{
    int k;
    for(k=1; k < numElts; k++)
    {
        list[k] += list[k-1];
    }
}

void Print(const int list[], int numElts)
// precondition: list contains at least numElts cells
// postcondition: all elements of list printed
{
    int k;
    for(k=0; k < numElts; k++)
    {
        cout << list[k] << endl;
    }
}
```

```
                              OUTPUT

before
---------
1
2
3
4
5
6
7
8
9
10

after
---------
1
3
6
10
15
21
28
36
45
55
```

The identifier `numbers` is used as the name of an array; its value is the location of the first array cell (which has index zero). In particular, `numbers` does *not* change as a result of being passed to `Change`, but the *contents* of the array `numbers` do change. This is a subtle distinction, but the array name is passed by value, as are all parameters by default in C and C++. The name is used to access the memory associated with the array, and the values stored in this memory can change. Since it is not legal to assign a new value to an array variable (e.g., `list = newlist`), the parameter `list` cannot be changed in any case, although the values associated with the array cells can change.

Program Tip: An array name is like a handle that can be used to grab all the memory cells allocated when the array is defined.

The array name cannot be changed, but it can be used to access the memory cells so that they can be changed.

---

const **Parameters**

The parameter for the function Print in Prog. 8.10 is defined as const or a constant array. The values stored in the cells of a constant array *cannot* be changed; the compiler will prevent attempts to do so. The values stored in a const array can, however, be accessed, as is shown in Print. If the statement list[k] = 0 is added in the while loop of Print, the g++ compiler generates the following error message:

```
fixlist.cc: In function 'void Print(const int *, int)':
fixlist.cc:46: assignment of read-only location

Compilation exited abnormally with code 1 at Sat Jun  4 14:02:18
```

Program Tip: Using a const **modifier for parameters is good, defensive programming—it allows the compiler to catch inadvertent attempts to modify a parameter.**

A const array parameter protects the values of the array cells from being modified.

Array size as a parameter The number of elements in an array parameter is *not* included in the formal parameter. As a result, there must be some mechanism for determining the number of elements stored in an array parameter. This is commonly done by passing this value as another parameter, by using a global constant, by using the array in a class that contains the number of entries, or by using a sentinel value in the array to indicate the last entry. As an example, the following function Average returns the average of the first numScores test scores stored in the array scores.

```cpp
double Average(const int scores[], int numScores)
// precondition: numScores = # of entries in scores
// postcondition: returns average of
//                  scores[0] ... scores[numScores-1]
{
    int total = 0;
    double average = 0.0;           // stores returned average
    int k;
    for(k=0; k < numScores; k += 1)
    {
        total += scores[k];
    }

    if (numScores != 0)  // guard divide by zero
    {
        average = double(total)/numScores;
    }
    return average;
}
```

Some other section of code might read numbers, store them in an array, and call the function `Average` to compute the average of the numbers read. Alternatively, the numbers stored in the formal parameter `scores` might be data generated from a simulation or some other computer program.

In the following program segment, numbers representing grades (in a hypothetical class) are read until the input is exhausted or until the number of grades would exceed the capacity of the array. The average of these grades is then calculated using the function `Average`.

```
const int MAX_GRADES = 100;              // maximum # of grades
int grades[MAX_GRADES];
int numGrades = 0;                       // # of grades entered

while (cin >> score && numGrades < MAX_GRADES)
{
    grades[numGrades] = score;
    numGrades += 1;
}
cout << "average grade = " << Average(grades,numGrades)
     << endl;
```

This example is meant to illustrate how an array might be used. The approach of storing the grades in an array to calculate the average is not a good one. Because the size of an array is determined at compile time, the code in this example is limited to manipulating at most `MAX_GRADES` grades. Since it is possible to calculate the average of a set of numbers without storing all the numbers, the approach used above is unnecessarily limiting.

The value of `numScores` in `Average` is exactly the number of values stored in the array `scores` but is one more than the largest index of an array cell with a valid value. This off-by-one difference is potentially confusing, so be careful in writing loops that access all the elements in an array.

8.10. Write a function `ReadValues` that reads integer values entered by the user and stores the values in an array. The input should stop when the user enters the character signaling end of file. The header for the function should be

*Pause to
reflect*

```
void ReadArray(int values[], int & numValues)
// postcondition: all integers entered by user
//                stored in values
//                number of integers is stored
//                in numValues
```

8.11. Write a function to print all the names of the months passed in an array of `strings`, as given in the example of the array `monthName` in Sec. 8.5.

8.12. Write two functions: one to shift all array elements one cell to the left, losing the value in the zeroth cell and decreasing the number of elements in the array by 1, and one to shift all elements to the right, storing zero in the zeroth cell. Use the function headers below as guides. Think carefully about at which end of the array the loops will begin:

```
void ShiftLeft(double a[], int & numElts)
// shift all elements to the left
// precondition: a[0] = val₀, a[1] = val₁,...,
//                   a[numElts-1] = valₙᵤₘₑₗₜₛ ₋ ₁, numElts = k
// postcondition: a[0] = val₁, a[1] = val₂,...,
//                   a[numElts - 2] = valₙᵤₘₑₗₜₛ ₋ ₁, numElts = k-1

void ShiftRight(double a[], int & numElts)
// shift all elements to the right
// precondition: a[0] = val₀, a[1] = val₁,...,
//                   a[numElts-1] = valₙᵤₘₑₗₜₛ ₋ ₁, numElts = k
// postcondition: a[0] = 0.0, a[1] = val₀, a[2] = val₁,...,
//                   a[numElts] = valₙᵤₘₑₗₜₛ ₋ ₁, numElts = k+1
```

Why is `numElts` a reference parameter and the array `a` not a reference parameter?

8.13. Write a function `Total` that computes the total of all the entries in an array of `doubles`. The prototype for the function is

```
double Total(double list[], int numElts)
// precondition: numElts = # of entries in list
// postcondition: returns list[0] + ... + list[numElts - 1]
```

8.14. What changes should be made to *badsub.cc*, Prog. 8.9, so that the value 10 is defined as a `const int` rather than being used as a literal in the definition of `list`?

8.15. How can Prog. 8.9 be changed so that the size of the array used is entered by the user?

8.16. The error in the `while` loop in Prog. 8.9 is typical of mistakes made in storing and retrieving values in an array: There is no test of whether the array is full. Using `&&`, change the test of the loop so that no invalid array accesses are made, by causing the loop to terminate when the array is full.

Alternatively, use an `if` statement to break out of the loop if the array is full.

8.6   Chapter Review

We studied the class `Vector` used in place of built-in arrays to store collections of values accessible by random access. Vectors can store thousands of values, and the fifth, five-hundredth, and five-thousandth values can be accessed in the same amount of time. Vectors and their built-in counterparts, arrays, are very useful in writing programs that store and manipulate large quantities of data.

The important topics covered include the following:

- Vectors can be used as counters, for example to count the number of occurrences of each ASCII character in a text file or the number of times a die rolls each number over several trials.

- Vectors are constructed by providing the size of the vector (the number of elements that can be stored) as an argument to the constructor. Like arrays, vectors are indexed beginning at zero, so a six-element vector has valid indices 0, 1, 2, 3, 4, 5.

- Vectors of all built-in types can be defined, and vectors of programmer-defined types (like `string`) can be defined if the type has a default constructor.

- Vectors can be initialized to hold the same value in every cell by providing a second argument to the constructor when the vector is defined. Alternatively, the function `Fill` can be used.

- Vectors can be resized. All resizing operations should double the size of the vector.

- Vectors should always be passed by reference to save memory and the time that would be required to copy if pass by value were used. There are occasions when a copy is needed, but in general pass by reference is preferred. Use `const` reference parameters to protect the parameter from being altered even when passed by reference.

- Initializer lists should be used to construct vectors that are private data members of class objects.

- Sequential search is used to find a value in an unsorted vector. Binary search can be used to find values in sorted vectors. Binary search is much faster, needing roughly 20 comparisons to find an item in a list of one million different items. The drawback of binary search is that its use requires a sorted vector.

- Built-in arrays are cumbersome to use but are often more efficient than vectors. Nevertheless, you should use vectors and switch to arrays only when you've determined that speed is essential and that the use of vectors is making your program slow (which is probably not the case).

- Built-in arrays can be initialized with several values at once. Built-in arrays cannot be resized, cannot be assigned to each other, and do not support range-checked indexing. The size of a built-in array must be known at compile time (although we'll see in Chapter 12 that an alternative form of array definition does permit array size to be determined at run time).

8.7   Exercises

8.1 Modify Prog. 8.3, *letters.cc,* so that a vector of 26 elements, indexed from 0 to 25, is used to track how many times each letter in the range `'a'–'z'` occurs. To do this, map the character `'a'` to 0, `'b'` to 1,..., and 'z' to 25. Isolate this mapping in a function `CharToIndex` whose header is

```
int CharToIndex(char ch)
 // precondition: 'a' <= ch and ch <= 'z'
 // postcondition: returns 0 for 'a', 1 for 'b', ... 25 for 'z'
```

(Note that `'a'` - `'a'` == 0, `'b'` - `'a'` == 1, and `'z'` - `'a'` == 25.)

8.2 Write a program that maintains an inventory of a CD collection, a book collection, or some other common collectible. The user of the program should have the choice of printing all items, deleting items, adding information about specific items (e.g., all works by a specific artist), saving to a file, and reading from a file. You can start from scratch or with the thousands of CDs in the file *cd.dat*.

8.3 Write a modified version of the program from Exercise 6.6 in Sec. 6.6, but use a `Vector` to keep track of the different items stored. When the user is prompted to enter an item, the available items should be listed. (Ideally the user could select the item by number; e.g., 1 for coat, 2 for shirt, and so on.) Print a summary of all items sold before prompting the user for wholesale information.

8.4 Implement a new version of the `WalkObserver` class used in *frogwalk3.cc*, Prog. 7.8, that keeps track of how many times a one-dimensional random walker visits every location in the range −100 to 100. You can either use one `Vector` with 201 elements or two `Vector` instance variables: one for nonnegative locations and one for negative locations. The `WalkObserver` class should also track the number of times the random walker goes past the boundaries of the range [-100..100] tracked by the observer.

You may want to add to the `WalkObsever` class a member function `Print` or `ShowInfo` that you call after the simulation is finished. Print at least the counts for each location, or use a histogram to print a graphical representation of the number of visits to each location (see Exercise 8.6).

8.5 Write a program to implement the guess-a-number game described in Sec. 8.4 on binary search. The user should think of a number between 1 and 100 and respond to guesses made by the computer. Make the program robust so that it can tell whether the user cheats by providing inconsistent answers.

OUTPUT

```
prompt> guessnum
Think of a number between 1 and 100 and I'll try to guess it.

Is the number 50 [y/n]? no
Is the number less than 50 [y/n]? no
Is the number 75 [y/n]? no
Is the number less than 75 [y/n]? no
Is the number 87 [y/n]? no
Is the number less than 87 [y/n]? yes
Is the number 81 [y/n]? yes

I guessed your number using 7 questions.
```

8.6 Design and implement a `Histogram` class for displaying quantities stored in a `Vector`. A **histogram** is like a bar graph that displays a line relative to the size of the data being visualized. The `Histogram` class should have a private instance variable that is a reference to a `Vector` of integers in a similar way as the `RandomWalkO` class has a reference to a `WalkObserver` object.

For example, the results of using *letters.cc*, Prog. 8.3, to find occurrences of each letter in *Hamlet* can be displayed as a histogram as follows:

```
                              OUTPUT

prompt> letters
enter name of input file: hamlet
    a (   9950 )  *********************************
    b (   1830 )  ******
    c (   2606 )  ********
    d (   5025 )  ****************
    e ( 14960 )  **************************************************************
    f (   2698 )  *********
    g (   2420 )  ********
    h (   8731 )  *****************************
    i (   8511 )  ***************************
    j (    110 )
    k (   1272 )  ****
    l (   5847 )  *******************
    m (   4253 )  **************
    n (   8297 )  **************************
    o ( 11218 )  *************************************
    p (   2016 )  ******
    q (    220 )
    r (   7777 )  *************************
    s (   8379 )  ***************************
    t ( 11863 )  ***************************************
    u (   4343 )  **************
    v (   1222 )  ****
    w (   3132 )  **********
    x (    179 )
    y (   3204 )  **********
    z (     72 )
```

The absolute counts for each letter are shown in parentheses. The bars are scaled so that the longest bar (for the letter *e*) has 50 asterisks and the other bars are scaled relative to this. For example, the letter *h* has 29 asterisks and $8731/14960 \times 50 = 29.15$ (where we divide using floating-point or `double` precision but truncate the final result to an integer).

Member functions for the `Histogram` class might include setting the length of the longest bar, identifying labels for each bar drawn, plotting a range of values rather than all values, and grouping ranges; for example, for plotting data in the range 0–99, you might group by tens and plot 0–9, 10–19, 20–29, . . . , 90–99.

It's difficult to write a completely general histogram class, so you'll need to decide how much functionality you will implement. The following histogram tracks 10,000 rolls of two six-sided dice and scales the longest bar to 40 characters:

```
                            OUTPUT

prompt> rollem
how many sides for dice: 6
how many rolls: 10000
     2 (    282 ) ******
     3 (    522 ) ************
     4 (    874 ) ********************
     5 (   1106 ) *************************
     6 (   1376 ) *********************************
     7 (   1650 ) *******************************************
     8 (   1431 ) **********************************
     9 (   1131 ) **************************
    10 (    815 ) ******************
    11 (    545 ) *************
    12 (    268 ) ******
```

8.7 Reimplement the histogram class from the previous exercise to draw a vertical
histogram rather than a horizontal histogram. For example, a graph for rolling two
six-sided dice is shown here (scaled to 10 asterisks in the longest bar):

```
     2 (    243 ) *
     3 (    594 ) ***
     4 (    827 ) ****
     5 (   1066 ) ******
     6 (   1327 ) *******
     7 (   1682 ) **********
     8 (   1465 ) ********
     9 (   1091 ) ******
    10 (    807 ) ****
    11 (    606 ) ***
    12 (    292 ) *
```

The same graph drawn vertically follows:

```
                        *
                        *
                        *    *
                   *    *    *
              *    *    *    *    *
              *    *    *    *    *
         *    *    *    *    *    *    *
    *    *    *    *    *    *    *    *    *
    *    *    *    *    *    *    *    *    *
    *    *    *    *    *    *    *    *    *    *    *
    ------------------------------------------
    2    3    4    5    6    7    8   9  10  11  12
```

It's harder to get labels drawn well for the vertical histogram, so first try to
determine how to draw the bars and don't worry initially about the labels.

8.8 Implement a *Sieve of Eratosthenes* to find prime numbers. A sieve is implemented using a `Vector` of `bool` values, initialized so that all elements are `true`. To find primes between 2 and N, use `Vector` indices 2 through N, so you'll need an $(N + 1)$-element `Vector`.

1. Find the first entry that is `true` (initially this entry has index 2, because 0 and 1 do not count in the search for primes). We'll call the index of the `true` entry p, since this entry will be prime.
2. Set each entry whose index is a multiple of p to `false`.
3. Repeat until all `Vector` elements have been examined.

The process is illustrated in the following figure for the numbers 2 through 18. Circled numbers are true. In the topmost view of the array the first `true` cell has index 2, so all the even numbers (multiples of 2) are changed to `false`. These are shown as shaded entries in the diagram. The next `true` value is 3, so all multiples of 3 are changed to `false` (although 6, 12, and 18 have already been changed). In the third row no more new entries will be set to false that are not already false, and the primes have been determined (although the steps are repeated until all `Vector` elements have been examined).

8.9 Write a program that determines the frequently used words in a text file. We'll define **frequently used** to mean that a word accounts for at least 1% of all the words in a file. For example, in the file *melville.txt* used in the output of Prog. 8.8, *allword4.cc* (page 395), there are 14,353 total words, so any word that occurs more than 143 times is a frequently used word. For *melville.txt* the frequently used words are shown in the following table with their number of occurrences.

334	a	196	my
376	and	151	not
218	he	359	of
219	his	194	that
519	i	603	the
265	in	432	to
164	it	195	was

8.8   A Computer Science Excursion: Large Integers

Arithmetic operations are fundamental in computing and programming. In many programming environments the largest value of an integer is much too small to represent quantities such as the population of the world, the U.S. national debt, and even the number of occurrences of the letter *e* in Melville's *Moby Dick.* Although `double` values can be larger than `int` values, it is not always possible to use `double` values, because they're represented only approximately in the computer (see Prog. 5.9, *newton.cc*, page 199).

In this section we'll provide a brief overview of a class `BigInt`, which can be used interchangeably with the built-in type `int` but represents arbitrarily large integer values limited only by computer memory and the time to process these large values.

Developing a Test Program

We should first specify the operations that the `BigInt` class will implement. Ideally, `BigInt` values will be used interchangeably with `int` values, but some arithmetic operations may be harder to implement than others. Rather than implement all arithmetic operations and then test the implementation, we should implement a minimal number of operations and test these thoroughly. We can then design and implement new operations a few at a time, adding them and testing them with a working implementation. By modifying a well-tested existing program and class, we can concentrate on small sections of code rather than trying to debug a large class at once.

However, we know we'll need to test all the arithmetic operations. We can implement a test program using `int` values and then use the test program to test the `BigInt` class. Implementing the test program with a proven class (the built-in type `int`) allows us to concentrate on the logic of the test program rather than worrying about the interplay between the testing program and the `BigInt` class. Ideally we want to debug the `BigInt` class—not the test program.

> **Program Tip: Debug small parts of a program or a class at one time.**
>
> **Try to minimize the dependencies between classes and programs when you're designing, implementing, and testing code.**
>
> This will let you concentrate on one piece of the puzzle at a time.

I implemented *testbig.cc*, Prog. 8.11, before I had implemented the complete `BigInt` class. I tested *testbig.cc* using `int` values, although the following listing shows the final program using `BigInt` values.[9] An enum is used to represent

---

[9]The same program can be used to test `int` values by using a `typedef` (see Sec. 11.6) at the beginning of the program: `typedef int BigInt;` to make `BigInt` a "synonym" for `int`.

Program 8.11 *testbig.cc*

```
#include <iostream.h>
#include "bigint.h"

// Owen Astrachan 7/5/96
// illustrates parsing arithmetic expressions with BigInt values

// define enumerated type and string equivalent of each value

enum   Optype { add, subtract, multiply, divide, stop, no_op };
string OPSTRINGS[] = {"+", "-", "*", "/", "=" };

const int NUMOPS = 5;     // # valid operations

Optype StringToOp(const string & s);
Optype Getop();

int main()
{
    BigInt accumulator(0);  // accumulate in this object
    BigInt current;         // value to be operated with
    Optype op = add;        // so first value is added to zero
    cout << "starting value: ";
    cin >> current;
    do
    {
        switch (op)
        {
          case add :
              accumulator += current;
              break;
          case subtract:
              accumulator -= current;
              break;
          case multiply:
              accumulator *= current;
              break;
          case divide:
              accumulator / current;
              break;
          default:
              cerr << "error with operator" << endl;
        }
        cout << "--> " << accumulator << endl;
        op = Getop();
        if (op != stop)
        {
            cout << "enter number: ";
            cin >> current;
        }
    } while (op != stop);
}
```

```
Optype StringToOp(const string & s)
// precondition:   s is a valid operator
// postcondition: returns Optype equivalent, e.g., add for "+"
{
    int k;
    for(k=0;k < NUMOPS; k++)
    {
        if (s == OPSTRINGS[k]) return Optype(k);
    }
    return no_op;   // not found, return no-operator
}

Optype Getop()
// postcondition: reads a white space-delimited operator from
//                cin and returns the operator
{
    string s;
    Optype retval;
    do
    {
        cout << "enter + - * / ( = to quit) ";
        cin >> s;
    } while ((retval = StringToOp(s)) == no_op);

    return retval;
}
```

```
                            OUTPUT

    prompt> testbig
    starting value: 25
    --> 25
    enter + - * / ( = to quit) +
    enter number: 7
    --> 32
    enter + - * / ( = to quit) *
    enter number: 4
    --> 128
    enter + - * / ( = to quit) −
    enter number: -8
    --> 136
    enter + - * / ( = to quit) /
    enter number: 16
    --> 8
    enter + - * / ( = to quit) −
    enter number: 13
    --> -5
    enter + - * / ( = to quit) *
    enter number: -5
    --> 25
    enter + - * / ( = to quit) =
```

valid operations, and a string equivalent for each `enum` is defined to facilitate conversion from typed operators to the internal enum used in the program. Built-in arrays are used to store the string equivalents, because built-in arrays can be initialized more simply than vectors. With this program tested, we can turn to the problem of implementing the `BigInt` class.

The `BigInt` Class

Rather than dwell on how the `BigInt` class is implemented, we'll study an elementary use of the class, provide exercises to explore more advanced uses, and use the source code to study implementation issues.

A `BigInt` value is represented internally by a vector of characters; the type `char` is studied thoroughly in Sec. 9.1. All the dependencies on the use of a `char` vector are isolated in three private member functions: `getDigit`, `changeDigit`, and `addSigDigit`. The `BigInt` member functions manipulate digits and numbers using these helper functions as abstractions to set and retrieve individual digits of a `BigInt` value. This isolates the somewhat complicated implementations of addition, subtraction, multiplication, and division from the concrete method used to store digits. You could, for example, reimplement the `BigInt` class using the `List` class from Sec. 6.7 by changing only the private helper functions.

Input and output of `BigInt` values are facilitated by conversion to and from `string` values. A member function `toString` converts a `BigInt` to a `string` representation; for example, the value 12345 is converted to `"12345"`. The `BigInt` constructor that has the following prototype constructs a `BigInt` from a `string`.

```
BigInt(const string & s);
```

For example, you can enter a `BigInt` from the keyboard by reading a string and constructing the `BigInt` from the string. If you study the source code, you'll see how this is done.

Program 8.12, *bigfact.cc*, computes factorials using the `BigInt` class.

Program 8.12   *bigfact.cc*

```
#include <iostream.h>
#include "bigint.h"
#include "prompt.h"

// Owen Astrachan
// illustrates rudimentary BigInt calculation of Factorial

BigInt Factorial(int num);
int main()
```

```
{
    int k;
    BigInt answer;
    int limit = PromptRange("max value for factorial",1,100);
    for(k=0; k <= limit; k++)
    {
        answer = Factorial(k);
        cout << k << "! = " << answer << endl;
    }
    return 0;
}

BigInt Factorial(int num)
// precondition: 0 <= num
// postcondition: returns num! (num factorial)
{
    BigInt product = 1;
    int count;
    for(count=1; count <= num; count++)
    {
        product *= count;
    }
    return product;
}
```

OUTPUT

```
prompt> bigfact
max value for factorial between 1 and 100: 30
0! = 1
1! = 1
2! = 2
3! = 6
4! = 24
5! = 120
6! = 720
7! = 5040
8! = 40320
9! = 362880
10! = 3628800
11! = 39916800
12! = 479001600
13! = 6227020800
14! = 87178291200
15! = 1307674368000
16! = 20922789888000
17! = 355687428096000
18! = 6402373705728000
```

```
19! = 121645100408832000
20! = 2432902008176640000
21! = 51090942171709440000
22! = 1124000727777607680000
23! = 25852016738884976640000
24! = 620448401733239439360000
25! = 15511210043330985984000000
26! = 403291461126605635584000000
27! = 10888869450418352160768000000
28! = 304888344611713860501504000000
29! = 8841761993739701954543616000000
30! = 265252859812191058636308480000000
```

The header file, *bigint.h,* is Prog. 8.13:

Program 8.13   *bigint.h*

```
#ifndef _BIGINT_H
#define _BIGINT_H

// author: Owen Astrachan
// 8/23/95, modified 7/5/96
//
// implements an arbitrary-precision integer class
//
// constructors:
//
// BigInt()              -- default constructor, value is 0
// BigInt(int n)         -- initialize to value of n (C++ int)
// BigInt(const string & s) -- initialize to value specified
//   by s; it is an error if s is an invalid integer, e.g.,
//   "1234abc567".  In this case the bigint value is garbage
// BigInt(const BigInt & b)  -- copy constructor
//
//
// *****  arithmetic operators:
//
// all arithmetic operators +, -, *, /, % are overloaded both
// in form +=, -=, *=, /=, %=, and as binary operators
//
// multiplication and division also overloaded for
// *= int and /= int; e.g., BigInt a *= 3 (mostly to facilitate
// implementation)

//   ***** logical operators:
//
// bool operator == (const BigInt & lhs, const BigInt & rhs)
// bool operator != (const BigInt & lhs, const BigInt & rhs)
```

```
// bool operator <  (const BigInt & lhs, const BigInt & rhs)
// bool operator <= (const BigInt & lhs, const BigInt & rhs)
// bool operator >  (const BigInt & lhs, const BigInt & rhs)
// bool operator >= (const BigInt & lhs, const BigInt & rhs)
//
//  ***** I/O operators:
//
//  ostream & Print()
//        prints value of BigInt (member function)
//  ostream & operator << (ostream & os, const BigInt & b)
//        stream operator to print value
//


#include <iostream.h>
#include "CPstring.h"          // for strings
#include "vector.h"            // for sequence of digits

class BigInt
{
  public:

    BigInt();                    // default constructor, value = 0
    BigInt(int);                 // assign an integer value
    BigInt(const string &);      // assign a string
    BigInt(const BigInt &);      // copy constructor
    ~BigInt();                   // destructor

    ostream & Print(ostream & os) const;  // so << isn't a friend

    BigInt & operator = (const BigInt &);

    // operators: arithmetic, relational

    BigInt & operator += (const BigInt &);
    BigInt & operator -= (const BigInt &);
    BigInt & operator *= (const BigInt &);
    BigInt & operator *= (int num);
    BigInt & operator / (const BigInt &);
    BigInt & operator / (int num);
    BigInt & operator %= (const BigInt &);

    string toString() const;    // convert to string

    friend bool operator == (const BigInt &, const BigInt &);
    friend bool operator < (const BigInt &, const BigInt &);

  private:

    enum BigError{
    underflow, overflow, not_a_number,infinity,no_error
    };

    // private state/instance variables
```

```
    bool myIsNegative;
    Vector<char> myDigits;
    int myNumDigits;
    BigError myError;

    // helper functions

    bool IsNeg() const;   // return true iff number is negative
    int getDigit(int k) const;
    void addSigDigit(int value);
    void changeDigit(int digit, int value);
    int size() const;
    void Normalize();
    void DivideHelp(const BigInt & lhs, const BigInt & rhs,
    BigInt & quotient, BigInt & remainder);

};

// free functions

ostream & operator <<(ostream &, const BigInt &);
istream & operator >>(istream &, BigInt &);

BigInt operator +(const BigInt & lhs, const BigInt & rhs);
BigInt operator -(const BigInt & lhs, const BigInt & rhs);
BigInt operator *(const BigInt & lhs, const BigInt & rhs);
BigInt operator *(const BigInt & lhs, int num);
BigInt operator *(int num, const BigInt & rhs);
BigInt operator /(const BigInt & lhs, const BigInt & rhs);
BigInt operator /(const BigInt & lhs, int num);
BigInt operator %(const BigInt & lhs, const BigInt & rhs);

bool operator != (const BigInt & lhs, const BigInt & rhs);
bool operator >  (const BigInt & lhs, const BigInt & rhs);
bool operator >= (const BigInt & lhs, const BigInt & rhs);
bool operator <= (const BigInt & lhs, const BigInt & rhs);


#endif   // _BIGINT_H not defined
```

bigint.h

Excursion Exercises

8.10 Write a program to determine whether a BigInt is prime. Use *primes.cc*, Prog. 5.8, as a model. To compute the square root of a BigInt modify the code in *newton.cc*, Prog. 5.9, to compute square roots of BigInt values. Alternatively, you can use binary search to find the square root of a number, using the same kind of high-low logic described for guessing a number in Sec. 8.4.

8.11 Write a function to compute x^n for BigInt values x and int values n. Test the program by computing 2^{500}, whose value is

32733906078961418700131896968275991522166420460430647894
83291368096133796404674554883270092325904157150886684127560
0710092172565458853930533285275893766

8.12 *(requires Excursion Section 4.9)* Write two functions to compute x^n for `BigInt` values of x and `int` values of n. Base one function on *logexpo.cc*, Prog. 4.15, and the algorithm that requires a logarithmic number of multiplications for exponentiation. Base the other on *itpower.cc,* Prog. 4.13. Time both versions of the program to compute a range of powers. Can you explain the differences in timings compared to the timings observed in Fig. 4.6?

## PART 3

DESIGN, USE, AND ANALYSIS: BUILDING ON THE FOUNDATION

Characters, Strings, and Streams: Abstraction and Information Hiding

9

He was a poet and hated the approximate.
RAINER MARIA RILKE
The Journal of My Other Self

Computer programs require precision even
when abstraction is required to make them
intelligible.
J.A. ZIMMER
Abstraction for Programmers

Abstraction . . . is seductive; forming generic
abstract types can lead into confusing excess . . .
MARIAN PETRE
Psychology of Programming, 112.

In 1936 Alan Turing, a British mathematician, published a famous paper titled
"On Computable Numbers, with an Application to the Entscheidungsproblem."
This paper helped lay the foundation for much of the work done in theoretical
computer science, even though computers did not exist when the paper was
written.[1] Turing invented a model of a computer, called a **Turing machine,** and
he used this model to develop ideas and proofs about what kinds of numbers
could be computed. His invention was an abstraction, not a real machine, but
it provided a framework for reasoning about computers. The **Church–Turing
thesis** says that, from a theoretical standpoint, all computers have the same
power. This is commonly accepted; the most powerful computers in the world
compute the same things as Turing's abstract machine could compute. Of course
some computers are faster than others, and computers continue to get faster
every year,[2] but the kinds of things that can be computed have not changed.

How can we define abstraction in programming? The American Heritage
Dictionary defines it as "the act or process of separating the inherent qualities
or properties of something from the actual physical object or concept to which

---

[1]At least, computers as we know them had not yet been invented. Several kinds of calculating
machines had been proposed or manufactured, but no general-purpose computer had been built.

[2]No matter when you read this sentence, it is likely to be true.

427

they belong." The general user's view of a computer is an abstraction of what really goes on behind the scenes. You do not need to know how to program a pull-down menu or a tracking mouse to use these tools. You do not need to know how numbers are represented in computer memory to write programs that manipulate numeric expressions. In some cases such missing knowledge is useful, because it can free you from worrying unnecessarily about issues that aren't relevant to programming at a high level.

Abstraction is a cornerstone of all computer science and certainly of our study of programming. The capability that modern programming languages and techniques provide us to avoid dealing with details permits more complex and larger programs to be written than could be written with assembly language, for example.

In this chapter we'll discuss characters, strings, files, and streams. These form an abstraction hierarchy with characters at the lowest level and streams at the highest level. A character is a symbol such as 'a'. Strings and files are both constructed from characters. We'll see that streams can be constructed from strings as well as from files. Although a character lies at the lowest level, we'll see that characters are also abstractions. We'll discuss programming tools that help in using and combining these abstractions.

9.1   Characters: Building Blocks for Strings

From the beginning of our study of C++ we have worked with the class `string`. Although we haven't worried about how the `string` class is implemented or about the individual characters from which strings are built, we have used the `string` class extensively in many programs. We have treated strings as abstractions—we understand strings by their use and behavior rather than by their construction or implementation. If we understand the `string` member functions (such as `length`, `substr`, `operator ==`, and `operator <<`), we do not need to understand the details and idiosyncrasies of the implementation. However, some programs manipulate the individual characters used to build strings, so we'll need to expand our understanding of characters.

The Type `char` as an Abstraction

We have discussed strings as sequences of characters but have not yet dealt with how a character is implemented in C++. The type `char` is used for characters in C++.[3]

A `char` variable stores legal character values. The range of legal values depends on the computer system being used and even the country in which the system is used. The range of legal characters that is supported in a computing system is called the **character set.** The most commonly used set is the ASCII set (pronounced "askee," an acronym for American Standard Code for Information

---

[3]Some people pronounce `char` as "care," short for "character." Others pronounce it "char" as in "charcoal." A third common pronunciation is "car" (rhymes with "star"). I don't like the "charcoal" pronunciation and use the pronunciation that has character.

Table 9.1   The ASCII Character Set

Decimal	Char	Decimal	Char	Decimal	Char	Decimal	Char
0	^@	32	Space	64	@	96	' (back quote)
1	^A	33	!	65	A	97	a
2	^B	34	"	66	B	98	b
3	^C	35	#	67	C	99	c
4	^D	36	$	68	D	100	d
5	^E	37	%	69	E	101	e
6	^F	38	&	70	F	102	f
7	^G (bell)	39	' (apostrophe)	71	G	103	g
8	^H (backspace)	40	(	72	H	104	h
9	^I (tab)	41	)	73	I	105	i
10	^J (line feed)	42	*	74	J	106	j
11	^K	43	+	75	K	107	k
12	^L	44	, (Comma)	76	L	108	l
13	^M (carriage return)	45	–	77	M	109	m
14	^N	46	.	78	N	110	n
15	^O	47	/ (slash)	79	O	111	o
16	^P	48	0	80	P	112	p
17	^Q	49	1	81	Q	113	q
18	^R	50	2	82	R	114	r
19	^S	51	3	83	S	115	s
20	^T	52	4	84	T	116	t
21	^U	53	5	85	U	117	u
22	^V	54	6	86	V	118	v
23	^W	55	7	87	W	119	w
24	^X	56	8	88	X	120	x
25	^Y	57	9	89	Y	121	y
26	^Z	58	:	90	Z	122	z
27	Escape	59	;	91	[	123	{
28	File separator	60	<	92	\	124		
29	Group separator	61	=	93	]	125	}
30	Record separator	62	>	94	^	126	~ (tilde)
31	Unit separator	63	?	95	_	127	Delete

Interchange); all programs in this book are run on a system with this character set. An emerging standard set is called Unicode, which supports international characters, such as ä, that are not part of the ASCII set. Chinese, Japanese, Arabic, and Cyrillic character sets may also be represented using Unicode. You must try to isolate your programs as much as possible from the particular character set being used in the program's development. This will help ensure that the program is **portable**—that is, useful in other computing environments than the one in which it was developed.

The type char is the smallest built-in type. A char variable uses less (actually, no more) memory than any other type of variable. A char literal is identified by using single quotes, as shown in the first two of the following examples:

```
char letter = 'a';
char digit = '9';
string word = "alphabetic";
```

Note that string literals use double quotes, which are different from two single quotes.

As an abstraction, a char is very different from an int. Unfortunately, in almost all cases a char can be treated as an int in C++ programs. This similarity has the potential to be confusing. From a programmer's view, a char is distinguished from an int by the way it is printed and, perhaps, by the amount of computer memory it uses. The relationship between char and int values is determined by the character set being used. For ASCII characters this relationship is given in Table 9.1.

Program 9.1 shows how the type char is very similar to the type int but prints differently. The char variable k is incremented just as an int is incremented, but, as the output shows, characters appear on the screen differently than integers.

The output of Prog. 9.1 shows that capital letters come before lower-case letters when the ASCII character set is used. Notice that the characters representing the digits '0' through '9' are contiguous and come before any

---

Program 9.1   charlist.cc

```
#include <iostream.h>

// illustrates use of char as an integral type

int main()
{
    char first,last;
    cout << "enter first and last characters" << endl;
    cout << "with NO SPACE separating them: ";
    cin >> first >> last;
    cout << first;    // print first char (fence post problem)
    char k;
    for(k=first+1; k <= last; k++)
    {
        cout  << " " << k;
    }
    cout << endl;
    return 0;
}
```

```
                        OUTPUT

prompt> charlist
enter first and last characters
with NO SPACE separating them: AZ
A B C D E F G H I J K L M N O P Q R S T U V W X Y Z
prompt> charlist
enter first and last characters
with NO SPACE separating them: 2B
2 3 4 5 6 7 8 9 : ; < = > ? @ A B
prompt> charlist
enter first and last characters
with NO SPACE separating them: Zz
Z [ \ ] ^ _ ' a b c d e f g h i j k l m n o p q r s t u v w x y z
prompt> charlist
enter first and last characters
with NO SPACE separating them: &F
& ' ( ) * + , - . / 0 1 2 3 4 5 6 7 8 9 : ; < = > ? @ A B C D E F
```

alphabetic character. If we change the output statement to cast the character to
an `int`,

```
        cout << " " << int(k);
```

the program will display the internal numeric representation of each `char`
rather than its symbolic character representation.

```
                        OUTPUT

prompt> charlist
enter first and last characters
with NO SPACE separating them: AM
65 66 67 68 69 70 71 72 73 74 75 76 77
```

Using the cast makes it more difficult to verify that the output is correct,
because the symbolic form of each character isn't used. In general, there isn't
any reason to be concerned with what the numerical representation of each
character is, because C++ provides many mechanisms that allow programs to
use the type `char` abstractly without regard for the underlying character set.
You can make the following assumptions about character codes:

1. The digit characters `'0'` through `'9'` (ASCII values 48 through 57) are
   consecutive with no intervening characters.
2. The lower-case characters `'a'` through `'z'` (ASCII 97 through 122) are
   consecutive, and the upper-case characters `'A'` through `'Z'` (ASCII 65
   through 90) are consecutive.

These assumptions are true for the ASCII character set and the Unicode character set, but not necessarily for all character sets.[4] In almost all programming environments you'll use either ASCII or Unicode. In the next section we'll study utility functions that help in writing portable programs.

The Library `<ctype.h>`

To be portable, your code must not rely on a specific character set. Just as the functions in the math library `<math.h>` make writing mathematical and scientific programs easier, a library of character functions helps in writing portable character-manipulating programs. This character library is accessible by using `#include <ctype.h>`.

Table 9.2 lists the prototypes for several functions in the header file `<ctype.h>` and a description of each function (these descriptions are based on those given in [Pla92]). You would expect functions with the prefix `is`, such as `islower` and `isalnum`, to have return type `bool`. They may, in environments that are exclusively C++ rather than C and C++. However, to ensure compatibility with both C and C++ code, many libraries use integer values for the return type of these predicates in `<ctype.h>`. These boolean-valued functions return some nonzero value for true, but this value is not necessarily one.

Although the formal parameter for each function is an `int`, these functions are intended to work with `char` arguments. Thus `isalpha('9')` evaluates to

Table 9.2   Some Functions in `<ctype.h>`

Function prototype	Returns
`int isalnum(int c)`	Returns true when `c` is alphabetic or a digit ("alnum")
`int isalpha(int c)`	Returns true when `c` is alphabetic (upper- or lower-case)
`int iscntrl(int c)`	Returns true when `c` is a control character
`int isdigit(int c)`	Returns true when `c` is a digit character `'0'–'9'`
`int islower(int c)`	Returns true when `c` is a lowercase letter
`int isprint(int c)`	Returns true when `c` is a printable character including space
`int ispunct(int c)`	Returns true when `c` is a punctuation (printable, not space, not alnum)
`int isspace(int c)`	Returns true when `c` is any white-space character
`int isupper(int c)`	Returns true when `c` is an upper-case letter
`int tolower(int c)`	Returns lower-case equivalent of c; if `!isupper(c)` then returns c unchanged
`int toupper(int c)`	Returns upper-case equivalent of c; if `!islower(c)` then returns c unchanged

---

[4]The C++ standard requires that `'0'` through `'9'` be consecutive, but in the EBCDIC character set the letters `'a'` through `'z'` and `'A'` through `'Z'` are not consecutive.

zero (false), because ′9′ is not an alphabetic character. In an ASCII environment isdigit(57) evaluates to nonzero (true), because 57 is the ASCII value for the character ′9′. You should avoid using these functions in such a manner; treat characters as symbolic abstractions.

To write portable programs, use the functions in <ctype.h> rather than writing equivalent functions. For example, if the ASCII character set is used, the following function could serve as an implementation of tolower:

```
int tolower(int c)
// postcondition: returns lowercase equivalent of c
//                if c isn't upper case, returns c unchanged
{
    if ('A' <= c && c <= 'Z')        // c is uppercase
    {
        return c + 32;
    }
    return c;
}
```

This function works only when the ASCII character set is used, and it relies on two properties of the character set:

- The uppercase letters occur in order with no intervening characters.
- The difference between a lower-case letter and its corresponding upper-case equivalent is always 32.

You can isolate some dependencies on ASCII by subtracting characters:

```
int tolower(int c)
// postcondition: returns lowercase equivalent of c
//                if c isn't upper case, returns c unchanged
{
    if ('A' <= c && c <= 'Z')        // c is uppercase
    {
        return c + ('a' - 'A');
    }
    return c;
}
```

The correctness of this code depends only on a character set in which ′a′ through ′z′ and ′A′ through ′Z′ are consecutive ranges. Since char values can be manipulated as int values, you can subtract one character from another, yielding an int value. However, although you can multiply ′a′ * ′b′, the result doesn't make sense; using ASCII, the result is 97*98 == 9506, which is not a legal character value. Although you can use char variables as integers, you should restrict arithmetic operations of characters to the following:

1.   Adding an integer to a character—for example, ′0′ + 2 == ′2′
2.   Subtracting an integer from a character—for example, ′9′ - 3 == ′6′ and ′C′ - 2 == ′A′
3.   Subtracting two characters—for example, ′8′ - ′0′ == 8 and ′Z′ - ′A′ == 25

You can use a `char` value in a `switch` statement, because `char` values can be used as integers. You can also compare two `char` values using the relational operators `<`, `<=`, `>`, `>=`. Character comparisons are based on the value of the underlying character set, which will always reflect lexicographic order.

Now that we have covered the lowest level of the character–string–file–stream hierarchy, we'll see how characters are used to build strings and files. We'll investigate strings first.

Strings as `char` Sequences

The class `string`, accessible using the header file `"CPstring.h"`,[5] is an abstraction that represents sequences of characters with certain properties. However, we haven't yet studied any mechanism for extracting individual characters from a `string`. Although the `substr` member function extracts strings and `operator +` concatenates strings, we cannot alter the individual characters of a string.

The characters in a `string` s are numbered from 0 to `s.length()-1`. Each number is called an **index.** For example, if `str` represents the string `"computer"`, then `'c'` has index 0 and `'r'` has index 7:

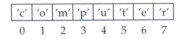

$$\begin{array}{cccccccc} 'c' & 'o' & 'm' & 'p' & 'u' & 't' & 'e' & 'r' \\ 0 & 1 & 2 & 3 & 4 & 5 & 6 & 7 \end{array}$$

Individual characters in a `string` are accessed using the **indexing** operator `[]`. It is used in *spreader.cc,* Prog. 9.2, to print a string with spaces between each character.

Program 9.2   spreader.cc

```
#include <iostream.h>
#include "CPstring.h"

// demonstrates string indexing by "spreading a string"
// by inserting spaces between each character

int main()
{
    string s;
    cout << "enter a string: ";
    cin >> s;
```

---

[5]The C++ standard string class is accessible using the header file `<string>`. You may be using this header file rather than the `CPstring.h` header file. You may also be using `apstring.h`.

```
    int k;
    int limit = s.length();        // # of chars in s

    // fence post problem: need to print
    // character ' ' character ' ' character ... ' ' character

    if (limit > 0)                 // at least one character
    {
        cout << s[0];              // first character
        for(k=1; k < limit; k++)   // then loop over the rest

        {
            cout << " " << s[k];
        }
        cout << endl;
    }
    return 0;
}
```

OUTPUT

```
prompt> spreader
enter a string:   longwinded
l  o  n  g  w  i  n  d  e  d
prompt>  spreader
enter a string:  !@#$%
!  @  #  $  %
```

Because the expression `s[k]` is used for output, and because the compiler can determine that the expression `s[k]` is a `char`, the symbolic form of each character is printed; that is, an `'o'` instead of 111 (the ASCII value of `'o'`). The indexing operator can also be used to change an individual character in a string. For example, the following sequence of statements would cause `taste` to be displayed:

```
string s = "paste";
s[0] = 't';
cout << s << endl;
```

A program that uses the `[]` operator with an index that is **out of range** (i.e., less than 0 or greater than or equal to the number of characters in a string) generates a runtime error. For example, if the `<` in the loop test in *spreader.cc*, Prog. 9.2, is replaced by `<=` as follows, the output will change as indicated:[6]

```
for(k=1; k <= limit; k += 1)
{
    cout << " " << s[k];
}
```

---

[6]The error message displayed on your system may be different, but the program will terminate.

OUTPUT

```
prompt> spreader
enter a string:  hello
h  e  l  l  o  index out of range: 5 string: hello
failed assertion
```

The statement `cout << endl` following the loop in *spreader.cc*, Prog. 9.2, is *not* executed. The out-of-range index generates the error message, and the program aborts.

JOHN VON NEUMANN (1903–1957)

John von Neumann was a genius in many fields. He founded the field of game theory with his book *Theory of Games and Economic Behavior* (cowritten with Oskar Morgenstern). He helped develop the atomic bomb as part of the Manhattan Project. Almost all computers in use today are based on the von Neumann model of stored programs and use an architecture that he helped develop in the early years of computing.

In 1944, von Neumann was working with the ENIAC (Electronic Numerical Integrator and Computer),

Figure 9.1   John von Neumann.

a machine whose wires had to be physically rearranged to run a different program. The idea of storing a program in the computer, just as data are stored, is generally credited to von Neumann (although there has been a history of sometimes rancorous dispute; see [Gol93, Mac92]).

Hans Bethe, a Nobel Prize–winning physicist, graded academic seminars on a scale of one to ten:

> Grade one was something my mother could understand. Grade two my wife could understand. Grade seven was something I could understand. Grade eight was something only the speaker and Johnny von Neumann could understand. Grade nine was something Johnny could understand, but the speaker didn't. Grade ten was something even Johnny could not yet understand, but there was little of that.

Von Neumann's powers of memory and calculation were prodigious, as were his contributions to so many fields. For a full account of von Neumann's life see [Mac92].

Pause to reflect

9.1. The following function is intended to return the decimal equivalent of a digit character; for example, for '0' it should return 0, and for '3' it should return 3.

```
int todigit(int c)
// precondition: c is a digit character: '0',
//                   '1', ..., '9'
//                   requires that digit characters
//                   be contiguous
// postcondition: returns digit equivalent,
//                   e.g., 3 for '3'
{
    if (isdigit(c))
    {
        return c - '0';
    }
}
```

This function does return the correct values for all digit characters. The function is not robust, because it may cause programs to crash if the precondition isn't true. How would you make it more robust?

9.2. The underlying numeric value of a character (in ASCII and other character sets) reflects lexicographic order. For example, 'C' < 'a', since upper-case letters precede lower-case letters in the ASCII ordering. Why does this help to explain why "Zebra" < "aardvark" but "aardvark" < "yak"?

9.3. Explain why the statement cout << 'a' + 3 << endl generates the integer 100 as output. Why does the statement cout << char('a' + 3) << endl generate the character 'd'?

9.4. If the ASCII set is used, what are the values of iscntrl('\t'), isspace('\t'), and islower('\t')?

9.5. Write a function isvowel that returns true when its parameter is a vowel: 'a', 'e', 'i', 'o', or 'u' (or the upper-case equivalent). What is an easy way of writing isconsonant (assuming isvowel exists)?

9.6. Write a boolean-valued function IsPalindrome that returns true when its string parameter is a palindrome and false otherwise. A **palindrome** is a word that reads the same backwards as forwards, such as "racecar," "mom," and "amanaplanacanalpanama" (which is "A man, a plan, a canal—Panama!" with no spaces, capitals, or punctuation).

9.7. Write the body of the following function MakeLower so that all upper-case letters in s are converted to lower case. Why is s a reference parameter?

```
void MakeLower(string & s)
// postcondition: all letters in s are lower case
```

9.8. There are several functions in the library "CPstring.h" for converting strings to numbers: atoi converts a string to an int and atof converts a string to a double. (The "a" is for "alphabetic"; "atoi" is pronounced "a-to-i.")

Write a function with prototype int atoi(string s) that converts a string to its decimal equivalent; for example, atoi("1234") evaluates to 1234, and atoi("-52") evaluates to −52.

9.2   Streams and Files as Lines and Characters

A string variable is a sequence of characters, but we manipulate strings abstractly without knowing the details of how the characters are stored or represented. When information is hidden in this way, and a type is used independently of the underlying representation of the data, the type is sometimes called an **abstract data type,** or **ADT.** The data type is abstract because knowledge of its underlying implementation is not necessary to use it. You probably don't know how individual 0s and 1s are stored to represent int and double values, but you can still write programs that use these numeric types.

In this section we'll see that a stream is also an abstract data type. Until now we have viewed a stream as a sequence of words or numbers. We extract words or numbers from a stream using >> and insert onto a stream using <<. We have developed programs using the standard streams cin and cout, as well as streams bound to files using the classes ifstream and ofstream. In this section we'll study functions that let us view streams as a sequence of lines rather than words and numbers. Other functions let us view streams as sequences of characters; different views are useful in different settings. We'll see some applications that are most easily implemented when streams are viewed as sequences of lines and others where a sequence of characters is a better choice.

Input Using getline()

Input operations on strings using >> result in word-at-a-time input, where words are treated as any sequence of non–white space characters. In some applications other methods of input are needed. In particular, an ifstream variable bound to a file may require line-oriented input. Consider, for example, processing a file in the following format, where an artist/group name is followed by the title of a compact disc (CD) by the artist:

```
The Black Crowes
The Southern Harmony and Musical Companion
10,000 Maniacs
Blind Man's Zoo
Spin Doctors
Pocket Full of Kryptonite
The Beatles
Sergeant Pepper's Lonely Hearts Club Band
Strauss
Also Sprach Zarathustra
```

```
The Grateful Dead
American Beauty
```

There is no way to read all the words on one line of a file using the stream-processing tools currently at our disposal. Since many text files are arranged as a sequence of lines rather than white space–delimited words, we need a method for reading input other than the extraction operator `>>`. The function `getline` allows an entire line of input to be read at once. When we view a stream as line-oriented rather than word-oriented, we need to be able to include white space as part of the line read from a stream.

If the line `cin >> s` in *spreader.cc*, Prog. 9.2, is replaced with `getline(cin, s)`, the user can enter a string with spaces in it:

OUTPUT

```
prompt> spreader
enter a string:   Green Eggs and Ham
G   r   e   e   n       E   g   g   s       a   n   d       H   a   m
```

In the original program the only word read by the program is `Green`, because the space between "Green" and "Eggs" terminates the extraction operation when `>>` is used. The characters `"Eggs and Ham"` will not be processed but will remain on the input stream.

The function `getline` is used in Prog. 9.3 to count the total number of lines in a file. This gives a better count of the number of characters in a file too, because a line can contain white space characters that would not be read if `>>` were used.

Program 9.3   lines.cc

```
#included <iostream.h>
#include <fstream.h>
#include <stdlib.h>
#include "CPstring.h"
#include "prompt.h"

// cout # of lines in input file
// Owen Astrachan, written: 7/11/94

int main()
{
    ifstream input;
    string s;                       // line entered by user
    long int numLines = 0;
    long int numChars = 0;
    string filename =
        PromptString("enter name of input file: ");
    input.open(filename);
```

```
    if (input.fail() )
    {
        cout << "could not open file " << filename << endl;
        exit(1);
    }

    while (getline(input,s))
    {
        numLines++;
        numChars += s.length();
    }

    cout << "number of lines = " << numLines
         <<", number of character = " << numChars << endl;
    return 0;
}
```

OUTPUT

```
prompt> lines
enter name of input file: macbeth.txt
number of lines = 2849, number of characters = 110901
prompt> lines
enter name of input file: hamlet.txt
number of lines = 4463, number of characters = 187271
prompt> lines
enter name of input file: lines.cc
number of lines = 34, number of characters = 725
```

The function `getline` extracts a line, stores the line in a `string` variable, and returns the state of the stream. Some programmers prefer to test the stream state explicitly:

```
while (getline(input,s) && ! input.fail())
```

However, it is fine to use `getline` in a loop test, both to extract a line and as a test to see whether the extraction succeeds, just as the expression `infile >> word` can be used as the test of a `while` loop to process all the white space–delimited words in a stream.

These examples show that `getline` has two parameters: an input stream and a string for storing the line extracted from the stream. The stream can be a predefined stream such as `cin` or an `ifstream` variable such as `input`, as used in Prog. 9.3. The prototype for `getline` is given below.

Syntax: getline

```
        istream & getline(istream & is,
                          string & s,
                          char sentinel = '\n')
```

The `string` function **getline** extracts one line from the stream passed as the first parameter. The characters composing the line are stored in the `string` parameter s. The state of the stream after the extraction is returned as the value of the function. The return value is a reference to the stream, because streams should not be passed or returned by value.

Normally, the end of a line is marked by the newline character `'\n'`. However, it is possible to specify a different value that will serve as the end-of-line character. An optional third argument can be passed to `getline`. This `char` parameter, `sentinel`, is used as the end-of-line character. The end-of-line character is extracted from the stream but is *not* stored in the string s.

Program Tip: Be very careful when using both `getline` **and the extraction operator** >> **with the same stream.**

Extraction skips white space, but it can leave the white space on the stream. For example, if you enter something and press Enter when >> is used, the newline character that was input by pressing the Enter key is still on the `cin` stream. A subsequent `getline` operation reads all characters until the newline, effectively reading nothing. If your programs seem to be skipping input from the user, look for problems mixing these two input operations. You can use `getline` for strings, and you can skip newline characters using an extra `getline` or using the `ignore` member function, described in Table 9.3.

The value returned by `getline` is the same value that would be returned if the stream member function `fail` were called immediately after the call to `getline`. As we've seen, some programmers prefer to make the call to `fail` explicitly rather than to use the value returned by `getline`.

A `getline` operation will fail if the stream cannot be read, either because it is bound to a nonexistent file or because no more lines are left on the stream.

A stream variable can be used by itself instead of the function `fail`. For example,

```
input.open(filename);
if (input.fail() )
{
    cout << "could not open file " << filename << endl;
    exit(1);
}
```

can be replaced by the statements

```
input.open(filename);
if (! input)
{
    cout << "could not open file " << filename << endl;
    exit(1);
}
```

The use of ! input in place of input.fail() is common in C++ programs. I'll use fail most of the time, because it makes it clear how the stream is being tested, but occasionally I'll use the name of a stream instead.

Parsing Line-Oriented Data Using String Streams

Data is often line-oriented, because people find it easy to edit and read lines of words, numbers, and other data. Reading data is straightforward when the number of items per line is the same for an entire data set, since a for loop can be used to iterate a set number of times for each input line. Another approach is needed when the number of items per line varies. For example, we might want to access the individual words in the titles of the CDs stored in a file:

```
The Black Crowes
The Southern Harmony and Musical Companion
10,000 Maniacs
Blind Man's Zoo
...
```

We might need to write a program to average students' grades, where each student has a different number of grades stored in the following format (firstname lastname grades):

```
Dave Reed 55 60 75 67 72 59
Mike Clancy 88 92 91 97
Stuart Reges 99 94 98 91 95
```

In general, parsing input and reading data often make up the hardest part of developing a program. Reading data is not an algorithmically challenging problem, but dealing with badly formed data and different kinds of data can be an unpleasant part of programming.

We already know how to process stream input a word at a time using the extraction operator >>. We need a tool that lets us use >> on one line of a file. The class istrstream (for **input string stream**), accessible by including the file <strstream.h>, is just the tool we need. The istrstream class constructs a stream bound to a string as the source of the input, much as the ifstream class constructs a stream bound to a disk file as the source of input. Because an istrstream object is a stream, it supports the same functions and operators as ifstream objects and the standard input stream cin.

The code in *readnums.cc*, Prog. 9.4, uses an istrstream variable to read line-oriented numerical data where the number of integers on each line varies. The average of the numbers on each line of input is calculated and printed.

Program 9.4   readnums.cc

```
#include <iostream.h>
#include <strstream.h>
#include "CPstring.h"
```

```cpp
// illustrates use of string streams
// Owen Astrachan, 1/25/96

int main()
{
    string s;
    cout << "program computes averages of lines of numbers."
        << endl;
    cout << "to exit, use end-of-file" << endl << endl;

    while (getline(cin,s))
    {
        int total = 0;
        int count = 0;
        int num;
        istrstream input(s);
        while (input >> num)
        {
            count++;
            total += num;
        }
        if (count != 0)
        {
            cout << "average of " << count << " numbers = "
                << double(total)/count << endl;
        }
        else
        {
            cout << "data not parsed as integers" << endl;
        }
    }
    return 0;
}
```

OUTPUT

```
prompt> readnums
program computes averages of lines of numbers.
to exit, use end-of-file

10 20 30
average of 3 numbers = 20
1 2 3 4 5 6 7 8
average of 9 numbers = 4.5
1 -1 2 -2 3 -3 4 -4 5 -5
average of 10 numbers = 0
apple orange guava
data not parsed as integers
2 4 6 8 10
average of 5 numbers = 6
^D
```

The `getline` function is used to read one line of input into the `string` s, and the `istrstream` variable `input` is constructed from s. Then `input` is used as a stream: integers are extracted using `>>` until the extraction fails. The variable `input` *must* be defined (and hence constructed) inside the `while (getline(cin,s))` loop of *readnums.cc*. The source of data in an `istrstream` object is the `string` passed as an argument to the `istrstream` constructor. It is not possible to define `input` before the loop and then rebind `input` to a string entered by the user within the loop. The `istrstream` variable `input` is constructed anew at iteration of the `while (getline(cin,s))` loop.

An `istrstream` must be constructed from a C-style string, but it will work correctly when constructed from a `string` object from `"CPstring.h"`.[7] Changing the value of the `string` used to construct an `istrstream` object while the stream is being used can lead to trouble.

Stream Member Functions (Optional)

We've seen that characters are used to build strings and that streams can be bound to both files and strings. Although we've increased the number of tools we have for programming with streams, a few more member functions will make our stream toolkit complete. For example, we have used expressions with `>>` and with `getline` as loop tests to read stream data. If an input operation fails, we have no method for determining whether the failure is due to reaching the end of file or because the string `"flop"` is entered when an integer is expected. In this section we'll cover stream member functions that can be used to determine why a stream operation fails.

The function `fail` returns true if a stream operation has just failed. The member function `eof` returns true if end of file was reached with the last input operation. You should never use `eof` unless you know that an input operation failed and you need to determine whether the failure is due to encountering the end-of-file state.

If an input operation fails, subsequent input operations will fail as well. Use the member function `clear` to clear the stream so that subsequent input operations can succeed. When an operation fails because of malformed input (e.g., reading `"purple"` when extracting an integer), the malformed input should be skipped or removed from the input stream. The function `ignore` can be used to skip characters until a sentinel character is found. Normally, the newline character `'\n'` is used as the sentinel to skip all characters on a line. Alternatively, you can use `getline` to read the characters into a `string` variable.

A complete explanation of these and other stream member functions can be found in [Tea93]. For our purposes we summarize stream member functions in Table 9.3. The use of `clear` and `ignore` is shown in *fixinput.cc*, Prog. 9.5.

---

[7]If the standard `string` class is used, you'll need to use the `c_str()` member function when constructing an `istrstream` variable. In the proposed ANSI C++ standard the class `istrstream` has been replaced by the class `istringstream`, which does support stream iteration using the `string` class. At the time of this writing, very few compilers support a class `istringstream`.

Table 9.3   Some Stream Member Functions

Function	Description
`fail()`	Returns true if a stream operation has failed but characters have not been lost. It is possible to recover from such a state (see `clear`).
`eof()`	Returns true if the end-of-file condition of a state has been detected; that is, if all input has finished. Use this function only when `fail` is true and you want to determine whether the failure is due to encountering end of file. Detecting when the end-of-file condition is true is very system-dependent.
`clear()`	Restores stream to a good state. Use `clear` after `fail` returns true because of an error such as attempting to read an `int` when the next character in the stream is `'z'` and you want to continue to extract input.
`open(char *)`	(with `ifstream`) Binds stream to file specified by `string` parameter. The type char * will be studied in Chapter 12; a `string` parameter can be used as the argument to `open`. (*Note:* If the standard `string` class is used, the member function `c_str()` must be used as described in Section 6.2.)
`close()`	Closes an output stream; that is, it takes care of managing system resources associated with a stream. Many systems limit the number of streams that can be open at one time. Also flushes the stream so that all buffered output is written (e.g., to a file).
`ignore(int numChars, char sentinel)`	Reads as many as `numChars` characters from the stream or until the character `sentinel` is read. In essence, these characters are skipped (the sentinel is read). As a side effect, the stream is returned.
`good()`	Returns true if a stream is in a good state; that is, if a stream operation has the potential to succeed. For all practical purposes, this is a pretty useless function.

You must use `clear` after a stream operation has failed, or all subsequent operations will fail as well. For truly robust input, you'll need to enter everything as a string and convert the string to the appropriate form of input (e.g., an `int` or a `double`). Making program input errorproof is a surprisingly difficult task.

Program 9.5   fixinput.cc

```cpp
#include <iostream.h>
#include "CPstring.h"

int main()
{
    int    intvalue;
    double doubvalue;
    string s;

    cout << "enter int and double pairs: ";
    while (cin >> intvalue >> doubvalue)
    {
        cout << "int = " << intvalue << " double = "
            << doubvalue << endl;
    }
    cin.clear();     // clear stream
    getline(cin,s);  // can use cin.ignore(INT_MAX,'\n')

    cout << "extraction failed, skipping line " << s
        << endl;

    cout << "enter int and double: ";
    cin >> intvalue >> doubvalue;
    cout << "int = " << intvalue << " double = "
        << doubvalue << endl;

    return 0;
}
```

OUTPUT

```
prompt> fixinput
enter int and double pairs: 2 3 4 5
int = 2 double = 3
int = 4 double = 5
2.5 3.7
int = 2 double = 0.5
int = 3 double = 0.7
1 2e7 -3 4e-9
int = 1 double = 2e+07
int = -3 double = 4e-09
3 pi 7 e-squared
extraction failed, skipping line pi 7 e-squared
enter int and double: 2 3
int = 2 double = 3
```

Strings, Streams, and Characters

Sometimes it is useful to regard a file (and its associated stream) as a collection of characters rather than as a collection of lines. Of course, we could read a file a line at a time using getline and then access each character of the extracted string, but sometimes character-at-a-time input is more appropriate than line-at-a-time input. The stream member function get is used to read one character at a time. White space is *not* skipped when get is used. Program 9.6 uses get to count the characters in a file one at a time.

Program 9.6   lines2.cc

```
#include <iostream.h>
#include <fstream.h>
#include <stdlib.h>
#include "CPstring.h"
#include "prompt.h"

// count # of lines in input file
// author:        Owen Astrachan,  7/11/94, modified 6/30/96

int main()
{
    long int numChars = 0;
    long int numLines = 0;
    char ch;
    string filename =
        PromptString("enter name of input file: ");
    ifstream input;
    input.open(filename);

    if (input.fail() )
    {
        cout << "could not open file " << filename << endl;
        exit(1);
    }

    while (input.get(ch))                    // reading char succeeds?
    {
        if ('\n' == ch)                      // read newline character
        {
            numLines += 1;
        }
        numChars++;
    }

    cout << "number of lines = " << numLines
         << ", number of characters = " << numChars << endl;
    return 0;
}
```

```
                                OUTPUT

prompt> lines2
enter name of input file: macbeth.txt
number of lines = 2849, number of characters = 113750
prompt> lines2
enter name of input file: hamlet.txt
number of lines = 4463, number of characters = 191734
```

Note that getline is not a stream member function but that get is.

The number of lines printed by *lines2.cc*, Prog. 9.6, is the same as the number of lines calculated by *lines.cc*, Prog. 9.3, but the number of characters printed is different. If you look carefully at all the numbers printed by both programs, you may be able to determine what the "missing" characters are. In the online version of *Hamlet*, both programs calculate the number of lines as 4,463, but Prog. 9.3 calculates 187,271 characters, compared to the 191,734 calculated by Prog. 9.6. Not coincidentally, $187,271 + 4,463 = 191,734$. The newline character '\n' is not part of the total number of characters calculated by Prog. 9.3. This points out some subtle behavior of the getline function. getline reads a line of text, terminated by the newline character '\n'. The newline character is read but is *not* stored in the string parameter to getline. An easy way to fix Prog. 9.3 is to change the calculation of numChars as follows:

```
numChars += s.length() + 1;    // add 1 for newline stripped by getline
```

The comment is important here; the reason for the addition of + 1 may not be apparent without it.

NIKLAUS WIRTH (B. 1934)

Niklaus Wirth is perhaps best known as the inventor/developer of the programming language Pascal. He also was an early adherent of a methodology of programming he called "stepwise refinement," writing a paper in 1971 that called for developing programs in a style I've called *iterative enhancement* in this book.

Pascal was developed in the early 1970s; it was not, as conventional wisdom would have it, developed solely as a language for educational use. In his 1984 Turing Award lecture Wirth says:

Occasionally, it has been claimed that Pascal was designed as a language for teaching. Although this is correct, its use in teaching was not the only goal. In fact, I do not believe in using tools and formalisms in teaching that are inadequate for any practical task. By today's standards, Pascal has obvious deficiencies for programming large systems, but 15 years ago it represented a sensible compromise between what was desirable and what was effective.

Wirth continued to develop languages that were successors of Pascal, notably Modula-2 and Oberon. In discussing the difficulties of developing hardware and software, Wirth has this to say about the complexity of these tasks:

It is true that we live in a complex world and strive to solve inherently complex problems, which often do require complex mechanisms. However, this should not diminish our desire for *elegant* solutions, which convince by their clarity and effectiveness. Simple, elegant solutions are more effective, but they are *harder* to find than complex ones, and they require more time, which we too often believe to be unaffordable.

Most of this material is taken from [Wir87].

9.9. Write a small program that prompts for the name of an artist and prints all CDs by the artist. Assume input is in the format

Pause to reflect

```
The Black Crowes
The Southern Harmony and Musical Companion
10,000 Maniacs
Blind Man's Zoo
The Beatles
Rubber Soul
...
```

For example, if the user enters `The Beatles`, the output might be

```
Sergeant Pepper's Lonely Hearts Club Band
The White Album
Revolver
Rubber Soul
```

depending on what CD titles are stored in the file.

9.10. From its use in *lines2.cc*, Prog. 9.6, the `char` parameter to `get` must be a reference parameter. Why is this the case?

9.11. Program 9.6, *lines2.cc*, can be modified so that it copies a file by writing every character (using `<<`) that is read. What modifications are necessary so that the user is prompted for the name of a new file to be written that will be a copy of the file that is read?

9.12. How can the copy program from the previous exercise be modified so that all upper-case letters in the input file are converted to lower-case letters in the output file? (*Hint:* The change is very straightforward.)

9.13. Explain why the input `1 2e7 -3 4e-9` to *fixlist.cc*, Prog. 8.10, results in two lines of output, and why entering `2.5 3.7` also results in two lines of output, as shown in the sample run of the program.

9.3   Case Study: Removing Comments with State Machines

With the stream and string functions we have studied, we now have the choice of reading streams in several ways:

- A word at a time, using >> and `string` variables
- A line at a time, using `getline` and `string` variables
- A character at a time, using `get` and `char` variables

In this section we'll develop a program to remove all comments from a file. We'll see that character-at-a-time input facilitates this task, and we'll study an approach that extends to other parsing-related problems.[8]

Problem Specification: What Is a Comment?

The first step in writing almost any program is to specify the problem properly. We must decide what a comment is, and we should try to identify potential problems in our definition. We'll write a program that removes comments beginning with `//`. These comments extend to the end of a line and are simpler to remove than `/* ... */` comments, which can extend over several lines. We'll read and echo all characters except those that are part of a comment.

A State Machine Approach to I/O

Our comment-removing program will prompt for the name of a program (actually any text file) and print the program with all the comments removed. Our first program will output using `cout`, but we'll design the program so that output to an `ofstream` object will be a simple change. We must decide whether to read a program a line at a time or a character at a time. Since `//` comments are line-oriented, reading input a line at a time makes sense. We could use the string member function `find` to determine whether each line contains the string `"//"` and, if so, where the `"//"` begins. However, this approach cannot be extended to removing `/* ... */` comments, which can extend over several lines, so we'll use character-at-a-time input instead.

We'll use a state machine approach in reading and removing comments. In a **state machine** program, each input character causes the program to change its behavior depending on the program's state. We'll use a three-state program to remove comments. The program will be in one of three states as it reads each

---

[8]A program is **parsed** by the compiler in the process of converting it into assembly or machine language. "Parse" usually refers to the process of reading input in identifiable chunks such as C++ identifiers, reserved words, etc.

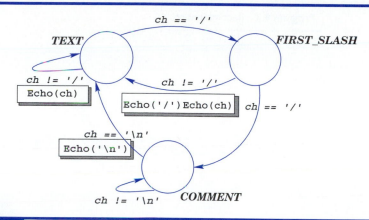

Figure 9.2 State diagram for removing comments.

character:

1. Processing regular, uncommented text
2. A slash ' / ' has just been read
3. Processing commented text

In Fig. 9.2, these states are labeled as *TEXT, FIRST_SLASH,* and *COMMENT.* Each state is shown as a circle, and state changes are shown with arrows. The program can change state each time a character is read, although it's possible to stay in the same state. Some state changes (or state transitions) are accompanied by an action, shown in a shaded box. In the text-processing state *TEXT,* nonslash characters are echoed; a slash character is not echoed but causes a state transition to the state labeled *FIRST_SLASH.* In the state *FIRST_SLASH* we don't know yet whether a comment follows or whether the division operator / was just read. The answer depends on the next character read. If a slash character is read, we know a comment follows, so we change state to *COMMENT;* otherwise there was only one slash, so we echo the slash and the character just read and return to *TEXT,* the state of parsing noncommented text. Finally, in the *COMMENT* state, we ignore all characters. However, when a newline character ' \n' is read, we know the comment has ended, so the newline is echoed and the state changes back to *TEXT.*

The advantage of the state approach is that we simply read one character at a time and take an action on the character depending on the current state of the program. In a way, the states serve as memory. For example, in the state *FIRST_SLASH* we know that one slash remains unprocessed. If the slash doesn't begin a comment, we'll echo the unprocessed slash and change to reading regular text.

Program 9.7, *decomment.cc,* implements this state machine approach to removing comments. An enumerated type `States` is used so that symbolic

Program 9.7   decomment.cc

```cpp
#include <iostream.h>
#include <fstream.h>
#include "CPstring.h"
#include "prompt.h"

// Owen Astrachan 7/4/1996
// state machine approach for removing // comments from file
// (doesn't handle // in a string, e.g., " test // comment "

const char SLASH = '/';
const char NEWLINE = '\n';
void Echo(char ch);

int main()
{
    enum ReadState {
        TEXT, FIRST_SLASH, COMMENT
    };

    ReadState currentState = TEXT;
    string filename = PromptString("enter filename: ");
    ifstream input;
    string extra;  // for storing extra chars on a comment line
    char ch;
    input.open(filename.c_str());

    while (input.get(ch))           // read one char at a time
    {
        switch(currentState)
        {
          case TEXT:
            if (ch == SLASH)        // potential comment begins
            {
                currentState = FIRST_SLASH;
            }
            else
            {
                Echo(ch);
            }
            break;

          case FIRST_SLASH:
            if (ch == SLASH)
            {
                currentState = COMMENT;
            }
            else    // one slash not followed by another
            {
                Echo(SLASH);        // print the slash from last time
                Echo(ch);           // and the current character
```

```
                currentState = TEXT;      // uncommented text
            }
            break;

        case COMMENT:
            if (ch == NEWLINE)      // end of line is end of comment
            {
                Echo(NEWLINE);       // be sure to echo end of line
                currentState = TEXT;
            }
        break;
        }
    }
}

void Echo(char ch)
{
    cout << ch;
}
```

OUTPUT

```
prompt> decomment
enter name of input file: commtest.cc
#include <iostream.h>

int main()
{
    int x = 3;
    cout << x / 3 << endl;
    return 0;
}
```

---

names can be used as the values of the variable `currentState`. Otherwise
the logic is precisely illustrated in Fig. 9.2. The input is the following file, named
commtest.cc:

```
#include <iostream.h>
// this is a sample program for comment remove
int main()
{
    int x = 3;               // this is a meaningful identifier
    cout << x / 3 << endl;   // complex math is fun
    return 0;                // this is a useful comment
}
```

The program *decomment.cc* does remove all comments properly, but there is
a case that causes text to be removed when it shouldn't be. When the two-
character sequence `//` is embedded in a string, it is not the beginning of a

comment:

```
cout << "Two slashes // but not a comment" << endl;  // tricky?
```

This situation causes problems with the state machine used in *decomment.cc,* but it's possible to add more states to fix the problem.

Pause to reflect

9.14. Modify *decomment.cc,* Prog. 9.7, so that the output goes to a file specified by the user.

9.15. Draw a state transition diagram similar to Fig. 9.3 but for removing /* ... */ comments. Don't worry about // comments; just remove the other kind of comment.

9.16. It's possible to use two states to remove // comments. Instead of using the state *COMMENT* in *decomment.cc,* use getline to gobble up the characters on a line when a slash is read in the state *FIRST_SLASH.* Modify *decomment.cc* to use this approach.

9.17. Add states to either the diagram or the program *decomment.cc* to avoid removing the // sequence when it is embedded in a string.

9.18. Write a state transition diagram for word-at-a-time input that you could use to find all int variables. Solve a simple version of the problem, assuming that every variable is defined separately—that is, there are no definitions in the form

```
int x, y, z;
```

What other situations can cause problems for your approach?

9.4   Formatting Output

Most of the programs we have covered have generated unformatted output. We did use the stream member function width in *windchill.cc,* Prog. 5.11 (page 217), to force column-aligned output, but we have concentrated more on program design and development than on making output look good.

In addition to well-formatted code, good programs generate well-formatted output. The arrangement of the output aids the program user in interpreting data. However, it is altogether too easy for a programmer to spend an inordinate amount of time formatting output trying to make it "pretty." The objective of this book is to present broad programming concepts, which include documenting code and formatting output. You should strike a balance between the objectives of producing working programs and writing programs so that users can understand both the program and the output.

There are two methods for altering an output stream to change the format of values that are inserted into the stream: using stream member functions and using an object called a **manipulator,** accessible via the include file <iomanip.h>; the stream member functions and manipulators are listed in Table 9.4. Program 9.8, *precise.cc,* shows how to specify the number of digits of precision with the stream member function precision.

Table 9.4   Stream Formatting Functions

Member Function	Manipulator	Description
width(int w)	setw(int w)	Sets width to w; pads with fill spaces as necessary (will not truncate to fit in width); affects only next value output
setf(long int f)	setiosflags(long int f)	Sets flags according to argument; for a summary of flags, see Table 9.5
precision(int p)	setprecision(int p)	Sets precision of output to p
fill(char c)	setfill(char c)	Sets fill character to c; the default fill is a space, used when padding needed with width

As we'll discuss later in this chapter, numbers are represented internally in computers with a limited precision. As can be seen from the output of Prog. 9.8, specifying a precision larger than 15 generates more digits, but the digits aren't correct (see the definition of MY_PI in Prog. 9.8).

Stream output is governed by many different **flags.** A flag is a variable or quantity that can have one of two values. Typically these values are on and off,

---

Program 9.8   precise.cc

```
#include <iostream.h>
#include <iomanip.h>

// illustrates output formatting using manipulators and
// stream member functions
// author: Owen Astrachan, 8/2/94

void Print(double num, int digits);

int main()
{
    const double MY_PI = 3.14159265358979323846264338327950; // too much PI
    const MAX_DIGITS = 25;                      // max digits to print

    cout << "default PI = " << MY_PI << endl;

    cout.setf(ios::fixed);         // don't use scientific notation
    cout.setf(ios::showpoint);     // show all decimal places

    int digits;
    for(digits = 0; digits <= MAX_DIGITS; digits += 1)
```

```
    {
        Print(MY_PI,digits);
    }
    return 0;
}

void Print (double num, int digits)
// precondition: digits >= 0
// postcondition: num printed with precision = digits
{
    cout << "precision = " << digits << "\t";

    cout.precision(digits);
    cout << num << endl;
}
```

OUTPUT

```
prompt> precise
default PI = 3.14159
precision = 0    3.
precision = 1    3.1
precision = 2    3.14
precision = 3    3.142
precision = 4    3.1416
precision = 5    3.14159
precision = 6    3.141593
precision = 7    3.1415927
precision = 8    3.14159265
precision = 9    3.141592654
precision = 10   3.1415926536
precision = 11   3.14159265359
precision = 12   3.141592653590
precision = 13   3.1415926535898
precision = 14   3.14159265358979
precision = 15   3.141592653589793
precision = 16   3.1415926535897931
precision = 17   3.14159265358979312
precision = 18   3.14159265358979311160
precision = 19   3.1415926535897931160
precision = 20   3.14159265358979311600
precision = 21   3.14159265358979311600
precision = 22   3.141592653589793115998
precision = 23   3.1415926535897931159980
precision = 24   3.14159265358979311599796
precision = 25   3.141592653589793115979635
```

Table 9.5 Stream Flags

Flag	Purpose/use
ios::fixed	Force floating-point numbers to have set number of digits as specified by precision
ios::scientific	Force output of floating-point numbers in scientific notation; e.g., 6.023e23 for 6.023×10^{23}
ios::showpoint	Force decimal point in output; e.g., the number 7 will be printed as 7.0 or as 7.000000 (with number of 0s as specified by precision)
ios::left	Print numbers left-justified, padding as specified by fill
ios::right	Print numbers right-justified, padding as specified by fill

up and down, or some similar opposition. The stream member function setf is used to set output flags. The flags are specified using an enum that is part the class ios. For example, the flag ios::fixed specifies a **fixed decimal** format, as opposed to a scientific format such as 31.4259e-1. Some common flags are described in Table 9.5.[9]

Setting the width using the member function width affects only the next value inserted in a stream. Consequently, each value inserted must have a width specified, or the default width is used. In contrast, the number of significant digits as specified by the member function precision is persistent and affects all subsequent values inserted until the precision is reset.

The other mechanism for setting flags is invoked within an output statement itself, using the class of I/O manipulators accessible from the header file <iomanip.h>. The following statement illustrates how the manipulator setprecision can be used to format output:

```
cout << setprecision(4) << MY_PI << " " << setprecision(9) << MY_PI << endl;
```

OUTPUT

```
3.1416 3.141592654
```

The manipulator setw changes the width of the field used to output the next value just as the width member function is used. We won't include an exhaustive set of examples at this point; rather, consult Table 9.4 to see the

___

[9]Flags can be combined in a single call to setf if each flag is separated from the others by a vertical bar: cout.setf(ios::fixed | ios::showpoint). The vertical bar | is the bitwise-or operator.

different member functions and manipulators available. Many of these affect input as well as output; we'll study these in more detail in Prog. 9.12.

9.5   Case Study: Manipulating Compact Discs

Often the hardest part of writing a program is reading the data. This can be difficult because data are often stored in a form that is inconvenient from the point of view of the programmer. In general, this sentiment is aptly stated as

I/O is messy.

In this section we'll develop a program that calculates the total playing time for all the music stored on a compact disc (CD). The program could be extended with more options such as those found on typical CD players: select some specific songs/tracks or play all songs/tracks after randomly shuffling them. We could also use the program to determine how to record songs onto a 30-minute cassette tape. The program will illustrate many of the stream and string functions we've covered in this chapter in addition to extending our knowledge of how classes are constructed in C++.

The input to the program is a file in the format shown here. Each line of the file consists of the duration of a track followed by the name of the track. For example, for the compact disc *The Best of Van Morrison* (1990, Mercury Records) the input is

```
3:46    Bright Side Of The Road
2:36    Gloria
4:31    Moondance
2:40    Baby Please Don't Go
4:19    Have I Told You Lately
3:04    Brown Eyed Girl
4:21    Sweet Thing
3:22    Warm Love
3:57    Wonderful Remark
2:57    Jackie Wilson Said (I'm In Heaven When You Smile)
3:14    Full Force Gale
4:28    And It Stoned Me
2:46    Here Comes The Night
3:04    Domino
4:05    Did Ye Get Healed
3:32    Wild Night
4:40    Cleaning Windows
4:54    Whenever God Shines His Light
4:54    Queen Of The Slipstream
4:44    Dweller On The Threshold
```

For Handel's *Water Music (Suite in F Major, Suite in D Major)* (Deutsche Grammophon, 1992, Orpheus Chamber Orchestra) the input is

```
3:12    Ouverture
1:49    Adagio e staccato
```

```
2:23    Allegro
2:11    Andante
2:25    da capo
3:22    Presto
3:26    Air.Presto
2:33    Minuet
1:38    Bourree.Presto
2:17    Hornpipe
2:53    (without indication)
1:52    Allegro
2:42    Alla Hornpipe
1:01    Minuet
1:37    Lentement
1:10    Bourree
```

To determine the total playing time of a CD, the following pseudocode provides a good outline.

```
total = 0;
while (more input)
{
    read track_time, read track-name;
    total += track_time;
}
cout << "total playing time = " << total;
```

There are several details that must be handled to translate the pseudocode into a working program. Most of these details involve getting the data from a file into the computer for a program to manipulate. Although algorithmically this is a simple problem, the details make it hard to get right.[10] There are enough sticky details in the I/O that developing the program takes patience, even if it seems easy at first.

Throw-Away Code vs. Class Design

We'll be able to read the input using the string and stream functions we've covered in this chapter, but if we read the data as strings, we'll need to decide how to convert the strings into numbers to accumulate the total playing time.

At this point we face a decision as developers of the program. We could develop code specifically for this program that correctly accumulates the total time for a CD. The program would work well for the task at hand, but the code would not be very general. At another extreme, we could develop a class for manipulating time stored in hours, minutes, and seconds with overloaded arithmetic and I/O operators; the class would provide code that could be reused in other contexts. Code reuse is a goal of object-oriented design and programming, but it takes more effort to develop reusable code than to develop program-specific code. The decision as to which approach to take is

---

[10]David Chaiken, a computer scientist trained at MIT, uses the acronym SMOP to refer to this kind of problem—it's a *Simple Matter Of Programming*. Usually those who claim it's simple aren't writing the program.

not always simple; often a "quick and dirty" programming approach is quite appropriate.

In this case we'll design a class for manipulating time as stored in the format: hours, minutes, and seconds. We'll name the class `ClockTime` and write functions that permit times in this format to be added together and output to streams.

A `ClockTime` Class

In designing a class, two major decisions influence the development process.

1.   What is the class behavior? This helps in determining appropriate public and private member functions.
2.   What is the class state? This helps in determining what instance variables are needed for the class.

For the `ClockTime` class the instance variables, or data fields, are straightforward: hours, minutes, and seconds. These are each integer fields, although the minutes and seconds fields are constrained to have values in the range 0 through 59. Member functions include appropriate constructors, access functions to enable "telling time," and arithmetic and I/O operators.

Because all that's needed for the CD problem is addition and output, we won't develop all the arithmetic operators at this time. However, by developing the structure for the class, we will have provided a foundation for future modifications. Further use of the `ClockTime` class will be explored in the exercises.

An instance (object) of the class `ClockTime` might be constructed by specifying just the seconds, or just the hours. For the preliminary development we'll provide a default constructor, which will initialize a time to 0 hours, 0 minutes, and 0 seconds, and a three-parameter constructor, which specifies all three quantities.[11] We'll see that a careful design of the three-parameter constructor allows it to be used with fewer parameters.

The first step in implementing the class requires implementing a constructor and some mechanism for determining the value of a `ClockTime` object. For example, we could implement accessor functions for obtaining hours, minutes, or seconds. We could also implement a function to print a `ClockTime` object. After we can construct and print an object, we can turn to the arithmetic operators.

The code for `operator +=` must check for overflow of minutes and seconds and adjust the other fields accordingly. Alternatively, a **normalizing** function could be written to ensure that all minutes and seconds were within proper range, as a **data invariant** of the class `ClockTime`. Just as a loop invariant is a statement that is true on every pass through a loop, a class data invariant is a property of class state that is always true. In this case the data

---

[11]By providing a default constructor, we ensure that arrays of `ClockTime` objects can be defined.

invariant would be that minutes and seconds are between 0 and 59. A clock time that obeyed the invariant, so that the minutes and seconds were both constrained to be between 0 and 59, would be said to be in a **normal form.** With this approach a function would be written that **normalized** times like 0:11:74 into 0:12:14. This normalizing function would be called after adding two times and, perhaps, after construction in case a time is constructed with 79 seconds. You might think about how you would write the code before examining the code provided as part of Prog. 9.9. The header file clockt.h follows:

Program 9.9   clockt.h

```
#ifndef _CLOCKTIME_H
#define _CLOCKTIME_H

#include <iostream.h>

// class for manipulating "clock time", time given in hours, minutes, seconds
// class supports only construction, addition, Print(), and output <<
//
// Owen Astrachan: written May 25, 1994
//                 modified Aug 4, 1994, July 5, 1996
//
// ClockTime(int secs = 0, int mins = 0, int hours = 0)
//                 -- default values of 0 for all three
//
//         access functions
//
//         Hours()     -- returns # of hours in ClockTime object
//         Minutes()   -- returns # of minutes in ClockTime object
//         Seconds()   -- returns # of seconds in ClockTime object
//         Print()     -- print time in format h:m:s
//                        (with :, no space, zero padding)
//
//         operators (for addition and output)
//
//         ClockTime & operator +=(const ClockTime & ct)
//         ClockTime operator +(const ClockTime & a, const ClockTime & b)
//
//         ostream & operator <<(ostream & os, const ClockTime & ct)
//             inserts ct into os, returns os, uses Print()

class ClockTime
{
  public:
    ClockTime(int secs = 0, int mins = 0, int hours = 0);

    int Hours()    const;        // returns # hours
    int Minutes()  const;        // returns # minutes
    int Seconds()  const;        // returns # seconds
    void Print(ostream & os)  const;   // prints ClockTime object
```

```
    ClockTime & operator +=(const ClockTime & ct);

  private:
    int mySeconds;          // constrained: 0-59
    int myMinutes;          // constrained: 0-59
    int myHours;
};
// free functions, not member functions

ostream &  operator << (ostream & os, const ClockTime & ct);
ClockTime operator + (const ClockTime & lhs, const ClockTime & rhs);  _____

#endif
```

clockt.h

Overloaded Operators

> It is not so much our friends' help that helps us
> as the confident knowledge that they will
> help us.
> Epicurus

Only member functions have access to an object's private data. This makes it difficult to overload the stream insertion operator <<, which for technical reasons cannot be a member function of the ClockTime class. Instead, we implement a member function Print that can be used to print a ClockTime object. We can then overload the insertion operator << using Print.

Sometimes, however, it is useful for nonmember functions to have access to private data fields. You can design functions (and even other classes) that have access to private data by declaring the functions as **friend** functions (or friend classes). However, granting nonmember functions access to private data violates the principles of encapsulation and information hiding that we've upheld in our programs. You should be very careful if you decide you need to implement a friend function. In our example, implementing Print and the overloaded operator += makes it possible to implement operator << and operator + without making them friend functions.

Careful coding in the implementation of Print ensures that 5 seconds is printed as 05 and that 1:02:03 is printed for one hour, two minutes, and three seconds. Two digits are always printed for each number, and a leading zero is added when necessary. The stream function width specifies a field width of 2, and a fill character '0' is specified using the stream function fill. Note that fill is also used to remember and restore the stream state before the fill character is changed to '0'. If we didn't do this, the stream passed to Print would be permanently changed, having a different fill character than it had before—an unexpected and very undesirable side effect.

When implementing arithmetic operators, it is much simpler to implement operator += first and then call += when implementing operator +. The implementation of operator + is the same for almost any class:

```
ClockTime operator + (const ClockTime & lhs, const ClockTime & rhs)
// postcondition: return lhs + rhs
// (normalized for myMinutes, mySeconds)
{
    ClockTime result(lhs);
    result += rhs;
    return result;
}
```

Compare this implementation, for example, to `operator +` for the `Date` class in Excursion Sec. 5.9.

For the moment we'll ignore the return statement `return *this`[12] used in `operator +=`; it will be explained in Chapter 12.

Program 9.10   clockt.cc

```
#include <iostream.h>
#include <iomanip.h>
#include "clockt.h"

ClockTime::ClockTime(int secs, int mins, int hours)
  : mySeconds(secs), myMinutes(mins), myHours(hours)
// postcondition: all data fields initialized
{
    // work done in initializer list
}

int ClockTime::Hours() const
// postcondition: return # of hours
{
    return myHours;
}

int ClockTime::Minutes() const
// postcondition: return # of minutes
{
    return myMinutes;
}

int ClockTime::Seconds() const
// postcondition: return # of seconds
{
    return mySeconds;
}

void ClockTime::Print(ostream & os) const
// postcondition: insert object in format h:m:s onto stream os
{
    char saveFill = os.fill();    // previous fill character
    os.fill('0');                 // pad with zeros
```

---

[12]Since assignment expressions can be chained together, as in `first = two += 3`, the operator `+=` must return something. The value returned is the object added to, which has the special name `*this`.

```
        os << Hours() << ":"
            << setw(2) << Minutes() << ":"
            << setw(2) << Seconds();

        os.fill(saveFill);              // reset stream fill character
}

ostream & operator << (ostream & os, const ClockTime & ct)
// postcondition: inserts ct onto os, returns os
//                   format is h:m:s
{
        ct.Print(os);
        return os;
}

ClockTime & ClockTime::operator += (const ClockTime & ct)
// postcondition: add ct, return result (normalized for myMinutes, mySeconds)
{
        mySeconds += ct.mySeconds;      // add mySeconds
        myMinutes += mySeconds / 60;    // overflow from secs to
                                        // myMinutes
        mySeconds %= 60;                // now between 0 and 59

        myMinutes += ct.myMinutes;      // add myMinutes
        myHours += myMinutes / 60;      // overflow from myMinutes to myHours
        myMinutes %=  60;               // now between 0 and 59

        myHours += ct.myHours;

        return *this;
}

ClockTime operator + (const ClockTime & lhs, const ClockTime & rhs)
// postcondition: return lhs + rhs (normalized for myMinutes, mySeconds)
{
        ClockTime result(lhs);
        result += rhs;
        return result;
}
```

clockt.cc

Testing the `ClockTime` Class

Before proceeding with the development of the program to manipulate CDs, we must test the ClockTime class. In testing the program we'll look for cases that might cause problems such as adding 59 seconds and 1 second. It may seem like too much work to develop a program just to test a class, but this kind of work pays dividends in the long run. By constructing a simple test program it's possible to debug a class rather than debug a larger application program. This will make the development of the client program easier as well, because (we hope) the class will be debugged.

In the sample run following this program, a complete set of test data is not used. You should think about developing a set of test data that would test important boundary cases.

Program 9.11   useclock.cc

```
#include <iostream.h>
#include "clockt.h"

// test program for ClockTime class

int main()
{
    int h,m,s;

    cout << "enter two sets of 'hour minute second' "
         << "with white space separation.  " << endl
         << "Enter nonintegers to terminate program." << endl << endl;

    while (cin >> h >> m >> s)
    {
        ClockTime a(s,m,h);
        cin >> h >> m >> s;
        ClockTime b(s,m,h);

        ClockTime c = a + b;

        cout << a << " + " << b << " = " << c << endl;
    }

    return 0;
}
```

OUTPUT

prompt> *useclock*
enter two sets of 'hour minute second' with white space separation.
Enter nonintegers to terminate program.

1 40 20 1 15 40
1:40:20 + 1:15:40 = 2:56:00
0 59 59 0 0 1
0:59:59 + 0:00:01 = 1:00:00
22 2 55 2 5 8
22:02:55 + 2:05:08 = 24:08:03
done

The use of setw and fill in the implementation of the operator << makes the output easy to read, which helps in determining whether it is correct.

The Final Program

Each track for a CD is stored in the following format:

```
4:19     Have I Told You Lately
2:46     Here Comes The Night
```

Because white space is used to delimit strings when reading input using the extraction operator >>, we'll need to use getline to read the title of a CD track, since the number of words is different for each track. We'll also use the optional third parameter of getline to signal a sentinel other than newline when we read the minutes and seconds that make up the time of a CD track. We'll read all the characters up to the ' : ' as the minutes, then all the characters up to a space as the seconds. The remaining characters on a line are the track's title. Since getline reads strings, we'll convert the strings for minutes and seconds to integers using the function atoi, whose prototype is in "CPstring.h".[13]

The third parameter for getline has a default value of ' \n' . This means that if no value is specified for the third parameter, a **default value** of ' \n' is used. The ClockTime constructor also has default values. The prototype in *clockt.h* shows that all three parameters have default values of zero. We make use of these default values in *cdsum.cc*, Prog. 9.12, where only minutes and seconds are used to construct the ClockTime object track. The number of hours gets the default value of zero.

Program 9.12   cdsum.cc

```cpp
#include <iostream.h>
#include <fstream.h>          // for ifstream
#include <stdlib.h>           // for exit, atoi
#include "CPstring.h"
#include "clockt.h"
#include "prompt.h"

// reads file containing data for a CD in the format
//         track time (Min:Sec) Title of Track
// (one line/track) and sums all track times
//
// Owen Astrachan, August 4, 1994

int main()
{
    ifstream input;
    string filename = PromptString("enter name of data file: ");
    input.open(filename);

    if (input.fail())
```

---

[13]atoi, read as "a to i," stands for "alphabetic to integer."

```
    {
        cerr << "could not open file " << filename << endl;
        exit(0);
    }

    string minutes,            // # of minutes of track
           seconds,            // # of seconds of track
           title;              // title of track

    ClockTime total(0,0,0);  // total of all times

    while (getline(input,minutes,':') &&
           getline(input,seconds,' ') &&
           getline(input,title))             // reading line ok
    {
        cout << minutes << " " << seconds << " " << title << endl;
        ClockTime track(atoi(seconds),atoi(minutes));
        total += track;
    }
    cout << "-----------------------------" << endl;
    cout << "total = " << total << endl;
    return 0;
}
```

```
                              OUTPUT

prompt> cdsum
enter name of data file: vanmor.dat
3 46    Bright Side Of The Road
2 36    Gloria
4 31    Moondance
2 40    Baby Please Don't Go
4 19    Have I Told You Lately
3 04    Brown Eyed Girl
4 21    Sweet Thing
3 22    Warm Love
3 57    Wonderful Remark
2 57    Jackie Wilson Said (I'm In Heaven When You Smile)
3 14    Full Force Gale
4 28    And It Stoned Me
2 46    Here Comes The Night
3 04    Domino
4 05    Did Ye Get Healed
3 32    Wild Night
4 40    Cleaning Windows
4 54    Whenever God Shines His Light
4 54    Queen Of The Slipstream
4 44    Dweller On The Threshold
-----------------------------
total = 1:15:54
```

If you review the specification for `getline`, you'll see that the sentinel is read but is not stored as part of the string `minutes`. The second `getline` uses a space to delimit the number of seconds from the title. Finally, the third use of `getline` relies on the default value of the second parameter: a newline `'\n'`.

The function `atoi` converts a string to the corresponding integer. If the string parameter does not represent a valid integer, then zero is returned.

Pause to reflect

9.19. In *cdsum.cc,* Prog. 9.12, the title read includes leading white space if there is more than one space between the track duration and the title. Explain why this is and describe a method for removing the leading white space from the title.

9.20. Provide three sets of data that could be used with *useclock.cc,* Prog. 9.11, to test the `ClockTime` implementation.

9.21. Explain why the `ClockTime` parameters for operators `<<`, `+`, and `+=` are declared as `const` reference parameters.

9.22. What is output by the statement `cout << ct << endl` after each of the following definitions?

- `ClockTime ct(71,16,1);`
- `ClockTime ct(5,62,1);`
- `ClockTime ct(12);`
- `ClockTime ct(21,5);`
- `ClockTime ct;`

9.23. If operators `-=` and `-` are implemented for subtracting clock times, which one is easiest to implement? Write an implementation for operator `-=`.

9.24. After reading the number of minutes using `getline(input, minutes)`, is it possible to replace the expression `getline(input, seconds)` with `input >> seconds`? What if `seconds` is defined as an `int` rather than as a `string`?

9.6   Chapter Review

In this chapter we discussed details of streams and characters and how these abstractions are implemented in C++. For example, we saw that a low-level understanding of how strings are implemented is not necessary in order to use strings in programs.

The following are some of the important topics covered:

- The type `char` represents characters and is used to construct strings. Most systems use ASCII as a way of encoding characters, but you should try to write code that is independent of any particular character set.

- The library `<ctype.h>` has prototypes for several functions that can be used to write programs that do not depend on a particular character set such as ASCII.

- Except for output and use in strings, char variables can be thought of as int variables. In particular, it's possible to add 3 to 'a' and subtract 'a' from 'z'.

- String variables are composed of char values. Individual characters of a string are accessible using [], the indexing operator.

- The function getline is used to read an entire line of text and doesn't use white space to delimit one word from another. The sentinel indicating end of line is an optional third parameter.

- Several stream member functions are used to set stream state and to obtain information about the state of a stream. In particular, the function fail is used to determine whether a stream operation has failed (such as if input failed, a stream bound to a file could not be opened).

- Side effects occur when a function has another action in addition to returning a value. As an example, extracting using >> stores a value in a variable (the value comes from a stream) but also returns the state of the stream; that is, whether the extraction succeeded.

- State machines can be useful when parsing data one character at a time.

- String streams (variables of type istrstream) are useful in reading line-oriented data.

- Formatting output can be done with stream member functions and with I/O manipulators (accessible using #include<iomanip.h>).

- A friend class (or function) has access to another class's private data members. Friendship must be granted by the class whose private data members will be accessed.

- It is possible to overload output (and input) operators for classes that you write.

- Class development and testing should be done together, with testing helping the development process and increasing confidence in the correctness of the class implementation (whether the class works as it should).

- The function atoi can be used to convert a string value to an integer value; for example, atoi("123") == 123.

9.7 Exercises

9.1 Modify *decomment.cc,* Prog. 9.7, so that removed comments are output to a separate file. Use string functions so that the name of the output file has a .ncm (for no comments) suffix with the same prefix as the input file. For example, if the comments are removed from *frogwalk.cc,* the removed comments will be stored in *frogwalk.ncm.* Each comment should be preceded by the line number from which it was removed. For example:

```
 3   // author: Naomi Smith
 4   // written 4/5/93
10   // update the counter here, watch out for overflow
37   // avoid iterating too many times
```

9.2 The constructor for the class `ClockTime` does not check the values of the parameters to see whether they represent a valid clock time (e.g., seconds between 0 and 59). Write a private member function `Normalize` that will convert a time such as 1:63:71 to 2:04:11. The code for `Normalize` is very similar to the code used in the implementation of the operator `+=`. The function `Normalize` should be called from the constructor and after adding numbers (the code for `+=` can simply add numbers without checking for overflow if `Normalize` is called).

9.3 Add several operators to the `ClockTime` class and develop a test program to ensure that the operators work correctly. For example, implement some of the following:

- `operator  -`   for subtraction of two times
- `operator ==`   to see if two times are equal
- `operator  <`   to see if one time is less than another
- Other relational operators: `<=`, `>`, `!=`, etc. These can often be implemented in terms of `==` and `<`.

9.4 Modify Prog. 9.4, *readnums.cc,* so that all integers on a line are parsed and added to `total` but nonintegers are ignored. To do so you'll need to change the type of the variable `num`. If you use the function `atoi`, it will be difficult to determine when an integer is read and when a noninteger string such as `"apple"` is read. However, all valid integers in C++ begin with either a +, a -, or a digit 0–9.

9.5 Design, implement, and test a class for fractions, or rational numbers, like $\frac{2}{3}$ and $\frac{7}{11}$. Overload operators so that fractions can be added, subtracted, multiplied, and divided. You should also write functions so that rational numbers can be printed. You'll need to write a normalizing function to reduce fractions to lowest terms (i.e., so that $\frac{1}{4} + \frac{1}{4} = \frac{1}{2}$). See Euclid's algorithm for finding greatest common divisors in Sec. 5.8 for help with the normalizing function.

9.6 Design, implement, and test a class for complex numbers. A complex number has the form $a + b \times i$, where $i = \sqrt{-1}$. Implement constructors from `double` values and from complex values. Overload arithmetic and output operators for complex numbers.

9.7 Write a program to play hangman. In hangman one player thinks of a word and the other tries to guess the word by guessing one letter at a time. The guesser is allowed a fixed number of missed letters, such as 6; if the word is not guessed before 6 misses, the guesser loses. Traditionally each missed letter results in one more part being added to the figure of a person being hanged, as shown in Fig. 9.3. When the figure is complete, the guesser loses.

Rather than use graphics (although if you have access to a graphics library, you should try to use it), the program should tell the user how many misses are left and should print a schematic representation of what letters have been guessed correctly. For example:

OUTPUT

```
prompt> hangman
# misses left = 6   word =   * * * * * * * * * *
```

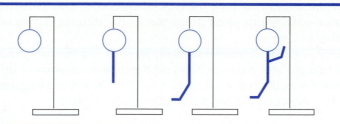

| **Figure 9.3** | Slowly losing at hangman. |

```
enter a letter: e
# misses left = 6   word =   * * * E * * * * E *
enter a letter: a
# misses left = 5   word =   * * * E * * * * E *
enter a letter: i
# misses left = 4   word =   * * * E * * * * E *
enter a letter: r
# misses left = 4   word =   * * R E * * * * E *
enter a letter: o
# misses left = 3   word =   * * R E * * * * E *
enter a letter: n
# misses left = 3   word =   * * R E N * * * E N
enter a letter: t
# misses left = 3   word =   * T R E N * T * E N
enter a letter: l
# misses left = 2   word =   * T R E N * T * E N
enter a letter: u
# misses left = 1   word =   * T R E N * T * E N
enter a letter: p
YOU LOSE!!! The word is STRENGTHEN
```

Your program should permit letters to be entered in either upper or lower case and should not count previously guessed letters again if the user forgets what letters have been guessed. If you have access to an online dictionary, use it for a source of words.

9.8   A Computer Science Excursion: Numerical Representation

Just as we could use streams and strings without being aware of many of their low-level characteristics, we have written and studied many programs using numbers without knowing how the types `int` and `double` are implemented. In this section we'll study some properties of the different types of numerical data available in C++.

You have already seen several examples showing the differences between conceptual integers and real numbers and the implementation of these kinds of numbers in C++ as the types `int` and `double`. In writing programs that use numbers, it is important to keep these differences in mind.

Roundoff Error

One way in which numbers differ in their implementation in C++, as compared to their existence in mathematics, is that programs do not always perform arithmetic exactly. Program 9.13 illustrates that arithmetic using the type `double` can lead to unexpected behavior.

Program 9.13   doubloop.cc

```
#include <iostream.h>
#include "prompt.h"

// illustrates roundoff error

int main()
{

    int count = 0;
    double val = 0.0;
    double increment = PromptRange("what increment",0.0,1.0);

    for(val = 0.0; val < 2.0; val += increment)
    {
        count += 1;
    }

    cout << "increment = " << increment << " expected iterations = ";
    cout << 2.0/increment << endl;
    cout << "actual # of iterations = " << count << endl;
    cout << "final value = " << val << endl;
    return 0;
}
```

OUTPUT

```
prompt> doubloop
what increment?  0.0002
increment = 0.0002 expected iterations = 10000
actual # of iterations = 10001
final value = 2.0002
```

```
prompt> doubloop
what increment?  0.00001
increment = 1e-05 expected iterations = 200000
actual # of iterations = 200000
final value = 2
```

The number $1e-05$ is printed using a form of scientific notation; it is the same as $1 \times 10^{-5} = 0.00001$. Often the scientific form is used when printing `doubles` to make the numbers easier to read. For example, the number printed as $2e-11$ is easy to distinguish from the number $2e-12$. If the numbers were printed using their full decimal expansion as 0.00000000002 and 0.000000000002, respectively, it would be much more difficult for humans to distinguish them.

Because of **roundoff** errors that accumulate during the repeated addition of `val`, the number of iterations of the `while` loop depends on whether all the floating-point numbers can be accurately represented within the computer. Incrementing a value that is initially zero by 0.0002 for 10,000 times should result in the value 2.0. However, because of the way numbers are stored in the computer, the number 0.0002 can only be approximated, and the accumulation of the approximations results in the small roundoff error shown in the run above. The branch of computer science known as **numerical analysis** includes the study of such roundoff errors and the development of algorithms to cope with the limited precision of computer arithmetic.

Modified Types: Float, Short, Long

The type `double` is so named because it is a double-precision floating-point number. "Double-precision" means that the range of real numbers representable by `double` is larger than can be represented using another type in C and C++, named `float`. If the variables of type `double` are changed to `float` in Prog. 9.13, different behavior results:

OUTPUT

```
prompt> doubloop
what increment?  0.00001
increment = 1e-05 expected iterations = 200000
actual # of iterations = 199766
final value = 2.00001
```

There are fewer iterations in this run than expected, and the results are different from those of the run when the type `double` is used. Arithmetic operations using `double` can take longer than when the type `float` is used, and a variable of type `double` typically requires more memory than a variable of type `float`. If there is a compelling reason to be concerned with memory and speed with floating-point operations, it may be prudent to use `float` variables.

However, as can be seen by the runs above, the roundoff error introduced when the type float is used can be much larger than when double is used. In this book we'll use double exclusively.

Just as float and double both represent real numbers, the type int has other forms that represent potentially different integers. The type long int includes at least the same integers as the type int and may include more. Typically, the long modifier has no effect as a modifier of int on workstations, but it does extend the range of integers when personal computers (at least, older models) are used. On such systems the type long int requires more memory and more time for arithmetic operations than the type int.

The type short int may represent a range of integers that is smaller than the set that is representable by an int. As is the case with long, a short int may also represent exactly the same range of integers as is representable by an int. The draft C++ standard requires that a short int be able to represent values[14] between −32,767 and 32,767 and that a long int be able to represent values between −2,147,483,647 and 2,147,483,647 (at least). An int is typically equivalent to either a short or a long int. In this book we'll use the type int for most programs. If you use a personal computer, however, you should use long int as the default type, since the typical range of an int on such machines is too limited for many arithmetic calculations. For example, the number of characters in each of Shakespeare's plays that are available online as part of this book is more than 90,000. The number of words in *Hamlet* is 31,956—very close to the largest value that can be represented by an int on personal computers.

Numerical Details: Representation

In this section we'll briefly explore how integers are represented in computer languages. This explanation will give you some background for how numbers are implemented without too much detail. For most programs you write, this knowledge isn't necessary, because treating the numerical types as abstractions works well. Sometimes, however, knowledge of the low-level details is necessary (and even interesting).

As was noted earlier (page 11), the switches that are used in computers are in one of two states: on or off (or 0 or 1). This **binary** system causes information to be stored in computers as sequences of zeros and ones, called **bits**.[15] Consider the integer 697 and its representations in Fig. 9.4 as a decimal number (base 10) and a binary number (base 2). Note that to represent the number 697 requires 10 bits in the binary system but only three decimal digits.[16] In particular, using 3 bits yields a total of 8 different values (0 through 7), as shown in Table 9.6, and using 10 bits yields a total of 1024 different values (0 through 1023). The

---

[14]Because most computers use what is called a *two's complement representation* for negative numbers, the smallest negative number is −32,768 on most systems.

[15]The term **bit** is short for *bi*nary dig*it* and was (apparently) coined by the statistician John Tukey.

[16]The term *dit* is not in widespread usage for decimal digit.

base 10				6	9	7
	10^4	10^3	10^2	10^1	10^0	
	10000	1000	100	10	1	

$$6 \times 100 + 9 \times 10 + 7 = 697$$

base 2	1	0	1	0	1	1	1	0	0	1
	2^9	2^8	2^7	2^6	2^5	2^4	2^3	2^2	2^1	2^0
	512	256	128	64	32	16	8	4	2	1

$$512 + 128 + 32 + 16 + 8 + 1 = 697$$

Figure 9.4   Representing numbers.

details of how numbers are represented in binary are not nearly as important as is the concept that *a limited range of integers can be represented with a fixed number of bits.* In particular, the number of different values that can be represented with n bits is 2^n, as shown for $n = 10$ in Table 9.6. Whether a computer uses 16 bits to represent an integer (as do most personal computers), 32 bits (as do most workstations), or 64 (as do some supercomputers) does not alter the constraint that there is a limit as to the largest integer that can be represented; the type of computer affects only what the limit is.

In later courses in computer science you may study different methods for representing integers in a computer. However, at this point we will note that, because integers can range over positive and negative numbers, the leftmost (most significant) bit of an integer normally distinguishes whether the integer is positive or negative. This effectively cuts the range of an n-bit integer in half,

Table 9.6   Counting in Binary

Base 2	Base 10	Base 2	Base 10
000	0	0000000000	0
001	1	0000000001	1
010	2	0000000010	2
011	3	0000000011	3
100	4	0000000100	4
101	5	0000000101	5
110	6	0000000110	6
111	7	0000000111	7
		. . .	
		1111111110	1022
		1111111111	1023

decimal	binary
1	1 0 0 1
1 3	0 1 1 0 1
+ 9	+ 0 1 0 0 1
2 2	1 0 1 1 0

Figure 9.5   Adding in different bases.

since both positive and negative numbers must be represented. Suppose, for example, that five bits are used to represent integers and that the numbers 13 and 9 are added together as shown in Fig. 9.5. The small numbers represent what is *carried* from one digit addition to the next, as is used in the normal method of addition learned in grade school. Note that the sum of the two numbers (the decimal number 22) is represented as 10110 in binary. If, as discussed above, the leftmost digit identifies the number as positive or negative, then this answer will be a negative number.[17] Finally we have an explanation as to why earlier runs of several programs generate negative numbers when positive numbers are expected.

We also see why the largest value of a `short int` is 32,767 (this is the size of a `int` on most personal computers). Since 16 bits are used for a `short int`, and one bit is reserved for the sign, the maximum value that can be represented is $2^{15} - 1 = 32,767$. For the same reason, the largest value representable by a `long int` that uses 32 bits is $2^{31} - 1 = 2,147,483,647$.

In addition to the modifiers `short` and `long`, there is a modifier `unsigned` that can be used with the integral types `char`, `short`, `int`, and `long` in C++. Variables defined as `unsigned` have nonnegative values (i.e., values that are zero or positive) and therefore need no sign bit and can use all of their bits for the absolute value. For example, on machines that use 32-bit integers, the maximum value of a variable defined as `unsigned int big` is 4,294,967,295, which is $2^{32} - 1$.

The range of integer values. The system header file `<limits.h>` defines several integer constants[18] that isolate the limits in a system-independent manner. These constants are printed by *limits.cc*, Prog. 9.14.

---

[17]We are not concerned with what the value of the negative number is; that depends on how negative numbers are represented in the machine being used. The most common method is called two's complement representation.

[18]These are **preprocessor** constants similar to the kind used in our header files defined with the `#define` directive, as opposed to constants defined using `const`.

Program 9.14   limits.cc

```cpp
#include <iostream.h>
#include <iomanip.h>              // for setw
#include <limits.h>
#include "CPstring.h"

// illustrates range of values for integral types
// author: Owen Astrachan, date: 8/2/94

const int FIELD_SIZE = 13;                  // size of field for output chunk

void Print(string type, long int low, unsigned long int high);

int main()
{
    cout << setw(FIELD_SIZE) << "type"
         << setw(FIELD_SIZE) << "low"
         << setw(FIELD_SIZE) << "high" << endl << endl;

    Print("char",CHAR_MIN,CHAR_MAX);
    Print("uchar",0,UCHAR_MAX);
    Print("short",SHRT_MIN,SHRT_MAX);
    Print("ushort",0,USHRT_MAX);
    Print("int",INT_MIN,INT_MAX);
    Print("uint",0,UINT_MAX);
    Print("long",LONG_MIN,LONG_MAX);
    Print("ulong",0,ULONG_MAX);
    return 0;
}

void Print(string type, long int low, unsigned long int high)
// postcondition: values printed in field width FIELD_SIZE
{
    cout << setw(FIELD_SIZE) << type
         << setw(FIELD_SIZE) << low
         << setw(FIELD_SIZE) << high << endl;
}
```

OUTPUT

```
prompt> limits
        type         low         high

        char        -128          127
       uchar           0          255
       short      -32768        32767
      ushort           0        65535
```

```
  int  -2147483648    2147483647
 uint           0    4294967295
 long  -2147483648    2147483647
ulong           0    4294967295
```

The types of the formal parameters of the function `Print` have a significant effect on the values printed. For example, if the type is `int` rather than `long int`, different—and incorrect—values will be printed. It isn't always possible to copy a `long int` value into an `int` variable. Since the parameters are passed by value, such copying is done when the values are passed to `Print`.

Memory used by integer types. The standard C++ operator `sizeof` calculates the amount of memory used by a built-in or user-defined type. The value returned is in units expressed as a multiple of the memory used by the type `char`, where `sizeof(char)` is 1 and other types are integral multiples of this value. Typically, memory is measured in **bytes;** a byte is eight bits.[19] On most systems a `char` is one byte (eight bits) and must be at least this big so that it can represent 256 different unsigned values.

Program 9.15 illustrates the use of the `sizeof` operator.

Program 9.15   size.cc

```cpp
#include <iostream.h>
#include "CPstring.h"

// print sizes of many types

int main()
{
    cout << "char = "   << sizeof(char)   << endl;
    cout << "short = "  << sizeof(short)  << endl;
    cout << "int = "    << sizeof(int)    << endl;
    cout << "long = "   << sizeof(long)   << endl;

    cout << "float = "  << sizeof(float)  << endl;
    cout << "double = " << sizeof(double) << endl;
    cout << "long double = " << sizeof(long double) << endl;

    string s = "smart";
    cout << "string = " << sizeof(s) << endl;
    cout << "string = " << sizeof(string) << endl;
    return 0;
}
```

---

[19]Like "bit," "byte" is a partial acronym; it stands for *binary term*.

```
                        OUTPUT

char = 1
short = 2
int = 4
long = 4
float = 4
double = 8
long double = 8
string = 8
string = 8
```

The output shown was generated on a Sun workstation. On a PC-compatible machine, the number of bytes in an `int` is 2, and the number of bytes in a `string` is 4. Note that the size of a `string` does *not* include the characters that make up the string. In Chapter 12 we'll study why the size of a `string` is eight (or four) bytes; at this point we'll note it and move on. The argument of the `sizeof` operator can be either an object or a type, as shown in Prog. 9.15.

Binary Printing: A Small Case Study

Although it is possible to determine the binary representation of any number with pencil and paper, we would like to develop a computer program to assist with this task. The program will accept a positive integer input by the user and print the binary representation of the integer. A function `PrintBinary` with prototype `void PrintBinary(int n);` will print its integer parameter in binary, using recursion to process the entire number digit by digit.

Since we want to process a number digit by digit (whether decimal digit or binary digit does not matter), we must determine which of the methods we know for manipulating integers will be useful. The arithmetic operations, `+ – / * %`, may be useful in this situation. Another tool to use when solving problems is to think of similar problems or simpler problems. In this case you may have solved one of the previous exercises (Problem 5.24 on page 209) that asks for a loop to determine how many times a number can be divided by two.

Such a function might yield a first attempt at a function `PrintDecimal`; we use decimal rather than binary (base 10 rather than base 2) because it is easier to understand; we won't have to do any number conversion to recognize whether the output is correct.

```
void
PrintDecimal(int n)
// precondition:  n >= 0
// postcondition: n printed in decimal
{
    while (n >= 0)
    {
        cout << n << endl;
```

```
                    n = n / 10;
                }
        }
```

```
                        OUTPUT

    1234
    123
    12
    1
```

However, rather than printing the entire number in each loop iteration, only the rightmost (least significant) digit is printed. This digit can be obtained using the C++ modulus operator `%`. Changing the output statement in the loop body to `cout << n % 10` causes the call `PrintDecimal(1234);` to generate 4321 as output; note that there is no `endl` in the new output statement. This represents the correct sequence of digits, but printed in the wrong order. To print the least significant (ones) digit last, it is necessary to use a recursive implementation of the function `PrintDecimal`.

The fundamental requirements for recursive functions given in Sec. 4.9 indicate that there must be a test that prevents the function from calling itself forever. This test identifies a **base case:** a case that generates no further recursive calls and that may be simple to process.

The intuition behind such a recursive function is that it is possible to print the current digit (either in decimal or in binary) only *after* all the preceding digits are printed. The loop in the modified `PrintDecimal` above prints a digit and then prints the preceding digits—thus, the number 1234 is printed as 4321. The following recursive implementation prints 1234 when invoked with `PrintDecimal(1234)`, but it prints these digits one at a time.

```
        void
        PrintDecimal(int n)
        // precondition:  n >= 0
        // postcondition: n printed in decimal
        {
            if (n < 10)
            {
                cout << n;
            }
            else
            {
                PrintDecimal(n/10);
                cout << n % 10;
            }
        }
```

A chain of recursive calls is illustrated in Fig. 9.6. Each clone of the function `PrintDecimal` first checks its base case to see whether a recursive call is made. As shown, a recursive call is made for the clones whose parameters have

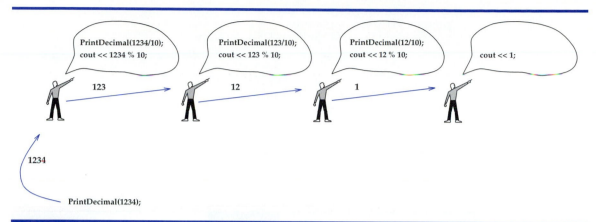

Figure 9.6   Printing one digit at a time.

values 123, 12, and 1. The clone in the figure that is passed an argument of 12 makes a recursive call of `PrintDecimal(12/10)`, which generates the last call shown in Fig. 9.6. This clone, with a parameter of 1 (the value of `12/10`), executes its base case. Note that this is the first value printed.

When the clone executing the base case is finished, control of the program returns to the clone that made the call (this is the clone to the left of the last clone in Fig. 9.6). The recursive call has just finished executing, and the output statement shown is executed. This process continues, with each clone returning control to the calling clone.

Changing the function to use base 2 rather than base 10 yields Prog. 9.16, which meets the goal of printing positive integers in binary:

Program 9.16   binary.cc

```
#include <iostream.h>

// print numbers in base 2

void PrintBinary(int n);

int main()
{
    int num;

    cout << "enter a number (to be printed in binary) ";
    cin >> num;
    PrintBinary(num);
    cout << endl;
    return 0;
}
```

```
void PrintBinary(int n)
// precondition:  n >= 0
// postcondition: n printed in binary
{
    if (n < 2)
    {
        cout << n;
    }
    else
    {
        PrintBinary(n / 2);
        cout << (n % 2);
    }
}
```

OUTPUT

```
prompt> binary
enter a number (to be printed in binary)   255
11111111
prompt> binary
enter a number (to be printed in binary)   103
1100111
prompt> binary
enter a number (to be printed in binary)   11
1011
prompt> binary
enter a number (to be printed in binary)   5329
1010011010001
```

Pause to reflect

9.25. How can you be sure that the function `PrintBinary` in Prog. 9.16 works as intended? Specifically, can you come up with a small number of test cases whose (correct) output you would view as conclusive as to the correctness of the program? The problem of developing data to test a program or function is a difficult one.

9.26. How many different values can be represented using 16 bits? Using 32 bits? Using 64 bits?

9.27. Write the numbers 9 and 11 in binary and add them using the method illustrated in Fig. 9.5.

9.28. What is the minimum number of bits needed to represent one million different values?

9.29. What happens when a negative number is entered by the user when running Prog. 9.16? Why?

9.30. What happens if the output statement `cout << (n % 2)` is interchanged with the recursive call `PrintBinary(n / 2)`?

9.31. What happens if the manipulator `setw(3)` is added in the output statements of the function `PrintBinary`?

Excursion Exercises

9.8 Find the ranges of values for the types `int`, `long int`, `float`, and `double` on your system. Write a program to time how long it takes to add `float` values compared to `double` values and how long to add `int` values compared to `long int` values. You'll need to design the program carefully to get valid timings.

9.9 An integer is printed with commas inserted in the proper positions similarly to the way in which binary numbers are printed. That is, to print the number 12345678 as 12,345,678, the 678 cannot be printed until *after* the preceding part of the number is printed. Write a recursive function `PrintWithCommas` that will print its `int` parameter with commas inserted properly. The outline of the function is

```
if (number < 1000)
    print normally, no commas needed
else
    recursively print the number without the last three digits
    print a comma and the last three digits
```

You'll need to be careful with leading zeroes to ensure, for example, that the number 12,003 is printed properly.

9.10 Change `PrintBinary` in Prog. 9.16 so that numbers are printed in base 10 rather than base 2. Change the function so that it has an extra parameter that indicates what base should be used when printing the first parameter. Allow the user to enter both a number and a base.

Recursion, Scope, and Lifetime

> Art, it seems to me, should simplify. That,
> indeed, is very nearly the whole of the higher
> artistic process; finding what conventions of
> form and what detail one can do without and
> yet preserve the spirit of the whole—so that all
> that one has suppressed and cut away is there
> to the reader's consciousness as much as if it
> were type on the page.
> WILLA CATHER
> *On the Art of Fiction*

In this chapter we focus on two areas relating to how functions and classes are used to solve problems using a computer. The first area is a technique called **recursion,** used to design functions that solve self-referential problems. The second area relates to properties of variables that determine the **scope** of a variable, or where a variable can be accessed, and the **lifetime** of a variable, or the duration of a variable's memory during program execution. We'll see that recursive functions seem to "call themselves," but they are better understood as functions that solve problems whose solution can be expressed by combining solutions to problems that are similar, but smaller. Some problems have terse and comprehensible solutions expressed as recursive functions but have convoluted nonrecursive solutions. Other problems seem to be suitable for recursive solution but are better solved nonrecursively. We'll also see that scope and lifetime are related to recursion but are more general concepts used in many different ways in writing computer programs. Unfortunately, the terminology used in C++ for expressing the general concepts relating to scope and lifetime is potentially confusing since the same word often has different meanings in related but different contexts.

10.1   Recursive Functions

As a first example of a problem whose solution is elegantly expressed using recursion, we turn to the problem of outputting an English version of an integer by printing each digit's spelled-out English equivalent. For example, 1053 should be output as "one zero five three." We solved this problem with *digits.cc*, Prog. 5.10, using `string` concatenation. Now we limit ourselves to a solution using only `int` variables. To make the problem simpler, we'll initially limit the input to four-digit numbers. However, the recursive solution will work for all `int` values.

Similar and Simpler Functions

When we solved this problem using strings, we concatenated digits to the front of a string as it was built up from each digit in an `int`. To convert 123, we first concatenated `"three"` to an empty string called s. Then we concatenated `"two"` to the front of s, forming `"two three"`. Concatenating `"one"` to the front of s now yields the desired string (see *digits.cc* on page 205). Since we aren't using `string` functions, we must rewrite the program to print string literals for each digit of an `int`. This is done in *digits2.cc*, Prog. 10.1.

Program 10.1   digits2.cc

```
#include <iostream.h>
#include "CPstring.h"
#include "prompt.h"

// prelude to recursion: print English form of each digit
// in an integer: 123 -> "one two three"
// Owen Astrachan, 7/11/96

void PrintDigit(int num)
// precondition: 0 <= num < 10
// postcondition: prints english equivalent, e.g., 1->one,...9->nine

{
    if (0 == num)       cout << "zero";
    else if (1 == num)  cout << "one";
    else if (2 == num)  cout << "two";
    else if (3 == num)  cout << "three";
    else if (4 == num)  cout << "four";
    else if (5 == num)  cout << "five";
    else if (6 == num)  cout << "six";
    else if (7 == num)  cout << "seven";
    else if (8 == num)  cout << "eight";
    else if (9 == num)  cout << "nine";
    else cout << "?";
}
```

```cpp
void PrintOne(long int number)
// precondition: 0 <= number < 10
// postcondition: prints English equivalent of number
//                e.g., 1 -> "one"
{
    if (0 <= number && number < 10)
    {
        PrintDigit(number);
    }
}

void PrintTwo(long int number)
// precondition: 10 <= number < 100
// postcondition: prints English equivalent of number
//                e.g., 12 -> "one two"
{
    if (10 <= number && number < 100)
    {
        PrintOne(number / 10);
        cout << " ";
        PrintDigit(number % 10);
    }
}

void PrintThree(long int number)
// precondition: 100 <= number < 1000
// postcondition: prints English equivalent of number
//                e.g., 123 -> "one two three"
{
    if (100 <= number && number < 1000)
    {
        PrintTwo(number / 10);
        cout << " ";
        PrintDigit(number % 10);
    }
}

void PrintFour(long int number)
// precondition: 1000 <= number < 10,000
// postcondition: prints English equivalent of number
//                e.g., 1234 -> "one two three four"
{
    if (1000 <= number && number < 10000)
    {
        PrintThree(number / 10);
        cout << " ";
        PrintDigit(number % 10);
    }
}

int main()
{
    int number = PromptRange("enter an integer",1000,9999);

    PrintFour(number);
```

```
    cout << endl;

    return 0;
}
```

```
prompt> digits2
enter an integer between 1000 and 9999: 8732
eight seven three two
prompt> digits2
enter an integer between 1000 and 9999: 7003
seven zero zero three
prompt> digits2
enter an integer between 1000 and 9999: 1000
one zero zero zero
```

The function `PrintFour` prints a four-digit number. We know how to peel the last digit from a number using the modulus and division operators, `%` and `/`. In *digits2.cc*, a four-digit number is printed by printing the first three digits using the function `PrintThree`, then printing the final digit using the function `PrintDigit`. For example, to print 1357 we first print 135, which is `1357/10`, by calling `PrintThree`, and then print `"seven"`, the last digit of 1357 obtained using `1357%10`. Printing a three-digit number is a similar process: first print a two-digit number by calling `PrintTwo`, and then print the last digit. For example, to print 135 we first print 13, which is `135/10`, and then print `"five"`, which is `135%10`. Continuing with this pattern we call `PrintOne` and `PrintDigit` to print a two-digit number. Finally, to print a one-digit number we simply print the only digit.

The code in *digits2.cc* should offend your emerging sense of programming style. Each of the functions `PrintFour`, `PrintThree`, and `PrintTwo` are virtually identical except for the name of the function, `PrintXXXX`, that each one calls (e.g., `PrintThree` calls `PrintTwo`). We can combine the similar code in all the `PrintXXXX` functions. Rather than using four separate functions, each one processing a certain range of numbers, we can rewrite the nearly identical functions as a single function `Print`. This is shown in *digits3.cc*, Prog. 10.2.

Program 10.2   digits3.cc

```
#include <iostream.h>
#include "CPstring.h"
#include "prompt.h"
```

```
// recursion: print English form of each digit
// in an integer: 123 -> "one two three"
// Owen Astrachan, 7/11/96

void PrintDigit(int num)
// precondition: 0 <= num < 10
// postcondition: prints english equivalent, e.g., 1->one,...9->nine
{
    if (0 == num)       cout << "zero";
    else if (1 == num)  cout << "one";
    else if (2 == num)  cout << "two";
    else if (3 == num)  cout << "three";
    else if (4 == num)  cout << "four";
    else if (5 == num)  cout << "five";
    else if (6 == num)  cout << "six";
    else if (7 == num)  cout << "seven";
    else if (8 == num)  cout << "eight";
    else if (9 == num)  cout << "nine";
    else cout << "?";
}

void Print(long int number)
// precondition: 0 <= number
// postcondition: prints English equivalent of number
//                e.g., 1235 -> "one two three five"
{
    if (0 <= number && number < 10)
    {
        PrintDigit(number)
    }
    else
    {
        Print(number / 10);
        cout << " ";
        PrintDigit(number % 10);
    }
}

int main()
{
    int number = PromptRange("enter an integer",0,1000000);

    Print(number)
    cout << endl;
    return 0;
}
```

OUTPUT

```
prompt> digits3
enter an integer between 1 and 1000000: 13
one three
prompt> digits3
```

```
enter an integer between 1 and 1000000: 7
seven
prompt> digits3
enter an integer between 1 and 1000000: 170604
one seven zero six zero four
```

The if statement in Print from *digits3.cc* corresponds to the equivalent if in the function PrintOne from the previous program, *digits2.cc*. A number in the range 0–9 is simply printed by calling PrintDigit. In all other cases, the code in the body of the else statement in Print from *digits3.cc*, Prog. 10.2, is the same code in the functions from *digits2.cc*, Prog. 10.1.

Although you may think that the function Print is calling itself in *digits3.cc*, it is not. As shown in Fig. 10.1, four separate functions named Print are called when the user enters 1478. These functions are identical except for the value of the parameter number stored in each function. The first Print, shown in the upper-left corner of Fig. 10.1, receives the argument 1478 and stores this value in number. Since the value of number is greater than 10, the else statements are executed. A function Print is called with the argument

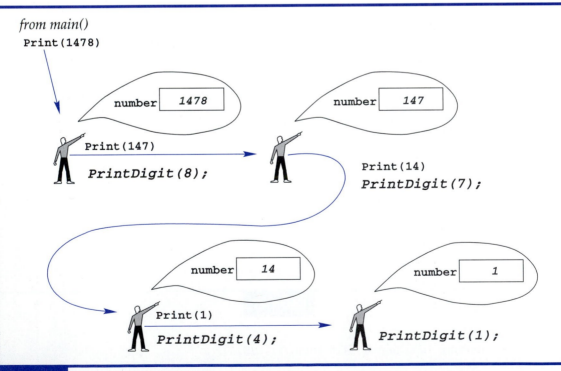

Figure 10.1   Recursively printing digits.

`1478 / 10`, which is 147. This is not the same function as in the upper left, but another version of the function `Print`, in essence a clone of `Print`, except that the value of `number` is different. Altogether there are four clones of the `Print` function, each with its own parameter `number`. The last clone called (lower-right corner of Fig. 10.1) does not generate another `Print` call, since the value of `number` is between 0 and 9. The `if` statement is executed, and the function `PrintDigit` is called with the argument 1. It's important to realize that this is the first call of `PrintDigit`, so the first digit printed is "one." Although each clone executes the statement `PrintDigit(number % 10)`, this statement is executed only after the recursive clone function call to `Print`. Each clone waits for control to return from the recursive call, except for the last function, which doesn't make a recursive call. The first clone called is the last clone to print a digit, so the last digit printed is `1478 % 10`, which is 8. This means the last word printed is "eight."

You'll need to develop two skills to understand recursive functions.

1. The ability to reason about a recursive function so that you can determine what the function does.
2. The ability to think recursively so that you can write recursive functions to solve problems.

Developing the second skill is more difficult than the first, but practice with reasoning about recursive functions will help with both skills.

General Rules for Recursion

When you write a loop, you reason about when the loop will stop executing so that you don't write an infinite loop. You must take the same care when writing recursive functions to avoid an infinite succession of recursively called clones. Each clone uses space, so you won't be able to actually generate an infinite number of clones, but you can easily use up all the memory in your computing environment if you're not careful. To avoid an infinite chain of recursive calls, each recursive function must include a **base case** that does not make a recursive call. The base case in `Print` of *digits3.cc*, Prog. 10.2, is a single-digit number identified by this test:

```
if (0 <= number && number < 10)
```

A function's base case is usually determined by finding a value, or a set of values, that does not require much work to compute. We'll reuse an example from an earlier Excursion Section (Sec. 4.9) that computes a^n, the value of one number raised to a power, as another example of recursion (see Prog. 4.15, *logexpo.cc*, page 164, but the code will be reproduced in the function `Power` that follows).

If you're asked to calculate 3^8, you could multiply $3 \times 3 \times 3 \times 3 \times 3 \times 3 \times 3 \times 3$. You could also calculate $3^4 = 81$ and then calculate $81 \times 81 = 6561$, since $3^8 = 3^4 \times 3^4$. The second method uses far fewer multiplications to calculate a^n than the first. The method is summarized in the following.

$$a^n = \begin{cases} 1 & \text{if } n = 0 \\ a^{n/2} \times a^{n/2} & \text{if } n \text{ is even} \\ a \times a^{n/2} \times a^{n/2} & \text{if } n \text{ is odd (note that } n/2 \text{ truncates to an integer)} \end{cases}$$

For example, to calculate 4^{11} using this method, we first calculate $4^{11/2} = 4^5 =$ 1024 and then multiply $4 \times 1024 \times 1024 = 4,194,304$. The base case requires no power calculation and no recursion. The base case in the formula corresponds to an exponent of zero. For nonzero exponents, the recursion comes from the calculation of $a^{n/2}$ in the formula. We'll write a function Power with two parameters: one for the base a and one for the exponent n in calculating a^n. A recursive implementation of the formula is given in the function Power (note that there is one recursive call and the value returned by the call is stored in a local variable semi):

```
double Power(double base, int expo)
// precondition: expo >= 0
// postcondition: returns base^expo (base to the power expo)
{
    if (0 == expo)
    {
        return 1.0;                        // correct for zeroth power
    }
    else
    {
        double semi = Power(base,expo/2);  // build answer from this

        if (expo % 2 == 0)                 // even exponent
        {
            return semi*semi;
        }
        else                               // odd exponent
        {
            return base*semi*semi;
        }
    }
}
```

The calculation of 3^{21} using Power(2,21) generates six clone Power functions with expo values 21, 10, 5, 2, 1, 0. Since the recursive call uses expo/2 as the value of the second argument, the total number of recursive calls is limited by how many times the original argument can be divided in half.

The six clones are shown in Fig. 10.2, where the value of expo can be used to determine the sequence of recursive calls. The result of each recursive call is stored in the local variable semi of the function that made the call and is used to calculate the returned result. Just as each iteration of a loop body changes values so that the loop test eventually becomes false and the loop terminates, each recursive call should get closer to the base case. This ensures that the chain of recursively called clones will eventually stop. In general, recursive functions are built from calling similar, but simpler functions. The similarity yields recursion; the simplicity moves toward the base case.

```
cout << Power(3.0,21) << endl;
```

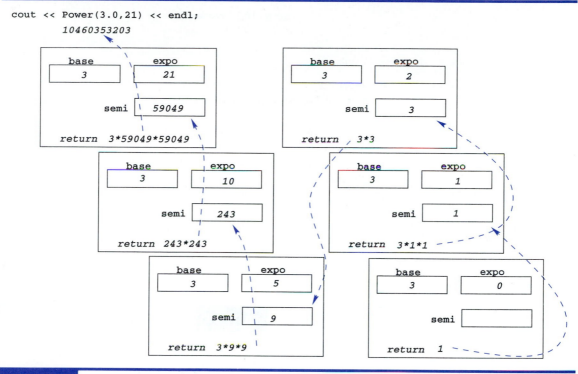

Figure 10.2   Recursive calls to calculate 3^{21}.

Program Tip: Keep two rules in mind when developing recursive functions:

1.   Identify a base case that does not make any recursive calls.
2.   Solve the problem by making recursive calls that are similar, but simpler, i.e., that move towards the base case.

Infinite Recursion

You must guard against writing functions that result in infinite recursion, that is, functions that generate a potentially endless number of recursive calls. When you forget a base case, infinite recursion results, as shown in *recdepth.cc*, Prog. 10.3. The output for Prog. 10.3 came from a Sun workstation using the g++ that compiler; it shows that nearly 75,000 recursive memory calls are made before memory is exhausted.

Program 10.3   recdepth.cc

```
#include<iostream.h>

// Owen Astrachan
// illustrates problems with "infinite" recursion

void
Recur(int depth)
{
    cout << depth << endl;
    Recur(depth+1);
}

int main()
{
    Recur(0);
    return 0;
}
```

OUTPUT

```
prompt> recdepth
0
1

some output removed

74867
74868
Segmentation fault (core dumped)
```

The maximum number of clones, or recursive calls, is limited by the memory of the computer used and on certain settings of the programming environment. For example, using Turbo C++ yields an illegal instruction error after making 530 calls. Borland C++ generates a *General Protection Exception* after roughly 225 calls.[1] As a programmer you must be careful when writing recursive functions. You should always identify a base case that does not make any recursive calls.

You may study methods in more advanced courses that involve changing a recursive function to a nonrecursive function. This is often a difficult task.

---

[1] If the *Test Stack Overflow* compiler option is checked, 178 calls are made when the stack size is 100,000.

Sometimes, however, it is possible to write a simple nonrecursive version of a recursive function. Nevertheless, some functions are much more easily written using recursion; we'll study examples of these functions in the next section.

10.2   Recursion and Directories

In this section we'll use recursion to solve problems that cannot be solved without recursion unless auxiliary data structures are used. The recursive functions find information about files and directories stored on disk. Almost all computers have an operating system in which directories help organize the many files you create and use. For example, you may have a directory for each of the computer courses you have taken, a directory for the electronic mail you receive, and a directory for your homepage on the World Wide Web. Using directories to organize files makes it easier for you to find a specific file. Directories contain files as well as **subdirectories,** which can also contain files and subdirectories. For example, the hierarchical arrangement of directories enables you to have a `courses` directory in which you have subdirectories for English, computer science, biology, and political science courses. A diagram of some of my directories and files for this book is shown in Fig. 10.3. Directories are shown as file folders, and files are shown as rectangles.

In this section we investigate classes that use recursion to process directory hierarchies. For example, we will develop a program that mimics what some operating systems do (and some don't) in determining how much space files use on disk. We will also develop a program that scans a hierarchy of directories to find a file whose name you remember but whose location you have forgotten.

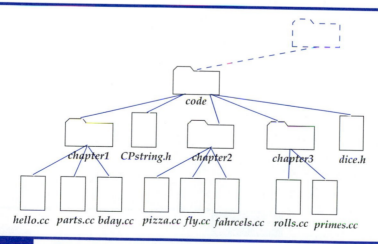

hello.cc parts.cc bday.cc   pizza.cc fly.cc fahrcels.cc   rolls.cc primes.cc

Figure 10.3   Hierarchy of directories and files.

Classes for Traversing Directories

Program 10.4, *files.cc*, prompts the user for the name of a directory and then prints all the files in that directory. This kind of listing is often needed when opening files from within a word processor; you must be able to type or click on the name of the file you want to edit. The variable `dir` is a class `DirStream` object. The `DirStream` class supports iteration using `First`, `IsDone`, `Next`, and `Current` similarly to other classes (e.g., the class `RandomWalk` from *walk.h,* Prog. 7.3.)

Program 10.4   files.cc

```
#include <iostream.h>
#include "direct.h"
#include "CPstring.h"
#include "prompt.h"

// illustrates use of the DirStream and DirEntry classes
// Owen Astrachan

int main()
{
    DirStream dir;                      // directory information
    DirEntry entry;                     // one entry from a directory
    int num = 0;                        // each file is numbered in output

    string name = PromptString("enter name of directory: ");
    dir.open(name);

    if (dir.fail())
    {
        cerr << "could not open directory " << name << endl;
        exit(1);
    }

    for(dir.First(); ! dir.IsDone(); dir.Next())
    {
        entry = dir.Current();
        if (! entry.IsDir() )
        {
            num++;
            cout << "(" << num << ") " << entry.Name() << endl;
        }
    }
    return 0;
}
```

OUTPUT

```
prompt> files
enter name of directory: chap1
```

```
(1)  hello.cc
(2)  hello2.cc
(3)  makehead.cc
(4)  bday.cc
(5)  bday2.cc
(6)  oldmac1.cc
(7)  oldmac2.cc
(8)  order.cc
(9)  order2.cc
(10) names.cc
(11) sqname.cc
(12) names2.cc
(13) names3.cc
(14) bigname.cc
(15) parts.cc
prompt> files
enter name of directory: chap22
could not open directory chap22
```

The member function `DirStream::Current()` returns a `DirEntry` object. Repeated calls of `Current`, in conjunction with the iterating functions `IsDone` and `Next`, return each entry in the directory. These directory entries are either files or subdirectories. In *files.cc*, the member function `DirEntry::IsDir()` differentiates files from directories, returning true when the `DirEntry` object is a directory and false otherwise. If the `if` statement is removed, so that the name of every entry returned by `Current` is printed, then the output changes slightly as shown in the following output:

OUTPUT

```
prompt> files
enter name of directory: chap1
(1)  .
(2)  ..
(3)  hello.cc
(4)  hello2.cc
same files as previous run
(16) bigname.cc
(17) parts.cc
```

The filename . (a single period) represents the current directory. The filename .. (a double period) represents the parent directory. This convention is followed by many operating systems. The member functions for the class `DirEntry` and the class `DirStream` are diagrammed in Fig. 10.4.

The header file, *direct.h*,[2] that contains declarations for the classes `DirEntry` and `DirStream`, is provided online. Program 10.5 lists the comments that describes each member function. The iterating functions `First`, `IsDone`, and `Next` work as they do in the class `WordStreamIterator` (*countw3.cc*, Prog. 6.4, page 270); it is an error to call `Current` when `IsDone` returns true.

Recursion and Directory Traversal

Program 10.4, *files.cc*, prints all the files in a given directory. Some applications require lists of subdirectories, and the files within the subdirectories, as well. For example, to calculate the total amount of disk space used by all files and directories, a program must accumulate the sum of file sizes in all subdirectories. We'll modify *files.cc*, Prog. 10.4 (page 496), so that it prints both files and subdirectories (and files and subdirectories of the subdirectories, and so on). As a first step, we'll move the `for` loop that iterates over all the files in a directory

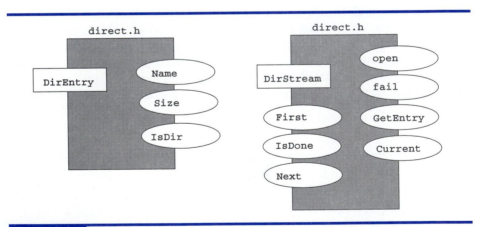

Figure 10.4   `DirEntry` and `DirStream` classes.

---

[2]On some systems the file may be named *directory.h.*

Program 10.5   direct2.h

```
#ifndef _DIRECTORY_H
#define _DIRECTORY_H


//
// author: Owen Astrachan
// date:  9/21/93
//
// modified 11/28/94
// modified  4/5/95
// modified 1/18/96
//
// classes for manipulating directories
// provide a standard interface for directory
// queries from C++ programs that can, in theory, be implemented
// on several platforms
//
// currently supported: UNIX, DOS, Mac in development
//
// the class DirEntry provides directory information
// accessible via methods Name, Size, and IsDir
// the private fields should really be in a handle-class hidden
// in directory.cc
//
// the class DirStream does I/O on directories
// it supports "standard" (for the Tapestry book)
// iterator methods/member functions
//


// *********  DirEntry member functions:
//
// string Name() -- returns name of file
// int Size()    -- returns size of file (in bytes)
// bool IsDir()  -- returns false if NOT directory, else true
//
// DirEntry()    -- constructor, directory entry undefined attributes

// *********  DirStream member functions:
//
// DirStream(string name) -- constructor (pass name of directory)
// DirStream()            -- default constructor (use current directory)
// void open(string name) -- opens directory stream with given name
// bool fail()            -- returns true if directory operation has
//                           failed, else returns false
// void close()           -- close stream
//
// bool GetEntry(DirEntry &)  -- get an entry
//                           (returns true if success, false if not)
//                           each call gets the "next" entry
//
```

```
// void First()          -- set DirStream so first entry is accessible
// bool IsDone()          -- returns true if done, false if not
//                           when false, accessing current entry is ok
// void Next()            -- advance to next entry
// DirEntry Current()     -- return current directory entry
//                           call only when IsDone == false
//
```

direct2.h

into a function `ProcessDir`. The final program, *subdir.cc*, Prog. 10.6, appears after a sample run of the the program, and Fig. 10.5 contains a diagram of the files and subdirectories that generate the sample run.[3]

OUTPUT

```
prompt> subdir
enter directory name tapestry
(1) chap2
        (1) chapter2.tex
        (2) progs
                (1) hello.cc
                (2) bday.cc
                (3) oldmac1.cc
        (3) oldmac.eps
(2) chap1
        (1) chapter1.tex
        (2) finalbigpic.eps
(3) chap3
        (1) chapter3.tex
        (2) progs
                (1) fly.cc
                (2) macinput.cc
                (3) pizza.cc
(4) book.tex
(5) library
        (1) CPstring.h
        (2) dice.h
        (3) dice.cc
```

---

[3]The suffixes in Fig. 10.5 represent different kinds of files: .cc for C++ source code, .tex for LaTeX files (a document-processing system), .eps for PostScript files, and so on.

```
#include <iostream.h>
#include "CPstring.h"
#include "direct.h"
#include "prompt.h"

// Owen Astrachan, 4/18/95
// print all entries in a directory (uses recursion)

void Tab(int count)
// postcondition: count tabs printed to cout
{
    int k;
    for(k=0; k < count; k++)
    {
        cout << "\t";
    }
}

void ProcessDir(const string & path, int tabCount)
// precondition: path specifies pathname to a directory
//               tabCount specifies how many tabs for printing
// postcondition: all files and subdirectories in directory 'path'
//                printed, subdirectories tabbed over 1 more than parent
{
    DirStream indir;
    DirEntry entry;
    int num = 0;                    // number of files in this directory
    indir.open(path);

    if (! indir.fail())        // directory opened successfully?
    {
        // check every entry in directory 'path'

        for(indir.First(); ! indir.IsDone(); indir.Next())
        {
            entry = indir.Current();   // either file or subdirectory

            // don't process self: ".", or parent directory: ".."

            if (entry.Name() != "." && entry.Name() != "..")
            {
                num++;
                Tab(tabCount);                      // print spaces
                cout << "(" << num << ") "
                     << entry.Name() << endl;     // and name

                if (entry.IsDir() )                 // process subdir
                {
                    // set path to subdirectory for recursive call
```

```
                    ProcessDir(path + DIR_SEPARATOR + entry.Name(),
                               tabCount+1);
                }
            }
        }
    } // end if (! fail)
}

int main()
{
    string dirname = PromptString("enter directory name ");
    ProcessDir(dirname,0);
    return 0;
}
```

subdir.cc

The files in a subdirectory are indented and numbered after the name of the subdirectory is printed. For example, the subdirectory named chap2 contains one subdirectory, progs, and two files, chapter2.tex and oldmac.eps. The subdirectory progs of chap2 contains three files: hello.cc, bday.cc, and oldmac1.cc. The directory tapestry, whose name is entered when the program is run, contains four subdirectories: chap1, chap2, chap3, and library, and one file: book.tex. Notice that the files in a subdirectory are numbered starting from one. We cannot control the order in which files and subdirectories are processed using First, Next, and Current. For example, the operating system may scan the files alphabetically, ordered by date of creation, or in some random order.

We'll investigate the function ProcessDir from *subdir.cc* in detail. One key to the recursion is an understanding of how a complete filename is

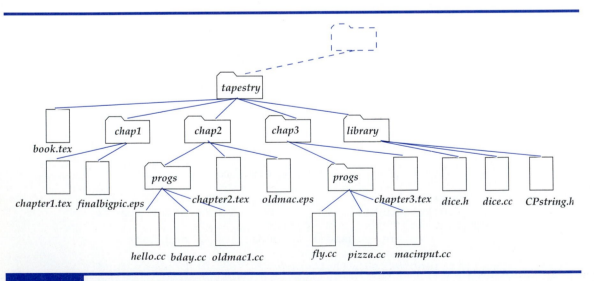

Figure 10.5   Files and subdirectories used in run of *subdir.cc*.

specified in hierarchical file systems. Most systems specify a complete file-name by including the directories and subdirectories that lead to the file. This sequence of subdirectories is called the file's **pathname.** The subdirectories that are pathname components are separated by different delimiters in different operating systems. For example, in UNIX the sep-arator is a forward slash, so the pathname to `fly.cc` shown in the output run of *subdir.cc* is `tapestry/chap3/progs/fly.cc`. On Win-dows and DOS computers the separator is a backslash, so the pathname is `tapestry\chap3\progs\fly.cc`. The string used as a separator is specified by the constant `DIR_SEPARATOR` in *direct.h*.

The `for` loop that iterates over directory entries in the function `ProcessDir` is similar to the loop used in *files.cc*, Prog. 10.4 (page 496). However, when the information stored in the `DirEntry` object `entry` represents a directory, the function `ProcessDir` makes a recursive call by constructing a pathname for the subdirectory. For example, the call `ProcessDir("tapestry",0)` directly generates four recursive calls for the subdirectories `chap2`, `chap1`, `chap3`, and `library`, as diagrammed in Fig. 10.5. The pathname for the subdirectory `chap3` is formed from the expression `path + DIR_SEPARATOR + entry.Name()`, where `path` is `"tapestry"` and `entry.Name()` is `"chap3"`. The value of `tabCount` is calculated from the expression `tabCount+1` so that the arguments for the recursive call are

```
ProcessDir("tapestry/chap3",1);
```

This recursive call will, in turn, generate a recursive call for the subdirectory `progs` by concatenating the value of parameter `path`, `"tapestry/chap3"`, with the value of `entry.Name()`, `"progs"`.

Examine the output run of *subdir.cc* on the directory `tapestry` (page 500), diagrammed in Fig. 10.6. Each clone of the function `ProcessDir` is shown as a stick figure. The call `ProcessDir(dirname,0)` from `main` is shown in the upper-left corner of Fig. 10.6 as `ProcessDir("tapestry",0)`; `dirname` has the value `"tapestry"`. Each recursive clone of `ProcessDir` has its own formal parameters `path` and `tabCount` and its own local variables `indir`, `entry`, and `num`. The execution of *subdir.cc* shown above is diagrammed in Fig. 10.6, where each clone is labeled with the values of parameters `path` and `tabCount` and local variable `num`. Only the recursive clones and calls are diagrammed; each recursive clone will print all the files in the subdirectory specified by the clone's `path` parameter. For example, the four clones generated by calls from the upper-left clone of `ProcessDir` are shown with `num` values 1, 2, 3, and 5. When `num` is 4, the file `book.tex` is printed as shown in the output from *subdir.cc*.

As shown in the output of the program, the files and subdirectories in `tapestry` are processed by `Next` and `Current` in the following order.

1. chap2
2. chap1

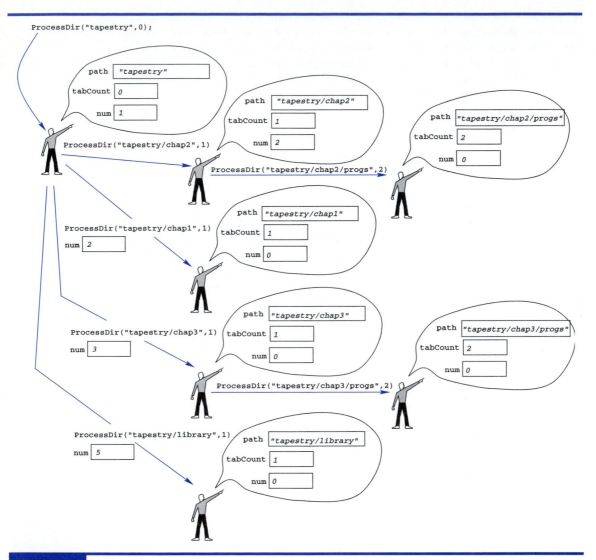

Figure 10.6   Recursive calls of `ProcessDir`.

3. chap3
4. book.tex
5. library

The first file/subdirectory printed and processed is (1) `chap2`. The number 1 is the value of local variable `num` shown in the stick figure in the upper left corner. The files/subdirectories of `chap2` are shown indented one level. The indentation level is determined by the value of parameter `tabCount`, which is

1 because of the recursive call of `ProcessDir`:

```
ProcessDir(path + DIR_SEPARATOR + entry.Name(),tabCount+1);
```

The value passed as the second parameter is `tabCount+1`, which in this case is `0+1=1`. Because the value passed is always one more than the current value, each recursive call results in one more level of indentation. The output of *subdir.cc* shows that the `progs` subdirectory is the second entry printed in the `chap2` directory. The first entry printed is `chapter2.tex`. The recursive call generated by `progs`, shown in Fig. 10.6 as the call `ProcessDir("tapestry/chap2/progs",2)`, shows that `num` has the value two when the call is made reflecting that `progs` is printed as the second entry under `chap2: (2) progs`.

Like all functions, the recursively called functions communicate only via passed parameters. There is nothing magic or different in the case of recursively called functions; each function just happens to have the same name as the function that calls it.

Properties of Recursive Functions

At most, three clones of function `ProcessDir` exist at one time, as shown in Fig. 10.6. The three clones at the top of the figure exist at the same time (with `path` values of `"tapestry"`, `"tapestry/chap2"`, and `"tapestry/chap2/progs"`). When the recursive call that process, the `chap2/progs` subdirectory finishes executing, the clone with `path` parameter `"tapestry/chap2"` still has one more entry to process: `oldmac.eps` (see the output). Then this clone finishes executing, and only the first version of `ProcessDir`, invoked by the call `ProcessDir("tapestry",0)`, exists.

A recursive call for the `chap1` subdirectory is then made. When the clone invoked by the call `ProcessDir("tapestry/chap1",1)` finishes executing, a recursive call is made for the `chap3` subdirectory. This, in turn, makes a recursive call for the `chap3/progs` subdirectory. Note that at this point the value of `num` for the original `ProcessDir` is 3, as shown in Fig. 10.6. Finally, after printing `(4) book.tex`, the subdirectory `library` generates the final recursive call `ProcessDir("tapestry/library",1)`; the value of `num` is 5 as shown.

10.1. Based on the output generated by *subdir.cc*, Prog. 10.6 (page 504) for the directory `tapestry`, what would be the output of the program *files.cc*, Prog. 10.4 (page 496) if run on `tapestry`? If the `if` statement checking for a directory is removed from `files.cc` and the program run on `tapestry`, what would the output be?

10.2. The `for` loop used in *files.cc* and *subdir.cc* for iterating over all directory entries can be replaced by a `while` loop that uses the member function `GetEntry` and a call `indir.GetEntry(entry)`. What

Pause to reflect

is the loop test, and what single statement should be removed from the `for` loop?

10.3. Why is the `if` statement with test `if (entry.Name() != "."` `&& entry.Name() != "..")` used in *subdir.cc* necessary? Describe what would happen if the comparison `entry.Name() != "."` were removed, but the other comparison remained. What would happen if the comparison with `".."` were removed (but the other remained)?

10.4. Describe how the output of *subdir.cc* will change if the expression `tabCount+1` in the recursive call is replaced with `tabCount+2`.

10.5. If the call of `Tab` and the `cout << ...` statement in function `ProcessDir` of *subdir.cc* are moved *after* the `if (entry.IsDir())` statement, how will the output change (e.g., if the directory `tapestry` is used for input)?

10.3   Comparing Recursion and Iteration

As an apprentice software engineer and computer scientist you must learn to judge when recursion is the right tool for a programming task. We've already seen that recursion is indispensable when traversing directories. As an apprentice, you should learn part of the programming folklore of recursion. We'll use two common examples to investigate tradeoffs in implementing functions recursively and iteratively.

The factorial function. In *fact.cc,* Prog. 5.7 (page 192), the function `Factorial` computes the **factorial** of a number where $n! = 1 \times 2 \times \cdots \times n$. A loop accumulated the product of the first n numbers. An alternative version of the factorial function is defined mathematically using this definition:

$$n! = \begin{cases} 1 & \text{if } n = 0 \\ n \times (n-1)! & \text{otherwise} \end{cases}$$

According to the definition, $6! = 6 \times 5!$. What, then, is to be done about $5!$? According to the definition, it is $5 \times 4!$. This process continues until $1! = 1 \times 0!$ and $0! = 1$ by definition. The method of defining a function in terms of itself is called an **inductive** definition in mathematics and leads naturally to a recursive implementation. The base case of $0! = 1$ is essential since it stops a potentially infinite chain of recursive calls. As we noted in the first section of this chapter, the base case is often a case that requires little or no computation, such as the calculation of zero factorial, which, by definition, is one. Recursive and iterative versions of the factorial function are included and tested in *facttest.cc,* Prog. 10.7. Statements are included to check if the values returned by the recursive and iterative functions are different, but the values returned are always the same when I run the program.

Program 10.7   facttest.cc

```cpp
#include <iostream.h>
#include "ctimer.h"
#include "prompt.h"

const int FACT_LIMIT = 35;

long int RecFactorial(int num)
// precondition: 0 <= num
// postcondition: returns num! (num factorial)
{
    if (0 == num)
    {
        return 1;
    }
    else
    {
        return num * RecFactorial(num-1);
    }
}

long int Factorial(int num)
// precondition: 0 <= num
// postcondition: returns num! (num factorial)
{
    long int product = 1;
    int count;
    for(count=1; count <= num; count++)
    {
        product *= count;
    }
    return product;
}

int main()
{
    CTimer rtimer,itimer;
    int j,k;
    long int val1,val2;
    int iters = PromptRange("enter # of iterations",1,1000000);

    for(k=0; k < iters; k++)    // compute factorials specified # of times
    {

        for(j=0; j <= FACT_LIMIT; j++)
        {
            rtimer.Start();                        // time recursive version
            val1 = RecFactorial(j);
            rtimer.Stop();

            itimer.Start();                        // time iterative version
            val2 = Factorial(j);
            itimer.Stop();
```

```
         if (val1 != val2)                          // note any differences
         {
              cout << "calls differ for " << j << endl;
              cout << "recursive = " << val1
                   << " iterative = " << val2 << endl;
         }
      }
   }
   cout << iters << " recursive trials " << rtimer.CumulativeTime() << endl;
   cout << iters << " iterative trials " << itimer.CumulativeTime() << endl;
   return 0;
}
```

OUTPUT

prompt> *facttest*
enter # of iterations between 1 and 1000000: *1000*
1000 recursive trials 2.09
1000 iterative trials 0.95
prompt> *facttest*
enter # of iterations between 1 and 1000000: *10000*
10000 recursive trials 22.02
10000 iterative trials 9.31

run on another computer (Pentium/100)

enter # of iterations between 1 and 1000000: *10000*
10000 recursive trials 3.52
10000 iterative trials 2.51

The `CTimer` class provides stopwatch capabilities for timing sections of a program. The interface is diagrammed in Fig. 10.7, and a listing of *ctimer.h*, Prog. 4.16, is given on page 167. The member function `CTimer::CumulativeTime` returns the total number of seconds recorded by the timer (since the last use of `Reset`). The function `CTimer::ElapsedTime` returns the seconds between the most recent uses of `Start` and `Stop`.

The recursive function `RecFactorial` is similar to the inductive definition of factorial given earlier. You will get better at understanding recursive functions as you gain more experience, but two ideas are helpful.

1. Believe the recursion works. This means that you *assume* that the recursive call works correctly, and you examine the code to see that the result of the recursive call is *used* correctly. For example, in calculating 4!, you assume that the call to calculate 3! yields the correct result: 6. The statement that uses this result

```
         return num * RecFactorial(num-1);
```

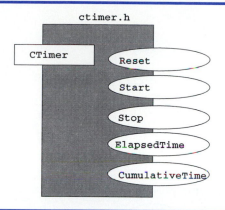

ctimer.h

CTimer

Reset

Start

Stop

ElapsedTime

CumulativeTime

Figure 10.7 Interface diagram for CTimer class (reproduced).

will then return 4×6, the value of num times the result of the recursive call. This is the correct answer for 4!.

2. Trace the recursive calls to see that the clones produce the correct results. This can be a tedious task, but some people like the assurance of understanding precisely how the recursively called functions work together. (A trace is shown in Fig. 10.8 for the computation of 5!).

To compute 5!, six clones of the factorial function are needed (and exist at the same time), as shown in Fig. 10.8. The first call, e.g., from main, is shown in the upper left as RecFactorial(5). The recursive calls are shown as solid arrows. The value passed to parameter num is shown in each clone. The return value is calculated by the expression num * RecFactorial(num-1); this is shown by the dashed lines. For example, the last clone called generates no recursive calls and returns 1. This value is used to calculate 1×1 so that 1 is returned from the clone with parameter num == 1. Each returned value is plugged into the expression num * RecFactorial(num-1) as the value of the recursive call, finally yielding $5 \times 24 == 120$, which is returned to main.

Based on the sample runs, which of the recursive and iterative functions is best? The answer is—as it is so often—"*it depends.*" It depends on (at least) how many times the factorial function will be called, it depends on what kind of computer is used, and it depends on what compiler is used. When run on the Pentium computer, the difference between the two versions is less than one second for 10,000 calls, whereas the results on the other computer (a SUN Sparc 20) are more drastically different.

Fibonacci Numbers

Fibonacci numbers (used in an Excursion Exercise on page 173) are integral in many areas of mathematics and computer science. These numbers occur in

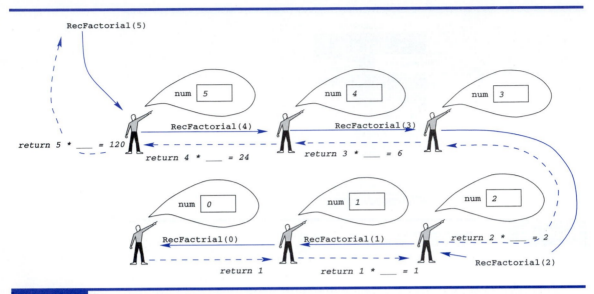

RecFactorial(5)

num 5

num 4

num 3

RecFactorial(4)

RecFactorial(3)

return 5 * ___ = 120

return 4 * ___ = 24

return 3 * ___ = 6

num 0

num 1

num 2

RecFactrial(0)

RecFactorial(1)

return 2 * ___ = 2

return 1

return 1 * ___ = 1

RecFactorial(2)

Figure 10.8 Recursive calls of `RecFactorial`.

nature as well [PL90]. For example, the scales on pineapples are grouped in Fibonacci numbers. In [Emm93], Fibonacci numbers are cited as the conscious basis of works by the composers Bartok and Stockhausen. Knuth [Knu73a] describes the mathematical constant $\phi = \frac{1}{2}(1 + \sqrt{5})$ as "intimately connected with the Fibonacci numbers," and the ratio of ϕ to 1 is "said to be the most pleasing proportion aesthetically, and this opinion is confirmed from the standpoint of computer programming aesthetics as well." The first 20 Fibonacci numbers are given below; this sequence originated in 1202 with Leonardo Fibonacci, whom Knuth calls "by far the greatest European mathematician before the Renaissance."

1 1 2 3 5 8 13 21 34 55 89 144 233 377 610 987 1597 2584 4181 6765

In general, each number in this sequence is the sum of the two numbers before it; the first two Fibonacci numbers are the exception to this rule. In keeping with tradition in C++ numbering schemes, the first Fibonacci number is $F(0)$; i.e., we start numbering from zero rather than one. This leads to the inductive or recursive definition of the Fibonacci numbers:

$$F(n) = \begin{cases} 1 & \text{if } n = 0 \text{ or } n = 1 \\ F(n-1) + F(n-2) & \text{otherwise} \end{cases}$$

As is the case with the recursive definition of factorial, the recursive definition of the Fibonacci numbers can be translated almost verbatim into a C++ function. The function `RecFib` is shown in *fibtest.cc,* Prog. 10.8. The function `Fib` computes Fibonacci numbers iteratively. The difference in this case between the recursive and iterative functions is much more pronounced than it was for the factorial function. If the constant FIB_LIMIT is changed, the difference is magnified. The runs in the following output use a limit of 30, but only 10 trials are run. Note that $F(30) = 1,346,269$.

```
                          OUTPUT

prompt> fibtest
enter # of iterations:   10
10 recursive trials 35.75
10 iterative trials 0

run on another computer (Pentium/100)

enter # of iterations:   10
10 recursive trials 22.97
10 iterative trials 0
```

Program 10.8   fibtest.cc

```cpp
#include <iostream.h>
#include "ctimer.h"
#include "prompt.h"

// Illustrates "bad" recursion for computing Fibonacci numbers
// Owen Astrachan 7/28/95

const int FIB_LIMIT = 20;              // largest fib # calculated

long int RecFib(int n)
// precondition: 0 <= n
// postcondition: returns the n-th Fibonacci number
{
    if (0 == n || 1 == n)
    {
        return 1;
    }
    else
    {
        return RecFib(n-1) + RecFib(n-2);
    }
}

long int Fib(int n)
// precondition: 0 <= n
// postcondition: returns the n-th Fibonacci number
```

```
{
    long int first = 1;
    long int second = 1;
    long int temp;
    int k;
    for(k=0; k < n; k++)
    {
        temp = first;
        first = second;
        second = temp + second;
    }
    return first;
}

int main()
{
    CTimer rtimer,itimer;
    int j,k;
    long int val1, val2;
    int iters = PromptRange("enter # of iterations",1,100000);

    for(k = 0; k < iters; k++)
    {
        for(j=0; j <= FIB_LIMIT; j++)
        {
            rtimer.Start();
            val1 = RecFib(j);
            rtimer.Stop();

            itimer.Start();
            val2 = Fib(j);
            itimer.Stop();
            if (val1 != val2)
            {
                cout << "calls differ for " << j << endl;
                cout << "recursive = " << val1
                    << " iterative = " << val2 << endl;
            }
        }

    }
    cout << iters << " recursive trials " << rtimer.CumulativeTime() << endl;
    cout << iters << " iterative trials " << itimer.CumulativeTime() << endl;
    return 0;
}
```

OUTPUT

```
prompt> fibtest
enter # of iterations: 1000
1000 recursive trials 29.53
1000 iterative trials 0.25
```

run on another computer (Pentium/100)
```
enter # of iterations: 1000
1000 recursive trials 18.72
1000 iterative trials 0.09
```

run on another computer (486/33)
```
enter # of iterations: 1000
1000 recursive trials 77.8
1000 iterative trials 7.32
```

The timer is not precise enough to capture the time for the iterative function. However, 1000 trials of the iterative function calculating $F(30)$ takes roughly 0.3 second. Extrapolating the result of 35.75 seconds for 10 trials of the recursive function shows that 1000 iterations would take 35,750 seconds, or nearly 10 hours, for what is done in less than half a second using the iterative function. What are the differences between calculating $n!$ and $F(n)$ that cause such a disparity in the timings of the recursive and iterative versions? For example, is the time due to the recursive depth (number of clones)? As we will see, the depth of recursive calls is not what causes problems here. Only 30 clones exist at one time to calculate $F(30)$. However, the total number of clones (or recursive calls) is 2,692,637. This huge number of calls is illustrated in Fig. 10.9 for the calculation of $F(6)$, which requires a total of 25 recursive calls.

If you examine Fig. 10.9 carefully, you'll see that the same recursive call is made many times. For example, $F(1)$ is calculated eight times. Since the computer is not programmed to remember a number previously calculated,

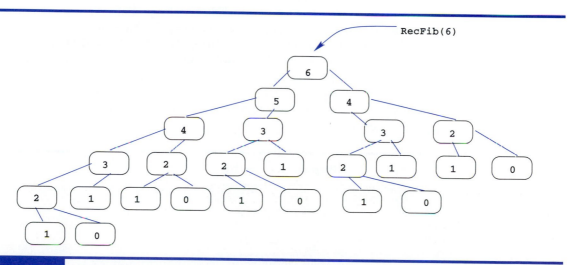

Figure 10.9   Recursive calls of `RecFib(6)`(numbers show value of num).

when the call $F(6)$ generates calls $F(5)$ and $F(4)$, the result of $F(4)$ is not stored anywhere. When the calculation of $F(5)$ generates $F(4)$ and $F(3)$, the entire sequence of calls for $F(4)$ is made again. The iterative function `Fib` in *fibtest.cc* is fast because it makes roughly n additions to calculate $F(n)$; the number of additions is **linear** (see Excursion Section 2.10 for a discussion of linear growth). In contrast, the recursive function makes an **exponential** number of additions. In this case the speed of the machine is not so important, and the recursive function is *much* slower than the iterative function.

In later courses you may study methods that will permit you to determine when a recursive function should be used. For now, you should know that recursion is often very useful, as with the directory searching functions, and sometimes is very bad, as with the recursive Fibonacci function.

10.4   Scope and Lifetime

In this section we'll discuss methods that are used to alter the lifetime of a variable in a class or program and the scope of declaration. We'll use two simple examples that extend the computation of Fibonacci numbers from *fibtest.cc*, Prog. 10.8, and then use these examples as a springboard to explore general principles of lifetime and scope. We touched on scope in Sec. 5.5; the scope of a declaration determines where in a function, class, or program the declaration can be used. *Lifetime* refers to the duration of storage associated with a variable. To be precise, scope is a property of a name or identifier (e.g., of a variable, function, or class) that determines where in a program the identifier can be used. Lifetime is a property of the storage or memory associated with an object.

Global Variables

Suppose we want to calculate exactly how many times the function `RecFib` is called to compute `RecFib(30)` in *fibtest.cc*, Prog. 10.8. We can increment a counter in the body of `RecFib`, but we need to print the value of the counter in `main` when the initial call of `RecFib` returns. The **global variable** `gFibCalls` in *recfib.cc*, Prog. 10.9, keeps this count. The scope of a global variable is an entire program as opposed to a local variable that can be accessed only within the function in which the variable is defined. In C++ a global variable has **file scope** since it is accessible in all functions defined in the file in which the global variable appears.

Program 10.9   recfib.cc

```
#include <iostream.h>
#include "vector.h"
#include "prompt.h"

// Illustrates "bad" recursion for computing  Fibonacci numbers
// and a global variable to count # function calls
// Owen Astrachan 7/28/95
```

```
const int FIB_LIMIT = 40;
int gFibCalls = 0;

long int RecFib(int n)
// precondition: 0 <= n
// postcondition: returns the n-th Fibonacci number
{
    gFibCalls++;
    if (0 == n || 1 == n)
    {
        return 1;
    }
    else
    {
        return RecFib(n-1) + RecFib(n-2);
    }

}

int main()
{
    int num = PromptRange("compute Fibonacci #",1,FIB_LIMIT);
    cout << "Fibonacci # " << num << " = " << RecFib(num) << endl;
    cout << "total # function calls = " << gFibCalls << endl;
    return 0;
}
```

OUTPUT

```
prompt> recfib
compute Fibonacci # between 1 and 40: 10
Fibonacci # 10 = 89
total # function calls = 177
prompt> recfib
compute Fibonacci # between 1 and 40: 20
Fibonacci # 20 = 10946
total # function calls = 21891
prompt> recfib
compute Fibonacci # between 1 and 40: 30
Fibonacci # 30 = 1346269
total # function calls = 2692537
```

I use the prefix g to differentiate global variables from other variables. Global variables are declared outside of any function, usually at the beginning of a file. Unlike local variables, global variables are automatically initialized to zero unless a different initialization is specified when the variable is defined. There are rare occasions when global variables must be used, as with gFibCalls in *recfib.cc*. However, using many global variables in a large program quickly leads to maintenance headaches because it is difficult to keep track of what identifiers have been used. In particular, it's possible for a global declaration to be hidden or **shadowed** by a local declaration, as shown in *scope2.cc*, Prog. 10.10. The local variable funCounter in Dummy hides, or shadows, the global variable of the same name so that the function calls are not counted correctly.

Program 10.10   scope2.cc

```
#include <iostream.h>

// illustrates difference between global and local scope
// Owen Astrachan, 7/29/94

int funCounter;                              // count function calls

void Dummy();

int main()
{
    int loop;
    cout << "how many iterations ";
    cin >> loop;

    int k;
    for(k=0; k < loop; k++)
    {
        Dummy();
        cout << "in main = " << funCounter << endl;
    }
    return 0;
}

void Dummy()
// postcondition: tracks number of times function is called
{
    int funCounter = 0;

    funCounter++;                // which funCounter is this?
}
```

OUTPUT

```
prompt> scope2
how many iterations 5
in main = 0
in main = 0
in main = 0
in main = 0
in main = 0
```

The local variable `funCounter` defined in `Dummy` is incremented each time `Dummy` is called rather than the global variable because the most recent declaration hides all other declarations using the same identifier. However, the global variable is printed in `main`, so the count appears as zero each time the loop executes. It is possible to access global variables even when they're shadowed. If the increment of `funCounter` in `Dummy` is changed as shown in the following, a run of the program shows the effect of the change.

```
::funCounter++;
```

OUTPUT

```
prompt> scope2
how many iterations 5
in main = 1
in main = 2
in main = 3
in main = 4
in main = 5
```

The scope resolution operator `::`, applied to an identifier, references a global object (or function) with that name. In *scope2.cc* the local variable defined and initialized to zero within `Dummy` is not accessed again after the initialization. Of course, the convention of using the `g` prefix with global variables makes it unlikely that a local variable will hide a global variable, but you should avoid using global variables in general.

Hidden Identifiers

Even nonglobal identifiers can be shadowed, as illustrated in *scope.cc*, Prog. 10.11. Because the braces, `{}`, that delimit function bodies and compound statements cannot overlap, there is always a scope "closest" to an identifier's declaration. It is possible for an identifier to be reused within a **nested scope.** A scope is nested in another when the braces that define the scope occur within another set of braces. When a variable is used, it may seem unclear in which scope the variable is declared, but the "nearest" definition is the one used.

The variable `first` defined within the scope of the `if` statement is accessible only within the `if` statement. Assignments to `first` within the statement do not affect the variable `first` defined at the beginning of `main`, as shown in the output where `first` is printed as 4, 8, 16, and 32 except for the indented values, which show `first` within the `if` statement. It is also apparent from the output that the value of `second` defined in `main` is not affected by assignments to `second` in the `while` loop since these assignments are made to a variable defined within the loop. Schematically the scopes are illustrated

Program 10.11   scope.cc

```cpp
#include <iostream.h>

// illustrates scope

int main()
{
    int first = 2;
    int second = 0;

    while (first < 20)
    {
        int second = first * 2;                  // shadows previous second
        cout << "\tsecond = " << second << endl;
        first *= 2;
        if (first > 10)
        {
            int first = second;                  // shadows previous first
            first = first/10;
            cout << "\tfirst = " << first << endl;
        }
        cout << "first = " << first << endl;
    }
    cout << "second = " << second << endl;
    return 0;
}
```

OUTPUT

```
prompt> scope
        second = 4
first = 4
        second = 8
first = 8
        second = 16
        first = 1
first = 16
        second = 32
        first = 3
first = 32
second = 0
```

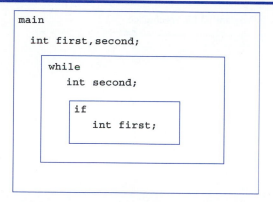

Figure 10.10 Boxing to illustrate scope.

in Fig. 10.10, in which a variable is known within the innermost box in which it appears. The variable `second` defined within the `while` loop shadows the variable defined at the top of the function `main`. In general, shadowing leads to unexpected, although well-defined, behavior.

> **Program Tip: Avoid using identifiers with the same name in nested scopes.** Hidden and shadowed identifiers lead to programs that are difficult to understand and ultimately lead to errors.

10.5 Static Definitions

Global variables maintain their value throughout the execution of a program; they exist for the duration of the program. In contrast, a local variable defined in a function is constructed anew each time the function is called. We can change the lifetime of a local variable so that the variable maintains its value throughout a program's execution by using the word **static** as a modifier when the variable is defined. This is illustrated in *recfib2.cc*, Prog. 10.12. A static `Vector` is defined to keep track of recursive calls so that the same recursive call is never made more than once. For example, the first call of `RecFib(4)` results in recursive calls of `RecFib(3)` and `RecFib(2)`. When these values are calculated, the values are stored in the `Vector storage` so that the values can be retrieved, for example, when `RecFib(2)` is called again. The key idea is that a recursive call is made once. All subsequent recursive calls with the same argument are evaluated by retrieving the stored value from `storage` rather than by making a recursive call. Notice how many fewer calls are made compared to the calculations of *recfib.cc*, Prog. 10.9.

Program 10.12   recfib2.cc

```
#include <iostream.h>
#include "vector.h"
#include "prompt.h"

// Illustrates "bad" recursion for computing  Fibonacci numbers
// but made better using a static Vector for storing values
// Owen Astrachan 7/28/95

const int FIB_LIMIT = 40;
int gFibCalls = 0;

long int RecFib(int n)
// precondition: 0 <= n
// postcondition: returns the n-th Fibonacci number
{
    static Vector<int> storage(FIB_LIMIT+1,0);

    gFibCalls++;
    if (0 == n || 1 == n)
    {
        return 1;
    }
    else if (storage[n] == 0)
    {
        storage[n] = RecFib(n-1) + RecFib(n-2);
        return storage[n];
    }
    else
    {
        return storage[n];
    }
}

int main()
{
    int num = PromptRange("compute Fibonacci #",1,FIB_LIMIT);
    cout << "Fibonacci # " << num << " = " << RecFib(num) << endl;
    cout << "total # function calls = " << gFibCalls << endl;
    return 0;
}
```

OUTPUT

```
prompt> recfib2
compute Fibonacci # between 1 and 40: 10
Fibonacci # 10 = 89
total # function calls = 19
```

```
prompt> recfib2
compute Fibonacci # between 1 and 40: 20
Fibonacci # 20 = 10946
total # function calls = 39
prompt> recfib2
compute Fibonacci # between 1 and 40: 30
Fibonacci # 30 = 1346269
total # function calls = 59
```

Like global variables, static local variables are automatically initialized to zero. However, it is a good idea to make initializations explicit. Static variables are constructed and initialized when a program first executes, *not* when a function is first called. The variable `storage` must be static in *recfib2.cc*, or the values stored will not be maintained over all recursive calls. For recursive functions like `RecFib`, only one static variable is defined for all the recursive clones. The variable `storage` is local to `RecFib` but maintains its values for the duration of the program *recfib2.cc*.

10.6. The code segment shown here illustrates shadowing. Describe an input sequence that causes the words `Banana yellow Banana red Apple` to be printed (one per line).

 Pause to reflect

```
string last = "Apple";
string word;
while (cin >> word && word != last)
{
    string last = "Banana";
    cout << last << " " << word << endl;
}
cout << last << endl;
```

Describe an input sequence that causes the single word `Apple` to be printed. If the definition of `last` within the `while` loop is removed, what input sequence generates `Banana yellow Banana red Apple`?

10.7. In the code fragment in the previous problem, if the definition of `last` before the `while` loop is removed, will the segment compile? Why?

10.8. If the statement `cout << funCounter << endl` is added after `funCounter` is incremented in the original version of Prog. 10.10 (in which the local variable is incremented), what will be printed if the function is called 10 times? Why?

10.9. If every function in a program begins with the statement

```
::funCounter++;
```

will the variable funCounter correctly keep track of the number of function calls (to any function) made? Is there a situation in which this will yield an incorrect count of the number of function calls? What about a recursive function?

10.6   Chapter Review

In this chapter we discussed recursion, a useful programming technique that can be misused. A recursive function does not "call itself," but calls a clone function, an identical copy of itself. Each recursively called function has its own parameters and its own local variables. We also covered variable scope and lifetime. A variable's scope is the part of the program in which the variable can be accessed. A variable's lifetime is how long the variable exists.

Important topics covered include:

■   Recursion is an alternative to iteration using loops. Recursive functions iterate by making recursive calls.

■   Recursively called functions use memory; there is a limit on the number of recursive calls or recursively called functions. This limit depends on the amount of memory in the computer.

■   Some problems are naturally solved with recursive functions and would be difficult to solve using loops.

■   Some functions should not be coded recursively. One example is computing Fibonacci numbers.

■   Recursive functions are often divided into two cases: a base case that does not involve a recursive call and a recursive case that makes a recursive call. The recursive call should get closer to the base case so that there are a finite number of recursive calls.

■   A variable's scope determines in which part of the program the variable can be accessed. Variables can be defined globally, accessible in all functions, or locally, accessible in the function in which the variable is defined.

■   Variables can be defined within the braces, { and }; this means a variable's scope can be restricted to any compound statement, e.g., accessible only within a loop.

■   The scope resolution operator, ::, is used to access global variables when the variable identifier is shadowed by a local variable.

■   Static variables maintain values throughout program execution, unlike non-static variables, whose lifetime is for the duration of the function in which the variable is defined.

MAURICE WILKES   (b. 1913)

Figure 10.11

Maurice Wilkes is one of the elder statesmen of computer science. He was a peer of Alan Turing and worked in England on the EDSAC computer. Wilkes was awarded the second Turing award in 1967.

In work written in 1955 and published in 1956 [Wil56], Wilkes offers advice for team programming projects. It is interesting that the advice still seems to hold 40 years later. "It is very desirable that all the programmers in the group should make use of the same, or substantially the same, methods. Not only does this facilitate communication and cooperation between the members of the group, but it also enables their individual experience more readily to be absorbed into the accumulated experience of the group as a whole... the group should be organized to produce, on a common plan, the input routines, basic library subroutines, and error-diagnosis subroutines... it will be much easier, once they are prepared, for an individual programmer to make use of them rather than to set about designing a system of his own." Wilkes wonders where computer science fits—whether it is more closely tied to mathematics or to engineering [Wil95]:

> Many students who are attracted to a practical career find mathematics uncongenial and difficult; certainly it is not the most popular part of an engineering course for the majority of students. Admittedly, mathematics trains people to reason, but reasoning in real life is not of a mathematical kind. Physics is a far better training in this respect.
>
> The truth may be that computer science does not by itself constitute a sufficiently broad education, and that it is better studied in combination with one of the physical sciences or with one of the older branches of engineering.

Wilkes pioneered many of the ideas used in current computer architectures including microprogramming and cache memories. In 1951 he published the first book on computer programming. He has this to say about object-oriented programming:

> [Object-oriented programming is] in my view, the most important development in programming languages that has taken place for a long time. ... Object-oriented programming languages may still be described as being in a state of evolution. No completely satisfactory language in this category is yet available.

For more information, see [Wil87, Wil95, Wil56].

10.7   Exercises

10.1 Modify Prog. 10.6, *subdir.cc,* so that instead of printing the names of all files and subdirectories, the size of each subdirectory is calculated, returned, and printed. Use the member function `DirEntry::Size()` to calculate the size (usually expressed in bytes) of each file. Print the size of each subdirectory in a format that makes it easy to determine where large files might be found. Do *not* print the names of every file; just print the names of the subdirectories and the size of all the files within the subdirectory.

10.2 Pascal's triangle can be used to calculate the number of different ways of choosing k items from n different items. The first seven rows of Pascal's triangle are

$$
\begin{array}{ccccccccccccc}
 & & & & & & 1 & & & & & & \\
 & & & & & 1 & & 1 & & & & & \\
 & & & & 1 & & 2 & & 1 & & & & \\
 & & & 1 & & 3 & & 3 & & 1 & & & \\
 & & 1 & & 4 & & 6 & & 4 & & 1 & & \\
 & 1 & & 5 & & 10 & & 10 & & 5 & & 1 & \\
1 & & 6 & & 15 & & 20 & & 15 & & 6 & & 1
\end{array}
$$

If we use C_k^n to represent the number of ways of choosing k items from n, then $C_0^n = 1$ and $C_n^n = 1$ as shown in the outside edges of the triangle. For values of k other than 0 and n, the following relationship holds.

$$C_k^n = C_{k-1}^{n-1} + C_k^{n-1}$$

Viewed in the triangle, each entry other than the outside 1's is equal to the two entries in the row above it diagonally up and to the left and right. For example,

$$C_2^5 = 10 = (C_1^4 + C_2^4) = (4 + 6)$$

Write a function *Choose,* with two parameters n and k, that returns the number of ways that k items can be chosen from n. Use this function to print the first 15 rows of Pascal's triangle.

10.3 Repeat the previous exercise, but try to develop a mechanism for storing the results of each recursive call using a static local variable so that no calculation is made more than once. This is tricky using `Vector` variables, but it is possible if you can develop a method for calculating a unique index for each pair of values used in the recursive calls. (You can also use a `Matrix`, described in the next chapter.)

10.4 The value C_k^n can also be computed using the factorial function and this equation:

$$C_k^n = \frac{n!}{k! \cdot (n - k)!}$$

Write two versions of a function to compute the value of C_k^n, one based on the factorial function (where factorial is computed iteratively, *not* recursively) and one based on the recursive definition in the previous exercise. Time how long it takes to compute different values of C_k^n.

10.5 The towers of Hanoi puzzle is traditionally studied in computer science courses. The roots of the puzzle are apparently found in the Far East, where a tower of golden disks is said to be used by monks. The puzzle consists of three pegs and a

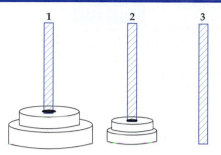

Figure 10.12   The towers of Hanoi.

set of disks that fit over the pegs. Each disk is a different size. Initially the disks are on one peg, with the smallest disk on top, the largest on the bottom, and the disks arranged in increasing order. The object is to move the disks, one at a time, to another peg. No disk can be placed on a smaller disk.

If four disks are used and all disks are initially on the leftmost peg, numbered **1** in Fig. 10.12, the following sequence of disk moves shows how to reach the configuration of disks shown. A move is indicated by the pegs involved since the topmost disk is always moved.

```
Move 1 to 3
Move 1 to 2
Move 3 to 2
```

To finish moving all the disks from the left peg to the middle peg, the top disk is moved from 1 to 3, then (recursively) the disks are moved from peg 2 to peg 3. The largest disk is then moved from peg 1 to peg 2. Finally (and recursively), the disks from peg 3 are moved to peg 2. Pegs are numbered 1, 2, and 3. To move 7 disks from peg 1 to peg 2, the function call Hanoi(1,2,3,7) is used. To move these seven disks, two recursive calls are necessary: Hanoi(1,3,2,6), which moves six disks from peg 1 to peg 3 (with peg 2 as the auxiliary peg), followed by a nonrecursive, plain disk move of the largest disk from peg 1 to peg 2, followed by a recursive Hanoi(3,2,1,6) to move the six disks from peg 3 to peg 2 (with the now empty peg 1 as the auxiliary peg).

Consider a function Hanoi using the following prototype.

```
void Hanoi(int from, int to, int aux, int numDisks)
// precondition:  top numDisks-1 disks on 'from' peg
//                are all smaller than top disk on
//                'aux' peg
// postcondition: top numDisks disks moved from
//                'from' peg to 'to' peg
```

Write the function Hanoi. The base case, and the single-disk case, should print the peg moves. For example, the output for a 4-disk tower is shown on the next page.

```
                               OUTPUT


prompt> hanoi
number of disks:   between 0 and 30: 4
move from 1 to 3
move from 1 to 2
move from 3 to 2
move from 1 to 3
move from 2 to 1
move from 2 to 3
move from 1 to 3
move from 1 to 2
move from 3 to 2
move from 3 to 1
move from 2 to 1
move from 3 to 2
move from 1 to 3
move from 1 to 2
move from 3 to 2
```

10.6 Modify the *hanoi.cc* program from the previous exercise to time how long it takes
for different numbers of disks from 1 to 25. Comment out (put // before each
statement) the statements that print disk moves so that the number of recursive
calls is timed. Use a global variable that is incremented each time `Hanoi` executes.
Print the value of this variable for each number of disks so that the total number of
disk moves is printed, along with the time it takes to move the disks. This can lead
to a new measure of computer performance: **DIPS,** for "disks per second."

Sorting, Algorithms, and Matrices

No transcendent ability is required in order to
make useful discoveries in science;
the edifice of science needs its masons,
bricklayers, and common labourers
as well as its foremen, master-builders,
and architects. In art nothing worth doing can
be done without genius;
in science even a very moderate capacity can
contribute to a supreme achievement.

BERTRAND RUSSELL
Mysticism and Logic

Many human activities require collections of items to be put into some particular order. The post office sorts mail by ZIP code for efficient delivery; telephone books are sorted by name to facilitate finding phone numbers; and hands of cards are sorted by suit to make it easier to go fish. Sorting is a task performed well by computers; the study of different methods of sorting is also intrinsically interesting from a theoretical standpoint. In Chapter 8 we saw how fast binary search is, but binary search requires a sorted list as well as random access. In this chapter we'll study different sorting algorithms and methods for comparing these algorithms. We will also extend our study of arrays and vectors to include two-dimensional vectors.

11.1 Sorting an Array

There are several elementary sorting algorithms, details of which can be found in books on algorithms; Knuth [Knu736] is an encyclopedic reference. Some of the elementary algorithms are much better than others, both in terms of performance and in terms of ease of coding. Contrary to what some books on computer programming claim, there are large differences between these elementary algorithms. In addition, these elementary algorithms are more than good enough for sorting reasonably large vectors,[1] *provided that the good elementary algorithms are used.*

In particular, there are three "classic" simple sorting algorithms:

- Selection sort
- Insertion sort
- Bubble sort

We'll develop selection sort in this section and insertion sort as part of a program that counts words. However, a few words are in order.

> **Program Tip: Under *no* circumstances should you use bubble sort.** Bubble sort is the slowest of the elementary sorts, for reasons we'll explore as an exercise. Bubble sort is worth knowing about only so that you can tell your friends what a poor sort it is.

Selection Sort

The basic algorithm behind selection sort is quite simple and is similar to the method used in shuffling tracks of a CD explored and programmed in *cdshuffl.cc*, Prog. 8.4 (page 375). To sort from smallest to largest in a vector named A, the following method is used:

1. Find the smallest entry in A. Swap it with the first element A[0]. Now the smallest entry is in the first location of the vector.
2. Considering only vector locations A[1], A[2], A[3], ..., find the smallest item and swap it with A[1]. Now the first two entries of A are in order.
3. Continue this process by finding the smallest element of the remaining vector elements and swapping it appropriately.

This algorithm is outlined in code in *sort.cc*, Prog. 11.1. The function Sort will sort a Vector of ints. Each time through the loop in the function Sort, the

---

[1]What is "reasonably large"? The answer, as it often is, is "It depends"—on the kind of element sorted, the kind of computer being used, and on how fast "pretty fast" is.

Program 11.1   sort1.cc

```
int MinIndex(Vector<int> & a, int first, int last)
// precondition: 0 <= first, first <= last, a[first]...a[last]
//               are initialized
// postcondition: returns index of smallest entry in a between
//                first and last inclusive
{

}

void Swap(int & a, int & b)
// postcondition: swap a and b
{
    int temp = a;
    a = b;
    b = temp;
}

void Sort(Vector<int> & a, int numElts)
// precondition: a contains numElts ints
// postcondition: elements of a are sorted in nondecreasing
//                order
{
    int k;
    int index;
    for(k=0; k < numElts - 1; k+=1)
    {
        index = MinIndex(a,k,numElts - 1); // find smallest from k to end
        Swap(a[k], a[index]);
    }
}
```

sort1.cc

index of the smallest entry of those not yet in place (from k to the end of the vector) is determined by calling the function `MinIndex`. This function (which will be shown shortly) returns the index, or location, of the smallest element, which is then stored/swapped into location k. This process is diagrammed in Fig. 11.1. The shaded boxes represent vector elements that are in their final position. Although only five elements are shaded in the last "snapshot," if five out of six elements are in the correct position, the sixth element must be in the correct position as well.

Note that each time the loop test `k < numElts - 1` is evaluated, the statement "All vector elements in positions $0 \ldots k-1$ are in their final position" is true. Recall that any statement that is true each time a loop test is evaluated is called a **loop invariant**. In this case the statement is true because the first time the loop test is evaluated, the range $0 \ldots k-1$ is $[0 \ldots -1]$, which is an empty

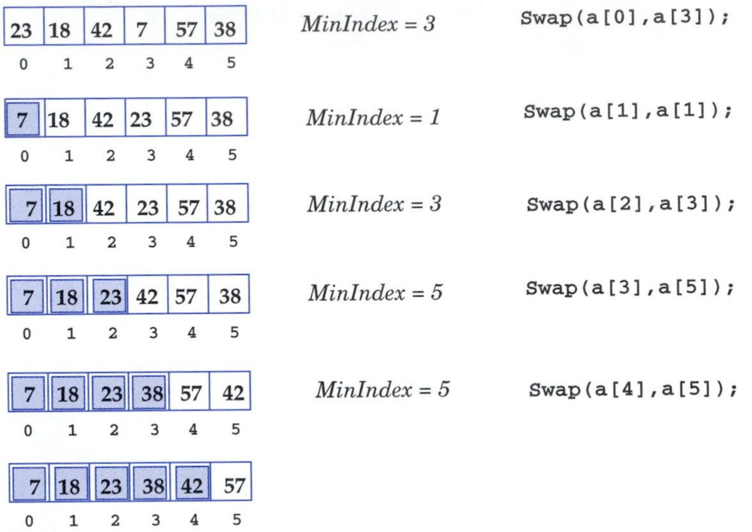

23	18	42	7	57	38	$MinIndex = 3$	`Swap(a[0],a[3]);`
0	1	2	3	4	5		

7	18	42	23	57	38	$MinIndex = 1$	`Swap(a[1],a[1]);`
0	1	2	3	4	5		

7	18	42	23	57	38	$MinIndex = 3$	`Swap(a[2],a[3]);`
0	1	2	3	4	5		

7	18	23	42	57	38	$MinIndex = 5$	`Swap(a[3],a[5]);`
0	1	2	3	4	5		

7	18	23	38	57	42	$MinIndex = 5$	`Swap(a[4],a[5]);`
0	1	2	3	4	5		

7	18	23	38	42	57	
0	1	2	3	4	5	

Figure 11.1   Selection sort.

range, consisting of no vector elements. As shown in Fig. 11.1, the shaded vector elements indicate that the statement holds after each iteration of the loop. The final time the loop test is evaluated, the value of k will be numElts - 1, the last valid vector index. Since the statement holds (it holds each time the test is evaluated), the vector must be sorted.

The function MinIndex is straightforward to write; its body is

```
int MinIndex(const Vector<int> & a, int first, int last)
// precondition: 0 <= first, first <= last, a[first]...a[last]
//               are initialized
// postcondition: returns index of smallest entry in a between
//               first and last inclusive
{
    int smallIndex = first;
    int k;
    for(k=first+1; k <= last; k++)
    {
        if (a[k] < a[smallIndex] )
        {
            smallIndex = k;
        }
    }
    return smallIndex;
}
```

This function illustrates a fence post problem. The first location of the vector a is used to initialize smallIndex, and then all other locations are examined. If a smaller entry is found in a, the value of smallIndex is changed to record the location of the new smallest item.

```
void Sort(Vector<int> & a, int numElts)
// precondition: a contains numElts ints
// postcondition: elements of a are sorted in nondecreasing
//                order
{
    int j,k,temp,minIndex;

    for(k=0; k < numElts - 1; k++)
    {
        minIndex = k;  // smallest item from k to end of a
        for(j=k+1; j < numElts; j++)
        {
            if (a[j] < a[minIndex])
            {
                minIndex = j;  // new smallest item
            }
        }
        temp = a[k];  // swap smallest item and kth item
        a[k] = a[minIndex];
        a[minIndex] = temp;
    }
}
```

sort2.cc

The function MinIndex, combined with Swap and Sort, yields a complete implementation of selection sort. Sometimes it's convenient to have all the code in one function rather than spread over three functions. This is certainly possible and leads to the code shown in *sort2.cc*, Prog. 11.2. However, as you develop code, it's often easier to test and debug when separate functions are used. This allows each piece of code to be tested separately.

The code in Prog. 11.2 works well for sorting a vector of numbers, but what about sorting vectors of strings or some other kind of element? If two vector elements can be compared, then the vector can be sorted based on such comparisons. A vector of strings can be sorted using the same code provided in the function Sort; the only difference in the functions is the type of the first parameter and the type of the local variable temp, as follows:

```
void Sort(Vector<string> & a, int numElts)
// precondition: a contains numElts strings
// postcondition: elements of a are sorted in nondecreasing
//                order
{
    int j,k,minIndex;
```

```
string temp;

// code here doesn't change

}
```

Both this function and the function `Sort` in *sort2.cc* could be used in the same program, because the parameter lists are different. In previous chapters we overloaded the + operator so that we could use it both to add numbers and to concatenate strings. In the same way, we can overload function names. That is, different functions with the same name can be used in the same program using C++ provided that the parameter lists of the functions are different.

In the examples here the function `Sort` is overloaded using three different kinds of vectors. The function `DoStuff` is overloaded, since there are two versions with different parameter lists. The names of the parameters do not matter; only the types of the parameters are important in resolving which overloaded function is actually called. It is *not* possible, for example, to use both functions `FindRoots` with the following prototypes in the same program, because the parameter lists are the same. The different return types are not sufficient to distinguish the functions:

> **Syntax: Function overloading**
>
> ```
> void Sort(Vector<int> & a,
>     int numElts)
> void Sort(Vector<string> & a,
>     int numElts)
> void Sort(Vector<double> & a,
>     int numElts)
>
> int DoStuff(int one, int two)
> int DoStuff(int one, int two,
>     int three)
> ```

```
int FindRoots(double one, double two);
double FindRoots(double first, double second);
```

Pause to reflect

11.1. What changes are necessary in Prog. 11.2, *sort2.cc*, so that the vector a is sorted into decreasing order rather than into increasing order? For example, why is it a good idea to change the name of the identifier `minIndex`, although the names of variables don't influence how a program executes?

11.2. Why is the test of the outer `for` loop in the sorting functions `k < numElts - 1` instead of `k < numElts`? Could the test be changed to the latter?

11.3. If the vector `counts` from Prog. 8.3, *letters.cc* (page 369), is passed to the function `Sort`, why won't the output of the fingerprint program be correct? What happens when the vector of counts is sorted in terms of the relationship of each vector entry to the corresponding letter? That is, if `counts['a'] = 103` indicates 103 occurrences of the character `'a'`, what happens when the 103 is moved?

11.4. How would a vector of `Date` be sorted (e.g., so that the earliest date track appears in the first vector cell of such a vector)?

SHAFI GOLDWASSER (b. 1958)

Figure 11.2 Shafi Goldwasser.

Shafi Goldwasser is Professor of Computer Science at MIT. She works in the area of computer science known as **theory,** but her work has practical implications in the area of secure cryptographic protocols—methods that ensure that information can be reliably transmitted between two parties without electronic eavesdropping. In particular, she is interested in using randomness in designing algorithms. She was awarded the first Gödel prize in theoretical computer science for her work.

So-called **randomized algorithms** involve (simulated) coin flips in making decisions. In [Wei94] a randomized method of giving quizzes is described. Suppose a teacher wants to ensure that students do a take-home quiz, but does not want to grade quizzes every day. A teacher can give out quizzes in one class, then in the next class flip a coin to determine whether the quizzes are handed in. In the long run, this results in quizzes being graded 50 percent of the time, but students will need to do all the quizzes.

Goldwasser is a coinventor of **zero-knowledge interactive proof protocols.** This mouthful is described in [Har92] as follows:

> Suppose Alice wants to convince Bob that she knows a certain secret, but she does not want Bob to end up knowing the secret himself. This sounds impossible: How do you convince someone that you know, say, what color tie the president of the United States is wearing right now, without somehow divulging that priceless piece of information to the other person or to some third party?

Using zero-knowledge interactive proofs it is possible to do this. The same concepts make it possible to develop smart cards that would let people be admitted to a secure environment without letting anyone know exactly who has entered. In some colleges, cards are used to gain admittance to dormitories. Smart cards could be used to gain admittance without allowing student movement to be tracked.

Goldwasser has this to say about choosing what area to work in:

> Choosing a research area, like most things in life, is not the same as solving an optimization problem. Work on what you like, what feels right. I know of no other way to end up doing creative work.

For more information see [EL94].

11.2   Function Templates

Although it is possible to overload a function name, the sorting functions in the previous sections are not ideal candidates for function overloading. This is because the code that would appear in each function is nearly identical. For example, if one program required functions to sort vectors of `ints`, `doubles`, and `strings`, the functions could be written and used, but the only differences in the code would be in the definition of the variable `temp` and in the kind of `Vector` passed to the function. Consider what might happen if a more efficient sorting algorithm is required. The code in each of the three functions must be removed, and the code for the more efficient algorithm inserted. Maintaining three versions of the function makes it much more likely that errors will eventually creep into the code, because it is difficult to ensure that whenever a modification is made to one sorting function, it is made to all of the sorting functions.

Fortunately, a mechanism exists in C++ that allows code to be reused rather than replicated. We have already used this mechanism behind the scenes in the implementation of the `Vector` class. A **function template**, sometimes called a **templated function,** is used when only the types of variables in a function need to be changed for different versions of the function. Program 11.3, *usesort.cc,* has a templated sort function to sort all the words read from a file specified by the user. Notice in the output that punctuation characters come before upper-case characters, which in turn come before lower-case characters.

Program 11.3   usesort.cc

```
#include <iostream.h>
#include "vector.h"
#include "worditer.h"

// Owen Astrachan, 7/30/95
// illustrates templated function for sorting
// reads file of words, sort words, prints words

template <class Type>
void
Sort(Vector<Type> & a, int numElts)
// precondition: a contains numElts ints
// postcondition: elements of a are sorted in nondecreasing
//                order
{
    int j,k,minIndex;
    Type temp;

    for(k=0; k < numElts - 1; k++)
```

```
    {
        minIndex = k  // smallest item from k to end of a
        for(j=k+1; j < numElts; j++)
        {
            if (a[j] < a[minIndex])
            {
                minIndex = j;  // new smallest item, remember where
            }
        }
        temp = a[k];  // swap smallest item and kth item
        a[k] = a[minIndex];
        a[minIndex] = temp;
    }
}


int main()
{
    int SIZE = 2000;                    // size of wordlist

    WordStreamIterator iter;            // to iterator over file
    Vector<string> list(SIZE);          // to store words
    int numWords = 0;                   // to count words
    string filename;
    int k;

    cout << "file name: ";
    cin >> filename;

    iter.Open(filename);
    for(iter.First(); ! iter.IsDone(); iter.Next())  // read words
    {
        if (numWords >= SIZE)
        {
            SIZE *= 2;
            list.SetSize(SIZE);
        }
        list[numWords] = iter.Current();
        numWords++;
    }

    Sort(list,numWords);                // sort words

    for(k=0; k < numWords; k++)         // print words
    {
        cout << list[k] << endl;
    }
    return 0;
}
```

usesort.cc

The templated sort function can be used with many different kinds of vectors. For example, each of the following `Sort` calls is correct C++ code.

```
Vector<int> numlist(2000);   // code assigns values to entries of numlist
Sort(numlist,2000);

Vector<double> readings(500);  // code assigns values to entries of readings
Sort(readings,500);
```

OUTPUT

```
prompt> usesort
file name: poe.txt
!ugh!-ugh!
A
A
A
A
A
A
Against
Allan
Amontillado
Amontillado

2,304 words removed

you
you.
your
your
your
your
your
your
your
```

Not all types of vectors can be sorted, however. The code in `Sort` compares vector elements using the < operator. Vector elements are also assigned with the = operator. If vector elements are not comparable or assignable, then the templated function `Sort` cannot be used. For example, it is not possible to sort vectors of `RandGen` elements, because it doesn't make sense to compare

RandGen variables to see which is larger. The following code generates an error message:

```
Vector<RandGen> vlist(30);
Sort(vlist,30);
```

The error message using the g++ compiler provides an indication of why the templated function will not work:

```
usesort.cc: In function 'void Sort(class Vector<RandGen> &, int)':
usesort.cc:11: no conversion from 'RandGen' and 'RandGen' to types
              with default 'operator <'
make: *** [usesort] Error 1
```

Syntax: Function template

```
template <class Type>
```
return type
function name (... Type *param-name* ...)

A function is defined as a templated function when it is preceded by the word **template** followed by an angle bracket delimited list of class identifiers that serve somewhat as type parameters. The identifier Type can be any identifier, for example <class Foo>. Then the identifier Foo can be used as a stand-in for a parameter type, the return type of the function, or a local variable type.

It is possible to have more than one template class parameter; for example, template <class VecType, class Number>. Then the identifiers VecType and Number can both be used as stand-ins for types in the templated function.

Although we will not use function templates extensively, you will certainly use them in later courses and more advanced programming projects. It is very common, for example, to use a templated Swap function to interchange the values of two parameters. In Prog. 11.4 a templated function swaps int, double, string, and ClockTime values.

Program 11.4   swap2.cc

```
#include <iostream.h>
#include "clockt.h"
#include "CPstring.h"

// illustrates use of template functions
// Owen Astrachan, 10/11/94

template <class Type>
void Swap(Type & a, Type & b)
//generic swap routine
{
    Type temp;
    temp = a;
```

```
        a = b;
        b = temp;
}

int main()
{
        int i1 = 1, i2 = 2;
        double d1 = 3.1415, d2 = 2.718;
        ClockTime c1(1,2,3), c2(4,5,6);
        char ch1 = 'a', ch2 = 'b';
        string s1 = "hello", s2 = "world";

        Swap(i1, i2);
        Swap(d1, d2);
        Swap(c1, c2);
        Swap(ch1, ch2);
        Swap(s1, s2);

        cout << i1 << " " << i2 << endl;
        cout << d1 << " " << d2 << endl;
        cout << c1 << " " << c2 << endl;
        cout << ch1 << " " << ch2 << endl;
        cout << s1 << " " << s2 << endl;
        return 0;
}
```

OUTPUT

```
prompt> swap2
2 1
2.718 3.1415
4:05:06 1:02:03
b a
world hello
```

11.3   Analyzing Sorts

We examined selection sort in Sec. 11.1 and mentioned two other sorts: bubble sort and insertion sort. Which of these is the best sort? As with many questions about algorithms and programming decisions, the answer is, "It depends"[2]—on the size of the vector being sorted, on the type of each vector element, on how critical a fast sort is in a given program, and many other characteristics of the application in which sorting is used. You might, for example, compare different sorting algorithms by timing the sorts using a computer. The program *timesort.cc*, Prog. 11.5 (page 544), uses the templated Sort function from *usesort.cc*, Prog. 11.3, to time two sorting algorithms. The graph in Fig. 11.3 pro-

---

[2]Note that the right answer is *never* bubble sort.

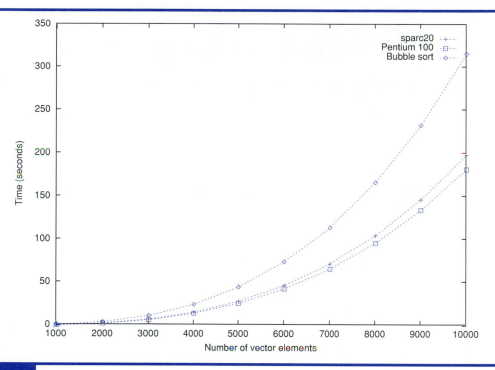

Figure 11.3 Timing selection sort on two computers (`int` vectors).

vides times for selection sort on two different computers for sorting `int` vectors; for purposes of comparison, a plot of bubble sort on the SPARC20 is included.

Although the timings are different, the curves have the same shape. The timings might also be different if selection sort were implemented differently; as by another programmer. However, the general shapes of the curves would not be different, since the shape is a fundamental property of the algorithm rather than of the computer being used, the compiler, or the coding details. The shape of the curve is called **quadratic,** because it is generated by curves of the family $y = ax^2$ (where a is a constant). To see (informally) why the shape is quadratic, we will count the number of comparisons between vector elements needed to sort an N-element vector. Vector elements are compared by the `if` statement in the inner `for` loop of function `Sort`:

```
if (a[j] < a[minIndex])
{
    minIndex = j;          // new smallest item, remember where
}
```

We'll first consider a 10-element vector, then use these results to generalize to an N-element vector. The outer `for` loop (with j as the loop index) iterates 9 times for a 10-element vector, because j has the values $0, 1, 2, \ldots, 8$. When $j = 0$, the inner loop iterates from $k = 1$ to $k < 10$, so the `if` statement is executed nine times. Since j is incremented by 1 each time, the `if` statement will be executed 45 times, since the inner loop iterates nine times, then eight times, and so on:

$$9 + 8 + 7 + 6 + 5 + 4 + 3 + 2 + 1 = \frac{9(10)}{2} = 45$$

The sum is computed from a formula for the sum of the first N integers; the sum is $N(N + 1)/2$. To sort a 100-element vector, the number of comparisons needed is $99(100)/2 = 4{,}950$. Generalizing, to sort an N-element vector, the number of comparisons is calculated by summing the first $N - 1$ integers:

$$\frac{(N - 1)(N)}{2} = \frac{N^2 - N}{2} = \frac{N^2}{2} - \frac{N}{2}$$

This is a quadratic, which at least partially explains the shape of the curves in Fig. 11.3.

O Notation

When the execution time of an algorithm can be described by a family of curves, computer scientists use *O* **notation** to describe the general shape of the curves. For a quadratic family, the expression used is $O(N^2)$. It is useful to think of the O as standing for **order,** since the general shape of a curve provides an approximation *on the order of* the expression rather than an exact analysis. For example, the number of comparisons used by selection sort is $O(N^2)$, but more precisely is $(N^2/2) - (N/2)$. Since we are interested in the general shape rather than the precise curve, coefficients like $\frac{1}{2}$ and lower-order terms with smaller exponents like $N/2$, which don't affect the general shape of a quadratic curve, are not used in O notation.

In later courses you may learn a formal definition that involves calculating limits, but the idea of a family of curves defined by the general shape of a curve is enough for our purposes. To differentiate between other notations for analyzing algorithms, the term **big-Oh** is used for O notation (to differentiate from little-oh, for example).

Algorithms like sequential search (see Table 8.2 on page 391) that are linear are described as $O(N)$ algorithms using big-Oh notation. This indicates, for example, that to search a vector of N elements requires $O(N)$ time. Again, this describes the shape of the curve, not the precise timing, which will differ depending on the compiler, the computer, and the coding.

Binary search, which requires far fewer comparisons than sequential search, is an $O(\log N)$ algorithm, as discussed in Sec. 8.4.

## 11.4	Quicksort

The graph in Fig. 11.3 suggests that selection sort and bubble sort are both $O(N^2)$ sorts.[3] In this section we'll study a more efficient sort called **quicksort**. Quicksort is recursive and is a three-step process.

---

[3]To be precise, the graph does not prove that bubble sort is an $O(N^2)$ sort; it provides evidence of this. To prove it more formally would require analyzing the number of comparisons.

1. A pivot element of the vector being sorted is chosen. Elements of the vector are rearranged so that elements less than or equal to the pivot are moved before the pivot. Elements greater than the pivot are moved after the pivot. This is called the **partition** step.
2. Quicksort (recursively) the elements before the pivot.
3. Quicksort (recursively) the elements after the pivot.

The partition step bears an explanation. Suppose a group of people must arrange themselves in order by age, so that the people are lined up, with the youngest person to the left and the oldest person to the right. One person is designated as the pivot person. All people younger than the pivot person stand to left of the pivot person and all people older than the pivot person stand to the right of the pivot. This is diagrammed in Fig. 11.4. In the first step, the 27-year-old woman is designated as the pivot. All younger people move to the pivot's left (from our point of view); all older people move to the pivot's right. It is imperative to note at this point that the 27-year-old woman *will not move again!* In general, after the rearrangement takes place, the pivot person (or vector element) is in the correct order relative to the other people (elements). Also, people to the left of the pivot always stay to the left.

After this rearrangement, a recursive step takes place. The people to the left of the 27-year-old pivot must now sort themselves. Once again, the first

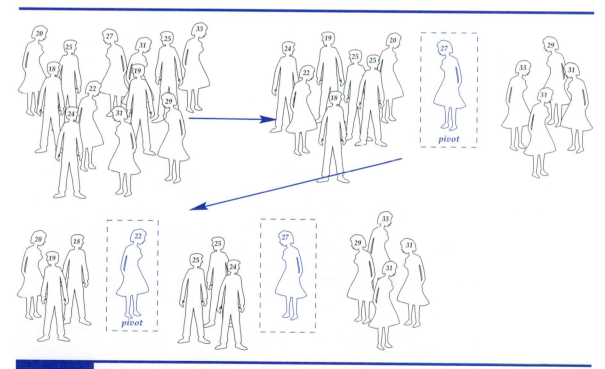

Figure 11.4   Partition step of quicksort.

step is to partition the group of seven people. A pivot is chosen—in this case, the 22-year-old woman. All people younger move to the pivot's left, and all people older move to the pivot's right. The group that moves to the right (two 25-year-olds and a 24-year-old) are now located between the two people who are in their final positions. To continue the process, the group of three (20, 18, and 19 years old) would sort themselves. When this group is done, the group of 25-, 25-, and 24-year-olds would sort themselves. At this point, the entire group to the left of the original 27-year-old pivot is sorted. Now the group to the right of this pivot must be recursively sorted.

The code for quicksort is very short, given a function to do the partitioning. For example, to sort an n-element int vector a, the call Quick(a,0,n-1) works, where Quick is

```
void Quick(Vector<int> & a,int first,int last)
// postcondition: a[first] <= ... <= a[last]
{
    int piv;

    if (first < last)
    {
        piv = Pivot(a,first,last);
        Quick(a,first,piv-1);
        Quick(a,piv+1,last);
    }
}
```

The three statements in the if block correspond to the three parts of quicksort. The function Pivot rearranges the elements of a between positions first and last and returns the index of the pivot element. This index is then used recursively to sort the elements to the left of the pivot (in the range [first... piv -1]) and the elements to the right of the pivot (in the range [piv+1... last]).

The Partition/Pivot Function

There are many different ways to implement the partition function. All these methods are linear, or $O(N)$, where N is the number of elements rearranged. We'll use a partition method described in [Ben86] that is simple to remember and that can be developed using invariants.

The diagrams in Fig. 11.5 show the sequence of steps used in partitioning the elements of a vector between (and including) locations first and last. Understanding the second diagram in the sequence is the key to being able to reproduce the code. The second diagram describes an invariant of the for loop that partitions the Vector. The for loop examines each vector element between locations first and last once; this ensures that the loop is linear, or $O(N)$, for partitioning N elements. The loop has the following form, where the element with index first is chosen as the pivot element:

```
for(k=first+1; k <= last; k++)
{
```

```
        if (a[k] <= a[first])
        {
            p++;
            swap(a[k], a[p])
        }
    }
```

As indicated by the question marks "???" in Fig. 11.5, the value of a[k] relative to the pivot is not known. If a[k] is less than or equal to the pivot, it belongs in the first part of the vector. If a[k] is greater than the pivot, it belongs in the second part of the vector (where it already is!). The if statement in Fig. 11.5 compares a[k] to the pivot and then reestablishes the picture as true, so that it is an invariant (true each time the loop test is evaluated).

This works because when p is incremented, it becomes the index of an element larger than the pivot, as shown in the diagram. The statement Swap(a[k],a[p]) interchanges an element less than or equal to the pivot, a[k], and an element greater than the pivot, a[p]. This informal reasoning should help convince you that the picture shown is an invariant and that it leads to a correct partition function. One more step is necessary, however; the invariant needs to be established as true the first time the loop test is evaluated. In this situation, the part of the vector labeled ??? represents the entire vector, because none of the elements have been examined.

In this case, the first element is arbitrarily chosen as the pivot element. Setting k = first+1 makes k the index of the leftmost unknown element,

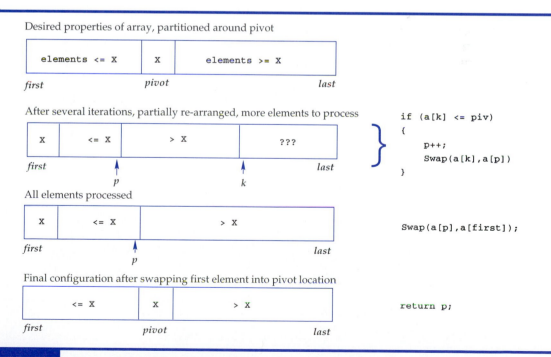

Figure 11.5   Picture of partition invariant.

the ??? section, as shown in the diagram. Setting p = first makes p the index of the rightmost element that is known to be less than or equal to the pivot, because in this case only the element with index first is known to be less than or equal to the pivot—it is equal to the pivot, because it *is* the pivot.

The last step is to swap the pivot element, which is a[first], into the proper location indexed by the variable p. This is shown in the final stage of the diagram in Fig. 11.5.

The partition function, combined with the three-step recursive function for quicksort just outlined, yields a complete sorting routine that is included in *timesort.cc*, Prog. 11.5. A function QuickSort calls the function Quick that actually does the work. This makes the parameter list of QuickSort the same as that of SelectSort. Such a dummy function, used to provide the user a more convenient or familiar interface, is called a **wrapper** function.

Program 11.5   timesort.cc

```
#include <iostream.h>
#include "ctimer.h"
#include "vector.h"
#include "rando.h"

// Owen Astrachan, 7/30/95
// time sorts, compare quick sort and selection sort

template <class Type>
void Swap(Type & a, Type & b)
// generic swap routine
{
    Type temp;
    temp = a;
    a = b
    b = temp;
}

template <class Type>
int Pivot(Vector<Type> & a, int first, int last)
// postcondition: returns piv such that
//                  first <= k <= piv, a[k] <= a[piv]
//                  piv < k <= last, a[piv] < a[k]
// (from Bently, Programming Pearls)
{
    int k,p=first;
    Type piv;

    piv = a[first];       // first element is pivot

    for(k=first+1; k <= last; k++)
    {
        if (a[k] <= piv)    // belongs in first "half"
        {
            p++;            // p now indexes "greater" elements
```

```
                Swap(a[k],a[p]);   // swap smaller and greater!
            }
    }
    Swap(a[p],a[first])    // put pivot in proper location
    return p;
}

template <class Type>
void Quick(Vector<Type> & a, int first, int last)
// postcondition: a[first <= ... <= a[list]
{
    int piv;

    if (first < last)
    {
        piv = Pivot(a,first,last);   // find pivot and divide vector
        Quick(a,first,piv-1);        // sort first "half"
        Quick(a,piv+1,last);         // sort other half
    }
}

template <class Type>
void QuickSort(Vector<Type> & a, int size)
// precondition: size = # of elements of a
// postcondition: a is sorted
{
    Quick(a,0,size-1);
}

template <class Type>
void SelectSort(Vector<Type> & a, int numElts)
// precondition: a contains numElts
// postcondition: elements of a are sorted in nondecreasing
//                order
{
    int j,k,minIndex;

    for(k=0; k < numElts - 1; k++)
    {
        minIndex = k;   // smallest item from k to end of a
        for(j=k+1; j < numElts; j++)
        {
            if (a[j] < a[minIndex])
            {
                minIndex = j;   // new smallest item, remember where
            }
        }
        Swap(a[k],a[minIndex]); // swap smallest item and kth item
    }
}

void Load(Vector<int> & a, int numElts)
// precondition: numElts < a.Length()
// postcondition: 0 <= a[k] = random integer <= INT_MAX
{
    int k;
```

```
    RandGen rando;

    for(k=0; k < numElts; k++)
    {
        a[k] = rando.RandInt();
    }
}

int main()
{
    Vector<int> list;                   // stores numbers to sort
    int minSize,maxSize;                // size range of vector
    int incr;                           // increment between sizes
    CTimer timer;
    int trials;                         // number of sorting trials
    int size,k;

    cout << "min and max size of vector: ";
    cin >> minSize >> maxSize;

    cout << "increment of size for each sort: ";
    cin >> incr;

    cout << "number of trials: ";
    cin >> trials;

    for(size=minSize; size <= maxSize; size += incr)
    {
        list.SetSize(size);

        for(k=0; k < trials; k++)
        {
            Load(list,size);
            timer.Start();
            QuickSort(list,size);
            timer.Stop();
        }
        cout << "size = " << size;
        cout << " time = " << timer.CumulativeTime()/trials
             << endl;
    }
    return 0;
}
```

OUTPUT

```
prompt> timesort
min and max size of vector: 1000 10000
increment of size for each sort: 1000
number of trials: 3
```

```
size = 1000   time = 0.0166667
size = 2000   time = 0.0566667
size = 3000   time = 0.106667
size = 4000   time = 0.18
size = 5000   time = 0.28
size = 6000   time = 0.403333
size = 7000   time = 0.546667
size = 8000   time = 0.713333
size = 9000   time = 0.923333
size = 10000  time = 1.14
```

You may get the idea from the sample runs that quicksort is *much* faster than selection sort. The plots in Fig. 11.6 show how much faster quicksort is; it takes 32 seconds to sort a 50,000-element vector, whereas 72 seconds are required for selection sort to sort a 7,000 element vector.

Analysis of Quicksort

With the limited analysis tools we have, a formal analysis of quicksort that provides a big-Oh expression of its running time is difficult. The choice of the

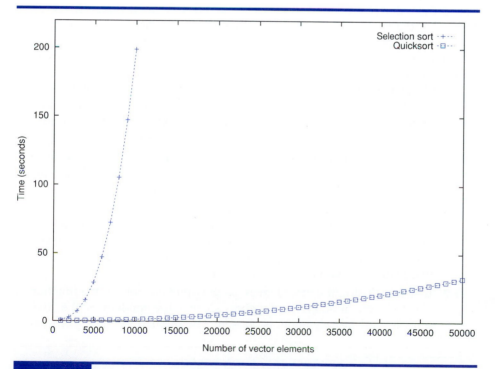

Figure 11.6 Timings for selection sort and quicksort (SPARC20).

pivot element in the partition step plays a crucial role in how well the method works. Suppose, for example, that in Fig. 11.4 the first person chosen for the pivot is the 18-year-old person. All the people younger than this person move to the person's left; all the older people move to the person's right. In this case there are no younger people. This means that the two subgroups that would be sorted recursively are not even approximately the same size. If a "bad" partition continues to be chosen in the recursively sorted groups, quicksort degenerates into a slower, quadratic sort. On the other hand, if the pivot is chosen so that each subgroup is roughly the same size (i.e., half the size of the group being partitioned) then quicksort works very quickly.[4]

Since the partition algorithm is linear, or $O(N)$, for an N-element vector, the **computational complexity,** or running time, of quicksort depends on how many partitions are needed. In the best case the pivot element divides the vector being sorted into two equal parts, as shown in Fig. 11.7.

If the vector shown in Fig. 11.7 has 16 elements, it is recursively partitioned into vectors of size 8, 4, 2, and 1 elements. There are 2, 4, 8, and 16 vectors of these respective sizes. This requires a total of $4 \times 16 = 64$ operations for the partitioning of a 16-element vector. In general, the number of operations needed is $\log_2(N) \times N$, since the number of times N can be divided in half is $\log_2(N)$. This makes quicksort an $O(N \log N)$ algorithm in the best case. It can be shown that on the average[5] quicksort is an $O(N \log N)$ algorithm. However, as we've noted, the worst case of quicksort is $O(N^2)$ for an N-element vector. It's possible to choose the partition in such a way that the worst case becomes extremely unlikely, but there are other sorts (that we will not cover here) that are always $O(N \log N)$ even in the worst case. Nevertheless, quicksort is not hard to code, and its performance is extremely good in general.

Table 11.1 provides data for comparing the running times of algorithms whose complexities are given by different big-Oh expressions. The data are for a (hypothetical) computer that executes one million operations per second.

Pause to reflect

11.5. Write a templated function `Print` to print the values in any kind of vector. Make the vector a `const` reference parameter, and pass the number of items stored in the vector as a parameter.

11.6. Write a templated function that reverses the elements stored in a vector so that the first element is swapped with the last, the second element is swapped with the second to last, and so on (make sure you don't undo the swaps; stop when the vector is reversed). Do not use extra storage; swap the elements in place.

11.7. Instead of using the first element as the pivot element in the function `Partition`, modify the function so that the median of the first, middle, and last elements is chosen. The median of three elements

---

[4]It's not an accident that C.A.R. Hoare named the sort quicksort.

[5]The average is hard to define; one common measure of average is to take all possible orderings of N elements and compute the average time to sort them all.

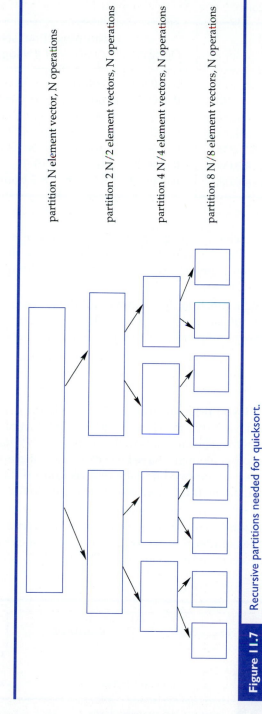

partition N element vector, N operations

partition 2 N/2 element vectors, N operations

partition 4 N/4 element vectors, N operations

partition 8 N/8 element vectors, N operations

Figure 11.7 Recursive partitions needed for quicksort.

549

Table 11.1 Comparing big-Oh expressions on a computer that executes one million instructions per second

N	Running time (seconds)			
	$O(\log N)$	$O(N)$	$O(N \log N)$	$O(N^2)$
10	0.000003	0.00001	0.000033	0.0001
100	0.000007	0.00010	0.000664	0.1000
1,000	0.000010	0.00100	0.010000	1.0
10,000	0.000013	0.01000	0.132900	1.7 minutes
100,000	0.000017	0.10000	1.661000	2.78 hours
1,000,000	0.000020	1.0	19.9	11.6 days
1,000,000,000	0.000030	16.7 min	8.3 hours	318 centuries

is the element in the middle if the elements are arranged in order. The simplest way to use the median as the pivot is to find the median element, swap into the first position, then use the existing `Partition`.

11.8. Write a function that removes all the zeros from a vector of integers without using an extra vector. The function should run in linear time, or have complexity $O(N)$ for an N-element vector.

```
void RemoveZeros(Vector<int> & list, int & numElts)
// postcondition: zeros removed from list,
//                numElts = # elements in list
```

If you're having trouble, use the picture in Fig. 11.8 as an invariant. The idea is that the elements in the first part of the vector are nonzero elements. The elements in the section "???" have yet to be examined (the other elements have been examined and are either zeros or copies of elements moved into the first section.) If the kth element is zero, it is left alone. If it is nonzero, it must be moved into the first section.

11.9. After the vector of words is sorted in *usesort.cc*, Prog. 11.3, identical words are adjacent to each other. Write a function to remove copies of identical words, leaving only one occurrence of the words that occur more than once. The function should have complexity

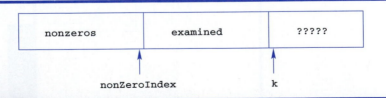

Figure 11.8 Invariant for removing zeros.

$O(N)$, where N is the number of words in the original vector (stored in the file). Don't use two loops. Use one loop and think carefully about the right invariant. Try to draw a picture similar to the one used in the previous exercise.

11.5   Two-Dimensional Arrays

An array is a one-dimensional structure; an index accesses an element of the array by ranging from zero to one less than the number of elements stored. In some applications two-dimensional arrays are necessary. For example, the pixels on a computer screen are usually identified by a row and column position. Mileage tables that provide distances between cities on a road map, as shown in Fig. 11.9, also use two dimensions. Positions of pieces in a chess game are also given by specifying a row and a column.

A two-dimensional array is sometimes called a **matrix** (the plural is matrices). The Cartesian (x, y) coordinate system uses two dimensions to specify a point in the plane. The system of latitude and longitude uses two dimensions to specify a location on the earth. Two-dimensional arrays, as we will implement them using the class `Matrix`, use row and column indices to specify an entry of the matrix. The program *matdemo.cc*, Prog. 11.6, defines a seven-by-nine matrix of integers, initializes each cell of the matrix, and prints the matrix. There are seven rows, pictured as going horizontally across the screen from left to right, and nine columns.

	Youngstown, OH	Yankton, SD	Yakima, WA	Worcester, MA	Wisconsin Dells, WI	Winston-Salem, NC	Winnipeg, MB	Winchester, VA	Wilmington, NC
Youngstown, OH									
Yankton, SD	966								
Yakima, WA	1513	2410							
Worcester, MA	2964	1520	604						
Wisconsin Dells, WI	1149	1817	481	595					
Winston-Salem, NC	927	729	2742	1289	494				
Winnipeg, MB	1611	686	1833	1446	550	1279			
Winchester, VA	1510	290	826	466	2641	1197	250		
Wilmington, NC	390	1823	214	1139	765	2956	1500	637	

Figure 11.9   Intercity distances from a road map, as given in the file `cities.dat` from [Knu93].

Program 11.6   matdemo.cc

```cpp
#include <iostream.h>
#include "matrix.h"
#include <iomanip.h>                        // for setw

// simple code to show two-dimensional arrays/ matrices
// Own Astrachan, 7/13/95

int main()
{
    const int ROWS = 7;
    const int COLS = 9;
    Matrix<int> mat(ROWS,COLS);

    int j,k;

    for(j=0; j < ROWS; j++)                 // fill matrix
    {
        for(k=0; k < COLS; k++)
        {
            mat[j][k] = 10*j + k;
        }
    }

    for(j=0; j < ROWS; j++)                 // print matrix
    {
        for(k=0; k < COLS; k++)
        {
            cout << setw(4) << mat[j][k];
        }
        cout << endl;
    }
    return 0;
}
```

OUTPUT

```
   0   1   2   3   4   5   6   7   8
  10  11  12  13  14  15  16  17  18
  20  21  22  23  24  25  26  27  28
  30  31  32  33  34  35  36  37  38
  40  41  42  43  44  45  46  47  48
  50  51  52  53  54  55  56  57  58
  60  61  62  63  64  65  66  67  68
```

As with `Vector` variables, the type used to define the element stored in each matrix cell can be any built-in type or any programmer-defined type that has a default (parameter-less) constructor. When no parameters are used when a `Matrix` is defined, the matrix has zero rows and zero columns. In that case the member function `SetSize` should be used to set the number of rows and columns. As with the `Vector` class, the `SetSize` function can be used to resize an existing matrix too. The number of rows and columns can be specified when a matrix is defined, as shown in Prog. 11.6, *matdemo.cc*. The first parameter is the number of rows, and the second parameter is the number of columns. Rows and columns are numbered starting with zero as with `Vector` variables.

A third parameter can be used to provide initial values for all the cells of a matrix just as a second parameter provides values for `charCounts` in *letters.cc*, Prog. 8.3 (page 369). For example, the definition `Matrix<double>` `chart(3,5,1.0);` defines a three-by-five matrix of 15 `doubles`, all initialized to 1.0.

Complete documentation for the `Matrix` class is found in the header file *matrix.h*. Part of this file follows:

```
#include "vector.h"

// templated matrix class,
//
// extends vector.h to two dimensional "safe" (range-checked)
// matrices
//
// written 4/17/95
//
//
// for a matrix of Items use Matrix<Item>, e.g., Matrix <int> intmatrix;
//
//                         note: Item must have a default constructor
//
// constructors:
//    Matrix()                    -- default, matrix of size 0x0
//    Matrix(int rows,int cols)   -- matrix with dimensions rows x cols
//    Matrix(int rows,int cols
//            Item fillValue)      -- matrix w/ entries all == fillValue
//    Matrix(const Matrix & vec)  -- copy constructor
//
//    int Rows()                  -- returns # of rows (capacity)
//    int Cols()                  -- returns # of columns (capacity)
//
//    void SetSize(int rows, int cols) -- resizes to rows x cols
//                                 can lose entries if size is smaller
//                                 in either dimension
```

```
//     void Fill(Item fillValue)   -- set all entries == fillValue
//
//     operator =                  -- assignment operator works properly
//     operator []                 -- indexes const and non-const matrixs
//
//
//   examples of use:
//          Matrix<double> dmat(100,80);       // 100x80 matrix of doubles
//          Matrix<double> dzmat(100,80,0.0);  // initialized to 0.0
//
//          Matrix<String> smat(300,1);        // 300 strings
//
//          Matrix<int> imat;                  // has room for 0 ints
```

11.6   Class Study: A RoadMap

In [Knu93] data are provided for 128 different cities in the United States. The data include latitude and longitude, the 1980 population of each city, and the distances between each pair of cities. Storing and manipulating the data can be done by an application using the Matrix class. The class *RoadMap*, as implemented and used in *roadmap.cc*, Prog. 11.7, supports the member functions shown in Fig. 11.10.

Program 11.7   roadmap.cc

```cpp
#include <iostream.h>
#include <fstream.h>
#include "matrix.h"
#include "vector.h"
#include "CPstring.h"
#include "iomanip.h"

// program to read intercity distances into a matrix
// of distances
// illustrates two-dimensional arrays, file processing
// Owen Astrachan, 7/11/95

// the RoadMap class stores city names and the distances between
// cities:
//
//            city A    city B     city C
// city A       0         15         20
// city B      15          0         17
// city C      20         17          0
//
// currently the Read member functions assumes data are in the
// format given in the files cities.dat from the Standford
// Graphbase as given in Knuth, The Standford GraphBase,
// Addison-Wesley, 1993
//
```

```
// city-name[latitude,longitude]population-in-1980
// d1 d2 d3 ... d(n-1)
//
// where d's are distances to cities appear earlier in the file.
// The first three cities from cities.dat are reproduced below:
//
//     Youngstown, OH[4110,8065]115436
//     Yankton, SD[4288,9739]12011
//     966
//     Yakima, WA[4660,12051]49826
//     1513 2410
//
// in general, the distances do NOT appear on a single line
// but are separated by white space
//
class RoadMap
{
    public:
      RoadMap();
      void Read(const string & filename);  // read from specified file
      void PrintCities();                  // all cities printed
      void PrintDistances();               // all distances printed
      void FindMaxDistance();              // max distance between cities
      int NumCities();                     // return number of cities
      int Distance(const string & c1,
                   const string & c2);
      // return distance between named cities

    private:
      int CityIndex(const string & name);  // find index of given city
      const int MY_MAX_CITIES;             // maximum capacity (# cities)
      Matrix<int> myDistance;              // 2-d array of distances
      Vector<string> myCities;             // list of city names
      in myCityCount;                      // # of cities stored
};


RoadMap::RoadMap()
  : MY_MAX_CITIES(130),
    myCities(MY_MAX_CITIES),
    myDistance(MY_MAX_CITIES,MY_MAX_CITIES),
    myCityCount(0)
// postcondition: all fields initialized, # cities = 0
{
    // all work done in initializer list
}


void RoadMap::Read(const string & filename)
// precondition: filename is name of readable file
// postcondition: data read from file and stored
{
    int count=0;
    ifstream input;
    input.open(filename);
    if (! input)
```

```
        {
            cerr << "could not open " << filename
                << " for reading" << endl;
        }
        else
        {
            string dummy;
            int j;
            while(getline(input,myCities[count],'['))  // city name and state
            {
                getline(input,dummy);       // discard rest of line
                for(j=count-1; j>= 0; j--) // once for each city
                {
                    input >> myDistance[count][j];  // read/store distance
                    myDistance[j][count] = myDistance[count][j];
                }
                if (count != 0)
                {
                    getline(input,dummy);  // discard last '\n'
                }
                myDistance[count][count]=0 // no garbage values
                count++;                   // another city read
            }
            myCityCount = count;
        }
}


void RoadMap::PrintCities()
// postcondition: all cities printed
{
    int j;
    for(j=0; j < myCityCount; j++)
    {
        cout << myCities[j] << endl;
    }
    cout << endl << "total # cities: " << myCityCount
        << endl;
}


void RoadMap::PrintDistances()
// postcondition: distances between each two cities printed
//                (triangular form)
{
    int j,k;

    for(j=0; j < myCityCount; j++)
    {
        for(k=0; k <= j; k++)
        {
            cout << setw(5) << myDistance[j][k];
        }
        cout << endl;
    }
}
```

```cpp
void RoadMap::FindMaxDistance()
// postcondition: maximal distance between two
//                cities calculated and printed with
//                names of cities

{
    int j,k;
    int maxfrom = 0;              // index of 'from' city
    int maxto = 0;                // index of 'to' city
    int maxdistance = 0;          // maximal distance between two cities

    for(j=0; j < myCityCount; j++)
    {
        for(k=0; k < j; k++)
        {
            if (myDistance[j][k] > maxdistance)   // update from/to/dist
            {
                maxfrom = j;
                maxto = k;
                maxdistance = myDistance[j][k];
            }
        }
    }
    cout << endl << "maximal distance in map: "
         << myDistance[maxfrom][maxto] << endl;
    cout << "from " << myCities[maxfrom> << " to "
         << myCities[maxto] << endl;
}


int RoadMap::NumCities()
// postcondition: returns # of cities in RoadMap
{
    return myCityCount;
}


int RoadMap::Distance(const string & c1, const string & c2)
// precondition: c1 and c2 are names of cities for which data
//               are stored
// postcondition: distance between c1 and c2 returned
//                if c1 or c2 not stored, then -1 returned
{
    int fromIndex = CityIndex(c1);
    int toIndex = CityIndex(c2);

    if (fromIndex != -1 && toIndex != -1)   // both cities found?
    {
        return myDistance[fromIndex][toIndex];
    }
    else
    {
        return -1;
    }
}
```

```
int RoadMap::CityIndex(const string & name)
// precondition: name is stored in RoadMap
// postcondition: returns index in vector myCities of name
//                returns -1 if not stored
{
    int j;
    for(j=0; j < myCityCount; j++)
    {
        if (myCities[j] == name)
        {
            return j;
        }
    }
    return -1;
}

int main()
{
    string name;
    string city1,city2;
    RoadMap map;

    cout << "name of input file: ";
    getline(cin,name);

    map.Read(name);
    map.PrintCities();
    map.PrintDistances();
    map.FindMaxDistance();

    while(true)
    {
        cout << "enter name of city (stop to exit) ";
        getline(cin,city1);

        // *** loop exit **
        if (city1 == "stop") break;

        cout << "enter another city name ";
        getline(cin,city2);

        cout << "distance between " << city1 << " and ";
        cout << city2 << " = " << map.Distance(city1,city2)
             << endl;
    }
    return 0;
}
```

roadmap.cc

The function FindMaxDistance determines and prints the two cities in the road map that are farthest apart. The function Distance determines the distance between two cities whose names are parameters to the function. Since the distance between each pair of cities is an int, a matrix will be used to store these data (schematically diagrammed in Fig. 11.9). However, the names of the cities are used too, so a string Vector stores the names. A diagram of the

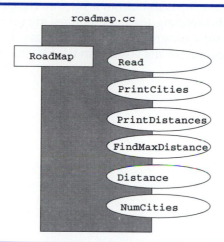

Figure 11.10 Interface diagram for RoadMap class.

RoadMap class is given in Fig. 11.11 showing the three private data members that are part of the class: a matrix of intercity distances, a vector of city names, and the number of cities in the roadmap.

As we'll see, most of the member functions are implemented using code patterns from previous programs. For example, finding the cities that are farthest apart is a slight modification of the pattern introduced in Sec. 6.3 for finding extreme values. Finding the distance between two cities requires finding the row and column index of each city using sequential search in the list of city names, and then looking up the distance in the matrix of distances.

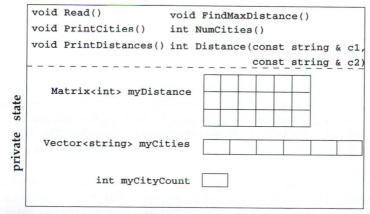

Figure 11.11 Class diagram for RoadMap class.

The function `Read` reads data from a file into the private `RoadMap` data variables. The code for reading the data requires attention to detail; often the hardest part of writing a program is getting the data into the program. Data from the first six cities and for the last city in the file *cities.dat* are

```
Youngstown, OH[4110,8065]115436
Yankton, SD[4288,9739]12011
966
Yakima, WA[4660,12051]49826
1513 2410
Worcester, MA[4227,7180]161799
2964 1520 604
Wisconsin Dells, WI[4363,8977]2521
1149 1817 481 595
Winston-Salem, NC[3610,8025]131885
...
...
Ravenna, OH[4116,8124]11987
348 2541 1570 2343 691 1943 246 413 405 723 272 457 1618 533 1581 558
2482 280 1012 861 661 322 807 554 786 2587 1498 987 2660 473 1814 1488
1470 2367 2425 93 2576 2602 2411 2514 1615 2585 1220 552 816 473 1304 363
2456 739 842 1080 1555 1164 1092 869 920 282 2161 504 575 788 182 337
1263 80 613 2522 388 682 805 351 2486 981 1167 384 1038 140 870 307
430 418 1439 2039 986 765 799 1984 1174 136 402 954 1094 2574 966 1449
431 1308 2321 144 325 552 638 405 996 406 646 910 2629 2328 1257 105
1024 1255 352 270 1451 370 660 270 1249 506 565 619 2380 936 34
```

The general format for the kth city's data is

$$Cityname \,, \; State \; [\; latitude \,, \; longitude \;] \; population$$
$$distance_1 \; distance_2 \; distance_3 \; \ldots$$
$$distance_{k-2} \; distance_{k-1}$$

The name, latitude and longitude, and population are read using `getline` in conjunction with different line delimiters (using ' [' to get the city name and the default ' \n' to discard location and population data, which are not used here). Reading data for the kth city requires reading $k - 1$ intercity distances. This is done using >>, the extraction operator, and then using `getline` to discard the ' \n' before reading the next city name. If this seems complicated, it is, to a degree. Reading the code and looking at the sample data should help in determining how each member function works. The distances are stored in the text file in a kind of reverse order; the first distance listed is the distance to city $k - 1$ and the last distance stored is the distance to city 1 (the first city in the file). Consider the entry for Worcester, Massachusetts, as shown above. The entry shows that Worcester is 604 miles from Youngstown, Ohio; 1520 miles from Yankton, South Dakota; and 2964 miles from Yakima, Washington.

```
                            OUTPUT

prompt> roadmap
name of input file: cities2.dat
Youngstown, OH
Yankton, SD
Yakima, WA
Worcester, MA
Wisconsin Dells, WI
Winston-Salem, NC
Winnipeg, MB
Winchester, VA
Wilmington, NC
Wilmington, DE
Williston, ND
Williamsport, PA
Williamson, WV
Wichita Falls, TX
Wichita, KS
Wheeling, WV
West Palm Beach, FL
Wenatchee, WA

total # cities: 18
    0
  966    0
 2410 1513    0
  604 1520 2964    0
  595  481 1817 1149    0
  494 1289 2742  729  927    0
 1279  550 1446 1833  686 1611    0
  250 1197 2641  466  826  290 1510    0
  637 1500 2956  765 1139  214 1823  390    0
  345 1305 2749  299  934  430 1618  168  466    0
 1481  663 1061 2035  888 1813  428 1712 2027 1820    0
  239 1203 2647  369  832  491 1516  201  567  172 1718    0
  353 1071 2539  843  724  240 1408  378  452  544 1610  504    0
 1284  724 1887 1848 1044 1246 1252 1432 1363 1574 1313 1500 1179    0
 1054  416 1774 1618  748 1192  944 1220 1360 1344 1068 1270 1002  308    0
   85  998 2442  605  627  416 1311  203  589  327 1513  255  269 1247 1017    0
 1252 1794 3280 1459 1515  760 2175 1048  718 1160 2375 1249  965 1432 1550 1167    0
 2358 1461  117 2912 1765 2690 1394 2589 2904 2697 1009 2595 2487 1948 1783 2390 3250    0


maximal distance in map: 3280
from West Palm Beach, FL to Yakima, WA
enter name of city (stop to exit) Yankton, SD
enter another city name Wilmington, NC
distance between Yankton, SD and Wilmington, NC = 1500
enter name of city (stop to exit) Wilmington, DE
enter another city name Wilmington, NC
```

```
distance between Wilmington, DE and Wilmington, NC = 466
enter name of city (stop to exit) stop

prompt> roadmap
name of input file: cities.dat
(List and table output not shown)

total # cities: 128
maximal distance in map: 3496
from Vancouver, BC to West Palm Beach, FL
enter name of city (stop to exit) stop
```

In the member function `RoadMap::Read()` a value is read and then duplicated, since the distance from city x to city y is the same as the distance from y to x.

```
input >> myDistance[count][j];   // read/store distance
myDistance[j][count] = myDistance[count][j];
```

This means that almost half of the entries in `myDistance` are redundant. If `myDistance` had a triangular shape, as shown by the numbers in Fig. 11.9, memory could be saved for a large road map. For example, when data for all 128 cities in `cities.dat` are stored, $128 \times 128 = 16,384$ `int` values are stored. Storing only nonredundant data requires only 8256 values, or 50.4 percent of the values stored when a full matrix is used, because there is only one value needed in the first row, two in the second, and k in the kth row. This is a total of $1 + 2 + \cdots + 128 = (128 \times 129)/2 = 8256$ values. Modifying the `RoadMap` class to save memory in this way requires a new method of storing values in `myDistance` and modifying the member function `RoadMap::Distance()` to avoid out-of-range array accesses.

Initializer Lists

Initializations of the `Vector myCities` and the `Matrix myDistance` are done with an initializer list in the `RoadMap` constructor:

```
RoadMap::RoadMap()
  : MY_MAX_CITIES(130),
    myCities(MY_MAX_CITIES),
    myDistance(MY_MAX_CITIES,MY_MAX_CITIES),
    myCityCount(0)
// postcondition: all fields initialized, # cities = 0
{
    // all work done in initializer list
}
```

As noted in Sec. 7.3, private instance variables should be constructed using an initializer list when possible. For matrices and vectors, using initializer lists is much more efficient than relying on the default constructor and then using `SetSize`.

Vectors of Vectors

The Matrix class is implemented using a vector of vectors. In a matrix each row has the same number of entries. To modify the RoadMap class to save memory, we want the kth row to have $k + 1$ entries; the zeroth row will have one entry, the first row will have two entries, and so on. This can be done by redefining the private data member myDistance as follows and changing the constructor to set the number of entries in each row appropriately.

```
    // missing public declarations

        private:
            typedef Vector<int> IntVector;
            Vector<IntVector> myDistance;

            // missing data members
        };

        RoadMap::RoadMap() : MAX_CITIES(130)
        // postcondition: all fields initialized, # cities = 0
        {
            int k;
            myCityCount = 0;

            myDistance.SetSize(MAX_CITIES);          // one for each city
            for(k=0;  k < MAX_CITIES;  k++)
            {
                myDistance[k].SetSize(k+1);          // minimize storage
            }
            myCities.SetSize(MAX_CITIES);
        }
```

Syntax: typedef

```
typedef   type alias;

typedef int Integer;
typedef Vector<int>
  IntVector;
typedef Vector<Vector<int> >
  RaggedIntMatrix;
typedef Matrix<int>
  ScreenPixels;
```

A **typedef** defines an alias—another name—for a type. It is never necessary to use a typedef, but the new name introduced by a typedef often helps in reading and understanding code. Using typedefs also results in code that is easier to modify.

For example, you might use the new name Integer, introduced by typedef int Integer, in a program, when you think it could become necessary to use some long int variables later. Changing the typedef, typically found at the top of a file so that it affects all uses in the file, to typedef long int Integer means that all definitions like Integer num; are automatically updated.

Complicated declarations are often easier to understand when typedefs are used. For example, the definition Vector<Vector<int>> list will not compile, because the compiler misinterprets the >> as the insertion operator; you must include a space, as shown in the typedef for RaggedIntMatrix in the syntax display. Using a typedef, as shown for IntVector in the preceding

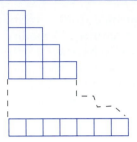

Figure 11.12   Triangular matrix as vector of vectors.

code for the modified `RoadMap` class, helps avoid this kind of problem. Some programmers use `typedef`s extensively, especially with C, where no class mechanism exists. In the program *roadmap2.cc* (on the disk, but not shown here) I use the following definition in defining `myDistance`—a `typedef` is not used:

```
Vector<Vector<int> > myDistance;          // 2-d array of distances
```

In the revised `RoadMap` class the `RoadMap` constructor uses the `Vector::SetSize()` member function to set the number of entries in each row with the statement `myDistance[k].SetSize(k+1)`. Reviewing the definition of `myDistance` shows that it is a `Vector`, so indexing it is appropriate. Furthermore, `myDistance[k]` is one element of the vector; in this case an element is an `IntVector`, which is an alias for `Vector<int>`. Since this is a `Vector`, it supports the `SetSize` function. The `for` loop in the constructor sets the number of entries in each row, so a kind of triangular matrix results, as illustrated in Fig. 11.12.

11.7   Built-In Multidimensional Arrays (Optional)

As we noted at the beginning of Chapter 8, arrays act differently than other types in C++. As a reminder, arrays are not copied when passed as parameters, and arrays cannot be assigned to one another using the assignment operator =. It is possible, however, to have an array of arrays; this is precisely how two-dimensional arrays are defined as follows (for the example of a 12-student class with each student having 10 scores):

```
int classScores[12][10];
```

This definition allocates 120 array cells, each storing an `int`. Conceptually, the array cells in this two-dimensional array are laid out in 12 rows of 10 columns.

Accessing values in a built-in two-dimensional array is the same as accessing with the `Matrix` class. Like all arrays in C and C++, indices begin with 0. Initializing all the cells of a two-dimensional array is typically done with nested `for` loops. To set all the entries in the array `scores` to zero, the following loop can be used:

```
int j,k;
for(j=0; j < 12; j += 1)
{
    for(k=0; k < 10; k += 1)
    {
        classScores[j][k] = 0;
    }
}
```

In this code all the entries in a row are set to zero before any of the entries in the next row are set to zero. One description of these loops is that the **column index varies more rapidly.** In this case the inner-loop index, k, varies from 0 to 10 while the outer-loop index, j, is fixed.

Two-Dimensional Arrays as Variables and Parameters

As is the case with one-dimensional C-style arrays, the size of each dimension of a two-dimensional array must be specified at compile time. When passed as parameters, only the first dimension of a two-dimensional array can be left out; the second dimension must be specified in the parameter list. The following function finds the average of all the scores on test number `testScore`. Using the array `classScores` just defined, the statement `cout << AverageScore(classScores,1,12) << endl` prints the average of all 12 student scores for the test with index 1 (the second column, because the first column has index 0).

```
double AverageScore(int scores[][10], int testScore, int numStudents)
// precondition: 0 <= testScore < 10, 0 < numStudents
// postcondition: returns average of scores[k][testScore] for
//                the number of students specified by numStudents
{
    int total = 0;
    int k;
    for(k=0; k < numStudents; k++)
    {
        total += scores[k][testScore];
    }
    return double(total)/numStudents;
}
```

You should study this function carefully. The column index (the second array index) does *not* vary inside the `for` loop, because the scores for a given test (e.g., the second test) are averaged. The row index varies from 0 to numStudents – 1, where the number of rows (students) is passed a parameter. In a class of 150 students, each of whom had 10 scores, stored in a variable `bigClass`, the average score for the class on the test with index

1 could be calculated using the same function as shown:

```
int bigClass[150][10];

double average = AverageScore(bigClass,1,150);   // average of test 1
```

Notice that *no* dimensions appear in the function call to `AverageScore`. Unfortunately, using the built-in two-dimensional array type in C++ it's not possible to write a function like the one above that would work with an array with 20 test scores as well as one with 10 test scores. Since the number of columns (the second dimension) *must* appear in the formal parameter list, this isn't possible.

Program Tip: When a multidimensional array is a formal parameter, all dimensions except the first dimension must be given as constants in the function header/prototype.

It is *not* possible to write a function that will work with any-sized two-dimensional (and higher-dimensional) built-in arrays. Only the first dimension is "free" in the sense that its value can be left out of the header/prototype.

This is the case with one-dimensional arrays as well, but the single "free" dimension is the only dimension. This means that one-dimensional arrays are more flexible as parameters than multidimensional arrays are.

Arrays of arrays. The discussion of multidimensional arrays began with the question of whether it is possible to define an array of arrays. Let's consider again the two-dimensional array of test scores defined previously:

```
int classScores[12][10];
```

It is possible to access one row of this array as a single entity. For example, the expression `classScores[3]` is an array of 10 scores corresponding to the fourth row of the array (remember that the first row has index zero). Thus, if a function to calculate student averages had the following prototype, the call shown could be used to calculate the average of the student for whom scores are stored in the row with index 3.[6]

```
double Average(int scores[], int numScores)
// postcondition: returns average of numScores entries in scores
{
       // implementation here
}

// ... program here
```

---

[6]This kind of convoluted sentence is often needed to distinguish between indices starting at 0 and a human preference to begin starting at 1. If I use "third row," I mean the physically third row, which will be the row with index 2 in a C++ array.

```
int classScores[12][10];   // class of 12 students, 10 scores each

double avg = Average(classScores[3],10);    // get average
```

The array parameter to `Average` does not need to have its size specified, because one dimension is "free." The number of entries that store meaningful values must be passed, however. In this example that number is 10, because there are 10 scores for each student. To print the average for each of the 12 students in the class, a `for` loop could be used in which each successive row of the array `classScores` is passed to `Average`.

Initialization. A two-dimensional array can be initialized with values as a one-dimensional array is initialized. For example, an array storing the names of the days of the week in three languages could be initialized as follows:

```
string weekdays[3][7] = {
    {"Sunday", "Monday", "Tuesday", "Wednesday", "Thursday",
     "Friday", "Saturday"},
    {"Dimanche", "Lundi", "Mardi", "Mercredi","Jeudi",
     "Vendredi","Samedi"},
    {"Domingo","Lunes", "Martes", "Miercoles","Jueves",
     "Viernes","Sabado"}
};

string dwarfs[7] = {"Sneezy", "Doc", "Dopey", "Bashful",
    "Grumpy", "Sleepy", "Happy"};
```

To print the days of the week in French, the second row (index 1) can be printed using the code.

```
int k;
for(k=0; k < 7; k++)
{
    cout << weekdays[1][k];
}
```

Because the dimensions of the array `weekdays` are given (as 3 and 7), it's not necessary to use the inner sets of curly braces in the initialization statement above. Instead, it's possible to list 21 comma-separated strings within one set of curly braces. The compiler will ensure that the strings are stored in the array appropriately. This works only because the dimensions of `weekdays` are supplied. In this case, the number of rows (3) could be left out and the beginning of the initialization specified by `weekdays[][7]`. The number 7 is needed in this case so that the compiler can determine how many entries appear in each row of the two-dimensional array.

11.8   Chapter Review

We discussed sorting, two-dimensional arrays, and elementary analysis of algorithms in this chapter. There are many, many sorting algorithms; we only covered two in depth.

Topics covered include the following:

- Selection sort, an $O(n^2)$ sort that works fast on small-sized vectors (where small is relative).
- Insertion sort is another $O(n^2)$ sort that works well on nearly sorted data.
- Bubble sort is an $O(n^2)$ sort that should rarely be used. Its performance is much worse, in almost all situations, than that of selection sort or insertion sort.
- Overloaded functions permit the same name to be used for different functions if the parameter lists of the functions differ.
- Templated functions are used for functions that represent a pattern, or template, for constructing other functions. Templated functions are often used instead of overloading to minimize code development.
- O-notation, or big-Oh, is used to analyze and compare different algorithms. O-notation provides a convenient way of comparing algorithms, as opposed to implementations of algorithms on particular computers.
- Quicksort is a very fast sort, $O(n \log n)$ in the average case. In the worst case, quicksort is $O(n^2)$.
- Two-dimensional arrays, or matrices, are useful for representing and manipulating data. We use a `Matrix` class for two-dimensional arrays, rather than using the built-in C-style two-dimensional arrays, which are very limiting.
- The `typedef` language construct can be useful as a shorthand for types whose names are cumbersome to reason about and type.

11.9   Exercises

11.1 The following code implements another sorting algorithm, called *insertion sort*. This algorithm works by keeping the first $k-1$ elements in sorted order. The kth element is placed in the correct position relative to the first $k-1$ sorted elements by sliding each of these sorted elements to the right, creating a "hole" in which the kth element is placed. The inner `while` loop in the following code shifts the elements to the right until the correct spot for `a[k]` is found.

Trace the code and provide a diagram similar to Figure 11.1 for the same initial vector of six elements given in that figure.

```
void InsertSort(Vector<int> & a, int numElts)
// precondition: a contains numElts ints
// postcondition: elements of a are sorted in nondecreasing
//                 order
{
    int k,loc;
    int hold;

    for(k=1; k < numElts; k+=1)
    {
        hold = a[k];                    // "keep" the kth element
        loc = k;                        // shift other elements right
        while (0 < loc && hold < a[loc-1])
```

```
    {
        a[loc] = a[loc-1];
        loc -= 1;
    }
    a[loc] = hold;  // store kept element in hole created
    }
}
```

In the code for `InsertSort`, why are two boolean expressions used in the inner `while` loop test? Does the order of the two expressions in the `while` loop test matter, or can the conditions be switched (so that `0 < loc` is the second condition)? Write a loop invariant for the insertion sort algorithm.

 Add this sort to the timing function *timesort.cc*, Program 11.5. Time the n^2 sorts for vectors of different sizes and either plot or chart the different times.

11.2 You may have seen the word game Jumble in your newspaper. In Jumble the letters in a word are mixed up, and the reader must try to guess what the word is (there are actually four words in a Jumble game, and a short phrase whose letters have to be obtained from the four words after they are solved). For example, *neicma* is *iceman,* and *cignah* is *aching*.

 Jumbles are easy for computers to solve with access to a list of words. Two words are anagrams of each other if they contain the same letters. For example, *horse* and *shore* are anagrams.

 Write a program that reads a file of words and finds all anagrams. You can modify this program to facilitate Jumble-solving. Store each word along with a sorted version of the letters in the word. For example, store *horse* together with *ehors*. To find a jumbled word, sort the letters and look up the sorted version. A word with anagrams will have more than one Jumble solution. You should sort the list of words by using the sorted word as the key, then use binary search when looking up the jumbled word.

11.3 In Exercise 6.6 in Sec. 6.6 an algorithm was given for calculating the variance and standard deviation of a set of numbers. Other statistical measures include the **mean** or average, the **mode** or most frequently occurring value, and the **median** or middle value.

 Write a class or function that finds these three statistical values for a `Vector` of `double` values. The median can be calculated by sorting the values and finding the middle value. If the number of values is even, the median value can be defined as either the average of the two values in the middle or the smaller of the two. Sorting the values can also help determine the mode, but you may decide to calculate the mode in some other manner.

11.4 The bubble sort algorithm sorts the elements in a vector by making *N* passes over a vector of *N* items. On each pass, adjacent elements are compared, and if the element on the left (smaller index) is greater it is swapped with its neighbor. In this manner the largest element "bubbles" to the end of the vector. On the next pass, adjacent elements are compared again, but the pass stops one short of the end. On each pass, bubbling stops one position earlier than the pass before until all the elements are sorted. The following code implements this idea.

```
template <class Type>
void BubbleSort(Vector<Type> & a, int n)
```

```
// precondition: n = # of elements in a
// postcondition: a is sorted
//                      note: this is a dog of a sort
{
    int j,k;
    for(j=n-1; j > 0; j--)
    {
        // find largest element in 0..k, move to a[j]
        for(k=0; k < j; k++)
        {
            if (a[k+1] < a[k])
            {
                Swap(a[k],a[k+1]);
            }
        }
    }
}
```

Bubble sort can be "improved" by stopping if no values are swapped on some pass,[7] meaning that the elements are in order. Add a `bool` flag variable to the preceding code so that the loops stop when no bubbling is necessary. Then time this function and compare it to the other $O(n^2)$ sorts: selection sort and insertion sort.

11.5 Merge sort is another $O(n \log n)$ sort (like quicksort), although unlike quicksort, merge sort is $O(n \log n)$ in the worst case. The general algorithm for merge sort consists of two steps to sort a vector of N items.

- Recursively sort the first half and the second half of the vector.
- Merge the two sorted halves together.

The key idea is that merging two sorted vectors together (into a sorted vector) can be done efficiently in $O(n)$ time if both sorted vectors have $O(n)$ elements. The two sorted vectors are scanned from left to right, and the smaller element is copied into an auxiliary vector. The scanning index is incremented only when an element is copied.

The merge operation requires an auxiliary vector to copy values into; these values are then copied back into the original vector.

The following code implements merge sort, except for the function `Merge`. Implement this function, then time this sort and compare its performance to quicksort.

```
template <class Type>
void DoMerge(Vector<Type> & a, int left,int right)
// postcondition: a[left] <= ... <= a[right]
{
    if (left < right)
    {
        int mid = (left+right)/2;
        DoMerge(a,left,mid);
```

---

[7]This improvement can make a difference for almost-sorted data, but it does not mitigate the generally atrocious performance of this sort.

```
        DoMerge(a,mid+1,right);
        Merge(a,left,mid,right);
    }
}

template <class Type>
void MergeSort(Vector<Type> & a,int n)
{
    DoMerge(a,0,n-1);
}
```

11.6 A square matrix a is symmetric if `a[j][k] == a[k][j]` for all values of j and k; that is, the matrix is symmetric with respect to the main diagonal from (0,0) to $(n-1, n-1)$ for an $n \times n$ matrix. Write a `bool`-valued function that returns true if its matrix parameter is symmetric and false otherwise.

11.7 An image can be represented as a 2-dimensional matrix of pixels, each of which can be off (white) or on (black). Color and gray-scale images can be represented using multivalued pixels; for example, numbers from 0 to 255 can represent different shades of gray. A **bitmap** is a two-dimensional matrix of 0s and 1s, where 0 corresponds to an off pixel and 1 corresponds to an on pixel. For example, the following matrix is a bitmap that represents a 9×8 picture of a < sign.

```
0 0 0 0 0 1 1 0
0 0 0 0 1 1 0 0
0 0 0 1 1 0 0 0
0 0 1 1 0 0 0 0
0 1 1 0 0 0 0 0
0 0 1 1 0 0 0 0
0 0 0 1 1 0 0 0
0 0 0 0 1 1 0 0
0 0 0 0 0 1 1 0
```

Implement the class `Pixmap` whose partial declaration is given at the end of this exercise. Then write a client program that provides the use with a menu of choices:

- Read an image from a file
- Write an image to a file
- Invert the current image (change black to white and vice versa)
- Enlarge an image
- Enhance the image using median filtering (described below)
- Count the "blobs" in an image (described below)

Enlarging an Image. A bitmap image can be enlarged by expanding it horizontally, vertically, or in both directions. Expanding an image in place (i.e., without using an auxiliary array) requires some planning. In Fig. 11.13 an image is shown partially expanded by three vertically, and by two horizontally. By beginning the expansion in the lower right corner as shown, the image can be expanded in place—that is *without* the use of an auxiliary array or bitmap.

Enhancing an Image. Sometimes an image can be "noisy" because of the way in which it is transmitted; for example, a TV picture may have static or "snow." Image enhancement is a method that takes out noise by changing pixel values according to the

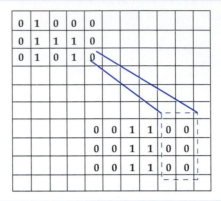

Figure 11.13   Enlarging a bitmap by three rows and two columns.

3-neighborhood

10	12	28
10	28	25
25	32	32

5-neighborhood

10	12	12	10	10
10	10	12	32	32
25	10	28	18	18
25	25	32	32	18
32	32	32	25	25

Figure 11.14   3- and 5-neighborhoods.

values of the neighboring pixels. You should use a method of enhancement based on setting a pixel to the median value of those in its "neighborhood." Figure 11.14 shows a 3-neighborhood and a 5-neighborhood of the middle pixel whose value is 28. Using **median filtering,** the 28 in the middle is replaced by the median of the values in its neighborhood. The nine values in the 3-neighborhood are (10 10 12 25 25 28 28 32 32). The median, or middle, value is 25—there are four values above 25 and four values below 25. The values in the 5-neighborhood are (10 10 10 10 10 10 12 12 12 18 18 18 25 25 25 25 25 32 32 32 32 32 32 32), and again the median value is 25, because there are 12 values above and 12 values below 25. The easiest way to find the median of a list of values is to sort them and take the middle element.

Pixels near the border of an image don't have "complete" neighborhoods. These pixels are replaced by the median of the partial neighborhood that is completely on the grid of pixels. One way of thinking about this is to take, for example, a 3 × 3 grid and slide it over an image so that every pixel is centered in the grid. Each pixel is replaced by the median of the pixels of the image that are contained in the sliding grid. This requires using an extra array to store the median values, which are then copied back to the original image when the median filtering has finished. This is necessary so that the pixels are replaced by median values from the original image, not from the partially reconstructed and filtered image.

Figure 11.15   Noisy image (*a*) before and (*b*) after median filtering.

Figure 11.16   Image with 10 blobs.

Applying a 3×3 median filter to the image in Fig. 11.15*a* results in the image Fig. 11.15*b* (these images look better on the screen than they do on paper).

Blob Counting. A **blob** is a contiguous black pixel region. In this case "contiguous" means adjacent, either horizontally, vertically, or diagonally. Writing this routine will require some ingenuity and the use of an auxiliary recursive function. For example, in Fig. 11.16, there are 10 blobs. This function might be useful in processing slides in biology, for example.

One method to count blobs is to use a nested loop to visit every pixel in an image. When a pixel is black (part of a blob), count the blob and then erase it by turning all contiguous black pixels to white. The erasing is done recursively, with eight recursive calls: one for each possible neighbor. If the neighbor is black, it is erased and it calls its neighbors. If the neighbor is white, no processing is needed:

```
Erase(int j, int k) // erase image

if (LegalIndexes(j,k) && image[j][k] == black)
{
    image[j][k] = white;
    Erase(j-1,k);            // above
    Erase(j+1,k);            // below
    Erase(j-1,k-1);          // up-left
    Erase(j-1,k+1);          // up-right
    // etc. etc.
}
```

If you use this method you'll need either to make a copy for erasing, or to store some other value in place of the erased pixels and then restore these values after all blobs have been counted.

A draft of a class Pixmap follows. If you have access to a graphics program, you should use it for displaying these images. The shareware program *XV* can be used to display a variety of image formats.

```cpp
#include "matrix.h"

class Pixmap
{
  public:
    Pixmap();                // constructor (0-sized bitmap)

    void Read(istream &); // read pixmap from file
    void Invert();        // invert pixmap

    void Write(ostream &) const;    // write bitmap
                                    // to file
    void Expand(int rowExp, int colExp);  // expand pixmap row x column
    int BlobCount() const;          // count blobs
    void Enhance(int size);         // median filter

  private:
    Matrix<int> myImage;
    int myRows;
    int myCols;
};
```

Information Hiding and Dynamic Data

Something deeply hidden had to be
behind things.
ALBERT EINSTEIN
autobiographical handwritten note
The Einstein Letter That Started It All
NY Times Magazine, August 2, 1964, Ralph E. Lapp

Although `Vector` variables can be resized and increase (or decrease) in capacity, excess storage is often allocated when vectors are used. Since vectors typically double in size when grown, memory will be wasted unless all vector cells are used. For example, *allword4.cc*, Prog. 8.8, counts 3,125 unique words in the text file `melville.txt` (*Bartleby, the Scrivener*). The `WordList` object used in the program defines a `Vector` of 1000 elements. Because the vector grows to 2000 elements and then to 4000 elements, and because the resizing operation throws out the old vector after allocating a new vector, more than 3000 elements are literally thrown away when the vector is resized. Although the `Vector` class takes the necessary step to reclaim the storage thrown away, some applications require more precise memory allocation. In this chapter we'll study a data structure called a *linked list*, which is an alternative to using vectors. Linked lists support different operations than do vectors and in some applications are more efficient. We'll also study how pointers, which are used in implementing linked lists, can be used in conjunction with vectors to make programs more memory-efficient and often faster too.

Pointers are essential in working with large object-oriented programs in C++. We won't begin to cover all applications of pointers in this chapter, but we will cover several basic uses of pointers. These basic uses can be divided into three categories:

1. Pointers are used to allocate memory dynamically, on an as-needed basis during program execution rather than when the program is compiled.

2. Pointers are indirect references that permit resources to be shared among different objects in the same way that reference variables maintain relationships in the `WalkObserver` class.

3. Pointers are used to implement linked data structures which are used in many applications.

12.1   Pointers as Indirect References

At a basic level, a **pointer** stores an address in computer memory. More abstractly, a pointer refers to something indirectly. If you look up *pointer* in the index of this book, you'll see a reference, or "pointer," to this page. Forwarding addresses also serve as indirect references. Suppose someone named Dave Reed lives at 104 Oak Street. If Dave moves, he'll leave a forwarding address with the post office. If he moves to 351 Coot Lane, then mail addressed to him at 104 Oak Street will be delivered, with some delay, using the forwarding address. The forwarding address is a pointer, or indirect reference, to Dave's new address.

Our first use of pointers will be to change *allword4.cc*, Prog. 8.8, so that rather than storing `WordStat` structs, it stores pointers to the `structs`. Using pointers as indirect references will save memory and make the program run much faster. Pointers in C++ are defined by putting an asterisk, or star, between the variable's type and identifier. The code below defines three pointer variables; one points to an `int`, one to a `Dice`, and one to a `WordStat`.

```
int * intPtr;
Dice * diePtr;
WordStat * wordPtr;
```

Like any variable, a pointer variable must be initialized before use. Before exploring the modifications to *allword4.cc* using pointers, we'll look at basic pointer operations.

Pointers as References: A Closer Look

In *intpoint.cc*, Prog. 12.1, two variables are defined: an integer `number` and a pointer to this integer `intPointer`. The pointer `intPointer` is an indirect reference to the variable `number`. Each variable in a program has a name, a value, and a location in memory, which is given by the variable's address. The variables used in Prog. 12.1 are diagrammed in Fig. 12.1.

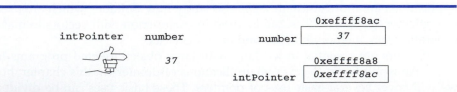

Figure 12.1   Conceptual pointer (on the left) and actual pointer.

Program 12.1   intpoint.cc

```cpp
#include <iostream.h>

// illustrates intPointer concept
// Owen Astrachan, 6/4/1996

int main()
{
    int number = 37;
    int * intPointer = &number;

    cout << "number = " << number << endl;
    cout << "address = " << &number << endl << endl;

    cout << "indirect number = " << *intPointer << endl;
    cout << "intPointer = " << intPointer << endl;
    cout << "intPointer address = " << &intPointer << endl;

    return 0;
}
```

OUTPUT

```
prompt> intpoint
number = 37
address = 0xeffff8ac

indirect number = 37
intPointer = 0xeffff8ac
intPointer address = 0xeffff8a8
```

In Fig. 12.1 the variable number has the value 37 and is stored in memory at location 0xeffff8ac. The variable intPointer has the value *0xeffff8ac* and is stored in memory at location 0xeffff8a8. Memory addresses are written using the base 16, or **hexadecimal**, number system, where the letter *a* corresponds to 10, *b* to 11, and so forth, with *f* corresponding to 15. Don't worry about trying to understand hexadecimal notation; you can think of addresses as having values like "101 Main Street." The important relationship is that the value of the variable intPointer is the address of the variable number.

The program shows how pointer values are assigned and accessed using two operators: *, the **dereference** operator, and &, the **address-of** operator. The dereference operator, *, yields the value of an object pointed to. This is like following a forwarding address to find the new address. Dereferencing a pointer variable requires three steps:

1. Find the value of the pointer that is an address, in this case `0xeffff8ac`.
2. Find the memory location with the given address, in this case the memory associated with the variable `number`.
3. Find the value in this memory location.

In *intpoint.cc* the expression `intPointer` has the value `0xeffff8ac`, but the expression `*intPointer` has the value 37 since `intPointer` "points" to the memory location associated with `number`, which has the value 37.

The address-of operator, `&`, yields the address of an object. This address serves as an indirect reference to the object and can be assigned to a pointer variable of the appropriate type. In *intpoint.cc*, `intPointer` is assigned the address of `number` using `&number`. In the output you can also see the address of `pointer`, `&intPointer`.

You must be careful when using indirect references since problems often arise when there is more than one way to access a specific memory location. For example, in Prog. 12.1, inserting the statement `*intPointer = 76;` changes the contents of the memory location pointed to by `intPointer` to have the value 76. This changes the value of `number` to 76 since `intPointer` points to the memory location associated with `number`.

Pointers as Parameters

When programming in C++, you seldom need to define pointers to built-in types. However, you would find this very necessary if you program in C, which does not have reference parameters. In C, all arguments are passed by value. This means that it is impossible for a function to change the value of a parameter so that the change will have an effect when the function has finished executing. Although this is done in C++ using reference parameters, in C changing the value of a variable requires passing a pointer to the variable rather than the variable itself.[1] Although a copy of the pointer is passed in C (since parameters are passed by value), the value of the pointer copy can access and change a value stored in memory.

Two versions of a function `Swap` are shown in the following code. The one on the left uses reference parameters to interchange the values of its parameters; the one on the right uses pointers.

```
void Swap(int & a, int & b)              void Swap(int * ap, int * bp)
//postcondition: swap values of a,b      //postcondition:  swap values of *ap,*bp
{                                        {
    int temp = a;                            int temp = *ap;
    a = b;                                   *ap = *bp;
    b = temp;                                *bp = temp;
}                                        }
```

---

[1] Reference parameters are implemented using pointers but have the advantage that programmers do not need to worry about addresses and dereferences.

```
int main()                              int main()
{                                       {
    int x = 4;                              int x = 4;
    int y = 8;                              int y = 8;
    Swap(x,y);                              Swap(&x,&y);
    cout << x << " " << y << endl;          cout << x << " " << y << endl;
    return 0;                               return 0;

}                                       }
```

In both cases, the output will be 8 4 since the values of the variables x and y are interchanged by the Swap function. In the code on the right, pointers, rather than reference parameters, achieve this change. In the code on the right, the parameters ap and bp are *pointers* to ints. The expression *ap is "the object pointed to by ap"; it represents the value of what ap points to. The reference parameters a and b on the left represent local names or aliases in the function Swap for the memory allocated for the variables x and y in main. In contrast, the parameters ap and bp on the right are *not* reference parameters (note that there is no & as part of the formal parameters). These value parameters are passed *copies* of the addresses of x and y in main. These differences are diagrammed in Fig. 12.2.

In Fig. 12.2, parameters a and b on the left are references to the memory locations passed as arguments; a references the memory location associated with the variable x in main, as shown. In contrast, the parameters ap and bp in the function on the right are pointers. The pointer variable ap's value is the location in memory associated with the variable x in main since the address-of operator & is used for both arguments to Swap on the right. The addresses of x and y are passed rather than the values of the variables. To find the value of the memory pointed to by ap, you must use the dereferencing operator, *, so that int temp = *ap stores 4 in temp since ap points to memory location 0x100 in main with the value 4 stored in it.

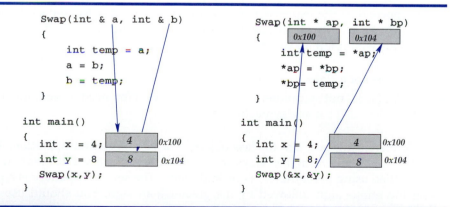

Figure 12.2   Pointers contrasted with references.

Some programmers prefer the C style of passing pointers to modify function parameters. Since the address-of operator, &, appears next to an argument in the function call, it is clear from the call what arguments can be modified. In contrast, you must examine a function prototype to see what parameters can be modified when using reference parameters. Since reference parameters exist in C++, why not dispense with pointers and avoid the problems that are associated with programming using pointers? There are several reasons for studying pointers. One reason is that at some point you may need to write programs in C rather than in C++. As we will see, pointers can result in more efficient memory use and in faster programs. Another reason is that using pointers is necessary in designing and implementing more advanced classes and programs when C++ is used.

Pointers to Class Objects

The dereferencing operator can be used with pointers to class objects as well as pointers to built-in types. The following code fragment shows two ways of calling the member function `Roll` of the `Dice` class.

```
Dice d(6);

Dice * dptr = &d;


cout << (*dptr).Roll() << endl;

cout << dptr->Roll()    << endl;
```

In the expression `(*dptr).Roll()`, the dereference of `dptr` is a valid use of `*`, because `dptr` is a pointer to the `Dice` object d. This means that `*dptr` is a six-sided die, in fact it is the six-sided die d. The dot operator then accesses the member function `Dice::Roll()` just as `d.Roll()` could be used to access the member function.

Because `.` has higher precedence than the dereference operator, parentheses are needed in the expression `(*dptr).Roll`. Otherwise, the expression `*dice.Roll` results in an attempt to dereference the `Roll()` function of `dptr`. This would fail for two reasons:

■ `dptr` is not a class object, so a dot can't follow it.

■ `Roll()` is not a pointer, so it can't be dereferenced (assuming that `dptr.Roll()` made syntactic sense).

Dereferencing pointers to class objects is a very common operation. The **selector** operator, `->`, makes accessing member functions via pointers much simpler than using parentheses, a dot, and a star. The selector operator is typed using the minus sign followed by the greater-than sign. You should use the selector operator rather than parentheses and the dereference operator, `*`; your code will be much more readable.

ALAN PERLIS (1922–1990)

In 1966 Alan Perlis became the first recipient of the Turing award. The award was given for his work in programming language design. In 1965 he established the first graduate program in computer science at what was then the Carnegie Institute of Technology and is now Carnegie-Mellon University. In the dedication of [AS85], Perlis is quoted with some important advice to novices and experts in computer science: "I think that it's extraordinarily important that we in computer science keep fun in computing.... I hope the field of computer science never loses its sense of fun.... What's in your hands, I think and hope, is intelligence: the ability to see the machine as more than when you were first led up to it, that you can make it more."

Figure 12.3   Alan Perlis.

In his Turing award address, Perlis looked ahead to parallel and distributed computation, a field that has been growing steadily and receiving increased attention in recent years. He also talked of the intellectual foundation of programming, from Turing's work to the languages LISP and ALGOL, which have had a profound impact on programming language design.

In [AS85] he writes about programming:

To appreciate programming as an intellectual activity in its own right you must turn to computer programming; you must read and write computer programs—many of them. It doesn't matter much what the programs are about or what applications they serve. What does matter is how well they perform and how smoothly they fit with other programs in the creation of still greater programs.

A list of Perlis epigrams has been gathered; these include:

- Most people find the concept of programming obvious, but the doing impossible.
- Once you understand how to write a program, get someone else to write it.
- The best book on programming for the layman is *Alice in Wonderland*; but that's because it's the best book on anything for the layman.

For more information see [Per87].

Table 12.1   Dereferencing and address of operators

operator/symbol	name/use	example
*	pointer to type	`Dice * dptr;`
&	address of operator	`dptr = &die;`
->	selector operator	`cout << dptr->Roll();`
*	dereference operator	`*numPtr = 25;`

Defining and Initializing Pointers

The pointer operators are summarized in Table 12.1.

There are four ways to assign a value to a pointer variable. They are described here and will be illustrated in Prog. 12.2.

1.   Assign a value allocated using the operator **new,** which allocates memory dynamically.

```
int     * intPtr    = new int;

string * stringPtr = new String;

Dice    * diePtr    = new Dice(6);
```

Variables like `number` in Prog. 12.1, *intpoint.cc*, are allocated storage when the program is compiled. The `new` operator allocates memory dynamically during program execution. For example, the `Vector` class uses `new` in implementing resizable arrays. When parameters are required for construction, as for the class `Dice`, the parameters are given as arguments to the class name when `new` is used. We'll study `new` in detail in Sec. 12.2.

2.   Assign the address of another variable using the address-of operator:

```
string name = "Fred";

string * ptr = &name;
```

Now `ptr` is an indirect reference to the storage allocated for the variable `name`.

3.   Assign the value of another pointer:

```
int * intPtr = new int;

int * otherPtr = intPtr;
```

Both `intPtr` and `otherPtr` are indirect references to the storage allocated dynamically using `new`. (Text continues on p. 584.)

Program 12.2   pointer.cc

```cpp
#include <iostream.h>
#include "CPstring.h"

// illustrates pointer definition, initialization, and use
// author: Owen Astrachan
//          11/27/94, modified 1/9/96

void Output(int & object,string name)
// postcondition: value and address of object are printed
{
    cout << name << "\tvalue = " << object
         << "\taddress = " << &object << endl;
}

void PointerOutput(int * & object,string name)
// postcondition: value and address of object are printed
{
    cout << name << "\tvalue = " << object
         << "\taddress = " << &object << endl;
}

int main()
{
    int first = 11;
    int second = 99;
    int * intPtr = 0;

    Output(first,"first");
    Output(second,"second");
    PointerOutput(intPtr,"intPtr");

    intPtr = &first;
    PointerOutput(intPtr,"intPtr");
    *intPtr = 32;
    Output(first,"first");

    intPtr = new int;
    PointerOutput(intPtr,"intPtr");
    *intPtr = second;
    PointerOutput(intPtr,"intPtr");
    Output(second,"second");

    delete intPtr;
    PointerOutput(intPtr,"intPtr");

    return 0;
}
```

OUTPUT

```
prompt> pointer
first    value = 11        address = 0xbffff844
second   value = 99        address = 0xbffff840
intPtr   value = 0x0       address = 0xbffff83c
intPtr   value = 0xbffff844     address = 0xbffff83c     contents = 11
first    value = 32        address = 0xbffff844
intPtr   value = 0x18ff8 address = 0xbffff83c     contents = 1718186611
intPtr   value = 0x18ff8 address = 0xbffff83c     contents = 99
second   value = 99        address = 0xbffff840
intPtr   value = 0x18ff8 address = 0xbffff83c     contents = 1768846416
```

---

4. Assign the special value 0, which can be assigned to any pointer:

```
int * intptr    = 0;

string * strptr = 0;

Dice * diePtr   = NULL;
```

Sometimes NULL is used instead of 0, but using NULL requires the use of some header file, e.g., <iostream.h> or <stdlib.h>, in which NULL is defined. Many programmers prefer to use NULL, but I'll use 0 more often than NULL in the programs in this book.

The pointer value 0 is useful since any pointer can be compared to 0. A pointer whose value is 0 does *not* point at a "good" memory location, but provides a means of comparing the value of a pointer to a known quantity. Many programmers initialize all pointers to 0.

Program 12.2 shows how pointers are accessed and assigned. The output will vary among different computers.

Figure 12.4 gives snapshots of how variable values change after each statement in *pointer.cc*. The value of a pointer like intPtr is an address, and addresses are usually printed in hexadecimal. No value is assigned to the integer dynamically allocated using new:

```
intPtr = new int;
```

However, the program prints a value, 1718186611, as shown in the run above. This value may be different on subsequent runs of the same program. There is no way of knowing what value will be stored in the memory allocated and returned when new is called.

You've probably made the mistake of using an uninitialized variable when programming. For example, some unknown (or garbage) value is printed as a

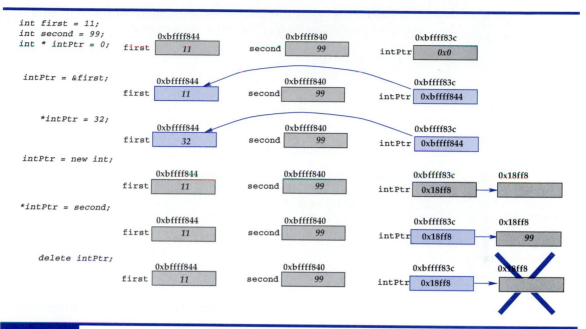

Figure 12.4 `int` values and pointer values.

result of executing the two statements

```
int x;
cout << x << endl;
```

A very small change in these statements can result in a program that crashes a computer because of a bad pointer dereference.

```
int * x;
cout << *x << endl;
```

In this case, x is a pointer to an `int`. In the output statement, the dereferencing operator accesses the value of the `int` pointed to by x. In this case, however, x does *not* point at any `int` since no value has been assigned to x. Executing the program will result in an attempt to dereference the garbage value stored in x. On many machines, dereferencing such undefined values results in an attempt to access some part of memory that is "out of bounds," crashing the machine. As a general rule, assign values to pointers as soon as possible to avoid such dereferencing errors. The pointer dereference in `PointerOutput` in *pointer.cc* could be guarded to protect against dereferencing a `NULL` or 0 pointer.

```
if (object != 0)
```

It's not possible to guard against a dereference of an illegal pointer value that is not `NULL`, so you should always initialize pointer variables.

12.1. The statements below are used in a program. What range of values might be printed by each of the `cout` statements?

```
Dice cube(6);
Dice octo(8);
Dice * pointer = &cube;
cout << pointer->Roll() << endl;
pointer = &octo;
cout << pointer->Roll() << endl;
```

Explain what the statement `pointer = &octo` does.

12.2. The function `Zero` below is intended to set its parameter to 0.0.

```
void Zero(double * d)
{

}
//...
double d;
Zero(&d);
```

What is the body of the function? Why is the address-of operator used in passing the actual parameter?

12.3. Explain why 13 3 13 is printed by the code fragment below.

```
double a = 3;
double b = 5;
double * d = &a;
b = *d;
a = 13;
cout << a << " " << b << " " << " " << *d << endl;
```

If the statement `d = &b` is inserted after `b = *d`, what is the output?

12.4. The code fragment below defines a variable `cube`, passes its address to `Mystery`, and then "rolls" `cube`.

```
void Mystery(Dice * d)
{
    Dice coin(2);
    d = &coin;
}

// ...
Dice cube(6);
Mystery(&cube);
for(k=0; k < 100; k += 1) {
    cout << cube.Roll() << endl;
}
```

Explain why the values printed when `cube` is rolled are between 1 and 6 (and not just 1 or 2).

12.2 Vectors of Pointers and Operator new

The C++ operator new allocates memory dynamically in response to program control rather than when the program is compiled. Operator new returns a pointer to the allocated memory. This memory comes from what is sometimes called the **freestore**, or the **heap**. When memory that has been allocated using new is no longer needed, it should be returned to the freestore for possible future use. This is done using the C++ operator **delete**.

To illustrate how pointers and dynamically allocated memory can result in faster programs that use less memory, we'll examine Prog. 12.3, *allword5.cc*,[2] a modified version of *allword4.cc*, Prog. 8.8. Instead of using a Vector of WordStat objects, *allword5.cc* uses a Vector of pointers and dynamically allocated WordStat objects. In contrast, a Vector of WordStat objects is used in *allword4.cc*. The difference between using a Vector of pointers and a Vector of WordStat objects is shown in Fig. 12.5.

There are two advantages to using a vector of pointers rather than a vector of structs in *allword5.cc*:

1. Exactly as many WordStat objects can be allocated as needed. There will be more pointers allocated than necessary; but pointers are smaller than WordStat objects, so less memory is required than when a vector of WordStat objects is used. This is shown in Fig. 12.5, where the Vector of pointers is smaller than the Vector of structs. Exactly as many WordStat objects are allocated as needed when pointers are used. In Fig. 12.5 the variable Vector<WordStat> myList—the Vector of structs—shows two extra WordStat elements allocated. The amount of unused memory can increase if the Vector is resized. In contrast, if the vector of pointers Vector<WordStat *> myList is resized, there will be unused memory; but each cell of the vector is a pointer rather than a struct containing a word and a count.

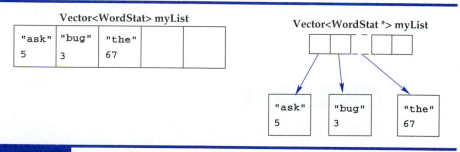

Figure 12.5   On the left is a Vector of structs, on the right a Vector of pointers to structs.

---

[2]In this chapter only part of *allword5.cc* is shown; the part shown is called *word5.cc*.

2.   When `Vector` elements are shifted to store words in alphabetical order, a pointer is shifted instead of a `WordStat` object. This saves lots of time since a `WordStat` object contains a `string` and an `int`. Copying these to shift elements is more time-intensive than copying pointers. When we examine the running times of *allword4.cc* and *allword5.cc*, we'll see this saving clearly.

Allocation and Access Using Vectors of Pointers

The code in *allword5.cc* is very similar to the code in *allword4.cc*. The main differences are in the declaration of the `Vector myList` and in how elements of the `Vector` are accessed. In a `Vector` of `struct`s, declared as `Vector<WordStruct> myList`, each field of the `struct` is accessed using dot notation. For example, the following statements store a word in *allword4.cc*.

```
myList[loc+1].info = word;
myList[loc+1].count = 1;
myCount++;
```

The corresponding statements in *allword5.cc* show how the code changes when a `Vector` of pointers, declared as `Vector<WordStat *> myList`, is used. Each element of `myList` is a pointer to a `WordStat` object.

```
myList[loc+1] = new WordStat;
myList[loc+1]->info = word;
myList[loc+1]->count = 1;
myCount++;
```

Initially, each vector element does *not* point to a `WordStat struct` but points to `NULL` or `0`. Each time a new word is added to `myList`, a `WordStat struct` is allocated dynamically using the operator `new`.

   The operator `new` allocates memory dynamically, or at **run time** as opposed to at compile time (when the program is compiled). By calling `new` only when necessary, a program can allocate memory precisely, without allocating too much as is done when a vector doubles in size. Operator `new` returns a pointer to the type specified by `Thing`, as shown in the syntax box. You can think of the type as a parameter to `new`. It's possible to allocate built-in types using `new`. For example, `int * iptr = new int` will make `iptr` point to a dynamically allocated `int`.

Syntax: operator `new`

```
Thing * thingPtr = new Thing;
Thing * thingPtr = new Thing(arguments);
Thing * thingPtr = new Thing[int expression];
```

   If the class (type) allocated by `new` uses a constructor, then arguments must be provided if the constructor needs them. Since `Dice` variables require a parameter when defined, a dynamically allocated `Dice` object is defined by `Dice * diePtr = new Dice(6)` for a six-sided die referenced by `diePtr`. It's possible to provide arguments for built-in types too: `int * iptr = new int(17)` makes `iptr` point to a dynamically allocated `int` with the value 17.

The third use of `new` is for allocating built-in arrays at runtime. We'll study this in detail in Sec. 12.5. As we'll see, the definition `int * list = new int[100]` makes `list` a pointer to memory that can store 100 contiguous `int` values. This makes `list` a built-in array.

Accessing a field of a `WordStat` struct pointed to by an element of `myList` requires use of the selector operator, `->`. The expression `myList[loc+1]->info` accesses the `info` field of the `struct` pointed to by `myList[loc+1]`. Dot notation can't be used because `myList[loc+1]` is not a `WordStruct`, but an indirect reference, or pointer, to a `WordStruct`. The selector operator dereferences a pointer to a `struct` or class to get to data or a member function.

The selector operator dereferences pointers to `struct`s or classes, but it does not dereference built-in types; it's used only when dereferencing to access a data member or a member function. As we saw in Sec. 12.1, the selector operator is a shorthand for what would otherwise be a cumbersome combination of the dereference operator `*` and the dot operator, e.g., `(*myList[loc+1]).info = Word`.

The differences between *allword4.cc* and *allword5.cc* are minor. All uses of `myList[k].info` are replaced by `myList[k]->info`. Instead of showing the entire program, only the class declaration, the constructor, the destructor, and the function `Update` are shown in *word5.cc*, Prog. 12.3. The destructor function returns storage allocated by `new` to the heap. We'll discuss destructors in the next section.

Program 12.3   word5.cc

```
// code from allword5.cc
// only the code that differs from allword4.cc
// is shown here, see allword5.cc for complete details
// 5-15-95

struct WordStat
{
    string info;                 // the string
    int count;                   // # of times string occurs
};


class WordList
{
  public:
    WordList(int size);          // constructor, specify size of list
    ~WordList();                 // destructor, free storage
    void Update(string word);    // update occurrences of word
```

```
      int GetUnique();              // return # of unique words in list
      int GetTotal();               // return # of total words in list
      void Print(ostream & output); // print all words in list
   private:

      int myCount;                  // # of entries stored in myList
      int mySize;                   // capacity of myList
      int myTotal;                  // # of words (non-unique)
      Vector<WordStat *> myList;    // storage for word stats

      int Search(const string & key); // returns index in myList of key
};

WordList::WordList(int size)
   : myCount(0),
     mySize(size),
     myTotal(0),
     myList(size,0)
{
    // all work done in initializer list
}


WordList::~WordList()
// postcondition: all new'd storage deleted
{
    int k;
    for(k=0; k < myCount; k++)
    {
        delete myList[k];
    }
}

void WordList::Update(string word)
// postcondition: updates occurrence of word
//                adds word to list if not already present
//                increments count of total # of words
{
    int loc = Search(word);

    myTotal++;

    if (loc == -1)                  // not already in list
    {
        if (myCount >= mySize)
        {
            mySize *= 2;
            myList.SetSize(mySize);
        }
        loc = myCount - 1;
        while (0 <= loc && word < myList[loc]->info)
        {
            myList[loc+1] = myList[loc];
            loc--;
        }
    }
```

```
            myList[loc+1] = new WordStat;
            myList[loc+1]->info = word;
            myList[loc+1]->count = 1;
            myCount++;
        }
        else
        {
            myList[loc]->count++;
        }
}
```

OUTPUT

```
prompt> allword5
enter name of input file: melville.txt
1        6
334      a
1        a--premature
1        abate
1        abated
1        aberration
1        abide
1        abiding
2        abode
23       about
...
...
4        yourself
2        youth
# of words = 3125
total words (non-unique): 14353
total time for update = 5.62
```

The time to find the words was almost cut in half compared to the time taken by *allword4.cc*, Prog. 8.8. Counting the words in *Hamlet* with *allword5.cc* takes 14.21 seconds and the nonpointer version in *allword4.cc* takes 25.34 seconds (on a Pentium 100 running Linux). The program is faster because rather than shifting WordStat structs to keep the list in alphabetical order, pointers to the structs are shifted. A pointer uses much less memory than a WordStat struct, so copying during the shifting operation takes less time.

The Destructor Member Function

Whenever a class object allocates memory from the freestore (heap) using new, the memory should be returned to the freestore using delete when the object no longer exists. A constructor is called automatically when an object is defined; similarly a special member function called the **destructor** is called automatically when an object goes out of scope.[3] In *word5.cc*, Prog. 12.3, the destructor is `WordList::~WordList()`.[4] The destructor in *word5.cc* iterates through `myList` deleting all `WordStat structs` allocated during the program's execution.

For any class named `Thing`, a member function named `~ Thing` is the class **destructor**. An object's destructor is called automatically when the object goes out of scope. All memory allocated by the object

> **Syntax: destructor and delete**
>
> ```
> class Thing
> {
> ~Thing();
> }
> Thing::~Thing(){ delete myPointer;}
> ```

using `new` should be returned to the freestore using `delete`. Often the destructor is used to return memory to the heap. You don't call the class destructor explicitly in a program. The destructor function `Thing::~ Thing()` is called automatically.

The operator **delete** returns memory allocated by `new`. The `delete` operator takes a pointer as an argument. The pointer should point to an object allocated by `new` or an error will occur. It is permissible, however, to delete a `NULL` pointer. An error can result if you delete an object twice, so careful programming is required when using pointers.

Pointers for Sorting on Two Keys

Program 12.3 (the shortened version of *allword5.cc*) prints words in alphabetical order. We could change the program to print words in order by frequency of occurrence by sorting the words on the `count` key. However, then the words cannot be listed in alphabetical order. To list the words sorted in two ways, we can use two vectors of pointers. One vector accesses the words in alphabetical order, the other vector accesses words ordered by frequency. This is shown in Fig. 12.6. In alphabetical order the structs are `"bear"`, `"dog"`, `"goat"`, `"lion"`, and `"monkey"`. In numerical order the words are `"dog"`, `"monkey"`, `"lion"`, `"goat"`, and `"bear"`. Using two vectors of pointers uses less storage than two vectors of `structs` and facilitates two orderings of the data.

To print the words sorted by frequency, the vector of pointers on the bottom of Fig. 12.6, are used. In Prog. 12.4, *word6.cc*, the vector `myNumList` points to words sorted by frequency. The vector `myList` points to words sorted alphabetically. Although it's possible to keep both vectors sorted after each call

---

[3]You can think of *going out of scope* as becoming undefined to contrast with definition and the constructor.

[4]The *tilde*, ˜, is sometimes pronounced "twiddle," but 'til-də is an acceptable pronunciation.

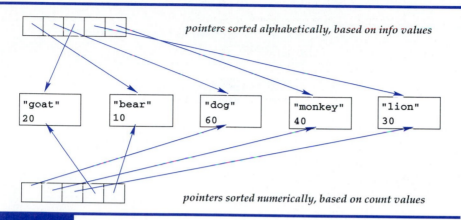

pointers sorted alphabetically, based on info values

pointers sorted numerically, based on count values

Figure 12.6   Sorting with different keys and pointers.

to `Update`, this is not the approach used in *allword6.cc*. Instead, a member function `WordList::Sort()` sorts these pointers. Rather than repeat the rest of the program, which is identical to Prog. 12.3, *word5.cc*, only the class declaration, constructor, print, and sort functions are shown in *word6.cc*. The entire program is stored online as *allword6.cc*. Note that the vector `myNumList` is empty until the `Sort` function is called.

Program 12.4   word6.cc

```
// extracted from allword6.cc, just those parts
// that differ from allword5.cc

struct WordStat
{
    string info;                    // the string
    int count;                      // # of times string occurs
};


class WordList
{
  public:
    WordList(int size);             // constructor,  specify size of list
    ~WordList();                    // destructor, free storage
    void Update(string word);       // update occurrences of word
    int GetUnique();                // return # of unique words in list
    int GetTotal();                 // return # of total words in list
    void Print(ostream & output);   // print all words in list
    void NumPrint(ostream & output);// print all words in list (by # occs)
```

```
    private:

        int myCount;                    // # of entries stored in myList
        int mySize;                     // capacity of myList
        int myTotal;                    // # of words (non-unique)

        Vector<WordStat *> myList;      // storage for word statistics
        Vector<WordStat *> myNumList;   // for sorting by # occurrences

        int Search(const string & key); // returns index in myList of key
        void DoPrint(ostream & output, const Vector<WordStat *> & list);
        void Sort();                    // sort by number
};

WordList::WordList(int size)
    : myCount(0),
      mySize(size),
      myTotal(0),
      myList(size),
      myNumList(0)
{
    // all work done in initializer list
}

void WordList::Sort()
// postcondition: list can be printed sorted by # of occurrences
{
    int j,k,min;

    myNumList.SetSize(myCount);        // allocate space for pointers
    for(j=0; j < myCount; j++)         // copy pointers to all words
    {
        myNumList[j] = myList[j];
    }

    for(j=0; j < myCount; j++)         // selection sort by # occurrences
    {
        min = j;
        for(k=j+1; k < myCount; k++)
        {
            if (myNumList[k]->count < myNumList[min]->count)
            {
                min = k;
            }
        }
        WordStat * temp = myNumList[min];
        myNumList[min] = myNumList[j];
        myNumList[j] = temp;
    }
}

void WordList::Print(ostream & output)
// postcondition: all elements of list printed, sorted alphabetically
```

```
{
    DoPrint(output,myList);
}

void WordList::NumPrint(ostream & output)
// postcondition: all elements of list printed, sorted by # occurrences
{
    Sort();
    DoPrint(output,myNumList);
}

int main()
{
    // code here removed (see allword6.cc)
    timer.Start();
    wlist.NumPrint(cout);
    timer.Stop();

    cout << "total words (non-unique): " << wlist.GetTotal() << endl;
    cout << "total time for update = " << processTime << endl;
    cout << "total time for sorting = " << timer.ElapsedTime() << endl;
    return 0;
}
```

OUTPUT

```
prompt> allword6
enter name of input file: melville.txt
...
...
219     his
265     in
334     a
359     of
376     and
432     to
519     i
603     the
# of words = 3125
total words (non-unique): 14353
total time for update = 5.85
total time for sorting = 5.4
```

The function Sort is a private helper function called from NumPrint. To sort by word counts, the vector of pointers myNumList is copied from myList. The function Vector::SetSize() allocates exactly the number of pointers necessary. The vector `myNumList` is initially constructed with zero entries so that no extra pointers are allocated when sorting by occurrence. The pointers are rearranged using selection sort based on the `count` field of each `WordStat struct`. The most frequently occurring word is referenced by the last pointer in `myNumList`. Because the user has the choice of printing in two ways, a private helper function `DoPrint` has the printing code and is called from public member functions `NumPrint` and `Print` as shown in *word6.cc*. You should try to factor common code into a private helper function rather than duplicate the common code in more than one member function.

Pause to reflect

12.5. Write a code fragment that defines a vector `dieVecPtr` of 30 pointers to dice objects, initializes `dieVecPtr[k]` to point to a (k + 1)-sided die (so that `dieVecPtr[0]` is a one-sided die and `dieVecPtr[29]` is a 30-sided die), rolls each dice object once, and then deletes all the dice objects.

12.6. Suppose that the following definition is made:

```
Vector<Vector<int> *> v(10);
```

so that `v[0]` is a pointer to a vector of integers. The following code fragment makes `v[0]` point to a vector of 100 integers, all equal to 2.

```
v[0] = new Vector<int>(100,2);
```

Since `v[0]` points to a vector of 100 integers, how is an element of this 100-integer vector indexed? That is, write a loop to print all elements of the 100-element vector.

12.7. It's possible to use vector indices as indirect references rather than pointers. For example, in *word6.cc*, Prog. 12.4, two vectors of pointers are used, one to index in alphabetical order and one in numerical order by number of occurrences. Suppose that the definition of `myNumList` is changed as

```
Vector<int> myNumList;
```

and that indices are stored in `myNumList` so that `myNumList[0]` is the index of the least frequently occurring word stored in `myList`. This means that if `myNumList[0] == 23`, then `myList[23]` stores a pointer to the word that occurs least often. To sort the indices in `myNumList`, the following statement is used:

```
if (myList[myNumList[k]]->
            count < myList[myNumList[min]]->count)
{
    min = k;
}
```

What other changes are needed in the `WordList::Sort()` function?

12.8. In *cdshuffl.cc*, Prog. 8.4, a vector of `TrackInfo` stores CD tracks. The declaration for `TrackInfo` and the definition of the vector in `main` are reproduced here.

```
struct TrackInfo
{
    string info;      // information about CD track
    int trackNumber; // the original track number
};

Vector<TrackInfo> allTracks(MAX_TRACKS);
```

What changes are needed in *cdshuffl.cc* if vectors of pointers are used, i.e., if `allTracks` is defined as in the following?

```
Vector<TrackInfo *> allTracks(MAX_TRACKS);
```

In particular, how is `tracks[numTracks].trackNumber` changed, how are the prototypes for `PrintTracks` and `ShuffleTracks` changed, and where is operator `new` called?

12.3 Linked Lists

A **linked list** stores a sequence of items as does an array or vector. However, arrays support random access to any element: the time needed to access `a[5]` is the same as the time needed to access `a[100]` when a is a `Vector`. In contrast, items that are stored near the front of a linked list are accessed more quickly than items near the end of a linked list. This is analogous to how the songs, or tracks, on a cassette tape are arranged. Accessing the fifth song requires skipping over the first four, and songs near the end of the tape take longer to access than songs near the front. Arrays are more like compact discs; it's as easy to play the last track of a CD as it is the first because CD players provide random access to the tracks.

Like any recording tape, linked lists permit new items to be "spliced" into the middle of a list. In the same way that tapes can become longer by splicing in new segments of tape and can be made shorter by cutting out segments of tape, linked lists can have items added and deleted from any location in the list without shifting other items in the list. In some sense, pointers link together the different items of a list in the same way that glue or tape is used to splice segments of magnetic tape.

If an array contains 100 items, the items must be allocated contiguously in memory. When linked lists are used, the different items (these items are usually called **nodes** in contrast with the cells of an array) do *not* need to be allocated contiguously. Each node of a linked list has a pointer to the node that follows it; these pointers are the "tape" used to splice nodes together. Figure 12.7 shows a linked list and an array that store the same values. The last node of a list usually points to 0 (NULL) so that a program can determine when the last node has been reached. This is diagrammed in Fig. 12.7 with the symbol for an electrical ground, three vertical bars.

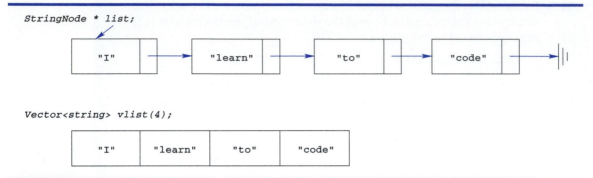

Figure 12.7   Linked list compared to vector.

A node in a linked list contains the information stored in the node, and a pointer to the next node in the list. In C++ a node storing a string is declared like this:

```
struct Node
{
    string info;
    Node * next;
};
```

The info field of the struct stores information, in this case a string. The next field stores a pointer to the next node in the list. This declaration is self-referential: the declaration for Node includes a pointer to a node. This is fine because a pointer can be declared without knowing completely how much memory the thing it points to uses. It would be illegal, for example, to declare Node as

```
struct Node
{
    string info;
    Node next;
};
```

Here the next field isn't a pointer, but a Node. This declaration is circular and will be rejected by the compiler. The g++ compiler generates an error message (in a program named *foo.cc*):

```
foo.cc:4: field 'next' has incomplete type
```

When the compiler parses the declaration for next, the declaration for the struct Node is not yet complete. The declaration can be incomplete for a pointer to a Node to be used, but not for a Node.

Program 12.5, *strlink.cc*, will show how a Vector and a linked list are initialized to contain the four strings "I", "learn", "to", "code". A Vector of strings is stored in the variable vec and a linked list based on the struct

StringNode is pointed to by a pointer variable list. When you write code that uses linked lists you'll need to maintain a pointer to the first node in the list. Often, you'll need to maintain a pointer to the last node to make it easier to add a node at the end of the list. You could write code to find the last node by starting at the beginning and traversing the list until the last node is found (the next field of the last node points to NULL). It's much faster, however, to maintain pointers to both the first and last nodes.

Three statements are needed to make list point to a node containing the string "banana".

```
StringNode * list;

list = new StringNode;        // allocate a node for list to point to
list->info = "banana";        // store a value in the info field
list->next = 0;               // make the next field point to 0
```

Once list points to a node, a pointer to the last node can be defined using StringNode * last = list. The assignment to last can be made only after list has been initialized to point to a new node. For example, the following code does not establish any relationship between list and last; it only makes both pointers have the value NULL.

```
StringNode * list = 0;
StringNode * last = list;
```

Creating Nodes with Linked Lists

The listing and output of Prog. 12.5, *strlink.cc*, are found on page 602; the discussion of the program follows here. The values stored in the built-in array storage are used to initialize the vector vec and the linked list pointed to by list. The initialization of the linked list is complicated since each new node except the first must be linked *after* another node. The first node doesn't follow a node, so it's treated separately, typical of fence post problems.

Program Tip: Creating a linked list often requires special-case code to manage the creation of the first node since this node is the only node that doesn't follow another node.

Sometimes creating a dummy first node (called a header node) avoids lots of special-case code.

Header nodes are used in the implementation of the class List discussed in Sec. 12.4.

In *strlink.cc*, three lines are needed to construct and initialize the first node of the linked list pointed to by list:

```
list = new StringNode;        // create new node
list->info = storage[0];      // info = "I"
list->next = 0;               // next points to 0
```

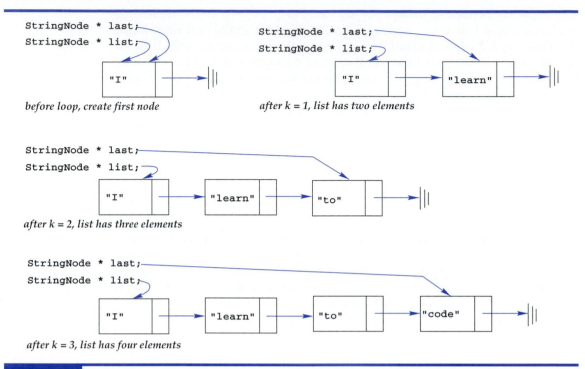

```
StringNode * last;
StringNode * list;
```
"I"

before loop, create first node

```
StringNode * last;
StringNode * list;
```
"I"   "learn"

after k = 1, list has two elements

```
StringNode * last;
StringNode * list;
```
"I"   "learn"   "to"

after k = 2, list has three elements

```
StringNode * last;
StringNode * list;
```
"I"   "learn"   "to"   "code"

after k = 3, list has four elements

Figure 12.8   Building a linked list.

Once the first node is constructed, a loop is used to add new nodes at the end of the list. The variable `last` always points to the last node created when the loop test is evaluated, so the statement "last points to last node in linked list" is a loop invariant. The formation of the linked list at each iteration of the loop is diagrammed in Fig. 12.8. Note that after each loop iteration the variable `last` points to the last node of the linked list. The variable `list`, initialized before the loop because of the fence post problem, never moves and always points to the first node of the linked list.

To add a new node to the end of the linked list, four statements are needed:

1. A node is allocated using `new` and is linked to the end of the list.
2. The pointer `last` is updated to point to the newly allocated node.
3. The `info` field of the new node is assigned a value.
4. The `next` field of the new node is assigned a value.

These steps correspond to the following statements, which are in the body of the `for` loop in `main` of *strlink.cc*:

```
last->next = new StringNode;    // create new node
last = last->next;              // advance to created node
last->info = storage[k];        // assign values
last->next = 0;
```

There are many ways to add a new node to the end of a list. For example, the statement `last = last->next` could be moved from the second statement to the last statement in the list of four statements above. The statement `last->info = storage[k]` would need to be changed to `last->next->info = storage[k]`. The pointer `last->next->info` can be read backward as "the info field of the thing pointed to by the next field of the thing pointed to by last." You should try to get comfortable saying this forward as: "last arrow next arrow info" since this is easier to say.

It's easy to forget to code an assignment to each field of the `struct` used to implement linked list nodes. Since a `struct` is a class in which all data are public by default, `struct`s can have constructors. It's very convenient to use constructors, so we'll use them in `struct`s designed for use with linked lists.

Iterating over a Linked List

The `while` loop that prints all the nodes of the linked list in the function `Print` of Prog. 12.5, *strlink.cc*, is the standard method for looping over all nodes of a linked list. The general format of such a loop is shown next, where `list` points to the first node of a linked list just before the first evaluation of the loop test.

```
while (list != 0)
{
    // process node *list
    list = list->next;
}
```

The statement `list = list->next` advances the pointer `list` so that it points at the next node, e.g., at the second node if it used to point to the first node. When the loop finishes, `list` is zero, or `NULL`. This is not a problem in `Print` of *strlink.cc* since `list` is a parameter that is passed by value and is thus a copy. Nevertheless, some people prefer to use a temporary pointer and rewrite the body of the function `Print` as

```
void Print(StringNode * list)
{
    StringNode * temp = list;
    while (temp != 0)
    {
        cout << temp->info << " ";
        temp = temp->next;          // move to next node
    }
    cout << endl;
}
```

You need not use a temporary pointer since `list` is a value parameter, and thus no changes to `list` are reflected in the calling code. However, there's nothing inherently wrong with using the temporary pointer, and we'll see that a temporary pointer is often required in a class-based use of linked lists.

Program 12.5   strlink.cc

```cpp
#include <iostream.h>
#include "CPstring.h"
#include "vector.h"

// illustrates linked list concepts with list of Strings
// compares to vector
// author : Owen Astrachan
//          11/26/94
//modified: 1/10/96

struct StringNode
{
    string info;                    // stores information
    StringNode * next;              // pointer to next node
};

void Print(StringNode * list);
void Print(const Vector<string> & list);

int main()
{
    StringNode * list=0;            // initialize to 0 for safety
    StringNode * last=0;
    int k;
    Vector<string> vec(4);

    string storage[] = {"I", "learn", "to", "code"};

    // assign values to each vector element

    for(k=0; k < 4; k++)
    {
        vec[k] = storage[k];
    }
    // assign values to each linked list element
    // fence post problem, create first node

    list = new StringNode;               // create new node
    list->info = storage[0];             // info = "I"
    list->next = 0;                      // node points to 0
    last = list;                         // invariant: last points to last node
    for(k=1; k < 4; k++)
    {
        last->next = new StringNode;     // create new node
        last = last->next;               // advance to created node
        last->info = storage[k];         // assign values
        last->next = 0;
    }

    cout << "vector:\t\t";
    Print(vec);
```

```
        cout << "linked list:\t";
        Print(list);
        return 0;
}

void Print(StringNode * list)
// precondition: list is 0-terminated (last node's next field is 0)
// postcondition: all info fields of list printed on one line
{
    while (list != 0)
    {
        cout << list->info << " ";
        list = list->next;          // move to next node
    }
    cout << endl;
}

void Print(const Vector<string> & list)
{
    int k;
    int len = list.Length();
    for(k=0; k < len; k++)
    {
        cout << list[k] << " ";
    }
    cout << endl;
}
```

OUTPUT

```
prompt> strlink
vector:         I learn to code
linked list:    I learn to code
```

Testing Linked List Functions

Program 12.6, *testlist.cc* (page 607), is a test program for checking and reasoning about linked list code. Nodes of lists are declared by the struct Node. The user has the option of adding a node to the front or back of a list, deleting a node, and printing the list. No pointer to the last node of the list is maintained. This forces a list traversal to add a new last node. In the next section we'll use some of the functions in *testlist.cc*, but we'll convert them to member functions of the class List.

The struct Node used in *testlist.cc* has two constructors: one is a default constructor (with no parameters) that initializes the string info to the empty string: "" and the pointer next to NULL; the other has two parameters, a string and a pointer, and initializes the fields of a node with these values. The pointer parameter in the second constructor has a default value of 0 so that the following two statements are equivalent ways of initializing a node pointed to by Node * list.

```
list = new Node("applesauce",0);
list = new Node("applesauce");
```

Although the pointer parameter in `Print` is a value parameter, the other list-manipulating functions use reference parameters. When new nodes are added or deleted, the parameter `list` may change and must be passed by reference. Although `list` points to the first node, and `Append` adds a new node to the end of a linked list, the last node is the first node of a one-element list, and so `list` must be passed by reference to `Append`. If you look carefully at the code for `Append`, `Prepend`, and `Delete`, you'll see that there is an assignment to `list` in each function that must be conveyed back to the calling statement. In contrast, although there is an assignment to `list` in the function `Print`, this assignment can be replaced with a temporary pointer since `list` is used only to traverse the linked list, not to change the contents of the linked list. The constructor is used in `Prepend` to add a new node to the front of the linked list whose first node is pointed to by `list`.

```
void Prepend(Node* & list, const string & s)
// postcondition: new node with s is added to front of s
{
    list = new Node(s,list);
}
```

You may find it easier to understand how this statement works by studying a two-statement equivalent that uses a temporary pointer:

```
Node * temp = new Node(s,list);
list = temp;
```

This two-statement equivalent is illustrated in Fig. 12.9, where a new node containing the string `"banana"` is added as the first node of a linked list.

In the statement `list = new Node(s,list)`, the right-hand side of the `=` operator is evaluated first. Both `s` and `list` are arguments used to construct a new node. The `next` field of this new node will point to `list`, which is the first node of the list. When the constructor is executing, there are two pointers to this first node: `list` and the `next` field of the new node being constructed. Since

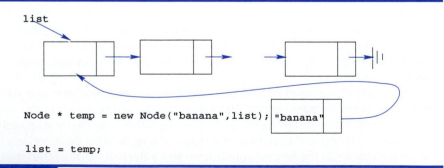

Figure 12.9   Adding a new first node to a linked list.

new returns a pointer to the constructed node, list is assigned this new pointer, and the former first node is now the second node of the list. You may decide that the explicit use of the temporary pointer is easier to understand. It's fine to use a temporary pointer, so you should if it facilitates your understanding of the code.

In the function Append, the list must be traversed to find the last node. As a special case we must check for the empty list. Because list might be empty, list must be a reference parameter since its value will change. Because list is a reference parameter, a temporary pointer must be used to traverse and find the last node of the list. If no temporary is used, using list to traverse the linked list would effectively lose all but the last node of the list, since the changes to list are reflected in the calling code because list is passed by reference.

Note the loop test to find the last node:

```
while (temp->next != 0)
```

When this loop terminates, temp must be pointing to the last node, since the loop test will be false and the next field of temp will be NULL. This loop test is potentially dangerous in other situations since temp is dereferenced in the expression temp->next. In general you should guard all pointer dereferences to avoid NULL-dereferences, which can cause the computer to crash. This loop test could be rewritten as

```
while (temp != 0 && temp->next != 0)
```

which, because of short-circuit evaluation, will not dereference temp if it is NULL. It's not necessary to use the explicit test against 0,

```
while (temp && temp->next)
```

since 0 is equivalent to false, which means that temp evaluates to true unless it is NULL. We do not need to check both temp and temp->next in the Append function because the while loop executes only when there is at least one node in the list.

Deleting Nodes in a Linked List

Deleting nodes in a linked list requires careful coding. We'll use recursion in the function Delete because it's much easier than writing a loop. As with all recursive functions, some base case must be identified. When linked lists are used, the base case is usually the empty list although sometimes a one-node can be used as a base case. Before examining the recursive function, we'll look at how the first node of a list is deleted. This requires a temporary pointer as shown in Delete and illustrated in Fig. 12.10.

Since the first node will be deleted, we must initialize a temporary pointer temp that points to the second node. After deleting the first node, the pointer list can be reassigned to point to the second node whose value was saved in temp. At first, you might think that a temporary isn't necessary and that the following code can be used to delete the first node pointed to by list:

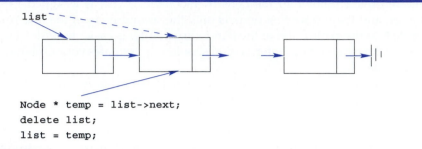

```
Node * temp = list->next;
delete list;
list = temp;
```

Figure 12.10   Deleting the first node of a linked list.

```
delete list;
list = list->next;
```

There is a problem with this code: you can't be sure what happens to the node pointed to by list after the deletion. Once deleted, the node is garbage and may be reclaimed by some other program or some other part of the system. Some programming environments may explicitly fill all deleted storage with garbage. In these cases, dereferencing list using list->next can result in a bad dereference, causing the program to abort. Although your code has not done anything with the storage that list used to point to, which was just deleted, you cannot be sure that the node still exists or that the next field has the same value. You must use a temporary variable.

If you can convince yourself that the first node is deleted properly when it contains a string equal to s, you've taken the first step toward verifying that the recursion works correctly. All nodes except the first node are deleted recursively by the statement

```
Delete(list->next,s);
```

Assuming this works correctly, the only node that may have an info field equal to s is the first node since all nodes after the first node have been treated recursively. We remove the first node if necessary and the function returns. Writing this function iteratively is very difficult; we'll explore this in the exercises. The key to the recursion is the use of a reference parameter.

```
void Delete(Node * & list, const string & s)
```

The parameter list is an alias for the pointer argument passed to Delete. In each function called recursively, the parameter list is an alias for the next field of some node in the list, since the recursive call is Delete(list->next,s). The argument list->next and the parameter list reference the same pointer. Assigning a value to list is the same as assigning a value to list->next, since list is a reference parameter. If list points to a node that should be deleted, it will be deleted after making a recursive call to take care of the rest of the list.

> **Program Tip:** Code that adds a new node to a list must assign a value to some next field or the new node will not be linked into the list. Similarly, deleting a node also requires an assignment to some next field.
>
> When recursion is used, the next field can be an argument passed recursively. The required assignment to a next field can be implemented by a recursive assignment to a parameter that is a reference to a next field.

Program 12.6   testlist.cc

```cpp
#include <iostream.h>
#include "CPstring.h"

// a program to test linked list code
// use a struct for Node so that all fields are public

struct Node
{
    Node() : info(""),  next(0)                  // default constructor
    { }
    Node(const string & val, Node * link=0)   // constructor
        : info(val), next(link)
    { }
    string info;                              // value stored
    Node * next;                              // link to next Node
};

void Append(Node* & list, const string & s)
// postcondition: new node with s is added to end of s
{
    if (list == 0)                      // empty list?
    {
        list = new Node(s);             // create first node
    }
    else
    {
        Node * temp = list;             // advance to end
        while (temp->next != 0)
        {
            temp = temp->next;
        }
        temp->next = new Node(s);
    }
}

void Prepend(Node* & list, const string & s)
// postcondition: new node with s is added to front of s
{
    list = new Node(s,list);
}
```

```cpp
void Delete(Node * & list, const string & s)
// postcondition: no node in list contains s,
//                 nodes removed are deleted
{
    if (list != 0)
    {
        Delete(list->next,s);
        if (list->info == s)
        {
            Node * temp = list->next;
            delete list;
            list = temp;
        }
    }
}

void Print(Node * list)
// postcondition: nodes of list printed, one per line
{
    cout << endl << "*****************" << endl << endl;
    while (list)
    {
        cout << "\t" << list->info << endl;
        list = list->next;
    }
    cout << endl << "*****************" << endl << endl;
}

void Menu()
{
    cout << "(a) append to end of list"            << endl;
    cout << "(p) prepend to front of list"         << endl;
    cout << "(d) delete all occurrences from list" << endl;
    cout << "(v) view/print the list"              << endl;
    cout << "(q) quit the program"                 << endl;
    cout << "(h) help, print choices"              << endl;
    cout << endl << "('a','p','d' prompt for a word)" << endl;
}

int main()
{
    string choice,word;
    Node * list = 0;
    char ch;

    Menu();
    do
    {
        cout << "enter choice: ";
        cin >> choice;

        switch((ch = tolower(choice[0])))
        {
          case 'a' :
            cout << "enter word to append: ";
            cin >> word;
```

```
            Append(list,word);
            break;
          case 'p':
            cout << "enter word to prepend: ";
            cin >> word;
            Prepend(list,word);
            break;
          case 'd':
            cout << "enter word to delete: ";
            cin >> word;
            Delete(list,word);
            break;
          case 'v':
            Print(list);
            break;
          case 'h':
            Menu();
            break;
          case 'q':
            cout << "thanks for list testing" << endl;
            break;
          default:
            cout << "unrecognized choice: " << ch << endl;
        }
    } while (ch != 'q');
    return 0;
}
```

OUTPUT

```
prompt> testlist
(a) append to end of list
(p) prepend to front of list
(d) delete all occurrences from list
(v) view/print the list
(q) quit the program
(h) help, print choices

('a','p','d' prompt for a word)
enter choice: a
enter word to append: banana
enter choice: a
enter word to append: cherry
enter choice: v

* * * * * * * * * * * * * * * *

        banana
        cherry

* * * * * * * * * * * * * * * *
```

```
enter choice: a
enter word to append: guava
enter choice: p
enter word to prepend: guava
enter choice: v

* * * * * * * * * * * * * * * *

        guava
        banana
        cherry
        guava

* * * * * * * * * * * * * * * *

enter choice: d
enter word to delete: guava
enter choice: v

* * * * * * * * * * * * * * * *

        banana
        cherry

* * * * * * * * * * * * * * * *

enter choice: d
enter word to delete: peach
enter choice: v

* * * * * * * * * * * * * * * *

        banana
        cherry

* * * * * * * * * * * * * * * *

enter choice: q
thanks for list testing
```

12.9. Write a function `Count` that counts the number of nodes in a linked list. Write the function recursively and with a `while` loop.

12.10. Describe the effects of the function `Change` in the following.

```
void Change(Node * list)
{
    while (list && list->next)
    {
        Node * temp = list->next;
        list->next = list->next->next;
        list = list->next;
        delete temp;
    }
}
```

12.11. Describe the effects of the function `Chop`, where `list` is a linked list storing `int` values:

```
void Chop(Node * & list)
{
    if (list != NULL)
    {
        Chop(list->next);
        if (list->info % 2 == 0)
        {
            list = list->next;
        }
    }
}
```

12.12. Write the function `CreateList` with header as shown. `CreateList` creates a linked list of *n* integers where the first node contains 1 and the last node contains *n*. The call `Print(CreateList(5))` should print 1 2 3 4 5, where `Print` is from *testlist.cc*, Prog. 12.6.

```
Node * CreateList(int n)
// precondition: 0<n
// postcondition: creates list 1->2->...->n
//                an n node list in which node k
//                contains the int k
```

12.13. Write a function `Reverse` that reverses the order of the nodes in a linked list. Reverse the list by changing pointers, not by swapping `info` fields.

```
void Reverse(Node * & list)
// precondition: list =  (a b c ... d)
// postcondition: list = (d ... c b a), list is reversed.
```

12.14. Write a function that doubles a linked list by duplicating each node; i.e., the list (*a b c d*) is changed to (*a a b b c c d d*). Use the header shown, where `list` is *not* passed by reference. (*Hint:* it's probably easier to write this recursively.)

```
void DoubleList(Node * list)
// precondition:  list = (a b c d)
// postcondition: list = (a a b b c c d d)
```

12.15. Rewrite the function `Delete` from *testlist.cc*, Prog. 12.6, using a `while` loop. Use two pointers to traverse the list, one that trails the pointer to the node that will be deleted. You'll probably need a special case to delete the first node.

Counting Words with Linked Lists

In the next section we'll develop a linked list class that can be reused in many programs. In this section we'll modify the `WordList` class from the *allword* group of programs (e.g., *allword4.cc*, Prog. 8.8, and *allword5.cc*, partially shown in Prog. 12.3.) We'll use a linked list of `WordStat` structs to keep track of words and occurrences.

```
struct WordStat
{
    string info;                // the string
    int count;                  // # of times string occurs
    WordStat * next;            // pointer to next node in list
};
```

Recoding the linked list routines from *testlist.cc*, Prog. 12.6, to fit into the `WordList` class is straightforward. We'll use a private instance variable `WordStat * myList` to point to the first node of the list used to store words and occurrences.

The functions that are substantively different from other *allword* programs are shown in Prog. 12.7, *word7.cc*. The destructor `~WordList` uses the coding techniques from Sec. 12.3 to delete nodes. As noted in that section, the use of the local variable `current` is essential. The only code substantially different from the code in *testlist.cc* is the code in `WordList::Update()` that adds a new node to the list. We'll keep the list ordered alphabetically since this makes nicer output and actually results in faster run times for many text files. Special cases include adding to an empty list and adding a new node to the front of the list. We'll see how to avoid many of these special cases in the next section.

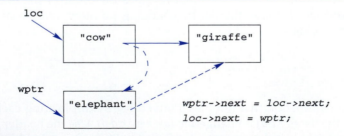

Figure 12.11   Adding a new node to a list.

The `while` loop in `Update` finds where to add a new node. By De Morgan's law (Sec. 5.6), when the loop terminates the following expression holds:

```
loc->next == 0 || loc->next->info >= word
```

If `loc->next == 0` then `loc` points at the last node of the list and the new word is the alphabetically last word in the list. Otherwise, the word in the node *after* `loc` is larger than the new word, but the word in the `loc` node is less than `word`. This means that `word` goes between nodes `loc` and `loc->next`. In either case, the new node `wptr` can be spliced into the list with two statements. Figure 12.11 shows this process when `"elephant"` is added between `"cow"` and `"giraffe"`.

Program 12.7   word7.cc

```cpp
// extracted from allword7.cc, just those parts
// that show important aspects of linked list code

struct WordStat
{
    string info;                    // the string
    int count;                      // # of times string occurs
    WordStat * next;                // pointer to next node in list
};

class WordList
{
  public:
    WordList();                     // constructor
    ~WordList();                    // destructor
    void Update(const string & word);  // update occurrences of word
    int GetUnique();                // return # of unique words in list
    int GetTotal();                 // return # of total words in list
    void Print(ostream & output);   // print all words in list
  private:
    int myCount;                    // # of entries stored in myList
    int myTotal;                    // # of words (non-unique)
    WordStat * myList;              // pointer to first node of list

    WordStat * Search(const string & key); // returns pointer
};

WordList::~WordList()
// postcondition: all new'd storage deleted
{
    WordStat * current = myList;
    while (current != 0)
    {
        myList = myList->next;      // advance to next
        delete current;             // delete current (first)
        current = myList;           // reset current
    }
}
```

```
WordStat * WordList::Search(const string & key)
// postcondition: returns pointer to struct with key
//                 returns 0 if key does not occur
// performance: O(n), n = # items in myList
{
    WordStat * current = myList;
    while (current != 0)
    {
        if (current->info == key)
        {
            return current;
        }
        current = current->next;
    }
    return 0;
}

void WordList::Update(const string & word)
// postcondition: updates occurrence of word
//                 adds word to list if not already present
//                 otherwise updates count of # occurrences
//                 increments count of total # of words
{
    WordStat * loc = Search(word);
    myTotal++;

    if (loc != 0)
    {
        loc->count++;
    }
    else
    {
        myCount++;
        WordStat * wptr = new WordStat; // create new node
        wptr->info  = word;             // store values
        wptr->count = 1;                // initialize all fields
        wptr->next  = 0;


        if (myList == 0)                // any nodes at all?
        {
            myList = wptr;
        }
        else if (word < myList->info)   // goes in front?
        {
            wptr->next = myList;
            myList = wptr;
        }
        else                            // find node before new word
        {
            loc = myList;
            while (loc->next && loc->next->info < word)
            {
                loc = loc->next;
            }
```

```
            wptr->next = loc->next;
            loc->next = wptr;
        }
    }
}
```

word7.cc

12.4   Making a List Class

The functions tested in `testlist.cc`, Prog. 12.6, are typical of C-style linked lists—they are not member functions of a class. You'll need to practice writing functions like the ones used in `testlist.cc` so that you're comfortable writing code that manipulates linked lists. For some applications, however, you'll be able to reuse linked list code created by you or someone else and stored in a library. We'll build on the ideas from the previous section to examine the implementation of a generic list class.[5]

The class is **generic** because it can store any kind of element, although all the elements must be the same type in any one list. We make the class generic by making it a templated class. Just as templates allowed us to design functions that sort vectors of many different types (see Prog. 11.3, *usesort.cc*), we can use templates to design classes that support many types.

Templated classes are not hard to use when writing code. For example, the `Vector` class is templated. The syntax for defining a vector, using angle brackets around the type, as in `Vector<int> ilist(20)`, is used in all templated classes. Unfortunately, the syntax for defining templated member functions is not as terse nor as easy to read. However, you'll find that definitions get easier to read as you become accustomed to reading and implementing them. Rather than start with the complex class `List`, we'll first examine a templated `struct` used to implement generic linked lists.

A Templated Node Class

A templated `struct` `TNode` is shown in Prog. 12.8, *tnode.cc*. A templated function `Print` prints a linked list constructed from templated `TNode` `struct`s. The definition of `TNode` is based on the `Node` `struct` from *testlist.cc*, Prog. 12.6.

A templated class is declared by including `template <class Type>` before the class declaration as shown for `TNode` in *tnode.cc*. Any identifier can be used instead of `Type`, but `Type` is often used.[6] Instead of using `TNode` to identify the struct, we must use `TNode<Type>` to indicate the kind of `TNode` used. For example, `ilist` is defined in `main` as `TNode<int> ilist`. A templated function is made by preceding the function definition with the same syntax: `template <class Type>` precedes the definition of `Print` in Prog. 12.8.

---

[5]The class was used in the Excursion Sec. 6.7.

[6]The most commonly used identifier appears to be `T`, but the brevity of the identifier does not make up for difficulty in reading definitions such as `TNode<T> * ptr`.

Program 12.8   tnode.cc

```
#include <iostream.h>
#include "CPstring.h"

// illustrates templated node class
// Owen Astrachan, 1/27/96

template <class Type>
struct TNode
{

    TNode() : next(0)              // default constructor
    { }
    TNode(const Type & val, TNode<Type> * link=0)
        : info(val),
          next(link)
    { }
    Type info;                     // information
    TNode<Type> * next;            // points to next node
};


template <class Type>
void Print(TNode<Type> * list)
// postcondition: all values in list printed on one line
{
    while (list != 0)
    {
        cout << list->info << " ";
        list = list->next;
    }
    cout << endl;
}

int main()
{
    TNode<string> * slist = new TNode<string>("apple");
    TNode<int>    * ilist = new TNode<int>(123);

    slist->next = new TNode<string>("guava");
    slist->next->next = new TNode<string>("orange");

    ilist->next = new TNode<int>(456);
    ilist->next->next = new TNode<int>(789);

    Print(slist);
    Print(ilist);
    return 0;
}
```

```
                           OUTPUT

prompt> tnode
apple guava orange
123 456 789
```

When variables such as `ilist` and `slist` are defined, the templated class is **instantiated**. Note the difference in how `new` is used when compared to a nontemplated `struct` such as `Node` used in *testlist.cc*, Prog. 12.6.

```
temp->next  = new Node(s);                    // from testlist.cc
slist->next = new TNode<string>("guava");     // from tnode.cc
```

Although this may be hard to read at first, try to remember that a templated `struct` or class name is *always* used in conjunction with the type of object stored in the class. The definition `TNode<double> * dlist` defines a pointer `dlist` to a `TNode` that can store `double` values.

A Templated List Class

Rather than examine every member function of the class `List` we'll concentrate on those functions that illuminate the use of linked lists in the construction of a robust, general class. For a simple use of the class see *wordlist.cc*, Prog. 6.13 (page 301). To see how using the `List` class facilitates code development, compare the function `Update` below to the version of `Update` in *word7.cc*, Prog. 12.7. In the version below, `myList` is defined as a `List` variable.

```
List<WordStat> myList;          // a list of WordStat objects
```

Like the `Vector` class, the `List` class requires the type that instantiates it to have a default constructor. Two `WordStat` constructors are shown in the following fragment

```
struct WordStat
{
    string info;                // the string
    int count;                  // # of times string occurs

    // make constructors
    WordStat() : info(""), count(0) {}
    WordStat(const string & s) : info(s), count(1) {}
};
```

Using `List` member functions specified in *list.h*, Prog. 12.9, yields the version of `Update` below. The list is maintained in alphabetical order just as it is in *allword7.cc*. To update the list, the list is traversed using `First`, `IsDone`, and `Next`. If the word being updated is found, its count is incremented. If a word is found that comes alphabetically after the word being updated, the new word is not in the list, so it's inserted before the word that comes after it. For example, if `"cow"` is found while searching for `"brown"`, then we can insert "brown" just before "cow". There is no helper function Search in this version of the program.

```
void WordList::Update(const string & word)
// postcondition: updates occurrence of word
//                adds word to list if not already present
//                otherwise updates count of # occurrences
//                increments count of total # of words
{
    myTotal++;
    bool inList = false;
    for(myList.First(); ! inList && ! myList.IsDone(); myList.Next())
    {
        if (myList.Current().info > word)      // stop and insert before
        {
            myList.InsertBefore(WordStat(word));
            inList = true;
            myCount++;
        }
        else if (myList.Current().info == word)  // stop and increment
        {
            myList.Current().count++;
            inList = true;
        }
    }
    if (! inList)     // not added, must belong at end of list
    {
        myList.Append(WordStat(word));
        myCount++;
    }
}
```

Implementing the List Class

The List class is implemented using a linked list of TNode objects. Private instance variables myFirst and myLast are pointers to the first and last nodes of the linked list, respectively. Because empty lists can require lots of special case code, the private linked list is implemented using a dummy header node. When a List variable is constructed, the pointer myList is initialized to point to a node that is *not* considered part of the List being constructed. The header node is a **dummy node** because no values are stored in it; it is used only to facilitate implementations of all the member functions. In particular, deleting nodes and inserting nodes are made much simpler by using a header node, since every node actually in the list has a node before it—the header node is the node before the first node actually in the list.

We do not have space to discuss all the List functions here, but we'll touch on the syntactic issues raised by the declarations in *list.h*, Prog. 12.9.

Const Member Functions and Reference Return Types

The accessor functions Front, Back, Contains, Size, and Print are declared as const **member functions** by following each declaration with the modifier const.

```
#ifndef _LIST_H
#define _LIST_H

// a list class that supports insertion at either the front
// or back.  Other operations include testing for containment
// and iterating over all elements of the list.  Iterator
// permits deletion and insertion before current item
//
// mutating functions, change list
//
// void Append(const Type & t)    -- add t to back of list
// void Prepend(const Type & t)   -- add t to front of list
// void ChopFront()               -- remove first element
// void Clear()                   -- make the list empty
//
// accessing functions, get values from list
//
// Type Front()       -- return copy of first element in list
// Type Back()        -- return copy of last element in list
// bool Contains(const Type & t) -- return true iff list contains t
// int Size(), int Length() -- return # elements in list
// void Print()               -- print list elements
//
// iterating functions:
// First(), IsDone(), Next() -- iterate through all elements
// Type & Current()              -- return element: can modify element
//                               (const version exists too)
// Delete()                  -- delete current item
// InsertBefore(const Type & t) -- insert t before current item

template <class Type>
class List
{
  public:

    List();                               // make an empty list
    List(const List & list);              // copy constructor
    ~List();                              // free memory

    const List& operator = (const List & list);   // assignment operator

    // mutators, add values to list

    void Append(const Type & t);          // new value at end
    void Prepend(const Type & t);         // new value at front
    void ChopFront();                     // chop off first value in list
    void Clear();                         // make the list empty

    // accessors, determine properties of list, get first/last values
```

```
    Type Front() const;                 // return copy of first element
    Type Back()  const;                 // return copy of last element

    bool Contains(const Type & t) const;   // true if t in list
    int Size() const;                      //  # of items in list
    int Length() const;                    //  # of items in list
    void Print() const;                    // print elements in list

    // iterator functions, traverse list, delete/modify

    void First() const;                 // set iterator to front
    bool IsDone() const;                // finished iterating?
    void Next() const;                  // advance to next item

    Type& Current();                    // return current item
    const Type& Current() const;        // return const current item

    void Delete();                      // delete current item
    void InsertBefore(const Type & t);  // add t before current item

  private:

    struct TNode
    {
        // data members
        Type info;              // value stored
        TNode * next;           // link to next TNode

        // constructors
        TNode()
            : next(0)
        { }
        TNode(const Type & val, TNode * link=0)
            : info(val),
              next(link)
        { }


    };

    TNode * myFirst;        // first node of list
    TNode * myLast;         // last node of list
    int myCount;            // # of items in list

    TNode * myCurrent;      // used by iterator
    TNode * myBefore;       // one before current
    bool myCurrentValid;    // true if current valid
};

#endif
```

```
bool Contains(const Type & t) const;     // true if t in list
int Size() const;                        // # of items in list
int Length() const;                      // # of items in list
```

Since programmers often write functions using const reference parameters, the compiler must have some way to determine which member functions can be used with const objects. Only member functions declared as const can be used with const objects. For example, the member function Append cannot be used with a const object. All const member functions can be applied to non-const objects, so any List object can have Contains and Print applied to it. However, only non-const List objects can have Append and Prepend applied, since they are not declared as const.

To facilitate traversal using the iterator member functions First, IsDone, and Next, two versions of the function Current are implemented. Each function returns a reference to an object in the list rather than a copy of the object. Returning a reference allows the object in the list to be updated. This behavior is essential if the List class can be used in place of a low-level, pointer-based linked list class. The return type is modified with an ampersand just as reference parameters and reference variables are modified. However, a const List object should not be modified. To ensure that this protection against modification is supported by the compiler, two versions of Current are implemented.

```
Type& Current();                         // return current item
const Type& Current() const;             // return const current item
```

The const member function returns a const reference. The compiler will catch attempts to modify a const object, so you will not be able to modify a const List object using the iterating functions.

Assignment Operator and Copy Constructor

(*The material in this section is not essential; it consists of advanced C++ details regarding class implementations.*)

When you design a class, you should aim for the behavior of the class to meet user expectations. For classes like List and Vector this means that users should be able to assign objects to each other and pass parameters by value if necessary, since the built-in types support these operations. What happens, for example, when one List object is assigned to another?

```
List<string> listOne, listTwo;

listOne.Append("tuna"); listOne.Append("shark");
listTwo = listOne;
listTwo.Print();
```

If List objects behave like built-in objects, then the object listTwo represents the list ("tuna","shark") after this code has executed. You should expect listTwo to maintain this value even after listOne.Clear() has executed. However, we know from experience with pointers that it's possible for storage to be pointed to by more than one pointer, which can cause problems. Although it's always possible for one object to be assigned to another in C++, an assignment can result in shared storage, especially when pointers are used.[7] To ensure this does not happen, classes that use pointers should implement `operator =`, the assignment operator. The assignment operator for the `List` class will be reproduced shortly. In the statement `listTwo = listOne`, the object `listOne` is passed as the argument to the parameter `list` in the assignment operator. The object `listTwo` is the object assigned to; its `myFirst`, `myLast`, and other instance variables get values from `listOne`.

First, the list assigned to (`listTwo` in the preceding example) is cleared so that it is empty. Then the values from `list` are added one at a time using `Append`. We could use low-level linked list routines instead of `Append`, but using `Append` will make it easier to modify the implementation if another kind of list is used. In any case, assignment using `Append` results in the allocation of new nodes for the underlying linked list so that no storage is shared.

One final detail remains for the assignment operator. Assignments can be chained together: `listOne = listTwo = listThree`. The chaining is possible because the assignment operator returns the object assigned to. The object that invokes a member function is pointed to by a pointer named `this`. The identifier `this` is a reserved word. For example, instead of using `Append` in the following code, we could use `this->Append()`. You do not declare or define `this`; it is part of the language and is always defined. Since `this` is a pointer, `*this` is the object it points to. The statement `return *this` thus returns the object assigned to.

```
template <class Type>
const List<Type> &
List<Type>::operator =(const List<Type> & list)
{
    Clear();

    myCurrentValid = false;    // don't copy iterator values
    myCurrent      = 0;
    myBefore       = 0;

        // append list values to myself: make me a copy of List

        for(list.First(); ! list.IsDone(); list.Next())
        {
            Append(list.Current());
        }
        return *this;
}
```

Arguments passed by value must be copied. Just as `operator = is` used to copy correctly when values are assigned, a special **copy constructor** is used to make a copy when arguments are passed by value or when one variable is constructed from another, e.g., `List<string> listThree(listOne)`. The copy constructor has a special prototype: the parameter is a `const` reference

---

[7]If the assignment operator is declared in the private section of a class, the compiler will prevent client code from assigning objects of the class. This was done in *heart.h*, Prog. 7.16.

object of the class:

```
template <class Type>
List<Type>::List(const List<Type> & list)
// postcondition: *this is a copy of list
```

For the `List` class, the body of the copy constructor is nearly identical to the assignment operator. In general, code is often duplicated and can be factored out for these two functions. However, the assignment operator assigns to an object that has previously been defined whereas the copy constructor constructs an object anew, for the first time.

Program Tip: When you implement one of the following three member functions, it is normally an indication that you should implement all three functions.

1. destructor
2. operator =
3. copy constructor

If this explanation has been less than perspicacious, do not worry. You do not need to master the topics in this section until you are designing and implementing more advanced classes.

12.5 Arrays and Pointers in C++ (optional)

The `Vector` and `Matrix` classes used in this book allocate and change the size of one- and two-dimensional arraylike classes at runtime. The implementations of these classes depend on low-level use of pointers to allocate contiguous blocks of memory that are treated as arrays by the C++ compiler. It's not essential that you understand the relationship between pointers and arrays, but you may read code that exploits this relationship and you may need to write pointer-based array code if you continue to use and study C++. In this section we'll investigate parts of the `Vector` class implementation, but we'll use some simplistic examples at first to see how pointers are used to implement dynamically allocated arrays.

Program 12.10, *dynarray.cc*, prompts the user for a value `size` and then defines an array with `size` entries setting the *k*th entry of the array to *k*.

Program 12.10   dynarray.cc

```
#include <iostream.h>

// illustrates (simplistically) dynamic allocation of arrays

int main()
```

```
{
    int size;
    cout << "enter size of array: ";
    cin >> size;

        // create array list with list[k] = k

    int * list = new int[size];
    int k;
    for(k=0; k < size; k++)
    {
        list[k] = k;
    }
        // print array

    for(k=0; k < size; k++)
    {
        cout << list[k] << " ";
    }
    cout << endl;

    delete [] list;

    return 0;
}
```

OUTPUT

```
prompt> dynarray
enter size of array: 10
0 1 2 3 4 5 6 7 8 9
prompt> dynarray
enter size of array: 21
0 1 2 3 4 5 6 7 8 9 10 11 12 13 14 15 16 17 18 19 20
```

The definition of `list` as `int * list` defines `list` as a pointer to an `int`. Traditionally this definition is read as "int star list"; the asterisk is pronounced "star" when used to indicate a pointer. As a pointer, `list` is an indirect address to an `int`. When a pointer is used as an array, the pointer will be used in conjunction with the indexing operator, `[]`, as shown in Prog. 12.10.

An array can be defined at run time using the operator `new`. This allows the number of array cells to be determined dynamically as opposed

---

Syntax: operator `new` and `delete` for arrays

```
Thing * thingPtr = new Thing[int expression]

delete [] thingPtr
```

to statically at compile time. When storage allocated by `new` for an array is no longer needed, it should be deallocated using the `delete` operator. The syntax for this is `delete [] thingPtr`, where `thingPtr` has been allocated using `new Thing[size]`. It's important to use brackets when deallocating a dynamically allocated array. For example, if an array is used in place of a `Vector` in *word5.cc*, Prog. 12.3, and the brackets aren't used to delete `myList`, the memory allocated dynamically for each `WordStat struct` will *not* be freed.

Once the memory for an array has been allocated and assigned to a pointer variable, the pointer can be treated as an array. This means that the pointer can be indexed using the operator `[]` and it can be passed to a function expecting an array as a parameter. In particular, the function prototype:

```
void Print(const int a[], int numElts);
```

indicates that the first parameter must be an array of `int`. Both calls of `Print` below are legal. The first passes a statically, or compile-time allocated array; the second passes a dynamically or run-time allocated array.

```
int list [100];
// fill list with values
int size;
cout << "enter size: ";
cin >> size;
int * dlist = new int[size];
// fill dlist with values

Print(list,100);
Print(dlist,size);
```

If the prototype is changed to `Print(const int * a, int numElts)`, then both function calls will still be legal! In this case, the prototype indicates that `a` is a (constant) pointer to an `int`. The compiler treats both declarations of parameter `a` in the same way.

> **Program Tip: For any array variable** `list`, **the following equivalence holds:** `list` **is treated identically to** `&list[0]`.
>
> Thus an array name is treated the same as the address of the first element of the array (the element with index zero).

The equivalence between pointers and arrays makes it possible to allocate a chunk of memory and then "divide" this chunk among several pointers, as shown in Prog. 12.11. The statically allocated `storage` stores a block of 60 contiguous integers. The pointers `first`, `second`, and `third` are assigned to point to cells at regular intervals in this block. Because pointers can be used as arrays, `third` is an array of 20 values (one-third of the block allocated for `storage`). The pointer `second` can be treated like an array of 40 values although in the program below, its size is treated as 20.

Figure 12.12 illustrates how one array is accessed by three different pointers in Prog. 12.11.

Program 12.11   arrayp.cc

```cpp
#include <iostream.h>

// illustrates pointer and array relationship
// author: Owen Astrachan
//         11/25/1994

const int SIZE = 60;

void Print(const int * list, int numElts);

int main()
{
    int storage[SIZE];
    int * first, * second, * third;
    int k;
    for(k=0; k < SIZE; k+=1)       // initialize all array cells
    {
        storage[k] = k;
    }

    first = &storage[0];           // first array cell
    second = &storage[SIZE/3];     // middle third of array cells
    third = &storage[2*SIZE/3];    // last third of array cells

    cout << "first = ";  Print(first,SIZE/3);
    cout << "second = "; Print(second,SIZE/3);
    cout << "third = ";  Print(third,SIZE/3);
    return 0;
}

void Print(const int * list, int numElts)
// precondition: list[0] ... list[numElts] have values
// postcondition: values are printed on one line
{
    int k;
    for(k=0; k < numElts; k++)
    {
        cout << list[k] << " ";
    }
    cout << endl;
}
```

OUTPUT

```
prompt> arrayp
first = 0 1 2 3 4 5 6 7 8 9 10 11 12 13 14 15 16 17 18 19
second = 20 21 22 23 24 25 26 27 28 29 30 31 32 33 34 35 36 37 38 39
third = 40 41 42 43 44 45 46 47 48 49 50 51 52 53 54 55 56 57 58 59
```

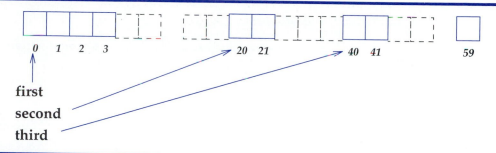

Figure 12.12   One array accessed by three pointers.

The definitions of the three pointers in Prog. 12.11 illustrates a potential source of confusion. When * is used as a type modifier, it binds only to the variable to its right, not to the type. Thus the definition

```
double * a, b;
```

defines a as a pointer to a double, but defines b as a double, *not* as a pointer.

Program Tip: Be careful when defining several pointer and nonpointer variables in a single statement.

In such a definition, the * binds to an identifier, *not* to a type. It's a good idea to define only one variable per statement to avoid this problem. This means you should write definitions like this.

```
double * first;
double * second;
```

Rather than trying to define two variables in one statement:

```
double * first, * second;
```

Implementing the Vector Class

Values stored in a Vector object are stored in a built-in array myList private instance variable. Resizing a Vector object requires allocating a new array, copying the values from the old array into the new array, and deleting the new array. The following code illustrates the use of pointers, new, and delete for built-in arrays.

```
template <class Item>
void Vector<Item>::SetSize(int newSize)
// precondition: vector has room for myLength entries
// postcondition: vector has room for newSize entries, the first
//                myLength of which are copies of original unless
//                newSize < myLength, then truncated copy occurs
{
  int numToCopy = myLength;    // copy all values unless ...
  if (numToCopy < newSize)     // truncating rather than growing
```

```
{
    numToCopy = newSize;
}
 Item * newList = new Item[newSize];      // allocate new storage
 int k;
 for(k=0; k < numToCopy;k++)
 {
     newList[k] = myList[k];
 }
 delete [] myList;                 //de-allocate old storage
 myLength = newSize;               // capacity changed
 myList = newList;                 // point to new array
}
```

The code for assigning one vector to another uses similar logic to copy values into a vector after allocating a new array.

Array Indexing and Pointer Arithmetic

The similarity between arrays and pointers extends to the manner in which the indexing operator, [], is implemented when arrays are used. If you review the definition of an array on page 362 you'll note that access to an array element should require time independent of which element is accessed—the zeroth element is as quickly accessed as the hundredth element. This is possible because the compiler can determine where any array element is, given its index and how much memory a single array element uses. For example, if an int uses 4 bytes of memory (see Sec. 9.8) then an array a of 7 ints requires 28 bytes of contiguous memory. If the memory location of the first int is 1000, then the second int begins at memory location 1004, assuming each memory location is one byte. The seventh int (which would be a[6]) begins at memory location $1024 = 1000 \times 6 * 4$. We can compute the location of any element given the beginning location of the array and the size of each array element. Figure 12.13 shows this calculation. In the figure, three arrays have been allocated using these definitions:

```
int a[7] = {100, 200, 300, 400, 500, 600, 700};
double b[6] = {1.1, 2.2, 3.3, 4.4, 5.5, 6.6};
String c[5] = {"ritz","spritz","nitz","quitz","glitz"};
```

We can add an int value to a pointer, and the compiler determines that "adding one" means something different for an int, a double, and a string. Figure 12.13 illustrates this difference, where the third cell of each array is accessed by adding 2 to the base location of the array. Because an int uses less memory than a double, the result of adding 2 to the location of the first array element is different for the array a and the array b. The physical address for an array element can be computed by multiplying the index by the value returned by sizeof(element). Fortunately, the compiler takes care of this arithmetic so that we can write an expression like c+2 to access the third element (index 2) of an array c regardless of the kind of element stored in c.

Just as the array name a is equivalent to the address &a[0], so is the value of the expression a+k equivalent to the address &a[k]. Thus in Fig. 12.13 the value of c[2] is "nitz," which can also be accessed as *(c+2).

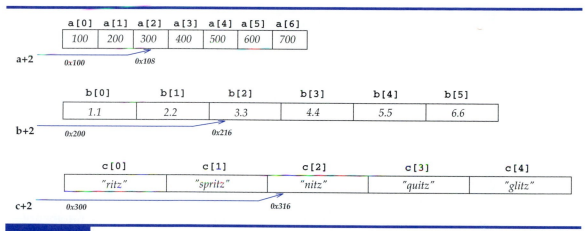

Figure 12.13   Pointer arithmetic and arrays.

Program Tip: Given the definition of a pointer p as `Type * p`, **the expression** `p + k` **is also a pointer to** `Type` **and is equivalent to** `&p[k]`, **a memory location** `k` **cells "away" from what** `p` **points to.**

This means that the dereferencing operator, `*`, can be used to access individual array cells and that the following equivalence holds.

```
p[2] = *(p + 2) = *(2 + p) = 2[p]
```

Although the expression `2[b]` has value 3.3 in the array diagrammed in Fig. 12.13 because of this equivalence, you should *not* use such an expression, since it does not convey that the cell with index 2 of an array `b` is being accessed in the same way that the expression `b[2]` does.

For user-defined classes like `Vector`, the indexing operator, `[]`, is defined in a different manner and the equivalence given above does *not* hold.

12.16. How can *arrayp.cc*, Prog. 12.11 (page 626), be modified so that the user can enter the size of the array `storage` at runtime? Does it matter if the user enters a value that is not a multiple of three?

12.17. Write the function `Copy`, which makes a copy of an array and returns the copy.

```
double * Copy(const double a[], int numElts)
// precondition: a contains numElts elements
// postcondition: returns a copy of a
```

12.18. The following function is designed to fill an array with zeros.

```
void Zero(int * a, int numElts)
// postcondition: a[0] == a[1] == ... a[numElts-1] == 0
```

Pause to reflect

```
{
    for(k=0;  k < numElts;  k++)
    {
        a[k] = 0;
    }
}
```

Why does this work when a is not a reference parameter?

12.19. Write a function HighLow that uses pointers rather than reference parameters to return the largest and smallest values in its array parameter. A call of the function HighLow(a,100,&big,&small) would set big to the largest of the first 100 values in array a and set small to the smallest of these values.

12.20. A char array with a special '\0' terminator is a C-style string. Explain why the following code can be used to count the number of characters in such an array a.

```
count = 0;
while (*a)
{
    a++;
    count++;
}
```

12.21. The classic way to copy a '\0' terminated C-style string a to a string b is shown here in a loop (note the semicolon after the loop). Both a and b are char * variables. Explain why the loop works. You may need to review how the postincrement operator, ++, works.

```
while (*b++ = *a++);
```

12.22. In Fig. 12.13, assume that the array a begins in memory at address or location 1000, array b begins at location 2000, and array c begins at location 3000. Assume that the size of an int is 4 bytes, and that the sizes of a double and a string are 8 bytes each. What are the addresses of a+2, b+2, and c+2? How many bytes of memory are allocated for each of the three arrays?

12.23. Consider this sequence of statements:

```
int one = 3;
int two = 5;
int * aPtr = &one;
int * bPtr = &one;

if (aPtr == bPtr) cout << "pointers equal" << endl;
bPtr = &two;
if (*aPtr == *bPtr) cout << "contents equal first" << endl;
two = 3;
if (*aPtr == *bPtr) cout << "contents equal second" << endl;
```

Explain why the second cout statement is *not* executed, but the other statements are. Explain why if the == is changed to a = in the second if statement the cout statement will be executed.

12.6   Chapter Review

In this chapter we discussed pointers. Pointers are indirect references, useful when data need to be accessed in more than one way and when data must be allocated dynamically.

Topics covered include:

- Variables have names, values, and addresses. The address of a variable can be assigned to a pointer.

- Several operators are used to manipulate pointers: `->`, `*`, `&`, `new`, and `delete`.

- Pointers can be used for efficiency since a `Vector` of pointers to strings requires less space than a `Vector` of strings, especially if the `Vector` is not full.

- The `new` operator is used to allocate memory dynamically from the heap. Memory can be allocated using `new` in conjunction with a constructor with arguments. Built-in arrays can also be allocated dynamically using `new`.

- Pointers are dereferenced to find what they point to. Pointers can be assigned values in four ways: using `new`, using `&` to take the address of existing storage, assigning the value of another pointer, and assigning 0 or `NULL`.

- A destructor member function is called automatically when an object goes out of scope. Any memory allocated using `new` during the lifetime of the object should be freed using `delete` in the destructor.

- Pointers can be used to change the values of parameters indirectly. This is how parameters are changed in C: addresses are passed rather than values. The indirect addresses are used to change values.

- Linked lists support splicing, or fast insertions and deletions (in contrast to arrays and vectors in which items are often shifted during insertion and deletion). However, items near the end of a linked list take more time to access than items near the front.

- Recursive linked-list functions with pointers passed by reference are often shorter than an equivalent iterative version of the function.

- Classes can be templated so that they can be used to generate literally thousands of different classes, just as templated functions represent potentially thousands of functions.

- A header node can be used when implementing linked lists to avoid lots of special-case code, especially when deleting and inserting elements into the list.

12.7   Exercises

12.1 Implement Quicksort for linked lists (see *timesort.cc*, Prog. 11.5). The partition function should divide a list into two sublists, one containing values less than or equal to the pivot, the other containing values greater than the pivot. The partition function can return three pointers:

- pointer to the pivot element (node)
- pointer to the list of items less than or equal to the pivot element
- pointer to the list of items greater than the pivot node

You'll need to be careful to break the original list so that all lists are properly NULL-terminated. You may find it useful to return pointers to the last nodes of the lists from the partition function; you'll have to see how the coding progresses.

When you've implemented the sort, develop a test program to verify that the original list is sorted. Then time the sort using either randomly constructed large lists or by reading words from a text file and sorting them. Consider writing a templated version of the sort as well.

12.2 In a **doubly linked** list, each node contains pointers to the preceding node as well as to the following node. Unlike singly linked lists, doubly linked lists can be traversed easily in both directions. Write a declaration for DNode, a node used to implement doubly linked lists. Then write a test program similar to *testlist.cc*, Prog. 12.6, to test your implementation of doubly linked lists.

12.3 In a **circularly linked** list, the last node points back to the first node rather than to NULL. A pointer is kept to the last node of a circularly linked list rather than to the first node, because the first node can be found in one step from the last node. Modify the code in **testlist.cc,** Prog. 12.6, so that the linked list is circular. Be careful when printing the list, you may need an extra local variable to determine when you get back to where you start.

12.4 The *Josephus problem* (see [Knu73b]) is based on a "fair" method for designating one person from a group of N people. Assume that the people are arranged in a circle and are numbered from 1 to N. If we count off every fourth person, removing a person as we count them off, then the first person removed is number 4. The second person removed is number 8, the third person removed is 5 (because the fourth person is no longer in the circle), and so on. Write a program to print the order in which people are removed from the circle given N, the number of people, and M, the number used to count off. The problem originates from a group determined to commit suicide rather than surrender or be killed by the enemy.

12.5 A **stack** is a data structure sometimes called a **LIFO** structure, for "last in, first out." A stack is modeled by cars pulling into a driveway: the last car in is the first car out. In a stack, only the last element stored in the stack is accessible. Rather than use insert, remove, append, or delete, the vocabulary associated with stack operations is

Push—add an item to the stack; the last item added is the only item accessible by the Top operation.
Top—return the topmost, or most recent, item pushed onto the stack.
Pop—delete the topmost item from the stack.

For example, the sequence Push(3), Push(4), Pop, Push(7), Push(8) yields the stack (3,7,8) with 8 as the topmost element on the stack.

Stacks are commonly used to implement recursion, since the last function called is the first function that finishes when a chain of recursive clones is called.

Write a (templated) class to implement stacks (or just implement stacks of integers). In addition to member functions `Push`, `Pop`, and `Top`, you should implement `Size` (returns number of elements in stack), `Clear` (makes a stack empty), and `IsEmpty` (determines if the stack is empty). Use either a vector or a linked list to store the values in the stack. Write a test program to test your stack implementation.

After you've tested the `Stack` class, use it to evaluate **postfix** expressions. A postfix expression consists of two values followed by an operator. For example: 3 5 + is equal to 8. However, the values can also be postfix expressions, so the following expression is legal.

```
3 5 + 4 8 * + 6 *
```

This expression can be thought of as parenthesized, where each parenthesized subexpression is a postfix expression.

```
( ( (3 5 +) (4 8 *) +) 6 * )
```

However, it's easy to evaluate a postfix expression from left to right by pushing values onto a stack. Whenever an operator (+, *, etc.) is read, two values are popped from the stack, the operation computed on these values, and the result pushed back onto the stack. A legal postfix expression always leaves one number, the answer, on the stack. Postfix expressions do not require parentheses; $(6 + 3) \times 2$ is written in postfix as 6 3 + 2 ×. Write a function to read a postfix expression and evaluate it using a stack.

12.8 A Computer Science Excursion: Hash Search and Tree Search

We've seen many versions of programs that read a text file and count how many times each word occurs. For example, *allword4.cc*, Prog. 8.8, uses a sorted vector of structs and binary search to look up each word. In *word5.cc*, Prog. 12.3, a vector of pointers to structs was used instead; binary search was still used to look up a word. In *allword7.cc*, Prog. 12.7, a linked list of structs was used to store words. Since linked lists do not support random access, it was not possible to use binary search. However, using linked lists means that no vector resizing is necessary and no shifting is needed to keep elements in alphabetical order. Timings are given in Table 12.2 for these different programs to process all the words in Melville's *Bartleby, the Scrivener* and in Hawthorne's *The Scarlet Letter*. As a base, the time needed to simply read the words, convert them to lowercase, and remove punctuation is also given. Note that this is *not* included in the timings of the *allword* programs, since these programs time only the member function `WordList::Update` in the different programs.

Program 12.3, which uses a vector of pointers to `struct`s, is the fastest of these programs. Is the program fast enough? Of course, the answer depends on what kind of machine the program is run on, on characteristics of the input data, and on what "fast enough" really means. For example, I'm willing to wait for 15 seconds, so all the programs are close to "fast enough" in processing Melville's *Bartleby, the Scrivener*, containing 3,125 unique words and 14,353 total words.

Table 12.2   These times are obtained on a Pentium 100-Mhz machine running Linux using the g++ compiler.

program	method	time (sec)	
		Melville	Hawthorne
read file	convert to lowercase and strip punctuation	1.2	7.2
read file	no `StripPunc`	0.5	2.6
allword4.cc	sorted vector of `struct`s with binary search	10.7	92
allword5.cc	sorted vector of pointers to `struct`s with binary search	5.78	53.1
allword7.cc	sorted linked list	15.9	287
allword8.cc	linked list, not sorted	17.7	349

However, I'm not willing to wait for a minute or longer, so the time needed to process Hawthorne's *The Scarlet Letter,* containing 9,164 unique words and 85,753 total words, is not fast enough. What options do I have if I really must process files of this size? There are three immediately obvious solutions:

1. Buy a faster machine.
2. Find a faster algorithm/data structure.
3. Learn to live with one minute as "fast enough."

Since processor speeds have been doubling at least every two years, I might not need to wait too long before faster machines become affordable. However, finding a better way of structuring the data would save money (I would not need to buy a new computer) and will also let us study some alternatives to using linked lists that result in dramatically faster search times.

In this Excursion Section we'll study two alternatives to structuring data that are amazingly fast. The first, called **hashing,** processes *The Scarlet Letter* in 1.5 seconds but does not maintain the list of words in alphabetical order. The second alternative, which uses a **search tree,** uses 2.3 seconds to process *The Scarlet Letter* but does maintain the list of words in alphabetical order. These programs take 13.4 seconds and 40.3 seconds, respectively, to process a 16,598–unique word and 755,231–total word online version of the Bible.

Hashing

In the form that we'll study it, **hashing** combines linked lists with the kind of indexed search associated with a dictionary that has thumb indices, which facilitate finding words according to the initial letter, like the *k* words and the *v* words. For example, when storing words as with the *allword* programs, instead of using one linked list, we will use 26 linked lists: one for each possible letter of

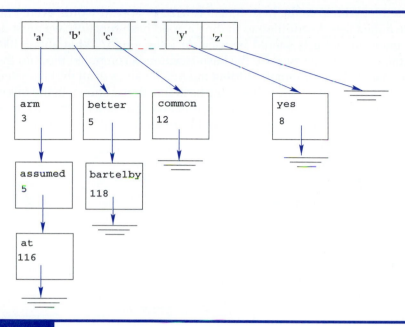

Figure 12.14   Using the first letter of a word as a hash function.

the alphabet. All the words beginning with *a* are stored in the *a* list, the words beginning with *b* are stored in the *b* list, and so forth. With this simple change to 26 linked lists, the time to process *The Scarlet Letter* is reduced to 25.5 seconds and the time to process Melville's *Bartleby, the Scrivener* is 1.6 seconds. This structure is shown in Fig. 12.14. To facilitate the generalization of this method, we'll speak of a **hash function** that maps a string to the linked list in which the string will be found or stored. The hash function returns an index into a Vector of 26 linked lists. In this example the hash function is shown in the following. The *a* words are stored in the first linked list (with index 0) and the *z* words in the linked list, whose index is 25.

```
int Hash(const string & word)
// precondition: 0 < word.length()
// postcondition: returns a hash index
{
    return tolower(word[0]) - 'a';
}
```

Rather than use only 26 linked lists, we can use a vector of 100 linked lists or 1000 linked lists. In general, the hash function maps a string to an index giving the linked list in which the string will be found. Even a "naïve" function using only the first letter of a word results in a large reduction in search time compared to when only one linked list is used (see Table 12.2). Many people have studied the problem of finding good hash functions. A good hash function spreads strings "evenly" among all the linked lists. Using the first letter of a string does not yield a good hash function, because many more words begin with *a* than with *q,* so the hash function will not spread words evenly among the 26 linked lists. In addition to finding a good hash function, we must decide how many linked lists should be used. Is 100 enough? What about 1000? In general, the value returned by the hash function is computed modulo the size of the hash table. For example, adding the ASCII values of all the characters in a string and using this as the value of the hash function is shown in the following, assuming that this is a private member function of a class WordList in which myList is a vector of pointers to linked lists (see *allword9.cc,* Prog. 12.12).

```
int WordList::Hash(const string & word)
// precondition: 0 < word.length()
// postcondition: returns a hash index
{
    int hval = 0;
    int k;
    int len = word.length();

    for(k=0; k < len; k++)
    {
        hval += s[k];
    }
    return hval % myList.Length();
}
```

This function is better than using just the first letter of a word, but words like "act" and "cat" still hash to the same value, resulting in a **hash collision**. There will always be some collisions, but we can alter the function slightly to yield a reasonably good hash function. We'll avoid the problem of collisions like "act" and "cat" by taking the index of each character into account as well as the value of the character. We'll use the same function above but include this line as the body of the for loop:

```
hval += s[k] * k;
```

Using this hash function and 1001 linked lists requires 2.4 seconds to process *The Scarlet Letter.* The complete program using this approach is shown in *allword9.cc,* Prog. 12.12. Most of the code is similar to the code in the linked list program *allword7.cc,* Prog. 12.7. For example, in the private member function WordList::Search(), the only difference is that the initialization

```
WordStat * current = myList;
```

from *allword7.cc,* is replaced by an initialization that finds the appropriate linked list to search. Note that myList is a Vector of pointers.

```
WordStat * current = myList[Hash(key)];
```

The Print function and the destructor are different because more than one linked list must be printed or deleted. The code from *allword7.cc* is nested in a for loop that visits every list in the Vector.

Using linked lists to store the strings hashed to the same value is called **chaining.**   Each linked list is sometimes called a **bucket,** with the metaphor that all strings that hash to the same value are stored in the same bucket. In the function `WordList::Update()` of *allword9.cc*, strings are stored in each chain by adding a new first node. Since `myList[index]` is a pointer to the linked list/chain, the following code adds a new first node:

```
WordStat * wptr = new WordStat; // create new node
wptr->info = word;              // store values
wptr->count = 1;
wptr->next  = myList[index];    // point at first node in chain
myList[index] = wptr;           // new first node in chain
```

In this example the `WordStat` `struct` does not have a constructor, so three statements are needed to create and initialize the `struct`.

Program 12.12   allword9.cc

```
#include <iostream.h>
#include <fstream.h>
#include <stdlib.h>             // for exit
#include "CPstring.h"
#include "vector.h"
#include "ctimer.h"             // for CTimer
#include "strutils.h"           // for StripPunc
#include "prompt.h"

// author: Owen Astrachan
//
// lists all words in an input file, with word counts
// uses class WordList to encapsulate behavior
//
// 5-15-95
//
// modified 6/10/96 to use hashing with chaining to store
// words/counts

struct WordStat
{
    string info;               // the string
    int count;                 // # of times string occurs
    WordStat * next;           // pointer to next node in list
};


class WordList
{
  public:
    WordList(int size);                 // constructor
    ~WordList();                        // destructor
    void Update(const string & word);       // update occurrences of word
    int GetUnique();                    // return # of unique words in list
    int GetTotal();                     // return # of total words in list
    void Print(ostream & output);       // print all words in list
```

```
  private:

    int myCount;                    // # of entries stored in myList
    int myTotal;                    // # of words (non-unique)
    Vector<WordStat *> myList;      // vector of pointers (chains) for hashing

    WordStat * Search(const string & key);  // returns pointer to node
    int Hash(const string & key);            // returns hash value
};

WordList::WordList(int size)
    : myCount(0),
      myTotal(0),
      myList(size,0)
{
    // all work done in initializer list
}

WordList::~WordList()
// postcondition: all new'd storage deleted
{
    int k;
    int size = myList.Length();
    for(k=0; k < size; k++)              // all chains
    {
        WordStat * current = myList[k];  // first node in chain,
        WordStat * temp;
        while (current != 0)
        {
            temp = current->next;        // store next node
            delete current;              // delete current first node
            current = temp;              // update to "new" first node
        }
    }
}

int WordList::Hash(const string & s)
// postcondition: returns hashed index, 0 <= index < myList.Length()
{
    unsigned int hval = 0;
    int k;
    int len = s.length();

    for(k=0; k < len; k++)
    {
        hval += s[k]*k;
    }
    return hval % myList.Length();
}

WordStat * WordList::Search(const string & key)
// postcondition: returns pointer to struct with key
//                returns 0 if key does not occur
// performance: O(1) average case (hashing with chaining)
```

```
{
    WordStat * current = myList[Hash(key)];
    while (current != 0)
    {
        if (current->info == key)
        {
            return current;
        }
        current = current->next;
    }
    return 0;
}

void WordList::Update(const string & word)
// postcondition: updates occurrence of word
//                adds word to list if not already present
//                otherwise updates count of # occurrences
//                increments count of total # of words
{
    WordStat * loc = Search(word);
    myTotal++;

    if (loc != 0)
    {
        loc->count++;
    }
    else
    {
        int index = Hash(word);
        myCount++;
        WordStat * wptr = new WordStat; // create new node
        wptr->info  = word;            // store values
        wptr->count = 1;
        wptr->next  = myList[index];   // point at first node in chain
        myList[index] = wptr;          // new first node in chain
    }
}

void WordList::Print(ostream & output)
// postcondition: all elements of list printed, sorted alphabetically
{
    int k;
    int size = myList.Length();
    for(k=0; k < size; k++)            // once for each chain
    {
        WordStat * current = myList[k];
        while (current != 0)
        {
            output << current->count << "\t" << current->info << endl;
            current = current->next;
        }
    }
    output << endl << "# of words = " << myCount << endl;
}
```

```
int WordList::GetUnique()
// postcondition: returns # unique words in list
{
    return myCount;
}

int WordList::GetTotal()
// postcondition: returns total # of words in list
//                same as # of times Update called
{
    return myTotal;
}

int main()
{
    string word;                        // word read from file
    string filename = PromptString("enter name of file: " );
    WordList wlist(1001);
    CTimer timer;
    double processTime;
    ifstream input;
    input.open(filename);

    if (input.fail())
    {
        cout << "could not open file " << filename << endl;
        exit(0);
    }

    while (input >> word)               // reading word succeeded
    {
        word = word.Downcase();
        StripPunc(word);
        timer.Start();
        wlist.Update(word);
        timer.Stop();
    }

    processTime = timer.CumulativeTime();
    wlist.Print(cout);

    cout << "total words (non-unique): " << wlist.GetTotal() << endl;
    cout << "total time for update = " << processTime << endl;
    return 0;
}
```

OUTPUT

```
prompt> allword9
enter name of file: hawthorne.txt
...
2        fellow-creature
```

```
1          measurement
4          faded
5          energies
5          supposed

# of words = 9164
total words (non-unique): 85753
total time for update = 2.4
```

There are other methods of resolving hash collisions that you may study if you continue your study of computer science. However, chaining is generally the preferred method, since linked lists can store an arbitrary number of nodes. It is important to have enough linked lists. Clearly, 26 is not enough. Changing the number of lists from 1001 to 10,001 reduces the time of *allword9.cc* to 1.8 seconds for *The Scarlet Letter*. This is roughly a 25% reduction in time. For reasons that are beyond what we can cover here, the number of linked lists should be a prime number. Since 1001 and 10,001 are not prime, prime numbers like 1009 and 10,007 should be used instead, although you probably won't notice any performance difference.

Complexity of Hashing

In the worst case, hashing performance is very bad. For example, a hash function that always returns the same number, 13, is the same as using one linked list. This is a most unlucky hashing function, since it does not distribute strings equally among different linked lists. However, in the average case,[8] hashing is extremely efficient. It can be shown that the complexity of hash search is $O(1)$, which is called **constant time.** This means that the time to search for a single value using hashing is independent of the number of values that have been hashed. In the average case, strings are distributed relatively evenly among all chains, so that the length of each chain is short compared to the total number of values stored in all the chains. To be more precise, the complexity of hashing depends on how full the chains are. If chains are short, hashing is fast. As you can determine from the data given in this section (using 1001 or 10,0001 chains) the performance of the hash search is very good. Even when only 101 chains are used for hashing *The Scarlet Letter*, a good hash function will distribute the roughly 9000 unique words evenly among all chains, resulting in approximately 90 nodes in each of the linked lists. Since searching a small list of 90 nodes is very fast, hashing can yield reasonable performance even when the number of chains is too small (with 101 chains, 5.7 seconds are needed to process *The Scarlet Letter*).

---

[8]It's difficult to define *average case* formally. However, for our purposes almost all data encountered are "average"; it's very difficult to make up "pathological" data, which perform badly when enough chains are used with a reasonably good hash function.

12.24. What modifications are needed in *allword9.cc*, Prog. 12.12, to add new nodes to the end of a chain instead of to the front?

12.25. Why is `hval` defined as an `unsigned int` in `Hash()` of *allword9.cc*? (*Hint:* Think about integer overflow.)

12.26. Use this statement in the function `Hash()` of *allword9.cc* and see if the timings change:

```
hval = hval * 256 + s[k];
```

12.27. Add a function `Statistics()` to *allword9.cc* used to output statistics of the chains in the hash table. Print the average chain length, the longest chain length, and the number of empty buckets. If you wrote code to calculate standard deviations (see Sec. 6.6), then print this statistic too.

12.28. Describe the modifications needed in *allword9.cc* to keep track of the line numbers on which each word occurs.

12.9   Tree Search

Hashing is usually the method of choice when a fast search is required. You may have noticed, however, that the output of *allword9.cc*, Prog. 12.12, is not sorted. The term *hashing* is derived from chopping each string up, or hashing it, and creating an integer index from the chopped-up string. Since hashing functions do not compare strings but map them to an index based on internal characteristics of the string characters, the strings will not be sorted. In some applications a fast search is required, but sorted data are also required. Although it's possible to sort the entries in a hash table, the addition of one new string necessitates resorting all the strings. In this section we'll study a method for storing data that combines the features of linked lists and binary search to yield fast search times and sorted data. The search times are not as fast as when hashing is used but are quite fast.

New nodes can be spliced into a linked list without shifting existing nodes. However, linked lists must be searched sequentially; binary search cannot be used since linked lists do not support random access. The key idea behind binary search is that after making one comparison, half the values stored are eliminated from consideration as potential matches. By adding another link to the nodes of a linked list we can achieve the same effect. The resulting data structure is called a **binary tree.** When the nodes of a binary tree are maintained in sorted order, the tree is called a **binary search tree.**

The declaration for a struct `WordStat` is modified to contain pointers to a left node and a right node:

```
struct WordStat
{
    string info;              // the string
    int count;                // # of times string occurs
    WordStat * left;          // pointer to left node in tree
    WordStat * right;         // pointer to right node in tree
};
```

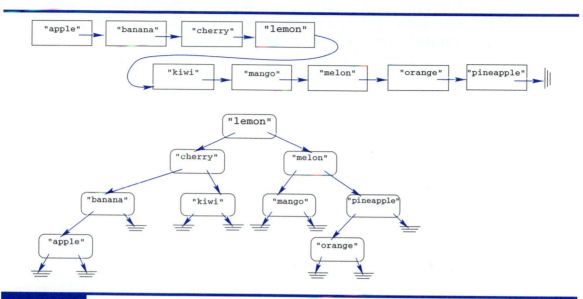

Figure 12.15   Linked list and binary search tree.

A sorted linked list and a binary search tree containing names of fruits are shown in Fig. 12.15. Each node in a search tree points to two **subtrees:** the left and right subtrees. In a binary search tree, all the values in a node's left subtree are less than the value in the node and all the values in the right subtree are greater than the value stored in the node. For example, in Fig. 12.15 the strings "apple," "cherry," and "banana" are all less than "lemon." The top node in a tree is called the tree's **root;** this is the node containing "lemon" in Fig. 12.15. A node's **children** are the nodes pointed to by the left and right pointers. The "mango" node is the left child of "melon," and "pineapple" is the right child of "melon" in Fig. 12.15.

Nodes with no children are called **leaf** nodes. The leaves in the tree in Fig. 12.15 are the nodes with the names "apple," "kiwi," and "orange." Binary search trees support efficient search because half the values in a tree can be eliminated from consideration with one comparison, just as with binary search in a vector. For example, in searching for the string "guava," we see that it is less than "lemon," the value stored at the root. This means that "guava" must be stored in the left subtree of the root if it is in the tree. No values in the right subtree should be examined in searching for "guava." The function Search below returns a pointer to the node containing key, or NULL if no such node exists. It is similar to the binary search code in the function Search from Prog. 12.3, *word5.cc*, but traverses the tree in the same way that Search in *allword7.cc*, Prog. 12.7, traverses a linked list. For example, in searching for "papaya" in the tree shown in Fig. 12.15, the following nodes are examined, in the order "lemon," "melon," "pineapple," "orange," NULL. This is because with the first comparison, "papaya" is greater than "lemon" so the statement `root = root->right` is executed. Then the search continues with right (melon), left (pineapple), right (orange), until a NULL node is found. Since "papaya" is not found, the function `Search` returns 0.

```
WordStat * Search(WordStat * root, const string & key)
// postcondition: returns pointer to node with key
//                returns 0 if key does not occur
{
    while (root != 0)
    {
        if (root->info == key)
            return root;
        else if (key < root->info)
            root = root->left;
        else
            root = root->right;
    }
    return 0;
}
```

Nodes are added to a search tree similarly, although we'll see in *allword10.cc*, Prog. 12.13, that using recursion makes the code very short. Ideally search trees are evenly balanced, with the number of nodes in each left subtree roughly equal to the number of nodes in the corresponding right subtree. However, adding words to a search tree in alphabetical order yields a very unbalanced tree. For example, the linked list in Fig. 12.15 could be viewed as a binary search tree if all the pointers are considered to be right-child pointers, with all left-child pointers being NULL. In advanced courses you may study methods for rebalancing a tree so that the tree is always short and bushy rather than long and stringy. Short and bushy trees support efficient searches, since many nodes can be eliminated from consideration with one comparison. However, on average, binary trees will be shaped so that searches are efficient.

We've seen how to search a tree; we also need to print the values stored in a tree in sorted order. Printing in sorted order is done most easily using recursion. For the tree in Fig. 12.15, where are all the strings less than "lemon" and when should they be printed? In general, two questions will help in reasoning about a recursive solution to printing a tree in sorted order.

1.   Where are all the strings less than the value stored in the root?

2.   Where are all the strings greater than the value stored in the root?

All the strings that are less than the root must be printed before the root is printed. All the strings that are greater must be printed after the root is printed. This leads to the following code for printing a tree in sorted order. This is called an **inorder tree traversal.**

```
void Print(WordStat * root)
// postcondition: all nodes printed using
//                inorder traversal
{
    if (root != 0)
```

```
    {
            Print(root->left);
            cout << root->count << "\t" << root->info << endl;
            Print(root->right);
    }
}
```

Rather than trace through a series of recursive calls, you should try to believe that it works based on the following argument. When is the value at the root of a tree printed? The value is printed after the entire left subtree is printed by the recursive call `Print(root->left)`. If you believe in the recursion, this means that all the values less than the root are printed, recursively, before the value at the root is printed. After the root value is printed, all greater values are printed by the recursive call `Print(root->right)`.

You can convince yourself more by reasoning about two different subtrees shown in Fig. 12.15.

1. A single-node tree, represented by any leaf, e.g., "kiwi" or "orange"
2. A tree with one child, such as "mango" or "pineapple"

The inorder traversal code in `Print` prints a leaf correctly. If the parameter `root` points to the "kiwi" node, then the recursive calls will not print anything, since both left and right children are `NULL`. This means that the only value printed is "kiwi." This reasoning generalizes so that you should be convinced that every single-node tree (i.e., a leaf) is printed correctly.

A tree with one child, such as "mango," is also printed correctly. The recursive call of the left subtree prints correctly because this is a leaf, and we've already argued that all leaves are printed correctly. This means that "kiwi" is printed, followed by the root value of "mango," followed by a recursive call for the right subtree, which prints nothing. You should try to convince yourself that this reasoning applies to the subtree with "pineapple" as a root too since this subtree has exactly the same shape as the "mango" tree. If you've convinced yourself that these trees print correctly using the inorder traversal in `Print`, you are ready to really believe.

Does the tree rooted at "melon" print correctly? We've just reasoned that both the left and right subtrees are printed correctly and from the code in `Print` it is clear that "melon" is printed after each value in the left subtree and before each value in the right subtree. This reasoning can be expanded into a mathematical proof that the code works correctly. You may have studied **mathematical induction,** which is strongly related to recursion in programming.

The public member functions of the `WordList` class in *allword10.cc,* Prog. 12.13, are the same as in previous versions of the program. There are several helper functions declared in the private section just as `Search` was declared in other versions of this program. These functions facilitate using recursion to process each node of the tree whose root is pointed to by private variable `myTree`. Each helper function `DoPrint`, `DoUpdate`, and `DoDelete` has a tree parameter. Since client programs of the `WordList` class are not aware that a search tree is used, the public member functions do not have tree parameters.

DoUpdate uses a reference parameter to add new nodes to the search tree. This function can be written without recursion using a trailing pointer as the tree is traversed to find the proper location for the new node. The resulting code is much more complicated. These same traits were seen in the function Delete in Sec. 12.3.

Program 12.13   allword10.cc

```cpp
#include <iostream.h>
#include <fstream.h>
#include <stdlib.h>              // for exit
#include "CPstring.h"
#include "vector.h"
#include "ctimer.h"              // for CTimer
#include "strutils.h"            // for StripPunc
#include "prompt.h"

// author: Owen Astrachan
//
// lists all words in an input file, with word counts
// uses class WordList to encapsulate behavior
//
// 5-15-95
//
// modified 6/10/96 to use a binary search tree to
// store each word/count

struct WordStat
{
    string info;                // the string
    int count;                  // # of times string occurs
    WordStat * left;            // pointer to left node in tree
    WordStat * right;           // pointer to right node in tree
};


class WordList
{
  public:
    WordList();                         // constructor
    ~WordList();                        // destructor
    void Update(const string & word);   // update occurrences of word
    int GetUnique();                    // return # of unique words in list
    int GetTotal();                     // return # of total words in list
    void Print(ostream & output);       // print all words in list
  private:

    int myCount;                        // # of entries stored in myTree
    int myTotal;                        // # of words (non-unique)
    WordStat * myTree;                  // pointer to root of search tree

    WordStat * Search(const string & key);  // returns pointer
    void DoDelete(WordStat * root);          // deletes tree
```

```
        void DoUpdate(WordStat * & root, const string & word); // adds node
        void DoPrint(ostream & output, WordStat * root);        // prints tree
};

WordList::WordList()
    : myCount(0),
      myTotal(0),
      myTree(0)
{
    // all work done in initializer list
}

WordList::~WordList()
// postcondition: all new'd storage deleted
{
    DoDelete(myTree);
}

void WordList::DoDelete(WordStat * root)
// postcondition: tree pointed to by root is deleted
{
    if (root != 0)
    {
        DoDelete(root->left);
        DoDelete(root->right);
        delete root;
    }
}

WordStat * WordList::Search(const string & key)
// postcondition: returns pointer to struct with key
//                returns 0 if key does not occur
// performance: O(log n), n = # items in myTree
{
    WordStat * current = myTree;
    while (current != 0)
    {
        if (current->info == key)
        {
            return current;
        }
        else if (key < current->info)
        {
            current = current->left;
        }
        else
        {
            current = current->right;
        }
    }
    return 0;
}

void WordList::DoUpdate(WordStat * & root, const string & word)
{
    if (root == 0)
```

```
    {
        root = new WordStat;
        root->info = word;
        root->count = 1;
        root->left = root->right = 0;
    }
    else if (word < root->info)
    {
        DoUpdate(root->left,word);
    }
    else
    {
        DoUpdate(root->right,word);
    }
}

void WordList::Update(const string & word)
// postcondition: updates occurrence of word
//                adds word to list if not already present
//                otherwise updates count of # occurrences
//                increments count of total # of words
{
    WordStat * loc = Search(word);
    myTotal++;

    if (loc != 0)
    {
        loc->count++;
    }
    else
    {
        myCount++;
        DoUpdate(myTree,word);
    }
}

void WordList::DoPrint(ostream & output, WordStat * root)
{
    if (root != 0)
    {
        DoPrint(output,root->left);
        output << root->count << "\t" << root->info << endl;
        DoPrint(output,root->right);
    }
}

void WordList::Print(ostream & output)
// postcondition: all elements of list printed, sorted alphabetically
{
    DoPrint(output,myTree);
    output << endl << "# of words = " << myCount << endl;
}


int WordList::GetUnique()
// postcondition: returns # unique words in list
```

```
{
    return myCount;
}
int WordList::GetTotal()
// postcondition: returns total # of words in list
//                same as # of times Update called
{
    return myTotal;
}

int main()
{
    string word;
    WordList wlist;
    CTimer timer;
    double processTime;
    string filename = PromptString("enter name of file: ");
    ifstream input;

    input.open(filename);
    if (input.fail())
    {
        cout << "could not open file " << filename << endl;
        exit(0);
    }

    while (input >> word)                    // reading word succeeded
    {
        word = word.Downcase();
        StripPunc(word);
        timer.Start();
        wlist.Update(word);
        timer.Stop();
    }

    processTime = timer.CumulativeTime();
    wlist.Print(cout);

    cout << "total words (non-unique): " << wlist.GetTotal() << endl;
    cout << "total time for update = " << processTime << endl;
    return 0;
}
```

OUTPUT

```
prompt> allword9
enter name of file: hawthorne.txt

...
10      youth
6       youthful
6       zeal
1       zealously
```

```
5        zenith
1        zigzag
# of words = 9164
total words (non-unique): 85753
total time for update = 2.9
```

We have discussed most of the code used in *allword10.cc,* but the code to delete a tree shows another kind of tree traversal. Deleting all the nodes in a tree requires a **postorder tree traversal**. First, all nodes in the left and right subtrees are deleted, then the root node of the tree is deleted. This is shown in the private member function `WordList::DoDelete()`.

```
void WordList::DoDelete(WordStat * root)
// postcondition: tree pointed to by root is deleted
{
    if (root != 0)
    {
        DoDelete(root->left);
        DoDelete(root->right);
        delete root;
    }
}
```

It is not possible to use an inorder traversal, where the `delete root` statement comes between the recursive calls, because the dereference `root->right` would be illegal after `root` is deleted.

Complexity of Search Trees

We have noted that in the worst case, binary search trees degenerate into linked lists, so that searching in an *n*-node tree is $O(n)$, or linear, in the worst case. However, in the average case, search trees are roughly balanced, meaning that the left and right subtrees are roughly equal in size for most nodes. This means that searching in a binary search tree has the same complexity as using binary search to search a sorted vector: $O(\log n)$ for an *n*-node tree. As we saw in Table 8.2 for binary search, searching in a million-node search tree requires only 21 comparisons if the tree is perfectly balanced. Although the constant time, $O(1)$, performance of a hash search is better than the $O(\log n)$ performance of a binary search tree, the search tree is maintained in sorted order (see, for example, the last part of the output of *allword10.cc*). Hashing also requires many chains to get reasonable performance, whereas a search tree uses exactly as many nodes as there are values in the tree, although each node does contain two pointers rather than the single pointer required for chaining with linked lists. Which search method is better? As with many answers, it depends on the problem being solved.

Pause to reflect

In all these problems, assume a `Tree struct` is defined with a constructor as shown here (note that both pointer parameters have default values).

```
struct Tree
{
    Tree(const string & data,
         Tree * lchild = 0, Tree * rchild = 0)
       : info(data), left(lchild), right(lchild)
    { }
    string info;
    Tree * left;
    Tree * right;
};
```

The following function NumNodes counts the number of nodes in a binary tree.

```
int NumNodes(Tree * t)
{
   if (t == 0) return 0;     // no nodes in empty tree
   else
   {
      return 1 + NumNodes(t->left) + NumNodes(t->right);
   }
}
```

12.29. Write an argument explaining why NumNodes is correct. Use the argument for inorder traversal as a model.

12.30. Write a function Copy that returns a copy of its Tree parameter. You must use recursion. Use NumNodes as a model: return an empty tree for a base case and construct one node using new whose fields are filled using recursive calls.

```
Tree * Copy(Tree * t)
// postcondition: returns a copy of t
```

12.31. A **preorder** traversal processes the root first and then recursively traverses the left and right subtrees. Write down the order in which nodes are visited for a preorder and a postorder traversal of the nodes in the fruit tree in Fig. 12.15.

12.32. Define the height of an empty tree as 0 and the height of a nonempty tree as the number of nodes on the longest root-to-leaf path.[9] What is the minimum height of a binary tree that contains 31 nodes? What is the maximum height of a binary tree that contains 31 nodes? Draw trees illustrating your answers.

12.33. Combine search trees and hashing by using search trees instead of linked lists to store values in each bucket. Compare the time to process large text files using both methods. Since chains must be short to realize good performance when hashing, using trees for chains is probably overkill but makes a good programming exercise.

---

[9]Sometimes the definition of height is based on tree edges that connect nodes rather than nodes. The number of edges on a path is always one less than the number of nodes.

Class Declarations and Implementations

A.1 Random Number Classes

The interface and implementation of the RandGen class are given here as Prog. A.1 and Prog. A.2. A static class variable, ourInitialized, is used in *rando.cc*. First we give the interface, *rando.h*:

Program A.1   rando.h

```
#ifndef _MYRAND_H
#define _MYRAND_H

#include <limits.h>                        // for INT_MAX

// designed for implementation independent randomization
// if all system dependent calls included in this class, then
// other classes can make use of this class in independent manner
//
// all random numbers are uniformly distributed in given range
//
// RandGen() ---          constructor sets seed of random # generator
//                        once per program, not per class/object
//
// RandInt(int max)
// RandInt(int low,int max) - return random integer in range [0..max]
//                     when one parameter used, [low..max] when
//                      two parameters used
//
//        examples:     rnd.RandInt(6) is random integer [0..5] or [0..6]
//                      rnd.RandInt(3,10) is random integer [3..10]
//                      rnd.RandInt() is random integer [0..INT_MAX)
//
// RandReal()        -- returns random double in range [0..1)
// RandReal(double low, double max)
//                   -- returns random double in range [low..max)

class RandGen
{
  public:
    RandGen();                           // set seed for all instances
    int RandInt(int max = INT_MAX);      // returns int in [0..max)
```

```
    int RandInt(int low, int max);        // returns int in [low..max]
    double RandReal();                     // returns double in [0..1]
    double RandReal(double low, double max); // range [low..max]
  private:
    static int ourInitialized;             // for 'per-class' initialization
};
```

```
#endif     // _MYRAND_H not defined
```

Here is the implementation, *rando.cc*. The system functions rand and srand are used to generate random numbers. On many systems these are not very good at generating "good" random numbers, but the results are acceptable for the simulations used in this book.

Program A.2   rando.cc

```
#include <time.h>               // for time()
#include <stdlib.h>             // for rand/srand
#include "rando.h"

int RandGen::ourInitialized = 0;

RandGen::RandGen()
// postcondition: system srand() used to initialize seed
//                once per program
{
    if (0 == ourInitialized)
    {
        ourInitialized = 1;      // only call srand once
        srand(time(0));          // randomize
    }
}

int RandGen::RandInt(int max)
// precondition: max > 0
// postcondition: returns int in [0..max)
{
    return static_cast<int>(RandReal() * max);
}

int RandGen::RandInt(int low, int max)
// precondition: low <= max
// postcondition: returns int in [low..max]
{
    return low + RandInt(max-low+1);
}

double RandGen::RandReal()
// postcondition: returns double in [0..1)
{
    return rand() / (static_cast<double>(RAND_MAX) + 1);
}
```

A.2   The string Class

The header file for "CPstring.h" is reproduced here. The implementation follows (the relational operators should return bool rather than int).

```
#ifndef _MYSTRING_H
#define _MYSTRING_H

#include <iostram.h>
#include <string.h>              // for strcmp, strlen, etc.
#include <stdlib.h>              // for exit,atof,atoi
#include <assert.h>              // for assert
#include <ctype.h>               // for tolower/toupper
//#include "bool.h"

// modeled (loosely) on Stroustrup 2nd edition, on Budd's String class,
// and Adams, Leestma, and Nyhoff Strings (and probably a host of others)
//
//
// written by Owen Astrachan April 1993 (with reference counts)
//      modified May 2, 1994
//      modified July 6, 1994 [fixed some inconsistencies found in DOS
//                             implementation]
//      modified October, 1994 [to re-use existing memory rather than
//                             than deleting when =, copy constructor used]
//
// provides a "standard" string class supporting operations given below
//
//   constructors:
//
//          string(const char * s = 0);
//              copies a C-style '\0'-terminated string
//          string(const string & x);
//              copy constructor
//          string (char ch);
//              make a string from a single character
//
//   destructor
//
//          ~string()    destructor frees memory associated with string
//   operators
//
//          string & operator= (const string & x);
//              assigns one string to another
//          string & operator= (const char * s);
//              assigns a C-style string to a string
//
//          operator const char * s () const
//              cast/convert string to C-style string
//
```

```
//          int length() const
//                  returns # of characters in string
//
//           char& operator[](int i)
//                  returns i-th char of string signals error if out-of-bounds)
//                      (char is assignable since reference)
//
//           const char& operator[](int i) const
//                  returns i-th char of string (signals error if out-of-bounds)
//
//  I/O operators
//      << and >>
//                  are "standard" for ostream and istream respectively
//          istream & getline(istream & is, string & s, char sentinel = '\n')
//                  mimics iostream.h getline for istreams and strings
//
//  relational operators
//              ==, !=, <, >, >=, <=
//                  for all combinations of C-style strings and string
//
//  concatenation operators and functions
//              string & operator +=(const string & x)
//                  catenates x to the right of the string
//              friend string operator +(const string & x, const string & y)
//                  catenates x to y and returns result
//
//
//  search/facilitator functions
//
//              string substr(int pos, int len)
//                  returns string of len chars starting at pos
//                  truncates if len too big, returns empty string
//                  if pos too big
//
//              string Downcase() const
//              string Upcase() const
//                  return lower/upper case versions of string, respectively
//
//              bool Contains(const string & s) const
//              bool Contains(char * s) const
//                  returns true if string contains s, else returns false
//
//  conversion functions
//
//              char * chars()
//                  similar to (char *) cast, but member function
//              char * c_str()
//                  identical to chars(), but ANSI compatible
//
//              int atoi(string &)
//                  like <stdlib.h> atoi, but has string parameter
//                  ensures that calling <stdlib.h> version is done
//                  correctly
//
```

```
//          int atof(string &)
//             like <stdlib.h> atof, but has string parameter
//             ensures that calling <stdlib.h> version is done
//             correctly
//
//          string itoa(int n)
//             returns string equivalent of number n
//             i.e., itoa(123) returns "123", itoa(-56) returns "-56"

extern const int NPOS;

class string{

  public:
    string(const char * s = 0);          // for literals and C-style strings
    string(const string & x);            // copy constructor
    string(char ch);                     // make string from char

    string& operator = (const char * s); // assign literal, C-style strings
    string& operator =(const string & x); // assign one string to another

    ~string();                           // free up memory

    // perhaps this cast should not be included

    operator const char *() const {return myCstring;}

    const char * chars() const {return myCstring;}    // explicit conversion
    const char * c_str() const {return myCstring;}    // to C-style

    int length() const {return strlen(myCstring);}  // returns # of chars
    char& operator[](int i);                  // index character (range checked)
    const char& operator[](int i) const;   // constant index  (range checked)

    string& operator +=(const string & x);

    string Downcase() const;

    string Upcase() const;

    string substr(int pos, int len) const;
    // precondition: 0 <= pos < s.length() && pos + len <= s.length()
    // postcondition: returns substring starting at char pos of len chars

    bool Contains (const string & s) const;

    bool Contains(const * s) const;

    int find(const string & s) const;
    int find(char * s) const;

// relational operators for string/string comparisons

    friend int operator ==(const string & x, const string & y)
        {return strcmp(x.myCstring, y.myCstring)==0;}
```

```
     friend int operator !=(const string & x, const string & y)
         {return ! (x == y);}

     friend int operator < (const string & x, const string & y)
         {return strcmp(x.myCstring, y.myCstring) < 0;}

     friend int operator > (const string & x, const string & y)
         {return strcmp(x.myCstring, y.myCstring) > 0;}

     friend int operator >=(const string & x, const string & y)
         {return x > y || x == y;}

     friend int operator <=(const string & x, const string & y)
         {return x < y || x == y;}

// relational operators for string/char * comparisons

     friend int operator ==(const string & x, const char *s)
         {return strcmp(x.myCstring,s)==0;}

     friend int operator !=(const string & x, const char * s)
         {return ! (x == s);}

     friend int operator < (const string & x, const char * s)
         {return strcmp(x.myCstring, s) < 0;}

     friend int operator > (const string & x, const char * s)
         {return strcmp(x.myCstring, s) > 0;}

     friend int operator >= (const string & x, const char * s)
         {return x > s || x == s;}

     friend int operator <= (const string & x, const char * s)
         {return x < s || x == s;}


// relational operators for char */string comparisons

     friend int operator == (const char * s, const string & x)
         {return strcmp(s, x.myCstring)==0;}

     friend int operator != (const char * s, const string & x)
         {return !(s == x);}

     friend int operator < (const char * s, const string & x)
         {return strcmp(s,x.myCstring) < 0;}

     friend int operator > (const char * s, const string & x)
         {return strcmp(s,x.myCstring) > 0;}

     friend int operator >= (const char * s, const string & x)
         {return s > x || s == x;}

     friend int operator <= (const char * s, const string & x)
         {return s < x || s == x;}
```

```
    enum {maxLength = 1024}; // maximum length of string read from input
  private:
    char * myCstring:            // private C-style string
    int myLength;
};

string operator +(const string & x, const string & y);
ostream& operator <<(ostream& os, const string& str);
istream& operator >>(istream& is, string& str);
istream & getline(istream & is, string & s, char sentinel = '\n');

int atoi(const string & s);          // returns int equivalent
double atof(const string & s);       // returns double equivalent
string itoa(int n);

//**************************************************************
//*************** pre/post conditions  ************************
/**************************************************************

string::string(const char * s)
// precondition: s is '\0'-terminated C-style string
// postcondition: object constructed to have same value as s
// assertion: fails if memory can't be allocated

string::string(const string & x)
// postcondition: object constructed has same value as x
// assertion: fails if memory can't be allocated

string::string(char ch)
// postcondition: object is string of one character ch
// assertion: fails if memory can't be allocated

string& string::operator = (const char * s)
// precondition: s is '\0'-terminated C-style string
// postcondition: assign object the value of C-style string s
// assertion: fails if memory can't be allocated

string& string::operator =(const string & x)
// postcondition: object assigned string x
//                memory allocated only if x.length() > length()
// assertion: fails if memory can't be allocated

string::~string()
// postcondition: dynamically allocated memory freed

char& string::operator[](int i)
// precondition: 0 <=i < length()
// postcondition: returns i-th character
// assertion: fails if index not in range

const char& string::operator[](int i) const
// precondition: 0 <= i < length()
// postcondition: returns i-th character (constant)
// assertion: fails if index not in range
```

```
ostream& operator <<(ostream& os, const string& str)
//precondition: os is writable
// postcondition: str is written to os (uses char * operator)

istream& operator >>(istream& is, string& str)
// precondition: is open for reading
// postcondition: string read from is, stored in str
//                  maximum of string::maxLength chars read

istream & getline(istream & is, string & s, char sentinel)
// precondition: is open for reading
// postcondition: chars from is up to sentinel read, stored in s
//                  sentinel is read, but NOT stored in s

string& string:: operator +=(const string & x)
// postcondition: concatenates x onto object
// assertion: fails if memory can't be allocated

string operator +(const string & x, const string & y)
// postcondition: returns concat(x,y)

string string::Downcase() const
// postcondition: returns lowercase equivalent of object
//                  non-lowercase chars not changed

string string::Upcase() const
// postcondition: returns uppercase equivalent of object
//                  non uppercase chars not changed

string string:: substr(int pos, int len)
// precondition: 0 <= pos < s.length() && pos + len <= s.length()
// postcondition: returns substring starting at char pos of len chars
//                  if len too large, takes s.length() chars

bool string::Contains (const string & s) const
// postcondition: returns true if s is a substring of object

inline int string::Contains(char * s) const
// postcondition: returns true if s is a substring of object

inline int atoi(string & s)
// precondition: s is a sequence of digits
// postcondition: returns integer equivalent of s
// exception: if s is not valid integer, 0 is returned

double atof(string & s)
// precondition: s is a sequence of digits
// postcondition: returns double equivalent of s
// exception: if s is not valid double, 0 is returned

*****************************************************************
*************** pre/post conditions    *************************
****************************************************************/

#endif /* _MYSTRING_H not defined */
```

CPstring.h

A.3   **The** Vector **Class**

A version of the Vector class is included here. All the code is in the header file, because that is the easiest way of instantiating templates with $g++$. Other compilers require separating the header file from the implementation.

Program A.4   vector.h

```
#ifndef _VECTOR_H
#define _VECTOR_H

#include <stdlib.h>
#include <assert.h>
#include <iostream.h>

// templated vector class, partially based on Budd,
//                      Classic Data Structures in C++
// written 11/5/93, modified 3/23/94
// changed on 3/9/95 to make all methods inline (defined in class decl)
//
// for a vector of Items use Vector<Item>, e.g., Vector <int> intvector;
//
//                       note: Item must have a default constructor
//
// constructors:
//    Vector()                    -- default, vector of size 0 (no entries)
//    Vector(int size)            -- vector with 5 entries
//    Vector(int size,
//            Item fillValue)      -- vector w/ size entries all == fillValue
//    Vector(const Vector & vec)  -- copy constructor
//
//    int Length()                -- returns size of vector (capacity)
//    void SetSize(int newSize)   -- resizes the vector to newSize elements
//                                   (can result in losing elements if
//                                   new size < old size)
//    void resize(int newSize)    -- synonym for SetSize
//
//    void Fill(Item fillValue)   -- set all entries == fillValue
//
//    operator =                  -- assignment operator works properly
//    operator []                 -- indexes both const and non-const vectors
//
//
//    examples of use:
//                Vector<double> dlist(100);     // a list of 100 doubles
//                Vector<double> dzlist(100,0.0); // initialized to 0.0
//
//                Vector<String> slist(300);     // 300 strings
//
//                Vector<int> ilist;             // has room for 0 ints
```

```cpp
template <class Item> class Vector
{
  public:
    Vector()                                    // default constructor 0 elts
    // postcondition: vector of zero items constructed
    {
        myLength = 0; myList = 0;
    }

    Vector(int size)                            // specify size of vector
    // postcondition: vector of size items constructed
    {
        myLength = size;
        myList = new Item [size];
        assert(myList != 0);
    }

    Vector(int size, Item fillValue)        // specify size and fill value
    // postcondition: vector of size items, each initialized to fillValue
    //                 constructed
    {
        myLength = size;
        myList = new Item [size];
        assert(myList != 0);
        for(int k = 0; k < size; k++){
            myList[k] = fillValue;
        }
    }

    Vector(const Vector<Item> & vec)          // copy constructor
    // precondition: Item supports assignment
    // postcondition: return copy of vec
    {
        // allocate storage

        myList = new Item [myLength = vec.myLength];
        assert(myList != 0);

        // copy elements
        for(int k = 0; k < vec.myLength; k++)
        {
            myList[k] = vec.myList[k];
        }
    }
    ~Vector ()                                  // free new'd storage
     // postcondition: dynamically allocated storage freed
     {
        delete [] myList;
        myList = 0;
        myLength = 0;                 // leave in "empty" state
     }
    Vector & operator = (const Vector<Item> & vec ) // overload assignment
    // precondition: Item supports assignment
    // postcondition: self is assigned vec
```

```
{
    if (this != &vec)          // don't assign to self!
    {
        delete [] myList;                 // out with old list, in with new
        myList = new Item [myLength = vec.myLength];
        assert(myList != 0);

        // copy vec
        myLength = vec.myLength;
        for(int k=0;  k < myLength;  k++)
        {
            myList[k] = vec.myList[k];
        }
    }
    return *this;
}

int Length() const                        // capacity of vector
{
    return myLength;
}
int length() const
{
    return Length();
}

void Fill(Item fillValue)
// postcondition: all entries == fillvalue
{
    int k;
    for(k=0;  k < myLength;  k++)
    {
        myList[k] = fillValue;
    }
}

void SetSize(int newSize)              // change size dynamically
// precondition: vector has room for myLength entries
// postcondition: vector has room for newSize entries
//                the first myLength of which are copies of original
//                unless newSize < myLength, then truncated copy occurs
{
    int numToCopy = newSize < myLength ? newSize : myLength;

    // allocate new storage
    Item * newList = new Item[newSize];
    assert(newList != 0);   // be sure storage allocated

    int k;
    for(k=0;  k < numToCopy;k++)
    {
        newList[k] = myList[k];
    }

    delete [] myList;              // deallocate old storage
```

```
            myLength = newSize;
            myList = newList;
        }

    void resize(int newSize)
    {
        SetSize(newSize);
    }

    Item & operator [] (int index)
    // safe indexing, returning reference
    // precondition:  0 <= index < myLength
    // postcondition: return indexth item
    // exception: aborts if index is out of bounds
    {
        if ((unsigned) index >= (unsigned)myLength || index < 0)
        {
            cerr << "Illegal vector index: " << index
                 << " (max = " << myLength-1 << ")" << endl;
            assert(index >= 0);
            assert(index < myLength);
        }

        return myList[index];
    }

    const Item & operator [] (int index) const // const index
    // safe indexing, returning const reference to avoid modification
    // precondition: 0 <= index < myLength
    // postcondition: return indexth item
    // exception: aborts if index is out of bounds
    {
        if ((unsigned) index >= (unsigned)myLength || index < 0)
        {
            cerr << "Illegal vector index: " << index
                 << " (max = " << myLength << ")" << endl;
            assert(index >= 0);
            assert(index < myLength);
        }

        return myList[index];
    }


  private:
    Item * myList;  // the array of items
    int myLength;   // # things in vector (array),0,1,...,(myLength-1)
};

#endif                          // _VECTOR_H not defined
```

vector.h

Bibliography

[AA85] Donald J. Albers and G. L. Alexanderson. *Mathematical People*. Birkhäuser, 1985.

[ACM87] ACM. *Turing Award Lectures: The First Twenty Years 1966–1985*. ACM Press, 1987.

[AS85] Harold Abelson and Gerald Jay Sussman. *Structure and Interpretation of Computer Programs*. MIT Press, McGraw-Hill Book Company, 1985.

[Asp90] William Aspray. *Computing Before Computers*. Iowa State University Press, 1990.

[Ben86] Jon Bentley. *Programming Pearls*. Addison-Wesley, 1986.

[Ble90] Guy E. Blelloch.*Vector Models for Data-Parallel Computing*. MIT Press, 1990.

[Boo91] Grady Booch. *Object Oriented Design with Applications*. Benjamin Cummings, 1991.

[BRE71] I. Barrodale, F. D. Roberts, and B. L. Ehle. *Elementary Computer Applications in Science, Engineering, and Business*. John Wiley & Sons, Inc., 1971.

[Coo87] Doug Cooper. *Condensed Pascal*. W. W. Norton, 1987.

[DR90] Nachum Dershowitz and Edward M. Reingold. Calendrical calculations. *Software—Practice and Experience*, 20(9):899–928, September 1990.

[EL94] Susan Epstein and Joanne Luciano, editors. *Grace Hopper Celebration of Women in Computing*. Computing Research Association, 1994. Hopper-Book@cra.org.

[Emm93] Michele Emmer, editor. *The Visual Mind: Art and Mathematics*. MIT Press, 1993.

[G95] Denise W. Gürer. Pioneering women in computer science. *Communications of the ACM*, 38(1):45–54, January 1995.

[Gar95] Simson Garfinkel. *PGP: Pretty Good Privacy*. O'Reilly & Associates, 1995.

[Gol93] Herman H. Goldstine. *The Computer from Pascal to von Neumann*. Princeton University Press, 1993.

[Gri74] David Gries. On structured programming—a reply to Smoliar. *Communications of the ACM*, 17(11):655–657, 1974.

[GS93] David Gries and Fred B. Schneider. *A Logical Approach to Discrete Math.* Springer-Verlag, 1993.

[Har92] David Harel. *Algorithmics, The Spirit of Computing.* Addison-Wesley, 2nd edition, 1992.

[Hoa89] C. A. R. Hoare. *Essays in Computing Science.* Prentice-Hall, 1989.

[Hod83] Andrew Hodges. *Alan Turing: The Enigma.* Simon & Schuster, 1983.

[Hor92] John Horgan. Claude E. Shannon. *IEEE Spectrum,* April 1992.

[Knu73a] Donald E. Knuth. *The Art of Computer Programming, Volume 1: Fundamental Algorithms.* Addison-Wesley, 2nd edition, 1973.

[Knu73b] Donald E. Knuth. *The Art of Computer Programming, Volume 3: Sorting and Searching.* Addison-Wesley, 1973.

[Knu81] Donald E. Knuth. *The Art of Computer Programming, Volume 2: Seminumerical Algorithms.* Addison-Wesley, 2nd edition, 1981.

[Knu93] Donald E. Knuth. *The Stanford GraphBase.* Addison-Wesley, 1993.

[KR78] Brian W. Kernighan and Dennis Ritchie. *The C Programming Language.* Prentice-Hall, 1978.

[KR96] Samuel N. Kamin and Edward M. Reingold. *Programming with* `class`; *A C++ Introduction to Computer Science.* McGraw-Hill, 1996.

[Mac92] Norman Macrae. *John von Neumann.* Pantheon Books, 1992.

[McC79] Pamela McCorduck. *Machines Who Think.* W.H. Freeman and Company, 1979.

[McC93] Steve McConnell. *Code Complete.* Microsoft Press, 1993.

[Mer94] Rick Mercer. *Computing Fundamentals with C++.* Franklin, Beedle & Associates, 1994.

[Mey92] Scott Meyers. *Effective C++.* Addison-Wesley, 1992.

[MGRS91] Albert R. Meyer, John V. Guttag, Ronald L. Rivest, and Peter Szolovits. *Research Directions in Computer Science: An MIT Perspective.* MIT Press, 1991.

[Neu95] Peter G. Neumann. *Computer Related Risks.* Addison-Wesley, 1995.

[Pat91] Richard E. Pattis. A philosophy and example of CS-1 programming projects. In *The Papers of the Twenty-first SIGCSE Technical Symposium on Computer Science Education,* pages 34–39. ACM Press, February 1991. SIGCSE Bulletin V. 23 N. 1.

[PAT96] Richard E. Pattis. *Get A-Life: Advice for the Beginning C++ Object-Oriented Programmer.* Turing TarPit Press, 1996.

[Per87] Alan Perlis. The synthesis of algorithmic systems. In *ACM Turing Award Lectures: The First Twenty Years.* ACM Press, 1987.

[PL90] Przemyslaw Prusinkiewicz and Aristid Lindenmayer. *The Algorithmic Beauty of Plants.* Springer-Verlag, 1990.

[Pla92]   P. J. Plauger. *The Standard C Library.* Prentice Hall, 1992.

[RDC93]   Edward M. Reingold, Nachum Dershowitz, and Stewart M. Clamen. Cal-endrical calculations, ii: Three historical calendars. *Software—Practice and Experience,* 23(4):383–404, April 1993.

[Rob94]   Eric S. Roberts. Loop exits and structured programming: Reopening the debate, *Proceedings of the Twenty-Sixth SIGCSE Symposium,* pages 268–272. ACM Press, 1995.

[Rob95]   Eric S. Roberts. *The Art and Science of C.* Addison-Wesley, 1995.

[Sla87]   Robert Slater. *Portraits in Silicon.* MIT Press, 1987.

[Str87]   Bjarne Stroustrup. *The C++ Programming Language.* Addison-Wesley, 1987.

[Str91]   Bjarne Stroustrup. *The C++ Programming Language.* Addison-Wesley, 2nd edition, 1991.

[Str94]   Bjarne Stroustrup. *The Design and Evolution of C++.* Addison-Wesley, 1994.

[SW89]   William Strunk Jr. and E. B. White. *The Elements of Style.* Macmillan Publishing Co., 3rd edition, 1989.

[Tea93]   Steve Teale. *C++ IOStreams Handbook.* Addison-Wesley, 1993.

[Tuc91]   Allen B. Tucker. *Computing Curricula 1991 Report of the ACM/IEEE-CS Joint Curriculum Task Force.* ACM Press, 1991.

[Wei94]   Mark Allen Weiss. *Data Structures and Algorithm Analysis in C++.* Benjamin/Cummings, 1994.

[Whi90]   Charles A. Whitney. *Random Processes in Physical Systems.* Wiley Interscience. John Wiley & Sons, Inc., 1990.

[Wil56]   M. V. Wilkes. *Automatic Digital Computers.* John Wiley & Sons, Inc., 1956.

[Wil87]   Maurice V. Wilkes. Computers then and now. In *ACM Turing Award Lectures: The First Twenty Years,* pages 197–205. ACM Press, 1987.

[Wil95]   Maurice V. Wilkes. *Computing Perspectives.* Morgan Kaufmann, 1995.

[Wir87]   Niklaus Wirth. From programming language design to compiler construction. In *ACM Turing Award Lectures: The First Twenty Years.* ACM Press, 1987.

Index